IOM International Organization for Migration

Academic Foundation New Delhi

WORLD MIGRATION

COSTS AND BENEFITS OF INTERNATIONAL MIGRATION 2005

VOLUME 3 – IOM World Migration Report Series

The opinions and analyses expressed in this book do not necessarily reflect the views and official policies of the International Organization for Migration or its Member States. The book is an independent publication commissioned by IOM. It is the fruit of a collaborative effort by a team of contributing authors and the editorial team under the direction of the editor-in-chief.

Unless otherwise stated, the book does not refer to events occurring after November 2004.

The maps do not reflect any opinion on the part of IOM concerning the legal status of any country, territory, city or area, or the delimitation of frontiers or boundaries.

This edition is published in India in 2006
by : ACADEMIC FOUNDATION
4772-73 / 23 Bharat Ram Road, (23, Ansari Road),
Darya Ganj, New Delhi - 110 002 (India).
Phones : 23245001 / 02 / 03 / 04.
Fax : +91-11-23245005.
E-mail : academic@vsnl.com
www.academicfoundation.com

World Migration 2005:
Costs and Benefits of International Migration
(Volume 3 — IOM World Migration Report Series)

ISBN 81-7188-550-0

Printed and bound in India.

IOM EDITORIAL TEAM

Editor-In-Chief And Concept	Irena Omelaniuk
Editorial Board	Gervais Appave, Clarissa Azkoul, Philippe Boncour, Jean-Philippe Chauzy, Denise Glasscock, Shahidul Haque, Charles Harns, Jill Helke, Frank Laczko, Heikki Mattila, Robert Paiva, Richard Perruchoud, Peter Schatzer, Erica Usher, Thomas Weiss
Editorial Assistance	Riad Al Khouri, Reginald Appleyard, Bimal Ghosh, Jill Helke, Franck Laczko, Rainer Münz, Robert Paiva, Ronald Skeldon, Valdis Thoman, Boris Wijkström
Executive Assistant	Dominique Jaud-Pellier
Statistics	Patrice Cluzant, Daphne Dadzie, Goran Grujovic, Mati Hashemee, Dejan Loncar, Heikki Mattila, Dario Muhamudo, Teodora Suter, Mariko Tomiyama
Cartography	Jana Hennig-Barthel
Bibliographic Research	Kerstin Lau
English Language Editor	Ilse Pinto-Dobernig

World Migration 2005 / Costs and Benefits of International Migration
is produced by IOM's Migration Policy, Research and Communication (MPRC) Department.

ACKNOWLEDGEMENTS

The editorial team wishes to thank all contributing authors and is especially grateful to **Brunson McKinley**, *IOM Director General, for his vision and encouragement to produce this book.*

The Editorial team wishes to thank the following persons for their kind assistance and support:

Maureen Achieng, Anelise Araujo-Forlot, Tamara Babiuk, Lars Bakker, Marthe Antoinette Balihe, Kerstin Bartsch, Diego Beltrand, Rosilyne Borland, Anne-Marie Buschmann-Petit, William Barriga, Giuseppe Calandruccio, Elizabeth Collett, Patrick Corcoran, Slavica Dimitrievska, Francoise Droulez, Christian Dustman, Sylvia Ekra, Nahreen Farjana, Berta Fernandez, Erin Foster, Keiko Foster, Cristiano Gentili, Nicoletta Giordano, Carmela Godeau, Danielle Grondin, Andreas Halbach, Mary Haour-Knipe, Bill Hyde, Vincent Keane, Michele Klein-Solomon, June Lee, Niusca Magalhaes, Davide Mosca, Neil Mullenger, Günter Müssig, Ndioro Ndiaye, Denis Nihill, Pierre Nicolas, Sophie Nonnenmacher, Jose-Angel Oropeza, Angela Pederson, Adela Pelegrino, John Rees, Abul Rizvi, Bryan Roberts, Redouane Saadi, Caroline San Miguel, Meera Sethi, Iuliana Stefan, Frances Sullivan, Teodora Suter, Istvan Szilard, Yorio Tanimura, Damien Thuriaux, Mariko Tomiyama, Michel Tonneau, Elisa Tsakiri, Zhao Jian, Jacqueline Weekers, Aida Zecevic, Justine Hsu.

Several organizations generously shared their data and other research materials:

Asian Development Bank (ADB), Australian Department of Immigration, Multicultural and Indigenous Affairs (DIMIA), Bertelsmann Foundation, China National Statistics Bureau, China Ministry of Public Security, Citizenship and Immigration Canada (CIC), European Commission Directorate, Global Commission on International Migration (GCIM), Global IDP Project, International Labour Organization, Migration Policy Institute, Washington D.C., New Zealand Immigration Service, Korean Ministry of Justice, Norwegian Refugee Council, Organization for Economic Cooperation and Development (OECD), Philippines Department of Labor and Employment, Statistical Office of the European Commission (EUROSTAT), Thai Ministry of Interior; Thai Ministry of Labour, UNAIDS (Joint United Nations Programme on HIV/AIDS), United Kingdom Home Office, United Nations Development Program (UNDP), United Nations High Commissioner for Refugees, UN Population Division (UNPD), United Nations Statistics Division, United States Census Bureau, United States Committee for Refugees, United States Department of Homeland Security, United States Department of State, World Bank, World Health Organization.

SECTION 2. COSTS AND BENEFITS OF MIGRATION

FOREWORD

When we issued the second World Migration report in 2003, I expressed the hope that it would shed more light on the challenges and responses for people on the move, and contribute towards enhancing migration management approaches that uphold the principle that "humane and orderly migration benefits migrants and societies". In the two years since then, the understanding of migration issues in migration management has broadened and deepened, and the examples of good practices have increased significantly.

It has become increasingly clear, however, that public perceptions of migration and migrants play a critical role in determining the policy choices available to governments – and the World Migration report series offers a sufficiently comprehensive range of facts and analysis to aid the accuracy and balanced nature of those perceptions.

This third edition, **World Migration 2005**, addresses the theme of the "costs and benefits" of international migration in an attempt to explain the opportunities and challenges in a manner which will inform, update and stimulate debate, and thus broaden the scope of policy choices. Rational and well-informed choices by migrants, governments, civil society, communities and the private sector can help maximize the benefits and minimize the costs of migration, in social, economic and political terms.

As with the last report, more than half the contributors are IOM staff members, drawing from the experiences of governments, migrants, NGOs and others working with migrants on the ground. The remaining sections have been contributed by authors from governments, universities, think tanks, international organizations and other sources of expertise. Each brings a different perspective to the discussion, but there is also a surprising convergence of interests, approaches and conclusions – particularly about the benefits of migration.

The report takes both a regional and thematic approach to charting and assessing the benefits and costs, and provides data, statistics and maps to offer both a snapshot of the situation and illustrate the trends. Due to its broad scope and unique combination of information, analysis and effective practice, the series has become a useful reference text for both policy makers and students of the subject.

We hope this report will succeed in illuminating further the complex issues which make up migration today and tomorrow, how they affect all of us every day in some way or another and how, together, we can manage migration better for the common good.

Brunson McKinley
Director General

INTRODUCTION
MIGRATION CHALLENGES IN THE 21ST CENTURY[1]

BACKGROUND

MIGRATION is a multifacetted and complex global issue, which today touches every country in the world. All 190 or so sovereign states of the world are now either points of origin, transit or destination for migrants; often all three at once. The UN's current official estimate remains at 175 million migrants globally. By extrapolating the growth of the known migrant stocks for the period 1990–2000, the UN Population Division predicted a total of between 185 million and 192 million migrants by early 2005 (UN, 2004a).[2]

At 2.9 per cent, the share of migrants in global population numbers is not high, though their presence and visibility in social, economic and political terms can be, particularly given the uncounted share of irregular migrants. The majority of migrants are concentrated in a relatively small number of advanced industrialized countries. Of these, almost half are women (49% in 2000), a proportion that has changed little in recent decades, despite an increase in the participation of women in migration, particularly in Africa or Asia, where women nevertheless remain under-represented (**see chapter 23**).

Migration flows have shifted in recent years with the changing poles of attraction for labour migration; for example more Asians are finding job opportunities within Asia itself, while more Latin Americans are moving to work in Europe. High labour force participation by migrants in Europe, the US and Australia confirms that economic incentives remain high for migration to those market economies. The UN also confirms the significant contribution of migration to population growth in Australia, the US and some European countries (ibid). Yet, reliable data on actual migration flows continue to be scarce.

The world is changing, and migration is contributing to that change. For instance, Ireland, traditionally a country of emigration, had one of the fastest growing immigrant populations in Europe in the early years of the 21st century (**chapter 7**); Germany, a country that until recently saw itself as a non-immigration country, has passed an Immigration Bill, to come into effect in 2005, and the UK recently elected its first local councillor of Somali origin.[3] Similar stories are recurring throughout the world. But the nature of migration is also changing. Taking the UK example, history and geographic proximity are no longer the primary drivers of migration, as more countries outside the British Commonwealth and the EU have become large net exporters of people to the UK.

World Migration 2005 examines these and other international migration trends from a geographic, thematic and statistical perspective with a view to updating and offering policymakers relevant data and models to inform policy decisions prompted by such developments. The thematic focus on costs and benefits of international migration points to the fact that policy decisions are determined by social,

1. *The authors of this chapter are Irena Omelaniuk, Editor-in-Chief, and Thomas Lothar Weiss, IOM Regional Representative, Helsinki.*
2. *These UN statistics are based on data from governments, which can include some irregular migrants (chapter 23).*
3. *In Toxteth, Liverpool, The Economist, October 9, 2004, p. 38.*

economic and political considerations of the causes and effects of migration. The report is accordingly organized into three sections:

1) *Regional Overview – Selected Geographic Regions:* a factual tour of the migration patterns and policy responses in the major regions of the world.
2) *Costs and Benefits of International Migration* – a selection of essays on how migration can benefit and cost migrants, societies and governments in social, economic and political terms, particularly at its interface with labour markets, development, integration, health and institutional structures.
3) *Migration Data and Statistics* – maps, tables and texts to illustrate a wide range of issues covered in this report.

EMERGING KEY TRENDS

Much has happened in the two years since World Migration 2003, for example international dialogue and cooperation on migration has intensified in the Western Mediterranean region through the "5+5" conferences; in Asia through the Labour Ministers' Consultations, the Bali Process workshops or Pacific Immigration Directors' conferences; in Africa through continent-wide consultations towards a strategic migration policy framework; in Geneva through the "GMG" meetings of heads of international organizations,[4] and the further globalization of the Swiss Government-led Berne Initiative; the founding of the Global Commission on International Migration (GCIM), and various global migration policy dialogues held by IOM in cooperation with WTO, the World Bank, WHO, DFID and others. These are just some examples of the burgeoning international dialogue around migration (chapter 22).[5]

At the same time, migration laws, institutional structures and procedures have tightened – particularly in the US and other immigration countries – as part of the broader efforts to combat terrorism. These are affecting migration patterns and the distribution of their costs and benefits, as well as relations between governments. Restrictive migration regimes contradict the increasingly open flow of goods, capital and foreign direct investments (UN, 2004b), an asymmetry that increasingly tries to correct itself through irregular and clandestine migration.

National and international development agencies are also more actively engaged today in evaluating and harnessing the benefits from migration for the development of countries and regions of origin with remittance management high on everybody's agenda.

While many of the usual pressures and motivations for migration remain – widening disparities in income and employment, low education and life opportunities, environmental degradation, political upheaval and armed conflict, poverty and human rights abuse – the types of migration are changing rapidly. More people today are moving temporarily, often staying longer, but then returning to their countries of origin. Overseas study options are expanding at a rapid and competitive pace among such countries as Australia, China, Japan, Germany, the UK and the US, increasingly opening ways into other, longer term skilled migration categories. Today, some 40 per cent of Australia's skilled migrants are drawn from the overseas student caseload, a trend noticeable also in Canada, the US and Europe.

With increased temporary migration, particularly of highly skilled persons, voluntary return has become a major feature of migration in recent years. As one author writes, today's migration of the highly skilled is characterized by "hypermobility involving remi-

4. *The "Geneva Migration Group" comprises the heads of ILO, IOM, OHCHR, UNCTAD, UNHCR and UNODC, and meets regularly to discuss how migration cross-cuts with trade, labour, development, health, security, crime et al.*

5. *For a comprehensive listing of meetings held under the auspices of ongoing regional integration processes - e.g. in the EU, Central and South America, Africa, Asia, the Middle East and Oceania, see chapters 1-7 and chapter 22. There are also regular international conferences and dialogues held by ILO, IOM, UNHCR, WHO, WTO and others.*

gration and return" (Hugo et al., 2001, p. 19). This is most widespread in countries experiencing vigorous economic growth, e.g. China, the Taiwan Province of China and Korea, or where there are financial and career incentives to return home **(chapter 16)**.

There is talk of a "new transnational model of skills sharing" **(chapter 8)**, and a new emphasis by both sending and receiving countries on return and circulation of skills **(chapter 11)**. For developed countries, particularly in Europe, North America, East Asia and Oceania, immigration offers an alternative source of people and labour at a time of declining population and labour supply, and a reassessment of policies towards migration (Chamie, 2003). For developing countries, it can help relieve surplus labour, unemployment and population pressures at home. The report explores the strategic and economic advantages of temporary foreign labour schemes **(chapters 9, 10)**, bilateral labour agreements to support these **(Textbox 12.2)**, and electronic visa systems to expedite cross-border business travel **(chapter 22)**. The General Agreement on Trade in Services framework could enhance the positive contribution of migration by offering more predictability and market access for temporary labour migrants **(chapter 9)**.

Alongside this is the complex networking between migrant *diasporas* and their home countries. Globalization has greatly expanded the means by which migrants can remain actively involved in the economic, cultural, social and political life of sending countries. Financial remittances, internet communications and travel, diaspora and hometown associations, and other mechanisms for expatriates to reside abroad and maintain ties with their country of origin are today creating powerful tools for development **(chapters 14 and 15)**. While not a new phenomenon, these are acquiring a new sophistication in Latin America, Asia and Africa, partly through policy and institutional adjustments by governments, partly through the initiatives of the migrants, and partly through internationally-supported programmes like IOM's MIDA.[6]

Another significant feature of contemporary migration is the large *emigration* flows out of traditional immigration countries, both of nationals and migrants. These are mostly temporary and work related, but can also lead to more permanent resettlement and reflect the general *laissez fairism* of skilled migration in a globalized world. For the first time, immigration countries like Australia, New Zealand and the UK are seriously examining their real or perceived "brain drain", with Australia considering its options for attracting back highly skilled and talented *émigrés* **(chapter 6)**.

Another pervasive theme of the report is gender, which in itself would warrant a separate report in the context of migration **(chapters 2, 6, 11, 13, 19, 23)**. Women and men circulate differently in the global economy (Kofman, 2003), women predominantly entering (or being entered into) the services and welfare sectors; and apparently featuring in skilled migration streams only if admission policies are specifically developed for their preferred occupations (e.g. the previous H1A visa to recruit nurses and carers for the US) **(chapter 11)**. Migrant women play increasingly important roles as family providers and development agents in parts of Africa, Southeast Asia and South Asia, yet few data are collected on their remittance patterns. They also make up the majority of victims of trafficking in persons in the world.[7] They comprise 70 per cent of the estimated 25 million persons internally displaced by conflict, yet are generally not invited to the peace negotiating tables **(Textbox 1.1)**. This report draws attention to the fact that there is insufficient gender analysis in the migration field.

The report also shows how changes in migration patterns can reflect changes in approach to managing and collecting information on migration. For example, the surge of immigration in Europe at the

6. *Migration for Development in Africa Programme launched in 2000 (see chapters 2 and 16).*

7. *US Victims of Trafficking and Violence Prevention Act, Section 102, 2000.*

beginning of the 21st century can be partly explained by some of the large-scale regularization initiatives in southern European states, which make migrant populations statistically more visible **(chapter 7)**.

Many of the current patterns can be ascribed generally to globalization, but have also been greatly influenced by government policies. In 2004, the UN called for greater investment in migration policies that are balanced and avoid unnecessary social costs.[8] For example, where integration policies are absent or inadequate, migrants' lack of access to welfare can cause immea-surable social and financial costs; just as early policy interventions against trafficking can help reduce the risks and accompanying costs for poorer migrants, in particular women in vulnerable circumstances.

With increasing visibility and importance, migration also attracts more controversy, in both sending and receiving states, which in turn influences policies. While migration from poor countries to wealthy countries, and the possible return of migrants to their countries of origin, can offer good opportunities for advancing welfare and income in both countries of origin and destination, the divergent interests of economics and politics can make it difficult, if not impossible, to evaluate the costs and benefits of international migration – and to explain them publicly. Effects that look like benefits from an economic viewpoint might look like costs from the political perspective (*The Economist*, May 6, 2004).

World Migration 2005 aims to fill the most common gaps of knowledge about migration, and to do so by evaluating social, economic and political costs and benefits of migration, and pointing to areas for further research, to foster balanced public debate and policymaking.

STRUCTURE OF THE WORLD MIGRATION 2005 REPORT

REGIONAL OVERVIEW OF MIGRATION

The report begins with overviews of recent migration trends in the major world regions. It highlights the new importance of migration as an engine for regional cooperation in Africa, and how the African Union's Vision and Strategic Plan 2004-2007 places the diaspora at the centre of its aspirations to maximize the benefits of migration for development in Africa. 2004 saw the start of implementation of the OAU/AU decision of 2001 (Lusaka Decision) to develop a strategic migration policy framework for Africa **(chapters 1 and 2)**. New attention is given to the Middle East and the western Mediterranean regions, and their complex, volatile intra- and inter-regional labour migration dynamics. Emerging cooperation within these and with other regions is seen as critical for future successful management of migration, for example through the current efforts of the "5+5" process between the Maghreb and southern European states **(chapters 3 and 4)**.

The vast and complex migrant sending-receiving dynamics of the Americas are explored in terms of the measures and institutional changes effected by the US and Canada in the wake of the September 11 events, many of which have come to fruition in 2003 and 2004. The region is an important crucible for regional cooperation such as under the "Puebla Process",[9] and for pioneering work in remittance management. Migration in that region has become more internationalized, with more people emigrating to Europe rather than intra-regionally **(chapter 5)**.

This is a recent pattern also in Asia, the primary source of most of the world's immigrant-receiving countries. Asia offers some important models of

8. *See the 92nd session of the International Labour Conference, June, 2004, and the UN Secretary General's lecture at Columbia University, 2003, where he observed that restrictive policies can inadvertently lead to human rights abuse (e.g. irregular migrants have less access to occupational health and safety) (Annan, 2003).*

9. *Regional Conference on Migration begun in 1996 in Mexico (see chapter 22).*

labour emigration and diaspora management (for example in the Philippines and China).The intensified trade and economic activities spur both large-scale labour migration and huge irregular movements, with all the attendant health and human rights problems. The Oceania region, with its large immigrant-receiving states Australia and New Zealand, is today working more cooperatively to manage the growing incidence of smuggling and trafficking into and through the region; and to strengthen the capacities of its members, such as Papua New Guinea and other Pacific states, to cope with new migration challenges **(chapter 6).**

The *Europe* chapter highlights the critical demography-migration interplay for Europe; and the difficulty of collecting and using migration data across a region where definitions and concepts vary widely. Statistics reveal much about the prevailing immigration policy culture of a state; for example, statistics on foreign nationals are usually much higher in countries with low naturalization rates. The chapter provides an update on current EU priorities such as integration and border management, and common EU policies on asylum and migration achieved by 2004. In spite of the EU enlargement after 1 May 2004, Europe will need to develop proactive immigration policies after 2010, and draw more migrants from outside Europe, in order to remain competitive with other major immigrant receiving regions in the world **(chapter 7).**

Common themes covered in the regional chapters include the feminization of migration in some regions, the growing challenges of migration health, in particular HIV/AIDS, and the need for urgent, joint measures to combat migrant smuggling and trafficking in persons. These issues are further contextualized in the thematic chapters.

COSTS AND BENEFITS OF INTERNATIONAL MIGRATION – THE THEMATIC CHAPTERS

THE THEMATIC section of the report looks principally at the impacts of migration in terms of social, economic and political costs and benefits, and the investments of migrants, governments and societies in their attempts to steer migration to their benefit. It shows that the costs and benefits of migration tend to be unequally distributed across sectors and between sending and receiving countries. Looking at impacts, some chapters also consider causes, as the two are closely interlinked, and early actions can minimize costs further down the migration track. (chapters 8, 9, 13, 19, 20). The impetus for this theme has come from governments themselves, which increasingly need to be accountable for their policy choices in this complex area, with inadequate information and tools at their disposal.[10]

The overview chapter of this section **(chapter 8)** cautions that economic considerations alone do not determine migration policies; but economic arguments, notably about benefits and costs of migration, can play a critical part in policy making. It explores those arguments, over time and through theoretical models and empirical studies, and shows how they confirm the all-round beneficial effect of migration, with gains to all, or nearly all, involved – depending on contextual factors. It laments the lack of a sound and comprehensive analytical framework for assessing the effects of migration, but shows how this assessment could be achieved by pulling together all available theories, analyses, and empirical evidence in a balanced way.

Migration can have a minimal negative effect on wages, employment and welfare systems in receiving countries, but this is highly variable and dependent on the timeframe and contextual factors, including government policies. For example, the extent to

10. *See Papademetriou, 2003: "policy-makers are ... asked to make virtually instant calculations about complex cost-benefit ratios across a maddening array of policy domains – and all that with grossly inadequate information and crude policy tools."*

which immigrants may use welfare systems depends heavily on the integration policy of the receiving society (ibid). But successful integration can also create an environment conducive to productive diaspora activity of mutual longer-term benefit to the migrants and sending and receiving countries.

As new patterns of transnational mobility emerge, governments need to consider the trade potential of migration in the context of GATS (**Textbox 9.1**).[11] The greater openness of some GATS signatories to temporary labour schemes, and the palpable support of immigration to population planning in those countries, challenges GATS negotiators to expand the scope, or interpretation of the GATS provisions for temporary labour migration. Market openness makes migration work best. Some economists even see a far greater potential for economic growth in migration than in new trade rounds or international financial structures (**chapter 9**). The question is how to value migration in order to understand its beneficial force, and devise appropriate policies to manage this.

LABOUR MIGRATION

International labour migration generates a complex set of economic and social costs and benefits for the receiving country, migrant workers and their countries of origin. Families often pool their economic resources to send one member into the world to improve their lot back home; and an intricate network of recruiters, employers, immigration authorities, relatives and friends abroad makes the rest of the process possible (ibid).

All chapters in this section demonstrate the overall benefits of migration for receiving countries and the potential gains for sending countries. Most economists welcome migration of all types of workers from lower to higher-wage countries, since it tends to allocate scarce labour resources to their highest value use, allowing maximal global production. The economic gains from immigration are small but positive, with the benefits however invariably distributed unequally. Most gains accrue to the migrants and owners of capital, and can have positive flow-on effects for global GDP levels. The "losers" are often the local workers with similar skills to the migrants, but again the overall losses seem minimal (ibid). It is also difficult to measure the longer-term integration or diversity costs of labour migration (**chapters 9 and 17**).

The consequences may sometimes conflict with each other and therefore policies cannot be decided without certain trade-offs. One expert concludes that this makes the design of labour immigration policy an inherently moral exercise, requiring a discussion of values and ethics rather than just facts. Policy makers often have to choose between economic efficiencies, unequal wage distribution and human rights, and determine the most sustainable policy options for the individual, society, the country, the region and the world. Sorting the potential from real trade-offs is an important task for empirical research (**chapter 10**).

A cogent and cost/benefits-based argument is made in favour of a new and expanded Temporary Foreign Workers' programme as a realistic, cost-effective and rights-based policy option for governments in a world of globalized economies on the one hand, and sovereign migration management cultures on the other (**chapter 10**). Bilateral labour agreements are one way of framing such an approach (**Textbox 12.1**). The Philippines offers an important model of a highly regulated large-scale and widely marketed labour export programme, with or without bilateral agreements. It supports the case for inclusive government approaches (involving ministries of labour, foreign affairs, finance, interior and justice), and for comprehensive policies to protect migrants and enhance their new role as growth and development agents at both ends of the migration spectrum (**chapter 12**).

Skilled migration patterns in the Asia-Pacific region demonstrate how sending and receiving countries with vastly different economies and approaches to

11. *General Agreement on Trade in Services (see the Textbox "Trade and Migration: GATS Mode 4" in chapter 9).*

migration, ranging from the giant growth economies of China, Japan, Korea and the Taiwan Province of China to the poorer economies of Bangladesh, plan and manage labour migration. The benefits for receiving countries, or for sending countries with large economies, are well documented. But the costs for smaller, economically weaker sending countries, or for migrants in vulnerable situations, are not sufficiently known and factored into migration policies. There is a call for more ethical approaches by migrant receivers (**chapter 11**).

MIGRATION AND DEVELOPMENT

The relationship between migration and development is complex and difficult to assess, yet many national and international development agencies are seriously exploring ways of reaping the development gains from migration.[12] Public perceptions are often negative: migration grows out of and causes further poverty both in the sending and receiving country. Experts have examined the cause-effect relationship between migration and poverty and concluded that sometimes, where poverty does seem to result from migration and displacements, it is rather the result of poor policy planning (**chapter 13**).

The report looks at some still neglected research areas such as the potential for migration-induced poverty to generate destabilizing social movements, i.e. through the vicious cycle of migration-poverty- destruction-more poverty- more migration. Despite the paucity of data, there is emerging evidence that emigration brings relative benefits in terms of reducing absolute poverty, although not necessarily lessening deprivation (or perceptions of it). It is not a panacea for broad-based poverty (UK, 2004).

Remittances – a pervasive theme in the report (**chapters 8, 9, 13, 14, 15**) – are high on the agendas of governments and development agencies around the world, as they now seriously rival official development aid in many countries. All authors agree that remittances can help alleviate poverty under certain circumstances. One expert on Latin America and the Caribbean sees migrant remittances as critical for drawing developing countries into the global economy, particularly through the intermediation of migrant communities (hometown associations) (**chapter 15**).

Household surveys conducted over the past two years in Latin America, Europe and Asia confirm the beneficial impact of remittances on vulnerable households (making up 80 per cent of household income for recipients in Armenia, for example (**chapters 13, 14, 15**)). Migration impacts sometimes play themselves out most significantly at the local level, and in the economic tensions between rural and urban development (**chapter 13**).

But the effect of remittances as development aids is often limited. For example, migrants who settle abroad and have their family join them are likely to contribute less to development through remittances. Experts warn against an over-reliance on remittances, and urge that they be seen as an initial investment in longer-term economic growth rather than a way of life (**chapters 13 and 14**). They should also not be concentrated in one sector to the disadvantage of others (e.g. construction over agriculture).

Some major growing economies in Asia are seeing a shift from *brain drain* to *brain gain*, also as a result of increasingly pro-active policies to attract back émigrés with newly acquired skills and education (China, Philippines, India). Governments ranging from Morocco to Bangladesh have esta-blished ministries/departments or agencies to deal with their *émigré* communities (including the Hassan II Foundation for Moroccans living abroad and the "amicales" (friendly associations) created by Maghreb countries to act on behalf of their governments as official or associated offices to manage expatriate affairs and relations with host countries (**chapter 4**).

Regarding the role migrants can play in supporting development of their home countries, one author

12. *See, for example: Newland, 2004; UK House of Commons, 2004; and the World Bank, 2004.*

corrects a frequently made complaint that remittance costs are too high. In fact, transfer costs can be quite low in some places, such as the Philippines where they range from less than one per cent to 2.5 per cent. High costs can also be caused by inefficiencies in the regulatory framework, e.g. ad hoc rules can often hinder competition in the remittance industry (**chapter 14**). Governments may need to be circumspect about imposing management strategies on migrants and their families at the expense of household survival strategies: obliging remittance recipients to save more and consume less could reduce their personal welfare. Regulatory and compliance requirements should as far as possible be harmonized between sending and receiving countries.

One chapter explores the potential for sending countries to gain from the improved human capital of their returning migrants. Given the vagaries of migration, and the vast differences in institutional capacities and approaches across sending and receiving countries, this requires careful planning and cooperation, particularly of incentives for return, and involving migrants and home communities in jointly drawing the benefits from this (**chapter 16**).

There is still insufficient analysis of the contribution of migrants to development – both skilled and unskilled; or of such social issues as gender and the economic participation of women; and the extent to which temporary labour migration schemes can factor in the potential gains of both virtual and actual return of migrants and their families.

MIGRANT INTEGRATION

At a time of growing resistance to migration in many receiving countries, effective policies aimed at socio-economic inclusion of migrants in their host communities can generate immediate and longer-term benefits for all involved. Better access to employment, education and support services can help migrants and their families adjust and become supportive members of their community; and mutual engagement of migrants, NGOs, community groups and government in activities to foster inclusion can strengthen a society's ability to withstand social shocks and conflicts. According to one study, the costs of integration are higher in those countries where there is less NGO involvement (**Textbox 17.1**).

One author notes that global pressures are levelling the differences among destination countries, and that over time, there will be convergences in the way governments and societies value integration as a strategy for social stability, and hence policies on migration and integration will also converge as a matter of necessity and expedience (**chapter 17**). Another compares the interfaces between migration and welfare across the different welfare regimes of a) Scandinavian countries, b) continental Europe and c) the US and the UK. He focuses on the policy dilemma of open versus exclusive approaches to migration, or how to keep unwanted migrants out while letting desired migrants in, from the perspective of how governments organize their welfare regimes (**chapter 18**).

The World Values Survey indicates that advanced industrial societies are becoming more open to diversity. The report looks at some existing and potential models and approaches to ensuring that diversity is managed to the mutual benefit of migrants and society.

MIGRATION AND HEALTH

Migration health is a critical issue for policymakers, yet few governments have included it in their public policies, either on health or migration. The report explains that the social and economic costs of neglecting migration health, also as a public health issue, can be immeasurable (**chapter 19**). It gives concrete examples of how targeted investment of migration policies and development aid can address this both in terms of prevention and assistance. Stigmas arising from perceptions of poor migrant health, for example, can cost society by undermining the benefits of migration. In developed countries, public health policies often target the general population but elude the migrants, yet ill health and even transmission of disease can occur after arrival in the receiving country (**chapter 20**). Policymakers need to understand how the immigration experience can increase vulnerability to ill health, yet migrants are often the last to seek medical attention for a variety of reasons ranging from socio-cultural habits to clandestine status. This is not just a migration but a public health issue.

HIV/AIDS is the starkest reminder today that public health is also a development issue, with the pandemic causing far greater long-term damage to national economies than previously assumed.[13] For example, by depleting families it wrecks an important mechanism for human capital formation, the basis for longer-term economic growth. But there is evidence that early, targeted investment in migration health can also have direct benefits for economic development **(chapter 20)**. Women are particularly vulnerable to risky behaviour resulting from migration, including those left behind by migrating men, and where the spouse does not send money home regularly. The risk of HIV infection among migrants and their families differs from region to region, but ultimately depends on good governance including migrant health in public health, education and information policies **(chapters 19 and 20)**.

INSTITUTIONAL MEASURES TO MANAGE MIGRATION

One of the key messages to emerge from the report is that policy and institutional environments are as important a determinant of the success of migration as, for example, the socio-economic performance of the migrants. Making the right policy choices is ultimately the best way for governments to steer migration in the direction of benefits over costs. A recent study comparing two traditional immigration countries with similar migration regimes found that, despite many similarities in their economies, political systems, living standards and broad approaches to immigration, one experienced a better labour market performance among recent migrants than the other, for reasons relating to a more centralized administration, more stringent selection criteria and more incentive-inducing social security policies.[14]

One of the chapters dealing with this issue asks whether traditional cost-benefit analysis in support of migration policies still makes sense in the wake of the September 11 events and the imperative for effective anti terrorism measures at any cost **(chapter 21)**. It shows how more efficient visa processing can benefit the governments and the migrants **(Textbox 21.1)**. The UK claims it is achieving real savings from its Biometric Identification Programme to check migrant access to social assistance; and the EU-wide electronic database Eurodac is helping to better manage and maintain the integrity of asylum systems across Europe. At a time when many governments are on high security alert regarding international terrorism, advanced computer information and visa systems, such as the APEC[15] Business Travel Card can be critical for raising confidence in joint migration management schemes **(Textbox 22.2)**.

The final thematic chapter deals with the crucial issue of how governments work together more efficiently today at regional and global levels **(chapter 22)**. It looks at old and new consultative and dialogue processes and how they have progressed in the past two years or so from dialogue to action. Regional processes can often leverage efforts at bilateral agreements, but also help place migration on the agendas of larger regional economic processes. Concrete projects have resulted from the "5+5" and Puebla processes, the Labour Ministers' conferences in Colombo and Manila and the Pacific Immigration Directors' Conference (PIDC) in the past two years, to name a few examples. In the Pacific, partner countries have started to develop a regional advanced passenger information system along ICAO standards (ibid).

13. *For example, South Africa could face progressive economic collapse within several generations unless it successfully combats the HIV/AIDS epidemic (ibid). A report recently completed for UNDP in Asia concludes that Asia may face a bigger AIDS pandemic than Africa in the coming years (chapter 11).*

14. *The study by Richardson and Lester, 2004, compared the different approaches and levels of effectiveness of Australia's centralized, federal system and Canada's de-centralized, provincial system in managing migration. It also compared the two countries' different systems for selecting migrants and dispensing social welfare entitlements, and the respective impact of these on migrant labour performance.*

15. *Asia Pacific Economic Cooperation.*

The UN is now attempting to correct a situation where migration has been lightly institutionalized within the UN system (UN, 2003). The independent Global Commission on International Migration (GCIM) will report in 2005 to the Secretary General on substantive questions related to current migration dialogues. Also, within IOM, the annual Council session has become an important venue for inter-governmental policy dialogue, and the 92nd session of the International Labour conference (ILC) in 2004 has pointed the way to a non-binding multilateral framework for a rights-based approach to labour migration.

MIGRATION DATA AND STATISTICS

The final section of the report tours the international migration trends recorded and analysed by the UN Population Division (UNPD), as supporting the discussion of key trends in the earlier chapters. Tables and maps derived from the UNPD, OECD, World Bank, Eurostat and others throw light on some of the less discussed issues such as population, female migration, regularization programmes, foreign students, IDPs, refugees and irregular migration.

IOM statistics also demonstrate the kind of data collected on the ground that may assist policymakers in the key areas of migrant resettlement, return migration, migration health and counter trafficking. These data are unique to IOM and serve to support many of the conclusions and policy pointers in the report.

CONCLUSION

Many of the chapters in this report bring to light the need for better management of public perceptions of migration, and by extension, for more results-oriented research and consistent data collection. Even some of the now well established regional consultative processes still lack reliable data collection mechanisms, also to evaluate their own effectiveness as migration policy-driving mechanisms (chapter 22). Despite excellent statistics collected by many governments and international agencies, there are still major disparities in methodology, which can hamper comparative analysis and far-sighted policy making.

Causes and impacts of migration and the policies to manage it are not easy to categorize, and even less easy to measure. The report aims to close some of the gaps of unpredictability about migration management, not for purposes of controlling migration, but to ensure maximum benefits derived from it for migrants, governments and society. It points to areas requiring more research, such as the real impact of remittances on poverty alleviation, the effect of the new liberalized forms of recruiting skilled immigrants from within a foreign community on future migration and emigration patterns; the emerging role of women diasporas as development agents, and what could today be useful indicators and determinants of costs and benefits of international migration. Recent studies and surveys in Europe, such as the European Social Survey (ESS) on the attitudes towards immigration, and behavioural patterns of its diverse populations, can be valuable guides for policy choices on such vital new areas of migration management as integration and social stability.[16]

Exploding the myths and establishing more clearly the facts about migration and its consequences is a sure way of enabling the debates and design of migration policies to be more informed and reasoned. With its focus on "costs and benefits" of migration, World Migration 2005 is intended to make a useful contribution to this end.

16. *See Dustmann and Preston, 2004, and the European Social Survey: www.europeansocialsurvey.org/*

SECTION 1

REGIONAL OVERVIEW SELECTED GEOGRAPHIC REGIONS

Africa and the Middle East

CHAPTER 1
MIGRATION: AN OPPORTUNITY FOR AFRICA?[1]

AFRICA[2] FACES enormous difficulties with the management of international migration: the issues are sensitive and give rise to heated debate, all too often swayed by negative attitudes and an excessive tendency towards protectionism, including in developing countries.

Africa is now the only continent in the world that still faces all of the classic obstacles to successful development:

- More than a third of the countries are experiencing armed conflicts or civil wars, a situation that has sometimes lasted for years and led to major forced population displacements.
- Education and health systems have continued to deteriorate under the combined impact of population growth (still close to 3% per annum) and structural adjustment plans.
- The AIDS pandemic is affecting Africa more than any other region in the world and is depriving it of the human resources it needs to advance economically, as well as to care for the younger generation, which includes millions of orphans.
- Natural hazards, especially drought, and the growing pressure on cities because of uncontrolled rural exodus, aggravate internal demographic imbalances and generate major social problems.
- The brain drain, which has continued steadily since the period of independence, is depriving African countries of a very significant part of their skilled human resources, which they have often trained at considerable cost.

The continent now has a population of around 680 million, of whom almost 50 per cent live below the poverty threshold. The 25 members of the European Union (EU) have a total population of 630 million, which, according to forecasts, should only grow to 632 million by 2050, due to falling birth rates, while Africa's population will grow to between 1.6 and 1.8 billion (UNPD, 2002; UNPD, 2001).

As all studies tend to show, the extreme poverty that affected the Asian continent for the greater part of the 20th century is now having its biggest impact on the African continent at the beginning of the 21st century.

During the 20th century, most developed countries introduced stricter laws, regulations and border controls for the admission and residence of foreigners. They took these measures to prevent a large-scale inflow of economic migrants and asylum seekers, but also to protect and regulate their labour markets better and enable them to actively select the qualified migrants required in many sectors of the western economies.

In Europe, the sub-Saharan diaspora has been mainly concentrated in France (274,538) and the UK (249,720)[3] and, to a lesser degree, in Germany (156,564) and Italy (137,780). In the US, there are a

1. *The authors of this chapter are Ndioro Ndiaye, Deputy Director General of IOM, and Philippe Boncour, Special Assistant to the Deputy Director General.*

2. *This chapter covers the regions and countries of sub-Saharan Africa: southern Africa (Angola, Botswana, Lesotho, Malawi, Mozambique, Namibia, South Africa, Swaziland, Zambia, Zimbabwe); East Africa and the Horn of Africa (Djibouti, Eritrea, Ethiopia, Kenya, Somalia, Sudan, Tanzania, Uganda); Central Africa (Democratic Republic of the Congo, Republic of Congo, Burundi, Cameroon, Central African Republic, Equatorial Guinea, Gabon, Rwanda, Sao Tome and Principe) and West Africa (Benin, Burkina Faso, Cape Verde, Chad, Côte d'Ivoire, Gambia, Ghana, Guinea, Guinea-Bissau, Liberia, Mali, Mauritania, Niger, Nigeria, Senegal, Sierra Leone, Togo).*

3. *Source: European Social Statistics (Eurostat), Migration, Luxembourg, 2002.*

total of 881,300 African residents,[4] divided fairly distinctly into three blocks: from the Horn of Africa plus Egypt and Morocco, the coastal countries of West Africa and South Africa. Migration flows are considerable and available data, which exclude migrants not reliably accounted for in consular or administrative statistics, do not truly reflect the full size of global immigration to the US. Lastly, intra-African migration concerns mainly Libya, the coastal states of West and Central Africa and South Africa, which have traditionally presented attractive destinations for migrants.

This demonstrates the importance of migration issues for international relations. Africa, which faces a huge challenge in managing population movements, both within the continent and between continents, finds itself at a crossroads at this critical time in its history. While it is still affected by negative structural trends, there are indications of change ahead.

- Regarding relations between the ACP countries and the EU, the current review of the Cotonou Agreement provides an opportunity to refine the articles dealing with migration (articles 13, 79 and 80) and adapt them to recent developments, in particular to achieve agreement on the conditions of legal migration, in terms both of content and estimated numbers. Only a joint approach supported by large-scale information campaigns can reduce irregular migration, improve governance in the countries of origin and rebalance technical cooperation arrangements between countries of the North and the South.

- NEPAD,[5] which is underwritten by heads of state, illustrates the ability of governments to come up with innovative, combined solutions for the development of the continent, including better use of migrants' know-how as a means of enhancing national human resources. This applies especially to the revival and improvement of social sectors like health and education, but also other areas such as conflict resolution and border control.

A general framework for progress is thus in place, aimed at sound economic and social governance, and the diasporas have a role to play in its implementation, both by making their know-how available and by contributing a proportion of their repatriated funds to development projects.

The full and complete integration of NEPAD into the institutional framework of the African Union is a significant step forward. This initiative has received the backing of the international community, precisely because of its underlying endogenous approach.

- Thus, in its Preamble, the new Constitution of the African Union,[6] adopted by the member states following the period of transition, recognizes the role of migrants, who are considered to be an integral part of national human resources, regardless of their place of residence. The African Union Commission is currently developing a Strategic Framework for the management of migration, and engaging in many consultations among member states.

This document provides a basis for genuine continental cooperation in the area of migration management, and facilitates a transversal understanding of the issue by encouraging vertical exchanges between sectors and horizontal exchanges between countries. Migration is now managed by a special unit within the African Union, which makes it easier to deal with all the various related problems.

4. *Source: Statistical Yearbook of the Immigration and Naturalization Service, Washington. D.C. 2002.*

5. *The New Partnership for Africa's Development (NEPAD) is a strategic vision and framework for Africa's renewal, formally adopted by the 37th Summit of the OAU in July 2001. It is also an African Union programme aimed at promoting its development objectives. It has been assigned several priorities, including peace and security, economic integration and regional cooperation, and capacity building.*

6. *The African Union, with headquarters in Addis Ababa, officially took over from the Organization of African Unity on 9 July 2002, in Durban, South Africa, with the goal of speeding up the process of integration on the continent. The AU is the continent's prime institution dedicated to socio-economic development and integration. Its aim is to promote peace, security and stability on the continent as a basis for implementing its programme of development and integration. In this respect, its Constitutive Act "invites and encourages the full participation of the African diaspora in the building of the African Union".*

- Among the Regional Economic Communities, the new awareness of the need to discuss migration has already led to informal, non-binding dialogues, involving especially member states of the Southern Africa Development Community (SADC) and the Intergovernmental Authority on Development (IGAD).[7] Several cooperation agreements already concluded are facilitating information exchange, joint training programmes and political consultations. Regional cooperation on migration can, in combination with other actions, contribute to the return of peace and stability in areas of unrest, as shown by several cases within ECOWAS.[8]

  This system of exchange and dialogue is now being applied, at different stages, among all the Regional Economic Communities of the continent (COMESA, EAC, IGAD, SADC, ECOWAS) as well as among member countries of the CENSAD and AMU.[9]

The systematic inclusion of migration issues in regional, subregional and national agendas in Africa should contribute towards better regional and continental integration, one of the main driving forces of development. If this new awareness is to have the desired effects on development, however, the African countries must take action aimed at:

- strengthening the technical capacities of personnel in charge of migration management;
- supporting legislative and regulatory provisions able to be adapted to key political priorities;
- taking account of the implications of mobility of persons for health and social issues;
- combating human trafficking, an issue which used to be taboo in African societies, but is now being taken up by politicians, both domestically and in relations with countries receiving emergency humanitarian assistance for persons displaced as a result of natural disasters, wars and crises;
- protecting migrants' rights by providing information on the international legal instruments that concern them and training;
- better valuing migrants' contributions, for example through programmes like IOM's Migration for Development in Africa (MIDA) programme,[10] which supports the positive contribution for both the North and the South of migrants, through the circulation of know-how and transfers of funds from abroad to countries of origin, to transform the "brain drain" into a "brain gain".

The notion of joint or shared development is now central to the improvement of relations between African countries and other continents and provides an interesting lead for future development aid. It is based on the idea of a genuine partnership in the sustainable development of traditional emigration areas through settling local populations in favourable environments equipped with basic services.

It is thus clear why migration issues are a vital component of national poverty reduction strategies and should be taken into account within the UN Millennium Development Goals. Apart from the technical capacities of migrants to compensate shortcomings in the home country, repatriation of migrant funds can significantly help finance development.

The sums transferred by migrant workers can be very large. It is estimated that in 2002 the equivalent of USD 4 billion was officially transferred to sub-Saharan Africa (Ratha, 2003). These sums account for a significant portion of GDP of African countries. One

---

7. *The Southern Africa Development Community (SADC), set up in Windhoek, Namibia, on 17 July 1992, has 14 member states. Its aims are free trade, free circulation of persons, democracy and respect for human rights.*
The mission of the Intergovernmental Authority on Development (IGAD), with headquarters in Djibouti, is to achieve regional cooperation and economic integration by promoting road safety, intraregional commerce and development.

8. *The Economic Community of West African States (ECOWAS) is a regional group of 15 countries set up in 1975 with the mission of promoting economic integration in all economic areas, such as industry, transport, telecommunications and energy.*

9. *COMESA: Common Market for Eastern and Southern Africa; EAC: East African Community; IGAD: Intergovernmental Authority on Development; SADC: Southern African Development Community; ECOWAS: Economic Community of West African States; CENSAD: Community of Sahelo-Saharan States; AMU: Arab Maghreb Union.*

10. *Endorsed by a decision of the Heads of State and Government at the Lusaka Summit in 2001, MIDA expands on the earlier, long-running Return of Qualified African Nationals programme (RQAN).*

example is Cape Verde, where fund transfers amount to USD 75 million a year, or 12.5 per cent of GDP. They also surpass the official development aid received by certain countries. In Eritrea, for instance, fund transfers amount to USD 141 million, while official development aid totals USD 148 million; hence the need to pay closer attention to the leveraging effects of such funds on development.

A major part of migrant transfers has always been used to meet the needs of families and relatives. Nevertheless, studies show that these funds are more constant than other financial contributions. They have increased steadily over the last 20 years, while official development aid has fallen for many countries; and the flows have been relatively immune to international financial crises or violent conflicts. Fund transfers potentially strengthen local and national economic growth in developing countries, while improving their balance of payments. But these benefits need to be balanced in a realistic way against other concerns about possible security risks involved in international fund transfers, and the need to render the immediate benefits more sustainable.

In the light of above considerations, increasing attention is paid by the World Bank and others to the creation of innovative remittance management instruments and the combining of fund transfers with ODA, and even with foreign direct investment. Efforts are being made to reduce transfer costs, and to channel part of the repatriated funds into income-generating activities and the creation of local wealth, and to involve migrants in the management of such funds.

African leaders should also look to Latin America, the Caribbean and Asia, and their experience regarding information, training and migration management programmes to strengthen the role of migrants, and of migration generally, in their development agendas. Through increased common action within the framework of the African Union and other regional processes, Africa can create stronger internal and external synergies and make the voice of developing countries heard in decision-making about the best options for Africa's future.

TEXTBOX 1.1

THE ROLE OF (MIGRANT) WOMEN IN POST-CONFLICT RECONSTRUCTION AND DEVELOPMENT

Of the estimated 25 million people displaced internally by conflicts around the world, more than 70 per cent are women and children (Cohen 1998; Rehn and Sirleaf, 2002). Many of these are inevitably victims at a number of levels – as survivors of psycho-social trauma, of sexual abuse, or simply struggling for economic survival while the men are at war.

Notwithstanding this, women can also be active and convincing partners for peace in post-conflict reconstruction efforts. During conflicts, they often have to assume sole responsibility for their household and develop creative survival strategies for themselves and their families, including medical, economic and administrative tasks. They are also frequently engaged in sensitizing communities to a culture of peace. Despite this, they are almost always absent from the peace negotiating tables, and all too often remain an untapped source for peace work.

In 1995, the Fourth World Conference on Women and the adoption of the Beijing Platform for Action highlighted the urgency and importance of involving women in all stages of post-conflict activities. In 2000, the twenty-third special session of the UN General Assembly devoted to Women 2000: Gender Equality, Development and Peace for the Twenty-first Century gave further impetus to women's full participation at all levels of decision making in peace processes.[11] The momentum intensified in October 2000 when, with Resolution 1325 on women, peace and security, for the first time in its history the UN Security Council acknowledged that women had a key role to play in promoting international stability and peace. The resolution called on all parties to ensure women's participation in peace processes, from the prevention of conflict, to negotiations and post-war reconstruction.[12] Yet, despite these international efforts, on the ground women and girls continue to be seen mainly as victims of conflict, not as potential actors or partners in peace.

For this reason, international organizations, NGOs and others have over recent years made substantial efforts to develop the role of women in post-conflict activities and social and economic reconstruction. For example, IOM has tried to empower women as sources for development by ensuring that post-conflict and demobilization programmes in, for instance, Mozambique and Angola, take account of nutrition, reproductive health and equality between the sexes, by training women to manage microenterprises in Armenia, Azerbaijan, Timor Leste, and Vietnam, through psycho-social counselling of women in post-conflict Kosovo (Serbia and Montenegro), and by engaging indigenous women in their own social reinsertion into community life in Guatemala.

Awareness-raising seminars are another strategy employed by IOM and others in post-conflict situations to strengthen women's role as actors in peace processes. One such memorable event was the Seminar on Conflict Resolution, Confidence-building and Peace Enhancement among Somali Women, organized by IOM in Hargeisa, Somaliland, in 2001, to promote awareness of the important role Somali women could play in the reconstruction of their country through constructive dialogue with belligerent clans.

In 2003, similar workshops were held on the role of women in reconstruction and development in Rwanda and the Democratic Republic of the Congo. Again, they aimed at empowering women socially and economically through engagement in microenterprises and as agents of change in achieving peace, ethnic reconciliation, economic development and conflict prevention. Each workshop brought together over 100 professional women, including ministers, judges, lawyers, law enforcement officials, businesswomen and journalists, to discuss among other topics, good governance, the influence of women in preventing conflicts through income-generating activities, access to microcredits, engagement of the diaspora in development, and women and the media. A third workshop held that same year in Guinea-Conakry focused on microcredit management and capacity building through the mobilization of women in the Guinean diaspora.

These are just a few examples of how awareness-raising and income-generating projects can promote the role of women, including migrant women, in the re-establishment of peace. IOM has specifically endeavoured to draw migrant women into such activities, to harness their potential honed through coping strategies developed in displacement or forced migration situations, to post-conflict reconstruction and development efforts.

Source: Denise Glasscock, Gender Coordinator, IOM Geneva.

11. *See the Report of the UN Secretary General on Women's equal participation in conflict prevention, management and conflict resolution and in post-conflict peace-building, E/CN.6/2004/10, 22 December 2003.*

12. *See the Women Waging Peace web portal: www.womenwagingpeace.net*

CHAPTER 2
MIGRATION TRENDS IN SUB-SAHARAN AFRICA (SSA)[1]

INTRODUCTION

AFRICA[2] accounts for one-quarter of the world's land mass and one-tenth of its population, and is the continent with the most mobile populations in the world (Curtin, 1997). In 2000, there were 16.3 million international migrants in Africa, accounting for some 9 per cent of global migrant stocks. Refugees have always been an important factor, but by 2000 both the numbers and the global share of refugees had declined from, respectively, 5.4 million or 33 per cent in 1990, to 3.6 million or 22 per cent. During that same period, the number of non-refugee migrants rose by nearly 2 million to reach 12.7 million in 2000 (UN, 2003). The proportion of females among the 16.3 million international migrants rose from 42 per cent in the 1970s to 46 per cent in the 1990s, and to 46.7 per cent in 2000 (Zlotnik, 2004).

Africa includes a large share of the world's poorest states, accounting for some 49 per cent of the total population, or 323 million people living below the poverty line (UNDP, 2003). Deteriorating living conditions and growing rural and urban poverty continue to push more and more people to move in search of livelihoods (DFID, 2004). The number of Africans living outside their country of origin has more than doubled in a generation, and African states are faced with the critical challenge of managing migration in the 21st century.

Migration flows within and out of Africa tend to display the following characteristics:

i) internal and cross-border migration as strategies to cope with ecological and economic problems;
ii) movements towards areas of relative prosperity and stability, triggered by intraregional disparities;
iii) increased transit migration through North Africa, the gateway to Europe;
iv) increased clandestine and irregular migration as a result of restrictive immigration policies of the North, but also involving trafficking of persons from within Africa;
v) higher international mobility of qualified and skilled persons from SSA to developed countries, and
vi) increased feminization of migration (although still under-represented when compared with other regions).[3]

Urbanization and population pressures, experienced as much more pressing than in other regions of the world, have serious implications for migration management and regional integration. The emigration of skilled individuals needs to be looked at afresh in the context of development cooperation benefiting both countries of origin and destination. Migration as a multi-sectoral issue barely features in national development strategies, and has not been adequately addressed in any of the development frameworks prescribed for Sub-Saharan Africa (MDGs, PRSP, NEPAD, TICAD).

1. *This chapter was written by Meera Sethi, Regional Adviser for Sub-Saharan Africa, IOM, Geneva.*

2. *In this chapter, the term "Africa is used as an abbreviated reference to Sub-Saharan Africa (SSA), which comprises the 47 African countries south of the Sahara, and does not include Egypt, Algeria, Morocco, Tunisia, Libya and Mauritania.*

3. *See also the discussion of this issue in the chapter on "International Migration Trends".*

This chapter looks broadly at recent and current migration challenges confronting Sub-Saharan Africa, including the feminization of migration, the spreading scourge of HIV/AIDS, the trafficking of women and children, and the evolving role of the African diasporas in the development efforts of sub-Saharan states. It discusses the new importance of migration as an engine for regional cooperation and integration, and the emerging cooperation between SSA, its northern African neighbours and European destination countries. It looks at actions taken across the continent in 2004 to start putting into effect the OAU/AU decision of 2001 (Lusaka Decision) to develop a strategic framework for migration policy in Africa, and identifies some broad future policy directions for African governments.

HISTORY'S LEGACY

Africa's colonization and post-independence links with former colonial metropolises have largely shaped the continent's prevailing migration trends (Miller 2003; Adepoju, 2004). With few exceptions, the volume and intensity of population movements were influenced by factors as diverse as long-distance trade, the needs of mining, plantations and agriculture, the search for pastures, the effects of droughts and land degradation. The "centres of economic activity and trade" that attracted a pool of labour to the more developed capital cities, the urban centres or the coastal towns created a circulatory migration of workers between home and plantations (East Africa), the mines (Southern Africa) and the coastal forest zones (West Africa). Today, these movements form the basis of the progressive pattern of migration from rural areas to the cities, and on to foreign destinations (Adepoju, 2004).

The ethnic and territorial configurations[4] that split members of ethnic, tribal and linguistic groups among two or more adjoining states, and often cited as the cause for many of the conflicts persisting in Africa today, have also had a bearing on traditional migratory movements. During the period 1993-2002, 27 of the 53 independent African states suffered from armed conflicts (Eriksson et al., 2003) resulting in massive forced migration. Sub-Saharan Africa accounts for about 13.0 million refugees and asylum seekers, and 21.8 million internally displaced persons (IDPs), a total of 34.8 million uprooted, and 4.28 million newly uprooted people around the world (USCR, 2003).

The Pan-Africanism that shaped the early development policies of African states is not without its ramifications for African migration as well. African states, driven by the conviction that development and emancipation cannot be achieved without also pooling natural and human resources, focused on the creation of regional groupings as homogeneous economic areas within which to move goods and persons around freely, and provide better access to economic opportunities inside common borders (Ricca, 1989).[5] While such regional entities as the Economic Community of West African States (ECOWAS) and the East African Community (EAC) have made considerable progress in establishing regional migration regimes, efforts in the South African Development Community (SADC) have been rather slow. Mobility is more restricted, pursued more on a country-to-country than a multilateral basis (ECA, 2004).

The significant outflows of SSA migrants were mainly directed towards Western Europe, but also to North America and the Arab region. Many were traditionally directed towards former colonial powers; for example Congolese emigrating to Belgium, Senegalese to France, Nigerians to the UK, Cape Verdeans to Portugal. Many migrants left for higher education and specialized training, thus contributing to the brain-

4. *This refers to the division of the continent into politico-administrative entities (which later became independent states) that split members of ethnic, tribal and linguistic groups into two or more adjoining states.*

5. *Pan-Africanism in its absolute form is the merger of two or more States. For over 25 years, there were a number of attempts at unity amongst various countries, which felt inhibited by the boundaries created by the colonial authorities. For example: the Ghana-Guinea Union; the Sudan and Egypt union; Tanganyika and Zanzibar joining to become the United Republic of Tanzania; the Federation of Mali, which grouped together Benin (Dahaomey), Burkina Faso, Mali and Senegal (and broke up twenty months later); and Rwanda Urundi dissolved to become Rwanda and Burundi. Attempts to secede and form new independent states were also rejected. Seventeen intergovernmental groupings of varying scope and size were formed, with some groups dissolving over time.*

drain on the continent. The recent crisis in the health sector caused by the out-migration of health care providers from Sub-Saharan Africa has once again brought the issue of "brain-drain" onto the development agenda. Intercontinental migration has since diversified, and increasingly includes poorly educated labour migrants, who migrate in significant numbers to destinations such as Spain, the Netherlands, Germany, Italy, Canada, the US and the Middle East.

THE FEMINIZATION OF SUB-SAHARAN MIGRATION

THE PROPORTION of females among international migrants in Africa has increased steadily and faster than at the world level. In the 1960s, Africa had the lowest proportion (42%) compared with Latin America and the Caribbean (45%) and Asia (46%). Today, female migrants account for almost 47 per cent of the stock of 16 million migrants in Africa, while in Asia the proportion has declined to 43 per cent (Zlotnik, 2003). More and more women are moving independently, not simply accompanying husbands or other family members, but to meet their own economic needs. They are becoming primary wage earners and taking jobs in domestic work, cleaning restaurants and hotels, child rearing, care of the elderly, but also as more specialized nurses and hospital aides (UN World Survey, 1999).

Women migrants are also sustaining families at home through their remittances. Indeed, they tend to remit more of their income than male migrants, both as international and internal migrants, as indicated in the World Survey. In Africa, a similar pattern has been observed in studies of remittance behaviour of internal migrants, particularly in rural South Africa, where it was concluded that "employed migrant men are 25 per cent less likely than employed migrant women to remit" (Collinson, 2003). As women migrants generally earn less than their male counterparts, their total available revenue is much lower. On the darker side, female migrants are more vulnerable to human rights abuses, since they frequently work in gender-segregated and unregulated sectors of the economy, such as domestic work, the entertainment and the sex industry, unprotected by labour legislation or social policy.

Most women move voluntarily, through legal channels. But, a significant proportion resort to irregular channels and become vulnerable to discrimination, exploitation and physical and sexual abuse. Many are forced migrants, who have fled conflict, persecution, natural disasters and other situations that affect their habitat and livelihood. Women and children today account for some 70 per cent of the African refugee and internally displaced populations and are subject to a wide range of problems, including security threats, sexual harassment, violence, abuse and breakdown of the family support system (UNHCR, 2002).

The feminization of migration is one of the most significant migratory patterns in Africa, as it is gradually changing the role of both female and male migrants as well as the traditional African family cultures. In particular, the migration of women is affecting the development processes on the continent, and "creating new challenges for public policy".[6]

INTERNAL MIGRATION AND URBANIZATION

AFRICA'S increasing urbanization is generating significant internal population movements (Simone, 2003). While insufficient data exist regarding the magnitude, available statistics indicate a current rate of urbanization in Africa of 3.5 per cent a year (UNCHS, 2001), the highest in the world, resulting in the rapid growth of urban agglomerations throughout the continent. By 2030, the proportion of Africa's urbanized population is expected to reach 54 per cent, compared

6. *According to the Fifth World Survey on the Role of Women in Development: Globalization, Gender and Work which addresses mobility from a gender perspective, the challenges related to immigration and refugee policies include: family reunification and formation, labour migration, trafficking, smuggling and forced migration.*

to 38 per cent today (UNPD, 2002). This urban explosion, a combination of rapid urbanization and high rates of natural population growth that affects both rural and urban areas, poses many social and economic challenges to African governments, including for migration management and regional integration.

While urbanization is an integral part of economic and social development in both the developed and developing countries, if rapid and unregulated, it can have adverse consequences for migrating and urban populations by straining the existing urban infrastructure and services and resulting in higher rates of urban poverty, lack of access to adequate housing, health care, education and other services, as well as environmental degradation. The heavy influx of people into urban areas increases socio-economic problems in the cities, but eventually also creates labour shortages in rural areas. These costs of migration may far exceed the benefits to migrants and societies (Todaro, 1997).

The movement of people from rural to urban areas to occupy positions vacated by persons having emigrated is considered a form of "replacement migration". In some instances, these "replacement" migrants could also be from neighbouring countries, as part of the village-city-foreign destination pattern mentioned above (Adepoju, 2004).

Internal migration in Africa has also been influenced by forced migration patterns. The endemic problems of IDPs and internal trafficking play a major role in internal migration in Africa. The development of high-risk corridors and their links to HIV, prostitution and trafficking are further characteristics of such migration trends. Few governments have established policies or strategies to effectively manage internal migration. The controls that are taken for granted at international borders are rarely acceptable (or applied) within countries (Gugler, 1996).

Promoting sustainable urbanization is therefore a priority concern for African governments and development partners in the years ahead, also for effective migration management. Some efforts to address the situation have been initiated by international agencies such as ILO, HABITAT and UNEP in the context of their mandates to address the rural-urban bias.

CROSS-BORDER MIGRATION

MOST OF THE 16 million or so migrants within Africa have crossed borders into neighbouring or other African countries. They are unevenly distributed among the regions. In 2000, 42 per cent were living in West Africa, 28 per cent in East Africa, 12 per cent in northern Africa, and 9 per cent in central and southern Africa (Zlotnik, 2003).

Populations along many border regions live in unstable circumstances, in part due to war, ethnic fighting and/or drought. Ethnic groups in Africa often inhabit areas on both sides of political borders (i.e. in East Africa, Somalis move between the border regions of north-east Ethiopia, southern Kenya and northern Djibouti, while Sudan shares borders and ethnic groups with nine countries; in West Africa, Tuaregs and Hausas live on the borders shared by Nigeria, Niger, Cameroon and southern Algeria; the Fulanis live along many common borders from the western to the southern region). The inhabitants of these border regions, which are fairly large, are engaged in a perpetual cycle of migration due to cross-border economic activity and pastoralist traditions.

These people often move within their ethnic areas, which frequently involves the crossing of international borders as the endemic cycles of drought and water shortages in the region cause population displacements. Linguistic and cultural borders between various ethnic groups are often stronger barriers than international political boundaries, and they are difficult for outsiders to know about or understand.

Cross-border migration is an important livelihood strategy in the face of ecological and economic disasters, and is key to understanding, and forecasting, the onset and evolution of humanitarian disasters caused by armed conflict, famine, drought and other difficulties in a given region. International migration management cannot afford to overlook the cross-border dimension of migration in Sub-Saharan Africa, as it has a major impact on irregular migration, HIV/AIDS and other communicable diseases, as well as smuggling and trafficking of women and children. Cross-border movements also impact on national, regional and international security and, as elsewhere, strengthening border systems and moving towards more integrated border management approaches are also gaining importance in the Africa region. (See also below on Intra-regional Labour Migration and Regional Integration.)

REFUGEES AND INTERNALLY DISPLACED POPULATION

Conflicts, human rights violations, and other emergencies together with weak or deficient democratic institutions, continue to pose pressing problems for many African states and often result in forced displacement of populations. The major sources and destinations of refugees and IDPs in Sub-Saharan Africa have shifted over time. Initially concentrated in the East African region, where environmental disasters, such as drought and desertification, and ethnic, border and guerrilla wars in the Horn of Africa (Somalia, Eritrea, Ethiopia and southern Sudan) gave rise to large movements of refugees and IDPs in the 1980s and 1990s, in recent years there has been a shift to Central and West Africa.

In Central Africa, the problem of refugees and population displacement has been acute as a result of ethnic violence and insurgencies that peaked in the mid-1990s following the genocide in Rwanda and the civil war in Burundi, which displaced more than three million people. Civil strife in the Republic of Congo and the disintegration of state authority in the Democratic Republic of Congo in 1997 (and the guerrilla warfare that followed) further generated massive flows of refugees and displaced persons in the sub-region, threatening regional security and long-term peace in the larger region. The Burundian peace process, begun in August 2000 with the signing of the Arusha Agreement for Peace and Reconciliation, has brought hope to the region. But increased tension between Rwanda and DRC, as a result of the recent events in the eastern part of DRC (African Union, 2004)[7] continues to threaten the peace and security of the sub-region.

In West Africa, the stretch of the coast covering Guinea Bissau, Sierra Leone, Liberia and now Côte d'Ivoire has been experiencing rebellions, the first signs of which began in Liberia in 1989, followed by Sierra Leone in 1991. A decade and a half later, the sub-region remains immersed in intractable conflicts and humanitarian disasters, notwithstanding the conclusion of peace agreements. The military uprising in Côte d'Ivoire in September 2002, that developed into a political and military crisis unknown in the history of the country, has led to the internal and external displacement of over 3.9 million (CAP, 2003). The escalation in July 2003 of Liberia's 14-year old war has affected some 3.1 million people (CAP, 2004).

The conflict in Côte d'Ivoire has had repercussions also for neighbouring countries, with those most affected being Liberia, Guinea, Burkina Faso, Mali and Ghana. An unknown number of civilians have been killed, more than 750,000 are believed to be internally displaced, and a further 400,000 have fled to neighbouring countries. Thousands of migrant workers, constituting about 30 per cent of the Ivorian population, also remain at risk. Burkinabes, Guineans and Malians have been displaced along with the refugees, forcing major return flows of foreign populations. Côte d'Ivoire's vibrant economy that once attracted its poorer neighbours is no longer able to serve as the economic engine of the sub-region. The deadlock in the Ivorian peace process continues to pose a threat to long-term peace and security in the sub-region (CAP, 2003).

7. *Dissidents of the new national army of the DRC, following a week of fighting, took control of the city of Bukavu in the South Kivu province on 2 June, 2004. There was an attempted coup d'état in Kinshasa on 11 June. African Union, Report of the Chairperson of the Commission on Conflict situations in Africa; July 2004.*

Southern Africa has experienced several phases of internal and international migration. These included large movements of unskilled labourers from Botswana, Lesotho, Swaziland, Mozambique and Malawi to the South African mines; mass displacements caused by wars of independence or liberation struggles in the region, e.g. in Angola, Mozambique, Zimbabwe and South Africa (against apartheid), and increasing inflows of skilled foreigners into Botswana, South Africa and Namibia over the past decade.

To manage these complex migration patterns, it is critically important to prevent, manage and resolve the conflicts in the region. Conflicts create massive population displacements, often across international borders, and involve great human suffering and socio-economic destabilization. These developments have led governments, international organizations and civil society to become more engaged in multilateral conflict management and post-conflict reconstruction. It is evident from the growing number of UN peacekeeping operations on the continent, the new focus of specialized agencies on conflict prevention and post-conflict peace building, as well as the initiatives recently launched by the African Union and the regional economic communities, that the international community is taking these challenges seriously.

INTERNATIONAL MIGRATION

Historical, cultural and linguistic ties have prompted large flows of skilled and unskilled migrants between African states and their former colonial powers. Many Sub-Saharan Africans who left in pursuit of higher education then stayed on in, e.g. Belgium, France, Portugal, Spain and the UK. (Sander et al., 2003). But intercontinental migration has diversified, and increasingly includes poorly educated labour migrants, who are emigrating in significant numbers to Europe, the Middle East and Asia. Overall, however, it appears that African people made up only about 5 per cent of the total foreign-born population in OECD countries in 2002 (OECD, 2002), while the US is home to fewer African migrants than in Europe.

Over the years, African transnational migration has evolved into a more complex and dynamic phenomenon fuelled by both "push" and "pull" factors and the demands of globalization (ACBF, 2004; Meeus and Sanders, 2003). The brain drain phenomenon, while not new to the continent, has intensified. As trade barriers come down and more developed countries adapt their immigration legislation to attract highly skilled manpower and compensate local skills shortages in certain sectors, the out-movement of all types of professionals will increase. Shrinking and ageing populations have led many industrialized countries to intensify the recruitment of well trained and educated workers and professionals from poorer countries. Aggressive and targeted international recruitment initiatives can be seen in several African states, for instance in Ghana and South Africa. As a result, a considerable part of the investment in training and education in Africa is never recovered.

MIGRATION OF HEALTH WORKERS

Migration of health workers has become a cause for concern in many countries in SSA because of its impact on African health systems. There is a global shortage of health workers, and Africa is one of the key suppliers. But there is already an unequal distribution of human resources in most SSA states because of the steady internal migration of health workers from rural to urban areas, public to private sector, and out of the health sector altogether (Meeus and Sanders, 2003), prompted by economic, social, professional and security factors.

The British Medical Journal estimated that 23,000 health-care professionals emigrate annually from Africa.[8] It is estimated that between 1993 and 2002, Ghana lost 630 medical doctors, 410 pharmacists, 87 laboratory technicians and 11,325 nurses. In 2002

8. *See also: South African Institute of International Affairs, "Africa's health care crises", September 2003.*

alone, 70 doctors, 77 pharmacists and 214 nurses left Ghana. In the UK, the main source countries for nurses issued with work permits in 2001 were South Africa and Zimbabwe. Statistics available from the Ministry of Health in Zimbabwe indicate that between 1998 and 2000 around 340 nurses graduated, while the number of Zimbabwean nurses registered in the UK in 2001 was 382. As there is no surplus of nurses in Zimbabwe, these figures represent a major loss of the human resources required in the country (Stilwell et al., 2003).

A study by the ad hoc group of the OECD Health Project[9] shows that while the proportion of general practitioners in the medical and nursing workforce in OECD countries fell between 1991 and 2000, the proportion of foreign-trained practising physicians and nurses in OECD countries is increasing. This is consistent with regional studies identifying the following countries as major destinations for health workers from Africa: UK, US, Canada, Australia, New Zealand, France and Belgium. As the global labour market strengthens, the migration of highly skilled and trained Africans will increase. According to the International Development Network (IDN), industrialized countries are the beneficiaries of the time and money invested by developing countries in the education and training of their health workers.[10]

It is critical that both developed and developing countries acknowledge the problem of brain drain resulting from "push" factors in countries of origin and "pull" factors of globalization, and focus on devising solutions beneficial to all concerned. Collaborative solutions should accept the fact of mobility, and build synergies between skill profiles of the migrants and the demand from countries, to ensure that the economies at both ends profit. Migrants often maintain a web of connections with their home countries with beneficial feedback effects such as the transfer of remittances, knowledge, skills and technology, as well as short and long-term return migration. Strengthening these feedback effects by enhancing collaboration with the African diaspora[11] would be key to fostering the migration-development nexus.

POVERTY REDUCTION THROUGH REMITTANCES IN AFRICA

Remittances represent an important financial flow with significant development potential, although recent claims by some that it is a panacea for all of Africa's problems seem exaggerated. African migrants have a long-established practice of sending money back to their country of origin. But it is helpful to distinguish between cross-border (or international) and domestic, as well as between officially recorded and unrecorded flows. Most published figures on migrant remittances are based on officially recorded flows that pass through banks or other formal financial institutions. In Sub-Saharan Africa, data are lacking for two-thirds of the countries and just one-third report official figures that include cross-border flows captured by banks as international transactions. *Domestic transfers* are not recorded anywhere as a

9. *The "Human Resources for Health Care" (HRHC) study is conceived as a component of the OECD Health Project, ref. www.oecd.org/document/54; see also Vujicic, Zurn, Diallo, Adams, Dal Poz "The role of wages in the migration of health care professionals from developing countries", Human Resources for Health, Vol. 2, No.3, BioMed Central, London, 2004 (www.pubmedcentral.nih.gov/articlerender.fcgi?artid=419378).*

10. *"It can be extrapolated that between 1985 and 1990 for the 60,000 professionals emigrating, the continent lost USD 1.2 billion. This represents the reverse of what development aid tries to achieve through 'transfer of technology and human resources'. This development paradox, combined with the inability of the African countries to build, retain and utilise indigenous capacities critical to Africa's growth and development, will deprive Africa of its vital development resources and make it more heavily dependent on foreign expertise", UNECA 2000: Debate on GATS- The Development Paradox.*

11. *In the past, the concept of "diaspora" has referred to three major historical events – the dispersal of the Jews, the movement of Africans in the slave trade, and the exodus of Armenians – but is today increasingly used in migration policy discourses to describe recent movements that have taken place for a wide range of reasons and with varied outcomes. In the African context, it is normally applied to sizeable African communities, living outside the continent, who are expected to stay for significant periods of time. A further perspective is given by IOM in its Migration for Development in Africa (MIDA) programme, which aims at enhancing the contribution of African expatriates to their home countries without returning permanently. See the chapter "Enhancing the Benefits of Return Migration for Development". Among expatriate communities, diaspora is gaining currency, both as a more acceptable alternative to "migrant" and an empowering term for the African migrant (Koser, 2003).*

separate category and can be captured only through household surveys. An unknown but substantial portion of overall remittances goes unrecorded, as they pass through informal channels, such as personal carriage by migrants, their friends, relatives or other trusted agents and the services of the *hawala* and the *hundi*[12] systems.

During the last ten years, while remittances to developing countries more than doubled (see also the chapter on Migrant Remittances as a Source of Development Finance), officially recorded flows to Africa grew very little, and as a result their relative share has declined, particularly in SSA (Ratha, 2003). In 2002, SSA received USD 4 billion, or 5 per cent of the global total, whereas the Middle East and North Africa together received USD 14 billion. North Africa alone accounted for about 8 billion (10%).

This picture is somewhat skewed, however, as the total amount remitted may be two or three times higher, if the large number of informal transactions were known. Informal remittance strategies are a reaction to weak or non-existent financial systems and barriers created by financial and monetary policies and regulations to cost-effective flows and investments of remittances. Experts report that throughout Africa financial and monetary policies and regulations have created barriers to the flow of remittances and their effective investment. A few governments, recognizing the valuable contributions of remittances, have facilitated foreign exchange transactions or provided investment incentives such as matching grants. More could be done, however, especially in the context of the regulation of the financial industry (Sander, 2003).

Remittances are primarily used by families to meet daily subsistence needs, but are also invested in improvements to land, homes, entrepreneurial and construction activities. As in Asia and Latin America/the Caribbean, they form part of the household strategy to escape poverty. A survey conducted in Burkina Faso found that about 15 per cent of households received international and domestic remittances, and these tend to benefit the rural, female-headed households most (Lachaud, 1999). In western Kenya, an area with poor climate for agriculture, remittances were found to fuel a sustained demand for local non-farm goods and services, such as construction and education.

According to the World Bank, remittances spent by rural households may thus have a larger multiplier effect than those spent by urban ones, as the former tend to consume more domestically produced goods and services (Ratha, 2003). In Ethiopia, remittances are commonly used by rural and urban families to pay the travel costs of an economically active household member to work abroad. Refugees are a key group of migrants that not only benefit from remittances, but are often able to remit money when they go abroad. In many instances, transactions extend beyond and across borders as well. This system of anchoring long-term support is expanding, and identifying ways to maximise the developmental effects of remittances, and to improve remittance transfer mechanisms, are therefore topics of growing importance to SSA.

INTRAREGIONAL LABOUR MIGRATION AND REGIONAL INTEGRATION

INTRA-REGIONAL migration also has far-reaching effects on the economies and societies of sub-Saharan African countries. In Africa, there are an estimated 20 million migrant workers and family members within and outside the continent. By most recent ILO calculations, some 7.1 million migrants are economically active in other African countries. Many millions more migrate seasonally or permanently within their own countries (ILO, 2004). The ILO estimates that the number of labour migrants in

12. Hawala *and* hundi *are terms that can be used interchangeably for informal cash transactions, typically* hawala *is used in the context of the Middle Eastern countries, and* hundi *is usually connected with South Asia.*

Africa today comprises one-fifth of the global total, and that by 2025 one in ten Africans will live and work outside the countries of origin.

Traditionally, labour migration in Sub-Saharan Africa has been directed towards a limited number of countries: Côte d'Ivoire, Senegal and Nigeria in West Africa; South Africa and Botswana in southern Africa; Gabon in Central Africa and Kenya in East Africa. But in recent years, these configurations have changed, and it is difficult to classify countries strictly as either origin or destination countries. Some serve as transit routes, while others are both origin and destination countries for migrant workers.

Intra-regional labour has increasingly become a concern for governments, i.a., because of the growing cross-border trade in goods and services, irregular migration and the linkage between mobility and HIV. In some countries, migrants have become scapegoats and targets of hostility and expulsions (Ricca, 1989),[13] particularly when governments are faced with economic and political problems. Migrants are often blamed for societal ills including taking jobs away from nationals. In the past two years, while many countries have made considerable progress in promoting migrant rights, xenophobic acts against migrants have been reported in Libya, Equatorial Guinea and South Africa. In Côte d'Ivoire, recent shifts in the country's liberal immigration policy have resulted in a "citizenship crisis", sparking discontent and mistrust between immigrants and local populations (UNDP, 2004).

Regional Economic Communities (RECs) are key to facilitating cooperation on labour mobility at the intra-regional level. Regional protocols on free movement of persons have made some progress in the ECOWAS and EAC communities. In the Southern African Development Community (SADC), however, member states have formulated and ratified several protocols but made little progress in developing appropriate policies and legislation. The reservations in SADC about free movement are illustrative of a dilemma faced by most governments: that more liberal policies could result in a one-way flow to countries with a stronger economy, whereas more restrictive policies could in turn lead to an increase in irregular migration.

Labour migration is likely to increase as the regional economic communities move towards further integration, and it is important that RECs address the issue in that context, as this requires harmonization of national and regional migration policies (Castles and Miller, 2003). This can contribute to socio-economic development by maximizing migration benefits in both sending and receiving countries, and enhancing the free movement of people as agreed in the Abuja treaty establishing the African Economic Community.

IRREGULAR MIGRATION FLOWS FROM SUB-SAHARAN AFRICA TO AND THROUGH THE MAGHREB

Another important aspect of intra-continental movements from Sub-Saharan Africa is the flow towards the Maghreb States (see also the Chapter on "Migration Dynamics and Dialogue in the Western Mediterranean"). This trend dates back many centuries, and remains a significant feature of African population movements. Nevertheless, distance and the cost of migration have largely limited any SSA movements to the north. But this has changed rapidly since the end of 1980's, and SSA movements northwards are growing for a number of reasons:

i) The deterioration of living conditions in parts of SSA due to conflicts, political instability and desertification, against which the Maghreb is an area of relative prosperity and stability.
ii) The increasing revenue and wealth differentials between the two regions.
iii) Restrictive immigration policies adopted by European countries in the last decade that have compelled SSA nationals to find illegal ways of migrating and/or alternative destinations.

13. *Ricca lists 23 expulsions by 16 different states between 1958 and 1991 in what has been called as "the era of mass expulsions". The most recent being the expulsion of Congolese and Guineans from Angola.*

Information about the numbers of Sub-Saharan migrants living in or transiting the Maghreb on their way to Europe is often piecemeal. However, available figures indicate that the SSA migrants who have reached the Maghreb in recent years across its Saharan borders number between 65,000 and 80,000 annually. The large movements from SSA to Libya, in particular, have been attributed to Libya's pan-African policy, that, since its inception some six years ago (Europa, 2003), has shifted its focus away from the Arab world towards Africa, and helped turn Libya into a country of immigration and transit for Africans from South of the Sahara (Boubakri, 2004; Al-Ali, 2004).[14]

Morocco has also become a final destination for growing numbers of West African nationals (ILO, 2002), many of them apprehended as irregular immigrants.

TABLE 2.1

SUB-SAHARAN MIGRANTS DETAINED IN MOROCCO IN 2001

Countries of Origin	Number of migrants arrested
Sierra Leone	2,245
Mali	1,625
Senegal	1,177
Nigeria	798
Guinea	519
Ghana	480
Congo	149

Source:
Identification mission in Morocco, July/October 2002, European Commission, final report.

Tunisia also has a considerable number of SSA migrants, many of them students, graduates and others who tend to work illegally in the service sector, leisure industry, catering and office work (Boubakri, 2004). In both Morocco and Tunisia, where the rate of unemployment varies between 15 and 18 per cent, a large number of migrants are working in the informal sector or engaged in basic services.

Migration in its many and various forms will continue to be an important element in the relations between Sub-Saharan Africa and the Maghreb countries as they introduce stricter border controls and rigorous measures to combat irregular migration. Migration dialogue and cooperation need to be extended southwards involving SSA and the Maghreb region.

TRAFFICKING IN PERSONS

In recent years, the incidence of trafficking of women and children has increased dramatically in Sub-Saharan Africa, sparing no region or country and involving hundreds of thousands of victims. Many African countries have become points of origin, transit and destination at the same time for the traffickers and trafficked. As in other regions, trafficking within Africa takes various forms, including large movements of children and young women from rural to urban areas for domestic work and forced prostitution. A study conducted in the south-western part of Tanzania found considerable local trafficking from rural areas, which increased during the months of October to December during which primary schools closed. The study also notes the existence of cross-border trafficking, where young girls from Malawi and Zambia are recruited by long-distance truck drivers or business people (GTZ, 2003).

Intra-regional trafficking is quite common among countries such as Nigeria, Ghana, Côte d'Ivoire, Senegal, Ethiopia, Kenya, Cameroon, Mali, Gabon and Niger. Outside Africa, countries in western Europe, North America and the Middle East have become frequent destinations for trafficked victims from the region. In 2004, IOM confirmed that trans-national criminal syndicates are also trafficking South African women to East Asia for sexual exploitation (IOM, 2003). Women have also been found to be trafficked to South Africa from well beyond the region, notably China, Thailand and parts of Eastern Europe, including Russia (IOM, 2003).

14. *As stated in the Europa Publications report,* The Middle East and North Africa 2004 *(Europa, 2003), Libya's decision dates back to 1998, when the government publicly took up the cause of self-determination of African states, and began to mediate in African conflict situations, which it continues today (e.g. in regard to the Sudan).*

Child trafficking presents very specific challenges in Africa. 32 per cent of all trafficked children worldwide are African (UNICEF, 2003). Some 16 million children work in Africa, often subject to extreme forms of exploitation such as slavery, sale, debt bondage, serfdom and prostitution. For example, 60 per cent of children trafficked to Italy come from Nigeria, 29 per cent of known cases of children trafficked to the EU for sexual abuse are from Africa. According to Human Rights Watch, Nigeria is a destination country for trafficked persons from Ghana, Togo and Benin. Children are trafficked both within Nigeria and to other West African countries such as Cameroon, Gabon, Guinea, Mali and Côte d'Ivoire (HRW, 2003).

A study in East Africa illustrates the impact of armed conflict on trafficking. In Uganda, large numbers of children in conflict areas are abducted by the rebel force, the Lord's Resistance Army (LRA), and are forced to work as child soldiers or slaves/wives to the LRA commanders. From June 2002 to July 2003, approximately 8,400 children were abducted in this way, bringing the total to well over 20,000 since the start of the 17-year conflict. To date, 6,000 children remain missing.

Regional economic communities have responded in different ways to the challenges of trafficking. Some have chosen not to prioritize it due to lack of resources, and others have stiffened visa requirements for nationals from neighbouring countries. South Africa expects to become the second country in the SADC region, with Tanzania, to criminalize trafficking in persons for sexual exploitation.

ECOWAS countries have adopted a Regional Protocol on Trafficking of Women and Children, while countries such as Ghana and Nigeria have made substantial progress in drafting anti-trafficking legislation at the national level as well. IOM has recently taken steps in collaboration with the East African Community to address the problem of trafficking in Kenya, Uganda, Tanzania, Eritrea and Ethiopia (IOM, 2003). European and African countries are also in the process of adopting a Plan of Action on trafficking of women and children under the auspices of the African Union which, for the first time, has included trafficking in its continent-wide Programme of Work (AU, 2004).

MIGRATION AND HEALTH

IN SUB-SAHARAN Africa, as in other regions, several studies show that migration per se is a key determinant of the increased vulnerability of communities and migrants to ill health and infections, such as HIV. They illustrate how people who are more mobile, or who have recently changed residence, tend to be at higher risk. People fleeing political instability, conflict or natural disasters have a high risk of contracting diseases due to the separation of families and the breakdown of social structures. This is further compounded by the lack of access to health care facilities and reproductive, mental and social health problems that are common among migrant populations.

In 2003, in SSA alone, there were between 25 and 28.2 million people living with HIV representing 65 to 70 per cent of the world's total. Between 2.2 and 2.4 million died from the virus, and between 3 and 3.4 million became newly infected in that year (UNAIDS, 2003).

In West and Central Africa, mobility is a key factor in the high prevalence of HIV/AIDS, particularly along the principal migration routes towards the three West African coastal countries that are the main centres of immigration – Senegal, Nigeria and Côte d'Ivoire – and in Central Africa, most notably between Cameroon, Congo, Gabon and the DRC. Truck drivers, itinerant traders, commercial sex workers, migrant labourers, trafficked women and children and refugees are of particular concern. Migration is one of the many social factors that have contributed to the AIDS pandemic in South Africa, where the prevalence of HIV infections increased dramatically from 0.76 per cent in 1990 to 26.5 per cent in 2002.

Migrants and mobile populations are often subject to discrimination, xenophobia, exploitation and harassment, and enjoy little legal or social protection in the host community. They often also have little or no access to HIV information, health services and means of prevention, such as condoms, or treatment of sexually transmitted infections (STIs). Migrants and mobile populations experience a multitude of risks. Often, preoccupied by more immediate challenges of physical survival and financial need, they regard HIV infection as a remote risk. In addition, the adverse working conditions and family separations lead some male migrant workers to seek solace and intimacy through multiple sexual encounters.

The devastating effects of HIV and AIDS have also increased cross-border movements in the Southern African region, and there is some evidence that the demographics of the movements are shifting significantly towards a younger, increasingly female population (IOM/SAMP, 2003).

CONCLUSION – MIGRATION ON THE AFRICAN UNION AGENDA

In 2001, recognizing the need to address the many migration challenges confronting the continent, the OAU/AU adopted a landmark decision[15] calling upon its member states to develop a strategic framework for migration policy in Africa. The Lusaka Decision exhorts governments to integrate migration into their national and regional agenda for security, stability, development and cooperation; to work towards the free movement of people; to strengthen intra-regional and interregional cooperation in matters concerning migration, and to create the necessary political, social and economic conditions in Africa to serve as incentives to curb brain drain and attract much-needed investment through its diaspora.

Following the decision, the AU embarked upon a process of consultations with governments in several fora in 2004. The draft framework was submitted for government comment at a Meeting of Experts in Addis Ababa (March 2004), at the AU Labor and Social Affairs Commission in Cotonou, Benin (April, 2004), and to the Africa Group during the International Labour Conference in Geneva (June, 2004). To further enrich this continental process and achieve complementarity between the various state policies, in the same year, the AU hosted regional consultations on the "Berne Initiative", a global process launched by the Swiss Government in 2002 (see the chapter 22).

The AU in its Vision and Strategic Plan, 2004-2007, has put the African diaspora at the centre of its work. and the AU Constitutive Act "encourages the full participation of the African Diaspora as an important part of the continent" (Art. 3). The strategic vision also envisages putting in place a special programme entitled "Citizens of Africa" with the objective of involving African citizens at large in this process, and promoting the talents of the African diaspora in particular (AU, 2004).

High-level dialogue on mobilization of the African diaspora for the development of their own countries/regions, as well as the role of remittances in poverty reduction, is ongoing across the continent. Notably, the New Partnership for Africa's Development (NEPAD) has identified "investing in human resource development, reversing the brain drain, as one of the priority areas for African development".[16] Efforts are ongoing to develop a continent-wide human resource development strategy and, under the leadership of the AU, to establish a human resource databank on the African diaspora.

As the AU moves towards regional integration within the context of the NEPAD and the AEC, migration is increasingly seen as an engine for regional cooperation and integration, as well as socio-economic development. It is thus critical for African states to elaborate appropriate mechanisms to better deal with this phenomenon and prevent its negative

15. *74th Ordinary Session of the OAU Council of Ministers, Lusaka, Zambia, July 2001.*

16. *See NEPAD: priority areas in the section "Human Resource Development Initiative" (including reversing brain drain), pp. 27-30.*

effects.[17] Migration policies for socio-economic development need to be implemented in a broader context – at the national, regional and continental levels, and with the participation of all stakeholders (governments, international community, civil society, private sector, migrant associations, etc.). Issues such as good governance and democracy, as well as other root causes of migration need to be addressed and action taken to translate commitments into concrete programmes.

17. *Cairo Plan of Action, p. 98, Africa-Europe Summit, Cairo, 3-4 April 2000.*

TEXTBOX 2.1

Migration Observatory in West Africa

West African emigration flows are large and closely linked to the migration policies of destination countries of the North, and influenced by the effects of globalization on the population's well-being and life options. There is, therefore, considerable interest in knowing more about the scale and motivations underlying these movements. But available data remain rare and unreliable.

As in other African countries most estimates are drawn from censuses that, however, were never intended to measure and analyse migration. But in the absence of more reliable data, they remain a principal source of information on immigrant and foreign populations in West Africa. These data need to be complemented by more far-reaching research into international migration, and the validation of national data, the value of which is often ignored or underestimated.

For this reason, an Observatory of West African international migration has been established in Dakar by IOM in partnership with the Institute of Research for Development (IRD) in Senegal, in pursuance of the agreement by West African governments at the Regional Conference on the Participation of Migrants in the Development of their Country of Origin in 2000. The objectives of the Observatory are to:

- establish within each ECOWAS Member State a standardized system of data collection and information on West African international migration, both regular and irregular (drawing on data supplied by the ministries of foreign affairs, the interior and justice);
- validate the national data at the regional (ECOWAS) and international levels;
- establish a centre for the collection, analysis and production of statistics in this field on the basis of continuously updated real-time data.

Data input from ECOWAS' ministries of interior and justice will enable a far broader analysis of migrant stocks and flows in the region than the national censuses are able to provide. It will facilitate a better understanding of the circular movements inside, through and out of the region, the effectiveness of border management within and around the region, and the interface between labour migration and the trafficking of migrants. A joint IRD-IOM research facility, established by the Framework Agreement of December 1999, is in charge of the scientific design and technical operation of the Observatory. For strategic and scientific reasons, Senegal was selected as the pilot host of the Observatory and is seen as a model for other countries of the sub-region.

The successful operation of the Observatory depends on the creation of three observatories (in the Secretariat of Senegalese abroad, and the Senegalese Ministries of Interior and of Justice) and their effective networking with counterpart observatories in other ECOWAS states. Access to data from the Ministry of the Interior and the Ministry of Justice, generally treated as highly confidential, is especially critical at a time when the migration challenges in the region, as elsewhere in the world, are also challenges to national, regional and international security. Migration, and the need for migration management, have become a central political concern for ECOWAS members.

Source: Nelly Robin, head of the unité mixte IRD/IOM, Dakar, Senegal.

TEXTBOX 2.2

MIDA PROJECT FOR GUINEAN WOMEN

Since the beginning of the 1990s, Guinea has received large numbers of refugees fleeing from conflicts in Sierra Leone, Liberia, Guinea Bissau, Casamance and, more recently, Côte d'Ivoire. The presence of a record number of refugees has had a major negative impact on the social well-being of the population. The long years of war have caused serious damage to physical, economic and social infrastructures, both in towns and in the countryside. Women, whose vulnerability is invariably increased in such circumstances, were the first victims of the effects of these regional crises.

Yet women have been largely excluded from attempts at economic recovery, even though in Guinea they are responsible for more than 70 per cent of subsistence production.[18] In addition, since women's illiteracy rate in Guinea is a record 73 per cent,[19] they are deprived of the basic knowledge needed to be able to raise their status in society and participate in socio-economic progress.

In response, and as part of its wider Migration for Development in Africa (MIDA), program IOM launched the MIDA Guinean Women's Project, financed by the US Government, to assist deprived women in the country through the dissemination of skills and experience of members of the Guinean diaspora. It provided technical and material support to 60 women beneficiaries for the development of micro-enterprises. In the selection process priority was given to poor women, who were engaged in small-scale activities to meet the needs of their families. None had previously received any micro-credits or training.

18. *Ibrahima Kaba, Diénabou Youla,* Les activités économiques des femmes en Guinée, *presentation made on 27 August 2000, Conakry. Subsistence farmers: 71.1 per cent; traders: 11.5 per cent; farmers/agricultural workers: 9.1 per cent. It should be pointed out that the document suffers from the fact that sources are not mentioned. However, the figures supplied may provide a guide and an order of magnitude to obtain a general picture of the situation of women in relation to employment.*

19. *Annual statistics, UNESCO, 1999.*

Members of the Guinean diaspora were recruited to provide the women with training in the creation and management of micro-enterprises. IOM started with the conviction that the Guinean diaspora included many highly qualified expatriates. Some of them have acquired the necessary knowledge and know-how for the creation and management of enterprises, which they can pass on to their fellow nationals in the home country, whose situation is becoming increasingly precarious.

Two women were selected from the Guinean diaspora in Senegal, and one man who had been part of the Guinean diaspora and had returned to Guinea and set up a development project consultancy. The three instructors worked hand-in-hand with instructors of Guinea's Rural Credit, acting as IOM's technical partner for the project. Through the preparatory activities conducted ahead of the training, IOM helped to strengthen the capacities of Rural Credit personnel, which has had a positive impact on all the institution's women customers.

The contents and execution of the training scheme were designed so that, by the end of their training, participants were fully familiar with the basic issues concerning the creation and management of micro-enterprises. Their personal experiences have been constantly incorporated into the learning process so that their acquired skills, which are rooted in scenarios based on their personal lives and the activities of their communities, may be directly applicable to the local situation and to their micro-enterprises.

The diaspora instructors, who had remained well acquainted with the realities of the home country, were able to adapt the knowledge they transmitted to the specific socio-economic conditions of Guinea, and to deliver the courses in the three main local languages (bearing in mind that most of the beneficiaries are either illiterate or semi-literate).

At the end of their training, the women received a low-interest loan (IOM negotiated lower interest terms at a regressive rate of 2 per cent per month). The amount of credit allowed was decided on a case-by-case basis according to the type of the project undertaken by individual women. The sums allocated ranged from 300,000 GF (approximately USD 155) to 650,000 GF (approximately USD 332), with average loans amounting to 475,000 GF or USD 242.

Thanks to this financial assistance and with the new knowledge they have acquired, the women have been able to either start up or further develop profitable micro-enterprises. The main activities created or improved included the sale of consumer products, dyeing, sewing, tapestry, small-scale catering, soap manufacture and weaving.

Source: Sylvia Ekra, Project Officer, IOM, Geneva.

CHAPTER 3
MIGRATION IN THE MIDDLE EAST[1]

IN RECENT YEARS the Arab Middle East has received over 10 per cent of the world's migrants (Dorai, 2000) with the oil-rich countries of the Gulf hosting the largest share of guest workers to indigenous populations anywhere (Milch, 1998). Both internally and within the region, this migration is highly diverse and involves legal workers and their families, irregular migrants, refugees and displaced persons.

This chapter highlights key trends and policy responses in the region, including "indigenization" of labour markets in the Gulf Cooperation Council (GCC) countries, replacement migration during and after the Gulf crisis and war of 1990-91, feminization of migration, irregular migration and trafficking, refugees, internally displaced persons (IDPs), stateless persons and the national measures adopted to protect migrants.

IOM estimates that there are about 14 million international migrants, mostly labourers, and six million refugees in the Arab Middle East.[2] Saudi Arabia has the biggest migrant population in the region, with large numbers also found in two other GCC countries, viz. the United Arab Emirates (UAE) and Kuwait. Egypt ranks second, with approximately three million migrants, due essentially to the presence of a large Sudanese community that began to arrive during the 1970s when the Egyptians opened the door to migrants from Sudan. The resurgence of the civil war in the Sudan in the 1980s created a large flow of refugees and asylum seekers, and prompted the government to reverse this policy and dramatically reduce Sudanese inflows. Today, the majority of Sudanese nationals settled in Egypt are those who moved during the 1970s and the 1980s.

Except for the Sudanese living in Egypt, Indians, Pakistanis, and Filipinos comprise the largest group of third-country nationals (TCNs) in the region. Within the region, Egyptians and Jordanians mostly move to GCC countries, particularly Saudi Arabia – Yemenis largely go there also, while Iraqis move mainly to Jordan and Syria. These migratory flows are mostly for labour purposes, typically temporary in nature and involving little expectation of permanent settlement or citizenship rights (Jureidini, 2004).

REFUGEES

VIOLENT conflicts are another major cause of migration in the Middle East. In 2003, there were an estimated six million refugees in the region, including some four million Palestinians, the largest refugee population in the world. The Arab Middle East is both a source and a haven for refugees, from within and beyond the region.[3]

1. *This chapter examines migration trends and issues in 13 Arab states, comprising those of a) the Arab Mashreq – Egypt, Iraq, Jordan, Lebanon, the Occupied Palestinian Territories (OPT), Syria, and Yemen – and b) the Gulf Cooperation Council (GCC) states – Bahrain, Kuwait, Oman, Qatar, Saudi Arabia, the United Arab Emirates (UAE). The authors include Riad al Khouri (see below), IOM Mission with Regional Functions, Cairo (Giuseppe Calandruccio), Professor Nasra M Shah (see below), Mohammed al Nassery (IOM, Kuwait City) and the staff of IOM Cairo. It is complemented by the chapter below on the West Mediterranean (Maghreb).*

2. *Data on international migrants compiled by IOM Cairo, 2003, from a variety of different sources. Data on refugees compiled from UNHCR, US Committee for Refugees and UNRWA, 2003.*

3. *Confirmed by IOM Cairo, UNHCR, US Committee for Refugees and UNRWA, 2003.*

Egypt and Yemen are signatories to the 1951 Convention relating to the Status of Refugees and its 1967 Protocol, establishing the legal standards for refugee protection. Yemen, the only signatory to this convention and protocol in the Arabian Peninsula, attracts large numbers of asylum seekers from sub-Saharan Africa, hosting over 85,000 refugees in both urban areas and camps. Though not signatories, Lebanon and Jordan also host significant numbers of refugees. More than a tenth of Lebanon's population are refugees, mostly Palestinian, who also make up a high percentage of the inhabitants of Jordan. The United Nations Relief and Works Agency for Palestinian Refugees in the Near East (UNRWA) assists the Palestine refugees, while UNHCR provides help to others.

THE PALESTINIAN ISSUE

According to UNRWA, as of mid-2003 there were more than four million Palestinian refugees in the region (Table 3.1).

TABLE 3.1

PALESTINIAN REFUGEES, 2003[4] ('000s)

Jordan	1,719
Lebanon	392
Syria	410
West Bank	655
Gaza Strip	907
Total	**4,083**

Source: UNRWA.

UNRWA is responsible for assisting registered Palestinian refugees in official camps, of which there are 19 in the West Bank, 8 in Gaza, 14 in Lebanon, and 10 each in Syria and Jordan (UNWRA, 2003). However, as the UN Conciliation Commission for Palestine (UNCCP) and its protection mandate collapsed in the mid-50s, UNRWA does not deal with protection issues, and no international agency currently has an explicit mandate regarding the protection of basic human rights of Palestinian refugees and the search for durable solutions to their problems. A protection gap is thus evident for Palestinians, with the most severe situations persisting in Lebanon, the West Bank and the Gaza Strip. In particular, UNRWA refugees are not protected against *refoulement* and do not enjoy other basic rights, including freedom of movement and acquisition of identity documents.

This also restricts UNHCR's role to assistance concerning travel documents, renewal of registration cards for refugees outside the area of UNRWA operations and facilitation of interim solutions for Palestinian refugees in case of forced departure (Badil, 2002). Following the 1993 Oslo peace agreement and transfer of control from Israel to the Palestinian Authority of portions of the Occupied Palestinian Territories (OPT), the refugees are considered IDPs not entitled to either UNRWA or UNHCR assistance.

An immediate consequence of the second Gulf War and the crisis leading up to it (1990-91) was the dislocation of large numbers of Palestinian migrants from their countries of residence. The Palestinian uprooting from the Gulf, especially from Kuwait, was calamitous, particularly for the second generation born and raised there. They did not enjoy permanent residence in the GCC states, yet, the length of service and residence of most would have qualified them for permanent residence, even if not citizenship, in many other countries. The Palestinian community in Kuwait prior to the Iraqi invasion numbered 400,000, but was reduced to just over an eighth of that in the mid-1990s (Ferghani, 2001).

In the Gulf as elsewhere, many of these Palestinians are actually holders of Jordanian passports. According to expert estimates for 2002, Jordanian citizens of Palestinian origin resident in the GCC countries for

4. Figures are based on UNRWA records that are regularly updated, but as registration and deregistration with the Agency is voluntary, these figures may not represent the true size of the refugee population.

work purposes numbered about 0.5 million, including 270,000 in Saudi Arabia, 110,000 in the UAE, 50,000 each in Qatar and Kuwait, and smaller numbers n Bahrain and Oman (Kapiszewski, 2003).

Palestinians remaining in their country also faced migration issues: in 1970-93, Palestinian labour flows to Israel were crucial for integrating the economy of the West Bank and the Gaza Strip into the Jewish state. These commuters represented a third of the employed Palestinian population and generated over a quarter of the West Bank and Gaza Strip GNP (Farsakh, 2001). With the advent of the Oslo peace accord in 1993, labour flows from the OPT into Israel no longer played the same integrating role as before. The number of Palestinian workers going to Israel on a daily basis dropped from its peak of close to 116,000 in 1992 to fewer than 36,000 in 1996. With the *Al-Aqsa* Intifada in September 2000, Israeli closures of the Occupied Territories brought the movement of labour and goods between Israel and the West Bank and Gaza Strip to a virtual halt for extended periods (Ruppert Bulmer, 2001).

THE IRAQI DIASPORA

Migration from Iraq has only become a noticeable phenomenon during the last 20 years, as by the mid-1980s, the impact of the Iranian-Iraqi war had started to push more people to look for security and prosperity outside the country. At least 517,000 Iraqis were dispersed all over the Middle East region by the early 1990s, prior to which Iraq had not been a big migrant exporting state (Kapiszewski, 2001). After the second Gulf War in 1991, migration from Iraq intensified owing to a crippling economic embargo and socio-economic hardships, compounded by the prevailing domestic political situation and the collective denial of access to public resources for marginalized groups and various religious and ethnic communities. Outflows resulted especially from the brutal treatment of the Kurds from the north of the country and the Shia from the centre and south by Saddam Hussein's Government, following uprisings by these groups.

It is estimated that a minimum of two million to a maximum of 4.2 million Iraqis (ABC, 2001) – the latter equal to about 20 per cent of the total population – were living abroad in 2001 as refugees (in camps or elsewhere), asylum seekers, illegal migrants, migrant workers, or naturalized citizens of various countries.

Migrations were also caused by fighting between rival Kurdish factions in the north, and the drainage of the marshlands in the southern Shia area of the Shatt al Arab. Inward migration also became an issue after the second Gulf War, as GCC countries expelled many Iraqis due to suspected collaboration with the Baath Party regime. A great number of them were faced with the option of returning to Iraq or migrating to other countries; many chose the latter option.

Some of them went to Jordan, which has been hosting one of the largest Iraqi expatriate populations in the world, and with up to 400,000 individuals the highest number in the region. However, Jordan tightened its borders at the end of 2002, prior to which many Iraqis had used Jordan as a transit point to other countries. After the third Gulf War in 2003, Jordan also adopted a semi-protectionist policy towards Iraqis, allowing them to stay for up to half a year, but without legal status or protection beyond that (Chatelard, 2002). Thus, many who were still in Jordan after six months became illegal, preferring to keep a low profile out of fear of deportation.

INTERNALLY DISPLACED PERSONS

Ethnic and religious strife in the Middle East has resulted in the internal displacement of some 1.5 million people. Compared to other areas of the world, however, the region has a relatively limited number of IDPs and is one of the few places where refugees by far outnumber the displaced. Iraq and Lebanon have the most significant IDP populations, the former hosting an estimated 700,000 to 1 million IDPs. The OPT also has an important displaced population (Norwegian Refugee Council, 2004).

In Iraq, due to the policies of the former government (and in some cases intra-Kurdish fighting), large numbers of Kurds, Assyrians, Turkmen, Marsh Arabs and others were displaced during the past two decades. At the end of the Iran-Iraq war in 1988, Saddam Hussein destroyed many Kurdish settlements because of their suspected collaboration with Iran, and tens of thousands of Kurds were also moved to "collective settlements" and detention camps. The regime's "Arabization" campaign in the strategic, oil-producing region of Kirkuk displaced more than 100,000 Kurds in 1991-2001. Similarly, some 200,000 Marsh Arabs have been displaced in the south of Iraq following the destruction of their villages and the construction of dams to depopulate the area and force out those who sought refuge in the marshes after a failed uprising in the early 1990s (Human Rights Watch, 2003).

In Lebanon during the civil war of 1975-90, almost a third of the country's population became displaced.[5] The displacement led to resettlements along religious lines and has exacerbated social tension in Lebanon. Of those displaced by the civil war, only about a third have returned to their homes as many IDPs do not wish to go back because of the new economic and social realities that have evolved in the country over more than 25 years.

In 1997, UNDP reported high unemployment and hardship among IDPs in Lebanon. About half of them were unable to meet their basic needs and 12.5 per cent lived in absolute poverty. The level of education of IDPs was below the national average, with half having only elementary schooling and 24 per cent only completing intermediary school. Families were experiencing severe social stress by having to move from a generally rural socio-economic environment to a mainly urban setting with poor housing conditions, and problems increased among displaced youth as a result (UNDP, 1997).

The Lebanese Government has made the return of IDPs a priority for the achievement of national reconciliation and peace. In 1993, it created the Ministry for the Displaced (MoD) to rehabilitate infrastructure and housing and improve the economic situation. With UNDP, the MoD launched a programme for the Reintegration and Socio-economic Rehabilitation of the Displaced to meet the socio-economic requirements for return of IDPs. The Central Fund for the Displaced was also created to finance IDPs going back to their homes. However, in November 2001, the fund stopped payments for lack of money. The year 2002 had been set for the return of all IDPs to their places of origin, but as of end-2003 there were still some 300,000 displaced persons in the country.[6]

As more than half of the IDPs in the Middle East have been displaced for at least twenty years, it is generally difficult to assess whether they have integrated into their new communities or should still be considered displaced.[7] At the same time, there is a lack of political will among the region's governments to tackle some complex IDP issues. For example, while the League of Arab States continues to address problems[8] of the Palestinians, the case of the Iraqi Kurds and other IDPs has not been given the same attention.[9]

5. *The largest wave of displacement of some 367,000 people took place in 1985 in Mount Lebanon. Further displacement was caused by Israeli interventions in Lebanon in 1978 with 200,000 Lebanese and 65,000 Palestinians displaced in the South. Israeli occupation of southern Lebanon in 1982 led to an even greater displacement than in 1978 (see Norwegian Refugee Council, 2002).*

6. *www.db.idpproject.org/Sites/IdpProjectDb/idpSurvey.nsf/wCountries/Lebanon*

7. *Norwegian Refugee Council, IDP Project, Internal Displacement in the Middle East, www.idpproject.org/regions/Middle_East_idps.*

8. *Ibid.*

9. *Ibid.*

TEXTBOX 3.1

The Bidun: Statelessness in a Volatile Region

In several Gulf countries (notably Kuwait, the UAE, Bahrain and Iraq), there is a population of stateless inhabitants known as *Bidun* – a term derived from the Arabic expression "*bidun jinsiya*", literally meaning "without nationality". Despite strong residence ties, the *Bidun* have no proof of citizenship of their home country. Many of them have not held any nationality for generations.

The *Bidun* typically originate from the territories of Iraq, Saudi Arabia, Syria, Jordan, and Iran. In the 1960s, some were allowed to settle permanently in Kuwait. Although they did not receive formal Kuwaiti citizenship, they enjoyed the same economic and social rights as citizens and by the 1980s made up approximately 80 per cent of the Kuwaiti military and police forces. In 1989, they were removed from "national" census data and added to the "non-national" population. (Because of this recategorization, the proportion of nationals dropped from 40 per cent to 28 per cent of the country's total population.) As a result of their changed status, the *Bidun* began experiencing difficulties in the labour market and also lost access to free health and education services.

Iraq's invasion of Kuwait complicated the situation of the *Bidun*. Thousands were asked to leave the country in 1991 and were not allowed back. Those who left were thus stateless for a second time, displaced to Iraq and other countries. There are an estimated 120,000 *Bidun* remaining in Kuwait – fewer than half of the pre-Gulf War population of approximately 250,000 (World Refugee Survey, 2003).

Bidun have also suffered elsewhere in the region: for example, in the UAE, some *Bidun* are nomads or descendants thereof, unable to prove that they are of UAE origin. Others who have been present in the country for more than a generation are originally from Iran or South Asia. By contrast, their situation in Bahrain appears to have improved: prior to 2001, Bahrain had a *Bidun* population of between 9,000 and 15,000, forbidden by law to buy land, start a business, or obtain government loans. In 2001, the government granted citizenship to the majority of them. These formerly stateless citizens of Bahrain are of Iranian rather than Arab origin. Most are Shiite, and some are Christian.

NATIONAL UNEMPLOYMENT AND JOB "INDIGENIZATION" IN THE ARAB MIDDLE EAST

Running at an average of 15 per cent, the Arab Middle East has the highest unemployment rate of all regions in the world (Fergany, 2001), about three times the global average (UNDP, 2002).

The UNDP Arab Human Development Report (AHDR) 2002 warns that "job creation, although rapid in some Arab countries from the mid-1980s to the early 1990s, has not matched the growth of the work force. Population growth is adding about six million labour-force entrants every year, a flow that is proportionately greater than in any other region of the world. Since the unemployment rate is also one of the highest among all regions, the task of job creation is probably more formidable in the Arab region than in any other" (UNDP, 2002).

Low productivity levels are also a feature in the region. According to the World Bank's World Development Report of 1998/9, the average GNP per worker in Arab Middle East countries was less than half the level in South Korea or Argentina. Output per person in the region is estimated to have been in decline since the 1980s, and the industrial labour productivity was estimated in the early 1990s to be approximately the same as in 1970 (Fergany, 2001). Moreover, according to the AHDR 2003, if we "compare the GDP indicator per worker in ten Arab countries with that of some faster growing countries over the relatively long period of 1980-97, the comparison is unflattering to the region. Productivity increased annually during that period by 15% in China, 8% in Korea and 6% in India. By contrast, productivity growth in the best performing Arab country was 4% (3-4% in Oman and Egypt, 2-3% in Tunisia, Mauritania and Morocco, 1-2% in Jordan and Algeria and less than 1% in the UAE and Saudi Arabia)" (UNDP, 2003).

Unemployment of nationals[10] is a recent phenomenon of the GCC labour markets (Fergany, 2001). Against that backdrop, the strong presence of migrant workers in the region takes on added significance, especially for the GCC countries that now have an expanding national labour force due to high indigenous population growth rates in the 1970s and 1980s (see section below on the GCC). In this context, the policy of job "indigenization" in the oil-producing countries of the Middle East will have an impact on unemployment levels in labour-exporting Arab countries that have traditionally used the GCC states as an economic safety valve for their surplus population. (It has been estimated that Egypt and Jordan will need to achieve a 7 per cent real growth rate per annum to make even a small impact on their unemployment.)[11]

FEMINIZATION OF MIGRATION IN THE MIDDLE EAST

THE GENDER dimensions of labour in general and migrants in particular are increasingly important in the Middle East, with the feminization of migration creating new economic and social realities. The last few decades have witnessed a growth of female migration to the region as Arab countries have undergone economic expansion and restructuring. The majority of female migrants work in the GCC and in Jordan and Lebanon (Khalaf, 2003).

The increased feminization of migration in the Arab Middle East reflects the fact that female Arab labourers have the lowest economic activity rate of the world. According to the UN Economic and Social Commission for Western Asia (ESCWA) in 2000, Arab women constituted only 29 per cent of the regional labour force and were more prone to unemployment than men, in spite of their enhanced educational, social and political position within Arab society (ESCWA, 2004).

It is interesting to notice that the lowest share of Arab women (13 to 21%)[12] in the labour force is registered in the five higher-income Arab countries of the GCC, where the presence of extra-regional female migrants is predominant.

The demand for female migrants in the Middle East has increased, particularly in the service industries, through the creation of low- and unskilled jobs that migrant women are willing to take, while the local population is reluctant to do so. These jobs are filled by women from the developing countries of Asia, principally Sri Lanka, the Philippines, Indonesia, Thailand, Bangladesh, Pakistan and India. The majority tend to work in private households as domestic workers, but also in the hotel and entertainment industries, the latter

10. *Here referred to as a person who has sought employment in the past month, but not actually worked in the seven days before interview with the authorities.*
11. *www.itp.net/features/print/103088283120751. "ECSWA Casts Dim Light on Arab Economies".*
12. *ILO, Labour Statistics Database (LABORSTA), www.laborsta.ilo.org/cgi-bin/brokerv8.exe*

sometimes being a euphemism for commercial sex. In Jordan, as of August 2000, over 98 per cent of female migrants were domestics, mainly from Sri Lanka and the Philippines (UNIFEM, 2000). Many were overqualified for this work; according to the ILO, 36 per cent of Filipino women who migrated for domestic work were either college graduates or persons with some college education (Raghavan, 1996).

The economic significance of female migration is so high for some Asian governments that female labour export targets are included in their development programmes.[13] In Bangladesh, for example, the remittances of women migrants are important not only for the survival of their families, but also for the economic stability of the country. Sri Lanka is unusual in that its expatriate labour force has more women than men. In 2000, 67 per cent of Sri Lanka's overseas workers were women, and the majority of them worked in the Middle East. In that year, remittances from the region made up 63 per cent of Sri Lanka's total.[14]

However, despite the increasing international visibility of female migrants and their contribution to the global economy, they remain vulnerable to marginalization and gender-based discrimination, and exploitation in the segregated labour markets of the Middle East. The key reasons for this are insufficient support from sending and receiving countries and policy gaps at both ends, as well as insufficient monitoring of employment agencies that act as middlemen (Mohsen, 2002). Prevailing labour laws and sponsorship systems, as well as the behaviour of employment agencies, all contribute to the particular vulnerability of female migrants in this region.

LABOUR LAWS OF THE HOST COUNTRY

While the labour laws of receiving countries provide legal guarantees to some categories of migrant workers, they often do not apply to domestic work and other low-skill jobs, which most migrant women in the Middle East undertake. The women are almost invariably paid less than the minimum wage and work beyond the legal maximum of hours prescribed in the labour laws of the host country. For instance, in Jordan, in the year 2000, more than 90 per cent of female migrant workers earned less than the minimum wage of eighty Jordan dinars (USD 120) per month (UNIFEM, 2000). The lack of legal guarantees to migrant workers in low-skill jobs has in some cases cast a shadow on the reputations of both the sending and receiving countries.

IRREGULAR MIGRATION

Irregular migration occurs throughout the Middle East, with all countries involved as origin, transit and destination points. There is sporadic evidence that both smuggling and trafficking of persons occur regularly and on a large scale. Reports of migrant smuggling and trafficking in persons appear frequently in the international media, and the local press also increasingly reports on the fate of Arab workers being moved by trafficking rings, as well as foreigners being trafficked into the region. More comprehensive research is needed to fully grasp the magnitude of these phenomena. **Table 3.2** shows the key smuggling routes of the region, as derived by IOM Cairo from cases apprehended and documented by governments and the media. (Note that intended transit states often become countries of destination.)

13. *IOM "Gender Mainstreaming in IOM"; www.iom.int/en/who/main_policies_gender.s*
14. *Women Migrant Workers of Sri Lanka, Center for Women's Research CENWOR, Colombo, www.cenwor.lk/migworkersstat accessed 8 July 2004.*

TABLE 3.2

PRIMARY SMUGGLING ROUTES FROM AND THROUGH THE MIDDLE EAST

Origin	Areas of Transit	Destinations
Iraq	Turkey	Europe, Indonesia, Australia
OPT	Lebanon, Turkey	Southern Europe
Jordan, Egypt	Tunisia, Southern Libya	Southern Italy
China, Eastern Europe	Egypt	Israel
Turkey	Jordan	Israel
Sub-Saharan Africa	Libya	Europe
Syria/Turkey/Iran/Iraq	Lebanon	Europe (esp. Cyprus, Greece, Italy)
Somalia	Yemen	GCC countries
Pakistan, Afghanistan, Iran, Yemen		GCC
Nigeria, Senegal	Egypt	Lebanon, S.Arabia, western Europe

Source: IOM Cairo.

The four main national groups originating in the Arab Middle East and smuggled and trafficked within and out of the region are: Iraqis taken across Lebanon and/or Turkey to Europe or Australia; Palestinians moved through Lebanon to Europe, and Jordanians and Egyptians who pass through Tunisia and Libya to Italy.

In the case of Egyptians smuggled through Libya, their journeys frequently end in capture and deportation, and sometimes drowning at sea. Many who are deported back to Egypt attempt the journey again after their return. Allegedly, the smugglers arrange with the migrants that, if they do not reveal their identity upon capture, they will smuggle them again. On average, a smuggler charges USD 2,000 per migrant for a journey and a promise of work in, e.g., Italy. The Egyptian Foreign Ministry recently warned all citizens to obtain work contracts certified by the Egyptian Ministry of Manpower and Emigration before going abroad. Egyptians are warned not to deal with "work permit agents" in Jordan, because they sell fake permits.

Primary transit countries of the Middle East are Egypt, Libya, Jordan and Lebanon. Jordan is said to be a transit country for women from Turkey going to Israel. Likewise, Lebanon is a main transit for Kurds smuggled from Syria, Turkey, Iran and Iraq *en route* to Europe (in particular to Cypriot, Greek and Italian shores). There has been a noticeable increase in the number of illegal migrants using Egypt as a transit station to nearby countries such as Israel. Egypt also serves as a transit country for Chinese job seekers and East European women entering Israel via the Sinai Desert. In November 2002, the Egyptian Government detained several Egyptian nationals in the tourism sector accused of smuggling foreigners to Israel, charging them with threatening the national security of Egypt (*Jordan Times*, 2002; *Middle East Times*, 2002).

In recent years, boats have been carrying irregular migrants mainly from Sri Lanka and Bangladesh through the Suez Canal towards Europe (Inter Press Services, 2002). The Egyptian position on passage through Suez is dictated by the 1888 Constantinople Convention on free passage in the Suez Canal, whereby the Egyptians cannot stop a boat on mere suspicion, even for random checks.

There is anecdotal evidence that Egyptian, Iraqi and Libyan nationals are involved in smuggling rings that transport national groups from outside the region, primarily Africans, through Libya and to Europe. Major smuggling destinations in the region are the GCC countries and, to a lesser degree, Jordan and Yemen, in particular for smuggled migrants from Pakistan, Afghanistan, Iran and Somalia. The permeable borders between Yemen, Oman and Saudi Arabia make the three countries major destinations for refugees and smuggled migrants. For instance, the frequent ship accidents in the Gulf of Aden shed light on the flows of migrants and refugees between Somalia and Yemen. The port of Bosaso in Somalia is a departure point for those who want to flee the Horn of Africa to Saudi Arabia (Al-Ahram, 2002; and AFP, 2002).

TRAFFICKING IN PERSONS

MANY women from the Philippines, Bangladesh, Pakistan, India, Thailand, Sri Lanka and Indonesia are attracted by promises of well-paid domestic jobs in the GCC countries. At destination, some experience physical and sexual abuse, under-or non-payment of wages, or are forced into sex work (Al-Najjar, 2002 and Sabban 2002). Women from Ethiopia, Madagascar, Sri Lanka and the Philippines have been taken to Lebanon, where they are subjected to mistreatment, under-payment and long hours of work without rest, at times sexually abused or forced into the sex trade (Jureidini, 2002 and Kebede, 2002).

In Saudi Arabia, cases of sexual harassment, humiliation, severe beatings and delayed salaries have driven a number of housemaids to escape from their employers. In December 2002, the King Fahd General Hospital in Jeddah received several cases of housemaids with serious fractures caused by falls sustained in attempts to flee employers by jumping out of windows in high-rise apartments. The press also reported cases of housemaids attempting suicide in the same year.[15]

Some Ethiopian, Sudanese, Somali and Kenyan women are also reportedly trafficked into Bahrain and Saudi Arabia, and Bahrain is a transit country for migrants trafficked to Kuwait. Nigerian and Senegalese women are also frequently taken to Lebanon, Saudi Arabia and Western Europe through Egypt and other North African countries for the sex trade. Lebanon, Bahrain and Saudi Arabia are considered both destination and transit areas of trafficked people going to Europe or to other Gulf countries. Egypt, on the other hand, is mainly a transit country for both smuggling and trafficking of migrants.

Women from Russia, Ukraine, Georgia, Kazakhstan, Uzbekistan, Azerbaijan, Kyrgyzstan and other countries of the former Soviet Union today represent the majority of sex workers in the UAE. Migrants to that country are required to be sponsored by a local guarantor, and the occasional manipulation of this system of sponsorship makes possible the arrival and stay of many women who are in effect irregular immigrants. These phenomena continue unabated as Gulf officials, jointly with western authorities, concentrate on the drug smuggling and money laundering aspects of the entertainment industry, while largely ignoring the sex trade.[16]

CHILDREN

ANOTHER trafficking trend peculiar to the Middle East is that of children from Bangladesh, Pakistan and India being sold (sometimes after having been abducted) in Qatar and the UAE to work as jockeys in camel races, a popular sport in parts of the region. Human rights groups have reported that child slaves from Sudan are also sold as camel jockeys in Qatar. **(See also Textbox 3.2 "Camel Jockeys in the Gulf Cooperation Council States".)**

15. *Arab News daily (Jeddah) "Indonesian maid attempts suicide" 9 January 2003.*

16. *For more information on sex-trade trafficking, see IOM Trafficking Reports: Armenia – Irregular Migration and Smuggling of Migrants from Armenia, IOM: Yerevan, 2002. www.iom.int//DOCUMENTS/PUBLICATION/EN/armenia_trafficking and Trafficking in Women and Children from the Republic of Armenia: A Study. IOM: Yerevan, Armenia, 2001. www.iom.int//DOCUMENTS/PUBLICATION/EN/Armenia_traff_report. Azerbaijan- Shattered Dreams: Report on Trafficking in Persons in Azerbaijan. IOM: Geneva, Switzerland, 2002. www.iom.int//DOCUMENTS/PUBLICATION/EN/Azerbaijan_Report Russian Federation- Hughes, Donna M. Trafficking for Sexual Exploitation:The Case of the Russian Federation. IOM No. 7 IOM Migration Research Series IOM: Geneva, Switzerland, 2002. www.iom.int//DOCUMENTS/PUBLICATION/EN/mrs_7_2002 and Tajikistan- Deceived Migrants from Tajikistan: A Study of Trafficking in Women and Children. IOM: Dushanbe, Tajikistan, 2001 www.iom.int//DOCUMENTS/PUBLICATION/EN/Tajikistan_study_august2001.*

THE IMPACT OF THE *KAFALA* SPONSORSHIP SYSTEM

COMPREHENDING the sponsorship system is pivotal to understanding some of the roots of trafficking in the Middle East. In the UAE and other Gulf countries, Kafala (Arabic for sponsorship) is the guarantee system for a guest worker vis-à-vis the authorities and the only means to legally enter and work in the country. Through this system the state delegates to its citizens certain functions that in other countries would remain with the authorities.

There are four types of visas available under the *Kafala* system: House Visas, Company Visas, Sponsorship by state institutions, and Sponsorship for business partnership. Of the four, House Visas and Company Visas are those that may result in hidden trafficking practices (Blanchet, 2002).

The House Visa, issued for domestic jobs, represents the most risky option. The sponsor, known as the Kafeel, provides the guest worker with an entry visa and a job, and is responsible to the authorities if the worker changes residence or employment. More important, the Kafeel has control over the worker's rights, freedom of movement, and labour and judicial actions.

According to many experts, the sponsorship rule "entails elements of servitude, slavery, and slavery-like practices, as defined in the UN Trafficking Protocol to Prevent, Suppress and Punish Trafficking in Persons, Especially Women and Children" (Mattar, 2002). For example, sponsors often cede employees to others without consent, and withhold passports to prevent possible escape (ibid).

In the case of Company Visas, or the "free visa" system, the worker purchases a visa from a sponsor without any expectations that he/she will work for that sponsor. If the police arrest a free visa holder, the sponsor is contacted but takes no responsibility for the migrant worker. Though illegal, the sale of "free visas" at a profit is widespread among the lower middle class GCC population. Some companies are granted permission for issuing visas without actually needing workers, which helps to make the scheme possible. Migrants frequently fall into debt to their employers or brokers and, unable to pay it back, are subjected to extortion because of their tenuous visa status – thereby becoming victims of trafficking (Jureidini, 2003). While governments are increasingly aware of this problem, work on solving it has only just begun.

CUSTOMARY MARRIAGE SCHEMES

CUSTOMARY marriage is a feature of the Middle East that is sometimes abused by wealthy nationals of GCC countries who marry young women from poorer Islamic countries in exchange for a dowry to the family. In such cases, a marriage contract can often be finalized in less than a week, and the families receive a false certificate from a doctor stating that their daughter is of legal age to marry. Once abroad, the brides can find themselves quickly divorced, forced into unpaid menial jobs or married to someone else by proxy. The young women are often unable to escape, communicate with their families, or contact their consulates.

LEGAL FRAMEWORK AND MEASURES FOR THE PROTECTION OF MIGRANTS

IN DECEMBER 2002, Saudi Arabia signed the UN Protocol against the Smuggling of Migrants by Land, Sea, and Air and the Protocol to Prevent, Suppress and Punish Trafficking in Persons, Especially Women and Children".[17] Among the signatories to both protocols are four other Arab countries: Algeria, Libya, Lebanon and Syria. Egypt has signed the Trafficking Protocol and Tunisia that against smuggling of migrants. Bahrain acceded to both protocols in August 2004. Egypt also signed the

17. *These Protocols supplement the UN Convention Against Transnational Organized Crime, adopted in 2000.*

International Convention on the Protection of the Rights of All Migrant Workers and Members of Their Families, albeit with reservations regarding article 4 concerning the definition of "members of family", and article 18 concerning compensation to migrant workers pardoned of a conviction after due legal process.

CHANGED ATTITUDES: MIGRATION TO THE GULF COOPERATION COUNCIL STATES (GCC)[18]

MIGRATION to GCC countries has, for the past three decades, been a major feature of regional labour markets, with millions of workers employed there coming from elsewhere in the Arab region and beyond. In 2000, the proportion of non-nationals in GCC country populations ranged from 76 per cent in the UAE to 23 per cent in Oman, while over half of the labour force in each country comprised expatriates (Table 3.3).

TABLE 3.3

PERCENTAGE OF NATIONALS AND EXPATRIATES IN THE POPULATION AND LABOUR FORCE OF GCC COUNTRIES, 2000

Country	Population		Labour force	
	Total ('000s)	Expatriates (%)	Total ('000s)	Expatriate (%)
Bahrain	652	40.0	272[a]	61.9
Kuwait	2,363	62.6	1,320	80.4[b]
Oman	2,442	22.7	859	64.3
Qatar	580	73.7	120[a]	81.6
Saudi Arabia	20,279	25.4	7,176	55.8
UAE	2,890	75.7	1,356	89.8
All GCC countries	29,322	34.9	11,103	70.0

Sources:
ESCWA, 2001, Demographic and Related Socioeconomic Data Sheets Economic and Social Commission for Western Asia
a. Data for 1997, Kapiszewski A, 2001, Nationals and Expatriates: Population and Labor Dilemmas of the Gulf Cooperation Council States, Garnet Publishing Ltd. UK
b. Data for 2003, Public Authority for Civil Information, Directory on Population and Labor Force, 2003, *Government of Kuwait*

While relations between host societies and guest workers have been generally good, attitudes to migrants in some of these richer oil-producing areas are starting to change. In response to UN global surveys on population and migration (ECOSOC, 2003), the four most populous GCC states – Kuwait, Oman, Saudi Arabia and the UAE – considered immigration levels excessive and wanted to lower them (with only Bahrain and Qatar seeing their immigrant situations as satisfactory).

An important reason for this new attitude is higher unemployment among GCC nationals, raising difficult economic and political questions for governments. Unemployment in Saudi Arabia, the largest GCC country, has risen to about 13 per cent among males and is estimated to be as high as 35 per cent among youth aged 20-24. The country also faces a demographic tidal wave, with 56 per cent of the population aged below 20. These cohorts will place a severe strain on the labour market in the next two decades, requiring for their absorption the creation of about 100,000 new jobs every year. Unemployment has already resulted in some political unrest in the region, such as the sit-ins outside the National Assembly in Bahrain in 2001 (*Agence France Presse*, 11 May 2001).

The overwhelming response of the host countries appears to have been to devise policies to limit the inflow of workers and enhance employment among nationals. At least four types of policies have evolved in recent years:[19]

i) Indirect taxes to raise revenue for the host country and make life more expensive for expatriates. A case in point are the health fees instituted in Kuwait in 1999, and in Saudi Arabia in 2001. A migrant worker in Kuwait must buy health insurance for him/herself and each member of the family residing with him/her. The employer does not pay a share of such insurance in the private sector, where 92 per cent of all

18. *The author of this sub-chapter on the GCC is Professor Nasra M Shah, Chairperson, Department of Community Medicine, Faculty of Medicine, Kuwait University: nasra@hsc.edu.kw*

19. *Some of these have been reported in the past two years in the* Arab News, *Saudi Arabia (e.g. February 3, 2003; July 10, 2002; Sept 26, 2002, and* The Gulf News, *UAE, December 30, 2002.*

expatriates work. Another example is the increased fee for the issuance and renewal of residence permits, driving licences and registrations in Kuwait. A more direct levy in Saudi Arabia consists of an annual payment of the equivalent of some USD 27 from each foreign worker towards the establishment of training programmes for indigenous workers.

ii) The phasing-out of reliance on foreign workers (at least planned). A decision was taken in 2003 in Saudi Arabia by the Manpower Council under the direction of Saudi Crown Prince Abdullah bin Abdulaziz to cap the level of expatriates and their dependants at 20 per cent of the population by 2013, while halving the number of expatriate workers (*Arab News*, 3 February, 2003). Kuwait is implementing a ceiling of less than 35 per cent expatriates employed in the public sector. Saudi Arabia and the UAE have identified occupations where phasing out of expatriates will occur on a priority basis. In Saudi Arabia, 25 such occupations have been identified thus far, including travel businesses, gold and jewellery shops, grocery stores, etc. Judging by the enforcement raids undertaken to ensure that guidelines for employment of nationals are being followed, the Saudi government is serious about implementing these policies.[20]

iii) Issuance of new work permits and the transfer of current ones from one employer to another (being seriously considered again). According to the current sponsorship system, each worker must have a local sponsor with a business requiring workers. A system of visa trading has emerged since the mid-1970s, when the demand for visas to the Gulf economies started to exceed the limited numbers issued by the authorities. Some nationals opened up fictitious companies, for which they procured work permits to sell to migrants; the work permit frequently not accompanied by a job. The migrant thus found employment with someone other than the sponsor, or remained unemployed. The numbers involved in these schemes are huge.[21] A fundamental difficulty in implementing this policy, however, is the ease with which an ordinary local sponsor can make money from workers in source countries, where many are eager to buy such visas.

iv) Amnesties, repeatedly declared by the Gulf Countries since the mid-1990s to encourage the departure of those residing in host countries in an irregular visa situation, largely as a result of being employed by a company not legally sponsoring the worker. For example, in the UAE, about 100,000 irregular migrants were deported under an amnesty in 2003 without penalty to them or their employers. However, deportees are banned from ever returning, and the companies employing them, while exempted under the amnesty from paying a fine equivalent to USD 3,700 per worker, come under greater scrutiny by the authorities.

Thus, the current tendency in the Gulf States, supported at the highest policy-making levels, is one of better regulating and limiting immigration. Policies are being fine-tuned and steps taken to implement them more actively and stringently. While the current policy is one of restricting the number of migrant workers, their sudden withdrawal would be catastrophic for both the GCC and the sending countries. Migrants are not only making a direct contribution to the economy as members of the workforce, but are also major consumers of goods and services produced in the host country. Some concern about the possible negative impact of a reduction in the foreign work force has occasionally been expressed by authorities within the host country, who feel that nationalization of the private sector may in fact reduce efficiency and result in a decline in job opportunities for nationals.

20. *In Jeddah, it was found that expatriates (with nominal Saudi sponsorship) owned 60 per cent of the shops selling gold, and many remained closed when the law came into effect. The authorities had warned the shops that violators would be fined a first and second time, and following a third violation, foreign workers would be deported and the shop closed. Hence, foreign workers did not open their shops, while the nominal Saudi sponsor who earns a fee for providing a business licence and visas for the workers is not trained to take over the business. Also, the sponsor does not have a ready and trained pool of Saudi workers to rely on. Implementation of such laws will therefore not be easy.*

21. *In the UAE, there are an estimated 600,000 workers (or 27 per cent of the total workforce) sponsored by these fictitious companies. The Saudi Minister of Labour said in early 2004 that 70 per cent of visas issued by the government are sold on the black market, and the government was determined to crack down on this. Authorities in other GCC countries repeatedly make similar statements.*

A DELICATE BALANCE: ARAB MASHREQ MIGRATION AND LABOUR MARKET SEGMENTATION[22]

SINCE the present state system emerged in the Mashreq[23] after the First Word War, cross-border movement of workers in the countries between the Nile and the Euphrates has been significant, as also between the region and the rest of the world. However, after the oil price adjustment of in 1973, Mashreq labour migration became crucial for many states in and outside the region.

The large outflow of workers from non-oil exporting Mashreq countries into the petroleum producing states of the Arabian Peninsula resulted in a boom in the Mashreq between 1974 and 1982. However, with the fall in oil prices in the mid-1980s, migration from Mashreq countries into the GCC economies began to slow. That was the result of mainly economic factors such as the price of oil, but further (political) change took place after Iraq's invasion of Kuwait in 1990. The crisis forced about two million Arab expatriate workers (mostly from the Mashreq) to leave the Gulf, and go either back to countries of origin, or to third states.[24]

Mashreq prosperity was thus reversed, dragging the region's economies down as rapidly as they had grown in the late 70s and early 80s. Following the second Gulf War in 1991, remittances from Mashreq migrants in the GCC states thus became relatively less important for a few years, but something of a revival took place with the return of a significant number of Mashreq workers to the Gulf economies in the late 1990s. This was partly the result of diplomacy by all sides seeking to repair damaged relations after the invasion of Kuwait, but the "re-migration" could not have been sustained without strong demand for labour in the Gulf.

GCC states thus continued to import labour from the Mashreq, as well as from other regions such as South and Southeast Asia, to fill the jobs that Gulf nationals are unable or unwilling to undertake. This is illustrated in one of the GCC's highest profile boom economies, Dubai, where recent statistics (**Table 3.4**) show that indigenization of jobs (i.e. giving them to citizens of the UAE), while progressing, still has some way to go.

What is not surprising about these figures is the overwhelming predominance of migrants in the lower labourmarket segment, which UAE nationals prefer not

TABLE 3.4

DUBAI MUNICIPALITY EMPLOYMENT BY NATIONALITY AND TYPE OF WORK, 1998-2002

	National staff	National labourers	Total national employees	Non-national staff	Non-national labourers	Total foreign employees	Total employees	Citizens as percentage of total employees
1998	1,038	10	1,048	3,557	4,274	7,851	8,899	11.8
1999	1,173	10	1,183	3,831	4,536	8,367	9,550	12.4
2000	1,452	10	1,462	4,063	4,801	8,864	10,326	14.2
2001	1,546	8	1,554	3,924	5,120	9,044	10,598	14.7
2002	1,829	7	1,836	3,787	5,303	9,090	10,926	16.8

Source: Dubai Municipality Statistical Yearbook 2002, p. 72.

22. *The author of this sub-chapter is Riad al Khouri, a Jordanian development economist and director of MEBA (MEBA@nets.com.jo, an economic and business consultancy). The information in this chapter derives from research undertaken for the publication "Arab Migration Patterns: The Mashreq" in* Arab Migration in A Globalized World, *IOM and League of Arab States, IOM, Geneva, 2004.*

23. *See footnote 1.*

24. *Some workers had to leave because of the conflict, others as a result of the political hostility caused by the decision of their governments not to support the anti-Iraq coalition.*

to hold, given abundant cheap migrant labour. Nationals tend to occupy the top jobs, with many of the middle and higher ranking ones also in the hands of non-nationals, some of whom are from the Mashreq.

The GCC job market is thus segmented, with nationals concentrated in the top jobs, other Arabs tending towards middle level, and South and Southeast Asian migrants largely occupying menial posts.

THE CASE OF JORDAN

THIS TREND towards labour market segmentation has been observed in the GCC countries for the past few decades, but is now also more evident in Mashreq economies, such as Jordan. At the same time, many Jordanians have returned to the GCC states and also continue to enter other labour markets outside the country (as per the travel figures in **Table 3.5**) with a significant benefit to Jordan's balance of payments (**Table 3.6**).

TABLE 3.5

JORDANIAN ARRIVALS IN AND DEPARTURES FROM JORDAN, 1999-2003 (IN '000s)

	1999	2000	2001	2002	2003
Arrivals in Jordan	1,452	1,599	1,723	1,627	1,401
Departures from Jordan	1,563	1,627	1,755	1,728	1,533
Annual net departures from Jordan	110	28	32	101	132
Cumulative net departures from Jordan since 1999	110	138	170	271	403

Source: Central Bank of Jordan Monthly Statistical Bulletin April 2004, pp. 78-9.

TABLE 3.6

WORKERS' REMITTANCES TO AND FROM JORDAN, 1999-2003 (IN USD '000s)

	1999	2000	2001	2002	2003
Incoming remittances	1,662	1,843	2,008	2,132	2,199
Outgoing remittances	204	197	193	194	183

Source: Central Bank of Jordan Monthly Bulletin of Statistics, April 2004, p. 58.

Large numbers of foreign workers live in Jordan, though their remittances are heavily outweighed by the money returning from Jordanian migrants (**Table 3.6**). Non-nationals with labour permits working in Jordan in 1998 totalled 114,000. In 2002, the number of those registered increased to 127,000, while in 2003 there were around 125,000 foreign workers with permits in the country, with the same number of non-registered foreign workers.[25] (By contrast, in 2003 the Jordanian resident labour force was estimated at around 1,150,000.)

Most of the country's non-Jordanian labourers come from other Mashreq states, especially Egypt and Syria. In these two cases in particular, migrants enter Jordan freely, without visa restrictions, and because of cultural and other factors, Mashreq workers integrate into Jordanian society relatively easily. Their presence in the country is thus more difficult to quantify and control.

That has posed a problem; with unemployment remaining high, the Jordanian Government has been striving to find more jobs for nationals, while reducing the country's overall dependence on foreign labour. In 1999, the state issued regulations restricting some jobs to local workers. Government strategies to cope with this situation also included more checks on the foreign labour force, pursuing stricter policies on importing labour, and enforcing relevant laws and agreements for Jordanian workers to gradually replace non-nationals. The government thus hopes to provide further job opportunities for the national labour force and thereby curb poverty, but this has not happened to a significant extent.

This approach seems to have led to a reduction in the net annual increase among some groups of migrant workers coming to Jordan but not others from Mashreq states, such as Egypt. **Table 3.7** below shows that numbers of Egyptians arriving in Jordan have been rising steadily in 1999-2003, despite state policies of labour indigenization.

25. *According to the then Jordanian Minister of Labour speaking in a public lecture, as quoted in* ad-Dustour *Arabic daily newspaper, Amman, 27 September 2003.*

TABLE 3.7

EGYPTIAN ARRIVALS IN AND DEPARTURES FROM JORDAN, 1999-2003 (IN '000s)

	1999	2000	2001	2002	2003
Egyptian arrivals in Jordan	270	215	325	355	410
Egyptian departures from Jordan	258	193	306	313	339
Annual increase in Egyptians remaining in Jordan	13	22	19	42	72
Cumulative increase in Egyptians remaining in Jordan since 1999	13	35	54	96	169

Source:
Central Bank of Jordan, Monthly Statistical Bulletin, April 2004, pp. 78-79.

Egyptians tend to do the more menial jobs in the Jordanian labour market, holding the highest number of permits to work in, for example, the agricultural sector. According to the Jordanian Ministry of Labour, a total of 4,860 Egyptians were given agricultural work permits in the first nine months of 2003, with only an additional 247 permits granted to migrants from Egypt to work in other areas.

However, many Egyptian migrant workers – as well as those of other Mashreq nationalities – are also working in Jordan illegally, something that the Jordanian Ministry of Labour has been trying to address with more or less success for the better part of a decade. The Ministry, which has been getting tougher on foreign labour for the past few years, tightened procedures further in 2004, when it started inspecting the country's private sector establishments more rigorously to check on their compliance with labour laws and regulations. Nearly 100 staff have been assigned to the inspection campaign, which will cover more than 55,000 companies and factories in the country. In particular, inspectors will ensure that non-Jordanian employees working in the private sector have legal permits and enjoy the full rights granted to them under labour regulations, such as health insurance and pensions. This is a sore point with unscrupulous employers, who, if not caught out, economize by hiring illegal migrants and then depriving them of their basic labour rights.

Meanwhile, for many Egyptians at home the unemployment problem continues. It has been estimated that Egypt needs to achieve a sustained real GDP growth rate of at least 6 per cent annually for joblessness to decline to manageable levels, but such expansion has not been forthcoming. For the time being, however, remittances by Egyptians abroad are among the country's largest foreign-revenue earners. Nearby Jordan remains a destination favoured by Egyptian migrants, especially those working in agriculture. That sector has seen more Jordanians abandoning it over the past few years, hence in 2003 the Ministry of Labour issued 31 per cent of its work permits for jobs in agriculture, more than any other area.

That was followed in importance by manufacturing at 20 per cent, where further labour market segmentation has occurred, and, with the introduction of the Qualifying Industrial Zone (QIZ) model into the Kingdom in the late 1990s, a further migration issue has arisen. The QIZ, an export processing zone, offers duty- and quota-free access to the US market for products manufactured by "qualifying" enterprises located in designated areas. Products must meet certain criteria to qualify under the programme. These include a 35 per cent minimum content rule, 11.7 per cent of which must be of Jordanian origin and 7-8 per cent from Israel, with the remainder to reach the 35 per cent requirement from US, Jordanian, Israeli or Palestinian sources. Many potential investors have been attracted by the privileges of investing under this model. Jordan's exports to the US are now much stronger, due in large part to the growth of QIZs. This has created jobs, as shown in **Table 3.8**.

TABLE 3.8

JORDAN QIZ WORKFORCE

	Local workers	Foreigners	Total	Foreigners as a % of total
2001	13,300	5,700	19,000	30
2002	13,900	9,600	23,500	41
2003 (to September)	17,300	13,600	30,900	44

Source:
2001-2 Ministry of Trade and Industry, Jordan; 2003 estimates by the Ministry of Labour.

However, while QIZs have created employment for Jordanians, there are also many non-Jordanian labourers working in the zones today. They are mainly from South Asian countries including India, Pakistan and Bangladesh, sometimes of the same nationality as the owners of the new factories. The reputed advantages of recruiting foreign workers are that guest labourers are generally easier to control, work harder and are already trained to do the jobs Jordanians are frequently unable or unwilling to perform. However, QIZ firms are apparently not adhering to an agreement made with the Jordanian authorities several years ago to limit foreign workers to 30 per cent of a QIZ factory's labour force, so foreigners appear to be taking more than their agreed share of jobs.

The persistence of double-digit unemployment in Jordan shows that it remains a labour-surplus economy with an urgent need for job creation. In that context, the question of foreign labour in QIZs is a new and sensitive issue that has arisen as Jordan integrates further into the global economy. QIZ jobs form an increasing share of total manufacturing employment in Jordan, but this has also resulted in the introduction of another group of foreign workers into the country. So far, that has happened without major incidents as, despite some objections by union groups, South Asian labour in QIZs has integrated smoothly into the economy and helped exports to boom. However, the sustainability of such a heavily segmented labour market remains questionable in an unstable region, with the 1990-91 expulsion of Mashreq labourers from the GCC countries still fresh in people's memory.

On the other hand, this segmentation goes along with the prosperity of Jordanians working abroad, who have played a key role in the Jordanian economy. In 2001, Jordan ranked as the ninth largest recipient of remittances among developing economies after such countries as Bangladesh (USD 2.1 billion), Lebanon (USD 2.3 billion), Turkey (USD 2.8 billion), Egypt (USD 2.9 billion), the Philippines (USD 6.5 billion) and India (USD 10 billion) (IMF, 2003).

Interestingly, all of these states also have workers in Jordan sending money home to their families. Businesses in Jordan are thus involved in paying wages to expatriates from a large number of countries, while Jordanians themselves work mainly in other places to send money home. Classical economic theory would show that this win-win situation is better than having closed labour markets with no migration. However, the problem with this increasingly complicated regional and international pattern of labour migration is that it is more vulnerable to economic and political shocks, like the oil price crash of the 1980s or the wars and political crises that have plagued the Mashreq and, more recently, the Gulf.

Remittances sent home by Jordanian expatriates rose to the equivalent of 23 per cent of GDP in 2003. This percentage is the highest in the Arab region,[26] followed by Yemen, where remittances account for 16 per cent of the country's GDP, Lebanon with 14 per cent, and Morocco with 10 per cent. Mashreq governments' efforts at diaspora management, and the degree to which remittances are actually or potentially contributing to unemployment alleviation, are considerable and increasing. Egypt has an active diaspora management strategy, as do Lebanon and, more recently, Syria. In Syria, an investment promotion law promulgated in the early 1990s was

26. *For Egypt, which has a large GDP (in the range of USD 80-90 billion), the percentage may be smaller. Still, remittances have represented 51 per cent of total financial inflow in the last 20 years. See IOM Migration Policy Issues No. 2, March 2003.*

specifically aimed at attracting Syrian migrant capital to the country, followed a few years later with the creation of a Ministry for Migrants, which is becoming very active.

On the other side of the equation, Saudi Arabia is the largest source of remittances in the Arab region (and the second in the world after the US), generating USD 15 billion in 2003. The second largest source of remittances in the region was the UAE (USD 4.5 billion), followed by Kuwait (USD 2.3 billion), Oman (USD 1.5 billion), Qatar (USD 1.4 billion) and Bahrain (USD 1.3 billion). In total, these account for around 8 per cent of the GDP of the six GCC states (IMF, 2003).

CONCLUSION

As GCC economies have been growing at high rates in the past two years, and are forecast to do well in 2005, demand for Mashreq labour in the Gulf is likely to rise over the rest of the decade. However, this will only happen if regional stability is maintained. Otherwise, the delicate balance of segmented labour markets, which brings prosperity to the Mashreq and the Gulf countries alike through specialization and the maximizing of their respective comparative advantages, will go into reverse and lead to serious economic disruption in the Arab region and beyond.

The closing of borders is no practical alternative to complex labour migration in a globalizing world context. However, a mixture of oil wealth, labour surpluses, and political crises will no doubt continue to interact with the increasingly complex segmentation of job markets in the Mashreq and the GCC. In such an atmosphere, indigenization of the labour force will no doubt remain on labour policy and migration agendas; but, in the end, the forces of supply and demand (sometimes pummelled by politics) are likely to prevail.

With more complex migration patterns in a volatile region, the need for a policy framework to manage regional labour mobility becomes more pressing. Jordan and other Mashreq countries have seen increasing cooperation with international agencies such as IOM to achieve this kind of migration management. But that still mostly occurs on a case-by-case basis, dealing with crises, or responding outside a regionally coordinated strategic framework to a national disaster. Whatever happens to labour markets in the Mashreq and the GCC over the next few years, a deeper, cross-border, strategic approach to migration is needed, preferably involving IOM and other international organizations, as well as regional bodies such as the League of Arab States (LAS).

TEXTBOX 3.2

CAMEL JOCKEYS IN THE GULF COOPERATION COUNCIL STATES (GCC): *THE CASE OF THE UNITED ARAB EMIRATES*

A large number of children are trafficked every year from southeast Asia and Sudan to the Gulf states to work as jockeys in camel races, a popular sport in Qatar, Bahrain and the UAE. Due to their light weight, children as young as 4 years of age are preferred, and are reportedly either kidnapped, or sold by their families and transported to the GCC region for this purpose. They are often sold by their own families for as little as USD 75, but more commonly in exchange for monthly payments of a few hundred dollars for one or two years. Traffickers can get as much as USD 5,000 for each child.

In camel races, children and/or minors are used as jockeys to spur the animals to win or to enhance their racing efforts. According to media reports, the children trafficked into the Gulf States for this purpose are denied adequate food and rest to ensure that they do not gain too much weight. They are kept in inhumane conditions, crammed in small rooms and often starved before a big race. Most of the children who have been returned to their families fail to remember or recognize their parents, as they were trafficked at a very early age. Many can no longer speak their mother tongue, and find it difficult to re-adapt to their cultures of origin, due to their prolonged stay in the Gulf region. As a result, they experience severe emotional traumas. If freed when they are older, they are cast aside and often become illegal.

Since the 1980s, reports have appeared in the national and international news media about children and/or minors being smuggled out of Bangladesh, Pakistan, India, Sri Lanka and Sudan to some Gulf countries, especially the UAE and Qatar. The use of children under 15 years of age as jockeys was banned in UAE in 1980 under section 20 of the Federal Labour Code No.8, after a number of children fell from camels during the races and died. However, media reports, including by the BBC, have shown that the practice still continues.

National reports have also pointed out that there is still a lot to be done to combat this practice. Thus, the UAE Minister of Foreign Affairs, who is also Chairman of the Emirates Camel Racing Federation, reiterated in July 2002 the prohibition on the employment of children who are under 15 years old or weigh less than 45 kilograms, as camel jockeys. The decision came into effect in September 2002. A fine of DHS 20,000 (USD 5,500) applies to a first offence; a second offence leads to a ban from camel racing for one year; and prison sentences are imposed for subsequent offences.

Despite the reactivation of the existing policy, child trafficking and the use of minors as camel jockeys in races continued throughout 2002 and 2003. The Karachi-based NGO, Lawyers for Human Rights and Legal Aid (LHRLA), made a study of all trafficking cases reported in Pakistan's newspapers during 2002, and documented 29 cases of child trafficking for camel racing in the UAE. This represents an increase from the 20 cases reported in the press during 2001. The Ansar Burney Welfare Trust International reported that it rescued two brothers, aged eight and 10, who were being used as camel jockeys in Abu Dhabi. The children were flown back to Pakistan in November 2002.

The use of children from Bangladesh as camel jockeys in the UAE also continued during 2002 and 2003. The Bangladesh Consulate in Dubai reported in June 2003 that in the previous few months it had rescued and repatriated approximately 20 Bangladeshi children working in the UAE as camel jockeys and domestics. The Consulate again intervened in November 2003 to rescue Zakir Mia (aged 10), who had been working as a camel jockey for some six years in the UAE. He was returned to Bangladesh and sent to the Bangladesh National Women's Lawyers Association for rehabilitation.

In 2003, the ILO Committee of Experts urged the UAE government to take immediate measures to eradicate "the trafficking of children for use as camel jockeys and punish those responsible through the strict enforcement of adequate penal sanctions".

In addition, the ILO Committee of Experts (2001), its Conference Committee on the Application of Standards (2002) and the UN Committee on the Rights of the Child (2002) concluded that employing children as camel jockeys constitutes dangerous work likely to jeopardize the health and safety of the young person. These bodies have asked governments to prohibit anyone under 18 to be engaged in this kind of work.

In a serious attempt by the UAE government to combat the problem, the Abu Dhabi Police Authority in April 2004 requested the International Organization for Migration to repatriate 69 Bangladeshi children to Bangladesh and provide them with comprehensive return and reintegration services. The main aim of the five-year project is to integrate the children socially and economically into their own families or communities. To avoid re-trafficking, the project will provide support services to ensure children acquire a formal education, and vocational or business management skills training, where appropriate, to help with economic, social and psychological integration. It is hoped that this initiative will open more doors in the future to work on the topic.

Source: IOM Kuwait City, 2004

ISRAEL: A COUNTRY OF IMMIGRATION[27]

MANAGING IMMIGRATION AND INTEGRATION

ISRAEL was established with the intention of creating a Jewish state that would provide a safe haven for Jews and a place for the national expression of the Jewish people. It became a multi-ethnic, multi-cultural, multi-lingual and multi-religious democratic state inhabited by Jews, Muslims, Christians, Bedouin and Druze, and immigrants from Europe, Africa, Asia, North and South America. In recent years, it has also become a recipient of migration flows of foreign workers, victims of trafficking, refugees and asylum seekers. Israel also maintains strong ties with its Jewish and Israeli diaspora communities, viewing them as an important resource to facilitate Israel's development.

Israel's diverse ethnic and religious population, high rate of immigration, commitment to facilitating immigrant integration and fast pace of development make it a source of instructive models on how to manage migration, multicultural integration, and diaspora-homeland ties. This chapter looks briefly at how Israel evolved as an immigrant state, the socio-economic benefits if immigration, the strong focus on integration, diaspora-homeland partnerships, and the emerging need to combat trafficking of persons, and more recently, adjustments to the labour migration policies in response to rising unemployment.

A COUNTRY OF IMMIGRATION

SOCIO-DEMOGRAPHIC FEATURES

When the state of Israel was recognized in 1948, its population comprised some 650,000 Jews and 160,000 non-Jews, most of whom were Muslim Arabs. Today, Israel's total population is 6,748,400, of which some 27.5 per cent are foreign born, hailing from the former Soviet Union, Europe, Asia, Africa, North and South America. 20 per cent of the population is comprised of Muslim Arabs, Bedouin, Christian Arabs, Druze and Circassians.

IMMIGRATION LAW

The right of immigration to Israel is primarily based on the Law of Return (1950), which entitles any Jew to become a citizen of Israel. A 1970 amendment extends this right to anyone with one Jewish parent or grandparent, and his/her spouse. Application of this law is not affected by the immigrant's financial status, educational background, age or general state

TABLE 3.9

IMMIGRANTS BY YEAR OF IMMIGRATION

Years	Asia	Africa	Europe	America & Oceania	Total*
1948-1951	237,000	94,000	327,000	5,000	687,000
1952-1960	35,000	146,000	103,000	10,000	294,000
1961-1970	49,000	151,000	139,000	45,000	384,000
1971-1980	27,000	16,000	213,000	73,000	330,000
1981-1989	10,000	23,000	60,000	40,000	133,000
1990-1994	6,000	32,000	554,000	17,000	609,000
1995-1999	39,000	12,000	276,000	20,000	347,000
Total	403,000	474,000	1,672,000	210,000	2,784,000

* The total for 1948-51 includes 24,000 immigrants whose last continent of residence is unknown; in later years it includes a small number of such immigrants. (CBS, 2003)

27. *The author of this sub-chapter is Rebecca Bardach, Director of Program Development at the Center for International Migration and Integration, established by the American Jewish Joint Distribution Committee.*

of health. This is in accordance with Israel's *raison d'etre* as a Jewish homeland and haven to Jews fleeing persecution. Citizenship paths for those who do not qualify under the Law of Return are fairly restrictive, and are issues of current public debate.

THE CONCEPTUAL FRAMEWORK

The Hebrew word for immigration to Israel is *aliyah*, which also means ascent. This is meant in both a spiritual and physical sense, as living in Israel is considered the ultimate expression of Jewish identity. The ideological view is that immigration is a form of "return migration" and so the state treats immigrants as repatriates. Governmental and non-governmental commitment to immigrant integration includes extensive planning and programme development in the areas of employment, housing, language, education, social and cultural integration.

However, even as these measures ease their transition, new immigrants to Israel must still cope with the challenges of integration that immigrants anywhere face in housing, employment, language acquisition, and social and cultural adjustment. Tensions between veterans and new immigrants also exist, in particular in cities suffering economic stress. Despite the ideological approach towards immigration, the daily challenges of integration are similar to other traditional immigration countries.

FROM MELTING POT TO MOSAIC

While the commitment to successful immigrant integration remains a national standard, the definition of integration has changed over time. In earlier decades, it was characterized by a "melting pot" approach. Immigrants were expected to reject their roots and assimilate fully into Israeli society. The absorption process became an even greater imperative as the young state focused on survival and nation-building. Between 1948 and 1951, the population doubled, becoming increasingly heterogeneous with the arrival of many new immigrants from Asia and Africa, as well as Europe. Cultural differences led to social tensions between the veterans and newcomers. Little knowledge and few resources were available to ease the integration process. The repercussions of these early social tensions continue to be felt today.

The melting pot approach changed gradually over the years. The 1960s and 1970s brought about liberation movements such as the Black Panthers, which represented the interests and demands of Israelis of North African origin (*Sephardim*). Immigrant groups gained greater political and social recognition. In the 1990s, immigrants from the former Soviet Union retained strong ties with their mother tongue, culture and sense of identity and pride. They formed Russian-language newspapers, radio and TV programmes. They became significantly involved in or formed their own theatres, symphonies, and other cultural fora. They made their political impact felt by organizing political parties represented in the Israeli Parliament.

Tens of thousands of new immigrants from Ethiopia have further changed the face of Israeli society. They brought with them unique cultural, social and religious traditions, that have enriched Israeli society. At the same time, they and the integration bureaucracies faced the challenge of adapting vocational skills from a rural lifestyle to a fast-paced, technologically- based society, learning Hebrew when many were illiterate in their own language, and bridging significant cultural gaps.

Population changes in Israel and globalization generally led to a new approach to immigrant integration. Immigrants maintain their original cultural identity while developing parallel ties to their new country. Service providers encourage a sense of membership in Israeli society, while also promoting the preservation of unique cultural heritages and identities.

GOVERNMENTAL AND NON-GOVERNMENTAL INSTITUTIONS RESPONSIBLE FOR INTEGRATION

As integration is primarily a government responsibility, a Ministry of Immigrant Absorption was founded in 1968 to determine and implement integration policies, in coordination with the

Ministries of Construction and Housing, Social Affairs, Education, Science, Culture and Sport and Health. Local municipalities also play a significant and often proactive role in this; as do non-governmental organizations such as the Jewish Agency for Israel, responsible for pre-migration and initial integration, local and international NGOs and migrant associations that assist with longer-term integration challenges of individuals and of immigrant communities in distress.

ADDRESSING INTEGRATION NEEDS

THESE government and non-governmental bodies are engaged in a variety of integration activities tailored to immigrant and community needs, including initially the following:

AIRPORT RECEPTION

New immigrants are received upon arrival at the airport by government officials and volunteers from relevant migrant associations. They are provided with information, initial documentation indicating their status, financial assistance for their first days in the country, and transportation to their first place of residence.

HOUSING

In the past, absorption centres were often used to ensure a soft landing for cultural adjustment. But from the 1990s, most immigrants have been offered a direct absorption path, and a variety of housing solutions such as rental subsidies, reduced rate mortgages and public housing.

ABSORPTION BASKET

Financial assistance referred to as the "absorption basket" is allocated to new immigrants in accord with their family size and composition, and in support of the direct absorption approach. While the benefits have recently been reduced, following budget cuts that affected a wide range of social services, the absorption basket continues to include assistance with initial rental and living expenses during the period of Hebrew-language study (Geva-May, 2000).

LANGUAGE ACQUISITION

New immigrants are entitled to attend five-month intensive Hebrew language acquisition programmes, known as *ulpan*. In addition to the standard courses, the government offers language courses designed for the needs of specific professional and immigrant populations.

IMMIGRANT EMPLOYMENT

Satisfactory employment is one of the main determinants of successful immigrant integration. Employment assistance has evolved considerably with the different flows of immigrants. For example, Soviet immigration increased Israel's adult-age workforce by 15 per cent, with a disproportionately high number of educated and skilled professional and technical workers; while Ethiopian immigration involved a high percentage of adults with agricultural and work experience, and illiterate in their own language.

Wide-ranging policies to meet these disparate needs include: accreditation of qualifications; job training, re-training and upgrading; employment referral and assistance centres; assistance in small business development; language acquisition tailored to different professional skill areas. The programmes are devised around the needs of both highly skilled and those with low skills, who lack even basic Hebrew and are illiterate in their mother tongue.

YOUTH AND EDUCATION

Schools receive government funding to provide additional, tailored educational assistance to immigrant children. Some groups, primarily the Soviet immigrants, have established a network of after-school enrichment programmes; government and non-governmental agencies have programmes to address the problems of immigrant youth-at-risk; and

Universities provide financial and educational assistance to immigrant students.

COMMUNITY DEVELOPMENT AND EMPOWERMENT

Immigrant groups have established their own associations and cultural centres to celebrate and preserve their culture and language and to facilitate the integration process. They also use radio, TV and newspapers to communicate with their own communities and broader society; and address their interests politically through immigrant-based parties.

Despite the significant expenditure on integration, immigration has had a positive effect on the macro-economic situation in Israel, bringing about a higher GDP and investment level. Immigrants from the former Soviet Union have had a powerful impact on various sectors: science, engineering, high tech. medicine (including dentistry, nursing and technician work), arts, culture and music. Immigrants generally complement rather than replace veteran workers in the labour market.

THE ISRAELI-JEWISH DIASPORA

Israel benefits from many forms of contributions from the Jewish diaspora – from financial, political and social support, to skills, infrastructure and support at both the national and community level. The diaspora community is committed to and engaged with Israel. Israel maintains a complex network of contacts, agencies and institutions to manage and strengthen its relationship with the Jewish diaspora worldwide. These bodies use a variety of practical models to deal with social, civil, population and education issues.

OTHER MIGRATION CHALLENGES

LABOUR MIGRATION

Until the outbreak of the first Palestinian uprising, or Intifada (1987-1993), Palestinians were the primary source of non-Israeli manual labour for sectors such as construction and agriculture. As security concerns increased, Palestinian labourers were no longer allowed to enter Israel regularly, and Israeli employers became increasingly reliant on labour from other source areas further afield. By 2001, there were an estimated 250,000 foreign workers in Israel, of whom some 150,000 were undocumented, accounting for approximately 13 per cent of the labour force in the private sector (Razin, 2002).

Foreign workers in Israel come from Romania, Ghana, Nigeria, Colombia, the Philippines, Turkey, the former Soviet Union, Thailand, China, and elsewhere. They are most prominent in agriculture (ca. 31.8 per cent in 2002) and construction (26.4 per cent), but also in domestic care (CBS, 2004).

For most of the 1990s, the government lacked a coordinated policy to effectively manage labour migration, though legal and social measures were gradually developed to cope with the issues that arose. Problems experienced by foreign workers, particularly the undocumented, include exploitation of their terms of employment, living conditions, social benefits, and denial of workers' freedom. The Foreign Workers Law of 1991 guarantees documented workers the right to decent working conditions, health insurance, and a written employment contract; and efforts are being made to improve enforcement of this law. Children of foreigners, including the undocumented, are entitled by law to attend school. The Tel Aviv municipality established a body in 1999 to address the social needs of both documented and undocumented foreign workers.

The high percentage of foreign workers in some fields, and the problem of rising unemployment in Israel, compelled the government to revise its approach to labour migration. An inter-ministerial Immigration Authority is being established under the umbrella of the Ministry of Interior and tasked with the responsibility of a) reducing the number of irregular foreign workers in Israel (achieved to date largely through a broad and controversial deportation scheme), and b) managing labour migration more effectively, via regulation, monitoring, enforcement, increased rights for the workers and other measures. By the end of 2003, the number of foreign workers was estimated at 189,000, a 16 per cent decrease from the previous year (CBS, 2004). The process of legislative and bureaucratic revision is still underway.

TRAFFICKING

As trafficking of women has reached global proportions, Israel too has become a recipient of victims of trafficking, usually compelled to work as prostitutes, often under terrible conditions. It is estimated that approximately 2,500-3,000 trafficked women are in Israel; most come from countries of the former Soviet Union (Gruenpeter Gold and Ben Ami, 2004). Israel is signatory to both the UN Convention Against Transnational Organized Crime and its supplementary Protocol on Trafficking in Persons. In 2000, a Parliamentary investigation committee on the Trafficking in Women was created, including members from all parties in the Parliament. NGOs active in the field are also invited to the committee sessions.

But these early efforts were insufficient to tackle the problem. In 2001, the US Department of State found Israel to be non-compliant with minimal standards set by the US Trafficking Victims Protection Act. Since then, Israel has increased its efforts to address this crime through the prosecution and conviction of traffickers; strengthened anti-trafficking legislation; a special Border Patrol unit to stem international trafficking by land; a shelter for victims willing to testify against their traffickers, and preparation of information campaigns for prevention in countries of origin.

REFUGEES AND ASYLUM SEEKERS

For many years Israel, party to the 1951 UN Convention Relating to the Status of Refugees, received a trickle of a few dozen asylum seekers per year. United Nations High Commissioner for Refugees (UNHCR) dealt with these cases in conjunction with the Ministry of Interior. As other international migration increasingly affected Israel throughout the 1990s, the number of asylum seekers also increased. In 2002, Israel hosted 703 asylum seekers and 4,180 recognized refugees.

In 2002, Israel established a National Status Granting Body, which works closely with UNHCR to determine refugee status. Asylum seekers come primarily from Africa (Ethiopia, Eritrea, Sierra Leone, Liberia, Congo, Côte d'Ivoire, etc.); but also from other regions, including the former Soviet Union.

CONCLUSION

ISRAEL faces different immigration challenges in the next decade from what it did in the last one. The flood of immigrants from the former Soviet Union arriving throughout the 1990s has begun to taper off, and the rate of emigration may increase. At the same time, the combined pressures of unemployment, and labour needs that are often met by foreigners today, will require a stronger set of coordinated solutions and policies regarding foreign workers beyond the current ad hoc approach. Trafficking continues to pose a complex international challenge. Israel will continue to face refugee issues, both in the form of an ongoing flow of asylum seekers and refugees, as well as at least a modest influx of Palestinian refugees, contingent upon developments in the peace process with the Palestinians. These various migration flows will pose social and economic challenges and demand further adaptation of Israel's ever-changing multicultural society.

CHAPTER 4
MIGRATION DYNAMICS AND DIALOGUE IN THE WESTERN MEDITERRANEAN[1]

WITH A POPULATION of close to 250 million (UNDP, 2002; 2004), the western Mediterranean[2] is a region that has been exposed to unusually complex migration dynamics because of demographic, economic, geographic, institutional and strategic factors.

The economic situation across the region varies broadly: in 2002, while France enjoyed a per capita income of USD 22,010, Mauritania's barely came to USD 340. However, this gap is not attributable to any North-South divide, since within the European Union (EU) the per capita income in Italy (USD 18,960) is almost double that of Portugal (USD 10,840). A similar pattern exists among the Maghreb countries, where Libya's per capita income (USD 7,570) is far ahead of that of all the other countries of the Arab Maghreb Union (AMU) (ibid).

There are huge contrasts in population and life expectancy across the region,[3] but also increasing similarities. For example, the general decline in the birth rates in western and southern Europe is now gradually also taking hold in the Maghreb as well. In Algeria, Morocco and Tunisia the drop in fertility in 25 years is equivalent to that in France over the last two centuries (INED, 2000). After three decades of steady decline, the fertility rate in Tunisia of 1.55 children per woman has now reached the same level as in western countries. However, the effects of this trend are unlikely to be felt in the labour market until 2010. Thus the pressure on the labour markets of the Maghreb countries is likely to continue and engender a relatively high emigration potential.

But, apart from economic and demographic considerations, migration in the western Mediterranean also plays a decisive role in the life of the region's states. It is also a major factor affecting bilateral and multilateral relations between them. This chapter looks at the growing and evolving nature of migration within this interdependent grouping of states across the north African and European continents, with a particular focus on the "5+5" dialogue that has emerged and found concrete expression among these states in recent years.

MIGRATION TRENDS

MIGRATION DYNAMICS IN THE SOUTH: FROM MIGRANT WORKER TO EMIGRANT COMMUNITY

THE 1960s saw the start of a significant flow of labour migrants from the Maghreb countries towards Europe (Brand, 2002).[4] These were mainly individuals coming with their families to work in selected sectors of the economy.[5] Between 1966 and 1972, the number of Algerians admitted to France increased by over 40 per cent (Tapinos, 1975).

1. *The author of this chapter is Redouane Saadi, Liaison Officer for the Western Mediterranean, IOM, Geneva.*

2. *Including the Maghreb countries, Algeria, Libya, Mauritania, Morocco and Tunisia; and the European Union countries, France, Italy, Malta, Portugal and Spain.*

3. *The population of Morocco (30 million) is much greater than that of Tunisia (10 million). Similarly, Italy (with 58 million inhabitants) is ahead of Malta (with only 0.4 million) and although life expectancy at birth for Spanish (78.5), Maltese (78.0) and Libyan people (70.5) is roughly comparable, the equivalent figure for Mauritania is only 51.5.*

4. *According to statistics of the French Ministry of the Interior (General Information Directorate), the net balance of Algerian migration to France from 1962 to 1964 stood at 110,213 (see Tapinos, 1975).*

5. *The main sectors employing such workers were heavy industry, construction, catering and tourism. Note, however, that the tertiary sector nowadays offers more jobs to migrants than the primary and secondary sectors (Salt, 2000).*

In 1973, however, a major economic recession was triggered in western Europe by the first oil price shock. In that year, Algeria stopped labour emigration to Europe and encouraged its expatriates to return.[6] In July 1974, France reacted to the oil price shock and the ensuing economic crisis by freezing labour immigration, a measure also adopted by other European countries.

This European freeze on immigration led to new migration strategies. Since the movement of workers slowed down after 1973, and only immigration for the purpose of family reunion remained legally possible, the two-way traffic of male workers tended to be replaced by a one-way immigration of women and children. After the flow of immigrant workers in the 1960s, family reunion reached a peak in 1975 and 1976, a trend that gave rise to a growing feminization of migration. While in the 1970s migrant women tended to be economically dependent on their spouses, they gradually became economic and social actors in their own right (Khachani, 1999).

Internal migration also plays a role in the Maghreb region. Mauritania, in particular, has had an interesting history of rural-urban migration, harking back to the society-building efforts of pre-colonial times.[7] The twin factors of migration and urbanization took a new turn following Mauritania's independence in 1960. Social change, development and the drought-related degradation of the environment led to intensified rural to urban migration and, by 1999 the urban population had increased from 40 per cent of the total population in 1992 to over 55 per cent[8] (80% currently in Nouakchott and Nouadhibou).

The Maghreb countries have set up a number of institutions, both in their own countries and in the host countries, to maintain close links with emigrant populations. Algeria, Morocco and Tunisia established "*Amicales*" (friendly associations), which act as official or associated offices to deal with expatriate affairs and manage relations with host countries, especially in regard to employment and social security. With the shift from labour migration to family reunion, the Maghreb countries were obliged to adapt their links with expatriate communities accordingly. After creating entities responsible for migrant labour quotas and subsequently relations with expatriates, they established institutions to manage the increasingly complex links with the diasporas, ranging from banking and legislative systems to facilitating investment in property in the countries of origin, to cultural instruments that help maintain and strengthen the identity of the home countries among expatriate communities.

Algeria established a National Labour Office to supervise the management of emigrant labour quotas and linkages with the diaspora. In 1996, the government set up a State Secretariat in charge of the National Community Abroad, attached to the Ministry of Foreign Affairs. At present, the Algerian government includes a Minister Delegate in charge of that community, who reports to the head of Government.[9]

In Morocco, the management of expatriate links had been shared between the Ministry of Labour and Ministry of Foreign Affairs. In 1990, a ministry dealing specifically with the affairs of Moroccan Communities Living Abroad was established and a Minister Delegate in charge of the communities duly appointed. The Hassan II Foundation for Moroccans Living Abroad[10] was also established that year, to help maintain and strengthen the links between Moroccans

6. *Algeria, an oil and gas producer whose energy resources were nationalized in 1971 by the late President Houari Boumedienne, aimed to relieve pressure on employment by creating jobs in the country with oil money instead of through emigration. Morocco and Tunisia, on the other hand, which at that time had essentially agriculture-based economies, had a more favourable policy towards emigration, and were more seriously affected by the European freeze on immigrant quotas. See also Collinson, 1996.*

7. *Traditionally, migration in Mauritania has been closely related to population movements in the region. The Saharan cities (like Chinguitti or Ouadane), whose power of attraction used to extend as far as Andalusia, became crossroads for the flow of people and products from large neighbouring empires, owing to their considerable influence, and supported by the dynamism of distant trade.*

8. *See Mauritania's Poverty Reduction Strategy Paper (PRSP), 2000 (refer footnote 13).*

9. *For more details, see www.mdccne.gov.dz.*

10. *See Act No. 19-89 promulgated by the Dahir of 13 July 1990, establishing the Hassan II Foundation for Moroccans Living Abroad. The Foundation is a "non-profit institution, pursuing social ends, under the responsibility of a financially independent legal entity", which plays an active part in social, cultural and religious affairs. It organizes courses in Arabic, civilization and religion for children of expatriates, and provides financial assistance to indigents.*

living abroad and the home country. More recently, the Minister Delegate at the Ministry of Foreign Affairs and Cooperation in charge of the Moroccan Community Living Abroad has been given the responsibility for developing a general policy on this.[11]

In Tunisia, the Office of Tunisians Abroad was set up in 1988 in the Ministry of Social Affairs and Solidarity with the general mandate of "providing the Government with elements and data to enable it to implement a policy for the guidance and assistance of Tunisians abroad". The Office operates at a national and a transnational level, by providing logistical support for the *Amicales* and associations of Tunisians abroad. It supervises economic, cultural and social aspects of relations with expatriates. In Tunisia, it is represented by regional delegations, which provide socio-cultural guidance to the families of emigrants that have remained behind in Tunisia (Brand, 2002).

The Libyan migration model is one of a kind in the Maghreb: similar to some guest worker-based labour migration systems, it does not expect migrants to become integrated locally. Immigrants play an extremely important role in all of the country's economic sectors (except in direct government service). The number of migrant workers in the country fell substantially, however, following the decline in oil price in the mid-1980s. The Libyan government manages migration through three bodies: the People's General Committee for External Relations and International Cooperation (migration diplomacy and consular affairs), the People's General Committee for Public Security (illegal migration and human trafficking) and the People's General Committee for Labour, Training and Employment (labour migration).

In Mauritania, the Office of the Commissioner for Human Rights, the Fight against Poverty and Integration has been dealing with the question of migration and development through special programmes since it was set up in 1998. Its actions are spelled out in the Mauritanian Poverty Reduction Strategy Paper (PRSP).[12]

MIGRATION DYNAMICS IN THE NORTH: FROM EMIGRATION TO IMMIGRATION

As amply discussed in other chapters,[13] most European countries have not traditionally been countries of immigration. France is an exception: in 1851, when the first general population census made a distinction between nationals and foreigners, it registered some 400,000 immigrants. Thirty years later, this number had grown to over a million. In the 19th century, the media in France included 19 newspapers in Arabic and dozens of others in Turkish, Armenian and Russian. Between the two world wars, in some years France took in more immigrants than the US (El Yazami and Schwartz, 2001).

Spain, Italy and Portugal, traditionally countries of emigration, have also recently become sizeable countries of immigration. Spanish migration, which since the 16th century was directed mainly at Latin America, has gradually turned towards western Europe. The new wave took on large-scale proportions after 1959, the year of the Economic Stabilization Plan.[14] Between 1960 and 1979, almost 2 million Spanish nationals migrated to what is now the EU (Rubio, 1974). The same pattern may be observed in the case of Italy, from where some 26 million nationals departed for America, Australia, and other European countries between 1876 and 1976. This peaked in 1913, when more than 800,000 Italians, or 2.4 per cent of the total population, left the country (Pastore, 2001).

Since becoming countries of immigration, these European countries have admitted a growing number

11. *See in particular the Strategy Paper proposed by Ms. Nouzha Chekrouni, Minister Delegate attached to the Ministry of Foreign Affairs and Cooperation in charge of the Moroccan Community Living Abroad, approved by the Council of Ministers on 13 March 2003 (www.marocainsdumonde.gov.ma).*

12. *The PRSP is linked to the initiative for reducing the debt of Highly Indebted Poor Countries (HIPC), for which Mauritania was declared eligible in 1999. The Mauritanian government prepared a poverty reduction strategy, which also involves local communities, employers and trade unions, civil society, Universities and others. The PRSP has given rise to a Steering Act on poverty reduction, which was passed by Parliament in July 2001.*

13. *See the chapters "Migrants in an Enlarged Europe" and "International Migration Trends".*

14. *Labour agreements were subsequently signed with the Federal Republic of Germany (1960), France, Switzerland, the Netherlands (1961) and Austria (1962).*

of migrants, also from the Maghreb region. In Spain, from 1991 to 1996, the average annual intake was 35,000 (EUROSTAT, 2000). Since then, the growth has been spectacular. For 1997 and 1998, the number of arrivals was estimated at, respectively, 64,000 and 123,000, and for 2000 and 2001, the figures are estimated to have risen to 360,000 and 250,000.[15] The proportion of foreigners living in Spain has increased substantially from about 0.5 per cent of the total population in 1980 to 1.1 per cent by the end of 1990, and 2.7 per cent by the end of 2001 (Fargues, 2002). One of the largest migrant communities in parts of Europe originates in the Maghreb countries. In Spain, there were 118,345 such immigrants in 1998 (EUROSTAT, 1998) and, having grown to 174,209 by 2002, they are at present the largest foreign community in the country (ibid).

Faced with growing immigration, many of the European states, particularly in the south, have tended to react along similar lines by trying to ward off the arrival of more foreigners through stricter border controls, more returns and new regulations affecting migrants already in the country. However, the restrictions imposed on legal admission channels have to some extent merely increased the incidence of illegal immigration into Europe.

TRANSIT MIGRATION: A NEW TREND

According to the highest estimates, there were just under 2 million irregular migrants in Europe in 1991, compared with 3 million in 1998. More than half of these appear to be living in France, Italy and Spain (IOM, 2000; 2004). These "Latin" European countries are the preferred gateway for irregular migrants from the Maghreb, as well as from Sub-Saharan Africa and Asia – and this is a growing trend.

Irregular migrants use several routes to enter Europe: some travel by air, the great majority by sea (Council of the European Union, 2003), which is less expensive. The extensive coastlines of Spain, France, Italy and Malta are the preferred options for entering Europe in an irregular manner, since they remain permeable despite stricter controls.[16] Italy, especially Sicily and the islands of Lampedusa and Pantelleria, has seen an increase in the arrival of irregular migrants from Libya (only 275 km from Italy) and Tunisia (a mere 113 km from Lampedusa). From Morocco, the Straits of Gibraltar are still the route most used by smugglers.[17] Owing to the closer watch on this route by Spain and Morocco, however, boats are now heading either farther east to the coast between Malaga and Almería, even as far as Murcia, or farther west, between Cadiz and Huelva. A route regularly followed by the *pateras*[18] runs from southwest Morocco to the Canary Islands.

At present, the Maghreb countries are both emigration and transit or destination points for migrants coming from Sub-Saharan Africa and Asia. Substantial population flows from Africa stretch between Sub-Saharan Africa and the Maghreb and, to a more limited extent, western Europe. They come mainly from West Africa, but also from the Sudan, the Horn of Africa and southern Africa.[19] Most migrants leave West Africa by a variety of means, including boats, buses, taxis, trucks and even on foot. They try to reach Tamanrasset either through the Niger or through Mali (Lahlou et al., 2002). Many then try to enter Morocco before attempting to cross to Europe. These journeys can last several years and are pursued by migrants in several stages, which give them a chance to take informal jobs *en route* to pay for the next stages of their journey. The number of irregular migrants in Libya, counting only those from Niger, the Sudan and

15. *See www.dgei.mir.es/fr/general/ObservatorioPermanente_index.html.*

16. *In 2003, the Spanish Guardia Civil intercepted more than 18,000 illegal migrants on the Spanish coasts, that is, 8 per cent more than in 2002.*

17. *Between 1996 and 2000, the number of immigrants arrested by the Spanish authorities in the Straits of Gibraltar rose from 7,741 to 16,885, according to Spanish Guardia Civil sources. See Pumares, 2002, p. 88.*

18. *Small boats (often fishing boats) equipped with 40-60 hp outboard motors, which can carry up to 30 passengers.*

19. *Several factors account for the rapid rise of irregular migration out of sub-Saharan Africa: population pressure, increasing poverty, reduced access to natural resources such as water, and lack of security. The tendency is further exacerbated by the strong attraction of the lifestyle and economic standards of western Europe.*

Mali, increased dramatically by 381 per cent between 2000 and 2003.[20]

The Maghreb countries have responded to this situation by introducing new measures to regulate migration. In June 2003, Morocco adopted a set of laws regulating the rights and conditions of admission and residence of foreigners in Morocco. The King of Morocco has undertaken to set up two new institutions, attached to the Ministry of the Interior, responsible for halting illegal migration. The first of these, the Migration and Border Control Directorate, will, inter alia, implement the national strategy to combat human traffic networks, as well as border controls. It will be run by a national research and investigation brigade responsible for combating illegal migration and dealing with all cases of human trafficking. The second body, the Moroccan Migration Observatory, will undertake research, gather information on migration, maintain a database of national statistics and submit proposals, including a national migration strategy, to the government for concrete measures to manage migration.

Recently, Tunisia has also made greater efforts to reduce the growing number of irregular migrants on its territory by imposing stricter conditions of admission.[21] A force of over 13,000 men, supported by 12,000 paramilitary guards, has been assigned to control the borders. Further backing for these forces is provided by joint Italian-Tunisian naval patrols. As a result of these harsher measures, Tunisia tends to be seen more as a transit than a residence option by irregular migrants (Commission of the European Communities, 2004).

Libya, on the other hand, has strengthened its institutional capacity to deal with irregular migration and human trafficking. In June 2004, the General Committee of the People for Security and IOM organized courses at the Police Academy in Tripoli to provide training for and strengthen the institutional awareness of 100 senior officials and officers of the Libyan police force. During the courses, participants studied issues such as border control, document fraud and assisted voluntary return of irregular migrants transiting Libya *en route* to southern Europe.

Actions taken by the countries of southern Europe have generally followed the policies of the European Union (EU). Since the introduction of the Schengen agreements, the EU has unified its immigration policy, by allowing free movement of persons within Europe, on the one hand, and stiffening controls around the Schengen borders, on the other.[22] EU governments have focused their efforts on strengthening border controls, maritime patrols and bilateral agreements, and on parallel diplomatic and operational dialogue with emigration countries. EU states have equipped themselves with a sophisticated computer network to share information on movements of persons within the common European space. They are also working on preventive measures to alleviate the causes of emigration in the countries of origin. Despite all these efforts, however, irregular immigration continues to grow.

REGIONAL COOPERATION ON MIGRATION ISSUES

THE EURO-MEDITERRANEAN DIALOGUE

The main objective of the Euro-Mediterranean Partnership (EMP), which was launched in Barcelona in 1995 by the governments of 27 countries,[23] is to turn the Euro-Mediterranean basin into an area of peace, stability and prosperity. This partnership, which

20. *In three years, the total number of illegal immigrants from Niger, the Sudan and Mali arrested by the Libyan authorities rose from 895 to 4,308. For more details see* Al Amn-Alam, *2004.*

21. *Act No. 2004-6 of 3 February 2004 amending Act No. 75-40 of 1975.*

22. *In 2002, Spain adopted an "Integrated External Surveillance System" (SIVE). Equipped with video and infrared cameras, it is already operational along some of the coastline of the Province of Cadiz and the Canary Islands, and is expected to be fully operational by 2005, when it should cover the whole of the country's southern border.*

23. *The signatory countries are: Algeria, Austria, Belgium, Cyprus, Denmark, Egypt, Finland, France, Germany, Greece, Ireland, Israel, Italy, Luxembourg, Jordan, Lebanon, Malta, Morocco, the Netherlands, Portugal, Spain, Sweden, Syria, Tunisia, Turkey, the UK and the Palestinian. National Authority.*

remains the most ambitious cooperation structure in the region to date, covers three main sectors: political and security; economic and financial and, lastly, socio-cultural. The latter sector has given rise to specific measures that recognize the important role played by migration in relations between host countries, countries of origin and transit countries, and the need for effective intergovernmental cooperation programmes. Continuity of the Euro-Mediterranean Dialogue is assured by the regular meetings of foreign affairs ministers of the Barcelona Process.

At the Malta meeting in 1997, it was agreed to intensify the Euro-Mediterranean dialogue and cooperation in the areas of migration and human exchanges, in particular, illegal immigration. At the fourth meeting in Marseilles in November 2000, the ministers stressed the need to extend this dialogue through a comprehensive, balanced approach. In 2002 in Valencia, a framework document was approved to implement a regional cooperation programme in the areas of justice, drug control, organized crime and terrorism, and to initiate cooperation on the social integration of immigrants, migration and the movement of people.

The ministerial conference in Naples in December 2003 concluded that, if correctly handled, migration can be a positive factor for socio-economic growth in the region. The ministers confirmed that there should be a balance between security concerns and the management of migration flows, on the one hand, and the need to facilitate legal movements and social integration of legal migrants, on the other. At the tenth and most recent ministerial meeting in Dublin in May 2004, on the eve of the tenth anniversary of the Barcelona Process, the emphasis was on how to manage irregular migration and trafficking of persons.

THE MIGRATION DIALOGUE IN THE WESTERN MEDITERRANEAN ("5+5")[24]

One of the most effective ways for western Mediterranean governments to jointly address the above-described complexities of migration in this broader region is through the "5+5" dialogue. This is an important new migration forum between the Maghreb grouping (Algeria, Libya, Mauritania, Morocco and Tunisia) and the European grouping (France, Italy, Malta, Portugal and Spain) that has been steadily consolidating itself in the past three years. The impetus was given at a meeting of the respective foreign ministers in Lisbon on 25 and 26 January 2001,[25] where the path was laid for closer regional cooperation on migration and more regular dialogue among the 5+5 countries. Annual meetings were programmed between foreign ministers, alternating between the northern and southern shores of the western Mediterranean.

This led to a first Summit of Heads of State and Government of countries of the western Mediterranean in Tunis in December 2003, at which delegates reiterated their wish to further strengthen trust, consultation and dialogue in all fields between their countries. The 5+5 partners continued their discussions on three main aspects of their partnership: i) security and stability, ii) regional integration and economic cooperation, and iii) cooperation in social and human affairs.[26] The Tunis summit marked the successful outcome of a long political process, involving similar attempts by a number of Mediterranean countries since 1983, and the 5+5 process was seen as a catalyst in this success.[27]

24. *See also Textbox 13.2, "Migration Dynamics in the Western Mediterranean",* World Migration 2003 *(IOM, 2003).*

25. *See the conclusions of the Portuguese President (item 4) of the Summit of Ministers of Foreign Affairs of the 5+5 Dialogue of the Western Mediterranean Forum, Lisbon, 26 January 2001, and the speech by Dr. Joe Borg, Minister of Foreign Affairs, Malta, entitled "Political, Cultural and Civilization Dialogue in the Western Mediterranean Area".*

26. *The Tunis Summit – particularly in the words of President of France, Jacques Chirac – recalled the promising results of the first ministerial conference on migration of the 5+5, in Tunis in 2002. The heads of state and government all agreed on the need for better cooperation, partly to combat illegal immigration and partly to improve the integration of legally established migrants by affording them better protection of their rights.*

27. *On a visit to Morocco in 1983, the late French President, François Mitterand, proposed a dialogue on the western Mediterranean involving Algeria, France, Italy, Morocco, Spain and Tunisia. This gradually took shape, with several pre-diplomatic meetings in Marseilles, Tangiers and Rome. From 1990 onwards, the meetings became more formal and were attended by the foreign affairs ministers of the countries concerned.*

FOUNDING CONFERENCE, TUNIS 2002

Following the recommendations of the Lisbon conference, Tunisia and IOM[28] organized the first 5+5 Ministerial Conference on Migration in Tunis in 2002. The meeting mostly confirmed the importance of regional dialogue on migration by the ten participating countries. Most importantly, however, it adopted by consensus the Tunis Declaration on the 5+5 Migration Dialogue (October 2002),[29] which reflects the willingness of partner states to consider multilateral approaches on common migration issues. Priority issues identified in the Tunis Declaration include: strengthening of regional consultation processes; exchange of information and analysis of migration trends; illegal migration and trafficking in persons; migration and development; migrant rights and obligations; management of legal migration flows; labour migration and vocational training; migration and health, and gender equality.

CONSOLIDATING CONFERENCE, RABAT 2003

While the Tunis Declaration established a framework for migration cooperation between the 5+5 partners, the Rabat Conference, held one year later in October 2003, consolidated that initial approach by focusing on several key areas of policy interest. The first of these included joint management of the movement of people, strengthening of human exchanges and the fight against migrant trafficking by combating networks of smugglers, and illegal immigration in general. The second concerned the rights and obligations of migrants and their integration in host societies. The third aspect was migration and joint approaches to development, involving the exchange of information about multilateral actions to combat poverty and local development measures in regions with a high migration potential, especially in cooperation with migrant associations.

OPERATIONALIZING CONFERENCE, ALGIERS 2004

Two achievements mark the third 5+5 conference in Algiers: first, the Migration Dialogue has now been accepted as part of the tradition of multilateral diplomacy between the countries concerned. Second, practical measures have been identified for follow-up, including the exchange of information and networking of national focal points on migration; training and seminars for experts of the region; awareness campaigns on migration and the risks and dangers of illegal immigration, and encouragement for the introduction of structures dedicated to research and analysis of data on migration flows. A dialogue with the countries of Sub-Saharan Africa on issues of illegal migration was also recommended.

CONCLUSION

THE 5+5 process reflects the extent to which governments across the western Mediterranean spectrum today embrace the need to work together on common migration challenges and strategies. Its forward-looking agenda for information exchange, joint management of international borders, agreed forms of labour migration, migration for development and protection of the rights of migrants is one of the best predictors of where this broad region is heading in regard to migration management over the coming years.

28. *Throughout the process, IOM has continued to act as a neutral facilitator of dialogue among the partner governments. For more information concerning these activities, see: www.iom.int/en/know/dialogue5-5/index.shtml.*

29. *For text see: www.iom.int/en/know/dialogue5-5/index.shtml.*

Americas

Chapter 5
Migration Trends and Patterns in the Americas[1]

INTRODUCTION

The complexity and scale of migration into, through and out of the Americas,[2] along with the notorious weaknesses in global migration data collection systems, make the study of migration patterns in this region more of an art than a science. Robust estimates and greater attention to the issue have begun to reveal how the powerful forces of regional integration, political disintegration, conflict and internal dislocation foster international migration throughout this vast area. Some estimates have placed nearly 20 million Latin American and Caribbean nationals outside their country of birth, most of them in North America (ECLAC, 2002). The United States (US) and Canada, largely because of their geographic proximity and economic strength, remain powerful magnets for migrants from the region, especially from Mexico, the Caribbean and Central America.

The role of migration in shaping the future of the region is uncertain. Many analysts hail the importance of remittances that pour back into countries of origin and provide a critical lifeline for communities and immigrant families. At the same time, there have been notable collaborative efforts to regionalize policies and infrastructure, and promote a greater role for migration in economic integration plans. Others point to intractable challenges in countries like Colombia and Haiti, where conflict and human rights abuses have led to seemingly perpetual displacement.

The greatest uncertainty, however, may result from two important developments in the past two years: the impact of the events of September 11, 2001, on US admissions systems in the light of increased security concerns, and the January 2004 announcement by US President George W. Bush about the possibility of a temporary worker programme.

This chapter examines the complex, evolving migration patterns and policy responses of the past few years across the region, in particular the burgeoning regional mechanisms to deal with them. Key changes relate to security, irregular migration, health, diaspora support to economic growth in Latin America and the Caribbean and the increasing internationalization of labour emigration.

1. *The authors of this chapter are: Dr. Kimberly A. Hamilton, Director, Program Planning and External Relations, MPI; Maia Jachimowicz, Research Assistant, MPI;Erin Patrick, Research Assistant, MPI and Dr Demetrios G. Papademetriou, Director of MPI. Additional input was provided by IOM Missions in Washington D.C., and Latin America and the Caribbean; and the Senior Regional Adviser for the Americas, IOM Geneva.*

2. *For the purposes of this chapter, the Americas include North America (Canada, Mexico and the United States (US)), Central America (Belize, Costa Rica, El Salvador, Guatemala, Honduras, Nicaragua, and Panama), South America (Argentina, Bolivia, Brazil, Chile, Colombia, Ecuador, Paraguay, Peru, Suriname, Uruguay and Venezuela) and the Caribbean (Independent: Antigua and Barbuda, Bahamas, Barbados, Belize, Cuba, Dominica, Dominican Republic, Grenada, Haiti, Jamaica, St. Kits and Nevis, St. Lucia, St. Vincent and the Grenadines, Suriname, and Trinidad and Tobago. Dependent territories or overseas departments include: Anguilla, Bermuda, Cayman Islands, Guadeloupe, French Guiana, Martinique, Netherlands Antilles, Puerto Rico, Turks and Caicos, UK Virgin Islands, and US Virgin Islands). Greenland and territories of foreign countries are not included in this discussion.*

DOMINANT MIGRATION TRENDS IN NORTH AMERICA

GIVEN their historical relationship to immigration, the countries of North America continue to be pre-occupied by migration-related issues, with differing areas of focus and concern, and differing commitments to addressing them.

IMMIGRATION AND SECURITY IN THE UNITED STATES OF AMERICA (US)

The US remains a dominant country of destination, home now to the largest number of immigrants in its history. As of the year 2000, 28.4 million foreign-born individuals (excluding most of the undocumented population) were living in the US, representing about 10 per cent of the entire population (US Census Bureau, 2000). Of these, some 14.5 million, or 51 per cent, are from Latin America, including Mexico and the Caribbean: 7.8 million from Mexico; approximately 2 million from Central America; 2.8 million from the Caribbean and 1.9 million from South America (ibid; SIEMCA, 2004). UN estimates place the total number of foreign-born individuals at 35 million,[3] including the growing undocumented population. This corresponds roughly to 11 per cent of the total population.

In 2002, more than 1,063,000 persons arrived in the US as legal permanent residents, primarily from Mexico (219,380), India (71,105), China (61,282), the Philippines (51,308) and Vietnam (33,627). Together, these five countries accounted for 40 per cent of all legal immigration. While the numbers continue to be significant, US government responses to the events of September 11, 2001, will significantly influence the management of future immigration flows.

In 2003, the security imperative continued to trump all other priorities in respect of cross-border movement of people. The US government continued its zero-based policy reviews of border security,[4] and scrutinized every avenue through which foreigners gain entry into the country. Several have already led to changes in administrative practices.

In this context, cooperation with Canada and Mexico, its contiguous neighbours and NAFTA partners, continued to occupy a great deal of the policymakers' attention. However, the discussions and gains in cooperation were bilateral, rather than trilateral. Each relationship moved at the pace and depth that pre-September 11, 2001 understandings and collaborative initiatives allowed. As a result, the bilateral progress on border management (both facilitation and controls), intelligence and police cooperation has been greater with Canada than with Mexico – although the gains in the depth of cooperation with Mexico have been impressive by any yardstick.

On December 12, 2001, Canada and the US signed a 30-point Smart Border Declaration in an effort to enhance security and facilitate information sharing along the border. As part of the agreement, the two governments signed a safe third-country agreement to require asylum seekers to seek status in the first country they enter (nearly one-third of Canada's annual asylum caseload was arriving from the US).[5] Three months later, the US and Mexico signed the 22-point Border Partnership Agreement which, while similar to the US-Canadian agreement in seeking improved security for the legitimate flow of goods and people, differed in many important ways.

While both agreements were based on previous bilateral discussions on border management, many of the initiatives outlined in the 22-point plan with Mexico were new. Creating compatible databases that allow for the electronic exchange of information,

3. *Cf. also the chapter in this report by the UN Population Division: "International Migration Trends".*

4. *Immediately following the September 11, 2001 terrorist attacks, and in keeping with the new heightened security environment, White House task forces were created to review and tighten border and visa admission policies.*

5. *On March 1, 2004, the Department of Homeland Security issued rules on the implementation of the US-Canada safe-third country agreement.*

implementing joint border-control training and conducting vulnerability assessments of border-related networks are some examples. Whereas the US-Canada agreement deepened and broadened specific pre-established cross-border efforts, the US-Mexico accord succeeded in opening the door to many new bilateral initiatives and was therefore more incremental by comparison (Meyers, 2003).

The most dramatic and, in many ways, most consequential 9/11-related action by the US Government has been in government reorganization. In January 2003, the US formally created a single agency, the Department of Homeland Security, to prevent future terrorist attacks and protect against, and respond to, damage from any that might occur. Pursuant to the Homeland Security Act of 2002, immigration services and enforcement, border patrol and visa policy authority, among others, are the responsibility of the new department – constituting the largest government reorganization since the creation of the Department of Defence in 1947 (Jachimowicz and McKay, 2003). Judicial review under the Board of Immigration Appeals, unaccompanied minors and the office of refugee resettlement, and visa issuance remain part of the Department of Justice, Department of Health and Human Services and the Department of State, respectively.

TEXTBOX 5.1

Enhancing US Security through Immigration Policy

Security has long been an element of US immigration policy, but it was the terrorist attacks of September 11 and their immediate aftermath that focused public and senior political attention on US borders and vulnerabilities in ways previously unimaginable. Government officials were forced to confront the reality that existing systems and processes were incapable of protecting security while also facilitating legitimate traffic. Furthermore, the narrow interpretation of border policy that had characterized the management of the US-Mexico border was deemed insufficient.

Consequently, the government undertook a number of policy initiatives designed to enhance US security in areas such as institutional restructuring, border enforcement and monitoring, interior enforcement and monitoring, and new requirements for visitors. These include the following:

- *USA Patriot Act of 2001:* Enacted on October 26, 2001, the law gives broad new government powers to monitor, detain and deport suspected terrorists, and includes provisions to strengthen border enforcement. Non-citizens (lawful permanent residents, temporary immigrants and foreign visitors) are particularly affected by some of these new provisions.
- *The US-Canada Smart Border Declaration of 2001:* This 30-point plan, signed on December 12, 2001, by then Director of the Office of Homeland Security, Tom Ridge, and Minister of Foreign Affairs, John Manley, pursues the broad goal of enhancing regional security while facilitating the legal flows of people and goods. The accord is structured around four broad pillars: the secure flow of people, the secure flow of goods, infrastructure security, and information sharing and coordination in the enforcement of these goals.
- *The US-Mexico Border Partnership Agreement of 2002:* Signed by Secretary of State, Colin Powell, and Interior Minister, Santiago Creel, on March 22, 2002, this 22-point agreement follows closely the objectives of the US-Canada declaration to create "smarter" borders. While the action items are more vague in comparison, the agreement still represents a significant step in the bilateral relationship.

- *The Enhanced Border Security and Visa Entry Reform Act of 2002:* Enacted May 14, 2002, this bill aims to further secure the nation by increasing immigration staffing, allocating new funds for technology and infrastructure improvements, and requiring the implementation of machine-readable documents with biometric identifiers. The act further expands the scope of information required and sets the implementation date for the Student and Exchange Visitor Information System (SEVIS) – a system designed to electronically track foreign students and exchange visitors during their stay in the US. Although mandated in previous legislation, the act instates new requirements such as biometric identifiers and interoperability with other law enforcement and intelligence systems to track the entry and exit of foreign visitors through the United States Visitor and Immigration Status Indication Technology System (US-VISIT).
- *Homeland Security Act of 2002:* Signed into law November 25, 2002, this piece of legislation establishes the Department of Homeland Security and incorporates, among other agencies, the Immigration and Naturalization Service. The Department's immigration-related functions are divided among the Bureau of Citizenship and Immigration Services, the Bureau of Immigration and Customs Enforcement and the Bureau of Customs and Border Protection.

Source: MPI, Washington.

As part of the continuing effort to collect information and know more about foreigners wishing to enter the US for any reason, additional changes have occurred. Two initiatives, in particular, stand out. The first is the tightening of the visa issuance process, primarily affecting nationals from Muslim and Arab countries through additional screenings. A new regulation issued by the State Department in July, 2003, requiring nearly all applicants to complete face-to-face interviews with consular officials suggests that this "tightening" is gradually spreading throughout the world.

Foreign students have been increasingly affected. Indeed, delayed and more time-consuming visa services, and new fears of discrimination regarding people applying from Arab and Muslim countries, may increase the appeal of, and add momentum to, growing competition from foreign educational institutions – all of which may have contributed to the recent decline in US academic admissions. To date, the delicate balance between enhanced security checks and timely visa issuance has not yet been struck.

Contributing to recent challenges is the new government-mandated electronic database designed to track all new and continuing foreign students and exchange visitors in the US. Fully implemented in August 2003, the Student and Exchange Visitor Information System (SEVIS) has faced tight deadlines, as well as data and access errors in its initial stages. Significant visa application backlogs and an increase in visa application fees, effective April 2004, in part attributable to additional security layers, are also the result of tightened visa policies.

The second major initiative has been the effort to track the entry and exit of all foreign visitors through the United States Visitor and Immigration Status Indication Technology System (US-VISIT), in effect since January 2004. Under the programme, foreign visitors with visas are required to have two inkless fingerprints and a digital photograph taken upon entry and verified upon departure. As of this writing, 115 airports and 14 seaports were operational for entry control, and pilot tests of exit controls were also being conducted. Beginning January 2005, US-VISIT is required to begin operating at the 50 busiest land ports of entry, but will apply to travellers requiring an Arrival-Departure Form (I-94). Mexicans holding Border Crossing Cards, not requiring the I-94, will not be subject to US-VISIT processing (as similar information is already captured). This may help allay concerns about what is regarded as the most difficult phase in the process. However, beginning in November 2004, nationals from all 27 visa-waiver countries[6] will be subject to US-VISIT, an administrative task that concerns many. Full implementation of the programme is slated for January 2006.

In this regard, it is also important to note two related efforts. The US Government had required all 27 so-called "visa waiver" countries to issue machine-readable passports with biometric identifiers to their nationals by October 2003, or lose the visa-free entry privilege. The deadline had to be extended by one year because virtually no country had the chance to comply fully. In August 2004, President Bush signed into law a one-year extension of the deadline to October 26, 2005. The second effort was a US demand that air carriers submit a full passenger information list to US authorities prior to take-off for a US destination. The European Commission had resisted this demand, but gave in under intense US pressure. In disagreement, the European Parliament has asked the European Court of Justice to rule on the issue on grounds that the agreement violates European Union and member state privacy protections.

The US also continued to experiment with domestic initiatives focused on non-citizens. Launched in December 2002, a domestic registration programme – a component of the National Security Entry-Exit Registration System (NSEERS) – required foreign visitors from designated countries staying in the US to register with immigration officials. Nationals from 25 predominantly Arab and Muslim countries, totalling over 80,000 individuals, were subject to this "special registration". Strong public and congressional criticism against the domestic registration programme, primarily on the grounds of nationality-based instead of security-based criteria, ensued as a result. The US government has since eliminated some re-registration requirements and ultimately hopes to fold the NSEERS programme into US-VISIT.

New security requirements have, in addition, affected refugee and asylum seeker inflows. Announced in March 2003, the Department of Homeland Security instated Operation Liberty Shield, which, among other things, detains all asylum seekers from countries thought to have ties to the Al Qaeda terrorist network upon entering the US, where they remain in custody until their application is processed. Refugee applicants and their identification documents are now subject to additional background checks as well. These actions have been criticized for unduly hindering the timely protection of those seeking refuge and possibly deterring new applicants. The number of refugees admitted to the US decreased from 68,426 in 2001 to 28,455 in 2003.

MEXICO, UNAUTHORIZED MIGRATION AND TEMPORARY EMPLOYMENT

Perhaps the initiative that has garnered most domestic and international attention was a Presidential announcement on January 7, 2004, addressing the issue of unauthorized immigration in the US. Containing some elements of previous discussions with Mexico on migration management, President Bush proposed to grant all unauthorized workers residing in the US temporary legal status. The temporary worker programme would also be extended to new foreign workers, provided there were no US workers to fill the positions. Incentives to return upon visa expiration and a "reasonable" annual increase in legal immigrant admissions were also mentioned.

Although reactions to the President's statement have been mixed, there is consensus that the current situation of having an estimated nine million irregular immigrants (the majority of whom are Mexican) living in the US is untenable (see **Figure 5.1**: Undocumented Population in the United States

6. *The US Visa Waiver programme enables citizens of certain countries to travel to the US for tourism or business for 90 days or less without obtaining a visa. At mid-2004, some 27 countries participated in the programme: Andorra, Australia, Austria, Belgium, Brunei, Denmark, Finland, France, Germany, Iceland, Ireland, Italy, Japan, Liechtenstein, Luxembourg, Monaco, the Netherlands, New Zealand, Norway, Portugal, San Marino, Singapore, Slovenia, Spain, Sweden, Switzerland, UK (www.travel.state.gov/visa/tempvisitors_novisa_waiver.html).*

by Country and Region of Origin, 2002). The security risks in having one-quarter of the resident foreign population without authorization, the inability of such foreign workers to avoid exploitation by their employers, and the need to reduce human smuggling and deaths along the border are just some of the reasons cited. The presence of immigrants (both legal and irregular) throughout the nation, including in new destination cities, and the increased attention to the need to effectively integrate newcomers into society have further spurred momentum for an overhaul of the US immigration system.

FIGURE 5.1

UNDOCUMENTED POPULATION IN THE UNITED STATES BY COUNTRY AND REGION OF ORIGIN, 2002

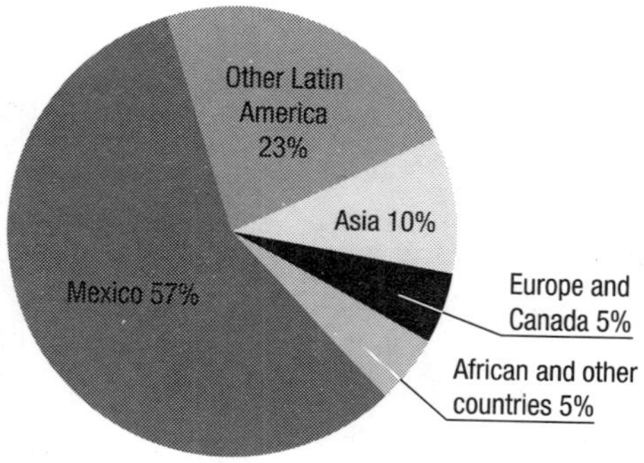

This initiative has been watched very closely by Mexico, whose government has made enormous political investments in the relationship with the US. In 2001, President Bush and Mexican President Vicente Fox initiated migration-related negotiations, important to the US and at the top of Mexico's foreign policy agenda. Progress towards a bilateral migration management strategy seemed near when the terrorist attacks of September 11 quickly halted all discussions. The US embarked on a security campaign, and the relationship suddenly became strained.

Later in 2002, the two countries signed the "smart" border accords to cooperate intensely on border security activities. However, migration discussions still did not resume. Instead, the Mexican Government decided to focus on strengthening its own immigration system (both enforcement and services) and on leveraging remittances sent from nationals working abroad. Although Mexican officials have responded favourably to US immigration reform discussions, they have approached public statements with care and caution.

Mexico, too, has seen its foreign-born population grow toward 500,000. More than half (63%) are children born in the US to Mexican immigrants (Alba, 2003). Another estimated 11 per cent come from other countries in Latin America and the Caribbean, over 60 per cent of these are from Guatemala. Despite the growing foreign-born population, Mexico is essentially a land of transit, especially for immigrants heading to the US from Guatemala, Honduras and El Salvador (CONAPO, 2000). (See Figures 5.2 and 5.3 for a US and Canadian comparison of foreign-born population by country of birth).

Even though offenders face high penalties and possibly jail, Mexico continues to be a source, transit and destination country for the smuggling and trafficking of persons. There are a number of diverse trafficking patterns in Mexico, including movement of 16,000-20,000 child sex victims and uncounted other labourers through the region. Baja California is considered to be the most vulnerable smuggling transit point (United States Department of State, 2004a). Mexico does not yet fully comply with the minimum standards for the elimination of trafficking, although it is making efforts to do so. For example, scattered criminal cases have resulted in 85 convictions of traffickers in 2003. Despite these efforts, there are still major concerns about Mexico's ability to protect victims, including the presence of corrupt government officials that are facilitating trafficking patterns, and the lack of a comprehensive anti-trafficking law (United States Department of State, 2004b).

ADMINISTRATIVE CHANGES AND SECURITY CONCERNS IN CANADA

Recent immigration trends in Canada show a rise in the foreign-born population, especially from Latin

America and the Caribbean, as well as Africa and the Middle East. In the forty-year time span between 1961 and 2001, the size of the Latin American and Caribbean-born population increased by a factor of 45 from 12,900 to 585,800, whereas those coming from Europe increased only by a factor of approximately eight from 809,330 to 1,478,230. In 2001, the foreign born represented 19 per cent of the total population (practically twice that of the US in 2000), approximately 5.5 million people (Statistics Canada, 2003). Because the majority of Canadian immigrants come for labour purposes, the level of immigrant education is highly polarized, immigrants are either very well educated or barely at all.

There have recently been important demographic shifts affecting Canadian policy developments in the immigration field. For example, the increasing immigrant density in large cities and declining labour skills of recently arrived migrants have affected the country's effort to stimulate economic growth through immigration (Beach et al., 2003). Other trends have removed pressure from the Canadian immigrant reception system. The number of refugees seeking asylum in Canada has been dropping significantly. If the country maintains its current pace, it will record 19,000 applicants, the lowest total since 1983 (Friscolanti, 2004).

Part of this reduction is due to the overarching reform of Canadian immigration policy with the Immigration and Refugee Protection Act of 2002. The legislation had three main goals: the strengthening of the Canadian economy, the facilitation of family reunification, and the fulfilment of Canada's legal and humanitarian obligations. The provisions of the legislation shifted the Canadian skills-based immigration system away from its focus on occupational shortages in favour of increased emphasis on long-term earnings potential as the basis of admission under the points system. The Act, in the interest of security concerns, also tightened the criteria for asylum application processing, including more thorough screening, reduced rights of appeal, and more explicit detention provisions (Beach et al., 2003).

In September 2003, Citizenship and Immigration Canada (CIC) revised the Act to decrease the number of points required to pass the skilled workers test from 75 to 67, citing the need to be more flexible to labour market needs. Canada has also actively recruited immigrants in other ways, from sponsoring recruiters in Mexico for agricultural and other low-wage jobs, to stepping up its recruitment of new university students from abroad in response to student visa complications across the American border (Perkins, 2004).

Another recent major development in Canada was the retirement of Prime Minister Chrétien and the ascension of Mr. Paul Martin to the Prime Ministership in December 2003. Mr. Martin's early decisions have focused on working even more closely with the US on the latter's security concerns. He showed his government's intentions first by committing to strengthening and upgrading the Prime Minister's relationship with US President Bush and, second, by reorganizing his government to focus more directly on internal security, in part by creating a new super-agency which, in many important respects, parallels that of the US Department of Homeland Security.

The new Department of Public Safety and Emergency Preparedness, headed by then Deputy Prime Minister Anne McLellan (whose position most closely corresponds to Secretary of Homeland Security) includes a Border Services Agency to consolidate border functions from various government agencies, and also consolidates all agencies with intelligence components through one chain of command. The Department, which created Canada's first national security policy, has been developed in conjunction with improved screening of immigrants, asylum seekers, and visitors.

Human trafficking has become a growing Canadian problem, warranting increased attention since the turn of the millennium. While the 2001 Immigration Act outlawed trafficking in persons and established severe criminal penalties for the offence, thousands of persons, including 15,000 Chinese, were smuggled into the country over the last decade. Canada has also been accused of deporting victims of human trafficking, especially those involved in prostitution (United States Department of State, 2004a). Recently, the country has improved its prosecution of human traffickers, with a new anti-trafficking law enforcement division of the Royal Canadian Mounted Police. However, the country is still under pressure because of accusations that trafficking victims are unable to finish complicated requests for asylum before being deported (United States Department of State, 2004b).

The Canadian national elections called for June 28, 2004, focused extensively on immigration reform. Conservative and New Democratic Party candidates alike published opinions on immigration reform, both indicating that employment-based immigration should be facilitated (Belgrave, 2004). The Prime Minister publicly responded to their proposals by expressing his desire to increase the number of immigration officers and reform the growing backlog of applications (Liberal Party of Canada, 2004). The future of Canadian immigration reform is very much tied to the more general future of Canadian politics and the electoral results. The Prime Minister established a minority government following the election, and retained both his Minister of Citizenship and Immigration, and Deputy Prime Minister. Further immigration reform will require a compromise in the absence of a majority in Parliament.

FIGURE 5.2

REGION OF BIRTH FOR THE FOREIGN-BORN POPULATION OF THE UNITED STATES, 2000

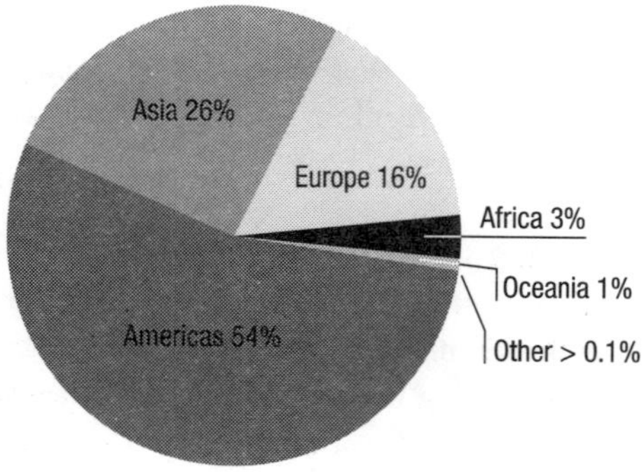

Source: "Comparing Migrant Stock", Migration Information Source, www.migrationinformation.org.

FIGURE 5.3

REGION OF BIRTH FOR THE FOREIGN-BORN POPULATION OF CANADA, 2001

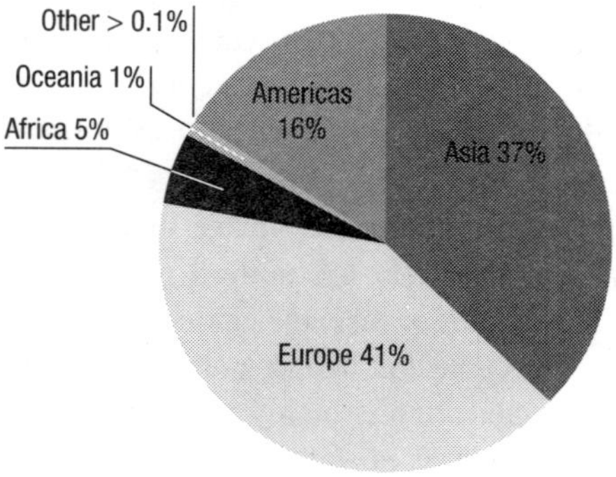

DOMINANT MIGRATION TRENDS IN LATIN AMERICA AND THE CARIBBEAN

As stated at the outset, there are estimates that, three years ago, 20 million of the total 175 million migrants globally were born in Latin America or the Caribbean: seven million residing legally in the US, three million within Latin America and the Caribbean, and ten million in other parts of the world. Popular destinations have been Spain, Italy, Canada, the Netherlands, the UK, Australia and Japan (ECLAC, 2002). In 2002, 5.9 million migrants representing 3.47 per cent of the world's migrant population lived in Latin America and the Caribbean (UN, 2003).

From the earliest days of colonization until the early 1970s, Latin America and the Caribbean attracted immigrants from around the world, especially from Spain, Italy, Portugal and Japan, but also other European countries. They carved out enclaves in the new and burgeoning economies. Today, that pattern is largely reversed, with many longstanding destination countries in Latin America seeing a marked decline in immigration due in part to economic problems, particularly in countries like Argentina and Venezuela. Over a five-year period from 1995 to 2000, the net emigration rate for Latin America and the Caribbean was the highest of any region in the world.

On average, one out of every 1,000 people emigrated annually (UN, 2003).

Today, migration is often interregional, and in some cases, migrants with demonstrated ethnic roots in former European and Asian sending countries are returning under preferential agreements. Spain's special agreement with Ecuador is particularly important in supplying labour.

For many decades, migration within Latin America was intraregional, shaped by a variety of political and economic forces. In Central America, political violence in Nicaragua and El Salvador led to mass flight in the 1970s and 1980s, especially to Costa Rica (SIEMCA, 2004). In 2000, the Costa Rican census counted nearly 300,000 immigrants. Nearly 75 per cent came from Nicaragua (Villa and Pizarro, 2002). In South America, dictatorships in the southern cone (Argentina, Brazil, Chile, Uruguay, Bolivia, Paraguay) forced many to leave, while the countries with more stable economic growth, including Argentina and Venezuela, encouraged immigration. Indeed, in 1990, these two countries hosted nearly two-thirds of the Latin American migrants living outside their country of birth (ibid).

A study by Alejandro Portes and Kelly Hoffman (Center for Migration and Development, 2004) reveals a series of major trends in the late 1990s that profoundly shaped regional flows. Public sector employment shrank across Latin America, as did opportunities in the formal economy, except in Argentina. Consequently, employment within the informal or small business sectors grew alongside rising poverty, even among workers. These and other trends affected the Andean region. A study by the UN Economic Commission for Latin America and the Caribbean (Solimano, 2002) finds that political instability, weak state institutions, and continued conflict spurred by growing inequality and ethnic diversity have created inhospitable conditions for economic stability.

In Central America, Costa Rica, Belize[7] and Panama[8] have been the three major immigrant-receiving countries. While for Costa Rica and Belize the main migrant flows are intraregional, in Panama most immigrants are from other regions like South America and the Caribbean, as well as Asia. In 2000, also, Central Americans represented almost 7 per cent of immigrants in the US. The total number of Central Americans in the US increased threefold during 1980-1990 and doubled between 1990-2000 (SIEMCA, 2004).

It is estimated that since the new intraregional destination countries, Costa Rica, Chile and the Dominican Republic have not been experiencing immigration flows equivalent to emigration from the region, intraregional migration has declined. Mexico and Colombia are the exceptions to this, the former because of growing illegal entries from Central America (The News – Mexico City, 12 June, 2003), the latter because of Colombians still attempting to escape the present conflict.[9]

Ecuador demonstrates the complexity of migration patterns in Latin America: a key destination country, it is also a significant country of origin and transit. According to the Ecuadorian Central Bank, 550,000 Ecuadorians have emigrated in the last five years, i.e., about a fifth of the working population. At the same time, Ecuador has received a substantial number of Colombians through the northern borders, and Peruvians on the southern borders (*El Comercio*, June 2003).

Within this context, the economic collapse of Argentina in early 2002 created a special set of

7. *Belize is less populated in the region and has a greater percentage of immigrant population: 15 of every 100 inhabitants were born abroad. During 2000, its population was 232,000, of which 34,000 were born abroad. In 1991, 74.3 per cent of immigrants were Central American. In 2000, this rose to 75.6 per cent, most of them from Guatemala (56 per cent) and El Salvador (23 per cent).*

8. *In Panama, in 2000, three out of every 100 persons living there were immigrants (82,000 of 2.8 million); approximately 16 per cent of them from Central America; almost half from South America (48.2 per cent), the Colombians being the most numerous local group (55 per cent). Immigration from the rest of the world, particularly Asia, increased from 21.9 per cent in 1980 to 30.8 per cent in 2000.*

9. *The Ecuadorian Immigration Police estimate that over 300,000 Colombians have entered and resided in Ecuador since 2000, while many Colombians still emigrate to Venezuela and Panama.*

international and regional migration patterns. Once counted among the wealthiest countries in Latin America, Argentina found itself on the brink of economic collapse. As a result, people from surrounding countries who had come to Argentina during its economic boom in the 1990s are returning to places such as Chile, Bolivia, Paraguay and Peru. In addition, some of its earliest settlers, including many Argentine Jews and descendants of European immigrants who made their way to Argentina early in the century, have left, taking advantage of the *ius sanguinis* citizenship systems in, e.g., Germany and Israel, to return to former countries of origin.

Spain, Portugal, Italy, Israel and the US are among the most popular destinations of Latin American emigrants. In early 2003, Spain anticipated receiving nearly 400,000 applicants for citizenship from Argentina alone (BBC News, 2003). Israel saw an increase in admissions from Argentina in 2002, when over 6,000 Argentines arrived, up 330 per cent from the previous year. Recent economic and political stability in Argentina, however, have stemmed outflows, which are now back to their pre-crisis level of around 1,500 departures in 2003 (MOIA, 2004).

Argentine immigration into the US increased to 3,685 in 2002 from 1,760 in 1995. Partially in response to the increasing numbers, as well as to managing immigration after September 11, the US removed Argentina from its visa waiver programme. Argentines wishing to travel there must now secure a visa before leaving (Lichtblau et al., 2002). In January 2004, the Argentine Government announced plans to reform its own immigration policy, simplifying the documentation process for citizens of the Mercosur region living in Argentina. While at the time of writing the specifics of the plan had yet to be determined, the reform was set to include a regularization programme for unauthorized immigrants from neighbouring countries, an estimated total of 700,000 individuals (Diario de la Sociedad Civil, 2004).

Despite this kind of strategy, however, when given the opportunity, migrants from the region choose to leave the region altogether. Immigration from the Dominican Republic to the US has continued to be strong since the mid-20th century. It was also important for Venezuela in the 1970s and 1980s, but the Venezuelan crisis caused a shift in other directions, principally to Spain. Approximately one out of every 200 Dominicans lives in Spain (Valiente, 2003). Unlike the flows to the US, which are primarily of urban origin, those who go to Spain are mostly from rural areas. But this extra-regional out-migration trend applies generally to the wider Latin American region (see **Graphs 5.4 and 5.5 below**).

GRAPH 5.4

TOP SOUTH AMERICAN SENDING COUNTRIES TO THE UNITED STATES, FY 1989-2002

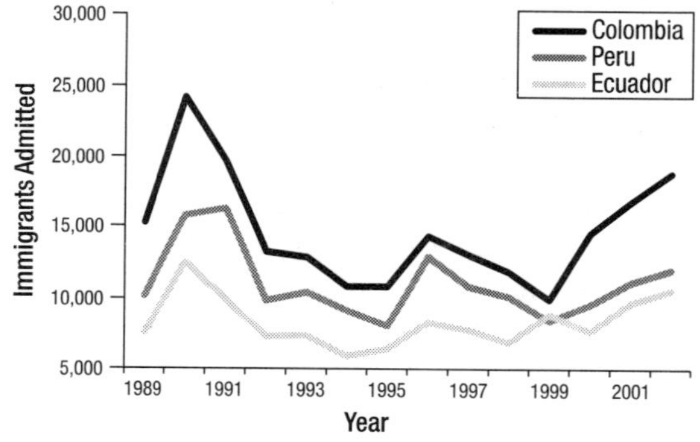

GRAPH 5.5

TOP CENTRAL AMERICAN SENDING COUNTRIES TO THE UNITED STATES, FY 1989-2002

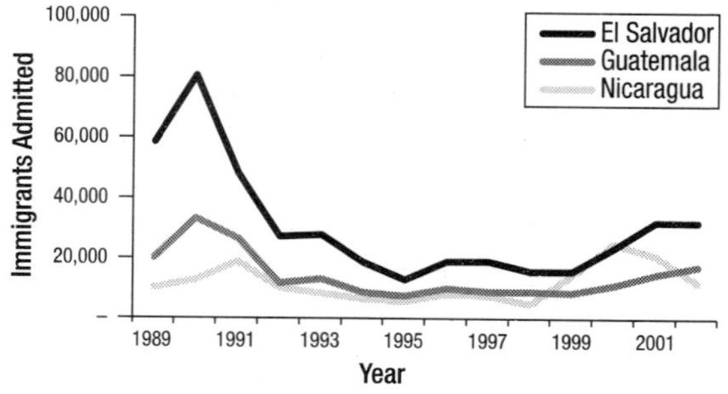

Source:
2002 Yearbook of Immigration Statistics. US Citizenship and Immigration Services: Washington, D.C.

The attraction of Venezuela as a destination country has also waned. An attempted coup in April 2002, combined with continued political and economic uncertainty, has encouraged emigration from that country. Fifty years ago, the country was a net importer of labour, especially from southern Europe, which supported its petroleum-based industrialization efforts. Of the estimated 335,000 immigrants at that time, roughly 70 per cent came from Portugal, Spain and Italy (Massey et al., 1998). Subsequent economic growth in the 1970s encouraged immigration from within the region, especially from Colombia and, to a lesser extent, from Ecuador and Peru. As with the Argentine population, Venezuelan immigrant flows to the US have increased considerably, rising from 2,630 in 1995 to 5,259 in 2002.

Like its northern neighbour, Brazil is also witnessing an emigration trend. The US has become one select destination, as legal and irregular immigrants make homes in states such as Florida, Massachusetts and New York. Inflows of Brazilian immigrants into the US have risen steadily since 1999, from slightly less than 4,000 to nearly 9,500 in 2002. According to US Census figures, the stock of Brazilians, too, has been rising from 82,500 in 1995 to 212,400 in 2000. (Note that the inflow numbers do not capture unauthorized entries.) Portugal is another primary destination; Brazilians now make up 11 per cent of the 191,000 legal immigrants in that country (Sopemi, 2001).

Brazilians as well as other Latin Americans of Japanese descent are also choosing to move to Japan, following the 1990 revision of Japan's Immigration Control Act (Papademetriou and Hamilton, 2000). In response to the growing number of visa overstayers, the Act increased opportunities for skilled and professional immigrants, provided for special technical training internships, and gave preferential access to descendants of Japanese emigrants. Brazil hosts the largest Japanese population outside Japan. The deteriorating economic situation in Brazil and elsewhere, however, combined with Japanese recruitment efforts, have also enticed more South American workers of non-Japanese origin to go to Japan. In 2000, Brazilians accounted for the largest foreign group in Japan, numbering 250,000. Peruvians, the second-largest group, numbered 46,000 (Kashiwazaki, 2002).

DISPLACED PERSONS AND REFUGEES

Intraregional displacements of persons is no longer a problem on the scale of the previous decade. In the past, such displacements gave rise to highly complex patterns of migration. These patterns ranged from short-distance movements (e.g. Nicaraguans to Honduras and Costa Rica, Salvadorans to Costa Rica, and Haitians to the Dominican Republic), medium-distance movements (e.g. Salvadorans and Guatemalans to Mexico) to long-distance movements (from various Central American countries to Mexico and the US, and Haitians to the US and Venezuela). Today, the numbers of refugees fleeing from these regions have dropped considerably from the 1980s and early 1990s. According to UNHCR, as of 1 January 2002 the list of "persons of concern" for Latin America numbered 765,400. This was the second-lowest number of persons of concern compared to 8,820,700 in Asia, 4,855,400 in Europe, 4,173,500 in Africa, 1,086,800 in North America and 81,300 in Oceania (UNHCR, 2004).

Conflict Spurs Continued Flight from Haiti

Haiti was in the news in 2004, as a rebel uprising in February forced President Jean-Bertrand Aristide to flee the country. Fears that the unrest would cause massive refugee flows to the US and throughout the Caribbean were for the most part unrealized. However, many believe the absence of Haitian refugees in 2004 (compared to 1994, for example) was due more to the restrictive policies of the US and some Caribbean neighbours than to a lack of desire on the part of Haitians to flee their troubled country.

For Haitians, the US maintains a policy of either summary return or mandatory detention. If intercepted Haitians express a clear fear of return, they may be interviewed and sent to the US naval base at Guantánamo Bay to have their case heard. Individuals who are deemed to have a well-founded fear of persecution if returned are held at Guantánamo, where they await resettlement; few Haitians are eligible for resettlement in the US. Those who do not express a clear fear of return upon interdiction are sent back to Haiti.

Estimates suggest that there are one million Haitians living in the Dominican Republic, many illegally. The Dominican government followed a harsh line during the most recent crisis; by most accounts either turning back Haitians at the border or forcibly returning those that arrived on Dominican territory. The Bahamas also hosts a large number of Haitians, who make up a significant proportion of its foreign-born population, but has in recent years followed the US policy of interdiction and return. Other neighbours, particularly Jamaica, have welcomed Haitian refugees to the extent that resources and international assistance allow.

The numbers of Haitians arriving in the US has steadily increased from over 16,500 arrivals in 1995 to more than 27,100 in 2001. That number declined to 20,270 in 2002, largely due to increased interdictions by US authorities. An estimated 497,000 Haitians live in the US, primarily in Florida and in New York (Migration Information Source).

Colombia's Internal Displacement Crisis

Over forty years of conflict in Colombia have uprooted millions of Colombians. Though historically displacement has tended to occur within rural areas, most of today's internally displaced Colombians flee from rural to urban areas, seeking better protection and, often, economic opportunities. They blend in with the urban poor and become more difficult to identify and assist. Internal displacement disproportionately affects Colombia's Afro-Colombian and indigenous populations, which make up only 18 per cent of the country's total population, but over one-third of the country's IDPs.

At the end of 2002, there were an estimated 2.5 million internally displaced Colombians, one of the world's largest IDP populations. In addition, more than 1.2 million Colombians have emigrated since 1997. This figure includes nearly 400,000 Colombian refugees or those living in refugee-like circumstances in countries in the region and in the US, as well as approximately 40,000 Colombians who sought or were granted asylum in 2002. According to the US 2000 Census, there are roughly 509,800 immigrants from Colombia in the US. In 2002, 18,845 Colombians immigrated to the US, up from 16,730 the previous year.

A significant increase in the number of Colombian asylum seekers has been noted in 2003-04 in Ecuador, which is finding it more and more difficult to absorb and integrate its Colombian refugee populations without additional international assistance. In recent years, Canada has started a "source country" resettlement programme for Colombians, under which Colombians who are in a refugee-like situation while still in Bogotá are resettled directly from there, a relatively uncommon policy within refugee resettlement processes. The existence of such a programme is, in effect, a recognition by the Colombian government that, in these cases at least, it cannot protect its own citizens.

KEY TRENDS IN THE CARIBBEAN

THE CARIBBEAN region, comprising 24 island states, has one of the highest net emigration rates in the world (some 72,000 persons emigrated annually between 1995 and 2000). While there is considerable intraregional migration, such as between Haiti and the Dominican republic, most Caribbean countries have developed specific labour migration ties to the US and, to a lesser extent, to Canada (Thomas-Hope, 2002; see **Graph 5.6**: Top Caribbean Sending Countries to the US, FY1989-2002). In 2000, Caribbean migrants in the US totalled 2,879,000 or 9.6 per cent of the foreign-born population (US Census, 2000) and these inflows into the US continue to be significant, even though in 2002 the numbers had fallen to 96,380 from 103,550 in 2001.

GRAPH 5.6

TOP CARIBBEAN SENDING COUNTRIES TO THE UNITED STATES, FY 1989-2002

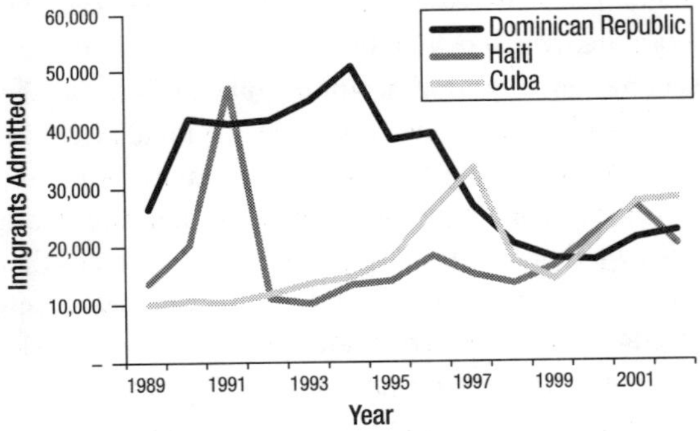

Source:
2002 Yearbook of Immigration Statistics. US Citizenship and Immigration. Services: Washington, D.C.

The US continues to be a prime destination for both Haitians and Cubans fleeing their countries. Sometimes arriving by boat and without authorization, the separate groups continue to be handled differently. Cubans who physically arrive on US soil are allowed to stay. Those who are intercepted at sea are returned. Beyond this, under agreements signed with Cuba in 1994 and 1995, the US admits roughly 20,000 Cubans annually either as refugees or through immigration channels. In return, Cuba works to prevent its citizens from departing illegally for the US. In 2002, some 28,270 Cubans entered the US. The stock of Cubans in the US as of 2002 was 919,000, the largest foreign-born group in Florida, where the majority of them reside

MIGRATION AND HEALTH

As Latin America is a prominent region for migration, there is concern about the health risks for migrants and the health problems that migration may cause or exacerbate. But it is difficult to find consolidated information across the region on this issue. Huge strides in public health policies and actions have been made by governments, but the inequalities regarding access to basic health services continue to persist across the region.

Migration and HIV/AIDS

UNAIDS reported in 2004 that around 1.6 million people were living with HIV in Latin America (UNAIDS, 2004). It concluded that HIV infection in this region tended to be highly concentrated among certain groups, such as injecting drug users and men who have sex with men. The most affected country is Brazil (660,000 people infected), although the national prevalence is less than 1 per cent. Marginal populations, including migrants in irregular status, are also at high risk.

Many of the same conditions that drive the spread of HIV also drive migration (IOM, 2004a), such as poverty, discrimination and exploitation, limited access to social, education and health services, separation from families and partners, and separation from the socio-cultural norms that guide behaviour in stable communities (IOM, 2004b). For example, one study found that HIV infection is spreading particularly among the poor and migrant communities in the interior of north-eastern Brazil (Kerr-Pontes et al., 2004). Structural factors, population mobility and migration patterns were strongly associated with the spread of HIV, and may explain the upward trend in infection rates among these populations.

The US National Institute of Health has noted that many immigrants entering a country are males who travel without their family in search of work. They are increasingly at risk of contracting HIV through sexual contact with women living in the host country, at times through engaging the services of sex workers. Recent studies indicate that women migrants are often sexually exploited, particularly when they require assistance or protection at border crossings, making them vulnerable to sexually transmitted diseases (Bronfman et al., 2004). Unauthorized immigrants often encounter difficulties accessing proper health care in the country of destination due to their illegal status, potentially harmful both to themselves and the host society. In many countries, being HIV positive or having AIDS can also be a cause for deportation.

Migration and Malaria in the Americas

Active malaria transmission is reported in 21 of the 35 countries members of the Pan American Health Organization (PAHO, 2003). Among these, 16 with a high risk of transmission identified human mobility as a major cause of persistent transmission (Bloland et al., 2002). In Colombia, the Ministry of Health knows that massive displacements in the regions with high transmission rates was one of the main hindrances to controlling the disease. They have created different stages of malaria transmission, including urban endemic malaria, stable malaria and epidemic malaria in reception zones.

International attention has recently focused on the health risks and increasing number of deaths among unauthorized immigrants attempting to migrate illegally. There are many health threats that unauthorized immigrants encounter as they travel through high-risk and unsafe areas where they are less likely to be caught by border patrol agents. Migrants face dehydration, serious injury, and even death when attempting to cross the US-Mexico border. At the destination, migrants with irregular status have great difficulty accessing health and social services, which further endangers their health and integration possibilities, and increases risks of stigmatization and marginalization.

The main causes of morbidity and mortality among the migrant and internally displaced populations are malnutrition, poor living condition (lack of clean water and basic sanitation and high population density), poor mental health[10] and lack of access to primary health care services. For example, in Colombia the IDP and migrant populations in neighbouring countries have a mortality rate 6 times higher than the general population.[11]

Government and International Responses

Governments in the region are attempting to address migration health issues in more cooperative ways. For example, Mexico and Canada jointly organized a seminar on migration health in Guatemala in October 2004, within the framework of the Regional Migration Conference (Puebla Process). Such initiatives provide a forum for dialogue between migration and health policymakers and experts, and strengthen partnerships needed to integrate migrant health into migration management strategies. The US and Mexico have also undertaken joint efforts to combat TB on both sides of the border (Waterman, 2004).

The UNFIP, UNDP and UNFPA are working together on a project "Protecting Migrant Populations in Central America from HIV/AIDS" to prevent the expansion of HIV/AIDS in Central America and Mexico (IMPSIDA, 2004). OPECP and UNFPA are also implementing a project on AIDS prevention and population mobility in Belize, Guatemala, Honduras, Costa Rica, French Guiana and Saint Lucia, that will help improve life skills and competencies in regard to STI/HIV/AIDS prevention among migrant and young mobile populations. Finally, in 2004 the ministries of health of Central America submitted a project "Mesoamerican Project in Integral Care for Mobile Populations: Reducing Vulnerability of Mobile Populations in Central America to HIV/AIDS" to the Global Fund to Fight AIDS, Tuberculosis and Malaria. This project will cover Belize, Costa Rica, El Salvador, Guatemala, Honduras, Nicaragua and Panama.

IRREGULAR MIGRATION

As in many other parts of the world, irregular migration in and out of the Latin American and Caribbean region is increasing. The well established migrant communities in some destination countries act as a "pull" and support for much of the irregular migration, particularly to North America and

10. *A Mental Health study conducted by PAHO in four cities in Colombia found depressive symptoms in 65.4 per cent of IDPs (Poncelet, 2004). A survey carried out in five localities in the city of Bogotáfound that the main health problems reported by IDPs are negative effects on their mental health and psychosocial stability, access to food and, to a lesser degree, gastrointestinal and respiratory disorders (Mogollon et al., 2003).*

11. *PMA, Vulnerability in IDPs in Colombia, June 2003.*

southern Europe. These networks are increasingly useful where legal channels for entry into desired destination countries are limited and selective.

The irregular movements that occur take different forms: a) exit from Latin American countries directly to destinations outside the region, mainly the US, Canada and western Europe; b) irregular movement within the region (e.g. Guatemalans to Mexico), and c) illegal entry into the region, notably through Caribbean and Central American countries, of persons from other regions (currently chiefly from China en route to the US). Irregular migration affecting Latin America is thus multi-directional and tends to follow the same pattern as regular migration.

Central American countries are the most immediate points of origin and transit for irregular migration northwards. Many Central Americans have migrated legally to the US and Canada, and their success, particularly in the labour markets, continues to draw others, often illegally. Recurrent droughts, failed internal and intraregional migration, and the devastations of Hurricane Mitch, have compounded the reasons for emigration and made people more vulnerable to human smuggling and trafficking activities as a result. Central American governments are increasingly looking for ways to make border movements into, through and out of their countries more secure, particularly in the context of the Regional Conference on Migration (RCM).[12] Pointing the way for others, Honduras, for example, is using cutting-edge technology to better secure its passport.

TEXTBOX 5.2

TRAFFICKING IN LATIN AMERICA AND THE CARIBBEAN

- According to the US Central Intelligence Agency (CIA), 50,000 women and children are trafficked to the US every year.
- Interpol estimates that 35,000 women are trafficked out of Colombia annually.
- Some 50,000-70,000 women from the Dominican Republic are working abroad in the sex industry. 75,000 are from Brazil.
- Over 2,000 children, mostly migrants from other Central American countries, were found in Guatemala's brothels in 2002.
- In Brazil, some 500,000 girls are in the prostitution business, many of them trafficked; many are also trafficked into the gold mining regions of the Amazon. (These are a combination of locals and migrants. The gold mines in the Amazon are in several countries: Perú, Colombia, Venezuela and Brazil.)
- In Costa Rica, Casa Allianza estimates that 2,000 girls are prostituted in San Jose, many of them migrants.
- Adolescents from Colombia, the Dominican Republic and the Philippines have been trafficked to Costa Rica for prostitution in areas known as sex tourism destinations.
- Sex tourism is on the rise in Latin America and the Caribbean. This implies that trafficking in these areas is likely to increase.

Source: Inter-American Commission of Women- Organization of American States, Facts-sheet 2001.

12. *The Regional Conference on Migration (RCM), also known as the "Puebla Process", is a multilateral regional forum on international migration begun in 1996. Member countries are: Belize, Canada, Costa Rica, Dominican Republic, El Salvador, Guatemala, Honduras, Mexico, Nicaragua, Panama, and the US. It has, inter alia, created a Liaison Officer Network to Combat Migrant Smuggling and Trafficking; established a matrix of national legislation relating to migrant smuggling and trafficking in persons and approved a Regional Work Plan to Combat Migrant Smuggling and Trafficking in Persons. See chapter 22.*

Migrant Smuggling and Trafficking in Persons

Migrant smuggling and trafficking in persons in Latin America and the Caribbean are high on regional agendas,[13] reflecting not only an increase in their incidence (at least the trafficking), but also the concern of governments, international organizations and civil society. Estimates are difficult, due to the clandestine nature of these crimes and the confusion between their definitions. Discussions and concrete actions are being taken by inter-governmental fora such as the RCM and the Central American Commission of Directors of Migration (OCAM).

Regional governments are increasingly working together with destination countries like the US and Canada, and with international organizations like IOM, to strengthen their legal and practical capacities to manage their borders and have sound documentation and information systems in place.[14] Regarding trafficking in persons, the focus has been on child trafficking, trafficking for sexual exploitation and migrant health. Together with IOM, ILO, UNICEF, IPEC and WHO governments are undertaking projects on collaborative training for migration officials, standardizing sanctions against offenders, capturing data on smuggling and trafficking and assisting the victims of trafficking.

TEXTBOX 5.3

"ATRAPADAS" – TRAFFICKING OF PERSONS IN THE CARIBBEAN

The Dominican Republic has been a major focus of trafficking activity for some years. The scale of the problem is unknown, but there is ample evidence of Haitian children working as beggars in the streets of Santo Domingo, South American women being trafficked through Santo Domingo to Europe, and Dominican women being trafficked to South America. The Government has been working with IOM since 2001 to enhance public awareness of the problem and strengthen institutional capacities to prevent it. New anti-trafficking legislation was passed in 2003, and a survey undertaken of Haitian migration, including irregular migration.

A new radio series called *Atrapadas* (*Trapped*) was co-produced by IOM and the Radio Netherlands Training Centre[15] in Costa Rica in 2004. Similar to a soap opera, it dramatizes 10 real-life stories related to human trafficking in the Caribbean: *Carmen in Curacao, Ana gets married to a Dutchman* (Aruba), *Alexa is indebted* (Argentina), *Maira does not want to be stared at* (Italy), *Norma and Dolores at the edge* (Slovakia), *Noemi is alone* (Germany), *Mireya on smashed crystals* (The Netherlands), *Francisca, living a different way* (Spain), *Margarita, tricked and prostituted* (Costa Rica), *Final chapter* (Sinopsis).

13. *As at July 2004, the following Latin American/Caribbean states have signed the UN* Convention Against Transnational Organized Crime, *2000: Argentina, Bolivia, Brazil, Chile, Colombia, Cuba, the Dominican Republic, Ecuador, El Salvador Guatemala, Haiti, Honduras, Mexico, Nicaragua, Panama, Paraguay, Peru, Uruguay and Venezuela. The following Latin American/Caribbean states have signed the* Protocol to Prevent, Suppress and Punish Trafficking in Persons*: Argentina, Bolivia, Brazil, Colombia, Dominican Republic, Ecuador, Haiti, Mexico, Panama, Paraguay, Peru, Uruguay and Venezuela. The following states have signed the* Protocol against the Smuggling of Migrants by Land, Sea and Air*: Argentina, Bolivia, the Dominican Republic, Ecuador; Haiti, Mexico, Panama, Peru, Uruguay and Venezuela.*

14. *For example, under the Central American Commission of Directors of Migration (OCAM), and the Central American Migration Integration Plan, a project is being established for joint control of the Penas Blancas border crossing between Costa Rica and Nicaragua. In Jamaica, IOM is assisting the government to improve the border management system and to deliver training as needed, in addition to updating its policy, legislative and regulatory frameworks. Similar assistance is being provided by IOM in the Bahamas, with added emphasis on human resources development and enhanced regional and extra-regional cooperation and information exchange.*

15. *(This is a Dutch institute of international education established in 1968 to contribute to development by increasing the informative and educational role of the media in developing countries. It is a part of Radio Netherlands, based in Hilversum, the Netherlands. The office in Costa Rica covers Latin America and the Caribbean. (English: www.rnw.nl/rntc/; Spanish: www.mediacommunity.org/campus/)*

Atrapadas was broadcast on more than 70 radio stations throughout the country, many of them in rural areas, over several months in 2004. The radio series is available in a kit containing five CDs, an information brochure, summaries of each chapter, and guidelines for use with radio presentations and student groups. In addition to disseminating these kits, IOM is using the radio soap opera in its education sessions in 90 secondary schools in the Dominican Republic.

To make this Spanish language counter-trafficking tool more widely available, the Organization of American States (OAS) began broadcasting the programme via satellite in February 2004 and has made the series available on its website at *www.oasradio.net/*.

At the regional level, the Inter-American Commission of Women of the Organization of American States (CIM/OAS) recently began working with IOM on governmental and non-governmental tools to combat trafficking in persons at national and regional levels. The project targets the Bahamas, Barbados, Guyana, Jamaica, Netherlands Antilles, St. Lucia, and Suriname. It seeks to research the scope and character of trafficking in the region, undertake legal reviews and strengthen the capacities of each state to prevent, prosecute and protect, as appropriate.

Source: IOM Santo Domingo and Washington D.C.

ECONOMIC DEVELOPMENT, REGIONAL COOPERATION AND SECURITY

ONE OF THE emerging stories of Latin American and Caribbean migration is the role that *remittances* play in economic development. By some estimates, one in twenty households in Latin America benefit from remittances (*International Herald Tribune*, 2004). The countries of Latin America and the Caribbean received more than USD38 billion in remittances in 2003 according to the Inter-American Development Bank (2004), an increase of 17.6 per cent over 2002. These financial flows outstripped foreign direct investment and net official development assistance in that year. According to the IDB, the multiplier effects of remittances on local economies could further enhance their actual impact by a factor of three (IDB, 2004). Similarly, a 2003 study by the Pew Hispanic Center estimated that remittances to Mexico and Central America saw a 28 per cent increase between 2000-2001, rising to USD13 billion (Suro, 2003).

Most of these remittances were sent by migrants in the US, followed by Japan, Spain, Italy, Canada and countries in the region itself. Mexico is in the lead, receiving some USD 13.2 billion, with other regional flows going to Central America (USD 6.5 billion), the Caribbean (USD 5.8 billion) and Andean countries (USD 6.2 billion).[16]

The sheer volume of remittances, combined with increasing regional migration, makes Latin America and the Caribbean one of the most interesting pilot regions to enhance the role of remittances in economic development.[17]

16. *In six countries of the region, remittances represented more than 10 per cent of total national income: Nicaragua (29.4%), Haiti (24.2%), French Guiana (16.6%), El Salvador (15.1%), Jamaica (12.2%) and Honduras (11.5%).*

17. *See also the chapter in this Report "Migrant Hometown Associations – the Human face of Globalization".*

The promise of development is also pinned on greater regional integration, manifested in such agreements as the North American Free Trade Agreement (NAFTA) and the Central American Free Trade Agreement (CAFTA). While not specifically designed to deal with the push and pull determinants of migration, such regional integration may facilitate cooperation on additional cross-border movements. Similarly, regional blocs such as Mercosur, the Andean Community and the Caribbean Community (CARICOM), whose goals extend beyond economic integration to issues of health, security and migration, among others, have focused efforts on increasing avenues for human mobility, particularly for labour migrants.

There are other regional and inter-regional migration efforts at play as well. The Regional Conference on Migration (RCM) and the South American Migration Conference are two such examples, where member states and relevant organizations meet annually to discuss migration management and other related issues from the varying perspectives of sending, receiving and transit countries. Successful cooperation on migration is promoted through an ongoing process of regional study, discussion and education. These fora make important contributions and often serve as inroads to the creation of bi- and multilateral migration policies.

LATIN AMERICA/CARIBBEAN AND THE EUROPEAN UNION

MIGRATION played an important role in both the agendas and final declarations of the Ibero-American Summit in Rio de Janeiro, 1999, and the Europe-Latin American Summits held in Madrid in 2002 and in Guadalajara in 2004.[18]

The inter-regional cooperation agreed at these meetings is reflected in the European Commission's strategic document "The Regional Strategic Report on Latin America and the Caribbean", which presents EU member states' programming plan for 2002-2006. Key points of cooperation are consistent with the rest of the EU's policies on Latin America, including sustainable development, adherence to the norms of the World Trade Organization, the fight against poverty and social exclusion, and the prevention of conflicts.

In this spirit, three bilateral cooperation agreements have recently been signed between Spain and Latin American countries (Colombia, Ecuador and the Dominican Republic), which aim to prevent clandestine migration and labour exploitation of foreigners with irregular immigrant status (Izquierdo, 2002), and regulate other types of labour situations, including social security rights. In 2003, Brazil and Portugal signed an agreement with similar objectives.

Agreements between European and Latin American countries with the central aim of achieving mutual benefits for communities of origin and destination through migration are expected to increase in coming years. Future agreements will cover issues related to the human rights of migrants, their rights as workers, and the preservation of their ties to countries of origin. The fight against irregular immigration in all its forms will continue to be a high priority. European policies are also seeking ways to strengthen diaspora networks and allow countries of origin to benefit from the training and skills that their nationals acquired during their stay in Europe.

18. *The Summit in Rio de Janeiro, Brazil, in 1999 was the first between the Heads of State and Governments of Latin America, the Caribbean and the European Union. The objective of the Rio Summit was to strengthen the political, economic and cultural understanding between the two regions, to encourage the development of a strategic partnership and establish a set of priorities for future joint action in the political and economic fields. The second EU-LAC Summit in Madrid, Spain, in 2002 assessed progress of the new strategic partnership in terms of: political dialogue, economic and financial relations and cooperation in a number of areas. New proposals were made to further strengthen this bi-regional partnership. The third EU-LAC Summit in Guadalajara, Mexico, in 2004 achieved a great deal in finding a common policy among the participating 33 LAC and 25 EU states. Concrete commitments were made in the areas of: social cohesion, multilateralism and regional integration.*

CONCLUSION

THE DIVERSITY of the Americas makes sweeping statements about policy recommendations almost meaningless. If nothing else, the region is a case study of root causes. Tremendous political and economic upheavals, along with grinding poverty in some countries, ensure that the pressures and incentives to migrate will be perennial. Likewise, migration is likely to continue to be characterized by individual and family survival strategies, and reflect the absence of necessary changes in governance, and of socio-economic and political equality in some Latin American countries. In Haiti and Colombia, the duration and the intensity of the continued conflict is sure to guarantee, at least in the short term, more displacement and flight.

Thus, the best predictors of future migration flows and patterns are those of today. With emigrants from Latin America and the Caribbean increasingly choosing to move to countries in Europe, that region, previously characterized by predominantly intra-regional movements is now internationalizing. Tolerance for increased immigration from Latin America and the Caribbean will certainly be tested, even as ageing industrial countries like Japan or those of Europe demand new workers. The expansion of Europe to include 10 new member states, changing patterns of migration within Europe that favour eastern European immigrants, and the difficulties of maintaining special bilateral relationships in a harmonized Europe, may quell the enthusiasm for Latin American immigrants in Europe. At the same time, the new security context in which migration occurs in the US and elsewhere may flatten the upward migration trend out of the region.

There is no doubt, however, that Canada and the US will remain the primary destinations for immigrants from the region who seek employment and security elsewhere. As the stock of Latin American and Caribbean immigrants continues to rise, especially in the US, the predominance of family reunification within US immigration streams practically ensures a constant inflow of migrants from the region. For the moment, however, one of the most significant contributions made by Canada and the US may simply be to provide opportunities for migrants to send remittances home. The epic story that is emerging of the size of remittances and their importance in providing a lifeline out of poverty for those who stay behind, speaks volumes about regional migration patterns. It also reveals a vast region that is becoming more and not less integrated and interdependent.

Asia and Oceania

Chapter 6
International Migration Trends and Patterns in Asia and Oceania[1]

INTRODUCTION

The Asian region[2] has been a primary destination for migrants since the 1960s, and today accounts for some 14 per cent of the world's total migrant stock (United Nations, 2003).[3] Many intra- or interregional migrants in Asia are driven by the need for gainful employment. Some seek refuge from persecution and conflict, others study abroad at higher education institutions. In all cases, the region receives a large share of Asian immigrants, while flows to the US, Europe and Australia are also continuing to rise.

Asia is currently the primary source of family and authorized economic migration of all forms to most of the world's immigrant-receiving regions and countries. Almost one-third of all immigrants in Australia are from Asia,[4] with China, the Philippines and India among the largest source countries. Similarly, 33 per cent of immigrants in Canada and 24 per cent of immigrants in the US are from Asia (Migration Information Source, 2004). In recent years there has also been a significant increase in Asian migration to Europe, especially from China (OECD, 2004; IOM, 2003). The nine largest Asian immigrant-exporting countries – the Philippines, India, Bangladesh, Pakistan, Indonesia, Thailand, China, Sri Lanka and Myanmar – together contribute between one-half and two-thirds of all legal immigrants and refugees to the international migration stream.

Asian migration flows display three distinctive features:

i) It is a more legally organized "industry", both publicly and privately, than in other world regions, involving migration-promoting government programmes in, for example, the Philippines[5] or South Asia, and innumerable legal and regulated immigration brokers throughout the region.
ii) Several countries are at the same time significant exporters and importers of foreign labour.
iii) The population size of the region's main sending states is vast, with China, India, Indonesia, Pakistan, Thailand, Bangladesh and the Philippines accounting for nearly half the world's population.[6]

1. *The authors of this chapter are Dr Demetrios G. Papademetriou, Director, Migration Policy Institute (MPI), Washington, and Ms Sarah Margon, Research Assistant, MPI. Additional input was provided by Mr Zhao Jian, IOM Geneva; Mr Shahidul Haque, IOM Dhaka; MHS Geneva; IOM Dhaka; IOM Manila; IOM Ho Chi Minh City, and IOM Bangkok.*

2. *For the purpose of this chapter, Asia includes East Asia [China (which includes China mainland, Hong Kong Special Administrative Region of China -- hereafter referred to as Hong Kong, Macao Special Administrative Region of China -- hereafter Macao, and Taiwan Province of China -- hereafter Taiwan), the Democratic People's Republic of Korea (hereafter North Korea), Japan, Mongolia, and the Republic of Korea (hereafter South Korea)]; Southeast Asia (Brunei, Cambodia, Timor Leste, Indonesia, Laos, Malaysia, Myanmar, Philippines, Singapore, Thailand and Viet Nam); and South-Central Asia (Afghanistan, Bangladesh, Bhutan, India, Iran, Maldives, Nepal, Pakistan and Sri Lanka). Countries in Western Asia and Central Asia are not included in this discussion.*

3. *According to the UNPD's 2003 revision of the global migrant stock in the year 2000, there were in that year some 43.8 million migrants in Asia, accounting for 25 per cent of the global stock. This, however, includes Western Asia, which, if removed in line with the geographic designation of this chapter, would leave 24.8 million migrants, representing 14 per cent of the global total.*

4. *In 2002, nearly 46 per cent (42,818) of immigrants to Australia came from Asia. Likewise, 33 per cent (351,344) of the inflows to the US in 2002 came from this region.*

5. *See also the chapter "Filipinos Working Overseas: Opportunity and Challenge".*

6. *According to the Institute of Population and Labour Economics at the Chinese Academy of Social Sciences, China is estimated to have eight million unemployed persons in urban areas alone (China Daily, 2003b).*

While much of the migration from the countries in the region is legal, increasing proportions of it are not. Economic reforms and the development of multilateral trade and investment arrangements have pressured governments to "multilateralize" discussions on immigration, while also fuelling the more traditional migration "push" and "pull" factors. The dominant "push" factors are still rapid population growth, inadequate economic opportunities and high unemployment, particularly in South Asia. "Pull" factors include expanding markets, labour shortfalls and ageing populations in the more industrialized countries of the region (Japan, Singapore, South Korea, Taiwan, and increasingly also China), and a continuing need for workers in the Gulf States (despite the current slowdown there). Increasingly, irregular forms of migration contribute to the expansion of migration flows, including the smuggling and trafficking of persons, as do the vast refugee populations generated by various conflicts. For these reasons, all forms of migration throughout Asia are expected to grow in the coming years.

This chapter reviews some of the most important patterns of international migration throughout Asia, and the government policy responses to them in the past few years. Examples in the chapter are drawn from various countries throughout the region. In considering recent patterns, it is important to note that as a result of globalization and the growth of the informal sector, traditional notions of "sending" and "receiving" countries have become quite blurred. Even a country like Australia, commonly described as a traditional country of immigration, is also a country of emigration (see the chapter on Oceania below).

The first section of the chapter focuses on trends in labour migration, both between states (external) and within national borders (internal), including irregular labour migration and its impacts, and the increased feminization of migration in Asia. The discussion of feminization draws on both regular and irregular variants of migration and discusses the implications of this trend for policy decisions. The second section focuses on refugee flows, while the third examines recent patterns of students seeking higher education and additional training abroad. The conclusion elucidates the importance of creating a regional framework for migration management, particularly in the light of increased security concerns.

LABOUR MIGRATION

THE EMIGRATION of workers from one country to another in search of economic opportunities is deeply entrenched in most Asian economies and is facilitated, in some ways even managed, by a system of labour recruiters and related agents. External labour migration has already been promoted for several decades by countries with a labour surplus and weak economies. Countries such as the Philippines or Indonesia, both with extensive experience in this regard, have created elaborate networks of government agencies and private contractors to facilitate the placement and travel of workers abroad. Others, like Vietnam, after experiencing fluctuations in recent decades, are planning and negotiating major expansions of their labour exports both within and outside Asia.[7]

Lately, two aspects of external labour migration in Asia have become particularly salient: a major shift in destinations and an increase in irregular migration throughout the region. The number of workers migrating within Asia has increased in proportion to the fewer numbers of migrants moving to the Middle East. There have also been significant increases in irregular migration between Asian countries, for

7. *Vietnam currently has some 350,000 migrant labourers abroad, mostly in Asia, and hopes to expand this to over 500,000 by 2005 (Vietnam Investment Review, 2003). Malaysia is Vietnam's largest export market, with over 72,000 Vietnamese employed there in manufacturing, construction and agriculture (*Vietnam News, *2004). Vietnam and South Korea signed an MOU for labour export in: electronics, information technology, computer programming, transport, commercial electronics, environment and energy (*Labor Newspaper, *Vietnam, 2004). The government also plans to expand its labour export market in Africa in the healthcare, education, agricultural and construction sectors; and to increase its share in the fishing industry, particularly in Japan and China, inter alia through better training of its fishermen (*Vietnam News, *2003). In 2004, labour export companies joined to form the "Vietnam Association of Manpower Supply" (VAMAS) to address future challenges of expanding the country's labour export markets (*Vietnam News, *2004).*

example from the Philippines to Japan,[8] from China to Japan and Korea, and from Myanmar to Thailand. Both elements add a new dimension to the more traditional labour movements and are illustrative of the impact of globalization on migration.

But Asia also offers some excellent examples of how the benefits of labour emigration can be reaped through remittances and proactive diaspora management. India and the Philippines are two of the largest beneficiaries of remittances globally, receiving between them more than USD 15 billion in 2000 alone;[9] and remittance flows are also increasingly important for Bangladesh, Pakistan, Sri Lanka and Vietnam. For some countries, remittance flows are a valuable strategic means to counteract the "brain drain" they may be experiencing.[10] These complex issues are discussed in greater detail in other chapters and in recent studies on migration and development.[11]

EXTERNAL LABOUR MIGRATION

While the war in Iraq and an increasing number of bilateral free trade agreements have substantially affected external labour migration, the SARS (Severe Acute Respiratory Syndrome) epidemic and its rapid spread throughout the region in early 2003 has apparently had little effect on this. Most Asian economies have continued to grow steadily, which is thought to have blunted the impact of SARS on labour migration. China's economy overcame formidable odds to grow at about 9.1 per cent in the third quarter of 2003, indicating that it had overcome any negative impact of the SARS outbreak (China Daily, 2003a), while Japan saw economic growth of over 6 per cent in the fourth quarter of 2003 (Bloomberg News, 2004). This economic growth has been underpinned by several trade agreements, such as between Singapore and Japan (2002), Australia and Thailand (2003), and a pending agreement between Japan and the Philippines (negotiations began in 2002). By expanding access to the signatories' markets, these agreements have increased business opportunities and facilitated the flow of goods and businesspersons within the region. The APEC Business Card Scheme also helps to facilitate business travel across the Asia-Pacific region.[12]

The combination of these factors has increased traffic of both business professionals and low-skilled workers in East and South Asia, and helped lessen the need for migrants to go to the Middle East and the Gulf States, which had been a principal destination for Asian labour migrants since the early 1970s. Initially, this shift was towards Indians, Bangladeshis and Pakistanis, but soon included migrants from China, Indonesia, Japan, South Korea, Malaysia, the Philippines and Thailand, among others. Between the mid-1970s and 1990s, the region's migrant stock quadrupled from about two million workers to some eight million, almost half of them employed in Saudi Arabia. In 1990, more than 40 per cent of the population of the Gulf States (72% for the UAE) and more than two-thirds of the workforce in those states was foreign-born.

Two further factors have caused economic migration to the Gulf States to slow down or, more accurately, to change proportionally, in comparison with labour flows elsewhere. The first is that the Gulf states have worked diligently to prevent temporary migration from turning into permanent settlement, and have been quite successful in this, *inter alia*, through the "indigenization" of labour selection.[13] Second, there is

8. *Japan is the third most popular destination for overseas Filipino workers after Saudi Arabia and Hong Kong, particularly for female entertainers; and the numbers are growing (source: Philipine Overseas Employment Administration (POEA)).*

9. *See also the chapter "Migration and Poverty: Some Issues in the Context of Asia".*

10. *While China mainland, Philippines and Taiwan already have brain drain correction strategies in place, countries like Iran, seen as having the highest rate of brain drain in the world (Esfandiari, 2004), are considering their best options.*

11. *See the chapters "Migration and Poverty: Some Issues in the Context of Asia" and "Migrant Remittances as a Source of Development Finance"; as well as Newland, 2004.*

12. *See chapter 21 in this report and the Textbox 22.1 "APEC Business Travel Card – Regional Cooperation in Migration".*

13. *There are a number of reasons for the slow-down in the Middle East: (1) more native labourers were available in the Gulf countries during the 1990s, young people have grown up and graduated from schools, (2) most of the basic construction projects in the Gulf countries had finished by the 1990s; (3) some of the Gulf countries took measures to restrict foreign labourers, encouraged employers to use local workers, (4) stricter control on the use of foreign workers by some countries (like Kuwait), where a work permit was needed if an employer wanted to use foreign workers.*

a rather unusual hierarchy among the region's workers. Outside the still small "ruling" class (in most instances the political class overlaps with the economic one), the hierarchy of workers finds western experts at top levels and ahead of most Asian workers. But, as discussed in the earlier chapter on "Migration in the Middle East", despite strong efforts in some of those countries to reduce their foreign labour intake, Middle East labour markets are likely to continue to need foreign workers.

There are huge labour migration flows between a number of Asian sending countries and receiving regions outside Asia and the Middle East, e.g. North America, Europe and Australia, either through labour agreements, or private contracts or under skilled visa categories. These range from Filipina caregivers bound for Canada, to Indian IT workers heading for the US. In 2002, the Chinese government estimated that more than 400,000 Chinese left for overseas employment (see also text below on "Migration in the People's Republic of China"). Philippines government estimates for mid-2004 point to around 7 million overseas Filipino workers abroad, and an annual outflow of contract labourers of around 44, 000 (see also the chapter below on "Filipinos Working Overseas: Opportunity and Challenge").

Iran, which in the past was principally a destination country, is also emerging as a proactive labour exporter, registering an annual outflow of skilled and specialized migrant workers from Iran of about 285,000[14] in the past three years, mainly to Europe and the Middle East. There are currently 3 million Iranians working abroad temporarily, mostly skilled and semi-skilled, mostly young and male. In 2003, the Ministry of Labour and Social Affairs established a new Development of Overseas Employment Department to manage the new and rapidly increasing emigration trend.

INTRAREGIONAL LABOUR MIGRATION

Today, many more Asian migrants are finding work closer to home. While South and Southeast Asian workers still travel to the Middle East, their share relative to those engaged in work closer to home has decreased. In part this is also due to the completion of many construction projects in the Middle East and the renewed economic growth in East and Southeast Asia (Wickramasekera, 2002). The new millennium saw more than 848,543 overseas Indonesian workers employed in Malaysia, Singapore, Taiwan, South Korea, Hong Kong, Brunei and Japan, among others, and only 504,656 in the Middle East (Hugo, 2002). India also sends large numbers of migrants to East and Southeast Asia, rather than to the Middle East, with Taiwan, Singapore and Hong Kong the key destinations. In recent years, workers from China, Malaysia, Thailand, Vietnam and Myanmar have also turned more to neighbouring destinations in East and Southeast Asia for employment, rather than the Middle East.

The recovery from the economic crisis of the late 1990s saw the resumption of large foreign direct investment (FDI) flows to Asia (particularly East and Southeast Asia) that, in turn, led to higher flows of skilled, professional and managerial workers (Manning, 2000). Despite traditionally tight controls on the entry of foreign workers, 2003 saw increased numbers of business professionals moving to Hong Kong and Singapore – notably from Malaysia, Japan and Australia. Many skilled Thais also left Thailand to find work in Japan, Singapore, Taiwan and Brunei. Similarly, Filipinos dominated the out-migration of skilled and professional migrants with the deployment of over 7,800 nurses and more than 99,000 high-tech professionals (Sizan, 2003).

In March 2002, the Japanese Ministry of Health, Labor and Welfare estimated the number of foreign workers in the country to be at least 710,000, up six per cent from the previous year, and accounting for just over one per cent of the Japanese workforce. This increase

14. *Society of Iranian Youth News Agency (SYNA), Tehran press conference, 12 April 2004.*

occurred despite a decade of economic stagnation in Japan, and is partly in response to Japan's ageing population and the low labour force participation of women. Many of these skilled workers come from South Korea and China (35.6% and 21.4%, respectively, of all foreigners in Japan) (Akaha, 2003).

As Korea experienced labour shortages in the 1980s, it, too, attracted hundreds of thousands of workers from the region, most of them undocumented, a pattern that continued for decades, despite the Asian financial crises of 1997. Today, Korea has relaxed its Immigration and Emigration Law to facilitate and simplify longer-term labour immigration.[15] Taiwan has attracted sizeable numbers of contract workers in the construction, manufacturing, health and domestic sectors, mostly from the Philippines, Thailand and Indonesia. Like Korea, Malaysia has continued to receive huge numbers of largely undocumented workers from neighbouring countries (see also the Chapter "International Migration Trends").

TEXTBOX 6.1

LABOUR MIGRATION IN SOUTH KOREA[16]

South Korea is a growing economy that needs more labourers than it can supply locally. As a result, it has had to revise its somewhat restrictive labour migration policies of recent years. A new Act on Foreign Workers' Employment was introduced in July 2003 and, since August 2004, the country has had a dual system in place for bringing low-skilled foreign workers into the country: the pre-existing industrial trainee system and an employment permit system.

Under the employment permit system, migrant workers may enter South Korea under bilateral memoranda of understanding (MOUs) signed with eight select countries of origin – the People's Republic of China, Indonesia, Kazakhstan, Mongolia, the Philippines, Sri Lanka, Thailand and Vietnam – and be granted equal labour rights alongside local workers. Quotas apply to those industries permitted to have foreign workers, namely, manufacturing, construction, coastal fisheries, agriculture, livestock farming and some parts of the service industry. The contract is initially for one year, but renewable for up to three years.

The scheme is designed to achieve three objectives:

First, to protect foreign workers from exploitation. In addition to labour rights, such as the right to join or form a trade union, the Labor Standard Act will be strictly applied to working conditions alongside the Minimum Wage Act and Industrial Safety and Health Act. Employers failing to uphold the terms of employment (stipulated in the recommended standard contract) can have their permit to employ foreign workers revoked. Unemployment insurance is optional for foreign workers. In exceptional cases, they may be permitted to change their workplace.[17]

Second, to ensure that foreign workers do not have to overstay to recuperate the exorbitant costs incurred when emigrating. Public agencies oversee the selection and immigration process in both Korea and the countries of origin.[18]

15. *See the Textbox "Labour Migration in South Korea" and the chapter "Balancing the Benefits and Costs of Skilled Migration in the Asia-Pacific Region".*

16. *The author of this Textbox is June Lee, Research Unit, IOM, Geneva.*

17. *For details, see www.eps.go.kr/wem/eh/inf/eh9901040b01.jsp*

18. *For the General Procedure of the Employment Permit System, see www.eps.go.kr/wem/eh/inf/eh9901030b01.jsp*

Third, to ensure there is no burden on Korean employers, and hence no migrant levy is imposed, as is the case in other parts of Asia (e.g., Hong Kong, Singapore). Instead, employers are expected to take out a number of insurance policies in order to avoid making lump-sum payments at the end of a contract period.[19] The workers in turn are required to place funds in a return expense trust fund, which they will receive when they return home, and to pay for accident insurance.[20]

Currently, foreign workers account for some 2 per cent of the total South Korean labour force. At the end of December 2003, there were 388,816 foreign workers residing in the country, among whom 35.5 per cent (138,056 persons) were presumed to be illegal. Of the total foreign workforce, only 5.2 per cent or 20,089 persons were skilled, while the rest were low-skilled labourers. This is a dramatic growth from a total of 81,824 at the end of 1994. The visa category distribution had also reversed dramatically, with only 6.4 per cent holding working visas and 34.6 per cent trainee visas in 1994, compared with 51.5 per cent of working visas and only 13 per cent trainee visas at the end of 2003 (South Korean Ministry of Justice).

But the government knows that the effectiveness of the new permit system will depend on how successfully the number of undocumented workers can be reduced. For the past decade, up to August 2003, the number of undocumented migrants has risen sharply from some 48,231 in 1994 to 289,239 in December 2002 (or 79.8% of the total foreign workforce in Korea).

The Addendum to the Foreign Workers' Employment Act foresees the legalization of undocumented migrants prior to the implementation of the new employment permit system in August 2004. A series of legalization measures was taken before the end of 2003, and the number of undocumented migrants had dropped to 138,056 by the end of 2003 (South Korean Ministry of Justice).[21]

Under the legalization programme, undocumented migrants resident in South Korea for less than three years as of March 31, 2003, will be permitted to work in an industry designated by the Minister of Labour for a maximum period of two years, if they voluntarily report to the relevant authorities and follow the specified procedure. Those who had lived in the country for three years or more, but less than four years, as of March 31, 2003, and departed from the country after voluntarily reporting to the competent authorities, are allowed to re-enter and work for up to a total of five years (including the residence period before departure). Persons who had been illegally in South Korea for four years or longer as of March 31, 2003, were required to depart voluntarily before November 15, 2003, or be deported thereafter.[22]

19. *These include: departure guarantee insurance and wage guarantee insurance, in addition to employment insurance, national health insurance, and industrial accident insurance that are required of any Korean employers.*

20. *See the Enforcement Decree of the Act on Foreign Workers' Employment, etc. Presidential Decree No. 18314, Articles 21, 22, 27, and 28.*

21. *By nationality, the largest group were Chinese, numbering 62,058, or 45 per cent (54.1% of them being Korean-Chinese), followed by Vietnamese (7.4%), Bangladeshis (6.9%), Filipinos (6.5%) and Indonesians (6.1%).*

22. *Per the Public Notice on the Legalization of Illegal Foreigners; in Korean, www.moj.go.kr/immi/04_data/statistics_f.html, accessed on 10 September 2004.*

It remains to be seen how successfully the employment permit system will work to achieve the goals of protecting migrant workers' rights while providing a viable source of labour to South Korean employers. Whether the number of undocumented migrant workers (approximately 181,000 at the end of August 2004) will be reduced as rapidly as hoped for is unclear, given the remaining hindrances such as a lack of incentive to return for those not eligible for legalization. But the government is clearly focused on a more comprehensive and managed approach to labour migration.

THE FEMINIZATION OF MIGRANT LABOUR

OFTEN thought to be male dominated, over the last decade migration in Asia has become increasingly feminized, and women now account for a growing share of migrant workers. Asian women already constitute the majority of migrant workers in several countries: one million Filipina, 500,000 Indonesian, and some 40,000 Thai women worked outside their countries in the late 1990s, and their numbers have continued to increase (Wille and Passl (Eds.), 2001). In 2001, women accounted for some 47 per cent of all migrants in Asia (Zlotnik, 2003). However, there are two sides to this coin: women who migrate and seek employment overseas by choice, and women who are "trafficked" around the globe. This dual situation regarding the migration of women calls for further clarification of migrant protection issues, particularly in such vulnerable sectors as domestic and entertainment work, and the sex industry.

For many years, most female migrants have come from the Philippines (see Table 6.1), Indonesia and Sri Lanka, where women make up between 60 and 80 per cent of all migrants (Asis, 2003). Large numbers of female migrants also originate in Thailand and Myanmar, and many have irregular status in the host countries. 70 per cent of the four million Indonesians working abroad are women. Half of the almost 500,000 foreign permanent residents living in Japan are women who work in both high and low-skilled professions, many of them second-, third- and fourth-generation Chinese and Koreans. Female migration flows tend to follow the main patterns, with increasing numbers of women going to work in Japan,[23] Hong Kong, Singapore, South Korea, Malaysia and Thailand. Female workers also fill the demand for medical personnel and domestic workers in many Middle Eastern countries.

South Asian women migrants mostly choose to work in the Middle East – the UAE, Kuwait, Bahrain, and Oman, but also in Malaysia and the Maldives. Women from Bangladesh are usually contracted as low-paid, semi-skilled garment workers and unskilled domestic workers and cleaners. Sri Lankan women accounted for 75 per cent of that country's total migration out-flow in 1997, and are mostly contracted as domestic workers.[24] Increasingly, South Asian women move independently.

Owing to their long-term absence from home, the traditional roles of Asian women are also changing. Often they assume the role of sole breadwinner and decisionmaker of the household, whether abroad or replacing the absent parent at home. Family allegiances and structures are breaking down, and governments, for instance in the Philippines, are confronting major policy challenges in regard to family health, counselling, reintegration assistance

23. *The Philippine Overseas Employment Administration (POEA) reports that in 2001, 99.6 per cent of Japan-bound overseas Filipino workers held entertainer visas, and 96.4 per cent of these were female.*

24. *Waddington, Clare; International Migration Policies in Asia; paper presented at the Regional Conference on Migration, Development and Pro-poor Policy in Asia, jointly organized by RMMRU, Bangladesh and DFID on 22-24 June 2003, Dhaka, Bangladesh.*

and jobs for returnees and their families. These challenges become even more acute when unskilled workers in informal sectors are exploited and abused, resulting both in human rights violations and costly treatment for health and other problems.

In response to highly publicized cases of abuse, the Governments of Bangladesh, Nepal, Pakistan and Iran banned certain categories of female workers from going abroad. However, as many women continued to migrate illegally, the barriers have again been relaxed, and applications for skilled, semi- and un-skilled migrant women are considered on a case-by-case basis. In 2004, the Bangladesh government relaxed the ban on a selective basis for unskilled women over the age of 35, married and accompanied by the husband. Nepal lifted its ban in 2003, after realizing that it was not stopping women from migrating, but rather making them more vulnerable to trafficking. Pakistan does not encourage female migration, and bans the migration of women under 45 as domestic workers,[25] hence only 0.04 per cent of total Pakistani migrant workers are women. Only Sri Lanka has an active policy to encourage female migration in the region.

But international labour contracts are highly gendered, with women migrants being mainly recruited to work in the domestic sector (Wille and Passl, 2001). Responding to the much-publicized abuse of migrants in the domestic sector many governments have introduced legislation to prevent such abuse. The Hong Kong authorities require that the minimum wage and one day of rest a week be included in standard contracts for domestic workers; in Singapore, lawmakers are attempting to curb the abuse of foreign domestic caregivers through tougher penalties (*Manila Times*, 2004).

IRREGULAR MIGRATION

AS THE FLOW of intraregional labour migrants continues to grow throughout Asia, so does irregular migration. Malaysia and Thailand currently appear to have the largest numbers of irregular workers, with estimates pointing to some 500,000 to one million unauthorized migrants working there (Migration News, 2001). Workers from Indonesia and Thailand, many of them unauthorized, fill rural labour shortages in Malaysia. Malaysian government records showed that only 65,329 of an estimated 102,555 foreign plantation workers were properly documented in 2004,[26] with a further estimated one million undocumented migrants in Malaysia driven there by poor economic conditions and internal conflicts in neighbouring countries.

Though itself a sending country of undocumented workers, Thailand also struggles with the implications of undocumented migration at home as well. Some estimates put the number of unauthorized workers in Thailand at 943,000, a figure three times that of legal immigrants (Inter Press Service, 1998). Thus, only about 35 per cent of all foreign workers in the country appear to be working there legally. The Ministry of Labour[27] estimates the number of irregular migrants in Thailand at around 1.7 million, including displaced persons, minorities and undocumented/unregistered migrant workers. The World Health Organization estimates the number of unregistered migrants in the border provinces with Myanmar at close to one million.[28]

In South Korea, the size of the foreign workforce has grown strongly over the past years, most of it in informal sector activities (79.8% of the total foreign work force at the end of 2002). But with the introduction of the new Foreign Workers'

25. *Labour Migration in Asia: Trends, challenges and policy responses in countries of origin; International Organization for Migration; Geneva, 2003, p. 21.*
26. *In January 2004, the Malaysian newspaper* The Star *reported that it had come to the attention of the Malaysian Immigration Department that nearly 40,000 plantation workers were not properly registered. The government plans to raid key regions to halt the practice of hiring unauthorized plantation workers.*
27. *Reported by IOM Bangkok.*
28. *Refer to WHO website: www.wc.whothai.org/EN/Section 3/Section39.htm*

Employment Act of 2003, and the concomitant crackdown on those not qualifying for the regularization programme, undocumented migrant workers only accounted for some 35.5 per cent of the foreign workforce at the end of 2003.[29]

In Taiwan, there were approximately 330,000 foreign workers in 2001 (Migration News, 2002). In order to reduce the number of runaways who become irregular migrants, the Taiwan authorities recently adopted a series of measures to restrict the number of foreign workers in major public construction projects and key manufacturing investment projects, in reaction to the estimated 10,400 legal foreign workers who have "run away" from their employer and lost their work visas (Migration News, 2003). As a result, the number of foreign workers fell to 302,000 by 2003. Of these, approximately 111,000 had come from Thailand, 80,000 from Indonesia, 72,000 from the Philippines and 40,000 from Vietnam (Migration News, 2003).

Vietnam recently introduced measures to reduce the incidence of irregular migration by its own nationals, and issued a directive for several of its agencies to help curb the flow of those attempting to enter and remain in foreign countries unauthorized. Revising labour laws, managing contractual labourers working abroad, enhancing exit controls and providing loans for returning Vietnamese nationals are among the actions proposed (SRV Official Gazette, 2004).

There is a considerable flow of irregular migrants from China into neighbouring countries like Russia, South Korea, Japan and elsewhere, also *en route* to other parts of the world. Irregular immigrants in China are mainly from neighbouring countries, primarily North Korea and Vietnam. Some North Koreans eventually find their way into South Korea. The Chinese government has adopted measures to combat smuggling and trafficking of persons (**see also the Textbox 6.3** "Migration in the People's Republic of China").

In South Asia, where all countries have long land borders with two or more neighbouring countries, irregular border crossings are both numerous and difficult to control. They include long-standing seasonal movements of Nepalese and Bangladeshi migrants to India during the harvesting season. Here, the notion of "borders" is vague, as everybody has either family or working relations with people on the other side. Poverty and unemployment are the principal driving forces of irregular migration, while ineffective border controls, increased labour demand combined with restrictive labour policies in some areas, and political tension between bordering countries also add to migration pressures. India and Pakistan are also major transit areas for irregular migrants from Bangladesh, Nepal, India and Pakistan on their way to the Middle East and Europe. Restrictive policies in countries of origin, such as Bangladesh and Nepal regarding the emigration of unskilled women, can also add to irregular migration.

High levels of irregular migration, together with intensified smuggling and trafficking of people and transnational crimes, such as drug trafficking and terrorism, have increased efforts by Asian governments to crack down on illegal immigration and visa overstayers. The terrorist bombings in Bali (October 2002) and Jakarta (August 2003) underscored the vulnerability of the region and further heightened security concerns. Such apprehensions have energized greater regional cooperation, which may become the nucleus around which institutions for a sustainable regional migration framework could eventually be built.

Many governments in the region have understood that terrorism and cross-border crime cannot be effectively fought alone or even through bilateral efforts, and that their complex and multi-faceted characteristics called for concerted, multilateral approaches. Considerable investment is being made particularly in Southeast Asia by governments, the international community and partner states to

29. *Ji-Young and Donho report a total of some 361,000 foreign workers in South Korea in 2003, of whom only 72,000, or about 20 per cent had legal status, while 80 per cent were unauthorized, most of them undocumented (2003).*

strengthen the area's institutional capacities to combat and prevent cross-border crime. The focus is mainly on strengthening national intelligence gathering, inter-agency cooperation, information sharing and joint cross-border operations. A number of technical cooperation projects addressing migration and security issues are being undertaken by IOM with the governments of Cambodia and Indonesia.

TRAFFICKING OF PERSONS

Trafficking of persons[30] is a huge and largely unreported problem in Asia. It is estimated that the region accounts for approximately one-third of the total global trafficking flow (close to one million), with 60 per cent of the women, men and children being channelled into major regional cities and 40 per cent to other destinations in the rest of the world (United Nations, 2003). Hong Kong is primarily a transit for individuals trafficked from China mainland and other Asian countries, but an estimated 20,000 foreign sex workers are thought to work there also. On average, about 70,000 Filipino entertainers move to other Asian countries each year, many legally through the Ministry of Labour. Some Thai women end up in Malaysia, Japan, South Korea and Taiwan, four major destinations for the sex industry, while the number of trafficked women in Malaysia is estimated between 43,000 to 142,000 (Human Rights Watch, 2000).

Vietnam's Ministry of Public Security (MPS) estimates that thousands of women are trafficked to China each year, with one in six girls being under the age of 18 (Vietnam Investment Review, 2004a). UNICEF reports that the women sold in China range from 15 to 45 years of age, the most vulnerable group being unmarried, divorced, widowed or unhappily married women. According to Vietnam's Ministry of Public Security, close to three-quarters of the brokers are themselves women.

UNICEF Vietnam lists several reasons for this flourishing trade: the 1,300 kilometre land border shared by the two countries; poverty, family conflicts, and the high demand by Chinese for foreign wives. China's 'one-child' policy has resulted in a disproportionately high number of men against women, with 118 male vs. 100 female births (China's 2000 census). In contrast, Vietnam is experiencing the reverse situation, particularly in rural areas in the north, mainly owing to the earlier war and traffickers capitalizing on the situation.

Vietnamese women who are trafficked tend to be poorly educated and are usually lured by the promise of a good job or marriage. In Mong Cai, a small Vietnamese town a few kilometres from the Chinese border, a Vietnamese woman can be purchased for USD 500-600, more than the average annual income in Vietnam (USD 430 in 2002, *Vietnam Investment Review*, 2004b). Some women agree to be sold when promised a decent, honest husband in China, ready to offer them a better life; others are simply abducted. Once in China, many are exploited and abused as sex workers or by their new families, putting them at high risk of contracting HIV. Many have no life outside their new homes, do not speak Chinese and are therefore unable to seek help, while their status in China is often irregular.

In South Asia, there is considerable trafficking activity, although exact numbers are not available. Bangladesh and Nepal are the main source countries for migrant trafficking, and India and Pakistan are considered countries of destination or of transit to other regions, most commonly the Gulf States, Southeast Asia or Europe. Women and children are trafficked to India, Pakistan, Bahrain, Kuwait and the UAE for commercial sexual exploitation, hard labour and domestic work. A small number of women and girls are transited through Bangladesh from Myanmar and Nepal to India and other countries. Boys are also trafficked, e.g. from Bangladesh to the UAE and Qatar

30. *As defined in the UN Protocol to Prevent, Suppress and Punish Trafficking in Persons, Especially Women and Children, defines trafficking as "the recruitment, transportation, transfer, harbouring or receipt of persons by means of the threat or the use of force or other forms of coercion, of abduction, of fraud, of deception, of the abuse of power or of apposition of vulnerability, or of the giving or receiving of payments or benefits to achieve the consent of a person having control over another person, for the purpose of exploitation".*

and forced to work as camel jockeys and beggars (**see also the Textbox 3.2** "Camel Jockeys in the Gulf Cooperation Council States (GCC)").

Nepalese women are trafficked to work as commercial sex workers. The main sources are the impoverished regions of Nepal, the street children and remote areas affected by the Maoist insurgency and where some girls and boys have been forcibly conscripted by the insurgents. In Bangladesh, the major areas of origin are in the impoverished north of the country, and it is also reported that Burmese women and children are trafficked through Bangladesh. Pakistan is a country of origin, transit and destination for trafficked women and children, who are also trafficked internally from rural areas to cities for the purpose of sexual exploitation and bonded labour. It is a source country for young boys who are trafficked to the UAE, Kuwait and Qatar as camel jockeys. Pakistanis travel to the Middle East in search of work and end up in situations of coerced labour and physical abuse. It is also a destination for women and children trafficked from Bangladesh, Myanmar, Afghanistan, Iran and Central Asia for commercial sexual and other labour exploitation, and a transit for women trafficked from East Asia and Bangladesh to the Middle East.

Sri Lanka is a country of both origin and destination for trafficked persons. Commercial sexual exploitation of children, especially of boys, occurs domestically, often in tourist areas. Children, especially girls, are lured by promises of job opportunities or overseas travel; family members or friends often introduce them to commercial sexual activity. Internal trafficking of persons for domestic servitude and other purposes has also been reported in Sri Lanka. In many cases, Sri Lankan women go to countries like Lebanon, Kuwait, Bahrain, the UAE, or Saudi Arabia to work, and end up in situations of coerced labour or sexual exploitation. Small numbers of Thai, Russian, and Chinese women have also been trafficked to Sri Lanka for sexual exploitation (US Department of State, 2004b).

India is a country of origin, transit and of destination for thousands of trafficked women, men and children. Indian men and women often find themselves in situations of coerced labour and exploitative conditions in countries in the Middle East and the West. Trafficking also occurs internally for sexual exploitation, domestic servitude and bonded labour. India is a destination for sex tourists from Europe and the US. Bangladeshi women and children are trafficked to India or transited through India on their way to Pakistan and the Middle East for the sex industry, domestic servitude, and forced labour. Women and girls from Nepal are trafficked to India for commercial sexual exploitation.

Most governments in the region have enacted laws against trafficking, but they are often not well enforced. Trafficked women are often considered illegal migrants, with the result that if they approach the authorities for help, they can face deportation with no further investigation of the traffickers (Human Rights Watch, 2000). In 2003, South Korea's newly established Ministry of Gender Equality (MOGE)[31] took up the issue and commissioned a survey of foreign women engaged in the South Korean sex industry. In September 2003, together with the Justice Ministry, the Ministry organized an international conference[32] to discuss with other governments in the Asia-Pacific region, international organizations, NGOs and other concerned parties the actions needed, particularly the need to raise awareness regarding the dimension and characteristics of trafficking in the region. Japan also announced in November 2004 that it would impose stricter work visa requirements on foreign entertainers in a bid to combat trafficking of persons (The Japan Times, November 24, 2004).

Therefore, a number of collaborative efforts against trafficking are under way. They began in 1996 with the "Manila Process", which brought together 17 participating members for an information exchange of experiences and countervailing measures regarding

31. *The Ministry of Gender Equality, Government of Republic of Korea was established on 29 January 2001.*

32. *The Expert Group Meeting on Prevention of International Trafficking and Promotion of Public Awareness Campaign was held in Seoul, South Korea, from September 22nd to 23rd, 2003. Meeting materials can be accessed at www.mogego.kr/eng/trafficking/index.jsp*

unauthorized migration and trafficking. This was followed by the "Bangkok Declaration" of 1999, which calls for regional cooperation on irregular and undocumented migration. In 2001, many Asian countries signed the 2000 UN Protocol to Prevent, Suppress and Punish Trafficking in Persons supplementary to the United Nations Convention against Transnational Organized Crime. A year later, the governments reiterated their commitment to this goal in the Bali Process, a ministerial conference dedicated to combating people smuggling, trafficking of persons and related transnational crime.[33] In 2002, the South Asia Association for Regional Cooperation (SAARC) adopted a regional convention to prevent and combat trafficking of women and children for prostitution. At the time of writing, that convention had not yet come into force.

The secretariat of the United Nations Inter-Agency Project on Human Trafficking in the Greater Mekong Region (UNIAP)[34] reinforced consultations on human trafficking at the ministerial level in the Mekong sub-region through a preliminary roundtable, held in Bangkok in November 2003, and a follow-up meeting in late 2004 in Myanmar. Notwithstanding such efforts, trafficking continues to be one of the major challenges in the region.

TEXTBOX 6.2

"THE POWER TO CHOOSE" – A VIDEO SERIES SUPPORTING SUCCESSFUL MIGRATION

The Philippine government has recognized that migrant education is key to managing successful migration, and has therefore made it compulsory for all Overseas Filipino Workers (OFWs) to attend a special Pre-departure Orientation Seminar (PDOS) to learn about overseas work and how best to cope with related problems. As part of this effort, the video series "*The Power to Choose*" uses multimedia techniques and real migrant situations to share key messages and responses to migration challenges. Migrant workers are shown that they can gain the power to choose success for themselves through learning and preparation. The seminar also helps migrant worker support organizations to deal with challenges to a successful migration experience.

The video provides migrants with practical information on how to adjust to their new environment abroad. But, a continuing gap in this pre-departure education programme is the absence of standard educational materials. PDOS is currently serviced by over 350 accredited migrant training centres, and the quality of implementation depends heavily on the training centres themselves, as there is no active government review or re-accreditation process at this time. IOM conducts all pre-departure and post-return interviews, and these have revealed that standardized education materials would ensure higher quality training.

The Philippines is experiencing strong feminization of migration, with women accounting for over 72 per cent of Overseas Filipino Workers (**Graph 6.1**). While women have always represented a large portion of the migrant population, their role as primary labour migrants has significantly increased in recent decades.

Thus the Philippines Overseas Workers Welfare Administration (OWWA) (Department of Labor) requested IOM to produce the first video on self-defence specifically aimed at women migrant workers. This was in response to the many cases of abuse against women

33. *The supplementary Protocol has been in force since December 2003. For all current signatories go to: www.unodc.org/unodc/en/crime_cicp_signatures_trafficking.html.*

34. *UNIAP is a regional counter-trafficking project: United Nations Inter Agency Project on Human Trafficking in the Greater Mekong Region.*

GRAPH 6.1

DEPLOYMENT OF NEWLY HIRED OFWs BY SEX

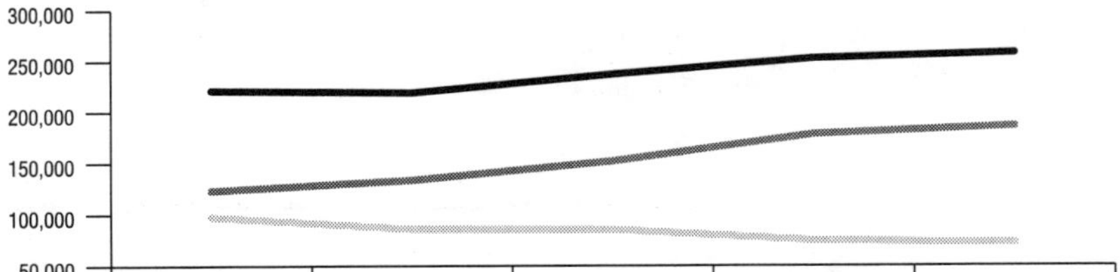

	1997	1998	1999	2000	2001
Female	123,399	133,458	151,840	178,323	186,018
Male	97,842	85,757	85,420	74,707	72,186
Total	221,241	219,215	237,260	253,030	258,204

Source: Philippine Overseas Employment Administration.

migrant workers reported to authorities and civil society organizations, including sexual harassment and rape. The status of a migrant woman as both a woman and a migrant makes her particularly vulnerable to various kinds of abuse.

The video raises women's awareness about personal security, both physical and mental. It begins with some statistics on abuse and an analysis of the factors leading to abusive behaviours, such as imbalance of power and racial/class/gender discrimination. Women migrants tend to avoid confronting or upsetting their employers in order to keep their jobs. Most of them work in private households and are isolated from the outside world, and so abuse can occur without anyone's knowledge. The video deals with the types of possible abuse, ranging from financial, verbal to physical and sexual abuse. After discussing risk avoidance, it explains some basic self-defence techniques for migrants who are already in a dangerous situation. Lastly, it explains the consequences of abuse, and the services available through embassies and other organizations to assist as needed.

Based on the success of this video, a second one was produced dealing with health and migration. According to OWWA, health is one of the most frequent problems and concerns among overseas workers. The link between migration and vulnerability to communicable diseases is recognized both nationally and regionally. Recent statistics from the Philippine Department of Health show that of the 1,385 Filipino nationals currently diagnosed as HIV positive, 480 (30%) are overseas workers.

The video conveys the following messages:

- It is the responsibility of the migrant worker to depart healthy, stay healthy and return healthy.
- Migrant workers should address issues of their health prior to departure with particular attention to health conditions prevailing in their country of destination.
- Failure to stay healthy is counterproductive to the migrant, the family and the home community.

Trainer and User Guides have been developed for both videos, that explain how to train with these tools. English and Filipino versions are designed for use in the Philippines, and Spanish and French versions are available for international use, e.g. in Latin America and Africa. IOM is exploring the possibility of using the video in post-arrival training in collaboration with colleagues in destination countries, such as Kuwait, to target Filipino diaspora communities. The video series will eventually also cover other migration themes, such as return and reintegration.

Source: IOM Manila, 2004; *MRFManila@iom.int*

INTERNAL DISPLACEMENT AND REFUGEE FLOWS

ASIA is host to nearly one half of the 20.6 million persons identified by UNHCR worldwide as "persons of concern" to the High Commissioner,[35] yet lacks sufficient means, resources and mechanisms to deal with the problem (UNHCR, 2003). Some states, for instance India and Afghanistan, are not party to the 1951 Convention relating to the Status of Refugees and the 1967 Protocol. The absence of such legal protection mechanisms and standards leaves the large refugee and IDP population in a precarious situation.

Internally Displaced Persons (IDPs) place huge strains on local infrastructure and government institutions. Five million people have been displaced in Asia by armed conflicts (Deng, 2000). In Indonesia alone, there are approximately 1.3 million IDPs, more than 50 per cent under the age of 18 (Norwegian Refugee Council, 2004a). Estimates of the total number of displaced persons in Myanmar range between one and two million, with over 600,000 located on the eastern border. At the end of 2003, there was no indication of any major returns in Myanmar (IDP Project, 2003).

In the Philippines, fighting between security forces and rebel groups in early 2003 displaced approximately 400,000 people, although all but 100,000 have now returned to their homes (IDP Project, 2004). In South Asia, continued attacks in Kashmir have prevented 350,000 displaced persons from returning to their homes, while conflicts in Northeast India have displaced more than 250,000 people. In Nepal, in the wake of the collapse of a ceasefire agreement between the government and Maoist rebels, hundreds of thousands of people have been uprooted across the country (IDP Project, 2004). Finally, in Sri Lanka, roughly 380,000 IDPs are still waiting to return home despite a 2002 peace agreement (Norwegian Refugee Council, 2004b).

Following the independence of Bangladesh, some non-Bengali Muslims who had migrated to Bangladesh (then East Pakistan) from India after 1947, known generically as "Biharies", wished to retain their Pakistani citizenship and demanded repatriation to Pakistan. Thousands had been settled officially in Pakistan after the 1971 Liberation War, and many went there clandestinely. But some 400,000 still remain as stateless people who are yet to be repatriated. The issue of the remaining "stranded Pakistanis" is still awaiting a solution by the Bangladesh and Pakistan governments.

For more than a decade now, Afghanistan has been the region's major generator of refugees. Despite the overthrow of the Taliban, tensions and fighting between warlords in the north has caused increased displacements and prevented the return of large numbers of refugees. The number of IDPs ranges from UNHCR's figure of 184,000 to the Afghan

35. *At the beginning of 2003, UNHCR counted 20.6 million "people of concern" around the globe – a number that includes 10.3 million refugees (51%), one million asylum seekers (5%), 5.8 million internally displaced persons (24%), 2.4 million returned refugees (12%) and 951,000 others of concern (4%). See also UNHCR's "Refugees by Numbers, 2003", Geneva, 2003.*

government's estimate of 340,000. The vast majority of these live in camps in the southern part of Afghanistan. In early 2003, 82,000 IDPs returned home with UNHCR and IOM assistance, but an unknown number have since been displaced again. By the end of 2003, some 200,000 to 300,000 IDPs were thought to have returned to their homes (USCR, 2003a).[36]

Currently, the IDP concept is under pressure to include individuals displaced by natural disasters or the impact of development projects. While the Guiding Principles on Internal Displacement submitted to the UN in 1998 suggest that those displaced by natural and man-made environmental events should be considered as IDPs, no document explicitly recognizes this category at present under international law (Robinson, 2004). For example, heavy monsoon rains caused severe flooding throughout Bangladesh in 1998, and the International Federation of the Red Cross and Red Crescent Societies reported that around 30 million people were affected, many of whom were left homeless. Relief efforts continued throughout 1999, but the situation in Bangladesh was further aggravated by unusual temperature shifts and cyclones (Reeds-Gildea, 1999). It is also estimated that some 64,000 Bangladeshi are displaced by riverbank erosion every year, and that 70 per cent of the slum dwellers in Dhaka are riverbank erosion-induced IDPs. In Pakistan, irrigation-related migration and displacement has a long history, and is closely bound up with issues of land distribution and ethnic demographics.[37] In South Bangladesh, displacements resulting from the construction of the Kaptai Dam (1957-1962) have given rise to long-standing conflicts among ethnic minorities in the Chittagong Hill Tracts, a region which, in the mid-1980s, had already experienced ethnic displacements to India because of settlers' appropriation of ethnic lands (UNHCR, 2002).

While the number of refugees throughout the Asia region has remained high over the past few years, the number of global asylum applications decreased in the aftermath of September 11, 2001, in part because the main refugee-accepting countries in the world tightened their asylum and refugee admissions programmes. Thus, refugee issues in Asia continue to be of concern.

The Afghan refugees in Pakistan and Iran continue to be of major concern in the Asian region. In mid-2004, there were some 2.5 million Afghans still living outside Afghanistan, with approximately 1.2 million living in Pakistan and 1.1 million in Iran (USCR, 2003a). Persistent insecurity outside Kabul and the near total absence of infrastructure have been a major impediment to the smooth return of Afghan refugees. Nonetheless, 612,000 refugees returned from Pakistan in 2003 with the assistance of UNHCR, and 269,400 returned spontaneously from Iran (UNHCR, 2004). According to UNHCR plans, one million Afghans were to be assisted to return in 2004. In 2003 about 14,500 Afghans applied for asylum worldwide (USCR, 2003b). Thailand has become a major receiving country of refugees and displaced persons from neighbouring countries. Many of these are classified as residing illegally in Thailand because the Thai government does not recognize them as refugees. The forced migration situation in Myanmar is of particular concern. In May 2003, the Thai Government signed an agreement to repatriate thousands of Burmese "illegal migrants". There are more than 277,000 Burmese refugees and asylum seekers in Thailand; among whom more than 125,000 are ethnic Karen and Karenni fleeing persecution (USCR, 2003b). In addition to the large numbers of Burmese, more than 13,000 Laotians have taken refuge on the northern Thai border. Many of them have been outside their country for nearly 15 years.

36. *IOM Kabul reports that at the time of writing, over 420,000 IDPs and refugees had returned under its IDP return and reintegration programme, carried out in close cooperation with the Ministry for Refugees and Repatriation and UNHCR.*

37. *For example, the "agricultural" migration of non-Muslim groups, such as the Bheels and Kohlis in the province of Sindh and in southern Punjab. They are seen as particularly vulnerable to become bonded agricultural labourers (Gazdar, 2003).*

In South Asia, more than 100,000 Bhutanese refugees are living in different camps in eastern Nepal. The country also hosts 20,000 Tibetan refugees (UNHCR, 2002a). The Maoist insurgency in Nepal has forced many people to move from the affected areas. At the end of 2001, UNHCR reported some 345,000 refugees living in India, including as many as 144,000 from Sri Lanka, 110,000 from China (Tibet Region), 52,000 from Myanmar, 15,000 from Bhutan, and 12,000 from Afghanistan. An estimated 40,000 Afghans were living in India in refugee-like conditions (UNHCR, 2002b).

ASYLUM SEEKERS AND DISPLACED PERSONS OUTSIDE ASIA

IN THE PAST, Asia has not been a major source of asylum seekers or displaced persons moving to the West when compared with other source regions in Europe, Africa and Latin America (UNHCR, 2004a). But, in the past few years, the number of Afghan, Chinese and Indian asylum seekers outside Asia has been more substantial, particularly in Europe. According to UNHCR, 13,820 asylum claims were lodged by Afghan nationals outside Asia in 2003 (UNHCR, 2004a). In Europe, China ranked fourth among the asylum seekers in 2003 with some 21,259 claims, and India ranked also among the top ten with 13,553 claims lodged that year (UNHCR, 2004a). Other source countries of asylum seekers to industrialized countries are Sri Lanka (5,183 in 2003), Bangladesh (5,083 in 2003) and Vietnam (4,471 in 2003).

However, asylum requests received from those source countries have also declined in recent years, most dramatically for Afghanistan (down by 46% between 2002 and 2003) and China (down 19% for the same period) and this trend continued in 2004 (UNHCR, 2004a).

UNHCR reports that in 2002 and 2003, some 3.5 million Afghan refugees were voluntarily repatriated from Pakistan and Iran (UNHCR, 2004a). Between March 2002 and June 2004, more than 2,000 Afghan asylum seekers and other migrants were assisted to return home voluntarily under IOM's assisted voluntary return (AVR) and reintegration assistance programmes (IOM Kabul), mainly from Europe, the Pacific region and Asia.[38]

MIGRATION HEALTH ISSUES IN ASIA

IN ASIA, as elsewhere, there are high inherent health risks in the complex migration patterns of the region. These are well documented (IOM, 2004[39]; Human Rights Watch, 2000a; UNHCR, 2001) and are as diverse as the types and circumstances of the movements that cause them. Though the risks and concerns related to migration health issues are being increasingly recognized and addressed by governments and the international community as a whole, the task is formidable and made even more so by pandemics such as HIV, and the difficulties of detection and control related to the clandestine nature of much migration.

Following the displacement of millions of people by the conflicts in Southeast Asia from the mid-1970s to the early 1990s, regular and orderly resettlement out of Asia has continued in recent decades under family reunification and other programmes in Australia, Canada, the US and other countries. These involve routine/standardized health checks of migrants, to assure receiving countries that medical conditions are documented and can be addressed, either before departure or after arrival. If infectious diseases such as, e.g., tuberculosis, syphilis or leprosy are detected, measures are taken to render them non-infectious prior to resettlement.

38. *UNHCR reported some 2.6 million returned either spontaneously or assisted in 2002, 646,000 returned voluntarily in 2003, and a further 1.3 million were expected to return in 2004 (UNHCR, 2003a).*

39. *See chapter 5, "Health – An Essential Aspect of Migration Management" of IOM, 2004.*

At the same time, large irregular migrant populations have continued to grow in some regions because of continuing conflicts, socio-economic upheavals, political unrest, poverty, corruption, high youth unemployment,[40] and the threatened survival of vulnerable populations. The push factors are very strong, causing irregular migration and its attendant negative health impacts for individuals and communities. These impacts can take various forms. Women may be exposed to particularly severe forms of physical and/or mental abuse and suffering, either as domestic servants or as trafficking victims. Lack of access to social networks/support and health services, conditions of enslavement, forced sex activities and unhygienic and unsanitary living conditions, can have serious health repercussions not only for the individual concerned, but for the larger community also.

Intensified trade and economic activities and the related movement of goods and people between countries can also dramatically influence the spread of communicable diseases. An example is the trans-Asia highway network currently under construction to bring trade and goods to the emerging economies of the region. In Vietnam and the Lao PDR, the HIV prevalence is well below 1 per cent in the general population; but neighbouring countries such as Thailand (1.8%), Myanmar (1.9%) and Cambodia (2.7%) are experiencing higher levels (UNAIDS, 2000). Southern China is also faced with an emerging epidemic. With the rise in regional mobility, the risk of contracting HIV also rises. Without pre-emptive action, the virus may be transmitted rapidly from high prevalence to lower prevalence areas. In response, governments, NGOs and international organizations in the region are working to develop proactive multi-sectoral approaches, emphasizing partnership, capacity building and the inclusion of persons living with HIV and AIDS.[41]

At present an estimated 6 million adults and children are living with HIV in South and Southeast Asia, and at least one in three of them will become infected with tuberculosis (WHO, 2001) and the disease may spread as they move from high to low prevalence populations. The capacity for dramatic change in HIV prevalence is well illustrated in Vietnam, which officially reported its first HIV case in 1990, and now has some 45 new cases every day (*Vietnam Investment Review*, 2004c). In the Philippines, over 30 per cent of HIV positive Filipino nationals are former overseas workers. This greatly concerns receiving countries such as Japan, although not yet considered an imminent public health threat in that country.[42]

Empowerment of the most vulnerable, particularly women, has been advocated in many international fora (UNIFEM, 2003) as an effective way of addressing this situation, but the need for practical and sustainable action will require a major shift in regional and national policy. Studies of the dynamics of transmission of epidemics such as tuberculosis, malaria and HIV within and across the region demonstrate the key role of irregular migration in the shifting high incidence patterns. While the forces driving irregular migration persist, the attitude towards those forced to move is becoming more mature. Increased access to health services is necessary to contain and make more manageable the negative impact on health of irregular migration.

An additional concern in the region has been the sporadic appearance of previously unknown infectious conditions, such as Severe Acute Respiratory Syndrome (SARS). The suddenness and impact of SARS caught regional and global health authorities off-guard and highlighted the role of migration in the rapid global dissemination of such conditions. It compelled governments to engage in local, regional and global cooperation to monitor and manage such conditions. WHO took the lead with investigative and

40. *Of the 90 million young people (aged 15 to 25) unemployed globally, i.e. nearly half of the world's jobless, 38 million are in the Asian region. In Southeast Asia, the number is almost 10 million, and growing (ILO, 2004). ILO estimates that the figure of 10 million in 2004 is almost double that of ten years earlier (ILO, 2004).*

41. *See also World Bank, "Addressing HIV/AIDS in East Asia and the Pacific" www.lnweb18.worldbank.org/eap/eap.nsf/0/00A1B68CE1D6FEDA85256ECA0058DC8E?OpenDocument*

42. *See also the website of the US Centers for Disease Control and Prevention www.cdc.gov/nchstp/od/gap/countries/vietnam.htm*

containment strategies, apparently eradicating the condition. Early awareness of the role of migration in disseminating SARS allowed the early detection, quarantine and isolation of known cases, and the containment of what could easily have developed into a global catastrophe (WHO, 2003).[43]

The Asian situation demonstrates that the negative health impacts of migration can best be managed by acknowledging irregular migration as both a key source, and solution, to the spread of health risks. Concerted collaborative action among governments, international organizations and NGOs can address the causes and controls involved in irregular migration on the one hand, while promoting tolerance and access of the vulnerable to national and targeted health services, on the other.[44]

The international community is increasingly investing in health prevention and care programmes regarding mobile populations in Asia. The ADB, UNESCO and Southeast Asian Ministers Education Organization are cooperating on a HIV/AIDS prevention project in the cross-border areas of the Greater Mekong Subregion (GMS). WHO is conducting a Border Health Program for the coordinated provision of health services in the ten Thai provinces bordering Myanmar. World Vision, Raks Thai Foundation, CARE International, Norwegian Church Aid, Health Unlimited, Population Services International, Family Health International (FHI) are among the local and international NGOs cooperating closely with government and international agencies on HIV programming in the region.

MIGRATION FOR EDUCATION

THE DEMAND to study abroad remains high, with roughly two million students per year studying outside their home countries. Asian students, especially from China, India and South Korea, make up a large portion of those studying abroad, especially in Australia, the UK and the US. In the 2002-2003 academic year, the number of students from the region grew rapidly: India: 74,603 (11.6%); China: 64,757 (2%); South Korea: 51,519 (5%) and Hong Kong: 8,076 (4%) (Education Travel, 2004).

Of the top 20 sending countries, however, 13 experienced a drop in enrolments in 2003, particularly Thailand, down 14 per cent to 9,982; Malaysia, down 11 per cent to 6,595, and Indonesia, down 10 per cent to 10,432 students. Factors contributing to the decline in enrolments from certain countries include increasing difficulties to obtain student visas, weaker local economies and parental concern over safety (ibid).

Overall, the number of foreign students studying in the US grew by just 0.6 per cent for the 2002/2003 academic year (Education Travel, 2004). Such weak growth may be attributed to the increased number of students from Asian countries that masked the decline in the number of applications from, or visa denials to, Arab and Muslim students, following increased security measures in the aftermath of September 11.[45] The main sources of foreign students from Asia in the US are China mainland, Japan, South Korea, India, Singapore, Malaysia, Thailand and Indonesia. While among all destination countries, the US hosts the highest number of Chinese graduate students, their numbers are down, and there are fewer self-funded students from China. Tighter security and entry

43. *See also the WHO case definitions for Surveillance of Severe Acute Respiratory Syndrome (SARS) www.who.int/csr/sars/casedefinition/en/*

44. *See also the report "Moving Across Borders", HDN Key Correspondent Team/Rapporteur Team, 2nd APCRSH: 6-10 October 2003, Bangkok, Thailand; correspondents@hdnet.org. It calls on governments to monitor compliance with the international convention on human rights, promote savings and insurance schemes, regulate labour recruitment, and provide legal, social and educational outreach to migrant workers (HDN, 2003).*

45. *In the academic year 2002/2003, the average number of Middle East students to the US dropped by 10 per cent over the previous year (the combined total was down to 34,803 from 38,545, Institute of International Education, 2003).*

controls, particularly following the September 11 attacks, have been a major deterrent in this regard. The US Embassy in Beijing anticipated some 22,000 applicants in 2004, with an expected visa issuance rate of 70 per cent, a drop from previous years.[46]

The number of students from Asia studying in the UK grew in 2003, in part because of an aggressive marketing campaign throughout Asia. The number of Chinese applications rose by 40.8, per cent, but the overall number of international students increased by only 2.3 per cent (Curtis, 2003). The overwhelming share of Chinese migrants in the UK are students; but, given the high incidence of fraud, the government has lowered its visa issuance rate in the past two years (in 2003/2004, there were 22,828 applications and an issuance rate of 63%).[47] Recent studies project continuing growth in Chinese and Indian demand for student visas over the next two decades. Australia and New Zealand have also marketed their universities more aggressively and enrolled more students from Asia.

In New Zealand, Malaysian students account for nearly one-third of all student entrants (OECD 2001). Australia experienced extraordinary growth in Chinese enrolments, up by as much as 69 per cent in 2000 (Education Travel, 2002). China is now the biggest and most rapidly growing source of overseas students in Australia, accounting for some 17,279 in 2003/2004 (cf. 14,215 in 2002/03) or 18 per cent of the 100,000 visas issued per year. Add to this some 30,000 Chinese students enrolled in Australian educational and training programmes in China as at 2004. In 2003, 43,000 Chinese students were studying in Australia and participating in 57,579 educational courses. Students from Malaysia, Singapore, Hong Kong and India comprise nearly 50 per cent of all foreign students in Australia (OECD, 2001).

Despite recent downturns in some student movements out of Asia, these are expected to grow rapidly again in the coming years, as is already the case between China and Australia. In fact, what might be referred to as "foreign education industries" are major export growth areas in Oceania, Europe and North America. Student pools are also being increasingly tapped to fill skilled labour market gaps, particularly in Australia.[48] At the same time, the countries of destination report high and sophisticated levels of document and other fraud in this area (e.g. the use of valid documents, for instance for MBA "refresher" courses, with subsequent breach of visa entitlements). Thus, immigration checks are being tightened, and government authorities require stricter monitoring and reporting by the universities and educational institutes on the behaviour and regular status of students – a method already applied in Australia.

For its part, China is also becoming a strong education hub, including for foreign students. It has been observed that fewer Chinese are going abroad for their education because of the increased opportunities offered by Chinese universities (owing also to the return to China of well educated former Chinese expatriate students and their placement in Chinese universities). Increasing numbers of foreign students, particularly from Thailand, have also begun to go to China for higher education, reflecting the country's increasing economic strength (China Education and Research Network, 2002). Japan is actively seeking to increase the number of foreign students studying in the country: in May 2002, over 95,550 foreign students were studying in Japan, 21.2 per cent increase over the previous year; in 2003 the number of foreign college students in Japan reached 109,508 (Japan Times, March 12, 2004).

46. *Information collected in discussions with US and other embassy staff by the CEME (Cooperative Efforts to Manage Emigration) team of migration experts in June 2004: www.migration.ucdavis.edu/rs/index.php*

47. *This information was collected by the CEME (Cooperative Efforts to Manage Emigration) team of migration experts during discussions with UK Embassy staff and other officials in Beijing in June 2004: www.migration.ucdavis.edu/rs/index.php*

48. *The Australian Skilled Migration programme allows overseas students, many of them Chinese, to change their status to permanent residence and work in Australia (some 55 per cent of Skilled Migration visas go to students).*

CONCLUSION

MIGRATION continues to be an immensely important political, economic, social and cultural issue throughout Asia, and one that is prone to rapid change, not only in terms of a shift of focus from the long dominant Middle East destinations. Labour migration is burgeoning within and beyond the region, and is being increasingly fostered and supported for the mutual benefit of Asian (and Pacific) states, particularly regarding the skilled and business levels. It will be instructive for other regions to observe the progress of highly organized labour emigration programmes of the region, and the growing sophistication and success of remittance and diaspora management strategies of the major migrant sending states.

Traditional characterizations of "sending" and "receiving" countries within the region no longer hold true, in particular if one considers China, for instance, as an emerging education hub, or Iran as a major labour exporter in the region. Similarly, there is little doubt that the feminization of migrant labour in Asia will continue to change the face of migration in the region and demand a regional system to safeguard the rights of workers, and the honouring of relevant international commitments.

The growing numbers and the pervasiveness of unauthorized migrants also calls for a mechanism that enhances the immigration management capacity of the region, as well as of individual countries within it. Intelligence cooperation and exchanges of practical management ideas must lead the way in this regard, as countries in the region seek out a better framework to maintain ease of movement while also enhancing security for everyone.

ECONOMIC MIGRATION IN SOUTH ASIA[49]

INTRODUCTION

IN SOUTH ASIA, one of the poorest regions of the world,[50] economic migration is a major livelihood option for many, and a possible tool to promote development and reduce poverty in the region. Migration for resettlement out of South Asia has been mostly to Europe, Australia or North America; contract labour migration has been to the Middle East, Southeast Asia and elsewhere, and seasonal labour migration has largely remained within the region (e.g. from Bangladesh and Nepal to India) (Skeldon, 2003). While international flows are high, internal migration far exceeds these, and is a growing policy priority for governments, because of the rural-urban and urban-urban migration impact on rapid urbanization in India, Pakistan and Bangladesh (Afsar, 2003).

The decision to move and work elsewhere is often taken within a household, sometimes a community, looking to minimize the risks of various markets (crop, capital, credit, insurance) and improve its conditions in regard to other households (Batistella, 2001). Gender discrimination and the low status of women across South Asia have also caused women and girls to move for employment, sometimes making them vulnerable to trafficking.[51] This chapter points to some of the complexities of labour migration, and ongoing efforts to manage it, in a region currently characterized by high emigration rates and some of the highest remittance returns in the world, but little in the way of general migration policies.

---

49. *The author of this sub-chapter is Shahidul Haque, IOM Regional Representative, South Asia.*

50. *About one-third of the populations of India (44.2%), Pakistan (31%), Bangladesh (29.1%) and Nepal (37.7%) are estimated to be living below the national poverty line, on incomes of USD 1 a day. Sri Lanka is close behind with 25 per cent of its people living on USD1 a day. (Skeldon, 2003; UNDP, 2001).*

51. *See the main chapter on "International Migration Trends and Patterns in Asia" for more details.*

THE COMPLEX DYNAMICS OF SOUTH ASIAN LABOUR MIGRATION

The Middle East remains the primary destination for migrants from South Asia, despite more recent diversification towards other Southeast Asian and European countries. This harks back to the early 1970s and the labour-intensive construction boom in the Middle East. By the mid-1990s, it peaked with an average 800,000 South Asians working there. Short-term seasonal migration in border areas during harvesting time is generally not documented or regulated as people have been migrating there already long before the borders existed. Most short-term labour migrants are low skilled and employed in the "informal sector" on a temporary basis. With the exception of Sri Lanka, they are mostly male.

Reliable data on emigrants, contract labour migrants or seasonal migrants in the region are difficult to come by. Some governments have official figures, but many migrants remain unrecorded. As data are not disaggregated by gender or skills, and methods of collection vary across countries, any comparative regional analysis is difficult. There is agreement, though, that the actual number of migrants far exceeds official estimates.

India's diaspora population around the world is estimated at some 20 million – the largest of the region, and the third largest in the world, after China and the UK (Rajan, 2003). Many Indians are working as short-term contract labourers, about 75 per cent of them in the Middle East. In 2002, contract labourers from India numbered 37 million, down from 44 million in 1993.

According to 2001 census data, 762,181 Nepalese were absent from their place of origin for more than six months, most of them in India because of historical ties. But this is declining, as more Nepalese turn to destinations like Saudi Arabia, Qatar, UAE, Hong Kong, China and the US (KC, Bal, 2003). Between 1991-2000, it is estimated that more than 250,000 Bangladeshis left their country annually to take up overseas employment,[52] but that the actual numbers are much higher. Major destinations for Bangladeshi labour migrants are the Middle East and Malaysia. It is roughly estimated that 1.05 million Bangladeshis are living abroad permanently, mostly in the UK, the US, Europe, South Africa, Canada and Australia (Siddiqui, 2004). Regarding Sri Lanka, some 158,287 migrants are believed to have left the country in 1998, 66.5 per cent of whom were women. Most migrate to the Middle East; but also to Lebanon, Libya, Jordan, Cyprus, Singapore, Hong Kong and Malaysia (INSTRAW-IOM, 2000).

The predominantly semi-skilled and unskilled nature of South Asian labour migration makes it difficult for both origin and destination countries to protect these migrants, particularly in the informal sectors. The migration trends also differ among South Asian countries; skilled worker migration from Bangladesh to the Middle East seems to have declined, and the movement of the unskilled increased, while the opposite appears to have occurred in India.

The labour recruitment industry is burgeoning in South Asia. In the 1970s and 1980s, when large numbers of contract labourers were migrating to the Middle East, recruitment was mostly dealt with by the state. Now, more than 90 per cent of it is conducted by private agencies in India, Pakistan, Sri Lanka and Bangladesh. The agencies normally require a licence from the government of the labour origin country. They find market employment opportunities abroad and facilitate the placement of the workers. Initially paid by the employer for the procurement of labour, they are now allowed to charge workers a regulated, but often illicit placement fee. Not all countries have adopted a standard labour contract, but even in countries that have, the standards are often disregarded (Batistella, 2001). Thus, while important for the expansion of migrant markets, recruiting agencies also play a role in the context of human

52. *Source: Bangladesh Bureau of Manpower, Employment and Training (BMET).*

rights and migrant workers rights abuses, as well as the rise in irregular migration.

Emigration of the highly skilled has boomed in recent years, along with the increase in investments in products and services related to IT. Indian IT professionals dominate this category of migration, and the Indian government has created the Ministry of Information Technology to organize this type of emigration. Return migration and its potential for the development of home communities is also gaining importance, and countries of origin like India are developing policies to facilitate diaspora investment in origin communities.

Some countries use foreign employment as a means of reducing local unemployment, but it is in particular an important source of foreign currency for many. Migration for economic purposes also raises the question, whether the highly educated and often wealthy people who leave create a space for less privileged people. There is a lively debate among development practitioners about whether migration reduces a country's skilled workforce, increases brain drain and consequently has a negative effect on the development process; and there are cogent arguments for the benefits that brain circulation can bring to the country of origin. But, as yet, there is inadequate information about this in South Asia.

REMITTANCES

REMITTANCES represent the most important impact of short-term or long-term international migration on South Asian economies and societies; an impact difficult to assess due to the unavailability of complete data. About 20 per cent of the annual global international remittances (close to USD 100 billion in 2004) flow into South Asia. India accounts for 78 per cent of this, which makes it the world's largest remittance receiving country (Kuddus, 2003). Bangladesh accounts for 12 per cent of the remittances flowing into South Asia; a notable 2 per cent of the global remittance flows. These figures vary according to the sources.[53]

The major impact of remittances in the areas of origin is the change in investment patterns, household expenditure, income and the labour market. While there is little research on this, it appears that remittances are able to markedly reduce the unemployment rate of the origin area (Anh, 2003).

GOVERNMENT POLICIES AND ACTIONS TO MANAGE MIGRATION

MOST POLICIES in the region relating to migration are *ad hoc* and focus only on temporary international contract labour migration, both nationally and regionally. Except for Sri Lanka, none of the countries has ratified the 1990 International Convention on the Protection of the Rights of All Migrant Workers and Members of Their Families.

Nevertheless, important steps are being taken in this direction. In Bangladesh, the government has set up a new ministry to deal with overseas contract labour and the diaspora, and is proactively negotiating with foreign governments and employers for a share of foreign labour markets (Waddington, 2003). Private recruiting agencies still handle more than 90 per cent of the labour migration. In India, where there has been no central structure to manage labour migration (ibid), and private recruiting agents operate within state structures, the government recently enhanced its

53. *According to World Development Indicators 2002, remittance figures vary because of the amounts flowing through unofficial channels. Pakistan and Sri Lanka, respectively receive 2.1 and 1.1 per cent of the total global remittance flow. However, such figures only reflect remittances coming through official channels and not those transmitted through unofficial channels. It is widely believed that a significant amount of remittance flows into South Asia through unofficial channels. A study carried out in Bangladesh suggested that only 46 per cent of remittances arrived through official channels, 40 per cent through the informal hundi or hawala system, 4.6 per cent were carried by friends and family and a further 8 per cent carried by the migrants themselves when they returned home. In India, estimates of the proportions sent informally vary between 25 and 30 per cent. However, investments in the origin countries by the non-resident Indians or Bangladeshis may not be included in the remittance data.*

capacity to respond to crises causing mass repatriations of expatriates,[54] and the new Ministry of Information Technology will have the capacity to deal with the emigration of IT professionals.

Pakistan's labour migration is managed by the state. It established its Bureau of Emigration and Overseas Employment in 1971, which worked through labour attachés in the Middle East and a network of 500 private licensed agents processing labour contracts (ibid). The Sri Lanka Bureau of Foreign Employment (SLBFE) was established in 1985. The main objectives of the SLBFE are the promotion of foreign employment, sound management of foreign employment and the welfare and security of migrant employees and their families (IOM, 2003). Sri Lanka is the only country in South Asia to have adopted a regional gender-based approach to labour emigration.

Nepal has no policy to deal with broad migration issues, which remain seriously under-researched, despite the fact that many socio-economic, demographic and political problems are closely linked to both internal and international migration (KC, 2001). However, the government's ninth five-year national development plan (1997-2002) did provide for the study of international migration, and for appropriate policies for its effective regulation (*New Era*, 2000).

In addition to strengthening the positive structural role that migration can play in the region, South Asian governments are increasingly working to identify the "root causes" of forced migration and trafficking, and the measures needed to control this type of migration. One such initiative to address trafficking is the SAARC[55] Convention on the Preventing and Combating Trafficking in Women and Children for Prostitution, adopted in 2002. In the labour migration area, the origin countries initiated the Colombo Process, a consultative mechanism for Ministers from Asian labour-sending countries, in Sri Lanka in April 2003. The major objectives of this process are: protection of migrant workers and migrant services, optimizing the benefits of organized labour migration, institutional capacity building and inter-state cooperation.

TEXTBOX 6.3

Migration in the People's Republic of China[56]

Since China started its reforms and open-door policy at the end of 1970s, migration flows from and into the country have gradually gained momentum. Both the numbers of Chinese migrants going abroad and the number of foreigners coming to China are steadily growing. China is experiencing multi-directional migration flows and multi-dimensional migration impacts, among these some brain drain and brain gain, which co-exist indivisibly.

China is one of the major migrant origin countries in the world. In 2000, some 62,000 Chinese nationals settled abroad, and in 2001 and 2002 that number reached 70,000 and 118,000, respectively, the number of those leaving temporarily as visitors, students or contract workers, are many times higher, with a total number of 20,204,600 exits last year alone.[57] The ratio between Chinese migrants going abroad for settlement and China's base population ranges between 1:21,400 to 1:10,700 in recent years (the base population was 1,295,250,352 at the time of writing). A number of migrants are also settling abroad in

54. *This followed the repatriation of several thousands of individuals under amnesty programmes from the UAE to Kerala (Waddington, 2003).*

55. *South Asian Association for Regional Cooperation.*

56. *The author of this Textbox is Zhao Jian, Regional Advisor for East and Southeast Asia and Oceania, a.i. IOM, Geneva.*

57. *See the publication of the Ministry of Public Security: www.edu.sinohome.com/oversea/papers/2793.htm, China Radio International: www.fpon.cri.com.cn/773/2003-2-6/118@153822.htm*

irregular ways. Although migrant settlers represent only an extremely small percentage of China's population, it is significant that the Chinese are increasingly participating in international migration, which some 30 years ago was unthinkable.[58]

At the same time, China has begun to accept more and more foreign workers and settlers in recent years. In 2001, about 119,900 foreigners (some of them may have multiple entries in the same year) entered China for employment, and in 2002 that number reached some 137,100.[59] Foreign workers are mainly concentrated in Shanghai, Beijing and other big cities. They are mostly employed by foreign companies, transnational companies or joint ventures in the country, most of them being skilled workers or managerial level personnel. A considerable percentage of them are also employed in academic institutions and the service sectors. The market has not yet officially been opened for unskilled migrant workers from outside.

In February 2003, China issued residence permits valid for two to five years and for multiple entries and exits, to non-diplomat foreigners investing or working in managerial or other skilled areas in China. In that month, Beijing issued 46 such permits, and other Chinese cities soon followed suit. Most notably on 15 August 2004, China issued and started to implement the Regulations on Examination and Approval of Permanent Residence of Aliens in China. This is commonly known as a "Green Card" for foreigners in China, by which qualified aliens could get permanent residence cards with 5 or 10 years validity; and the cards are renewable upon expiry. These are notable steps for China in revising its management of immigration, since, in the past, foreigners who were not diplomatic staff were only issued cards with one-year validity and only a few foreigners, who had been living in China for many years, were issued longer residence permits.

China encourages skilled overseas Chinese to return and work in China, and incentives (such as the choice of working place and equipment purchase) have been designed especially for such persons. Over the past 25 years, some 700,200 Chinese went to study abroad, and about 172,800 returned in the period 1978 to end-2003.[60] Some returnees have assumed leading positions in government agencies or academic institutions. About 80 per cent of the academics of the Academy of Sciences of China are former overseas Chinese students.[61] Some are now successfully running their own enterprises and contributing to local economic development.

China has made remarkable progress in attracting overseas Chinese to invest both money and expertise in the country's economic development and social progress. Over 60 per cent of all overseas investment in China in the past two decades was from overseas Chinese investors.[62] The number of such enterprises constitutes over 70 per cent of the total number

58. *Chinese emigration mainly started in the 19th century and the first half of the 20th century. Zhu Guohong (1999) estimated that about 10 million Chinese emigrated in the period 1840 – 1911, and 6 million in 1912-1949. In 1950-end of 1970s, there was little emigration from China.*

59. *See the website of the Ministry of Public Security: www.mps.gov.cn/webpage/shownews.asp?id=710&biaoshi=bitGreatNews*

60. *According to a senior official of the Ministry of Personnel of China (reported on 26 Feb. 2004 by Wang Li). For more details see: www.quanze.com/Job/News.asp?CID=42&ID=304*

61. *Ibid.*

62. *Chen Yujie, Director of the Overseas Chinese Affairs Office of the State Council said in an interview with the Chinese Press in USA on 6 Nov. 2003, that since China started its reforms and opened up to the outside world, the enterprises in China funded by overseas Chinese have made valuable contributions to economic development and social progress in China.*

of enterprises in China with funding from overseas. In 1979, China promulgated a law on joint venture management in China and, in 1980, the first joint venture "Hong Kong Beijing Air Catering Co. Ltd." was established. Until October 2003, the number of enterprises with foreign investment in China reached 456,892, and the aggregate total of foreign investment was USD 491,522 million (the amount of total foreign investment by contract was USD 916,743 million).[63] China has also benefited from the remittances sent by its workers abroad. In the first half of 2003, these amounted to more than USD5.5 billion, and by the end of the year had reached some USD 10 billion.[64] Thus, overseas Chinese have made considerable contributions to the development of China.

China has a surplus labour force, both in rural areas and in the cities. With continuing urbanization, more and more rural labourers are moving into the cities. In 2003, some 121 million people were migrating internally and stayed out of their household-registered places for over six months.[65] These internal migrants have made significant contributions to China's economic development and social progress, for instance through infrastructure building and service provision. Remittances and expertise from those migrants have helped to support the development of their hometowns and villages. In a number of provinces, internal migrants help fill the labour gaps left behind by those who have gone abroad. The income of these internal migrants amounted to over 30 per cent of the total income of all rural residents in recent years. The stock of surplus labour in rural areas was estimated to be over 150 million, and many of them are expected to move internally. Managing internal migration remains one of the biggest long-term challenges for China.[66]

Until a few years ago, documented migrant workers from China only comprised those of Chinese companies with projects in foreign countries. In recent years, China revised its regulations on the issuance of passports for work abroad. In April 2002, China promulgated a regulation on Chinese labour workers going abroad for employment, and some provinces and cities also passed local regulations simplifying passport application procedures for individuals to obtain passports "according to their needs". Individuals can now go abroad on their own volition for overseas employment. In 2002, total exits from China for overseas employment, including project-related and individual employment, numbered about 442,200.[67] By the end of 2003, about 550,000 Chinese migrant workers were working abroad,[68] most of them as construction workers with a small number of skilled workers in the medical, engineering and IT sectors. Unlike some labour-sending countries, China does not send migrant workers to labour receiving countries through official bilateral or multilateral agreements. Whether the government will change this in the future remains to be seen.

63. *Zhang Feng,* Study on the 2004 Prospects of Chinese Economy, *published by Beijing Chen Bao, 22 January 2004: www.xici.net/main.asp?doc=35192225*

64. *See Nan Ke, 2003; and B. McKinley, 2004.*

65. *See the website of the China National Statistics Bureau: www.happyhome.net.cn/read*

66. *Li Peilin,* Issues for the Economic Development of China in 2004, *published in Dec. 2003. www.bj.edu21cn.com/web_news/news.asp?id=1183&type=703*

67. *See the website of the Ministry of Public Security: www.mps.gov.cn/webpage/shownews.asp?id=1137&biaoshi=bitGreatNews*

68. *Figure from the speech by BU Zhengfa, Vice Minister of Labour and Social Security of China, at* the Second Labour Migration Ministerial Consultations for Countries of Origin in Asia *held in Manila on 22-24 September 2004.*

Irregular migration from and into China exists. The government has a stated policy and practice of taking back any Chinese irregular migrant found abroad, as long as the Chinese citizenship is established. It has also put measures in place to address irregular migration, including stronger laws against smuggling and trafficking, enhanced passport features, upgraded detention facilities, public information campaigns, creation of a marine police team and the establishment of a joint committee against illegal migration. In 2002 and 2003, Chinese police intervened in 4,623 and 6,907 irregular border crossings, respectively.[69] In 2003, Chinese police arrested 774 traffickers of human beings.[70] Most irregular migration to China is from its neighbouring countries, and largely for work purposes.

China is increasingly working together with other countries in the region and beyond to manage international migration through bilateral and multilateral cooperation. For example, the government hosted a workshop convened as part of the Bali Process in November 2002, held annual discussions with the EU in recent years, and participated in the IOM-organized Asian Labour Migration Ministerial Consultations in Colombo in April 2003, and in September 2004. The government has also signed a number of Approved Destination Status Agreements with other governments, to ensure greater cooperation between governments and travel agencies in the tourism industry.[71] By September 2004, Chinese tourists could go to over 50 countries/regions in accordance with those Agreements.

69. *Ibid.*

70. *See also Xinhuanet; www.qingdaonews.com/gb/content/2004-03/25/content_2908986.htm*

71. *Information by China National Tourism Administration (11 October 2004), www.cnta.com/chujing/chujing.htm*

OCEANIA – MIGRATION DYNAMICS[72]

BACKGROUND

Oceania[73] is a region of more than 10,000 islands (including Australia and New Zealand), where population numbers and population densities are relatively low, variously reflecting small land mass, water scarcity, unproductive soils or rugged terrain. A total population of 33 million is anticipated for 2005 (United Nations, 2003), of which over three-quarters will be living in Australia (over 20 million) and New Zealand (6 million) (ABS, 2004).

Migration in and through the region is significant, with almost 6 million international migrants in the region in 2000, the highest percentage per regional population globally, and growing at a rate of 2.1 per cent, the third highest after North America and Europe (United Nations, 2003). Only Papua New Guinea shares a land border with another state; so, for almost all of Oceania, border management challenges are limited to managing those who arrive by sea or air.

This chapter surveys the major migration trends and policy responses of this region, particularly of the past two years, with a focus on Australia and New Zealand, the largest migrant and refugee receiving countries, and the interplay between these two and others in the region, notably in strengthening cooperation on managing irregular migration. It shows how Australia and New Zealand will continue to be major hubs, particularly for visitors, students and temporary labour migrants, and how climate and demographic changes will influence the migration patterns of the future.

A HISTORY OF OCEANIA MIGRATION

Migration to Australia and New Zealand

For Australia and New Zealand, traditional immigration countries since the European settlements of the late 18th century,[74] migration has been a major contributor to population growth. The share of overseas-born in their population are high in comparison to other developed countries.[75] As at the 2001 census, 17.4 per cent of Australia's population was born overseas and 18.3 per cent of the Australian-born population had one or both parents born overseas (DIMIA, 2003a). In New Zealand for the same period, 19 per cent of the population was born overseas; a quarter of these came from the Oceania region (17% from the Pacific, 8% from Australia). In 2002-03, net overseas migration (125,300) contributed more to Australia's population growth than did natural population growth (115,200) (DIMIA, 2004h). In 2003-04, the reverse was true in New Zealand. Net natural population growth (29,750) contributed more to New Zealand's population growth than net overseas migration (22,000) (Statistics New Zealand, 2004a; 2004b).

Both Australia and New Zealand continue to operate the full range of skilled, business and family immigration programmes, together with humanitarian programmes to resettle refugees.

---

72. *The author of this sub-chapter is Jenny Bedlington, Principal, JennGen Consulting, Canberra, Australia.*

73. *For the purposes of this chapter Oceania includes: Australia, New Zealand, Melanesia [comprised of Fiji, New Caledonia, Papua New Guinea, Solomon Islands and Vanuatu], Micronesia (comprised of Guam, Kiribati*, Marshall Islands*, Micronesia,(Federated States of, Nauru*, Northern Mariana Islands* and Palau*), and Polynesia (comprised of American Samoa*, Cook Islands*, French Polynesia, Niue*, Pitcairn*, Samoa, Tokelau*, Tonga, Tuvalu*, and the Wallis and Futuna Islands*). Countries marked with an asterisk had a population of less than 100,000 in 2002. (Population Division of the Department of Economic and Social Affairs of the United Nations Secretariat, 2003.)*

74. *The indigenous peoples of both countries were probably also migrants about 50,000 and 1,000 years ago, respectively.*

75. *See also the other regional chapters in this section and the chapter "International Migration Trends" presenting UN data on global migrant stocks and flows.*

TABLE 6.2

IMMIGRATION INTAKE FOR AUSTRALIA AND NEW ZEALAND 2002-2003

Migration category	Australia (residence approvals 2002-03[76])	New Zealand (residence approvals 2002-03)
Skilled/Business	66,053	30,443
Family	40,794	14,809
Humanitarian	12,525	3,286
TOTAL	120,595	48,538

Source: NZIS, 2002-2003; DIMIA, 2003b

Australia and New Zealand are also experiencing high levels of emigration, mostly temporary and of educated young citizens seeking work experience overseas. However, 50,463 people left Australia permanently between 2002 and 2003, the highest number ever, mostly to the UK, the US and Asia. About half were Australia-born and just less than half were skilled; thus, for that year, skilled immigration added only around 11,000 skilled permanent settlers to Australia's population in net terms. New Zealand had a permanent emigration rate of 62,300 people in 2003-04, two-thirds of whom were citizens (Statistics New Zealand, 2004b); set against 84,300 permanent long-term arrivals, this amounted to a positive net migration balance of 22,000. An Australian study concluded that the high Australian emigration is a function of globalization, and a response to massive improvements in transportation and information flow (Hugo et al., 2001). A more recent study, however, shows that, given Australia's attractiveness in terms of quality of life, and strengthened skilled migration programme, the net gain of professionals in the past three years has been substantially higher than in the final years of the 20th century (Birrell et al., 2004).

Permanent Migration

Australia has shifted its programme emphasis in recent years to skilled and business migration, while still maintaining a commitment to family migration. About 60 per cent of permanent migration is skilled and business migration, and 40 per cent family migration – nearly three-quarters of which comprises spouses of Australian citizens and permanent residents. Demand for migration of spouses, dependent children and other close family members continues to increase. Migration programme numbers are planned over a three-year period, and will be around 100,000-110,000 for 2003-04, plus a parent contingency reserve (DIMIA, 2004b).

The New Zealand immigration programme is also set on a planning cycle of three years, with the major focus on skilled and business immigrants. In 2003/04, the level of approvals was set at 45,000-50,000 per annum, with 60 per cent of places reserved for the skilled/business stream[77] (nearly 50% of those approved come from the UK, India, China and South Africa).

Temporary Migration

A notable shift in Australia's immigration policy in recent years has been the increased intake of temporary migrants for work purposes. In mid-2000, there were more than half a million temporary labour migrants in the country, and 2002-03 saw the highest long-term temporary movements ever recorded for Australia (more than 500,000). New Zealand granted 27,426 temporary work permits in 2003-04 to fill identified skill shortages in the New Zealand workforce. Both countries have in recent years increasingly opened up avenues for temporary residents to remain long term and eventually gain permanent status through job opportunities.[78]

76. *Total includes 1,223 Special Eligibility visas covering the Former Resident and Close Ties categories, and excludes New Zealand migrants.*

77. *53 per cent were ultimately approved in this stream, 35 per cent in Family Sponsored stream (some 60% being partners of New Zealanders), and 13 per cent through the International/Humanitarian stream. At the end of November 2002, New Zealand placed more focus on settlement prospects for skilled and business migrants by requiring greater English proficiency. In 2003, the General Skills Category, the main category of the Skilled/Business Stream, was closed and a new Skilled Migrant Category (SMC) introduced, for which applicants were invited to apply following a selection from a pool containing those interested in gaining residence in New Zealand.*

78. *Some New Zealand visas are issued with the intention of granting residence after two years of working in New Zealand.*

Tourist and Student Entry

While there are a myriad of temporary visa categories ranging from visitors to executives offered by Australia and New Zealand, tourism and study bring major export earnings to both:

- Tourism – one of the largest export industries in both countries – generated over AUD 17.1 billion in Australia in 2000-01 (more than 11.2% of total export earnings) and over NZD 7 billion in New Zealand (NZIS, 2004a; 2004b). The overall number of visitor visas issued for Australia in 2003-04 (3,458,422) represented a 7 per cent increase over 2002-03.[79] Similarly, the number of visitors travelling to New Zealand rose by 10 per cent in 2003-04 to 2,250,000 in 2002-03 (Statistics New Zealand, 2004).[80]
- Overseas students are Australia's second largest group of temporary entrants, constituting an AUD 4 billion plus industry. A total of 171,619 student visas were issued in 2003-04, an increase of 8 per cent on 2001-02, the largest source being China (DIMIA, 2003c). Since 1997-98, the number of overseas students in New Zealand had increased by 390 per cent by 2002-03 again most of that increase coming from China (NZIS, 2003). Student visas issued in 2003-04 were 87,075 (including offshore visas).[81]

Australia's Working Holiday Maker arrangements also allow young people aged between 18 and 30 to holiday for up to twelve months in Australia and supplement their travel funds through casual employment of up to three months with each employer. These arrangements are conducted on a reciprocal basis with fourteen countries. The programme contributes positively to Australia's economy,[82] helps fill demand for seasonal labour and, in 2003, helped some 30,000 Australian and over 88,000 young foreigners to develop cultural understanding and associations (DIMIA, 2004b; Vanstone, 2004).

New Zealand has similar reciprocal arrangements with 20 countries or regions, and a unilateral working holiday scheme for the US, with a total annual quota of around 31,000.[83] These working holiday schemes also aim to strengthen international links, contribute to the economy[84] and encourage potential skilled migrants to choose New Zealand as a permanent home.

Visa Arrangements

Australia uniquely requires all persons seeking to enter the country to possess a valid visa. In this way, the government can capitalize on the geographic advantage for migration management of having no land borders. To ensure that these requirements operate efficiently and with the minimum of inconvenience on the traveller, Australia offers an electronic travel authority (ETA) – in effect, a "virtual visa" – through 300,000 travel agents and more than 75 airlines worldwide, and through the Internet (see also the Textbox 21.1 "Visa Systems in the 21st Century – the Australian Model"). The ETA is available to nationals of 33 countries and locations deemed to present a low risk of migration law violations. As at October 2004, over 15 million travellers had come to Australia on ETAs, which now account for 87.2 per cent of all tourist and short-term business visas issued worldwide.[85]

---

79. *Note that visitor visas issued to PRC nationals are increasing (162,116 in 2003-04, or up 25% from 2002-03; the Tourism Forecasting Council projects an increase of up to 620,000 visas to Chinese by 2010.*

80. *Australia is New Zealand's largest source of international visitors and visitor expenditure (NZIS, 2004c).*

81. *Updated data derived directly from the NZIS representative, New Zealand High Commission, Canberra, October, 2004.*

82. *Working Holiday Makers are estimated to spend around AUD 1.3 billion a year.*

83. *In addition to the unilateral US scheme, New Zealand has reciprocal agreements with Argentina, Canada, Chile, Denmark, Finland, France, Germany, the HKSAR, Ireland, Italy, Japan, Republic of Korea, Malaysia, Malta, the Netherlands, Singapore, Sweden, Taiwan Province of China and Uruguay. The New Zealand WHS for British nationals reflects the arrangement for New Zealanders in the UK, but is not directly reciprocal.*

84. *Working Holiday Makers are estimated to spend around NZD 309.1 million a year.*

85. *ETA visas have been available on the Internet since 2001. See the DIMIA website on ETAs: www.immi.gov.au/cgi-bin/AT-immisearch.cgi*

Visitors to New Zealand who are citizens from visa-free countries[86] need not apply for a visa if they intend to stay for up to three months.[87] New Zealand and Australian citizens or residents with a valid Australian Resident Return visa do not require a visa to visit, study or work in New Zealand. (People from Nuie, the Cook Islands and Tokelau are New Zealand citizens.)

TEXTBOX 6.4

TRANS-TASMAN TRAVEL ARRANGEMENTS (TTTA)

Australians and New Zealanders can visit, live and work in each other's country without restriction under the Trans-Tasman Travel Arrangement, which is a series of immigration procedures applied by each country and underpinned by joint expressions of political support. The Arrangement has its origins in an exchange of letters in 1920. Today, it applies to nearly two million Australian and New Zealand travellers crossing the Tasman Sea each year.

Citizens of either country are not subject to the usual visa processing for such visits, and need only present a valid passport upon arrival. Subject to a character clearance, they are then able to live and work in the other country. In view of its global visa requirements, Australia considers a New Zealand passport to be an application for a visa, and grants it electronically (subject to health and character clearance), entitling the person to stay and work as long as he/she remains a New Zealand citizen.

Agreements have also been concluded for reciprocal access to social welfare and health services for TTTA visitors. A bilateral social security agreement has existed since 1948 (updated several times, most recently in 2002, which entitles New Zealanders living in Australia to receive old-age pensions and disability benefits, and vice versa for Australians living in New Zealand). The reciprocal health care agreement was signed in 1986 and allows Australians and New Zealanders to make short-term visits to each other's country to receive "immediately necessary" hospital care on the same terms as residents of that country.

Approximately 60,000 Australian citizens live in New Zealand, and as of mid-2003, some 460,000 New Zealanders were living in Australia, 25 per cent of whom were born outside New Zealand. The demographic profiles on both sides are similar: young, working-age adults, living mainly in the cities (ABS, 2002). Their arrivals and departures tend to fluctuate in response to changing economic conditions in the two countries (DIMIA, 2004a).

Sources: DIMIA and NZIS.

86. *There are 49 visa-free countries. See the NZIS website, www.immigration.govt.nz, for the full list of countries. British citizens or residents who hold a valid British passport may be granted an entry permit valid for six months.*

87. *They are, however, required to show evidence of the ability to return to their country at the conclusion of their visit.*

OTHER INTRA-OCEANIA MIGRATION

Other intra-Oceania migration has made a significant, albeit minor, contribution to migration intakes by Australia and New Zealand.

Traditional movements between Australia and Papua New Guinea are governed by the Torres Strait Treaty. This enables indigenous peoples to move freely between the two countries without passports or visas, for traditional activities like hunting, fishing, ceremonies and social gatherings,[88] inside a "Protected Zone". The flow is managed by Movement Monitoring Officers on the inhabited islands in the Torres Strait, working closely with Island Chairpersons (DIMIA, 2004f).

New Zealand has two special categories to facilitate migrant intakes from smaller Pacific nations: the Pacific Access Category and the Samoan Quota scheme. Under the Pacific Access Category, the quotas for migrants are: Kiribati (75); Tuvalu (75); Fiji (250), and Tonga (250). The Samoan Quota scheme is facilitated by the Treaty of Friendship between New Zealand and Samoa and allows up to 1,100 Samoans to be granted residence each year (NZIS, 2004a).[89]

Humanitarian Migration

Australia and New Zealand are among the ten traditional refugee resettlement countries in the world. In the past 50 years, over 620,000 refugees and displaced people have been resettled in Australia and over 35,000 in New Zealand (New Zealand Ministry of Health, 2004). New Zealand was the first country in 1959 to accept 'handicapped' refugees; refugees with disabilities, and medical conditions continue to be a significant part of New Zealand's annual Refugee Quota, set at 750. In recent years, women at risk of violence and family members of refugees already resettled in New Zealand have made up a significant part of the Refugee Quota intake.[90]

In the 2002-03 programme year, Australia granted a total of 12,525 visas under its Humanitarian Program, 11,656 of these for third-country resettlement, a 38 per cent increase over 2001-02, and the highest number of offshore grants in the last five years. Australia explicitly ties its capacity for refugee third-country resettlement to unused "in-country protection" places within its overall humanitarian quota. Thus the size of its offshore resettlement programme is directly affected by the movements of refugees to Australia.

Secondary Movements of Asylum Seekers and Refugees

Governments in the region have in recent years become increasingly concerned with the phenomenon of "secondary" movements, or the migration of asylum seekers and others out of their region of origin, or countries where they could access effective protection, to gain entry to countries further afield through the asylum system. The issue has been the subject of extensive discussion by the international community in recent years.[91] Australia's position is that refugees should be able to seek and access effective protection in their region of origin, and avoid arduous, expensive travel and the risks of people smuggling. The government has thus introduced measures to discourage secondary movements of asylum-seekers and refugees from countries where they had, or could have, accessed effective protection.[92]

88. *Business dealings and gainful employment are not recognized as traditional activities under the treaty.*

89. *Applicants under these categories must meet certain requirements, including having a job offer in New Zealand and evidence of their ability to speak English.*

90. *In 2003-04, 115 people successfully claimed refugee status onshore. Over 50 per cent of these people came from Iran and Zimbabwe.*

91. *These issues were discussed at the Lisbon Expert Roundtable held on 9 and 10 December 2002 (UNHCR, 2002). The approach is now under serious consideration by the European Union (Vitorino, 2004).*

92. *States subscribing to this approach believe that interim protection (while awaiting a durable solution) in the region of origin minimizes cultural dislocation and enables refugees to engage in productive activities consistent with the local economy and their existing skills. This is likely to maximize the acceptability of repatriation, particularly if the refugee is able to keep contact with friends and family in the country of origin; and make 'go home and see' visits pending repatriation more feasible. Refugees can also use their personal resources for support during the period of asylum and for investment in a new life, whether repatriation, local integration or resettlement, rather than pay people smugglers.*

From late 1999, various changes to the law had made it progressively difficult for such persons to stay permanently in Australia: those found to be genuine refugees were granted Temporary Protection Visas (TPVs) for an initial protection period of 36 months; but those who, since leaving their home country, had resided for at least seven days in a country where they could have sought and obtained effective protection, could generally not access permanent protection visas. Thus local integration was available only to those who came directly to Australia from a country in which they had a well-founded fear of persecution, or were unable to access effective protection.

In July 2004, these provisions were relaxed through regulations that enable TPV holders to apply for regular migration status without leaving Australia. The amendments take account of the socio-economic contributions of TPV holders in regional areas in Australia; many having settled well in country towns and met local demand for unskilled labour. Other changes include the introduction of a 'return pending visa', which will give former TPV holders who no longer require protection up to 18 months to make their own arrangements to return home. Reintegration packages, including airfares and financial assistance, continue to apply (DIMIA, 2004f; DIMIA, 2004g).

Refugee status claimants in New Zealand can be issued temporary permits allowing them to work or study while their claim is assessed. In some cases, where there are issues surrounding identity or risk, refugee status claimants may be detained while their claim is assessed. Those recognized as refugees are entitled to apply for residence in New Zealand.

In an effort to reduce the incentive for false refugee status claims, New Zealand has recently focused on clearing the substantial backlog of claims that had built up in the 1990s and on removing failed claimants. From a high point of over 3,000 claims on hand in 1999, New Zealand only had 227 refugee status claims remaining as of 30 June 2004. In 2003-04, 311 failed refugee status claimants were removed, up from 185 in 2002-03.[93]

STRATEGIES TO COMBAT IRREGULAR MIGRATION

Australia's approach to border control has drawn considerable controversy from commentators in recent years. Irregular air arrivals are largely controlled by the combination of Airline Liaison Officers (ALOs) placed in all major air transport hubs, the universal visa requirement, and advanced passenger processing (APP) in countries of embarkation. Security measures have also been tightened to thwart smugglers' access to air travel through such tactics as boarding-pass swaps. New Zealand also has ALOs in place overseas, and introduced the APP in 2003 as part of its strategy to move its border offshore. APP allows immigration documentation checks to be carried out prior to travel to destination, and *mala fide* travellers to be denied boarding by airlines.

In respect of irregular arrivals by boat, there are some clear policy trends. Each time Australia has become the target of smuggled irregular movements by boat, the government of the day has responded quickly with new legislative tools, bilateral agreements to facilitate returns of rejected asylum seekers to the country of origin, or asylum-seekers and refugees to countries offering effective protection, and with interception and off-shore processing arrangements. Thus each surge in arrivals has been followed by a period of low irregular movement.

The boat arrivals in 1994-95 were predominantly ethnic Chinese Vietnamese who had been resettled in the People's Republic of China. At Australia's request, China agreed to re-admit them and provide them effective protection, and continued to cooperate in the return of Chinese nationals not in need of protection. After these returns, boats from China almost ceased.

The boat arrivals beginning in 1999 involved refugees and asylum-seekers from countries of first asylum, in

93. *This information was received from NZIS via the High Commission, Canberra, October, 2004.*

this case, the Middle East and Pakistan. A readmission agreement, such as Australia has with China, was not able to be concluded with countries of origin or transit, and the flows continued until Australia resorted to a combination of:

- interception strategies in Indonesia and the waters between Indonesia and Australia; and
- offshore processing centres established in Nauru and Papua New Guinea for persons intercepted in Australian waters. These have been managed by IOM on behalf of the Australian government; and have also involved UNHCR.[94] By mid-2004, most of the persons in the centres had either been resettled as refugees, had returned home voluntarily, or were awaiting return.[95]

These efforts successfully lowered unauthorized boat arrivals in Australia to zero in 2002-03, and to 53 in 2003-04, compared with 4,137 in 2000-01, and 1,212 in 2001-02 (DIMIA, 2004e).

Despite its high overseas-born population, New Zealand has not seen the same levels of attempted irregular entry. The sea voyage from Southeast Asia to New Zealand is long and dangerous; and Australia's interception presence in waters to the north of Australia is an added barrier to such irregular movement. Nevertheless, having signed the United Nations Convention Against Transnational Organized Crime, New Zealand also passed legislation in 2002 to increase penalties for those who assist people to enter New Zealand unlawfully. Other new measures include a transit visa requirement[96] for people transiting New Zealand to or from certain Pacific states,[97] and a response strategy for mass arrivals of would-be asylum claimants in New Zealand.[98] In July 2004, New Zealand also legislated to make Advanced Passenger Processing compulsory for all airlines flying to New Zealand (already used voluntarily by many airlines).

INTRAREGIONAL COOPERATION ON MANAGING IRREGULAR MIGRATION

Countries in the region are increasingly working together to manage irregular migration in and through the region. Australia and Indonesia have long-standing arrangements in respect of persons intercepted by Indonesia as being in breach of Indonesian migration laws and seeking to travel on to, and illegally enter, Australia.[99] As part of the so-called Bali Process, Indonesia and Australia co-chaired two regional ministerial conferences on people smuggling, trafficking in persons and related transnational crime in 2002 and 2003, in cooperation with IOM and UNHCR; New Zealand was the coordinator of the Ad Hoc Experts Group I, established to promote regional and international cooperation;[100] and Fiji, Kiribati, Palau, Papua New Guinea (PNG), Nauru, Samoa, Solomon Islands, Tonga and Vanuatu all participated in the process.

The other aspect of cooperation relates to strengthening the technical capacity of Oceania states. Oceania immigration officials come together

94. *Asylum processing has been undertaken by UNHCR for certain groups (i.e. those rescued from the* MV Tampa*) and by Australian officials, at the request of the Nauru or PNG Government. In August 1999, the MV Tampa rescued passengers on a boat attempting to smuggle people into Australia. Although the captain of the Tampa received authority from Indonesia to proceed to its port of Merak to disembark the passengers, the rescued asylum seekers put the captain of the Tampa under duress and forced him to turn around and head towards Christmas Island. Australia refused permission to disembark the asylum seekers and instead transferred them to Nauru for processing (Ruddock, 2002).*

95. *As of 15 October 2004, no intercepted persons remained in the PNG offshore processing centre, and 81 remained in Nauru awaiting return. All others had been returned home (482) or been resettled to seven countries (983). Of these, 536 refugees were resettled in Australia and 401 in New Zealand (DIMIA officials).*

96. *Persons already holding a valid visa for New Zealand or Australia, or from a visa-free state, are exempt from this.*

97. *The Cook Islands, Niue, Tokelau, Fiji, Samoa, Tonga, Kiribati, Nauru, Tuvalu, Marshall Islands, Solomon Islands, Vanuatu, New Caledonia and Tahiti. Nationals of the Cook Islands, Niue and Tokelau who are New Zealand citizens are, of course, exempt from this requirement.*

98. *As yet, these procedures have not been tested.*

99. *With funding support from Australia, IOM provides accommodation and support to such persons intercepted in Indonesia, and UNHCR processes any asylum claims made. Those found to be refugees have been resettled in a number of countries, and those found not to need protection have been assisted to return home voluntarily by IOM.*

100. *A second group, the Ad Hoc Experts Group II on law enforcement, was coordinated by Thailand.*

annually in the Pacific Immigration Directors' Conference (PIDC), whose principal objective is to promote consultation and cooperation among Immigration agencies within the Pacific region. The conference provides for the exchange of ideas, dissemination of information and mutual technical assistance. At the 2003 conference in the Kingdom of Tonga, discussions ranged widely over migration management issues, including strategies to strengthen integrity of data and reduce migration crime and fraud (PIDC, 2004).

Australia and New Zealand are closely involved, with the assistance of IOM, in supporting other states in the region to develop effective migration and border systems appropriate to their needs. For example, Australia and Papua New Guinea are working together to safeguard the national interest of PNG through more effective control over who may enter or remain in the country, and to help strengthen regional security through more efficient administrative frameworks and information management systems, the reform of legal frameworks and training and equipment.

FUTURE TRENDS

Climate Change

While the world's scientists debate the extent and impact of climate change and global warming, it is clear that many small island states in Oceania would be among the first to suffer the effects on their political and economic stability if world sea levels were to rise. Already, changes in sea temperatures and violent storms are damaging coral reefs, the basis of many of the states' tourist industries, causing beach erosion, contaminating drinking water and agricultural soil, and damaging fishing industries. With only small increases in sea levels, states such as The Marshall Islands, Kirabati and Tuvalu may face at the least relocation of their people from low-lying outer islands and beach-side areas and, at worst, relocation of their entire populations.

Demographic Change

As with other developed nations, population growth in Australia and New Zealand[101] is expected to continue to slow down, with the relative share of those older and out of the workforce increasing markedly. Australia's net migration inflow (arrivals minus departures) has for many years been younger on average than the resident population, so that the ageing of the population profile has been slowed to some extent. Migration will continue to be an important contributor to population growth and the supply of young, skilled workers. Australia and New Zealand, with long histories of migration, and highly diverse populations are well placed to attract migrants in what is expected to become a highly competitive global market, as populations age in all developed states (Commonwealth of Australia, 2002; 2003).

MANAGED MIGRATION

In view of the importance of tourism to regional economies, Oceania states will continue to seek ways to facilitate the movement of people, while ensuring that security concerns are addressed.

While largely protected by distance from people smuggling and trafficking and other forms of transnational crime, small island states without robust people management systems are increasingly likely to become targets of these criminal activities, particularly as other states tighten their controls (ibid). Through strong regional cooperation and technical capacity building, this richly diverse region can reap the rewards of managed migration, while avoiding the costs of irregular movement.

101. *Current projections suggest that, by 2035, deaths will outnumber births in New Zealand. If this occurs, population growth will become increasingly dependent on net migration (New Zealand Government, 2003).*

Europe

CHAPTER 7
MIGRANTS IN AN ENLARGED EUROPE[1]

Migration remains a key topic in public and political debates across Europe.[2] Despite the long-standing preoccupation with asylum issues, the focus has recently shifted to economic immigration, irregular migrants and the integration of newcomers. The latter, in part, reflects an often ignored reality in Europe: many immigrants are not fully integrated, some not at all.

The social and economic implications of demographic ageing and the eventual decline of Europe's local populations have also contributed to the migration debate. Demographic studies have, however, shown that, within realistic limits, higher immigration rates could deal with labour market shortages, but would not reverse the greying of the continent.

This chapter provides an update on current demographic and migration trends in Europe and discusses the conceptual and empirical gaps resulting from the use of different criteria to categorize the foreign-born residents vs. locally born non-citizens. The recent and foreseeable impact of EU enlargement, and the potential for further East-West migration in Europe are considered, along with the growing level of immigration to southern Europe. As noted above, the integration of third-country nationals has become a key subject of concern across Europe, and national policies are being adapted in response. Regarding integration, specific attention is given to Austria, Germany and the Netherlands. Finally, the chapter looks at actual and possible common EU policies on migration and frontier management, asylum, family reunification and health.

KEY DEMOGRAPHIC AND MIGRATION TRENDS

A DEMOGRAPHIC overview of Europe sends two clear messages. First, the number of countries with a shrinking local population is growing. Second, most European countries have a positive migration balance (Table 7.1). As a result, in many cases the size of net migration determines whether a country's population is still growing, or already on the decline.

In early 2004, the total population of Europe (also including Turkey, but excluding Russia and other CIS countries) stood at 594 million. The European Union (EU-25) counted 456 million inhabitants; of these, 382 million were either citizens or foreign residents of the 15 pre-enlargement members (EU-15), and the remaining 74 million either citizens or foreign residents of the ten new EU Member States. 34 million people were living in EU accession countries[3] and 71

1. *The authors of this chapter are Professor Rainer Münz, Senior Fellow at the Hamburg Institute of International Economics, and Dr. Joanne van Selm, Senior Policy Analyst at the Migration Policy Institute (MPI, with research assistance from Marjorie Gelin and Kevin O'Neil. Information was also provided by IOM Migration Health Department (MHD), Geneva; IOM Budapest and IOM Vienna.*

2. *The chapter covers the 25 EU Member States (since May 2004: Austria, Belgium, Cyprus, Czech Republic, Denmark, Estonia, Finland, France, Germany, Greece, Hungary, Ireland, Italy, Latvia, Lithuania, Luxembourg, Malta, the Netherlands, Poland, Portugal, Slovakia, Slovenia, Spain, Sweden, the United Kingdom (UK)), the additional 3 European Economic Area (EEA) countries: Iceland, Liechtenstein and Norway; as well as Switzerland. It also contains some information on the EU accession states Bulgaria, Croatia and Romania, and on the candidate (as of October 2004) country Turkey.*

3. *Bulgaria, Croatia and Romania.*

million in the candidate country Turkey, with another 12 million people living in the rest of Western Europe,[4] and 20 million in the rest of south-eastern Europe (i.e. the Western Balkans).[5]

TABLE 7.1

DEMOGRAPHIC INDICATORS IN EUROPE, 2003

	Population January 2003 ('000s)	Births	Deaths	Natural population De/Increase	Net migration	Total population change	Population January 2004 ('000s)
		per 1,000 population					
EU-25	**454,560**	**10.4**	**10.0**	**0.4**	**3.7**	**4.1**	**456,449**
Germany	82,537	8.6	10.4	-1.8	1.8	0.0	82,539
France	59,635	12.7	9.2	3.5	0.9	4.4	59,901
UK	59,329	11.6	10.2	1.4	1.7	3.1	59,516
Italy	57,321	9.5	10.0	-0.5	8.9	8.4	57,804
Spain	41,551	10.4	9.1	1.3	14.2	15.5	42,198
Poland	38,219	9.2	9.5	-0.3	-0.4	-0.7	38,191
Netherlands	16,193	12.4	8.7	3.7	0.2	3.8	16,255
Greece	11,006	9.3	9.4	-0.1	3.2	3.1	11,255
Portugal	10,408	10.9	10.5	0.4	6.1	6.5	10,475
Belgium	10,356	10.7	10.2	0.5	3.4	3.9	10,396
Czech Rep.	10,203	9.2	10.9	-1.7	2.5	0.8	10,212
Hungary	10,142	9.4	13.5	-4.1	1.5	-2.5	10,117
Sweden	8,941	11.0	10.4	0.6	3.2	3.8	8,976
Austria	8,082	9.5	9.5	-0.0	4.0	4.0	8,114
Denmark	5,384	12.0	10.7	1.3	1.3	2.6	5,398
Slovakia	5,379	9.6	9.7	-0.1	0.3	0.2	5,380
Finland	5,206	10.9	9.4	1.5	1.1	2.6	5,220
Ireland	3,964	15.5	7.3	8.2	7.1	15.3	4,025
Lithuania	3,463	8.8	11.8	-3.0	-1.8	-4.8	3,446
Latvia	2,332	9.0	13.9	-4.9	-0.4	-5.3	2,319
Slovenia	1,995	8.6	9.6	-1.0	1.7	0.7	1,996
Estonia	1,356	9.6	13.3	-3.7	-0.2	-4.0	1,351
Cyprus*	715	11.3	7.7	3.6	17.9	21.5	731
Luxembourg	448	11.8	9.1	2.7	4.6	7.3	452
Malta	397	10.1	8.0	2.2	4.3	6.5	400
Iceland	289	14.2	6.2	8.0	-0.8	7.2	291
Liechtenstein	34	8.8	5.0	3.8	10.0	13.8	34
Norway	4,552	12.0	9.4	3.1	2.4	5.5	4,578
EEA	**459,435**	**10.4**	**10.0**	**0.4**	**3.7**	**4.1**	**461,352**
Switzerland	7,318	9.7	8.5	1.2	5.6	6.8	7,368
EU accession countries	**34,061**	**9.2**	**12.5**	**-3.3**		**-3.1**	
Croatia[1]	4,442	9.0	11.4	-2.4	2.0	-0.4	n.a.
Bulgaria[2]	7,846	8.4	14.3	-5.7	n.a.	-5.7	7,799
Romania	21,773	9.6	12.2	-2.5	-0.3	-2.8	21,716
EU candidate country							
Turkey	70,173	21.0	7.1	13.9	1.4	15.3	71,254

1. Croatian data on birth, death and net migration and population growth rate are from 2002; no population size for January 2004 available.
2. No data on migration available for 2003; population size for January 2004 is an estimate without migration.

Source: EUROSTAT, Chronos Database

In 2003, Europe still registered population growth. In the 28 EU/EEA countries[6] and Switzerland, total growth was +1.97 million (2003). But in 12 of the 28 EU/EEA countries (as well as the three EU accession countries[7]) deaths exceeded births. The number of countries experiencing a decline in their domestic population will continue to rise in the coming years. The other 18 countries (analysed in **Table 7.1**) still show some natural population growth. Net migration was positive in 26 of the 33 countries. Relative to population size, Cyprus[8] had the largest positive migration balance (+17.9 per 1000 inhabitants), followed by Spain (14.2 per 1000), Liechtenstein (+10.0), Italy (+8.9), Ireland (+7.0), Portugal (+6.1) and Switzerland (+6.0). Only Lithuania (-1.8 per 1000 inhabitants), Iceland (-0.8), Poland (0.4), Latvia (-0.4), Romania (-0.3) and Estonia (-0.2) had a negative migration balance.

In absolute numbers, net migration was largest in Spain (+594,000) and Italy (+511,000), followed by Germany (+166,000), the UK (+103,000), Turkey (+98,000), Portugal (+64,000) and France (+55,000).[9]

Several countries, in particular Austria, the Czech Republic, Italy, Germany, Greece, Slovenia and Slovakia, only showed a population growth because of immigration. In 2003, the EU-25 recorded an overall net migration rate of +3.7 per 1000 inhabitants, and a net gain of +1.7 million people. This accounts for almost 90 per cent of Europe's total population growth.

CONCEPTUAL AND EMPIRICAL GAPS: FOREIGN RESIDENTS VS. FOREIGN-BORN POPULATION

In the second half of the 20th century, large parts of Europe experienced a historical shift from emigration to immigration. However, the exact number of migrants residing in Europe is still unknown. This is partly due to the fact that, in contrast to Australia, Canada, New Zealand and the US, many European countries use nationality, not the place or country of birth, as the standard criterion in their demographic, economic and social statistics. This means that in many instances it is not possible to differentiate between the foreign-born (= immigrants) and the locally born non-citizens, but it is always possible to distinguish between citizens of a particular country, and legal foreign residents. Usually the latter are subdivided into citizens of other EU member states and third-country nationals.

When using nationality as the main criterion, the rapidly growing number of (predominantly foreign born) naturalized citizens[10] can hardly be distinguished from the majority of native citizens. By the same token, locally born children of immigrant parents are registered as "foreigners" unless they acquire citizenship of the receiving country on the principle of *ius soli* at birth, or later through naturalization.

Only some European countries try to deal with irregular migrants through registration or regularization. Belgium, France, Greece, Italy, Portugal and Spain have offered quantitatively significant regularization programmes. Germany, Luxembourg and Switzerland have offered regular status at least to some irregular migrants. Since the 1980s, EU Member States (EU-15) have regularized a little below 3.2 million irregular foreign residents in total. Spain continues to allow irregular migrants access to basic medical services, if they register with local municipalities. As a result in 2002-2003 Spain had 2,664,000 registered foreign-born residents,[11] but only 1,324,000 legal foreign residents (**Table 7.2**).

4. *Iceland, Liechtenstein, Norway and Switzerland.*

5. *Albania, Bosnia-Herzegovina, Macedonia, Serbia-Montenegro (including Kosovo). See also the chapter in this Report on "South-eastern Europe – Stabilization and Association Dynamics".*

6. *The European Economic Area (EEA) consists of the EU-25 plus Iceland, Liechtenstein and Norway.*

7. *EU accession countries (as of October 2004) are Bulgaria, Croatia, Romania.*

8. *Greek part of Cyprus only.*

9. *Net flow of migrants (regardless of citizenship) according to Eurostat (Chronos data base).*

10. *In the decade 1992-2001 some 5,855,000 people were naturalized in one of the EU-15 Member States. (EU-15) (OECD/Sopemi, 2003).*

11. *Regular and irregular migrants based on the local municipalities' registers.*

BASIC CONCEPTS IN EUROPE AND THE US

European concept: *Citizenship*	US concept: *Place of birth*	Applied to the EU context
	Locally born population	Foreign-born population
Citizens of a particular EU Member State	Majority of domestic population in receiving countries; locally born children and grandchildren of foreign immigrants who either acquired citizenship at birth (*ius soli*), or later through naturalization.	Naturalized immigrants; people who immigrated as citizens of the receiving country.
Other EU citizens	Children/grandchildren of EU immigrants who did not acquire the receiving countries' citizenship either at birth or through naturalization.	Immigrants from other EU Member States.
Third-country nationals	Children/grandchildren of third-country immigrants who did not acquire the receiving countries' citizenship either at birth or through naturalization.	Immigrants from third countries.

In countries with high naturalization rates and/or *ius soli* birthright citizenship,[12] the official number of legal foreign residents largely underestimates the immigrant population. This is obvious for the US and Canada, but can also be demonstrated for a few EU countries with high naturalization rates. For example, in 2001 Sweden's foreign-born population stood at 1,028,000, while only 476,000 people were legal foreign residents. In the Netherlands, the respective figures for 2001 were 1,679,000 registered foreign-born residents against 690,000 legal foreign residents (Table 7.2).

A higher share of foreigners is to be expected in countries with low naturalization rates and where citizenship is conferred on the principle of *ius sanguinis*.[13] There the number of legal foreign residents can be of the same magnitude as the foreign-born population, since many immigrants are never naturalized, and most of their locally born children and grandchildren acquire the host country's nationality at birth. In 2001, Luxembourg's legal foreign residents numbered 167,000, but the size of the foreign-born population was only 145,000. Census results for Austria show 896,000 foreign-born residents in 2001 compared with 764,000 foreign nationals (Table 7.2).

FOREIGNERS AND MIGRANT STOCKS: WHAT DO WE KNOW?

ACCORDING to national population statistics, population registers and census data collected around 2000-2001, the 15 pre-enlargement EU Member States (EU-15) were home or host to some 18.7 million legal foreign residents. This is the number also reported by Eurostat's Chronos database (Table 7.2). Data collected by national correspondents of OECD's Sopemi network for 2000-2001 put the number of foreign nationals in the EU-15 at 20.1 million people (see also Table 7.2). Of these, some 6 million were EU-15 citizens living in another E-15 country, and some 14 million were third-country nationals.[14] In 2000-2001 the difference between Eurostat/Chronos and OECD/Sopemi was particularly visible for Greece, Spain, Ireland and Portugal (Table 7.2). This group of 18.7 million (Chronos DB) to 20.1 million (Sopemi) registered legal foreign residents in EU-15 consists of both foreign-born and locally born persons not holding the citizenship of the EU country in which they lived in 2000-2001.

12. Ius soli *confers nationality through the place of birth thus giving some, most or all children (and/or grandchildren) of foreign immigrants automatic access to citizenship of the receiving country applying that principle.*

13. Ius sanguinis *birthright citizenship bases citizenship on descent, thus automatically conferring the nationality of the foreign immigrant parents on their children and/or grandchildren (or leaving them stateless if the parents/grandparents are stateless themselves).*

14. *Some of them have since become EU citizens because their countries joined the EU in May 2004.*

TABLE 7.2

TOTAL, FOREIGN RESIDENT AND IMMIGRANT POPULATION (EU-15), 2000-2002, DIFFERENT DATA SOURCES COMPARED

EU-15	Total population Eurostat [1]	Foreign resident population, Eurostat, Chronos DB for 2000	Foreign resident population, OECD/ Sopemi for 2001	Foreign resident population with nationality known, LFS [2]	Immigrant/ foreign resident population, UN for 2000 [3]	Immigrant population according to national sources for 2001 [4]	Immigrant population with country of birth known, LFS [5]	Immigrant population with duration of stay known, LFS
Belgium	10,356	853	847	784	879	n.a.	974	1,034
Denmark	5,384	256	267	166	304	322	225	227
Germany	82,537	7,344	7,319	5,444	7,349	9,700	n.a.	8,915
Greece	11,018	161	762	362	534	n.a.	489	480
Spain	40,683	801	1,109	450	1,259	2,664	858	664
France [6]	59,629	3,263	3,263	2,724	6,277	5,868	4,605	1,327
Ireland	3,964	127	151	118	310	n.a.	232	263
Italy	57,321	1,271	1,363	n.a.	1,634	2,200	n.a.	511
Luxembourg	448	148	167	161	162	145	127	119
Netherlands	16,193	652	690	555	1,576	1,675	1,179	1,593
Austria	8,067	754	764	695	756	893	899	798
Portugal	10,408	191	224	106	233	n.a.	1,119	1,313
Finland	5,206	88	99	50	134	145	81	86
Sweden	8,941	487	476	295	993	1,028	681	933
UK	59,329	2,298	2,587	2,026	4,029	n.a.	3,307	4,467
Total (N)	379,484	18,692	20,088	13,936	26,429	24,640	14,776	22,730

1. Eurostat, year-end population 2002; **2.** European Labour Force Survey (LFS) 2002 (data for Italy not available); **3.** UN Population Division, Data for 2000 or latest available year (see UN 2002); **4.** Data for Denmark, the Netherlands, Finland and Sweden are from national population registers, data for Austria, France, Luxembourg and the Netherlands are from the most recent national censuses, data for Spain (2003) are from local municipalities' registers, data for Germany are rough estimates based on foreigners' registers, naturalization statistics and an Allbus survey estimate for ethnic German *Aussiedler*, taking only immigration after 1950 into account (see Münz and Ulrich 2003), data for Italy are based on the number of residence permits (2003, various categories) and an estimate for foreign-born children not required to hold residence permits (see Einaudi 2004); **5.** European Labour Force Survey (LFS) 2002 (data for Germany and Italy not available); **6.** Chronos data, Sopemi data and Census data for France are from 1999.

Source:
Münz and Fassmann (2004), Eurostat Chronos DB and European Labour Force Survey, OECD/Sopemi (2004), UN Population Division (2002), various national sources.

The European Labour Force Survey (LFS) is the sole EU-wide data source that provides information on people born outside their country of residence.[15] In 2002, according to the LFS, an estimated 22.7 million people (for whom the duration of stay is known) were born in another EU-15 or third country. For a partially overlapping group of 14.8 million people (except foreign-born residents of Germany and Italy),[16] there is information available on their country of birth.[17]

In order to calculate the total number of foreign-born residents in the EU, estimates are needed for Germany and Italy not fully covered by the LFS. For Germany, the best estimate combines the number of legal foreign residents not born in the country (5.7 million), the estimated share of the foreign-born among all naturalized persons (some 65 per cent out of 1.4 million) and the number of ethnic German immigrants (*Aussiedler* with German citizenship, still alive in

15. *The LFS does not cover people living in collective households, e.g. members of armed forces living in barracks, prison inmates, people in nursing homes, asylum seekers living in reception centres or hostels. In 2002, some 374 million out of 379 million residents of EU-15 were living in private households.*

16. *Data on foreign-born residents in Germany and Italy (by country of birth) are not available from the LFS as in Germany the country of birth is not asked, while Italy does not authorize the analysis or publication of this information.*

17. *The two groups overlap only partially as for some individuals only their country of birth or their duration of stay are known. For some we know neither their country of birth nor their duration of stay. The latter have been excluded from the calculation, though some of them may actually be migrants (see Münz and Fassmann, 2004).*

2002: 3.2 million). The estimated number of foreign-born residents for Germany is, therefore, 9.7 million (Münz and Ulrich, 2003). The assumed number for Italy is 2.2 million based on the number of residence permits (2003, various categories) and an estimate for foreign-born children not required to hold residence permits (Einaudi, 2004). Adding these 12.2 million to the number of immigrants whose country of birth is identified in the LFS (14.8 million) puts the foreign-born population at 27.0 million. A similar figure (26.4 million) is published by the UN Population Division for the EU-15 in 2002.[18] However, as shown below, this figure seems to be too low.

For ten of the 15 states that constituted the EU until the recent enlargement, data on the foreign-born (=immigrant) population are available from either population registers,[19] a recent census[20] or from other sources.[21] The aggregated results put the number of foreign-born residents in these ten countries at 24.6 million (Table 7.2).

Combining the information from the LFS[22] with that produced by the UN Population Division and data from national censuses and population registers (looking only at the highest available figure or estimate for each country), the number of statistically "visible" first-generation immigrants in the EU-15 (2002) can be put at 33.0 million. As published and unpublished data for some countries still underestimate the size of the foreign-born population to a certain extent,[23] one can presume the presence of 33 to 36 million legal immigrants, both foreign nationals and citizens, and irregular migrants[24] in the EU-15 (2001-02).

Adding another 1.7 million immigrants living in the other EEA countries and Switzerland[25] and some 1.5 million immigrants living in the new EU members in Central Europe[26] brings the size of western and Central Europe's migrant population to between 36 and 39 million people (or 8% of the total population). Given available information and the shortcomings mentioned, this could be seen as a best estimate.

EFFECTS OF EU ENLARGEMENT ON EUROPEAN MIGRATION

BASED on concerns in some of the 15 pre-enlargement EU Member States, the European Commission, in its accession agreements with eight of the ten new Member States established a transitional mobility regime potentially restricting free access to EU-25 labour markets (van Selm and Tsolakis, 2004). This means that access to employment and welfare benefits for the citizens of eight of the ten new

18. *Standard UN criteria define international migrants as persons residing outside their country of birth or citizenship for 12 months or more. But for its own statistics, the UN Population Division relies on national data sources. Some countries define migrants according to different criteria, others publish data on legal foreign residents, but not on the foreign-born population.*

19. *Denmark, Finland, Spain, Sweden.*

20. *Austria, France, Luxembourg, the Netherlands.*

21. *Data for Germany are from aliens' registers, naturalization statistics and an Allbus survey estimate for ethnic German* Aussiedler *(see Münz and Ulrich 2003); data for Italy are based on residence permits (see Einaudi 2004).*

22. *This calculation takes the foreign-born population by duration of stay or country of birth (whichever is higher).*

23. *Such an undercount has to be assumed for both foreign immigrants with short duration of stay and/or irregular status, as well as for naturalized immigrants with a fairly long duration of stay, in particular privileged co-ethnic immigrants (e.g., ethnic German* Aussiedler*, Pontian Greeks) and colonial return migrants (e.g., French pieds noirs).*

24. *Prior to recent regularization programmes in Italy, Greece, Portugal and Spain the number of irregular migrants was apparently more than 10 per cent of the total foreign-born population; for the UK 10 per cent might be a good estimate; figures for Denmark, Sweden and Finland could be lower than 10 per cent. We can estimate such differences both from recent regularization and amnesty programmes (Papademetriou et al., 2004) and from discrepancies between local registers and general census results or national registers (see the case of Spain; Table 7.2).*

25. *Besides the EU-25, the European Economic Area (EEA) includes Iceland, Norway and Liechtenstein; migration between the EU-25 and Switzerland is regulated through bilateral agreements.*

26. *New EU Member States in Central Europe are Estonia, the Czech Republic, Hungary, Latvia, Lithuania, Poland, Slovakia and Slovenia. Other new member states are Cyprus and Malta. In the new EU Member States, most labour migrants apparently come from neighbouring countries such as from the Balkans, Belarus, Moldova, Russia and Ukraine. Several countries are also home or host to labour migrants from Asian countries, notably China and Vietnam.*

member states (Czech Republic, Estonia, Hungary, Latvia, Lithuania, Poland, the Slovak Republic and Slovenia) can be restricted by each of the pre-enlargement EU-15 countries. Only Sweden chose to impose no restrictions. Greek Cypriots and Maltese citizens are exempt from this and free to work in any other EU-25 country. The new Member States are also entitled to apply similar measures and limit access to their labour markets.

Despite these transitional restrictions, the EU enlargement of May 2004 will in the short term lead to a certain increase in regular and irregular migration from new EU Member States in Central Europe to EU-15 + EEA states in western and southern Europe. This is mainly due to a combination of basic freedom of settlement and transitional restrictions on employment and welfare; while the citizens of new EU Member States in Central Europe have no immediate and general access to western European labour markets, they have the right to migrate for family reunion, educational purposes and to establish a business.

New EU members are gradually being incorporated into the Schengen area. They have adopted existing EU/Schengen visa regimes and started to police their eastern and southeastern borders. But border controls between old and new EU member states will only be abolished in 2007 or 2008, when the latter will fully join the Schengen area.

Concurrent with EU enlargement, some 750,000 citizens of new EU members now lawfully residing in one of the old EU-15 member state have acquired the right to bring in dependent family members (spouses, minor children) without major restrictions. The same will be true after 2007 for another 650,000 legal residents of Bulgarian, Croatian and Romanian nationality.[27] This represents a considerable potential for family reunion over the coming decade.

Today, some 730,000 citizens of new EU members and candidates (Bulgaria, Croatia, Romania) are gainfully employed in Western Europe (EU-15). Another 300,000 enter the EU-15 for a limited period of time as regular seasonal workers. And, since the 1990s a large number of people from Central Europe have become part of western Europe's temporary and semi-permanent irregular labour force. EU enlargement has led to a de facto regularization of irregular migrants from new EU Member States residing in another EU country. But in many countries, they remain part of the irregular work force.

In the immediate future, regular East-West labour migration within the EU-25 will be limited because most pre-enlargement EU members have imposed a transitional regime restricting potential migrants' access to their labour markets for the next 2 to7 years. Some EU-15 states, however, are less restrictive than others. Already during the period 2004-2006, citizens of new EU Member States have legal access to the labour markets of Ireland, Denmark, the Netherlands (contingent), Sweden and the UK. Other EU-15 Member States have indicated that they might follow this example in 2006. By contrast, Hungary and Poland have decided to reciprocate by restricting access to their labour markets for citizens of those old EU Member States that have implemented the transition regime. There is also a growing debate among policy makers and academics about the differentiated impact of these divergent approaches, and also the likely impact on a range of other areas such as wages and working conditions of local workers in the more open EU-15 states.

Restrictions imposed during the transitional period of 2-7 years might eventually lead to an increased migration of mobile and ambitious people from new EU members in Central Europe to traditional immigration countries overseas (Australia, Canada, New Zealand, US). This could be seen as a potential loss of human capital for Europe. Imposed restrictions will also lead to some increase in irregular labour migration as citizens of new EU Member States now have the right to reside in western Europe and do not face the threat of being expelled if they seek or accept

27. *According to data and information from Eurostat and OECD/Sopemi (2004).*

work in the informal economy. Citizens of new EU Member States belonging to western Europe's irregular work force will no longer be required to leave and re-enter the receiving countries every three months in order to qualify for tourist status.

In western Europe the demand for irregular labour migrants in agriculture, hotels, restaurants, private households and home-care for the disabled will remain, and possibly increase in the future. In the short term, this demand will continue to be covered by migrants from the new EU Member States, wherever they are already active. This will change, either following demands for higher wages and social security coverage, or after full access for citizens from Central Europe to the European labour market. People from other countries will then informally be recruited for such jobs. New EU citizens formerly belonging to western Europe's irregular work force may well bring legal action for better working conditions, as the threat of expulsion disappears.

POTENTIAL FOR FURTHER EAST-WEST MIGRATION IN EUROPE

Data from a recent Eurobarometer survey (Krieger, 2004) and a series of other studies (Fassmann and Münz, 2002) show that about one per cent of the population of the new EU Member States (i.e. some 700,000 people) firmly intend to migrate to a western country (Alvarez-Plata et al., 2003). The total migration potential over the next 20 years can thus be put at 3-4 million people (European Commission, 2003; Fassmann and Münz, 2002). Experience from earlier EU enlargements suggests, however, that emigration is more likely to decrease than increase after EU accession of countries with below-average GDP and a negative migration balance. This has been demonstrated by Greece, Ireland, Portugal and Spain.

Finally, mobility studies within the EU-15 reveal that, while eight per cent of the EU population indicated their intention to migrate within the next five years, only four per cent have actually done so in the past 10 years. This implies that intentions of spatial mobility exceed the actual number of mobile people (Krieger, 2004).

In the medium and long term, however, the new EU Member States that joined the union in 2004, and the accession countries for the 2007-08 enlargement, do not have the demographic potential for large-scale emigration to western Europe because most of them have more rapidly ageing and eventually shrinking populations. Economic growth following EU accession will not only reduce emigration pressure, but will sooner or later turn Central Europe into an area of large-scale immigration. Official statistics for 2003 already show a positive migration balance for the Czech Republic, Hungary, Slovakia and Slovenia (Table 7.1).

Because of enlargement, the new EU members have access to EU structural and cohesion funds and money for large infrastructure and environmental projects. This will create additional jobs in road works, construction, environment and the waste management industry. Many of these jobs are not likely to be taken by the underemployed, ageing rural population in the new EU countries, especially in Poland, eastern Hungary and northern Slovakia. It is therefore likely that new immigrants from Ukraine, Romania and Bulgaria will fill some of these jobs.

After many years of visa-free travel and intensive cross-border trade, implementation of the Schengen regime makes it more difficult for people from eastern Europe and Central Asia to enter Central Europe's new EU Member States. They are now required to apply for a visa before entering the Baltic countries, Poland, Slovakia, Hungary, Slovenia (or any other EU Member State). Such visas do not give access to the EU labour market.

For now, only citizens of Romania are exempt from the Schengen visa requirement. This does not improve their chances to be granted work permits in any of the 25 EU members, but makes it easier for them to become part of the irregular migrant work force. However, emerging economic opportunities in the new Member States, established social networks and the presence of co-ethnic minorities will help overcome such difficulties. Exceptions will be made for Russian citizens travelling to and from Kaliningrad. And Hungary grants ethnic Hungarians from neighbouring countries limited access to not only its domestic labour market, but also to its educational and health care systems. Further exceptions are expected for non-EU citizens of central and eastern Europe living in the vicinity of the external Schengen border.

RAPIDLY GROWING IMMIGRATION TO SOUTHERN EUROPE

IN THE FIRST years of the 21st century, southern Europe and Ireland had the fastest growing immigrant population. In 2003, relative to population size (the government-controlled, i.e. the Greek part of) Cyprus recorded Europe's largest net gain from migration, followed by Ireland, Portugal, Spain, Malta and Italy (Table 7.1). Some of this increase, however, not only reflects recent immigration but also large-scale regularization programmes, which made parts of the migrant population statistically visible.

In 2000-2001 Spain granted one-year residence and work permits to 399,000 irregular migrants (OECD/Sopemi, 2004; Papademetriou et al., 2004). In 2003, the net flow into Spain was apparently the largest among EU+EEA member states in absolute terms. In 2003, municipal population registers (accounting for irregular as well as legal immigrants) included 2.66 million immigrants. Compared with 2002, this represented an increase of nearly 700,000 people. Of these, some 850,000 seem to have been present without legal residence permits. EU nationals (in particular from Germany and the UK), many of them retired senior citizens, still represent a relative majority. The largest non-EU groups are Ecuadorians, followed by Moroccan, Colombian, Romanian and Argentine citizens (Baldwin-Edwards, 2004). In many cases Latin Americans have Spanish or other European ancestors and cultural ties with southern Europe.

In Italy the most recent regularization programme of 2003 led to applications from 705,000 irregular labour migrants, of whom 689,000 were granted residence and work permits (OECD/Sopemi, 2004; Papademetriou et al., 2004). This has been Europe's largest regularization programme so far. Almost 20 per cent of the applicants were Romanians, 15 per cent Ukrainians, eight per cent Albanians and eight per cent Moroccans (Baldwin-Edwards (2004).

Portugal's latest regularization programme, completed in 2001-2002, granted residence and work permits to 179,000 labour migrants (OECD/Sopemi, 2004; Papademetriou et al., 2004). Data for 2003 suggest that legally resident Ukrainians had displaced Brazilians as the largest group. But the large number of Brazilian applications for residence permits under current regularization programmes are expected to show that they actually remain the largest group (Baldwin-Edwards, 2004).

In 2001-2002, Greece's most recent regularization programme led to 351,000 applications for short-term residence and work permits.[28] Because of the short period of legal residence granted under these permits, many applicants are assumed to have again become irregular migrants. Census data from the same year (2001) show that Albanians are now by far the largest group of foreign residents, representing about 55 per cent of the (statistically "visible") total foreign population (Baldwin-Edwards, 2004).

INTEGRATION OF THIRD-COUNTRY NATIONALS

FOR MANY years, little attention was paid to immigrant integration. In the early 21st century, however, the integration of immigrants and refugees became a high-level political issue, at least in north-western Europe. As a result, there is also more discussion of this issue at the EU level. At the national level, the

28. *See OECD/Sopemi (2004); 6-month permits only.*

major focus so far has been on introductory programmes that orient newcomers and put them on a language training path. Some programmes involve examinations and disadvantages if they are not completed, others are of a more voluntary nature.

Three European countries have mandatory integration programmes for third-country nationals.

AUSTRIA[29]

Since 2003, third-country nationals who intend to stay in Austria for longer than six months and apply for a temporary (renewable) residence permit must sign an Integration Agreement. Exceptions to this ruling include newly arriving family members of Austrian and other EU citizens who enjoy preferential treatment, children, business executives and other skilled labour migrants remaining in Austria for less than two years. Those who can prove knowledge of German are also exempt. These provisions also apply retroactively to people who, in 1998-2002, were granted a temporary (renewable) residence permit, and who wish to renew their permit.

The Integration Agreement involves compulsory German language training of up to 100 hours. The immigrants pay 50 per cent of the costs if they finish it within 18 months, 75 per cent if the course is completed in 18-24 months, and 100 per cent if finished after 24 months. After this period, fines may be imposed by the authorities. Immigrants who do not successfully complete the course within four years can have the renewal of their residence permit denied.

GERMANY (BADE ET AL., 2004)

Following the Dutch example (see below), social integration is also a core element in Germany's new immigration law, due to come into force in January 2005. In Germany, this approach is not entirely untested. Since the 1980s, language training and integration programmes have existed for ethnic German immigrants (*Aussiedler*) from Central Europe, Russia and Central Asia and their non-German family members. As from 2005, attending such programmes will be mandatory for newly arriving third-country nationals. These include both language training and cultural orientation courses. The estimated additional annual cost of 235 million euros is covered through federal government funds. Only migrants without EU citizenship are obliged to attend language and integration classes. If they fail to attend, some of their social benefits may be denied. In extreme cases, their residence permits will not be renewed.[30]

THE NETHERLANDS (MINISTRY OF JUSTICE; INBURGER NET)

Since 1998, all non-EU/EEA citizens emigrating to the Netherlands are required to present themselves to local authorities who assess their individual need to attend an introductory programme. If considered necessary, a package of requirements is assembled, which the individual must follow. It includes Dutch language lessons, basic information about Dutch society, information about employment opportunities, basic orientation (usually conducted by the Dutch Refugee Council) in the locality where the migrant lives, and a test at the end with a certificate for those who pass. Those awarded the certificate are allowed to study or work in the Netherlands. There are no fines or other disincentives if the course is not completed (despite being compulsory), but the course must be repeated if the final test is not passed.

Discussions are underway in the Netherlands on changes in the law regarding introductory courses for newcomers, and for those who have been in the country a long time, but never followed such a programme. A commission appointed by the Minister for Immigration and Integration advised in June 2004 that the level of Dutch language required should be equal to the knowledge of English required of Dutch students completing a non-academic vocational high school. Other policy options under discussion are to

29. *See also the website of the* Österreichischer Austauschdienst*: www.oead.ac.at/_english/austrai/entry/integration.htm*

30. *At the time this chapter was written it was not possible to assess the implementation of these provisions.*

finance the programme through immigrant fees, and the requirement for some, including under family reunification, to learn Dutch before emigrating.

COMMON EU MIGRATION AND FRONTIER POLICIES

By 2004, several basic agreements had been reached on European migration and frontier issues. The EU focus on migration has primarily been on ensuring the right of citizens of the EU and their family members to move and reside freely within the territory of all member states. EU citizens, their spouses (regardless of nationality) and children (below the age of 21 or dependants of either spouse or partner) may move, reside and work without restrictions in any EU Member State. They may be required to register their presence in the country with the relevant authorities once they have been there for a three-month period. They do not need to obtain work permits, with the exception of the citizens of eight of the 10 new member states during the transitional period described above.

The EU members have also agreed to grant "long-term residence" status to third-country nationals lawfully present for five or more years in one EU Member State (European Council Directive, 2003b). Those to be granted this status must demonstrate that they dispose of a reasonable level of resources or income and are covered by health insurance. The "long-term residence" status allows third-country nationals to reside and work in any of the 25 EU Member States, with appropriate communication with the relevant authorities. An agreement has finally been reached on the conditions for admission of third-country nationals to study and participate in student exchanges, unremunerated training or voluntary service.[31]

Major policy decisions have finally been taken on further steps towards joint border management, and on common asylum standards and family reunion principles.[32]

BORDER CONTROL AND VISA ISSUES

Joint border management and visa issues have been prominent in European Union discussions. The Schengen system has seen the inclusion of Norway and Iceland – neither one a member of the EU – in the decision-making and implementation processes. Switzerland has also shown interest in participating in the Schengen system. The subject has been of particular importance in the light of European concern about illegal immigration and international attention on the security issues related to travel and borders following terrorist attacks in Europe and the US. EU Member States have agreed in principle to establish a joint border control agency, as well as maritime and air border centres to advance their cooperation.[33] These decisions now need to be implemented.

COMMON EU ASYLUM POLICY

By 2004, the EU Member States had reached agreement in the following areas:[34]

- Burden sharing and common temporary protection in situations of a political or humanitarian crisis leading to large numbers of people seeking protection in an EU Member State.
- Regulations deciding which state is responsible for examining an asylum application, and the technical procedures for the collection of data (including finger scans) from asylum seekers and the sharing of that data.
- Common minimum standards and procedures for asylum seekers throughout the EU, and,
- Common requirements defining qualification for refugee status and "subsidiary" protection.

31. *See the decision follow-up, including the Commission's proposal and all opinions and amendments 2002/0242/CNS at www.europa.eu.int/prelex/detail_dossier_real.cfm?CL=en&DosId=176790. The decision has not been entered in the Official Journal at the time of writing.*

32. *All of the documents and details on the progress of negotiations can be found at www.europa.eu.int/comm/justice_home/doc_centre/intro/doc_intro_en.htm.*

33. *See www.europa.eu.int/comm/justice_home/news/information_dossiers/external_border/links_en.htm.*

34. *See European Commission* "A single roof for asylum in the European Union", *www.europa.eu.int/comm/justice_home/doc_centre/asylum/doc_asylum_intor_en.htm for details of all the agreements reached and proposals tabled.*

Agreements on regulations and common standards in these areas had been reached by 14 of the 15 pre-enlargement EU states[35] before they were joined by the 10 new members, which would have made unanimity more difficult to achieve. The regulation determining the state responsible for assessing an asylum application, replacing the Dublin Convention, has directly become law. The other common standards listed above have to be implemented through national laws.

FAMILY REUNION

In 2003, most EU 15 Member States (excluding the UK and Ireland, which had both opted out, and Denmark, which does not participate at all) finalized a directive on family reunification (European Council Directive, 2003a). This has a "minimum standards" approach, and EU members can adopt their own more generous regulations. It permits nuclear families (spouses and dependent children) to reunite, if at least one member is a legal resident of an EU country. This right does not apply to asylum seekers and beneficiaries of temporary or subsidiary protection. EU members may apply the provisions of the directive to parents and adult unmarried children of legal foreign residents. But these family members are not automatically included. Family members are to be given individual independent status. Subsequently, their stay is no longer specifically linked to the sponsor or family member who first acquired residence in the EU. This is meant to facilitate the integration of the family members in their own right and to protect them against any loss of residence status in case of divorce.

The family reunification directive does include the derogation that children over the age of 12 arriving later than their parents may have to attend integration-related programmes already implemented, when the directive comes into force by October 2005. The European Commission is to report to the Council and the European Parliament on its application, and propose necessary amendments in 2007.

Reaching agreement on common family reunion standards was a difficult process. As in many EU countries, family reunion and formation both represent the most important reason for admission and lead to the admission of people whose integration has proven difficult over time. Austria and Germany had postponed the agreement for a long time.

Denmark,[36] which remains outside the European Union activity on asylum and immigration policy, has introduced restrictive regulations on family unity. Residence permits can be granted to spouses, cohabiting companions and registered partners, as well as children under the age of 18, but there is no legal claim to such permits. Several conditions must be met, including that both spouses must be over 24 years of age. This latter rule can be waived if the person to be joined in Denmark is a Danish citizen and has been both a citizen and resident of Denmark for an extensive period of time. It can also be waived if the joining person is a citizen of Denmark or another Nordic country. There are also housing and financial support requirements, as well as a requirement that the couple in question demonstrate greater overall attachment to Denmark than to any other country. These regulations, which impact on Danish citizens as well as third-country nationals, are intended to end forced and arranged marriages.

HEALTH/PUBLIC HEALTH ASPECTS OF CURRENT MIGRATION TRENDS IN EUROPE

AS AN ENLARGED Europe faces increased and more complex migration flows, governments will need to pay more attention to the health impacts of this phenomenon. The estimated 36-39 million migrants

35. *Denmark does not participate in the decision-making process in the area of migration and asylum, and therefore does not need to implement any agreements reached by the other EU member states.*

36. *See the Ministry of Integration* Bill amending the Aliens Act, the Marriage Act and other Acts (Abolition of the de facto refugee concept, streamlining of the asylum proceedings, more stringent conditions for the issue of permanent residence permits and tightening of the conditions for family reunification, etc.), *28 February 2002 File No. 2001/7310-81 www.inm.dk/images Upload/dokument/aliens_act_amending.pdf.*

in western and Central Europe alone would warrant such attention, particularly as a large proportion of them are engaged in the European labour market, which brings occupational health concerns into play. The health implications of irregular migration are even more complex, as explained below.

There is currently no European-wide health policy addressing this special need, not even for those persons already enjoying permanent or temporary resident status. Even at national levels, migrant health practices are rare and disparate across countries. Yet it is an indispensable part of any sustainable integration strategy, and should be factored into all efforts to harmonize migration policies and establish common denominators of welfare for both hosting and migrant communities. Actions should range from organized training and education of health professionals to access to needs-matched migrant health care for all migrants.

The need for general health attention to migrants may be best illustrated by two extreme examples relating to irregular migration: the rapidly increasing phenomenon of trafficking in persons, and apprehensions of irregular migrants at the new eastern EU borders.

TRAFFICKING IN PERSONS

Trafficked persons are exposed to a range of health-related problems regardless of whether their forced movement is for the purpose of labour, or sexual and other forms of exploitation. During captivity, they can experience physical violence, sexual exploitation, psychological abuse, poor living conditions and exposure to a wide range of diseases, which may have long-lasting consequences for their physical, reproductive and mental health.[37]

The number of trafficked women in the EU alone is estimated at 500,000, of whom some 300,000 are estimated to have either originated from, or transited through, the Balkans.[38] Despite the fact that humanitarian organizations like Save the Children (Carvel, 2000), academics (Willis and Levy, 2002) and the British Medical Association (BMA) have recently called for appropriate medical attention and harmonization of policies highlighting the risk of trafficking to public health (BMA, 2001), not much has happened in this regard.

In March 2003, a regional conference on Public Health and Trafficking was organized by IOM in Budapest to raise awareness of these issues. The resultant Budapest Declaration noted that "more attention and resources should be dedicated to the health and public health concerns related to trafficking", and added that "victims of trafficking must be given access to comprehensive, sustained, gender, age and culturally appropriate health care which focuses on achieving overall physical, mental, and social well-being." To this end, "minimum standards should be established for the health care that is provided to trafficking victims" with the understanding that "different stages of intervention call for different priorities" (IOM, 2003a). While the development of such minimum standards for mental health and psycho-social assistance is already underway,[39] the somatic, public health and data sharing aspects of care provision are still lacking.

APPREHENSIONS AT THE NEW EASTERN EU BORDERS – THE CASE OF SLOVAKIA

The new eastern borders of the EU (i.e. of the Baltics, Hungary, Poland, Slovakia) are also a front line for mobile pathologies, in particular carried by irregular migrants. The new EU members have become magnets

37. *Refer London School of Hygiene and Tropical Medicine. The health risks and consequences of trafficking in women and adolescents, findings from a European study. London: LSHTM. 2003.*

38. *Refer: US Department of State: Release of* 2002 Trafficking in Persons Report. *Statement of Ambassador Nancy Ely-Raphel, Senior Advisor to the Secretary, Office to Monitor and Combat Trafficking in Persons; the European Women's Lobby:* The Gender Divide in the EU *(Statistics).*

39. *As a first follow-up to the Conference, IOM has completed the* Mental Health And Trafficking: Development of Minimum Standards of Care and Regional Training of Trainers Workshop *project, funded by the Bureau for Population, Refugees and Migration of the US Department of State. A training handbook reflecting the minimum standards of psycho-social assistance has been published within the context of this project.*

for migrant smuggling and trafficking en route to western Europe, yet there is little on migrant health to guide governments in the Schengen protocols on border management. The Slovak Ministry of Interior, for example, reported that in 2002/2003, when Slovakia was preparing for EU membership, the number of intercepted and registered irregular migrants trying to cross the Slovak/Ukrainian border almost doubled from 2,399 to 5,483.[40] They hailed from many places – Vietnam, China, Afghanistan, India, the Caucasus, Iraq, Somalia, etc. – and carried a variety of respiratory tract infections, TB and scabies with them (no reliable data about HIV positive testing). This information was only available regarding asylum seekers subjected to medical screening after arrival at inland detention centres/refugee camps (IOM, 2004b). Official data about the health status of irregular migrants held in border guard facilities are not available.

Like all migrants, irregular migrants, regardless of whether they have committed an offence (illegal border crossing) or are victims of a criminal act (trafficked persons), are likely to have been exposed to a range of health-related problems during their travels. But if they are not caught, the dangers to themselves and to the public will not come to light.

When highlighting the need for a Europe-wide, harmonized health policy, it should be considered that health care services for irregular migrants are not only a humanitarian obligation, but also a public health concern for countries of transit and destination. This is not just a problem of spreading 'common' infectious diseases, such as the (re-) emerging TB, HIV/AIDS and Hepatitis B and C, or even sexually transmitted infections (STIs). Where public health systems are under-developed, or have been destroyed, which is often the case in developing countries of origin, diseases otherwise preventable by vaccination might spread to transit and destination countries, where physicians have not been confronted with these pathologies before (IOM, 2004a).

CONCLUSION

EUROPE, like most other regions of the world, faces demographic ageing due to increasing life expectancy. But, unlike other regions, almost all countries in Europe are experiencing below replacement fertility rates. As a result, the pace of demographic ageing is much more accelerated. And migration plays a more prominent role for population growth than in any other region.

Today, western and Central Europe are home or host to some 36-39 million international migrants. This represents a fifth of the world's migrant population, equal to the size of the foreign-born population in the US. One major difference remains, though; in western Europe economic and political integration of immigrants takes place at a slower pace than in either Canada or the US.

During the 21st century, for demographic and economic reasons, all present and future EU Member States will either remain or become immigration countries. After 2010, many countries will have to develop pro-active migration policies to meet those burgeoning demographic and economic needs. For a relatively short period of time, European East-West migration will continue to play a role. But in the medium and long term, potential migrants will inevitably have to be recruited from other world regions. In this context, Europe will have to compete with traditional countries of immigration, in particular Australia, Canada, and the US, for qualified migrants to fill their labour gaps. As a result, EU Member States and other countries in Europe will have to develop and implement more pro-active migration policies.

However, all attempts to develop and implement coherent migration regimes, and integration and citizenship policies, need public support among

40. *See the Slovak Ministry of Interior report coded* UHCP P PZ *(refer IOM Budapest).*

domestic populations and in the polities of sending and receiving societies. It is therefore necessary to explain why and how shaping – not preventing – future migration to Europe, influencing the characteristics of the migrants, and incorporating those who will (and should) stay for an extended period, can be managed in the best interests of both migrants and Europeans themselves.

MIGRATION IN EASTERN EUROPE AND CENTRAL ASIA (EECA)[41]

As external EU borders move east, they bring the EECA region increasingly into focus as a migration space with its own internal and external dynamics and policy developments. Compared with the 1990s and following the break-up of the former Soviet Union, issues of involuntary migration and displacement have faded into the background, except in the Caucasus region, and migration flows increasingly occur in reaction to economic and administrative changes. A predominant concern of the region is how best to plan and manage labour migration, also against the backdrop of increasingly diversified flows from other parts of the world, irregular migration (particularly trafficking), security and ongoing humanitarian needs of some displaced groups.

MIGRATION TRENDS

In recent years flows out of the region have decreased steadily, owing in part to new visa restrictions within the region and with third countries, the effects of EU enlargement, and the security agenda emerging after September 11, 2001. This decrease can also be attributed to positive factors, including improved economic growth and job opportunities within the region, particularly in those sectors of the Russian Federation and Kazakhstan that experience rapid economic growth.

Within EECA, relocation of persons to countries of their own nationality is no longer occurring with the disruptive momentum experienced just after the break-up of the former Soviet Union. The slow-down also favours opportunities for the integration of persons who have relocated, mainly to Russia and Ukraine. Conflicts in the Southern Caucasus that remain frozen have generated displacements, which

41. *This region comprises: Armenia, Azerbaijan, Belarus, Georgia, Kyrgyzstan, Kazakhstan, Moldova, the Russian Federation, Tajikistan, Turkmenistan, Ukraine and Uzbekistan. The chapter has been prepared by IOM, Vienna.*

likewise remain frozen or, in turn, generate secondary migration flows abroad in search of economic opportunities. The return of formerly deported peoples, such as Crimean Tatars, is largely completed, although full reintegration requires ongoing attention. The situation of many Meskhetians remains difficult, particularly in Russia's Krasnodar Region. As regards demographic trends, continuing population growth is expected for Azerbaijan and most parts of Central Asia, but Russia, Belarus and Ukraine face considerable demographic decline due to ageing populations and low birth rates (World Bank, 2004), which calls for immigration policies aimed at demographic stability.

In general, the mix of push and pull factors of the 1990s is today increasingly overshadowed by a major concern with economic opportunities. Russia, Belarus, Ukraine and Kazakhstan remain the primary destination countries for economic migrants within the region. Until 2002, Armenia, Georgia, Moldova, Tajikistan and Kazakhstan experienced an outflow of between 14 and 24 per cent of their population,[42] as did Kyrgyzstan, Uzbekistan and Azerbaijan although to a lesser extent. While this trend mostly continues, more recent developments in Kazakhstan indicate a reversal. Most migrants in the region have only one or two major migration destinations within the region – Russia being the preferred choice. In 2003, around half of Russia's foreign labour force was from former Soviet republics, the highest percentage from Ukraine, Moldova, Uzbekistan and Tajikistan. Neighbouring China accounted for 20 per cent of the share.[43]

Official statistics cannot capture the significant growth of irregular labour migration within and from the region. According to some estimates, up to ten million irregular migrants could be spread throughout the region, pushed by low living standards and rising poverty levels at home, and pulled by economic opportunities abroad. More than two-thirds of migrants are of working age. Every third household in Armenia, Moldova and Tajikistan has one or more family members working abroad (IOM, 2002). Besides being a source of irregular migrants, the region continues to be a convenient conduit for transit migration originating in third countries, mainly from South and Southeast Asia, China and Afghanistan.

The region also continues to be a hub for trafficking and smuggling activities, with the criminals operating mainly in an organized manner, and in rare cases individually (IOM, 2003). While there are no exact and reliable statistics owing to the illicit nature of the activity (Kelly, 2002), EECA is a major source region for trafficking in persons.[44] Besides being used for transit, some have also become countries of destination (Kazakhstan, Russia). Women and children from the western CIS[45] are trafficked mostly to western Europe, the Balkans and the US, while victims from Central Asian countries are channelled mainly to the UAE, Saudi Arabia, Turkey or South Korea (ibid).

POLICY RESPONSES

LABOUR MIGRATION is a key area of concern in EECA, yet the value of remittances in the development context is only slowly coming into focus. Governments are becoming more active in addressing labour migration issues through new institutional and policy frameworks. Tajikistan and Azerbaijan, for example, have included provisions for reducing the root causes of economic migration and regulating

42. *IOM,* Migration Trends in Eastern Europe and Central Asia*; 2001-2002 Review.*

43. *"Country Report, Russian Federation", High Level Review Meeting on "Refugee, Migration and Protection" serving the follow-up to the 1996 Geneva Conference on the Problems of Refugees, Displaced Persons, Migration and Asylum Issues, organized jointly by UNCHR, IOM, OSCE and the Council of Europe, Minsk, 26-28 May 2004.*

44. *See also the Trafficking in Persons Report 2004 by the US Department of State, which estimated the trafficking phenomenon worldwide at between 600,000 and 800,000 individuals a year.*

45. *The Commonwealth of Independent States (CIS) includes the twelve countries of the former Soviet Union. Western CIS refers to Belarus, Ukraine and Moldova.*

internal and external labour migration in their Poverty Reduction Strategy Programmes, adopted in 2002 and 2003, respectively.[46]

Regarding *labour migration*, a number of EECA countries have pursued bilateral agreements within and outside the region, as well as agreements on social protection and humane policies for return and readmission of their nationals. Kyrgyzstan's migration strategy for 2004 included a call for regional inputs to the development of a retirement insurance scheme for labour migrants, channelling labour migration remittances through a regional mechanism, and recommendations for facilitating the World Trade Organization's General Agreement on Trade and Services (Mode 4) as an instrument to regulate labour migration at the regional level. Dialogue between countries of origin and destination, and better legal regulation of employment or self-employment abroad, can help curtail fraudulent schemes ending in illegal migration and trafficking in persons.

A 1998 agreement among CIS countries to combat illegal migration was a first example of cross-border cooperation. In 2000, the CIS Conference[47] thematized irregular migration and trafficking in persons. Since then, migration management has moved up on the agendas of subregional fora such as the Eurasian Economic Community[48] and GUUAM,[49] and the combat of irregular migration, the trafficking in persons and other forms of organized crime has been declared common policy objectives. Ukraine, Moldova and Belarus share common concerns as increasing numbers of irregular EU-bound transit migrants are stranded at the now strengthened eastern borders of the enlarged EU. Seeking to address this situation, the "Soderkoping Process"[50] aims to enhance dialogue, cross-border cooperation and transfer of know-how in migration and asylum management with a view to mitigating the repercussions of the eastward expansion of the new EU border.

Public sector reform also affects border management. Border control entities are beginning to be converted from militarized structures into civilian agencies (e.g. in Azerbaijan and Kyrgyzstan). Border guard training facilities have been upgraded in Azerbaijan, Georgia and Kyrgyzstan. Revisions to curricula and instruction manuals reflect the efforts to modernize and the enhanced awareness of asylum, trafficking and human rights issues.

With *terrorism and extremism* dominating the political discourse, document security and the issuance of secure passports, visas and other identity documents used in local cross-border travel, have become critical. Ensuring integrity, quality and security of document design, and of registration and issuance systems, has become an important aspect of migration management. More sophisticated border management equipment and technology have been installed in a number of countries, systems for computerized exchange of passenger data (entries and exits) between the border services and ministries of interior and foreign affairs are being developed in, e.g. Azerbaijan, and new passports with modern security features are being introduced, such as in Kyrgyzstan.[51] Much remains to be done, including improvement of working conditions with a view to reducing graft and corruption.

Regarding *trafficking in persons*: as of August 2004, eleven out of twelve countries in the region had signed, and eight had ratified the 2000 UN Convention Against Transnational Organized Crime. Ten had signed and six

46. *Adopted within the framework of World Bank and UNDP technical assistance initiatives, with migration-related inputs from IOM.*

47. *Follow-up to the 1996 Geneva Conference on the Problems of Refugees, Displaced Persons, Migration and Asylum Issues.*

48. *The EEC covers Belarus, Kazakhstan, Kyrgyzstan, Russia and Tajikistan.*

49. *GUUAM covers Georgia, Ukraine, Uzbekistan, Azerbaijan and Moldova.*

50. *The Soderkoping Process consists of countries on either side of the new eastern border of the enlarged EU, namely Belarus, Ukraine and Moldova to the east, and Estonia, Latvia, Lithuania, Poland, Slovakia, Hungary and Romania to the west; it is facilitated jointly by the Swedish Migration Board, UNHCR and IOM, and funded by the European Commission.*

51. *US-funded project implemented with IOM support.*

had ratified its Protocol to Prevent, Suppress and Punish Trafficking in Persons, Especially Women and Children,[52] which came into force in December 2003. Considerable work is needed to fully align national legislation with it. Regarding the tier system used in the 2004 U.S. State Department *Trafficking in Persons Report*,[53] five of the twelve EECA countries were placed in the "Tier 2 Watch List" category.

Recognizing trafficking in persons as a major concern, most states have introduced legislative amendments to their criminal codes. Many have developed official action plans – the latest being the National Action Plan Against Trafficking decreed in May 2004 in Azerbaijan, which incorporates suggestions from both IOM and the OSCE.[54] Government and community awareness of trafficking as a critical social issue is now widespread in the region, including in Turkmenistan, where counter-trafficking measures were endorsed in late 2003 as part of an agenda to protect women and children. However, demand for cheap labour and sexual services, and the adaptive capacity of organized crime, remain a continuing challenge to prevention and law enforcement and underline the importance of strong cross-border, regional and international cooperation.

The situation of *refugees and IDPs* in the Caucasus region remains unresolved. Similarly, the needs of other vulnerable groups, such as migrant women and children or persons displaced by natural or man-made ecological disasters (such as around the Aral Sea), remain largely neglected apart from some capacity building in disaster preparedness. Ensuring minimum standards and good practices for reception or detention centres for asylum seekers or irregular migrants stranded on the borders of the expanded EU or elsewhere, remains an ongoing concerns. Likewise, mechanisms for the voluntary return of irregular migrants and their sustainable reintegration in countries of origin require much more attention.

The role of the non-governmental sector in migration management has evolved significantly. Networks of NGOs at the national and regional level, particularly in Ukraine, Moldova, the Southern Caucasus and Central Asia, are emerging to consolidate know-how in assisting vulnerable migrants or potential and actual trafficking victims, either directly or through hotline and referral services.

With accelerating mobility and ease of communication, migration within, into and out of the EECA region is likely to grow, mostly for economic reasons. As elsewhere, poverty and income differentials influence these flows. High economic growth rates attract migrants from almost all parts of the former Soviet Union to Russia, and from Central Asia to Kazakhstan. They are being increasingly joined by migrants from China and southern Asia. Farther to the West, the European Union, is the main destination area, especially for migrants from countries in its immediate neighbourhood. Management of these flows within, to, from or through the region calls for sustained regional and international cooperation, particularly along the EU-EECA trajectory.

52. *Armenia, Azerbaijan, Belarus, Russia, Tajikistan and Ukraine.*

53. *2004 U.S. State Department Trafficking in Persons Report. Available at www.state.gov/g/tip/rls/tiprpt/2004/.*

54. *IOM is party to the national working groups addressing trafficking in persons.*

MIGRATION IN TURKEY: FACING CHANGES AND MAKING CHOICES[55]

Turkey has long been a main actor on the Eurasian and Middle Eastern migration scene, first as a country of origin and more recently of destination and transit. Among the major migration challenges for Turkey and its neighbours have been the large irregular movements through the country, particularly from the Middle East, towards Europe. But the patterns are changing and diversifying, and Turkey's migration policies are evolving rapidly, particularly in the context of its candidature for EU accession.

CURRENT IMMIGRATION AND EMIGRATION TRENDS

By the early 2000s, there were over three million Turkish citizens in Europe, more than 110,000 in Arab countries, and some 40,000 Turkish workers in the CIS region (Icduygu, 2003a). Some 400,000 Turkish citizens have also been reported in other countries, 75 per cent of them residing in traditional immigration countries such as Australia, Canada and the US. The total number of expatriate Turks abroad is over 3.5 million, or five per cent of the nation's total population.

In the last two decades, Turkey has itself increasingly experienced large, diverse inflows of foreign nationals, including transit migrants, illegal labour migrants, asylum seekers, refugees and registered immigrants. These flows are often inextricably intertwined and the legal environment has not been sufficiently able to distinguish between, e.g., asylum seekers and irregular migrants,[56] or smuggled and trafficked persons. In the early 2000s, almost 100,000 illegal migrants were being apprehended in the country each year. The number of foreigners with residence permits in Turkey is over 150,000, and asylum seekers numbered more than 4,000 a year (ibid). The number of irregular migrants is unknown, but is estimated at between several hundred thousand and one million (Icduygu, 2003b).

Turkey has experienced high irregular immigration for several decades, with more than 300,000 apprehended irregular migrants recorded between 2000 and 2003.[57] This trend has increased more than tenfold in the last eight years (Icduygu and Koser-Akcapar, 2004). In notable contrast, there was a decline in 2003 when only 56,000 irregular migrants were apprehended, a drop of one-third from the previous year. This is no doubt partly due to the lower numbers of Afghans and Iraqis seeking asylum in Europe (and hence transiting Turkey) (UNHCR, 2004),[58] but also to the government's increased enforcement actions.[59]

The irregular migration flows are mostly transit migrants en route to other countries, notably western Europe, and foreign workers employed irregularly in the country. Four key factors appear to determine these irregular inflows (Icduygu, 2000):

- The ongoing political turmoil in neighbouring areas has forced people from their homes, in search of security and a better life.
- Turkey's geographic location between East and West, and South and North has turned the country into a transit zone for many migrants heading west and north.
- The policies of "Fortress Europe", with their restrictive admission procedures and immigration

55. *The author of this sub-chapter is Ahmet Icduygu, Bilkent University, Turkey.*

56. *Turkey's position on the 1951 Convention and its geographical limitation excluding non-European asylum seekers (the majority of migrants in Turkey) is a factor contributing to this (Icduygu, 2003a).*

57. *Figures related to the apprehended cases of irregular migrants in Turkey come from the Bureau for Foreigners, Borders, and Asylum (BFBA) at the Directorate of General Security of the Ministry of Interior. For the related Website see, for instance, www.egm.gov.tr.*

58. *An ICMPD survey of illegal migration in Europe also shows this trend for the CEECs (Futo et al., 2003).*

59. *For instance, the EU's 2003 Progress Report indicates that the trend in illegal migration via Turkey has shown a decrease, and international migration flows have been diverted away from Turkey to other routes; see www.europa.eu.int/comm/enlargement/report_2003/pdf/rr_tk_final.pdf.*

control, have diverted some flows to peripheral zones around Europe, including Turkey.
- Turkey's relative economic prosperity in the region is a magnet for migrants from everywhere.

The top ten source countries of apprehended migrants between 1995 and 2003 were Iraq (24%), Moldova (10%), Afghanistan (8%), Pakistan (7%), Iran (5%), Romania (4%), Ukraine (4%), Russian Federation (3%), Georgia (3%) and Bangladesh (3%). Fewer than half of those apprehended were transit migrants intending to leave Turkey for a third country. In recent years, as the numbers of transit migrants in the total apprehended caseload dropped, the numbers of those intending to work in the informal sectors in Turkey have increased (Icduygu and Koser-Akcapar, 2004).

Turkey has also recently become a destination for persons from transitional democracies searching for better life and job opportunities abroad in the face of conflicts or economic and social hardships at home. The main countries of origin are those neighbouring Turkey in the north and northeast, whose nationals can enter Turkey with a visa obtained at the border gates and stay for up to one month. Their purpose is twofold: most engage in "suitcase trading", which has reached huge volumes in the past years, but many also hunt for jobs, which until recently were only available on the illegal labour market.

While many of these migrants are in Turkey voluntarily, their illegal work and resident status make them vulnerable to exploitation. Some obtain legal residence through arranged marriages. Others end up in small workshops, the tourism and entertainment sectors or in private households, working illegally without job security, insurance or administrative and judicial safeguards. The majority of male workers (mainly Romanians and Moldovans) are employed in the construction sector, and the females (mainly Moldovans, Ukrainians and Russians) in domestic services and the sex and entertainment sectors (Icduygu and Koser-Akcapar, 2004).

Since the early 1980s, Turkey has also become a major country of asylum (Kirisci, 2001) receiving approximately 4,000-5,000 asylum applications a year in the past five years. In the past three years, asylum applicants in Turkey have come from more than 20 different countries, mainly in the Middle East, and parts of Africa and Asia.

POLICY RESPONSES

IN LINE WITH its candidature for accession to the EU, Turkey is actively harmonizing its migration legislation with the *acquis communautaire*, particularly on irregular migration and asylum-related issues. To this end, the government has recently taken important initiatives (or with the intention to change) its migration policies and practice, including:

- Ratification in March 2003 of the UN *Convention against Transnational Organized Crime and its two additional Protocols including the Protocol to Prevent, Suppress and Punish Trafficking, especially Women and Children.* (Turkey was among the first signatories of both in 2000.)
- Adoption by parliament of new legislation in August 2002, which adds some articles to *the Penal Code* and amends *the Law on Combating Benefits-oriented Criminal Organizations*, to introduce the definitions of human trafficking and smuggling in persons into the Turkish legal system and impose heavy penalties on traffickers and smugglers.
- Approval by parliament in February 2003 of the *Law on Work Permits for Foreigners.*
  With this law, Turkey established new rules for access of migrant workers to the Turkish labour market. Under these, foreigners can be employed in domestic work previously not available to them.
- Approval by parliament in June 2003 of an amendment to *Article 5 of the Citizenship Law*, precluding applications for citizenship for three years. (Previously, a foreign woman could acquire Turkish citizenship immediately after marrying a Turkish national.)

The strengthened laws against smuggling and trafficking of migrants have enabled the government to impose heavier penalties against criminal networks engaged in these activities, and to take a number of actions against perpetrators in the criminal courts.[60] Law enforcement agencies are today also referring more and more trafficking cases to IOM for assistance, rather than automatically deporting them (Icduygu and Toktas, 2002).[61] The government is also moving to adjust its administrative and legal systems on asylum in line with international asylum practices, which should help to resolve the complex irregular migration situation in Turkey.[62]

CONCLUSION

THERE ARE indications that Turkey will continue to experience modest reductions in irregular immigration, but the decline may be neither rapid nor uniform. The pace of change will be closely tied to the pace of social, political and economic developments in the Middle East, Asia and Africa, the strength of migration networks between potential migrants and their relatives and friends abroad, and the labour demands of destination countries. Equally critical, however, will be the migration policies and practices of Turkey itself. Harmonization with EU migration and asylum regimes will greatly help the evolution from irregular to regular migration.

60. *For example, 27 lawsuits were initiated, 12 of which have since been concluded and 15 carried over to 2004. The number of the accused is 76 and the total number of plaintiffs is 70. Obtained from the Website of the Ministry of Foreign Affairs, www.mfa.gov.tr.*

61. *If a victim is not immediately identified as such, she/he is likely to be deported by the Turkish authorities as an illegal migrant. Note also that IOM offices in Ukraine and Moldova have provided reintegration assistance to several women who had been trafficked to Turkey and then deported (refer to Counter-Trafficking Service Area, IOM, Geneva).*

62. *It is moving to lift the geographical limitation on the Refugee Convention (footnote 3) (Icduygu, 2003a).*

SECTION 2

COSTS AND BENEFITS OF MIGRATION

Chapter 8
Economic Effects of International Migration: A Synoptic Overview[1]

Globalization, particularly the inter-penetration of markets and economies, has added new dimensions to some of the old migration issues; just as it has profoundly influenced both the surroundings and the consequences of contemporary migration.

Economic considerations alone do not determine migration policies. But economic arguments, notably about benefits and costs of migration, can play a critical part in policy making. Unfortunately, the debate is often pre-emptively hijacked by negative, populist slogans, which can inhibit the formulation of sound and balanced migration policies. Current knowledge about the benefits and costs of migration also remains inadequate, diffuse and often confusing, which in turn aids the cause of those politicizing the debate, and helps to create a vicious circle.

The impressive volume of literature on the subject shows how complex and diverse the effects of international migration are. This chapter draws on some of this literature, including the available empirical evidence, to discern the major economic effects of migration. It refers to past and current theories, identifies points to be discussed further in ensuing chapters of this section of the Report, and highlights some of the issues for future consideration by policymakers.

THEORETICAL MODELS TO ASSESS MIGRATION IMPACTS

Given the complexity of migration, how helpful are the existing theoretical models in discerning its effects? At first glance, classical and neo-classical theories of economic migration seem to offer some straightforward answers.

According to these theories, migration has an all-round beneficial effect, with gains for all, or nearly all, directly involved. The receiving country (assumed to have a labour shortage) gains as immigration removes labour scarcity, facilitates occupational mobility and reduces wage-push inflationary pressure, leading to fuller utilization of productive capital, increased exports and economic growth. For the sending country, emigration can reduce unemployment and boost economic growth through access to strategic inputs such as remittances and returning skills. The migrants, in turn, can benefit from higher wages and productivity in the capital-rich receiving country. These theories also suggest that with wages rising in the sending country and falling in the receiving country, factor costs eventually become balanced, and migration between the two countries ceases.

At a time of increasing resistance to immigration, such a glowing assessment of the consequences of migration may not enjoy high credibility. But there is some historical evidence lending support to these theories. The massive trans-Atlantic migration of the late 19th century both helped to open up the US economy with its vast potential resources, and ease

1. *This chapter is prepared by Professor Bimal Ghosh, Emeritus Professor of the Colombian School of Public Administration, and international consultant on trade, migration and development. A longer version of this paper is to be found in his forthcoming publication* Migration and Development: Unveiling the Nexus.

poverty and population pressures in the sending European countries. The economic conditions of labourers in poorer countries like Ireland, Italy, Norway and Sweden improved as migrants left, both in absolute terms and relative to those in the UK and France in Europe and in the US (Williamson 1996). In 1882, the Swedish economist Knut Wicksell argued in favour of emigration to rid his country of paupers, because poverty, he reasoned, was a consequence of surplus labour and insufficient land.

Supposing these theories are right, how much can the world gain from free circulation of labour? In 1984, experts made an assessment of possible efficiency gains using a simple methodology to assess the differences in marginal productivity of labour between countries and across regions owing to barriers to inward mobility of labour (Hamilton and Whalley, 1984).[2] They concluded that if these barriers were removed, the efficiency gains could double world income. More recently it has been postulated that, since wages for similarly qualified workers in developed and developing countries differed sharply – by a factor of 10 or more, as against a difference for commodities and financial assets that rarely exceeds a ratio of 1:2 – the gains from openness could be enormous, roughly 25 times the gains from the liberalization of the movement of goods and capital (Rodrik, 2002).[3]

These theoretical models and analyses highlight the positive effects of migration in a given set of circumstances, but they fail to take into account the costs, or negative externalities, of migration. Huge inflows of foreigners could place a heavy strain on the receiving country's physical infrastructure and public services, including housing facilities, transport systems, schools and medical services. The costs of integration could be high when the ethnic, cultural and religious background of the migrants differ sharply from that of the resident population. If this overwhelms the overall capacity of the receiving society to integrate them, exceeding the margin of tolerance for foreigners, tension and even conflict could follow, threatening economic growth and social stability.

These theoretical models also suffer from another type of limitation. They are based on a set of fixed assumptions; for example, that migrant labour is homogeneous, that there is perfect competition and mobility in the labour markets, that full employment prevails in all countries, and there are no state interventions in respect of migration. The reality, as discussed later in this chapter, is often different.

There is a litany of other theories of economic migration. But they fail to provide a better or more adequate framework to capture the complex effects of migration in varying contextual circumstances. Those constructed on the general hypothesis that migration invariably takes place between economically and politically unequal geographical units (e.g. centre-periphery theory or conflict theory) are too rigidly deterministic, while those focused on limited economic aspects of migration (e.g. new economics of migration) do not reveal the complexities of the situation as a whole.

FRAMEWORK FOR CURRENT EMPIRICAL STUDIES: HOW ADEQUATE IS IT?

If there are limits to what we can learn from theoretical models, what about empirical studies? While empirical studies abound in migration literature, they have generally been designed as micro projects, confined to specific areas and time periods. Aside from differences in methodology, the diversity of settings has often led the studies to divergent and conflicting conclusions. The snapshots they provide are real and therefore valuable, but not a sufficient basis for rational generalizations on the benefits and costs of migration.

---

2. *See also the chapter in this report "Economic Costs and Benefits of International Labour Migration".*

3. *Rodrik estimated that even a modest relaxation of the restrictions on the movement of workers – temporary admission of poor country workers numbering no more than 3 per cent of rich countries' labour force – could yield a benefit of USD 200 billion for the developing world.* Feasible Globalizations, *Kennedy School of Government, Working Paper Series RWP02029, July 2002, pp.19-20.*

But the current empirical and analytical studies suffer from other shortcomings as well. As at 2000, just under 40 per cent of the world's migrant stock lived in developing countries.[4] Although the collective emigration flows from these countries exceed their collective inflows, the latter (mostly between developing countries) continue to be significant. More important, in addition to the oil-producing Gulf states, which host millions of contract migrant labourers, several developing countries, including Gabon, Malaysia and Singapore, have been receiving relatively large numbers of labour migrants, and others, such as Argentina, Côte d'Ivoire and Venezuela did so in the past. But little is known about the impact of immigration on these and other developing countries, as the empirical studies have so far focused almost exclusively on developed countries, notably Australia, Canada, Germany and the US.

If a rigid, mutually exclusive categorization of "emigration" and "immigration" countries is used in analysing the effects of migration, this will also leave some important knowledge gaps for those countries significantly affected by both emigration and immigration at the same time. A 1994 ILO survey of some 100 countries showed that nearly 25 per cent of them now fell into that category (ILO 1994; 1999), and that their numbers were increasing. To assess the consequences of migration inflows, analysts normally use net immigration figures. However, since persons entering and leaving countries are not necessarily the same, the method used fails to reveal the interactive effects, if any, of the simultaneous flows of immigration and emigration. For instance, if, as the ILO survey showed in 1994, Italy had some 500,000 economically active non-nationals on its territory and 600,000 economically active nationals abroad, were the two flows completely independent of each other? Or did the two flows interact in some ways; and, if so, what were the repercussions for Italy's labour market and economy?

In addition to the two-way migratory flows (when both are significant), it seems important to examine the effects of migration on a country's other economic flows, such as trade. A recent study by Columbia University showed that in the US the gains in output from labour immigration in 1998 were more than offset by a deterioration in its terms-of-trade amounting to 0.9 percent of GDP, or USD 80 billion, about nine-tenths of which (or USD 72 billion) were carried by US-born workers. These findings could be argued about and caveats issued, but the study unquestionably makes the important point that the effects of labour immigration can be fully assessed only in conjunction with other economic flows, such as trade and foreign investment, and not in isolation.[5]

GLOBAL CHANGES AND THEIR IMPACT ON THE CONFIGURATION AND CONSEQUENCES OF MIGRATION

The above arguments make the case for a broader analytical framework to assess the effects of migration. But, it is no less important that the framework also be sensitive to the global changes that impinge on migration. Globalization, particularly the interpenetration of markets and economies, has added new dimensions to some of the old migration issues; just as it has profoundly influenced both the context and the consequences of contemporary migration. For example, the conventional idea of trade-offs between remittances and "brain drain" is now being largely replaced by new models of transnational networking with the diaspora. In these models, emigration and migrant return can be seen less and less as discrete events and increasingly as part of a wider process of global mobility and international exchange. Similarly, freer temporary movement of persons providing skill- and knowledge-intensive services, as envisaged under the General Agreement on Trade and Services (GATS), has opened up the prospect of turning "brain drain" into "brain gain".

4. *See also the chapter "International Migration Trends".*

5. *Most of the existing studies on trade and migration assume, based on the Heckscher-Ohlin-Samuelson model, that they are substitutes. However, the relation between trade and migration is often much more complex, depending on such factors as the openness of the economies, differences in the levels of technologies and specialization of countries. In many cases, trade and migration could be complementary, or both complements and substitutes (as in the case of temporary movement of service providers under mode 4 of the GATS), see Venables, 1999.*

SHARING GAINS AND LOSSES

DOES the lack of a sound and comprehensive theoretical or analytical framework make it obsolete to assess the effects of migration? We think not. By following the conventional approach, we can still make a sensible, though not complete or perfect, assessment of these effects, provided full use is made of the available theoretical and analytical tools and the pieces of empirical evidence are pulled together in a balanced manner. Some of these effects, but not all, are discussed in this chapter.

There is ample evidence that migration brings both benefits and costs for sending and receiving countries, and that these are often shared differently by different groups – workers and employers/ owners of capital, skilled and unskilled workers and groups of consumers in the respective countries. The volume, skill composition and other characteristics of the migration flows critically influence these effects, as do other contextual circumstances in which the flows take place. These include labour market conditions and trends, the demographic profile, and the stage, strategy and rates of economic growth and development in each country. Additional important factors are: a) for the receiving country, its socio-cultural capacity to accept and integrate new immigrants, and b) for the sending country, the degree of its preparedness to respond to new economic stimuli such as remittances and returning skills, and to inspire confidence in the future of the economy.

For the distribution of gains and losses due to migration, a key issue is whether, or to what extent, immigrants complement, or compete with, local workers. An important point to note is that labour is not homogeneous within or across countries. Thus, when unskilled foreign workers directly compete with similar workers in the receiving country, all things being equal, the latter are likely to lose, owing to the likely downward pressure on their jobs and wages. On the other hand, employers/owners of firms engaged in labour-intensive production, consumers of their products, and the immigrants themselves, would gain. But so would skilled workers, if the unskilled immigrant workers complemented them. A 1995 study in Germany, for example, found that a one per cent increase in the share of foreign workers led to a small increase of 0.2 per cent in the wages of blue collar workers, but to a 1.3 per cent rise in the wages of white collar workers (Haisken-DeNew and Zimmermann, 1995). Also, if the economy is open and flexible, with elastic demand in external markets for its tradable, labour-intensive goods, a fall in wages of unskilled workers may induce employers to expand production and recruit some new ones. Thus, a change in output mix could eventually leave both wages and employment relatively unaffected.

For the sending country, the effects will, in principle, be the opposite. Unskilled workers left behind gain through a rise in wages, while employers lose. But this, too, is not automatic. In a typical labour-surplus country, outflows of unskilled workers may not necessarily lead to a general rise in wages given the vast pool of unskilled workers, many of whom may be unemployed or under-employed.

In a country that has abundant labour but a shortage of skills, skilled immigrants can also be a complement to unskilled workers. The latter can gain from the inflow of new skills leading to a better and fuller utilization of labour and other resources, though skilled workers are likely to lose from this. The situation is less than clear cut if skills brought by immigrants lead to innovation and the creation of new jobs. Even in a highly advanced economy, and depending on the type of new jobs, it could have a positive effect on skilled workers as well. In the US, the Cypress Semiconductor Corporation recently reported that about 40 per cent of the research and development jobs were held by immigrants and that each job created nine additional jobs.[6]

6. *Cited in* Migration News, *Vol.4, No. 2, Feb. 1997.*

A further important point is that even within the same skill category labour may not be fully homogeneous across countries. The immigrant workers may be substitutes for local workers, but only partially so. When Mexican workers move to the US, they may not be used at the same level of labour productivity as local workers, although they may belong to the same skill category. The immigrants could gain from higher wages than in Mexico, but if paid less than the US workers they are replacing, their gains will be correspondingly smaller than expected.

Finally, there is the question of contextual circumstances. Just as the volume and skill composition of migration flows change over time, so do the labour market conditions in particular countries or regions, and the interactive conditions of the world economy. These changes can in turn alter the migration effects, both real and perceived. This can be seen from the shifting international migration policies in different periods following World War II. In the early 1950s, there was an acute labour shortage in industrial countries, especially in war-ravaged western Europe, which, helped by massive inflows of US capital, was heavily engaged in reconstruction work. There were widespread calls to liberalize the movement of workers for the benefit of both migrant-receiving and migrant-sending countries. Formal declarations of international organizations such as the ILO in 1949, OEEC (now OECD) in 1953, and the EEC (now EU) in 1957 echoed these calls (Ghosh, 1992; ILO, 1981). But, by the early 1970s, as countries in western Europe faced the first oil crisis and suffered from widespread recession and high unemployment, they no longer needed imported labour. There was also a growing feeling that the social costs of immigration were rising fast.

In western Europe, labour immigration was virtually halted by 1973-74, with international organizations also highlighting the economic and social costs of migration. It was no longer perceived as a factor in world development.[7] The situation led to calls in 1976 for a new division of labour in trade, which would 'take work to the workers' and reduce emigration pressure, while promoting growth and welfare in both rich and poor nations. However, by the mid-1980s, amid a sharply deteriorating world trade and economic environment, it became apparent that the slogan 'trade in place of migration' had failed. Once more, there was a change in international migration policy. Reducing the need for migration was still the main objective, but the emphasis now shifted from a new international division of labour to wider economic cooperation between sending and receiving countries to achieve this goal (Ghosh, 1992a).

CURRENT CONCERNS IN THE RECEIVING COUNTRIES: MYTHS AND REALITIES

CONTEXTUAL circumstances can seriously influence the real effects of migration and shape the perception of it. In many receiving countries, where there is a growing sense that immigration is getting out of control, large sections of the public seem to have a negative perception of the effects of immigration. This expresses itself through three inter-related concerns:
1) migrants take away jobs from the local population;
2) immigration is driving down wages, and
3) immigrants are a heavy burden on the country's social welfare system. How valid are these concerns?

DO IMMIGRANTS TAKE AWAY JOBS AND DEPRESS WAGES?

Studies in western Europe show that the impact of immigrants on employment is weak or ambiguous.[8] As discussed above, the key issue is whether, or to what extent, foreign workers complement or compete with resident workers. In western Europe, there are at least three categories of jobs that largely eschew direct competition between foreign and local workers, and where the question of job displacement hardly arises.

7. *This was despite the new demands for immigrant labour in the oil-producing Gulf States.*
8. *See Herbert Brücker:* "The Employment Impact of Immigration: a Survey of European Studies", Table 3.7, *2002.*

First, many dirty, difficult and dangerous (so-called 3-D) jobs are being increasingly shunned by local workers in industrial countries.[9] Second, the current life-style of many Europeans is sustained by a wide variety of service jobs – childcare, house cleaning, pizza delivery etc. – undertaken by foreigners who cannot easily be replaced by locals.[10] Third, immigrants also respond to another type of unmet, but distorted labour demand – low-skilled jobs in the underground economy, which in the EU countries now engage between 10 and 20 million workers, many of whom are immigrants with irregular status (Ghosh, 1998).

There is still another category of jobs traditionally filled by immigrants, in sectors such as farming, road repairs and construction, hotel, restaurant and other tourism-related services, which, although not completely shunned by local workers, often suffer from seasonal shortages of labour. In the EU as in the US, lavish export subsidies, domestic support and import protection enhance production and thus labour demand in the farm sector. Far from taking away jobs from local workers, immigrants redress labour scarcities and help these businesses to flourish during the high seasons.

Finally, there are several skill and knowledge-intensive industries, notably in the fast-moving information technology sector, with an unmet demand for highly skilled immigrants in most industrial countries.[11] There is a scramble for additional skills to develop new technologies, enhance competitiveness and create new jobs. At the European Council meeting in Stockholm on 23 March 2001, Romano Prodi, President of the EU Commission, warned that the EU needed 1.7 million qualified workers in the technology sector alone (*The Economist*, 29 March 2001). Despite the recent downturn in the IT market (or partly because of it), Germany was hard pressed to recruit 20,000 software engineers from abroad. The UK National Skills Task Force said in 2000 that if the UK could close the skill gap on Germany, it would generate GBP 50 billion additional output in a decade (DIEE, 1998; *Financial Times*, 6 September 2000), and has since launched the Highly Skilled Migrant Programme, which is similar to the points assessment schemes of Australia and Canada.

Thus, in a wide variety of jobs in western Europe there is hardly any direct competition between immigrants and local workers. In the US, even when low-skilled immigrants compete with resident workers, they do so mostly with other immigrants possessing similar skills but other labour market (and ethnic) characteristics already in the country. A series of econometric studies showed that the impact of Hispanic immigrants (who arrived between 1975 and 1980, the majority of them "illegal") on wages and employment was insignificant, except for one category – other immigrants (DeFreitas, 1986). Earlier, this chapter had indicated that in some situations immigration may create, or help to create new jobs. Many people think or tacitly assume that there is always a fixed number of jobs in an economy. This notion is incorrect.

In view of the foregoing, it is not surprising that recent studies have found no correlation between migration and unemployment. The OECD, for example, carried out an exercise for a number of countries to establish if increased immigration in fact matched with increased unemployment. Of the five countries that saw a substantial increase in immigration in 1984-89 (the US, Germany, Japan, Switzerland and France), unemployment dropped in one, rose slightly in three and remained the same in the fifth (OECD, 1998). The contrasting experiences of Spain and Switzerland are also revealing. Spain has a migrant stock of some 3.2 per cent of its population,

9. *According to a recent study, two-thirds of foreigners in Germany who found employment in 1998 were working in jobs turned down by local workers* (Migration News, *1996).*

10. *In 1997 the World Bank reported, on the basis of data collected by OECD, that as many as 70 per cent of recent migrants from developing countries were active in unskilled labour sectors native workers prefer to avoid. World Bank,* World Development Indicators, *1997. In Spain in February 2000, at a high point of joblessness in the country, the Employment Minister declared "we need people to do the jobs Spaniards no longer want to do"* (The Economist, *6 May 2000).*

11. *According to a study in 2000, since 1998 western Europe had lost EUR 110 billion in gross domestic product due to skill shortages* (Financial Times, *7 March 2000).*

and an annual net immigration rate of less than 0.9 percent, but its unemployment has been hovering above 18 per cent. By contrast Switzerland, with a migrant stock of over 22 per cent and a net annual migration of 0.6 per cent, has had an unemployment rate of around 4 (3.7) per cent.

This does not mean that immigration has no effect on employment. When there is a high concentration of foreign workers in certain industries or geographical areas, it can cause pressure on jobs and working conditions of the local labour force. For example, in the construction industry in Germany, which employs large numbers of both regular and irregular foreign workers, trade unions have complained that the situation was endangering job prospects for regular German workers. The problem is aggravated by a rigid labour market and low mobility of German workers, who do not move away from immigration areas and wind up in times of recession competing directly with immigrants. This undermines their job prospects.[12]

The situation is somewhat different in the US where the labour market is less rigid and white workers have high (4-6 times higher than in Western Europe) mobility. New immigration, for example of low-skilled (and mostly irregular) Mexicans, may displace some resident workers, but, as noted above, this applies mostly to Mexican immigrants with similar skills, who had arrived earlier, and not the white workers (Ghosh, 1998; DeFreitas 1986; OECD, 1993).[13]

What about wages? There is a widespread belief that even if immigrants do not steal jobs, they depress wages. But the findings in a wide range of studies in Europe and the US tell a somewhat different story. In Europe some found small negative wage effects, ranging from -0.3 to -0.8 per cent, while others suggested that local wages, especially of the highly skilled, increased slightly (Hanson et al., 2002). In the UK, a recent study suggested that wages among existing workers there had not been affected; if anything, they had gone up (Dustmann, 2004; *The Economist*, 28 February, 2004). In the US, one study concluded that a 10 per cent increase in immigrants in a region lowers non-migrant wages by an amount close to zero (0.2%) (Brucker 2002).

Some of these differentiated effects on wages of skilled and unskilled local workers can also be influenced by the conditions of the labour market of the receiving country. The large contrasts in labour market situations in Western Europe and the US have already been noted. The fact that the US has a vast pool of black and Hispanic labour explains further how the recent streams of low-skilled Mexican immigrants have put downward pressure on wages (and jobs) due to direct competition at the low end of the local labour force, involving not only earlier Mexican immigrants with similar skills and other characteristics, but also low-skilled black and Hispanic workers.

Not surprisingly, in 1997 the US National Research Council concluded that American workers as a whole have gained from immigration, but wages of workers without a high-school education had declined – a conclusion in line with findings of the 1994 Report of the President. It also confirmed that those most affected were previous immigrants in low-wage jobs for which new immigrants were competing. A more recent study confirmed that those most affected by new immigrants who had arrived since the beginning of 2000 were resident immigrants, but that the group also included young, less educated American worker (Sum, 2003).

To complete the picture of labour market effects, in most countries of western Europe immigrants are more likely to be unemployed than the local labour force, and are generally first to be retrenched in times of recession. Both in western Europe and the US, they

12. *In the US, a few studies have shown how immigration can have a negative effect on jobs and wages of local workers. See, for example, G.Borjas "The labour demand curve is downward sloping: Re-examining the impact of immigration on the labour market,* The Quarterly Journal of Economics *118(4), 2003; and "Increasing the supply of labour through immigration, measuring the impact on native-born workers". Center for Immigration Studies, 2004.*

13. *More recently, they have also been found to compete with black workers in the same areas holding low-skilled jobs. Mexican immigrants, for example, are now doing the work black janitors used to do in Los Angeles (Martin and Midgley, 1994). It should be noted, however, that most blacks do not live in areas with large concentration of immigrants.*

are also found to earn less than local workers in comparable jobs. This may in part be due to lower levels of education and skills, but there is enough evidence to suggest that it is also due to discrimination against immigrants.

DOES IMMIGRATION RAISE SOCIAL WELFARE COSTS?

Immigrants are sometimes seen by host communities as profiting from benefits. The assumption is that they rely heavily on public welfare and social services, but pay relatively little in the form of welfare contribution and taxes. In the US, as in western Europe, the assumption is being widely used as an argument to restrict immigration or delay welfare benefits to certain categories of immigrants. The fear of being a "welfare magnet" has led countries like Ireland and the UK to delay such payments to immigrants from the new EU members, even while opening their borders to them. Once more, evidence from existing empirical studies is somewhat conflicting, and the reality is much more complex.

In the UK, a recent Home Office study calculated that in 1999-2000 migrants contributed GBP 2.5 billion (USD 4 billion) more in taxes than they received in benefits (Gott and Johnston, 2002). Another study revealed that the foreign-born population contributed around 10 per cent more to government revenue than they took in benefits, and that in the absence of their contribution either public services would have to be cut or taxes raised (ILO, 2004). Similarly, in Germany it was claimed that without the contributions from immigrants who came in 1988-91, the German social welfare system would have collapsed (UNHCR, 1992). In the US, a recent study at Rice University concluded that regular and irregular migrants who had arrived since 1970 cost the country USD 42.5 billion in 1992. But, more recently, the Urban Institute showed that, instead of a net cost of USD 42.5 billion, there was a net benefit for the US during the same period.[14]

A critical element in these cost estimates is the extent of immigrant dependence on public welfare. But again the picture is ambiguous. Across western Europe, in a number of countries (Austria, Belgium, Denmark, France, the Netherlands and Switzerland) migrants' welfare dependence seems to be higher than that of the local population. On the other hand, several other countries (Germany, Greece, Portugal, Spain and the UK) show that welfare dependence among migrants is similar to, or lower than that of EU citizens (Brucker, 2002). In Canada, too, a 1993 study showed that immigrant households were generally less dependent on welfare than non-immigrant households (Baker and Benjamin, 1993).

There is often also a general belief that irregular immigrants do not pay taxes. But, anxious to conceal their identity, many irregular immigrants do not claim welfare benefits. In the US, a most recent measure that seeks to link immigrant patients' legal status to federal government support of USD 1 billion to hospitals would make the situation even more complex (*New York Times*, 10 August 2004). Studies in the US show that a large percentage pays social security and income through the automatic withholding system. In 1984, the average irregular immigrant worker in the US had more than USD 1,000 withheld each year for federal income taxes and social security payments alone (Simon, 1989). In 1990-1998, employers paid the US government up to USD 20 billion in welfare contributions for the irregular immigrant workers they employed. But they did so with fake social security cards. Since these cards cannot be matched to legally recorded names, they do not entail any benefit expenditure (ILO 2004).

What then is the real situation? Some of the differences among these findings clearly stem from differences in the methodology used. For example, in the two US studies cited above, the Urban Institute treated social security on a pay-as-you-go basis (in keeping with US federal government practice), while Rice University did not. It excluded the 15 per cent of each worker's earnings paid as social security contribution on the grounds that these would be offset by the anticipated benefits to be returned on

14. *For a more detailed discussion on the public welfare costs of immigration, notably irregular immigration, see Bimal Ghosh,* Huddled Masses and Uncertain Shores: Insights into Irregular Migration, *1998.*

retirement. Also, in countries with a federal system (like the US), if the assessment is confined to a particular city or area, it would lead to distorted results. Clearly, for an overall assessment of the net welfare cost it is important to take into account all contributions made to, and benefits received from, different public authorities by the immigrants. In 1997, the US National Research Council (NRC) estimated that, measured in terms of net present value, while the states had a loss of USD 20,000 for every immigrant, the corresponding gain for the federal government was USD 80,000 (NRC, 1997).

Caution is also needed on how to calculate the value of the services provided. It can be argued that only the marginal costs should be taken into account for all those services that the host country will need to maintain, even if there were no immigrants. And the marginal cost could be lower than the average cost, if the migrants use only the spare capacity of existing services, or higher if new facilities are to be set up because of the arrival of immigrants.

Methodology aside, the main issue is the level of use of welfare services by immigrants and their families. And this, once more, depends on the characteristics of the immigration flows in a given time period. Skills and education, age, family status and cultural background as well as the original motive to migrate – all influence migrants' attitudes towards the use of public welfare. Studies in the US have shown that immigrants who came during 1965-69 used less public welfare than those who arrived in 1985-89. Why? At least part of the explanation lies in the differences in skills and education of the two groups (Borjas, 1994). The National Research Council similarly found that newly arrived immigrants with little education used more state and local public services than they paid in taxes. Experience in countries like Australia and Canada have shown that skilled immigrants have a lower propensity to depend on public welfare (Ghosh 1998; Baker and Benjamin, 1953).

Age and family status are also important factors: young, active, highly motivated and often single, most migrants in the initial stage are less likely to depend on welfare. But the situation evolves over time, especially as families grow and welfare transfers are likely to increase. After a relative decline, these could rise again as immigrant populations age. The importance of the age factor was brought into focus in a recent study in Germany, which showed that if someone immigrated at the age of 30, he or she will contribute EUR 110, 000 over his or her lifetime. By contrast, a person who immigrates before his/her first birthday will create a net burden of EUR 60,000 on public finances. Since 78 per cent of immigrants in Germany are of working age, an average immigrant makes a positive net contribution of EUR 50,000 in his or her lifetime (ILO, 2004).

Taking a longer, inter-generational view, the US National Academy of Sciences has concluded that immigrants in the early years do add to costs, particularly for education. Eventually, however, each immigrant, with his or her descendants paying taxes, would make a net positive contribution of USD 80,000 to the US budget (Smith and Edmonston, 1997).

Another important factor shaping immigrants' attitudes towards the use of public welfare is the integration policy of the host society. What matters particularly is their ease of access to training and economic opportunities, including scope for occupational mobility and advancement. Will they remain poor and continue to depend on public welfare? Or, will they have economic success and, as earnings rise, avoid dependence on public welfare, despite being eligible? Any policies or practices based on exclusion or discrimination are unhelpful. A separate, but related, factor is the attitude of the host society and its own citizens towards the use of public welfare. A general cultural aversion and social reticence of the host society towards public welfare dependence is likely to discourage immigrants from relying unduly on public welfare, and the reverse could be equally true.[15]

15. *See chapters "Benefits and Costs of Integration – International Convergence?" and "Migration and the Contemporary Welfare State".*

MIGRANT-SENDING DEVELOPING COUNTRIES: DOES MIGRATION HELP OR HINDER DEVELOPMENT?

FOR POLICYMAKERS in the developing countries a key question is whether migration helps or hinders development. Some of the general effects of emigration are discussed earlier in this chapter and in greater detail in other chapters of this Report.[16]

One of the most stubborn problems facing most developing countries is widespread unemployment. Emigration is sometimes seen, as was the case for several eastern Mediterranean countries in the 1960s and early 1970s, as a means to reduce joblessness and enhance industrial development through increased foreign exchange earnings (Ghosh, 1996; Korner, 1987). In Asia, similar considerations have led countries like Bangladesh, India, Pakistan, the Philippines and Sri Lanka to encourage labour emigration. There is little doubt that in over-crowded areas emigration can provide some temporary relief from unemployment. It can be particularly helpful in absorbing the increase in labour force, as has occurred in countries like Pakistan, the Republic of Korea and Sri Lanka at different times (ILO/UNDP, 1988; Korale and Gunapala, 1985; Kim, 1983).

Emigration can also serve as a temporary safety valve against mass discontent resulting from job losses during the transition following economic reform and restructuring. This was a major consideration prompting western European countries, notably Germany, to launch various temporary labour migration schemes from Central European countries in the early 1990s. By alleviating unemployment, emigration can also reduce the fiscal burden of welfare benefits. Egypt might have found it difficult to sustain its employment guarantee scheme in the 1970s without the massive movement of its workers to the Gulf states.

But emigration usually does not involve more than 2-3 per cent of the domestic labour force – too small to make a real dent in widespread unemployment and underemployment of many labour-abundant countries. Even a much higher level of emigration may prove relatively ineffective, when the problem is structural and the country continues to face high demographic pressures. In 1973, Turkey had one million expatriates abroad, or six per cent of its labour force at that time. Today, the Philippines has about six per cent of its labour force living abroad. But in neither case could emigration solve the problem of structural unemployment. In Sri Lanka, although the gross emigration flow represented roughly 86 per cent of its incremental labour force, unemployment remained 14 per cent in 1960. Mexico continues to face serious problems of joblessness, although around 8 million Mexicans – nearly 8 per cent of its total population of 108 million – are living in the US alone.

Reliance on emigration, even as a temporary relief to unemployment, also carries a potential risk. Should such relief encourage the sending country to postpone unpopular but essential economic reforms, it can over time only aggravate the unemployment situation and undermine sustainable growth. Also, the selection of migrants – whether by family decision (or, as in many cases in Africa, by clan heads) or at the behest of employers – tends to cream off some of the most enterprising and innovative workers of the sending country. As a result, both future economic growth and job creation could seriously suffer, especially in a country with a narrow human capital base.

The negative consequences of labour outflows on output and eventually on employment could be particularly disturbing when several types of outflows occur at the same time, causing production bottlenecks and economic dislocation. The immediate production and employment losses can be compounded by population redistribution, dislocation of inter-firm and inter-industry linkages and their

16. *See particularly the chapter "Migration and Poverty: Some Issues in the Context of Asia".*

negative spread effect. Empirical evidence in some countries, for example Pakistan in the 1970s and Jordan in the 1980s, also shows how labour outflows can create temporary labour shortages in certain industries or high emigration areas. This can lead to a substitution of capital for labour in the production process, reducing labour demand and thus job opportunities.

Some of the direct consequences of emigration on the labour market can have second-round effects owing to changes in the social and family structure of the sending country. Just as labour outflows can encourage the use of unemployed labour, they can also draw new people into the labour market, especially at the lower end. Examples include increased female participation in the labour force in the Philippines, Indonesia and Sri Lanka, and the Sahelian countries in Africa. In Yemen, following labour migration in the 1980s, children were inducted to fill the jobs previously handled by adult workers. In some countries, labour migration has also been found to encourage increased spatial mobility of the domestic labour force. When there are social or spatial barriers to such mobility, unemployment and labour shortages can co-exist in the same country (Ghosh, 1996).

How does emigration affect wages? Although in theory labour emigration should lead to a rise in real wages, in most developing countries this may not happen, since, as already noted, they generally suffer from a large backlog of unemployed and under-employed. This is one reason why employers normally do not oppose labour emigration. However, if large-scale emigration leads to temporary labour shortages in specific industries or high emigration areas, it could, at least temporarily, lead to a sharp rise in wages, as happened for example in Yemen between 1975 and 1977, and in Pakistan in the late 1970s (Ghosh, 1997).

SKILL MIGRATION: TURNING BRAIN DRAIN INTO BRAIN GAIN AND BRAIN CIRCULATION

Skill migration, a hotly debated issue in the 1960s and 1970s, has once more moved sharply up the migration agenda (see the next chapter). Globalization, including fast-evolving technological change, ascendancy of knowledge- and skill-based service industries, and intense market competition, have led to a worldwide scramble for skills. Although this concern is also shared by most industrial countries, poor nations are particularly worried about losing their best talents to rich countries with selective immigration policies for skilled workers. But the new global changes are gradually shifting skill migration away from its fixed, unidirectional pattern, which, in the past, generally resulted in a permanent loss of talent for the home country, into a new transnational model of skills sharing.

A recent estimate suggested that some 400,000 scientists and engineers from developing countries (between 30 and 50% of the total stock) were working in research and development in the industrial countries, compared with around 1.2 million doing the same at home (Meyer and Brown, 1999). In the US, immigrants from several developing countries had twice as much education as their counterparts at home in 1999 (ILO 2004). An extreme case is that of Jamaica in 2000, when there were nearly four times more Jamaicans with tertiary education in the US than at home. The percentage of such migrants in the US from several Central American countries – El Salvador, Guatemala and the Dominican Republic – varied roughly between 25 and 40 per cent of those at home (see Table 8.1). More Ethiopian doctors are practising in Chicago than in Ethiopia.

TABLE 8.1

MIGRANTS TO THE US BY LEVEL OF EDUCATION RELATIVE TO SIMILARLY EDUCATED COHORTS REMAINING AT HOME, 2000 (IN PERCENTAGES)

Country		Educational level		
	Total	Primary or less	Secondary	Tertiary
East Asia				
China	0.1	0.1	0.2	2.2
Indonesia	0.1	0.1	0.1	0.7
Philippines	3.6	0.6	2.2	11.7
Eastern Europe, Central Asia				
Croatia	1.2	0.4	1.2	4.7
Turkey	0.2	0.1	0.4	1.3
Latin America and the Caribbean				
Brazil	0.2	0.1	0.5	1.1
Colombia	2.1	0.4	4	9.9
Dominican Republic	12.9	5.3	42.4	24.8
El Salvador	24.3	12.4	114.8	39.5
Guatemala	7.6	3.8	29.9	25.8
Jamaica	33.3	4.7	40.9	367.6
Mexico	13.3	10.8	17.2	16.5
Peru	1.8	0.3	2.5	4.2
Middle East, North Africa				
Egypt	0.3	0.1	0.2	2.3
Tunisia	0.1	0.1	0.2	1.3
South Asia				
Bangladesh	0.1	0.1	0.3	2.3
India	0.2	0.1	0.2	2.8
Pakistan	0.3	0.1	0.5	6.4
Sri Lanka	0.2	0.1	0.1	5.6
Sub-Saharan Africa				
Sudan	0.1	0.1	0.3	3.4

Note: Immigrants defined as foreign-born population in the US aged 25 years or over ; primary education or less corresponds to 0-8 years of schooling, secondary to 9-12 years of schooling ; and tertiary to more than 12 years of schooling. Percentages represent ratio of numbers living in the US over those living at home with same educational attainment.

Source:
Reproduced from table 5, R.H. Adams : International Migration Remittances and the Brain Drain : A study of 24 labour-exporting countries, Working Paper No. 3069, 27 May 2003.

A disquieting aspect of skill migration from developing countries is that skilled individuals are disproportionately high among those who leave. Some 12 per cent of Mexico's labour force is in the US, but 30 per cent of Mexicans with PhDs are among these migrants. OECD estimates that between 1990 and 1999 the stay rates of foreign science and engineering PhD graduates in the US were as high as 87 per cent for China, and 82 per cent for India, followed by Britain (79%), Taiwan, China (57%) and the Republic of Korea (39%) (OECD, 2002b).

BRAIN DRAIN, REVERSE TRANSFER OF TECHNOLOGY AND POVERTY

Skilled labour is both a complement to, and an embodiment of, technology and capital. Not only does it have a cumulative or multiplier effect on production and economic growth, but it also has an impact on the pace and prospects of technological innovation and future human capital development. It is this nexus between human skills and technology that led the 1972 UNCTAD III conference to describe developing countries' "loss of brains" to developed countries as "reverse transfer of technology". A recent survey covering 14 countries revealed a clear link between skills development and a rise in both labour productivity and GDP growth (Coulombe et al., 2004). Given their importance as a key factor in production and growth, the outflow of skills, if not easily replaceable, may ultimately lead a fragile economy into stagnation, with a lowering of average incomes of the resident population. At the same time, the redistribution of income in favour of the skilled workers resulting from their outflows, may depress wages of unskilled workers. It can thus lead to a deterioration of income distribution, and aggravate poverty in the sending countries.

Long-term or permanent emigration of skilled individuals can involve a loss of large amounts of public funds directly and indirectly invested in them. South Africa claims to have spent USD 1 billion educating health workers who migrated – the equivalent of one-third of all development aid received between 1994 and 2000. In Ghana and Zimbabwe, three-quarters of all doctors leave within a few years of completing medical school (*Financial Times*, 16 July 2004).[17] The full magnitude of such losses cannot be easily estimated, but the gains for receiving countries are obvious.[18]

Rich nations' policies of draining scarce and expensive human resources from poor countries, which aggravate global inequality, have also been criticized on ethical grounds. Skill migration boosts the tax revenues of receiving countries, but depletes them in the sending countries. A study at Harvard University showed that the one million Indians living in the US accounted for 0.1 per cent of India's population but earned the equivalent of 10 per cent of India's national income. In India, their income would have been less, but they would still have been among the highest taxpayers[19] (Desai et al., 2001). The 50 million Chinese who live outside China (including Taiwan Province of China) earn an annual income equivalent to two-thirds of China's gross domestic product (Devan and Tewari, 2001).

BRAIN DRAIN, BRAIN OVERFLOW OR OPTIMAL BRAIN OUTFLOW?

There are also some well known counter arguments to the above approach. Since skill migration is not the cause but a consequence of lack of job opportunities, the phenomenon should be seen, it is argued, more as a "brain overflow" than a "brain drain". From this perspective, the outward movements actually reduce the supply-demand gap of skilled workers in sending countries and ensure a more efficient allocation of human resources, from which the world economy gains. It is further argued that the investment in education and training of skilled workers is more in the nature of a sunk cost, and that it is better to have "brain drain" than "brains in the drain". The experience of many European countries is also sometimes cited to counter the criticism of skill migration. Norway, Sweden and the UK in the 19th and early 20th century, and Italy, Spain and Portugal in the 1960s and 1970s sent their skilled (and unskilled) workers abroad, but none of them became the poorer as a result. Finally, there is the argument of the individual's freedom of movement and the right to market one's talent in the world market.

OPTIMAL BRAIN DRAIN?

Goldfarb, Havrylyshyn and Magnum (1984) used a model to analyse the impact of skill migration, in conjunction with the effects of remittances, in the case of Filipino physicians moving to the US. Their findings, based on a set of reasonable assumptions about the income differential between the US and the Philippines, the proportion of the US income to be sent to the Philippines, the multiplier effects and other relevant factors, were that those who remain will

17. *"Exodus of medical staff hampers aids programmes", based on a report by Physicians for Human Rights, presented at the International Aids Conference in Bangkok.*

18. *The UN Conference on Trade and Development (UNCTAD) estimates that for each developing country professional aged between 25 and 35 years, USD 184,000 is saved in training costs by developed countries. Considering that the 27 OECD countries have a workforce of approx. 3 million professionals educated in developing countries, this could result in a staggering USD 552 billion savings for the OECD countries (cited in Meeus and Sanders' presentation "Pull factors in international migration of health professionals'" at the Public Health 2003 Conference, Cape Town, 24-26 March, 2003.*

19. *As mentioned in the section on remittances, the fiscal loss is currently more than offset by the remittance flows to India.*

benefit from the physicians' emigration. More recent econometric analyses have put forward the concept of "optimal brain drain". They show that countries with emigration of over 20 per cent of all persons with tertiary education, and low levels of education (e.g. El Salvador, French Guyana, Jamaica, and Trinidad and Tobago), would benefit from reduced skilled emigration. On the other hand, countries with low levels of adult education and low emigration rates (e.g. Brazil and China) would benefit from increased skill emigration (Lowell, et al., 2004).

For countries with a broad and flexible human resources base and the capacity to easily replace the outflows, skill migration is not a major problem. However, when poor countries that are short of human capital lose some of their most talented workers, this can be a major impediment to future economic growth and technological progress. In Sub-Saharan Africa, as in the Caribbean and several countries in Latin America, the initial cost of skill migration has been compounded by a second round of negative effects, undermining the training of the intermediary cadres and inhibiting product and process innovation (Ghosh, 1996; Papademetriou et al., 1991).

Even for countries with a broader human resources base skill migration can create temporary skills shortages in specific sectors and occupations, and if these occur in key sectors, the problem can be more serious, as found in Sri Lanka, Jordan and Turkey.[20] On the other hand, sector-specific experience in several countries, including Pakistan and the Philippines, has shown that when skills can be rapidly replaced and the production processes easily adjusted, the losses from skill migration could be marginal (Ghosh, 1996).

In the past, a few countries tried to restrict skill migration, with little success. Others have sought to levy a tax on the migrant, and this, too, has had few positive results. It was also proposed to set up a global fund with contributions from skill-receiving countries to compensate for the loss suffered by the countries of origin, but it never took off. A more promising, but still problematic approach is to work out bilateral arrangements for sharing taxes paid by the skilled developing country expatriates. An alternative, but also doubtful approach is to give a "talent tax credit" to local companies employing workers returning from abroad (Devan, et al., 2001).

An excessive outflow of skills from a developing country often reflects the supply-demand gap of skilled workers. The response is either to reform the education and training system, or to increase the demand for skilled workers by creating opportunities for jobs through increased foreign and domestic investment. Interstate wage differentials, while important, are not necessarily a decisive factor in all circumstances. A 1999 global survey showed that, regardless of their stage of development, countries with an unfavourable future economic outlook tend to experience outflows of qualified people (IMD, 1999). This applies to a country's political and cultural environment as well. Scientists, academics and high-level researchers in particular, cherish intellectual freedom. As past experience has shown in countries like Argentina and Chile in Latin America or Ghana, Nigeria and Uganda in Africa, when political oppression and human rights abuse create a stifling intellectual and cultural environment, improvement of earnings or physical working conditions alone do not arrest the outflows of high-level talent (Adepoju, 1991; Ghosh, 1992).

TURNING BRAIN LOSS INTO BRAIN CIRCULATION

But skill migration need not be seen as a permanent loss for the sending country. Recent global changes, including closer economic and market integration, and spectacular progress in information and communication systems, make it possible for the

20. *In Sri Lanka, the loss of construction and engineering skills at the height of labour migration to the Gulf States led to a decline in output and delays in project implementation. Many small firms lost their workers to larger enterprises, involving the transfer of their training costs to the former (Korale et al., 1984). In Jordan, migration of highly skilled workers in the early 1980s and their replacement by rural-urban migration (often at lower levels of productivity) caused skill shortages in rural areas. In Turkey, skill migration led to a sudden worsening of safety conditions in mines on the Black Sea coast.*

sending country to establish transnational links with its diaspora and tap its skills and talents. A new pattern of increased transnational mobility of skilled personnel is thus emerging, presaging better sharing of knowledge and talents among nations.[21] International organizations, for example UNDP through its TOKTEN and IOM through its MIDA programmes, are facilitating temporary visits by qualified expatriates without requiring their permanent return, to help countries of origin meet their skills requirements.[22]

The potential available resources of the transnational diaspora network for the home countries are not limited to knowledge and talents; they are also a source of investment and new technology, market intelligence and business contacts. The diaspora can be a bridgehead for the penetration by home country enterprises of the markets of the host country, as exemplified by Korean Americans who helped to open markets in the US for Korean automobile, electronics and other industries (OECD, 2002 b).

However, only few countries have so far tapped the full potential of the diaspora network, and its impact has generally been limited to certain sectors. Its role in the development of the country of origin should not be taken for granted. Building transnational links is a two-way process. The home country environment needs to be friendly and supportive if expatriates are to be actively engaged in its development. Emotional bonds and nostalgia are important, but not sufficient for the purpose. The diaspora, if it holds key positions in transnational corporations (TNCs), can influence company decisions to set up operations in the country of origin, as Indian expatriates working in Hewlett Packard have done (Biers and Dhume, 2000). Some companies are recruiting young developing country graduates abroad and, after further training, post them in their country of origin to better exploit local market opportunities (*Financial Times*, 1 July 2004).

All this is unlikely unless, in addition to market openness, the country can provide macroeconomic stability, good governance, basic infrastructure and a generally favourable investment climate. Closer cooperation between migrant sending and migrant receiving countries, including mutual recognition of dual nationality and other rights and obligations of the migrants, can be of significant help.

BRAIN GAIN THOUGH TRADE-RELATED TEMPORARY MOVEMENT OF SKILLED PERSONS

A new and promising, but still largely unexploited approach to turn brain drain into brain gain lies in the freer temporary movement of persons providing skills and knowledge-intensive services across borders. Balance-of-payments data show that many developing countries have a "revealed comparative advantage", i.e. the ratio of a given export item to a country's total exports, divided by a similar ratio for the world, in a variety of sectors, including engineering, accounting, law, management consulting, nursing, software development and data processing. The same comparative advantage largely explains the increasing interest by industrial countries' service industries in outsourcing high-skilled jobs to developing countries (*Financial Times*, 31 March 2004).

The rapid development of these services and their increased exports in the global markets can give a powerful boost to the economy of a sending country and reduce the pressure for skill migration. It requires better market access, including freer temporary movement of persons as a mode or sub-mode of delivery of such services. The WTO's General Agreement on Trade in Services (GATS) provides precisely for such liberalization, although so far government commitments under the agreement are limited. A 1997 study shows that instead of depleting

21. *South Africa and several countries in Latin America have linked expatriate researchers to networks at home, leading to circulation of ideas and knowledge. The Indian government has been encouraging the development of such private networks by supporting organisations and events that actively involve the non-Indian nationals abroad.*

22. *See also the chapter "Enhancing the Benefits of Return Migration for Development".*

human capital such temporary movements among countries can raise the earnings of the skilled individuals involved and help broaden their knowledge and experience, thus leading to a "brain gain" for themselves and their country (Ghosh, 1997).[23] This can raise developing countries' earnings and employment rates, and alleviate long-term or permanent migration pressure. Importing countries also stand to gain from access to such services at lower cost and a more efficient allocation of their resources.

HARNESSING THE DEVELOPMENT POTENTIAL OF REMITTANCES

Remittances are widely seen as a litmus test of the benefits to be derived from migration by the sending country. As the subject is discussed in detail in other chapters of this report,[24] only a few points related to the development impact of remittances are highlighted here (Ghosh, 2004).

Many analysts use the gross amount of remittances to developing countries to highlight their importance relative to official development assistance and other financial flows. But this is misleading, since the gross figures do not take into account the transfers migrants make to rich countries, and those that take place between developing countries. When these "reverse flows" are taken into account, the net amount received by developing countries is much smaller – in 2002, around USD 50 billion, compared to the official gross amount of USD 93 billion.[25] On the other hand, the actual remittances to developing countries far exceed the amount officially recorded as many transfers take place through unofficial channels. No one knows the exact amounts involved, but an earlier study covering 11 different countries estimated that the unofficial transfers may, on average, represent 36 per cent of total flows[26] (Puri and Ritzema, 1999).

Remittances are not necessarily a net addition to the household budget or the economy. The opportunity cost of emigration – the possible earnings forgone in the home country if the migrant had stayed at home, and the output loss to the economy, needs to be taken into account, too. But, as other chapters show, migrants make their own rational cost-benefit calculations (Ghosh 1996, 2004) and, besides the high personal consumption fuelled by remittances, by boosting the household budget they also promote children's schooling, better health, housing and family welfare, and, hence, future human capital development (Ghosh, 1996).

High transfer costs reduce the size and thus the development impact of the flows. But this problem is being increasingly addressed and the costs, which can be as high as 20 per cent of the sum being remitted, are falling for some regions, such as Latin America (IADB, 2003). The later chapter "Migrant Remittances as a Source of Development Finance" explores measures to lower these costs and ensure the security of transfers.[27]

The criticism that remittances do not generally find their way into productive investments, first, because remittances are not capital flows, but rather a contribution to family income and, second, because of the migrants' alleged general lack of familiarity with investment instruments, is largely flawed. As demonstrated in the chapter "Migration and Poverty: some Issues in the Context of Asia", recipients of international remittances have a high propensity to save. Remittances can also open the way to credit for use as investment capital. When made through credit co-operatives or community-based microfinance institutions, they provide valuable capital for small business. By creating new demand for labour-intensive goods and services, they can boost

23. *The study also recommends a special, multilaterally harmonized visa regime both as a facilitating and a monitoring tool for such trade-related temporary movements.*

24. *See the chapters "Migrant Remittances as a Source of Development Finance" and "Economic Costs and Benefits of International Labour Migration".*

25. *Estimated on the basis of IMF balance of payment statistics (IMF, 2003).*

26. *The claim made by some transfer agencies that unrecorded remittances may be larger than official transfers seems exaggerated.*

27. *These can include electronic transfers and related innovative devices, such as prepaid debit cards, transfer agencies' easier access to state-owned service networks and development of credit unions (as already seen in Spain and Portugal) and community-based microfinance institutions.*

aggregate demand and therefore output and income, with a multiplier effect as high as 1: 3 or even more (in Bangladesh, for example, it was 3.3 for GNP, 2.8 for consumption and 0.4 for investment (Van Doorn, 2003)).

Remittances can help local community development projects and businesses in the home country and, as the chapter "Migrant Hometown Associations: the Human Face of Globalization" shows, migrant associations in the host country are increasingly active in pooling migrant funds and raising additional means from external sources to support such projects. For instance, the government of Mexico, among others, actively encourages the development of social assets through matching contributions.

Remittances are a valuable addition to GNP, an important source of foreign exchange (especially for small countries) and can alleviate temporary foreign exchange difficulties, but it is doubtful that they serve as a driving force for trade policy or economic reform. The overall development impact of remittances at the macro level has so far been less impressive than at the household or local community level. Cross-country comparisons do not show any direct correlation between inflows of remittances and economic performance.

In recent years, remittances have proven more stable than other forms of private financial flows to developing countries,[28] opening up the possibility of raising external funds by securitizing future flows, as is being done in Brazil, El Salvador, Mexico, Panama and Turkey (Ghosh, 2004; Ketkar and Ratha, 2001). They generally also have an anti-cyclical economic effect. Even so, undue reliance on remittances as an engine of development may be unwise, and could make emigration-dependent countries vulnerable to external shocks.[29] Excessive reliance on remittances to finance development can also be self-defeating, if necessary, but often politically painful structural reforms are postponed or avoided, as may have happened in some of the remittance-receiving eastern Mediterranean countries in the 1960s and 1970s (Korner, 1987).

Do remittances reduce poverty and inequality? A recent study covering 74 low and middle-income countries indicated a positive correlation between remittances and poverty alleviation. According to the findings, a 10 per cent increase in the share of remittances in country GDP would lead to a 1.2 per cent decrease in the percentage of persons living on less than USD 1 a day, and also reduce the depth or severity of poverty (Adams and Page, 2003).[30] The available evidence of the impact on equality is inconclusive. Some studies show that remittances have an equalizing effect on income distribution in Mexico (Taylor, 1999). In contrast, others found that, to the contrary, international remittances increased rural-urban inequality and economic asymmetry in Mexico, and also in Egypt (McCormick and Wahaba, 2002; Rubenstein, 1992). This finding is probably partly explained by the original (pre-migration) income levels and the location of the migrant households. To the extent that migrants come from above-average income households, remittances may exacerbate income inequality.

BENEFITS OF MIGRANT RETURN

Do sending countries gain from improved human capital when their migrants return? The answer could be positive, provided three main conditions are met: a) migrants return with more, or better skills than they would have acquired at home; b) the skills acquired abroad are relevant to the needs of the home country economy, and c) the migrants are willing and able to use the skills upon return. Empirical evidence

28. *See also the chapter "Migrant Remittances as a Source of Development Finance".*

29. *For example, Egypt faced a difficult budgetary situation when 1.5 million Egyptian workers and their dependants were suddenly repatriated during the 1991 Gulf crisis; and Turkey's 1973-77 Five Year Plan, which had anticipated an export of 350,000 labour migrants was in a shambles when western Europe put a sudden halt to labour immigration in the mid-1970s.*

30. *For an indication of the volatility of annual remittance flows to selected African countries, see IOM* World Migration Report *2003, Table 12.3. What is, however, less clear is how and to what extent the decline in poverty is influenced by the effects of remittances-induced economic growth and its distribution.*

suggests that only in a few cases are these conditions fully met (Ghosh, 1996).

Studies on return migration in several countries, including Greece and Turkey, show that more skilled and successful migrants are generally better integrated in the receiving society and hence less likely to return. Data relating to other migrants, such as e.g. from Bangladesh and Sri Lanka in the Gulf States, provide little evidence of skills upgrading during their stay abroad. On the contrary, available though limited evidence suggests that at least in a few cases there was actually some downgrading or de-skilling of migrants, as was also the case in regard to some Turkish workers in Germany during 1960-73. In such situations it is not just the immigrants but also the host country that fails to reap full benefits from the available human capital.

Moreover, new skills acquired by the migrants abroad are not always adaptable to local conditions. In Pakistan, 81 per cent of returnees and 84 per cent of employers felt that the skills acquired during overseas employment were largely irrelevant (Adams, 1998). Finally, when migrants return to the country of origin, they are not always willing to accept new challenges in the industrial sector. A general tendency among many returnees is to set up their own business or simply opt for retirement. The few who would like to take up the challenge have often been disillusioned by the negative attitude, even resistance shown by members of the local community, and have been handicapped by the lack of support and guidance of public authorities.

Even so, the benefits of return must not be completely discounted. The experiences of a significant number of countries, e.g., Colombia and Mexico in Latin America, Bangladesh, India, Pakistan and Sri Lanka in South Asia and Greece and Turkey in Europe, show that return migration can be a powerful factor for modernization and social change in small towns and villages, despite occasional tension in the initial stages. In several East African countries, return migration has contributed significantly to the growth of small business enterprises, the construction of modern houses and roads and overall development of local communities. Indian and Taiwanese returnees from Silicon Valley in the US have been a main driving force for the growth of the software industry in India and Taiwan, following liberalization[31] (*The Economist*, 28 September 2002; Luo and Wang, 2001; Ghosh, 1996).

As the past experiences of several southern European countries demonstrate, when conditions in the home country improve, the more enterprising and innovative migrants tend to return and participate in national development. This has already been happening in several East Asian countries, while similar prospects are opening up in Central European countries, such as Hungary and Poland. As suggested earlier, highly skilled and otherwise successful migrants can pay frequent short visits to the country of origin, without having to contemplate permanent return. Such multiple short visits are more problematic for unskilled or low-skilled migrants, especially if they do not have residence visas or citizenship status in the host country. They may even fear being denied re-entry once they leave.

A different kind of problem is faced by contract workers as they return home at the end of their contract period and have to wait for an indefinite period before getting new offers for jobs abroad, as, for instance in the case of Indian migrants from Kerala working in the Gulf states. Since they may have difficulty in getting jobs in the local market or a new contract abroad, they need special assistance (e.g. accelerated retraining to meet new skill needs).

Then there is the additional complex problem of voluntary and forced return of rejected asylum seekers and irregular migrants, and temporary refugees. This has serious implication for development, but is insufficiently discussed in

31. *Of the 312 companies in the Hsinchu industrial park near Taipei, 113 have been started by UDS-educated engineers with professional experience in Silicon Valley, where 70 of the park's companies have offices to pick up new recruits and ideas,* The Economist, *28 September 2002.*

existing migration literature, with the notable exception of the work done in this area by IOM (IOM, 2004).

HOW DOES DEVELOPMENT AFFECT MIGRATION?

To what extent can the economic development of sending countries contribute to managing migration? The basic objective of migration management is not to eliminate migration altogether.[32] Rather, the goal should be to make movement of people more orderly, safe and humane, and to ensure that it is voluntary. Greater economic convergence between countries should no doubt lower emigration pressure; it is also a welcome objective on ethical and other grounds. But, there are two important reasons why global economic convergence should not be overstated as a means of managing migration:

a) The income disparity, in dollar terms, between rich and poor countries has been increasing rather than decreasing, and the prospect of closing the gap in the near to medium term is slim. At its present GDP growth rate, it would take India some 62 years to reach the current per capita income of the US. If India grows at its pre-1980 rate, it would take 246 years (*Financial Times*, 17 August, 2004).[33] In terms of purchasing power parity (PPP), which is a better index of the real welfare situation, the gap is much smaller,[34] but it is still too large to be eliminated in the near term. Average per capita income figures do not, however, take into account the internal income distribution patterns (and therefore do not adequately reflect the real individual or family welfare gaps between countries). If instead of per capita income, we looked at the wage rates across countries, does the outlook for convergence seem any more promising? Clearly not. It has been estimated that average wages for similarly qualified workers in rich countries were 10 times higher or more than in poor countries (Rodrik, 2002).[35]

b) Income differential is clearly an important factor in international migration, but not the only one.[36] As one UN study observed, in the majority of cases, large wage differentials do not by themselves trigger migration. Indeed, a striking feature of international migration is that in the aggregate, its responsiveness to international income and wage differences is very low (UN, 1997). Moreover, historical and contemporary evidence demonstrates that when a migrant-sending country is successfully engaged in broad-based development involving job creation and economic growth, and people feel that things will improve for themselves and their children, migration pressure declines and it may even trigger some return migration despite higher earnings abroad. Clearly, it is the rate of economic growth and its fair distribution in the population rather than the absolute level of income that is of importance for the effective management of migration.[37]

This leads the discussion to another issue related to the development-migration nexus, namely the so-called migration hump theory, which argues that

32. *Clearly, the "right to stay" does not imply that people should never move.*

33. Financial Times, *17 August 2004. Similarly, an estimate made in 1994 suggested that even at three times the per capita GDP increase in the countries of Central America, it would take 150 years to overcome the income disparity between these countries and the US (Weintraub and Diaz- Briquets, 1994).*

34. *The ratio between high income and middle-income countries is: 27: 5.7 or less than 5 times and between high income and low income countries is 27:2 or slightly less than 14 times.*

35. *The World Bank estimated that the ratio between the wages of the richest and the poorest groups in the international wage hierarchy - skilled industrial country workers and African farmers - was 60:1 in 1992 and that it could rise to 70 by 2010, if things were to go badly,* World Development Report *1995.*

36. *See also the chapter "Economic Costs and Benefits of International Labour Migration".*

37. *Establishing a fixed threshold in terms of per capita income or international income disparity for migration transition to take hold (that is, for emigration to stabilize) is an elusive goal. Based on the experience in Western Europe in certain periods it is sometimes argued (see the chapter "Economic Costs and Benefits of International Labour Migration") that when interstate disparity is reduced to about 4/5:1, emigration pressure tends to decline. But this varies widely depending on the numerous other factors involved. Brazil, for example, has a per capita GNP of US 3,060, which is roughly one-tenth that of high-income countries; and yet, its net annual migration is nil. Aside from questions of distance and the direct and indirect cost of the move, the anticipated delay in getting a job in the destination country as well as the risks of subsequently losing it must be taken into account, alongside the question of access (or its absence) to unemployment benefits at home and abroad.*

development may be the only effective means of reducing emigration pressure, even though initially it would stimulate more migration. The transition period of high emigration – the "migration hump" – is supposed to span many years, even generations, for the process to run its course and turn full cycle.[38] But more needs to be known about the nature of the interactive process, the different variables that influence it and the time element involved for policymakers to be able to effectively use this paradigm.

While western and northern Europe's transition from emigration to immigration was the result of development sustained over several generations, newly industrializing economies in Asia, e.g. Singapore, Malaysia and, more recently, South Korea and Thailand, have brought emigration under control in less than 15 years and, in some cases, in only 10 years. The story of the erstwhile emigration countries of southern Europe is not much different. In the wake of the accelerating expansion of tourism and off-shore banking activities in the Caribbean, the turnaround was rapid in several island countries, such as the Bahamas, the Cayman Islands and the US Virgin Islands. Indeed, in some cases, it may have been too rapid and, instead of emigration pressure, excessive immigration has emerged as a serious problem.

To judge from available indications, the time element in the transition does not seem to be an independent variable, but rather closely correlated to the applied development strategy, and the causes of existing migration. It is also likely that the development strategy influences the types and characteristics of any new flows it may generate.

CONCLUDING REMARKS

THE DISCUSSION above and in other chapters of this section of the Report show how difficult it is to make generalizations about the complex effects of international migration. Existing knowledge bases are fragile and fragmentary and, combined with the lack of an adequate theoretical or empirical framework, increase the difficulty of assessing these effects properly. This can also feed the politicization of migration issues and polarize the debate.

Many of the receiving industrial countries' immigration-related concerns over jobs, wages and increased public welfare cost are exaggerated or ill founded. They are heightened by the fear that migration is getting out of control. Such fears are likely to remain unabated, unless the rising emigration pressure in most developing countries, and the opportunities for legal entry into destination countries, are brought into a dynamic equilibrium. This calls for closer international cooperation based on agreed principles and practices, that balance and harmonize the needs and interests of both groups of countries, and the migrants themselves (Ghosh, 2000).

In the past, migration-related issues, including the benefits and costs of migration, have often been perceived as an area where the interests of sending and receiving countries are largely in conflict. The framework used for assessing the benefits and costs has been narrowly unilateral. However, with migration becoming an integral part of global integration this needs to be changed to one of cooperation and partnership. A transnational framework is now more suitable to capture the benefits and costs of migration, as reflected in the discussion in this chapter on skill migration, remittances and return.

38. *See the discussion in the chapter "Economic Costs and Benefits of International Labour Migration" based on the findings of the 1990 US Commission for the Study of International Migration and Cooperative Development.*

A wider framework is also needed to assess the effects of the interaction between migration and other economic flows, such as trade and investment. The recognition of such interaction will help ensure adequate policy coordination between migration and other related fields, both domestically and internationally. Migration will be better factored into development policies.

Achieving global economic convergence, however desirable an objective, is not an essential pre-condition for effective migration management. What is needed is for migrant-sending countries to be engaged in dynamic and broad-based development, combining job creation and economic growth with a fairer distribution of income, thereby generating general optimism about the future of the country. The effective support by industrial countries of these efforts will enhance this process and contribute to its success.

LABOUR MIGRATION

CHAPTER 9
ECONOMIC COSTS AND BENEFITS OF INTERNATIONAL LABOUR MIGRATION[1]

Even a marginal liberalization of international labour flows would create gains for the world economy that are far larger than prospective gains from trade liberalization.

INTRODUCTION

LABOUR migration does not lend itself to an easy cost-benefit analysis, in part because of the immeasurable aspects of migration, such as integration "costs". The benefits of foreign labourers may be immediate and relatively easy to measure in terms of jobs filled, wages paid and economic output, but there can be disagreement over whether more diversity is either a benefit or cost, or whether educating the children of migrant workers is a pure cost or a productive investment in their future. For these and other reasons, optimal migration frameworks and flows are likely to vary over time and between regions.

This chapter discusses some of the key economic factors regarding international labour migration - the enduring economic disparities between countries that drive labour migration, the positive and negative impacts on sending and receiving countries, and also globally, and the migration policies that can ultimately help alleviate the very disparities that are one of the causes of labour migration, and the negative impacts. It poses some overarching policy questions for governments, including whether, and if so, what level of migration between developing and developed countries could be optimal, in whose interest international migration for employment should be managed, and whether labour migration management agreements should be bilateral, regional, or global.

Four major topics are covered: i) economic reasons for migration, ii) the economic impacts of migration in receiving countries, iii) its economic impact in the country of origin, and iv) the relationship of development and migration. The conclusion emphasizes that the "natural" solution to shrinking labour forces in developed countries and growing labour forces in developing countries is managed labour migration, which generally benefits individuals and the receiving countries. Underlying this is the danger that migration could lead to economic divergence instead of convergence, e.g. where some countries become "nurseries" and "nursing homes", when their working-age population goes abroad in search of jobs. Avoiding a world in which the long-run comparative advantage to some countries of this arrangement brings too high a cost for others adds urgency to the quest for a better migration management framework.

ECONOMIC IMPULSES FROM MIGRATION

IN AN IDEAL world, there would be little unwanted migration and few migration barriers. People move for many reasons, but economic differentials are still the main determinants of migration from developing

1. *The author of this chapter is Professor Philip Martin, Department of Agriculture and Resource Economics, University of California, Davis, CA 95616, plmartin@ucdavis,edu*

to developed countries (Ellerman, 2003). To achieve such an ideal world would require a greater reduction of economic differences between countries that encourage people to migrate than is at present the case. Governments and international organizations are striving to reduce these differences and, using migration, managed properly, as one means to speed development and convergence.

Experience shows that once per capita income differentials are reduced to about 4:1 or 5:1, as when per capita income is USD 20,000 in the receiving country, and USD 4,000 - USD 5,000 in the sending country combined with a higher economic and job growth rate, the anticipation of continued economic improvement would keep most persons, who might otherwise consider crossing national borders for economic reasons, at home.[2] Other factors also stimulate international migration for employment, including, e.g, relative deprivation, that is, individuals are not necessarily absolutely poor, but feel poor in comparison to others, for instance, when families with a migrant abroad are able to acquire additional valuable (and status-boosting) consumer items, such as a TV, stimulate other families to also send out migrants to keep up; or where some misfortune, such as a failed crop or a health emergency prompts emigration to bring quick money for survival or to repay an unexpected bill (Taylor and Martin, 2001).

But, we do not live in a world where per capita income differentials between countries tend to be reduced substantially. Instead, economic differences between many states are widening, increasing the motivation for international labour migration. Though the world's GDP was USD 30 trillion in 2000, yielding an average annual per capita income of USD 5,000, the actual income levels ranged from USD 100 per person per year in Ethiopia to USD 38,000 in Switzerland, a 380:1 difference. When countries are ranked according to per capita GDP and tracked over time, it becomes apparent that the gap between high-income countries (USD 9,300 or more per person per annum) and low-income countries (below USD 750 per person per annum) and middle-income countries (USD 750 to USD 9,300 per person per annum) has been widening, and that very few low and middle-income countries were able to climb into the high-income ranks over the past quarter of a century.[3]

Per capita GDP in the high-income countries in 1975 was on average 41 times higher than in low-income countries, and 8 times higher than in middle-income countries, but by 2000, high-income countries had a per capita GDP 66 times that of low-income countries and 14 times those in middle-income countries.[4] It should be emphasized that per capita income differentials by themselves do not necessarily trigger migration flows, but once they are started, flows tend to stop "naturally" when income differentials narrow to 4:1 or 5:1.

2. *There are exceptions to this, and important reasons for them. For example, Brazil has a per capita GNP of USD 3,060, roughly only one-ninth the per capita income of high income countries, but generates relatively few emigrants. The richest Brazilians who could get visas to migrate have much higher-than-average incomes, and are likely to remain at home, and poorer Brazilians have less opportunity to access higher-income countries. There is a significant migration of over 200,000 ethnic Japanese Brazilians to Japan for employment (Tsuda, 2003).*

3. *For example, Portugal and South Korea moved from the middle- to the high-income group between 1985 and 1995, while Zimbabwe and Mauritania moved from the middle- to the low-income group (World Bank World Development Reports, various years).*

4. *These numbers would change slightly if per capita income were measured in purchasing power terms, but would still be far more than 4 to 1. Note that inequality can also be measured across individuals rather than countries, e.g. by dividing the world's population of 6.4 billion into quintiles and seeing the share of global income accruing to each 20 per cent. Measuring inequality in this way shows, according to some studies, declining inequality, but largely because of rapid economic growth in a few countries like China and India.*

TABLE 9.1

GLOBAL MIGRANTS AND INCOMES, 1975-2000

	Migrants (mio)	World pop. (bio)	Migrant pop.	Year change (mio)	Countries grouped Av. p.c. GDP (USD) Low	Middle	High	Ratios High-low	High-middle
1975	85	4.1	2.1%	1	150	750	6,200	41	8
1985	105	4.8	2.2%	1	270	1,290	11,810	44	9
1990	154	5.3	2.9%	10	350	2,220	19,590	56	9
1995	164	5.7	2.9%	2	430	2,390	24,930	58	10
2000	175	6.1	2.9%	2	420	1,970	27,510	66	14

Sources:
UN Population Division and World Bank Development Indicators; 1975 income data are 1976. Migrants are defined as persons outside their country of birth or citizenship for 12 months or more. The estimate for 1990 was raised from 120 million to 154 million, largely to reflect the break-up of the former Soviet Union.

There is another dimension to the economic differences between states that contribute to international migration pressures. Agriculture remains the world's major employer, accounting for 43 per cent of the world's 3 billion workers. In poorer countries, where farmers account for the majority of labourers, those with below-average incomes are often taxed. In contrast, the relatively few farmers in rich countries are often subsidized to a point where they earn above-average incomes.[5] Low farm incomes in developing countries encourage rural-urban migration and international migration, in part because trade barriers for farm products sustain a demand for migrants in more developed countries, while reducing farm prices and farm employment in developing countries. The so-called "great migration" off the land in developing countries provides a ready supply of workers willing to accept "3D" (dirty, dangerous, difficult) jobs inside their countries, as in the People's Republic of China, or abroad, as when Mexicans migrate to the US.

Demographic differences also contribute to migration pressures. Developing countries add over 40 million workers to their labour force each year, while there is slow or no labour force growth in developed countries, where two-thirds of workers are employed in service industries. Labour costs are a high share of production costs in most service industries, encouraging some employers to turn to migrants to hold down costs, while others move the jobs offshore, or outsource them, to lower-wage countries. If current trends continue, many developed countries will experience a shrinking work force, while many developing countries will continue to have high levels of under unemployment. To maintain the labour supply in developed countries, workers could work more hours, more women could be induced to join the work force, retirement could be delayed to reflect longer lives, or migrants could be admitted to stabilize work forces at current levels. Some or all of these are being tried in many developed countries.

The role migration should or could play in this mix of policy options to stabilize the labour force and social security systems in developed nations is the subject of much debate. Migrants will clearly play a role, and most industrial countries have already made it easier for foreign students to enter, and graduates to remain as workers and settlers,[6] and have opened immigration doors more widely for highly skilled and professional migrants. However, most unemployed and under-

5. *The OECD reported that farmers in rich countries received USD 257 billion in subsidies and payments in 2003, making subsidies equivalent to a third of farm sales. But this varies: in Norway, for example, subsidies are the highest share of farm incomes, while in Australia and New Zealand they are the lowest (OECD, 2004).*

6. *For example, the Australian Skilled Migration Programme allows overseas students in the country to change their status to permanent resident and to work in Australia. Today, some 40 per cent of Australia's skilled migrants are drawn from the overseas student caseload, a trend growing also in Canada, the US and Europe, although not on the same scale.*

employed workers in developing countries are unskilled, and there is far more ambiguity in developed countries about their recruitment and settlement.

Since most developing countries welcome the opportunity to export their "excess" unskilled workers in order to relieve unemployment pressures and generate remittances, a critical dialogue is needed between developed and developing countries on the potential impacts of brain drain on development and the conditions under which "brawn drain" migrants can be employed abroad to mutual benefit.

THE ECONOMIC IMPACT OF MIGRATION ON COUNTRIES OF DESTINATION AND ON MIGRANTS

MOST economists welcome migration of all types of workers from lower to higher-wage countries, since it tends to allocate scarce labour resources to their highest value use, allowing maximal global production. In standard economic theory, the overall economic gain from migration in receiving countries are the net income gains to migrants, plus a (small) dividend that accrues to the owners of capital in the host country. Local workers most similar to the migrants tend to lose: their wages may fall, or rise more slowly, or their unemployment rates may rise, but these negative effects tend to be small.

For example, the wage and employment changes in the US due to an influx of migrant workers in the mid-1990s are illustrated in Figure 1. Without migrant workers, the US would be at E, with 125 million US-born workers earning USD 13 an hour. In fact, the US had 15 million migrant workers, which shifted the labour supply to the right, to 140 million at F, and lowered average hourly earnings by 3 per cent to USD 12.60, according to the National Research Council (Smith and Edmonston, 1997).

GRAPH 9.2

THE NET ECONOMIC EFFECTS OF MIGRATION

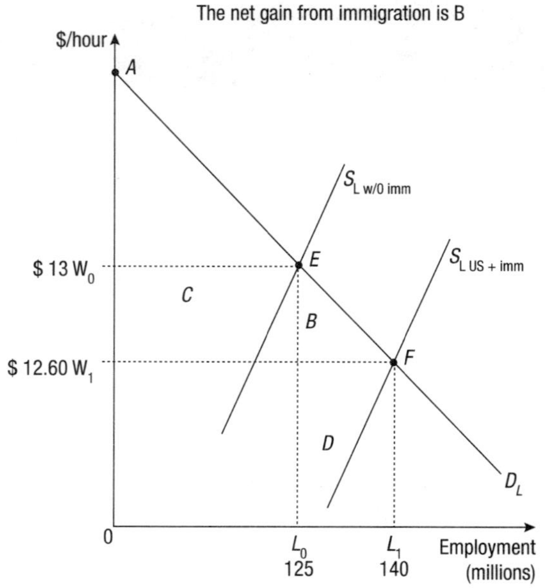

The movement from *E* to *F* creates two rectangles, *C* and *D*, as well as triangle *B*. Rectangle *C* represents the reduced wages paid to US workers. These reduced wages do not disappear into thin air, but are transferred to the (US) owners of capital and land in the form of higher profits and rents. Because of immigration, the US economy expands by rectangle *D* and triangle *B*, with migrant workers getting most of the benefits of this expansion in the form of their wages (*D*).

The net gain from immigration is triangle B, and its size can be estimated in percentage-of-national-income terms as 1/2 × the estimated 3 per cent decrease in US wages due to immigration × 11 per cent immigrant share of US labour force × 70 per cent share of labour in US national income, or 1/2 × 0.002 = 0.001, which means that US national income was about 1/10 of 1 per cent or about USD 8 billion higher in 1997 because of immigration (Smith and Edmonston, 1997).[7]

This economic gain from immigration is small but positive. To put it into perspective, if the USD 8 trillion US economy (1996) grows by two per cent a year, economic output rises by USD 160 billion a year, which means that the gain from immigration was equivalent to about 20 days of "normal" economic growth. The economic gain may be larger if there are positive externalities, as might occur if immigrants are entrepreneurial, or the risk-taking that encouraged them to migrate inspires Americans to work more productively. On the other hand, if there are negative externalities from migration, as when immigration is associated with crime or over-crowded schools, for example, the gains are smaller.

Most of the economic gains from migration accrue to the migrants, whose incomes rise after they cross borders; but there are also flow-on gains for global GDP. For example, if one million foreigners cross borders, and they achieve an average net income gain of USD 10,000, global income rises by USD 10 billion. This was the basis of UNDP's earlier calculations that, if an additional two per cent of the 2.5 billion strong labour force of developing countries in 1990 migrated to industrial countries, there would be 50 million additional migrants (UNDP, 1992). If each migrant earned an average USD 5,000 a year or a total of USD 250 billion, and remitted 20 per cent or USD 50 billion a year to countries of origin, the extra remittances would be equivalent to official development assistance (ODA).

Other estimates of the global economic gains of more migration between developing and developed countries reach similar conclusions. Free migration that equalized the marginal productivity of labour, and had all workers fully employed, and paid the value of their marginal productivity (contribution to economic output), is estimated to potentially more than double global GDP from USD 8 trillion (in 1977), to USD 16 trillion (Hamilton and Whalley, 1984).[8]

This suggests that even small increases in migration can help individuals enjoy higher incomes while significantly raising global GDP. Furthermore, since the first migrants gain the most because they move when the wage gaps between countries are greatest, one economist advises that "even a marginal liberalization of international labour flows would create gains for the world economy" that are far larger than prospective gains from trade liberalization, so that, "if international policy makers were really interested in maximizing worldwide efficiency, they would spend little of their energies on a new trade round or on the international financial architecture. They would all be busy (...) liberalizing immigration restrictions" (Rodrik, 2001).[9]

If economists agree that migration benefits receiving countries and increases global output, why do the richer destination countries keep their doors (at least partially) closed? Migration restrictions are especially surprising when the numbers favour openness - the benefits of migration tend to be immediate, measurable and concentrated, while the costs of migration, if any, tend to be diffuse, deferred and harder to measure. For example it is relatively easy to measure the wages paid and the value of additional output from additional migrant workers, but much harder to measure integration and diversity "costs", since there may not be agreement on which aspects of bilingual education and integrated housing are

7. *The increase in national income due to immigration - triangle B - will be larger if: 1) there are more migrant workers, and/or 2) the wage depression effect of migrant workers is larger. For example, if the migrant wage-depression impact doubled to 6 per cent, and the migrant share of the work force doubled to 22 per cent (e.g. California in the late 1990s), the income would increase due to migration by 1/2 × 0.06 × 0.22 × 0.7 = 0.005, or 5/10 of 1 per cent, four times larger.*

8. *Hamilton and Whalley assumed the world's labour supply was fully employed, producing a single output, and used CES production functions to estimate differences in the marginal productivity of labour across seven multi-country regions - these differences were assumed to be due to migration restrictions. They estimate the efficiency gains that would result from labour moving until MBPS and wages were equalized, that is, they assume factor-price convergence via migration, with workers losing and capital owners gaining in receiving areas and workers gaining and capital owners losing in sending areas. There are many problems with such estimates. For example, the full employment assumption is necessary to claim that wages are determined by marginal productivity; as is the assumption that capital does not move even as labour migrates.*

9. *Rodrik notes that most "artificial" barriers to cross-border flows of goods or capital lead to differences in prices or interest rates of 2 to 1 or less (differences in goods prices of more than 2 to 1 may reflect supply and demand, transportation, risk etc.), while wages for similarly qualified workers vary by 10 to 1 or more.*

benefits and which are costs.[10] The existence of triangle B means that the overall net economic gains from migration are positive, suggesting, much like the case for freer trade, that governments need to educate their residents about the virtues of increased migration and develop ways to compensate its losers.

The benefits and costs of migration are more ambiguous for developing emigration countries, and this ambiguity is reflected in the views of leading economists. At one end of the spectrum are the "internationalists", such as Johnson, who in the 1960s asserted that, because voluntary migration from poorer to richer countries increases the incomes of migrants as well as global income, economically motivated migration is good even if emigration countries are worse off; the global gains from moving workers into higher wage jobs offset any country-specific losses.[11] Johnson believed that there were few negative externalities from emigration for sending countries, and those often discussed could be handled with specific policy changes, such as having students rather than developing country governments pay for higher education, to counter the losses due to brain drain.

The opposite "nationalist" perspective uses the nation-state rather than the individual as the appropriate unit of analysis. Patinkin, for example, argued around the same time that developing countries need a critical mass of talent to achieve an economic take-off, and the emigration of "too much" human capital can keep a country poor, perhaps trapping it in a low-level equilibrium, where people are sustained by remittances, but where there is no stay-at-home development (Patinkin 1968). More recent endogenous growth theories support this perspective, emphasizing the positive externalities and spill-over effects of highly educated people on economic growth, and warning that increased movement of human capital from poorer to richer countries in the 1990s could slow growth in developing countries (Mayer, 1996; Straubhaar, 2000).

To sum up, immigration generally brings economic benefits for individual migrants and receiving countries, measurable in monetary terms. However, the benefits are relatively small, and tend to be concentrated among the relatively well off, who own capital in receiving countries. This, in combination with the already difficult socio-economic adjustments faced by immigrants, their families and the host communities, can make immigration very controversial.

Clearly, individual migrants benefit by moving elsewhere for higher wages; but it is less clear if their countries of origin benefit from the loss of human capital associated with their emigration.

THE ECONOMIC AND DEVELOPMENT IMPACT OF MIGRATION IN THE COUNTRY OF ORIGIN

THE EFFECTS of migration on sending countries are usually mixed, but in large measure can be seen as either virtuous or vicious for development. There can be virtuous circles in which *recruitment, remittances* and *returns* speed up growth in sending countries, accelerating convergence and reducing migration pressures; and there can be vicious circles when these "three *Rs*" interact in ways that widen the very gaps that motivate international migration.

International migration moves people from one country to another, and the three *Rs* summarize the impacts that migrants can have on the development of their countries of origin. *Recruitment* deals with who migrates, asking whether migrants would have been unemployed or underemployed at home, or key employees of business and government, whose departure leads to layoffs and reduced services. *Remittances* are the monies sent home by migrants abroad, and remittance questions include whether the volume of remittances can be increased by reducing the cost of transferring funds between countries. The more important question is how to invest remittances

10. *See also Borjas, 1994, for more discussion of the different use of public welfare by migrants with different skills.*

11. *Migration, "like any profit-motivated international movement of factors of production, may be expected to raise total world output." (Johnson, 1968, p. 75).*

in ways that create jobs and reduce migration pressures. *Returns* ask whether migrants return with new technologies and ideas of use to them and their country, or just return to rest and retire.

Migration is not random: young people are most likely to move across borders, because they have "invested" the least in jobs and careers at home, and the longest period to recover an "investment in migration" abroad. However, even among the youth, the question of who migrates is influenced by the recruitment efforts of employers in receiving areas, recruiting agents in sending areas, and networks that link them. For example, if employers are seeking IT professionals and nurses, recruiters will help young computer specialists and nurses to move abroad, and networks will evolve to make it easier for their friends and relatives to follow them. If foreign employers are seeking domestic helpers and farm workers, recruiters will find them, and networks will evolve to move unskilled migrants over borders.

The recruitment of migrants has been concentrated at the extremes of the education ladder, involving migrants with college education and unskilled migrants alike. However, different processes are involved. The overseas recruitment of well educated professional workers is often done openly, with employers and recruiters advertising for migrants in developing countries, and offering contracts to nurses and teachers before they travel abroad. Recruiters play a larger role in recruiting unskilled migrants, who are more likely to be abroad in an irregular status, often employed by contractors and other intermediaries.

The skilled worker flows tend to be of most concern to developing countries, and unskilled flows of most concern to developed countries. However, the impetus of both flows comes largely from inside developed countries - it is their approval or toleration of recruitment that brings the first migrant workers, and then networks allow the migration to take on a life of its own. By the time governments stop legal recruitment or announce that they will no longer tolerate unauthorized migrant flows, they are attempting to break networks that serve the interests of both migrants and employers. Governments that believe migrant flows can be turned on and off like a water tap are often disappointed. For example, stopping legal recruitment is assumed to stop the flow of migrants, just as closing a gate in a dam stops the flow of water in a river. But migration networks are like rivulets that form a delta, and blocking one migration channel often pushes migrants into other channels.

The problem in many developed countries is that irregular migrants outnumber regularly admitted migrant workers, and there is no agreement on how to deal with the irregular migrants. In the US, there were an estimated 9.3 million irregular migrants in 2003 (Passel, et al., 2004). There is general agreement that the irregular migrants should be converted into regular migrants, but no agreement on what should happen after regularization. For example, the US president's proposal in January 2004 for a Fair and Secure Immigration Reform (FSIR) plan that would, *inter alia*, allow US employers to legalize the irregular workers they employ, has had very mixed responses,[12] with no agreement on what status would represent an improvement for the US and for the migrants' countries of origin.

The second R stands for *remittances*, the portion of migrant incomes abroad that is sent home. Remittances to developing countries more than doubled between the late 1980s and the late 1990s, after experiencing drops in 1991 (Gulf war) and in 1998 (Asian financial crises), reaching USD 72 billion in 2001, and on track to surpass USD 100 billion by 2005. They have risen with the number of migrants, surpassed ODA in developing countries in the mid-1990s, and are approaching declining foreign direct investment flows to developing countries. It should be

12. *Most employers embraced the FSIR, but it was attacked by unions and migrant advocates for converting irregular migrants into guest workers, not immigrants. The Democrats countered with the Safe, Orderly, Legal Visas and Enforcement Act (SOLVE) in May 2004, which would give immigrant visas to unauthorized workers who have been in the US for at least five years, worked at least two years, and pass English, background and medical checks.*

noted that all these flows are gross flows, and that remittances also flow from developing countries to the expatriates employed there.[13]

A handful of developing countries receive most of the remittances. The three largest recipients, India, Mexico and the Philippines, received a third of total remittances to developing countries in recent years, and the top six recipients, these three plus Morocco, Egypt and Turkey, received half of all remittances to developing countries. Remittances are most important in smaller and island nations, where they can be equivalent to between 20 to 40 per cent of GDP, e.g., in 2001 remittances represented 37 per cent of GDP in Tonga, 26 per cent in Lesotho, 23 per cent in Jordan, and 15 to 17 per cent in Albania, Nicaragua, Yemen, and Moldova. The major sources of remittances were the US (USD 28 billion), Saudi Arabia (USD 15 billion) and Germany, Belgium and Switzerland (USD 8 billion each).[14]

The best way to maximize the volume of remittances is to have an appropriate exchange rate and economic policies that promise growth (Ratha, 2003). Since the September 11, 2001 terrorist attacks, many governments have tried to shift remittances into formal channels, such as banks, which migrants use if it is easy and cheap to do so. However, there must be enough banking outlets in migrant communities at home and abroad, and competition in order to lower transfer costs, and this is not always the case. Governments have become far more active regarding policies to reduce remittance transfer costs, and the June 2004 G-8 summit called for remittance transfer costs, today typically 10-15 per cent of the amount transferred (USD 30 to USD 45 of USD 300), to be reduced by 50 per cent within a decade.[15]

Most remittances are used for consumption, which helps to explain their stability,[16] even as exchange rates and investment outlooks change.[17] Migrant families are the chief beneficiaries, but their spending of remittances also generates jobs for non-migrants, with most studies suggesting that each USD 1 in remittance spending generates a USD 2 increase in local economic output, depending on whether remittances are used to purchase imported or locally produced goods (Taylor and Martin, 2001). The emigration of adult men initially leads to reduced output in local economies, but remittances prompt adjustments that maintain output. For example, many farming families with migrants abroad shift from crops to poultry or livestock, because they have less labour, and hire labour to produce crops or rent crop land to other farmers; incomes bolstered by remittances raise the demand for meat.

Remittances have many other socio-economic effects. They can change the social hierarchies in communities, creating a new class of moneylenders, such as women whose husbands are abroad. Women take on new roles in the absence of their husbands, making decisions that previously would have been made by their husbands, or jointly. If women have more income because of their husband's migration, there tends to be more spending on education and health for children, which can increase human capital in the long run (Taylor and Martin, 2001). However, there is also a danger of dependence, as the relatives of migrants do less work at home assuming that remittances will continue to arrive, and children assume that they will go abroad to work.

The third R in the migration and development equation stands for *returns*. In the ideal virtuous circle

13. *See also the figure "Resource Flows to Developing Countries" in the chapter "Migrant Remittances as a Source of Development Finance", and in Ratha, 2003.*

14. *See the World Bank's table "Remittances to Select Countries 1995-2001"; www.worldbank.org/prospects/gdf2003/gdf_statApp_web.pdf*

15. *Countries recounted their plans and activities to reduce remittance transfer costs. Canada intends to promote financial literacy among migrants to encourage them to open bank accounts. France pledged to expand its co-development strategy, which involves reducing remittance transfer costs and making loans to returned migrants. The US announced it would reduce the cost of remitting to the Philippines (receiving about half its USD 8 billion in remittances from the US in 2003) (www.g8usa.gov/).*

16. *Automatic stabilizers in developed countries, such as unemployment insurance, help to stabilize the flow of remittances to developing countries with the same economic cycles as the countries where their migrants work.*

17. *Ratha, 2003, noted that remittances to high-debt and less-transparent countries were more stable than those to middle-income open economies because the latter include more remittances destined for investment.*

scenario, migrants who have been abroad return to their origin countries with the entrepreneurial energy and ideas needed to start or expand businesses there, or with the skills and discipline needed to raise productivity as employees.[18] They generally tend to come from the ranks of the risk takers at home, and if their risk-taking behaviour is combined with skills and capital acquired abroad, the result can be an economic take-off. Take-off behaviour tends to be most common in countries poised for economic growth (including southern European countries in the 1960s and 1970s).

On the other hand, if migrants return to economies that have not changed, they may rest and retire rather than be a force for economic change, as has occurred in many African, Caribbean and Pacific island countries where improved housing is a visible sign of having worked abroad, but there are few migrant-inspired businesses that promise migrant children opportunities at home. Many migrants settle abroad and have their families join them, which limits their contribution to development in their country of origin.

As communications improve and transportation costs fall, migrants may engage in back-and-forth circulation, which can contribute to economic growth in both the sending and receiving countries (viz. the IT services in India). The General Agreement on Trade in Services (GATS) provides a framework to liberalize the temporary international migration of natural persons to provide services.[19] This sector accounts for up to 70-80 per cent of output and employment in the world's high-income economies, and tends to expand with economic development, e.g. when women work outside the home, they can generate a demand for day care.[20] Labour typically accounts for 70-80 per cent of service production costs versus 20 per cent for manufactured goods (Krueger, 1999). Thus, importing service providers could raise incomes in developing countries, and reduce service costs in developed countries.

GATS negotiations stalled in 2004 over issues not related to the labour mobility of service providers. However, the mobility of service providers promises to become more important in trade negotiations, justifying closer examination of the relationship between easier access for service providers, and irregular migration. More attention also needs to be paid to the provision of services across borders without migration, as services once considered to be immobile have become mobile (e.g. the processing of bank and medical records, and software development). That discussion covers a range of possibilities from distance learning in education, to diagnosis in medicine.[21]

Earlier in this chapter attention was drawn to the fact that the three "Rs" can produce vicious or virtuous circles. There is clearly a need to generate more virtuous circles and fewer vicious circles linking migration and development.

The virtuous circle is perhaps best exemplified by the case of Indian IT workers, whose emigration led to the creation of a significant service export industry, that has improved IT services in India and created jobs there. In the mid-1980s, India had about 7,000 IT specialists, and a government hesitant about supporting IT expansion. Recognizing their skills, multinationals began to employ the specialists abroad, as did Indian firms such as Tata. But the latter soon began to return some work to India, and persuaded the government to introduce measures to bolster this budding global service within the country. Following the increased engagement of government,[22] by 2003 there were around 700,000 IT workers in India, and the country had become world-renowned for low-cost, high-

18. *See also the chapter "Enhancing the Benefits of Return Migration for Development".*

19. *See also the Textbox 9.1 "Trade and Migration: GATS Mode 4".*

20. *The demand for services is income elastic, which means that if incomes rise 10 per cent, the demand for tourism or health care services rises more than 10 per cent.*

21. *See supra, ftn. 19.*

22. *The government supported the IT industry by reducing barriers to imports of computers, assuring reliable infrastructure, and allowing the state-supported Indian Institutes of Technology to use merit as a quality benchmark for education.*

quality IT services. The benefits of this emigration-led growth included a sharp jump in science and engineering graduates and the provision of world-class IT services to private firms and government agencies in India.

In some African countries, by contrast, a vicious circle seems to link migration and development. Many former British colonies train nurses and other health care workers to world-class standards, which makes it easier for them to emigrate to fill jobs in expanding health care sectors, including the British National Health System (NHS). For Malawi, the wage gaps in 2004 were 16 to 1 (USD 31,000 a year for an RN to start in the NHS, versus USD 1,900 a year at home), and nurses seeking higher wages are emigrating. African leaders argue that the loss of human capital via emigration erodes the value of foreign aid.[23] As a result of African grievances, the World Health Organization has urged developed nations to negotiate recruitment agreements with developing countries that avoid "aggressive recruitment" of health care workers and include compensation for the lost investment in training nurses.

Why do some migration flows lead to virtuous and others to vicious circles? There is no easy answer. Clearly, health care and IT services are different sectors. Governments strongly influence the demand for health care via the provision of clinics and hospitals, and charges for patients and drugs, and they affect the supply of health care workers via subsidized training and by setting salaries and working conditions. IT services are largely produced and consumed in the private sector, and IT can be provided with brains and ever-cheaper technology, while the cost for health care services tends to increase.

TRADE AND THE MIGRATION HUMP

FOR MANY years, poverty was seen as a root cause of migration, and development the solution for unwanted migration. When workers move from lower to higher wage jobs, wages should rise more slowly in receiving economies and faster in sending countries, and this convergence should make migration self-eliminating under the factor price equalization theorem. This is what occurred in the late 19th and early 20th centuries between Europe and North America, with one economic historian concluding that "mass migration by itself may explain about 70 per cent of the real wage convergence in the late 19th century Atlantic economy" (Williamson, 1998).

Migration involves workers crossing borders for jobs, but jobs can also cross borders to workers, as when investment creates industries that produce goods for local consumption and export. The US Commission for the Study of International Migration and Cooperative Economic Development, searching for "mutually beneficial" ways to reduce unwanted migration in the late 1980s, found that freer trade was preferable to more migration, concluding that "expanded trade between the sending countries and the United States is the single most important remedy" (US Commission, 1990).

Trade means that a good is produced in one country, taken across borders, and consumed in another. Economic theory teaches that trade dictated by comparative advantage increases global income. This means that if countries specialize in producing the goods they can produce relatively more cheaply, and import the goods needed that other countries are comparatively better at producing, the residents of all countries engaged in trade will be better off. Trade and migration are substitutes in economic theory, which is why former Mexican President Salinas

23. *South Africa says it has spent USD1 billion educating health workers who emigrated - the equivalent of a third of all development aid it received from 1994 to 2000 (Dugger, 2004).*

argued in favour of NAFTA on the grounds that North American free trade means "more jobs... (and) higher wages in Mexico, and this in turn will mean fewer migrants to the US and Canada. We want to export goods, not people." (quoted in the Bush letter to Congress, May 1, 1991).

Trade and migration are substitutes in the long run, but they can be complements in the short run. It is well known that there can be job-displacement in response to freer trade, as when TV factories in the US close, or Mexican farmers stop growing corn in response to a removal of trade barriers. The displaced US workers are not likely to migrate to Mexico, but since rural Mexicans were migrating to the US before freer trade in corn, some may migrate as a result of freer trade. The possibility that freer trade could be disruptive in emigration countries led the US Commission to warn that "the economic development process itself tends in the short to medium term to stimulate migration," producing a migration hump when migration flows are viewed over time (US Commission, 1990).

A *migration hump* – trade and migration acting as complements – can be a political dilemma for governments since the same economic policies that can reduce migration in the long run may increase it in the short run. In the words of the US Commission, the possibility of a migration hump produces "a very real short-term versus long-term dilemma" for a country such as the US trying to persuade a sceptical Congress and public that NAFTA is the best way to reduce unauthorized immigration (US Commission, 1990). In order to make its case, the Commission argued that the short-run increase in immigration associated with freer trade was a worthwhile price to pay for policies that would reduce unwanted immigration in the long run.[24]

The critical policy parameters in the migration hump are: a) how much does migration increase as a result of economic integration, b) how soon does this hump disappear; and c) how much migration is "avoided" by economic integration? Generally, three factors must be present to create a migration hump: a continued demand-pull in the destination country, an increased supply-push in the origin country, and migration networks that can move workers across borders (Martin, 1993).

The Mexico-US case provides an example of economic integration when per capita income differences are more than 8 to 1. Migration was the major relationship between Mexico and the US for most of the 20th century, but legal immigration remained low until recently - 36 per cent of 20th century Mexicans arrived in the 1990s (2,249,421) and 34 per cent of the apprehensions of unauthorized Mexicans also occurred in the 1990s (14,667,599). This compares with 7 per cent arrivals and 4 per cent apprehensions in the 1960s, or 10 per cent arrivals and 19 per cent apprehensions in the 1970s (INS Statistical Yearbook).

NAFTA came into effect in January, 1994, locking in place policies that lowered barriers to trade and investment in Canada, Mexico and the US. Most benefits of this freer trade were expected to accrue to Mexico in the form of more foreign investment, faster economic and job growth, and increased exports. The most cited study of NAFTA's likely effects concluded that Mexican employment figures, projected to be 30 million in 1995, would rise by 609,000, or two per cent, because of NAFTA. Mexican wages were projected to be 9 per cent higher with NAFTA, largely because of foreign investment (and Mexican money staying in Mexico), and it was expected to raise the value of the peso relative to the dollar, reducing the cost of imports (Hufbauer and Schott, 1992).

All studies agreed that most of the additional jobs due to NAFTA would be created in Mexico, and some anticipated simultaneous job creation and displacement in Mexico, predicting that the displacement of workers from previously protected

24. *For a more detailed explanation of the Hump Theory, see also Martin, 1993.*

Mexican sectors such as agriculture, could lead to additional Mexico-US migration (up to 600,000 illegally over 5-6 years).[25]

Trade and migration were complements in the Mexico-US case in the 1990s. The major reasons include Mexico's failure to create enough formal sector jobs for the million new labour force entrants each year, and extraordinarily rapid employment growth in the US, especially in the late 1990s. There were about 109 million Mexican-born persons in 2000, and 8 per cent lived in the US; more importantly, 30 per cent of Mexicans with formal-sector jobs were in the US.[26]

Past demographic growth presents Mexico with a major job creation challenge, but demography and economics offer hope that the migration hump may soon be past. The number of Mexicans turning 15, the age of labour force entry in Mexico, is expected to drop by 50 per cent between 1996 and 2010 from 1 million a year to 500,000 a year. At a sustained GDP growth of 5 per cent, employment growth is expected to rise from 0.9 to 1.3 per cent per year between 1996 and 2010, enabling formal sector job growth to average 3-4 per cent a year.

The combination of fewer work force entrants and rising employment forms an "X" when traced over time, with the intersection occurring where the falling number of labour force entrants equals rising employment growth. Projections made in the mid-1990s imagined the intersection would be reached in 2002, when labour force growth of 1.1 per cent matched employment growth of 1.1 per cent. GDP growth averaged less than 4 per cent, so the intersection is not likely to be reached until after 2005, but the larger point made by the X-diagram is clear – *emigration pressures in Mexico are likely to fall between 2005 and 2010 for demographic and economic reasons.* The lesson for governments is also clear: if the massive border enforcement build-up is completed just as emigration pressures fall for demographic and economic reasons, it is important to keep these fundamental reasons in mind when evaluating governmental expenditure on enforcement.

Similar detailed analyses would be needed in other countries to evaluate the possibility and nature of migration humps with closer economic integration, and to explore ways to manage them cooperatively. Migration humps are another reason why optimal migration management strategies may be most likely to be found in bilateral and regional settings, although the best practices they develop may be applicable globally.

CONCLUSION

LABOUR migration is a natural response to widening demographic and economic differentials. The challenge and opportunity is to manage the already occurring labour in a manner that reduces these differences, so that economically motivated migration comes to a "natural end" or falls to sustainable levels. Common sense and history teach that slower population growth and faster economic growth lead to convergence, but there is no global consensus about which migration management strategy is best to help achieve this desired convergence.

The Mexico-US case shows how economic integration under NAFTA has led to a migration hump, and left the US with perhaps 10 million Mexican-born residents, half of them with irregular status. There is

25. *Hinojosa and Robinson (1991), for example, estimated that NAFTA would displace about 1.4 million rural Mexicans, largely because NAFTA-related changes in Mexican farm policies and freer trade in agricultural products would lead some farmers to quit farming; and that 800,000 displaced farmers would stay in Mexico, and 600,000 would migrate (illegally) to the US over 5-6 years.*

26. *In 2000, 15 million of the 40 million-strong Mexican labour force were in formal sector jobs, with an additional 6 million Mexican-born workers in the US; 29 per cent of Mexicans in formal sector jobs are in the US. Many Mexican workers are self-employed farmers, unpaid family workers, or in the informal sector - the usual indicator of formal sector employment in Mexico is enrolment in the pension system (IMSS). (www.banamex.com/weblogic/svltC71930EstSE?LNG=1&SEQ=3&folio=5). With 5.5 million Mexicans employed in the US, and 13 million in IMSS in Mexico, 30 per cent of Mexicans with formal-sector jobs are in the US.*

agreement that having so many irregular Mexican migrants is not optimal, but there is disagreement on how their status should be changed - should irregular workers be converted into guest workers expected to leave, or to immigrants expected to settle? Perhaps the most important aspect of the Mexico-US migration hump is that, despite rising Mexico-US migration, there has been no backtracking on the economic integration that is expected to eventually lead to economic convergence and less migration.

Migration is an age-old response by individuals to different opportunities either within or across international borders, to be managed by governments as an opportunity, not solved as a problem. The ideal world is one where there are few migration barriers and enforcement expenditures, because there is little unwanted migration. The challenge for governments is to understand the fundamental forces motivating migration, the virtuous and vicious circles that labour migration can set in motion, and policies that can hasten the economic convergence that makes migration more manageable. This chapter has attempted to arm the policymaker with some key data, arguments and examples to meet this challenge with well researched and workable policies.

TEXTBOX 9.1

TRADE AND MIGRATION – GATS MODE 4

The General Agreement on Trade in Services (GATS) is a multilateral framework agreement covering the trade in services, which applies to all 148 WTO Members. It provides a framework for countries to decide which service sectors they want to open to foreign suppliers, and under what conditions. Mode 4 of GATS is the section most closely linked to some forms of temporary labour migration. Most significantly for the migration community, GATS Mode 4 represents the only multilateral treaty commitment concerning the movement of persons at the global level, albeit for a small range of persons. As such, it offers one approach to the international management of migration, even if limited in scope and applicability.

What is Mode 4?

For the purpose of making commitments to open markets, GATS divides trade in services into four modes of supply: cross-border supply (Mode 1); consumption abroad (Mode 2); supply via commercial presence (Mode 3), and supply via presence of natural persons (Mode 4). Mode 4 is defined as the supply of a service by a supplier of one WTO member, through the presence of natural persons in the territory of another member on a temporary basis. While there is some debate about what exactly this means, Mode 4 service suppliers generally:

- gain entry for a specific purpose (e.g., to fulfil a service contract, either as self-employed or as an employee of a foreign service supplier);
- are confined to one sector (as opposed to workers who enter a country under general migration or asylum programmes, who can move between sectors);
- are temporary – they are not migrating on a permanent basis, nor seeking entry to the labour market in the host country. The GATS does not define "temporary" but it does specifically exclude permanent migration. In practice, the timeframes set out in WTO member countries' commitments on Mode 4 range from several weeks to 3-5 years, depending on the countries, sectors and professions involved.

Mode 4 only covers movement of people supplying services; there are no parallel WTO rules covering movement of people in other areas, such as agriculture or manufacturing. And while in theory Mode 4 covers service suppliers at all skill levels, in practice WTO members' commitments are limited to the higher skilled. Generally, GATS Mode 4 is understood to cover:

- Business visitors: persons visiting the host country for the purpose of conducting or organizing business, but who receive no remuneration in the host country;
- Intra-corporate transferees: existing employees transferred within the same foreign controlled company;
- Contractual service suppliers (employees of companies): persons providing services where a foreign company obtains a contract to supply services to a host country client and sends its employees to provide the services;
- Contractual service suppliers (individuals/independent service suppliers): an individual who wins a contract to supply services to a host country client;

- Foreign employees of foreign companies established in the host country (but excluding nationals of the host country employed by these companies).

However, there is no agreement among WTO Members on whether Mode 4 covers *foreign employees* of domestic companies, as opposed to foreigners with a *contract to supply services* to domestic companies. This distinction can be complicated by the fact that some WTO Members deem almost all types of foreign temporary service suppliers to be employees for the purpose of bringing them under domestic labour law.

What is on the Table in the GATS Negotiations?

Even by the modest standards of services liberalization in the Uruguay Round, little was achieved on liberalizing Mode 4. GATS commitments are guaranteed *minimum standards*, so countries tended to be conservative, with most committing to a more restrictive regime than they were – or are – actually employing. There are high expectations among some WTO Members for progress on Mode 4 in the current Doha round of negotiations.

In general, proposals on the table in the WTO negotiations seek either to increase market access (mostly developing country proposals) or to increase the effectiveness of existing market access (supported by most major developed countries) and include:

- Greater clarity and predictability in WTO Members' commitments: e.g., by agreeing on common definitions for "managers, executives, specialists", and providing information on labour market tests, such as the criteria used and timeframe for decisions.
- Improving transparency: e.g., one-stop information points for all relevant procedures and requirements, prior consultation on regulatory changes.
- GATS visa: to facilitate entry to Mode 4 workers, the visa would be issued rapidly, be time-limited, include appeal rights and a bond, with sanctions for abuse.
- More market access: in sectors in high demand (e.g., ICT, professional services), better access for some groups, in particular intra-corporate transferees, and more access for other types of personnel, beyond the highly skilled.

What are Some of the Migration Issues Involved?

One major apprehension for both origin and destination countries, is that persons who move under Mode 4 will try to establish themselves permanently. Mode 4 can be a first step to permanent residence, either legally by changing visa categories, or illegally by overstaying. But overstaying is a risk with all temporary entry, including tourists, and increased Mode 4 movement could arguably help to discourage employers from using undocumented workers by making temporary foreign workers legally available for seasonal activities. Temporary workers legally applying to change status may serve as a useful pre-selection of candidates for future migration.

Second, while labour market conditions – and migration needs – fluctuate, GATS commitments do not. They guarantee minimum treatment from which a WTO Member will not deviate without compensating other members. Governments typically wish to maintain maximum flexibility to regulate the flow of temporary entrants according to their needs, and are reluctant to commit in perpetuity to existing regimes. Further, Mode 4 movement represents a small proportion of the people crossing borders every day. The additional resources required to give special treatment to this group may be hard to justify, also in terms of the administrative capacities of some countries.

Third is the issue of whether temporary foreign workers should receive the same wages and conditions as nationals employed in the same industry. In many developed countries, this is a legal obligation, but some developing countries argue that this undermines their comparative advantage. Others argue that there is no justification for lower wages, given that temporary workers in the host country have to meet host, not home, country costs of living. Unions fear both the exploitation of foreign workers and the undermining of their own conditions. Even where foreign workers are not actually paid less, their presence is seen by some as a brake on reform - the availability of temporary foreign nurses is argued to have enabled governments to ignore the root causes of their nursing shortages, such as the need for better wages and conditions.

However, equal treatment does not always result in equitable outcomes. Some foreign workers are required to contribute to social security programmes from which they receive no, or minimal, benefits. While exemption from contributions would impact the competitiveness of foreign workers compared to nationals, there is a basic iniquity in workers contributing to benefits that they will never be eligible to receive. One alternative is for these charges to be paid into separate funds and reimbursed upon the workers' return to their home country.

Finally, brain drain, or the emigration of highly skilled workers leading to skill shortages, reductions in output and tax shortfalls, is of significant concern to countries of origin. Brain drain can reinforce the development trap, with communities of skilled persons in developed countries attracting other skilled persons, leaving weaker communities in developing countries even further depleted. Where skilled persons are educated at public expense, these countries also suffer loss of public investment in education.

While Mode 4 could exacerbate fears of brain drain, it is only *temporary* migration, and as such may pose fewer costs than permanent migration. The costs of temporary movement of skilled people can be offset by the benefits to their home country, when they return with enhanced skills and contacts in the international business community, and through their remittances from abroad, an important revenue for developing countries, often larger than either FDI or ODA flows.

However, where the need is great and skills are scarce, even the temporary loss of skilled persons can be a problem. This has been a particular concern in the case of health workers. Here the Commonwealth countries have developed a Code of Practice for the International Recruitment of Health Workers intended to discourage the targeted recruitment of such workers from countries which are themselves experiencing shortages.

Opportunities in the home country can be an important determinant of whether skilled workers move and when they return to their home countries. Some countries, often with the assistance of international organisations such as IOM, are taking steps to encourage the return of skilled workers, including via tax breaks and other incentives. Further, some developing countries see international outsourcing as an increasingly important means of creating jobs at home and an alternative to sending their qualified people abroad.

The text of the GATS and the market-opening commitments of each WTO Member are available on the WTO website (*www.wto.org*).

Source: Julia Nielson, OECD.

CHAPTER 10
DESIGNING VIABLE AND ETHICAL LABOUR IMMIGRATION POLICIES[1]

The design of labour immigration policies has become one of the most contentious and divisive issues of public policy making in many countries. Public debates have been hampered by a lack, or distortion of facts about migration and its consequences, thus leaving policymakers in the difficult position of having to design labour immigration policies based on incomplete and highly contested evidence. Increasing the range and quality of information about the consequences of international labour migration must undoubtedly be one of the most important steps toward improving the quality of public debate and the policy choices for governments. It will, however, not be enough.

International labour migration generates a complex set of economic and social costs and benefits for the receiving country, migrant workers and their countries of origin. These consequences may sometimes be in conflict with each other, and therefore policies cannot be made without certain trade-offs. Difficult decisions need to be made about which of the multifaceted and interrelated consequences of international labour migration should be given more importance in the design of national labour immigration policies, and why. Labour immigration policymaking is an inherently moral exercise that requires a discussion of values and ethics, not just of facts.

There is therefore an urgent need for a framework for the comprehensive discussion of labour immigration policy that separates the normative from other aspects, and places the debates and design of labour immigration policies on a more informed and reasoned footing. To this end, it is useful to distinguish between three fundamental questions that require separate discussions in the debate and design of a country's labour immigration policy:

i) What *are* the consequences of international labour migration?
ii) What *should be* the objectives of labour immigration policy?
iii) What policies are best suited to achieve these objectives?

While some of the facts about migration and its consequences (question (i)), the values underpinning a country's labour immigration policy (question (ii)) and the resulting optimal national immigration policies (question (iii)) may be similar across countries, each of these questions requires answers that are country-specific. This is because the design and implementation of immigration policy remain principally the domain of *domestic* policymaking of sovereign and self-determining states.[2] Furthermore, there are significant contextual differences between countries that are manifest in differences in, for example, levels of economic development, regulation of labour markets, culture, establishment of democratic institutions, international relations with the migrant-sending countries and the world community as a whole, the role and independence of the judiciary, and the actual capacity of the state to act and implement certain policies.

1. *The author of this chapter is Dr Martin Ruhs, researcher at the Centre on Migration, Policy and Society (COMPAS) at Oxford University. martin.ruhs@compas.ox.ac.uk. The chapter draws on Ruhs and Chang, 2004 and Ruhs, 2003.*
2. *Note that the existing regional consultative processes on international labour migration are all informal and non-binding; see Klekowski 2001.*

Rather than suggest ready-made, one-size-fits-all answers based on "international experience" or "best practices", this chapter aims to provide a framework for discussion of each of these questions in a structured and comprehensive manner, and to suggest basic policy principles for a general "shell" or set of guidelines for country-specific policymaking.

The first part of the chapter categorizes the main consequences of international labour migration and identifies the most important potential trade-offs between them.

The second part outlines some ethical issues to be addressed when evaluating these consequences and choosing policy objectives. It suggests five core considerations for a balanced approach that is both realistic, by taking account of existing realities in labour immigration policy making, and idealistic, by striving to improve existing labour immigration policies and outcomes for all involved, especially for the migrant workers and their countries of origin.

Based on this approach, the third part makes a case for liberalizing international labour migration through new and expanded temporary foreign worker programmes, especially for low-skilled migrant workers. It argues that such programmes are both desirable from an ethical point of view, and feasible in the sense that new and innovative policies could help avoid the adverse consequences associated with many past guest worker programmes.

IMPACTS AND TRADE-OFFS IN INTERNATIONAL LABOUR MIGRATION

INTERNATIONAL labour migration generates a complex set of economic, social, political, cultural, environmental and other consequences for individuals, communities and countries as a whole. At the risk of over-simplification, **Table 10.1** categorises the major types of impact (each indicated by an "x") on non-migrants in the migrant-receiving country, non-migrants in the migrant-sending country, and on migrants themselves.

TABLE 10.1

TYPES OF IMPACTS OF INTERNATIONAL LABOUR MIGRATION

	RC	SC	M
Economic efficiency	X	X	X
Distribution	X	X	
National identity	X	X	
RC citizens' rights	X		
SC Citizens' Rights		X	
Migrants' Rights			X

(RC=Receiving Country; SC=Sending Country; M = Migrants)

A comprehensive discussion of the consequences of international labour migration would need to consider all types of impacts identified in **Table 10.1**.[3] In the context of this chapter, it suffices to explain their meanings and identify the potential trade-offs between them.

The consequences of international labour migration for *economic efficiency* and distribution in the receiving country and sending country include, *inter alia*, impacts on national income and its distribution among non-migrants (e.g. income per capita, economic growth, structural change, inequality, poverty rates); the national labour market (e.g. wage levels, unemployment rates, labour market participation rates, labour market segmentation), and the fiscal balance (e.g. public services, tax revenues, etc.). The "economic efficiency of migrants" is meant to capture migrants' economic welfare, as primarily reflected by their wages and employment prospects.

National identity may be loosely defined as the shared beliefs and values of a country's residents. The meaning and substance assigned to national identity – and thus the way in which international labour migration may impact on it – largely depend on how

3. *Other chapters of this Report provide further discussion on the state of knowledge about some of those impacts. See, e.g., the chapters "Economic Costs and Benefits of International Labour Migration" and "Migration and Poverty: Some Issues in the Context of Asia".*

countries "see themselves". For example, a receiving country that sees itself as culturally homogeneous, such as Japan and Korea, may view the immigration of people with different cultural backgrounds as "diluting" its national identity. In contrast, in countries with long histories of immigration, such as the US, Canada and Australia, national identity may, arguably, be partly defined by cultural diversity, thus making immigration a potential tool for preserving or even increasing that diversity.

At the same time, there is little doubt that large-scale emigration (such as from Mexico and the Philippines) also impacts on the national identity in sending countries, mainly through the return of emigrants who have acquired some of the receiving country's values and habits, the activities and influence of diasporas on social and political affairs in their home countries, and through imported consumer goods purchased with remittances.

More recently, the above listed considerations of national identity have been further conflated with considerations of public order and national security, especially in the receiving country. For example, since the 9/11 terrorist attacks, national security has been a major concern in the immigration policies of the US, and increasingly also of other high-income countries, such as the UK. Similarly, efforts to "localize" the predominantly foreign labour force in most oil-rich Gulf states are largely motivated by security concerns about hosting a foreign population that is larger than the citizenry.

In addition to impacting on collective notions of economic efficiency, distribution and national identity, international labour migration also affects the *rights of individuals*. Most obviously, by virtue of their change in location and legal status (from citizens in their countries of origin to foreigners in their countries of employment), migrant workers necessarily experience a change in the range and scope of their rights – and obligations. For example, a migrant worker employed abroad under a temporary foreign worker programme is usually required to work only for the employer specified in the work permit, which restricts the migrant's right to freedom of movement in the labour market – a right that most people enjoy in their home countries. In other cases, employment abroad may increase the number and scope of rights enjoyed by migrants. This is typically the case where migrants come from undemocratic regimes and gain permanent residence or citizenship in more democratic high-income countries.

Immigration may also positively or negatively affect the rights of citizens of the receiving country. For example, granting migrants the right to own certain types of property, such as land, may adversely affect the value of the corresponding right of a citizen, who needs to compete with non-citizens in the market for land, and may thus have to pay a higher price. Similarly, extending the right to certain social security benefits or public services, such as free public health care, to non-citizens may adversely affect the value of the corresponding right of a citizen, who may have to wait longer before receiving medical treatment unless the capacity of the medical system is also increased. At the same time, when effective control of the border is economically and politically too costly, legalizing illegal foreign workers, i.e. giving illegal migrant workers the right to legal residence and employment in the receiving country, could enhance the rights of citizens, as migrant workers with more rights are less likely to undercut citizens in terms of wages and working conditions.

The impacts of international labour migration identified above are likely to be *interrelated* and potentially *conflicting*, which means that the relationship between them may be characterized by *trade-offs*.

One of the most frequently discussed potential trade-offs is that between the impacts on economic efficiency and distribution in the receiving country. Analysis based on the most simple model in labour economics suggests that, in the short run, immigration marginally increases national income (the *efficiency effect*) and, more significantly, redistributes national income from workers to the owners of capital (the *redistribution effect*) (Borjas,

1995). In other words, local employers and capitalists gain from immigration at the expense of competing local workers, whose wages are depressed by the employment of migrant workers. Trade theorists argue that some of these effects may disappear in the long run, when the increase in labour supply, and the subsequent decline in real wages may be counterbalanced by an increase in labour demand (Trefler, 1997). Empirical labour economists also point out that, in practice, the impacts of immigration on local workers are minor or insignificant (Dustmann, 2003; Card, 2004). Nevertheless, most observers would agree that, just like aspects of international trade and investment flows, labour immigration has the *potential* to adversely affect wage and employment outcomes of some competing local workers in the short run (Borjas, 2003).

The level of immigration that maximizes economic efficiency may also differ from that considered socially desirable, based on the perceived impact on national identity. This may especially be the case where national identity is defined in terms of cultural homogeneity. It may, however, also apply to already diverse and multi-ethnic societies who view further immigration as a threat to social cohesion and solidarity. The UK has recently seen a fierce debate about whether immigration is making Britain too diverse to sustain the mutual obligations behind a good society and the welfare state.[4] A recent commentary by Samuel Huntington, entitled "The Hispanic Challenge", recently ignited a similar debate in the US.[5]

Trade-offs may also arise in the context of the migration of highly skilled workers from less to more developed countries. For example, while potentially increasing economic efficiency in the receiving country and improving the economic outcomes for migrant workers themselves, granting highly skilled workers permanent residence status may adversely affect the economy of the migrants' sending countries through the potential permanent loss of human capital ("brain drain") and likely decline in remittances usually associated with permanent emigration.

Another frequently ignored potential trade-off is that between the rights and economic welfare of migrant workers. In some cases, migrant workers experience significant restrictions of their rights in return for incomes that are multiples of what they would earn in their home countries. Two extreme examples are migrant workers from developing countries who choose to migrate temporarily to the oil-rich Persian Gulf states and Singapore, despite sharp restrictions of many of their employment-related and other rights. For a more recent example, since the recent EU enlargement on 1 May 2004, workers from the ten EU accession countries have been able to freely migrate and take up employment in the UK and Ireland.[6] However, mainly due to pressure from the tabloid media and the opposition parties in the weeks preceding EU enlargement, they face extended restrictions on accessing certain social welfare benefits. Arguably, the latter were the "political price" the UK and Irish governments had to pay in order to sustain their liberal migration policies toward workers from the accession states.[7]

Finally, as already mentioned, extending rights to migrant workers may, in some cases, adversely impact the rights of citizens. The discussion above showed how extending rights to migrant workers may negatively, or positively, affect the *value* of the corresponding rights of citizens (e.g. the right to buy land). A more direct infringement of citizens' rights may occur if the receiving country grants migrant workers access to the national labour market in the absence of an effective mechanism encouraging

4. *See Goodhart 2004 and responses.*

5. *See Huntington 2004 and responses.*

6. *Together with Sweden, the UK and Ireland were the only ones among the pre-enlargement EU countries to open up their labour markets to workers from the ten EU Accession states immediately on 1 May 2004.*

7. *Phil Martin (2003) refers to the migrants' welfare vs. migrants' rights trade-off as the numbers-rights dilemma. He cites the conclusion of a classic study by Fisher on Californian agriculture in the 1950s: "The brightest hope for the welfare of seasonal agricultural workers [in the US] lies with the elimination of the jobs upon which they now depend" (Fisher 1953, p. 148). In other words, according to Fisher, the only way of improving migrant workers' rights was to eliminate them from the workforce.*

employers to first ascertain the availability of equally suitable local workers. This is most obviously the case where migrant workers can be employed illegally and without much fear of detection. The UK's decision to grant nationals from EU accession states immediate and free access to its labour market is another case in point. It could be argued that the right accorded to migrant workers to take up employment in the UK is a direct trade-off against local workers' preferential access to the UK labour market.[8]

It is important to emphasize that these trade-offs are not inherent to international labour migration. Sorting out potential from actual trade-offs is an important task for empirical research. However, where they are real, the various trade-offs in international labour migration need to be acknowledged and considered in the debate and design of labour immigration policy.

A BALANCED APPROACH TO THE DESIGN OF LABOUR IMMIGRATION POLICY

Having discussed the multifaceted and interrelated consequences of international labour migration, the next step in the design of labour immigration policy is to define its policy objectives. This requires policy makers to assign weights to the ten types of impacts listed in **Table 10.1**.[9]

In practice, the decision about which consequences of migration are more important than others is usually observed, and typically analysed, as the result of political negotiations and power struggles between the key political stakeholders and various interest groups. It is important to realize, however, that any politics of migration[10] is conducted within a certain *ethical* framework. This means that, although played out in the political domain, the assignment of weights to the ten types of impacts in **Table 10.1** is, in the end, an inherently normative exercise. This opens up an important, but all too often neglected, discussion of the values and ethical considerations that inform, or *should inform*, the choice of policy objectives and the subsequent design of a labour immigration policy.

It is useful to distinguish between two key questions in this discussion of the ethics of labour immigration policy:
(i) to what extent, if at all, should the outcomes for collectives, such as economic efficiency, distribution and national identity, and the economic welfare of individuals be given priority over individuals' rights, and
(ii) to what extent, if at all, should the interests of citizens be given priority over those of migrant workers and their countries of origin?

The answers to these questions, which differ from one ethical theory to another, constitute an ethical framework. For a discussion of the desirable degree of consequentialism, i.e. the degree to which the ethical evaluation of public policies (or private action) should be made in terms of outcomes (ends) rather than processes (means), see, for example, Scheffler, 1998. For a discussion of the "moral standing" to be accorded to non-citizens, see, for example, Nussbaum, 1996 and Goodin, 1988. Different ethical frameworks naturally give rise to very different definitions of the objectives of a "desirable" labour immigration policy, as reflected in the different weights given to the impacts in **Table 10.1**. It could be argued that the policy principles espoused in the ILO's Migrant Worker Conventions or the UN's International Convention on the Protection of the Rights of All Migrant Workers and the Members of their Families (MWC) are based on an ethical framework of "rights-

8. *This trade-off is not necessarily undesirable, but it needs to be acknowledged.*

9. *One could argue that, if labour immigration policy is made at the national level, the process of assigning weights to the various migration impacts in Table 10.1 defines the "national interest". This framework for defining the national interest would be in line with Nye, who suggests that, "(...) global interests can be incorporated into a broad and far-sighted concept of the national interest". See Nye, 2002.*

10. *For a recent discussion of the politics of migration, see Spencer, 2003. Spencer argues that managing migration is about trying to balance the following high-level objectives (some of which may be conflicting): achieving labour market objectives, protecting national security, minimizing public expenditure, promoting social cohesion, honouring human rights obligations and promoting international development and cooperation.*

based cosmopolitanism", which emphasizes the individual's rights rather than the individual's economic welfare, or the consequences for society, and accords a very high degree of "moral standing" to non-citizens. The outcomes for citizens and non-citizens are given (almost) equal weight in the ethical evaluation.[11]

In contrast, the current labour migration policies of many migrant-receiving countries appear to be based on an ethical framework of "consequentialist nationalism", which focuses on the consequences for the community, rather than the rights of individuals, and accords a significantly lower moral standing to non-citizens than to citizens. In other words, the preferred labour immigration policies of most receiving countries tend to place most weight on economic efficiency, distribution and national identity (including security) of their citizenry as collectives, less weight on individual rights (related to the employment of foreign workers), and least weight on the impacts on migrants and non-migrant citizens of sending countries. This is perhaps best illustrated by the popular appeal of "manpower planning exercises" behind many countries' labour immigration policymaking,[12] and by the disappointingly low numbers of ratification of the three global legal instruments developed for the protection of migrant workers.[13]

Given the multitude of competing ethical theories, it needs to be recognized that there is no single most "correct" starting point for theoretical reflection in the ethical discourse on immigration (Carens, 1996). However, if the objective of the ethical discourse is to yield practical policy implications, as is the case in this chapter, there is a strong argument to be made for adopting a *balanced approach* that is both *realistic*, in that it takes account of existing realities in labour immigration policymaking (such as the consequentialist nationalism underlying many migrant receiving countries' current policies), and *idealistic*, by actively promoting the interests of migrant workers and their countries of origin (ibid). Such a balanced approach would be based on the following core considerations:

i) All the impacts in **Table 10.1** may be *potentially legitimate* determinants of a viable and ethical labour immigration policy. This implies that discussions about labour immigration need to address the impacts of international labour migration in an explicit, well informed and open manner. This requires, among other things, a thorough understanding of the consequences of international labour migration, including relevant trade-offs, and active discouragement of the kind of "polarization" of immigration debates currently occurring in many countries.

ii) If one accepts the legitimacy of notion states, national policy makers have an obligation to assign more weight in their policy decisions to the impacts on residents and citizens than to those non-citizens. Thus, a balanced approach to the design of labour immigration policy would, at a minimum, require policies that protect a citizen's right to preferential access to the national labour market;[14] ensure that the receiving country derives net economic benefits from the employment of migrant workers, and prevent

11. *In line with the Universal Declaration of Human Rights, the rights contained in the UN's MWC are intended to be* universal *(i.e. they apply everywhere),* indivisible *(e.g. political and civil rights cannot be separated from social and cultural rights), and* inalienable *(i.e. they cannot be denied to any human being and should not be transferable or saleable, not even by the holder of the right).*

12. *In immigration policy, manpower planning usually results in discussions about the number and type of migrant workers that will maximise economic benefits and minimise distributional consequences for the receiving country.*

13. *They include the Migration for Employment Convention of 1949 (ILO Convention No.97), the Migrant Workers (Supplementary Provisions) Convention of 1975 (ILO Convention No.143), and the International Convention on the Protection of the Rights of All Migrant Workers and the Members of their Families, adopted by the UN General Assembly in 1990 (MWC). ILO Convention No. 97 (which came into force on 22 January 1952) has been ratified by 42 member states, while ILO Convention No. 143 (which came into force in 1978) has been ratified by only 18 member states. As of February 2004, the MWC had been signed by only 25 member states, most of which are predominantly migrant-sending rather than migrant-receiving countries.*

14. *Of course, there are instances in which citizens may collectively decide to waive this right. The freedom of movement and employment within the countries of the pre-enlarged European Union is a case in point.*

immigration from adversely affecting national security, public order and the social and political stability of the receiving country.

iii) Migrant workers face particular vulnerabilities in international labour migration and their *interests* therefore need special promotion and protection. Furthermore, these interests are multifaceted, comprising both migrant workers' rights and economic welfare (see **Table 10.1**). Given that the promotion of migrant workers' rights and economic welfare may sometimes be negatively correlated, an extreme rights-based policy would imply that no level of improvement of foreign workers' welfare justifies the restriction of some of their rights. Considering that many migrant workers migrate for economic reasons, giving such minimal weight to their economic welfare seems unlikely to be in their overall interest.

At the same time, it is equally obvious that policies driven and justified by an almost exclusive concern for the economic welfare of migrant workers, with little or no regard to their most basic human rights (the voluntary slavery or sweatshop argument), would be equally objectionable in an approach that purports to be concerned with the overall interest of migrant workers. It is well known that international labour migration frequently takes place in an environment of exploitation, sometimes involving the violation of the most basic human rights of migrant workers.[15] Rather than insist on a very comprehensive set of inalienable rights for migrant workers, as the UN's MWC currently does, a balanced approach would first identify and effectively enforce a basic set of rights that cannot be violated, and then give migrant workers at least some voice/agency in, and the necessary information for, choosing whether and how to balance an increase in their income with a restriction of their rights while employed abroad.

iv) The vulnerabilities of sending countries are significant and stem from inherent asymmetries in the regulation of international labour migration. It is a human right to leave and return to one's country of origin, but there is no corresponding right to enter another country. As a result, there are relatively fewer opportunities for sending countries to regulate emigration than for receiving countries to regulate immigration. For example, receiving countries may effectively restrict the immigration of a highly skilled worker from a developing country if deemed necessary to protect the receiving country's labour market. In contrast, there is relatively little that sending countries can do to restrict the emigration of a highly skilled worker, even if the loss of human capital has significant adverse effects on the sending country's economy.

These asymmetries in the regulation of international labour migration create at least some obligation for receiving countries to make their labour immigration policies "development friendly" for sending countries. This could be achieved by creating legal and readily accessible channels for the flow of remittances, discouraging the permanent immigration of highly skilled migrant workers, where such migration would constitute a serious loss to the sending country, and by encouraging the return and/or circulation of migrant workers. The best way of promoting sending countries' interests in international labour migration would be to adopt a more inclusive approach in the design of labour immigration policies, and to cooperate with sending countries in at least some aspects of policy design.[16]

v) In order to avoid policy conflicts, the choice of the objectives of labour immigration policy should not be too dissimilar from those of policies regulating other aspects of a country's economic openness, such as international trade and capital flows.

International labour migration and international trade and capital flows are not symmetrical phenomena. While most of the purely economic

15. *For a discussion, see, for example, Taran, 2000.*

16. *Weil, 2002, makes the case for a coherent policy of co-development based on more cooperation between migrant receiving and sending states, and migrants themselves.*

effects could be similar, e.g. the labour market impacts of immigration could be similar to those of imports or investment abroad, the international flow of workers also generates a number of non-economic effects, e.g. on national identity and on the rights of individuals, generally not associated with international trade and capital flows. For this reason, there is no *a priori* inconsistency in receiving countries' policies of encouraging the liberalization of international trade and capital flows to a greater degree than that of international labour flows.

A balanced approach to the design of labour immigration policy would, however, ensure that the *degree* of asymmetry between the restrictions on international flows of labour and capital reasonably reflects the differences between their economic and non-economic impacts. Looking at the current globalization trends, it could be argued that the existing imbalances are significantly greater than such considerations of consistency would demand. As of 2000, the ratios of exports, and the stock of outward foreign direct investment, to world GDP were 22.1 and 18.7 per cent, respectively,[17] while the ratio of the estimated *stock* of total migrants to total world population was only about 3 per cent (based on an estimated global stock of 175 million migrants, the great majority of whom are migrant *workers*).[18]

A balanced approach would include policies to encourage a greater degree of liberalisation of international labour migration, especially of low-skilled workers whose international mobility is the most restricted, than is currently the case. This would enhance consistency between international trade, investment and migration policies. Because the integration of international labour markets is significantly lower than the integration of international markets for capital and commodities, such liberalization would also generate significantly higher economic benefits than those derived from a further liberalization of international trade and capital flows (Rodrik, 2002).

THE CASE FOR NEW AND EXPANDED TEMPORARY FOREIGN WORKER PROGRAMMES

THIS CHAPTER argues that a balanced approach to the design of labour immigration policy calls for the liberalization of international labour migration through *new types* of temporary foreign worker programmes (TFWPs) for skilled *and especially for low-skilled foreign workers*. In contrast to the widely held arguments against such programmes, it is suggested that new and expanded TFWPs are both *desirable* from an ethical point of view, and *feasible*, since innovative policy designs, if effectively implemented and enforced, could help avoid the adverse and unintended consequences of most past and existing guest worker programmes.[19]

DESIRABILITY

The ethical argument against TFWPs typically rests on universalistic rights-based theories that emphasize the universality and priority of migrants' rights over narrowly defined national interests of receiving countries. Rights-based theories tend to oppose the *active promotion* of new policies that are based on an explicit distinction between the rights and entitlements of different categories of residents (such as temporary residents, permanent residents, and citizens) and on the idea that it may be desirable to trade certain personal rights against increases in their

17. *In 2000, the ratio of FDI outward flows to total fixed capital accumulation was 17.8 per cent (UNCTAD, 2001). Of course, FDI figures are not strictly comparable to GDP and fixed capital accumulation figures. The idea here is to merely give an indication of the overall magnitudes under consideration, rather than identify the exact degree of the integration of international capital markets.*

18. *See UNPD, 2002. It is interesting to note that, while today's levels of international trade and capital market integration are roughly comparable to those prevailing in the early 20th century (Williamson, 2002; Baldwin and Martin, 1999; Taylor, 1996), the scale of international labour migration since 1950 has been significantly smaller (as a percentage of world population) than that prevailing in the "age of mass migration" of 1820-1913 (Hatton and Williamson, 1998).*

19. *Of course, the issues of desirability and feasibility are interrelated in practice. For example, it could be argued that it cannot be desirable (or ethical) to promote a policy which is clearly unfeasible to implement, i.e. desirability requires feasibility. The reason for separating the two concepts here is to facilitate a more structured discussion of the arguments for and against implementing new and expanded temporary foreign worker programmes.*

and other peoples' economic welfare.[20] Criticisms of TFWPs based on rights-based theories also point to the strong presumption in liberal democracies that residents acquire rights over time. Within this framework, it is immoral to invite foreign workers to immigrate and take up employment, without at the same time enabling them over time to acquire the rights and entitlements typically granted to citizens.

A very similar argument is also made by some communitarian writers. For example, Michael Walzer, a communitarian who argues that restricting immigration could be ethically justified,[21] suggests that if foreign workers are admitted into the political community, they must be given equal rights and opportunities and be set on the road to citizenship.[22] Any other arrangement would constitute a 'family with live-in servants'. Walzer summarizes the issue of guest workers as follows:

'Democratic citizens, then, have a choice: if they want to bring in new workers, they must be prepared to enlarge their own membership; if they are unwilling to accept new members, they must find ways within the limits of the domestic labour market to get socially necessary work done. And those are their only choices. Their right to choose derives from the existence in this particular territory of a community of citizens; and it is not compatible with the destruction of the community or its transformation into yet another local tyranny' (Walzer 1983, p. 61).

Based on the discussion in the above two sections, it can be seen that some arguments against TFWPs are well served by ethical references that are narrow and place their emphasis on a relatively small subset of the migration impacts in **Table 10.1**. For example, and as mentioned before, migrants' rights advocates who oppose TFWPs on the grounds that they restrict migrant workers' rights unacceptably, frequently fail to acknowledge that TFWPs typically increase the economic welfare of (often economically underprivileged) migrant workers. Similarly, communitarian arguments such as Walzer's are primarily concerned with the collective interests of the community in the receiving country, and less so with the interests of individual potential migrants (still in the sending country, and seeking employment abroad), or the interests of the sending country in general.

As a result of this narrow focus on a few selected migration impacts, critics of TFWPs have in fact contributed to maintaining the status quo, as characterized by restrictions on international labour migration, especially of low-skilled workers, and high levels of illegal immigration. Most illegally employed migrant workers are found in relatively low-wage jobs and have very few rights.

Based on a balanced approach, the ethical case *for* new and expanded TFWPs is motivated by the argument that a managed liberalization of international labour migration, especially of low-skilled workers for whom international migration restrictions and thus also international wage differentials are greatest, would benefit all sides; and that of all the possible ways to manage and liberalize labour immigration in a world of sovereign states, TFWPs are the most *realistic* policy option.

TFWPs could benefit receiving states by providing them with a highly motivated workforce that can carry out jobs in sectors and occupations where the following conditions are met: (i) local workers are unavailable to fill existing vacancies; (ii) existing

20. *This assertion holds as a general statement about the nature of rights-based ethical theories (such as libertarian theories based on Nozick, 1974). It needs to be acknowledged, however, that some rights-based approaches, including the one embodied in the international human rights treaties and migrant worker conventions, allow for a (limited) distinction between different categories of residents based on legal status and citizenship (for a discussion, see, for example, Ghosh, 2003).*

21. *Walzer, 1983, suggests that the political community can be thought of as a national 'club' or 'family'. As clubs can regulate admissions, but cannot bar withdrawals, there is a legitimate case for national immigration restrictions that serve to 'defend the liberty and welfare, the politics and culture of a group of people committed to one another and to their common life' (p. 39).*

22. *This includes the right to family reunion. Walzer argues that the notion of the country as a 'family' suggests that 'one cannot admit them (foreign workers) for the sake of their labour without accepting some commitment to their aged parents, say, or to their sickly brothers and sisters' (p. 41).*

vacancies are advertised at "decent" wages that are above the official minimum wage; (iii) a change toward less labour-intensive production technology is difficult in the short term; (iv) relocation abroad is difficult or impossible, and (v) the complete elimination of the occupation or sector is considered to go against the country's national interest. Arguably, the number of jobs in high-income countries meeting all of the five criteria is significant.[23] They exist at both the high and low-skill end of the labour market and include jobs in the IT sector, health care, agriculture, food processing, construction and a number of service industries, including cleaning and, especially, hospitality.

In addition to filling genuine labour shortages that meet the above five criteria, TFWPs could also enable receiving countries to minimize the potentially adverse impacts of the employment of migrant workers on the wages and employment opportunities of the local workforce. This could be done, for example, by restricting the employment of foreign workers to sectors that suffer from labour shortages (a restriction impossible to impose on foreign workers with permanent residence status). Because of the possibility of protecting local workers, and the general expectation of return, TFWPs are more likely to be politically feasible than large-scale permanent immigration programmes. If effectively implemented, they are also more desirable than a policy of benign neglect towards illegal immigration,[24] which could easily lead to a race to the bottom in the wages and employment conditions offered in certain jobs, thus adversely affecting local workers and potentially discouraging employers from modernizing production processes.

While they do not adequately address fundamental issues of poverty and economic development in low and middle-income countries, expanded TFWPs may benefit sending countries through the increased inflow of remittances and return of workers with potentially more skills and knowledge about modern technology. The temporary nature of migrant workers' employment abroad, and their eventual return home, prevents the permanent loss of human capital (brain drain[25]) and the decline in remittances (which often sets in after the family joins the migrant worker abroad). There is thus a convergence of interests of receiving and sending countries in *temporary* labour migration.[26]

From the migrant workers' point of view, the main benefit from new and expanded TFWPs lies in the prospect of increased access to legal (but temporary) employment in higher-income countries. In a way, the creation of new and expanded TFWPs would increase the "choices" for migrant workers, offering them the opportunity to legally earn higher wages abroad at the (potential) cost of restricting some of their rights. It is a trade-off, but it may be a welcome one, especially for workers with little or no other opportunities to economically better themselves and their families.

It could also be argued that temporary employment is desirable, as it maximizes the potential number of migrant workers able to benefit from employment abroad. Long or permanent stays of workers currently abroad naturally make it more difficult for potential newcomers to gain access to a given foreign labour market.

23. *The number of advertised vacancies in high income countries that meet only (i) is significantly greater than those meeting all five criteria cited in the text! This is why the extent of illegal immigration, or even the vacancy assessments by some employer associations, is likely to overstate the demand for migrant workers.*

24. *A frequently cited example of such benign neglect over the issue of illegal immigration is US policy towards undocumented workers in agriculture, where internal and border enforcement efforts have been systematically relaxed during periods of high labour demand (Hanson and Spilimbergo, 2001).*

25. *Note that encouraging return is not the only possible policy option to address the brain drain (although, if implemented successfully, it may be the most effective). Many recent contributions to the brain drain debate have focused on a "diaspora approach" that aims to mobilise migrants abroad to engage in activities that benefit their home countries (through, for example, remittances, investments and transfer of technology). For a discussion, see Wickramsekara, 2003.*

26. *It is important to recognise that – for the reasons mentioned in the text – sending countries are likely to prefer temporary emigration to a completely free international flow of labour.*

FEASIBILITY

The second charge against TFWPs is that they are simply unfeasible. This argument is based on the fact that many of the past and existing TFWPs, most notably the *Bracero* programme in the USA (1942-64) and the *Gastarbeiter* programme in Germany (1955-73), failed to meet their stated policy objectives and instead generated a number of adverse, unintended consequences. The three most important adverse impacts included the exploitation of migrant workers in both recruitment and employment; the emergence of labour market distortions, and the growth of a structural dependence by certain industries on continued employment of migrant workers and, perhaps most importantly from the receiving country's point of view, the non-return and eventual settlement of many guest workers.[27]

In light of these policy failures, it is indeed fair to say that past experience with TFWPs has been overwhelmingly negative. However, to conclude that such programmes are therefore inherently unfeasible ignores the fact that most failures of past guest worker programmes can be traced to a common set of mistakes in policy design. The remainder of this section identifies the three major policy mistakes of past programmes and proposes key policies to avoid them, and their adverse consequences, under new and improved TFWPs. It also acknowledges and addresses the significant challenges to implementing the proposed policies, including especially the need for effective enforcement of immigration and employment laws, especially those designed to combat illegal immigration and employment. Without the latter, any TFWP, including the policies proposed below, is bound to fail.

i) *First*, foreign workers' vulnerability to exploitation in employment mainly arises from the fact that work permits made available through TFWPs are usually specific to a job and employer. Programmes that allow migrant workers to change employers without leaving the country typically require the new employer to apply for a new work permit – a time and resource consuming process. Unless they are willing to return home, foreign workers may thus find it difficult or impossible to escape unsatisfactory working conditions. The problem may be exacerbated by some employers' illegal practices of retaining migrant workers' passports and by the provision of "tied accommodation", i.e. accommodation provided by the employer to their migrant workers on the condition that, and as long as, the migrant continues to work for that employer. This may naturally lead to employers gaining excessive control over migrant workers, and to exploitation.

A first core policy element of new and improved TFWPs is to grant migrant workers at least some freedom of movement (and thus the freedom to choose and change employers) in the receiving country's labour market. This could be done, for example, by issuing work permits specific to a certain sector or occupation (rather than to a certain job and employer), where the work permit holder is allowed to change employers at will. Important supplementary policies would need to include making it a criminal offence for employers to retain their workers' passports, and providing information to migrant workers about affordable housing opportunities, if they exist, other than those offered by the employer.

Importantly, in addition to reducing foreign workers' vulnerability, granting foreign workers more freedom of movement also benefits the receiving country. It increases the efficiency of that country's labour market by enabling foreign workers to better respond to wage differentials, thereby helping to equalize the value of the marginal product of all workers across labour markets. This point has been made by Borjas, who argues that, "immigration greases the wheels of the labour market by injecting into the economy a group of persons who are very responsive to regional differences in economic opportunities" (Borjas, 2001). Efficiency gains may be particularly pronounced

27. *There is a plethora of studies providing empirical evidence for these and other "policy failures" of past guest worker programmes. For overviews, see, for example, Castles, 1986; Martin and Teitelbaum, 2001; Martin, 2003; and Ruhs, 2003.*

where the mobility of native workers is relatively low (such as in the EU).[28]

None of the major existing and past TFWPs has ever experimented with granting migrant workers freedom of movement within certain occupations and/or sectors. The main obstacle appears to be resistance by employers who run the risk of losing migrant workers before the employers' recruitment costs have been recovered.[29] One way of addressing this problem could be to organize collective recruitment by all employers within the occupation and/or sector within which migrants are allowed to move freely.[30] A more modest policy alternative would be to offer migrant workers freedom of movement after a relatively short period of employment with the employer who initially recruited them (that period should reflect the time needed for the employer to recover recruitment costs).

ii) Labour market distortions and a structural dependence on the employment of migrant workers stem from the failure of many existing and past TFWPs to offer employers the right incentives to recruit migrant workers. Although under most existing TFWPs work permits for migrant workers can be issued only if an employer can reasonably demonstrate that no equivalent local workers are available, this so-called "labour market test", aimed at securing the important objective of protecting citizens' rights to preferential access to the national labour market, has typically failed in practice. Whenever necessary, employers have shown considerable ingenuity to ensure that no local workers are found to fill their vacancies (Martin, 2003).

In addition, the work permit fees employers pay under most past and existing TFWPs are relatively low.[31] As a result, migrant workers tended to be both easily accessible and available at relatively low cost to local employers. Although systematic empirical evidence on this issue is scant, an effectively "unlimited" supply of readily available and cheap workers may discourage some employers from modernizing production processes, and thus lead to a situation where inefficient companies and industries remain viable only because they are subsidized by a readily available and cheap immigrant workforce.[32]

Another key policy principle for new and improved TFWPs is, therefore, to "get the price of migrant workers right" by charging employers a monthly fee for each foreign worker they employ. The fee would need to be set at a sufficiently level high to provide local employers with the necessary incentives to: a) search for local workers and avoid paying the fee (this would effectively help to protect the local workers' right to preferential access to the labour market), and b) look for alternatives, such as the mechanization of the production process, or outsourcing, before considering the recruitment of migrant workers. Something similar is occurring in Singapore, where the government sets and regularly revises flexible "foreign worker levies" specific to the sector of employment and the skill level of the migrant worker.

In addition to levelling the playing field, the revenues from work permit fees could also be used to generate funds for enforcement and integration assistance (Martin, 2003). They could also be used as a tool of industrial policy. For example, fees could be raised in order to encourage mechanization or technological change in certain industries. Fees could be set at prohibitively high levels in industries considered to have lost their comparative advantage relative to those in low-income countries. For most high-income countries, labour-intensive manufacturing and, more

28. *In 2000, only 225,000 persons (0.1 per cent of the total EU population) moved their official residence to another EU country. This is only a fraction of the mobility observed in the US, where about 2.5 per cent of the population change states every year (European Commission, 2002).*

29. *Indeed, granting migrant workers freedom of movement within certain occupations and/or sectors may initially decrease the number of workers recruited, as employers become more careful about their "recruitment investments". It is, however, argued that this would be a desirable development as it would help to remove unacceptable risks of exploitation.*

30. *See Weinstein, 2002, for a discussion of this proposal.*

31. *The exception is Singapore, which is discussed immediately below.*

32. *See, for example, Martin and Olmstead's (1985) discussion of the mechanization controversy in US agriculture.*

controversially, parts of agriculture, may be cases in point.[33]

To charge a work permit fee could also serve another important purpose, namely, to reduce local workers' opposition to TFWPs by distributing part of the work permit revenues (e.g. through periodic hand-outs) to native workers in those sectors where the hiring of foreign workers has verifiably depressed wages and/or working conditions.[34] Under such a system, the government would need to carefully determine the appropriate level of such a fee able to compensate local workers while also leaving local employers better off.

Alternatively, in countries where union membership is high, a more market-based system under which native workers collectively decide on the compensation in exchange for their agreement to the employment of a certain number of foreign workers could be foreseen. Such a system would essentially be based on a bargaining process, where local employers, local workers and the government come together and collectively bargain over the number of foreign workers to be admitted and employed, and over the price (work permit fee) that native employers would pay to compensate local workers.[35] This system has, in part, been operating in Australia, where the government consults interest groups and the public about the size and composition of migrant intakes.

Where direct compensation of local workers is considered to be undesirable, for example, because of the potentially adverse impact on the perception of immigration as inherently threatening the employment prospects of local workers, the revenues raised through fees could still be used to mitigate the potential adverse impact on local workers by funding their retraining and skill development.

To implement fees effectively, two main challenges need to be overcome. First, the government of the receiving country needs to accept the proposition that the merits of micro-managing the employment of migrant workers by setting employer fees justify and outweigh the costs associated with increased government intervention. This may be difficult for governments with a strong preference for *laisser-faire* and minimal intervention in the domestic economy. Second, there is a danger that some employers will illegally deduct work permit fees from migrant workers' wages. If this happens, the fees will achieve none of their intended objectives and simply reduce the wages of migrant workers. To prevent this, work permit fees need to be effectively enforced with credible and stiff penalties for employers who pass the fees on to their workers.

iii) One of the biggest policy mistakes under past guest worker programmes, and especially in the German *Gastarbeiter* programme, was the assumption that guest workers were essentially available on tap, i.e. that their numbers could be increased or decreased at will, depending on the economic needs of the receiving country. This assumption was based on the idea that guest workers were labour units without agency, i.e. without the capacity to make independent decisions or revise their decisions based on new information and circumstances (Castles, 2004). In practice, changing expectations on the part of the foreign worker, and pressures on liberal and democratic receiving countries – by the judiciary and civil society – to grant workers employed for a certain number of years the right to family reunion, create dependencies that limit the receiving country's ability to reduce the number of admitted foreign workers at will.[36]

33. *European and US agriculture is heavily subsidized not only through price supports but also through cheap immigrant labour (sometimes from the very countries that would be most efficient at producing these agricultural products in the first place).*

34. *It should be acknowledged that, given disagreements within the theoretical and applied literature about the effects of labour immigration on the labour market outcomes for locals, this is likely to be a formidable and highly controversial exercise.*

35. *For a more detailed analysis of this mechanism, see Weinstein, 2002.*

36. *Compare the discussion in ILO, 2004.*

It should therefore be recognized already at the stage of policy design, that some foreign workers may apply to remain in the host country on a permanent basis and to bring their families. The implementation of new and improved TFWPs must therefore include transparent mechanisms and rules for a *regulated* and *conditional* (*i.e. non-automatic*) transfer into different and "better" programmes that grant *some* foreign workers permanent residence status and the right to family reunion. This could be done, for example, through a points system that places particular emphasis on criteria considered essential for the long-term integration and employability of the migrants in the receiving country. Proficiency in the receiving country's language may be a case in point.[37] Such points-based programmes have been tried and tested, as a means of direct entry, for decades in Australia and Canada, and have helped to give immigration policy a semblance of certainty and measurability.

At the same time, new and improved TFWPs must necessarily remain based on a *general expectation* of *temporariness* of employment and stay of the majority of migrant workers who join the programme. To make this a realistic expectation, policies should discourage a situation in which a foreign worker decides to overstay a temporary work permit because his/her savings target could not be achieved during the period of validity of the work permit. This requires strict enforcement measures against employers and recruiters who give foreign workers wrong information about employment conditions and living costs in the receiving country, and steps to prevent the illicit sale of visas.

A mixture of incentives and enforcement is needed to facilitate the return of migrant workers who exit TFWPs without changing their status to permanent programmes. For example, migrant workers with a valid work permit need to be given the right and opportunity to travel freely, or at least without too many restrictions, between the sending and receiving countries. This will help them maintain networks in the home country, which in turn will increase the probability of their return.

Financial return incentives could include the transfer of migrant workers' social security payments to the workers' sending country. Another policy would be to create special savings accounts which offer migrant workers the opportunity to save part of their wages at special high interest rates subject to the condition that the savings will only be released to migrant workers upon their return to their home countries. Such financial return incentives have been tried before with mixed success. The most infamous example is the Mexican *Bracero* programme that required a portion of migrants' earnings to be deducted for retirement in Mexico. The policy ultimately failed as migrants never received the money, and their claims for deferred wages have been under investigation for decades.

Clear and effective procedures to remove migrant workers who illegally overstay their temporary worker visas are needed, as well as to penalize employers who employ migrant workers without valid work permits. This is primarily a question of political will and depends on the resources made available for internal enforcement measures such as detection, persecution, enforcement of employer sanctions, and deportation. The record of most liberal and democratic receiving countries in enforcing employer sanctions is less than encouraging.

The success of any TFWP ultimately depends on the receiving country's willingness to strictly enforce the law against all parties, recruitment agents, employers and migrant workers, who circumvent the programme.[38] In the absence of effective law enforcement, employers and migrant workers may have very few incentives to join the TFWP and prefer

37. *Great sensitivity is needed to use proficiency in language as a criterion for improved status: the government has to provide adequate and accessible courses, and ideally insist that workers get time off to do them; and it must address the needs of special groups, especially women with child-care responsibilities.*

38. *In fact, some critics of TFWPs agree that the list of policies outlined above may, in theory, make a TFWP work. They argue, however, that the policies are simply impossible to enforce and, therefore, ultimately unfeasible.*

(the continuation of) illegal employment arrangements instead.[39] Also, the toleration of illegal immigration and employment will obviously undermine any policy to encourage the return of migrant workers upon the expiry of their work permits. Between 1998-2002, only eight employers were found guilty of illegally employing migrant workers under Section 8 of the UK's Asylum and Immigration Act 1996, the law preventing illegal work in the UK (Home Office, 2003). Similarly, in 2002, only 53 employers were fined for immigration violations in the whole of the US (Cornelius, 2004).

There are two compelling arguments in favour of effective enforcement of the proposed policies and measures against illegal immigration. First, the ethical case for new and expanded TFWPs – which includes a strong economic argument – could provide a politically powerful justification for devoting resources to law enforcement, and for implementing measures sometimes deemed undesirable in a liberal democracy, such as restricting some migrant workers' rights in exchange for greater access to legal employment opportunities abroad. In other words, if it can be successfully argued, as suggested in this chapter, that a well functioning TFWP is an ethical immigration policy in the interests of all actors involved, one could realistically hope for a more serious commitment to enforcement. This is why the discussion of the ethics of labour immigration policy is of critical importance.

Second, given the convergence of interests of migrant receiving and sending countries in ensuring the temporariness of migrant workers' employment abroad, those countries may find it mutually advantageous to cooperate in supporting and implementing immigration control measures necessary to make a TFWP work. The sending country could, for example, take measures to regulate its migrant worker recruitment industry and assist with the return of migrant workers who have been apprehended and deported by the authorities of the migrant receiving country. Receiving countries could only solicit such support from sending countries if they operate liberal and orderly TFWPs for migrant workers from those countries.

At a minimum, these are sufficient grounds for taking the idea of new and expanded temporary foreign worker programmes seriously, and for testing some of the above policy options. The UK's Sector Based Schemes (SBS) for employing migrants in selected low-skill jobs in hospitality and food processing are a welcome case in point. While lacking most of the policies outlined above, they are a welcome step towards experimenting with new policies for temporary migrant workers in low-skill jobs.[40]

CONCLUSION

In an effort to order what are currently fairly confused debates about labour immigration, this chapter identified three issues for consideration in the design of labour immigration policy: the *consequences* of international labour migration for the receiving country, the sending country and migrants themselves; the values and *ethical considerations* underlying any evaluation of these consequences and informing the choice of policy objectives; and the *policies* best suited to implement the objectives.

Having reviewed the main types of migration impacts and potential trade-offs between them, a case has been made for a balanced approach to evaluating the consequences of international labour migration and subsequent design of labour immigration policy. The key elements of such an approach include:

i) an open, transparent discussion of all economic, social, cultural and other impacts of international

39. *This has been one of the main criticisms voiced again President Bush's proposal of introducing a new guest worker programme-cum-amnesty for Mexican workers seeking employment, or already employed, in the US. The argument is that the policy will be ineffective unless illegal immigration is brought under better control.*

40. *For more information about the SBS, see www.workingintheuk.gov.uk/working_in_the_uk/en/homepage/work_permits/sector_based_schemes.html.*

labour migration for migrants and non-migrants in receiving and sending countries;
ii) the acknowledgement of the need for national policymakers to give at least some preference in their policy decisions to the interests of citizens;
iii) the recognition that the interests of migrant workers need to be actively protected and promoted, including both migrants' rights and economic welfare, two factors that may sometimes conflict;
iv) the responsibility of receiving countries to make their labour immigration polices "development-friendly" for sending countries, and,
v) the need to avoid policy contradictions by aligning the objectives of labour immigration policies more closely with those of international trade and investment policies.

It has been further suggested that these considerations can be used to make an ethical case to liberalize international labour migration through new and expanded temporary foreign worker programmes, especially for low-skilled migrants. To make such programmes feasible, the policy mistakes of past guest worker programmes must be avoided. Three key policies are needed:

i) some freedom of movement for labour migrants in the receiving country's labour market;
ii) regulation of employers' costs of migrant workers by setting flexible work permit fees, and,
iii) mixed incentives-enforcement measures to encourage the return of migrants on expiry of their work permits.

As stated, these policies will be difficult to implement, and their success will ultimately depend on effective enforcement, especially of the laws against illegal immigration and the illegal employment of migrant workers. While intensely contested, the feasibility of effective enforcement could be greatly enhanced by making a convincing ethical case for a well functioning and mutually beneficial Temporary Foreign Workers Programme, and by greater cooperation between receiving and sending countries in the design and implementation of appropriate migration laws and policies.

The discussion of the ethics of labour immigration policy, the potential trade-off between migrants' rights and their economic welfare, and the attendant feasibility of temporary foreign worker programmes raises questions that are inherently difficult and contentious. That is precisely why they are frequently avoided in labour immigration debates. It is important to close this "values gap" in the discussion. One may not agree with the policy recommendations made in this chapter, but it is important to address and answer these hard ethical questions, and to have the courage to follow through their policy implications, particularly for innovative temporary migrant worker programmes, that many countries already urgently need.

TEXTBOX 10.1

ILO Action Plan on Labour Migration

At its 92nd session in June 2004, the International Labour Conference adopted a resolution for a comprehensive Action Plan on Migrant Workers. This was prompted by government concerns about the growing numbers of migrants in an irregular status, the spreading menace of trafficking of persons, abuses against migrant workers in some countries, and the worrying signs of racism and xenophobia in others. International norms and standards, while relevant, were considered inadequate to ensure protection of migrant workers in these circumstances.

The Action Plan was seen by governments as a practical and timely way of responding to the emerging problems posed by growing cross-border movements of people. The ILO report to the Conference, "A Fair Deal for Migrant Workers in a Global Economy", argues that a sound rights-based management of labour migration is the key to effective protection of migrant workers.

The Action Plan lists a number of elements, including an expanded role for tripartism and social dialogue, capacity building and normative activities. But at its centre is a "non-binding multilateral framework for a rights-based approach to migration", which would comprise international guidelines based on best practices in the following areas:

- Expanding avenues for regular labour migration, based on labour market needs and demographic trends.
- Promoting managed migration for employment, and addressing such aspects as admission procedures, flows, social security, family reunification possibilities, integration policy and return.
- Supervision of recruitment and contracting of migrant workers.
- Preventing smuggling and trafficking of persons, and preventing and combating irregular labour migration.
- Promoting decent working conditions and protecting the human rights of all migrant workers, as well as promoting awareness of those rights.
- Promoting measures to ensure that all migrant workers benefit from the provisions of all relevant international labour standards.
- Improving labour inspections and creating channels for migrant workers to lodge complaints and seek remedies without intimidation.
- Reducing the cost of remittance transfers and promoting the productive investment of remittances.
- Ensuring that all migrant workers are covered by national legislation and applicable social laws.
- Encouraging return and reintegration into the country of origin and the transfer of capital and technology by migrants.
- Guidelines for ethical recruitment and mutually beneficial approaches to ensure adequate supply of health and education personnel that serve the needs of both sending and receiving countries.
- Reducing the specific risks for men and women migrant workers in certain occupations and sectors with particular emphasis on dirty, demeaning and dangerous jobs, and on women in domestic service and the informal economy.

- Promoting social integration and inclusion, reducing discrimination and combating racism and xenophobia.
- Facilitating the portability of social security entitlements, and
- Promoting recognition and accreditation of migrant worker's skills and qualifications.

While there was extensive debate about the interpretation of a "rights-based approach", or what was to be done regarding irregular migrant workers, the resolution marked a clear agreement on many issues that in the past had proven contentious. These include the need to expand avenues for regular labour migration; the need for all migrant workers, regardless of their legal status, to benefit from international standards and to be covered by national legislation and applicable social laws, and the need for "ethical recruitment guidelines" and bilateral and multilateral agreements to avoid negative consequences for sending countries.

The framework is intended to be non-binding, but is also part of a broader Action Plan that seeks to engage all parties – governments, workers and employers organizations, the ILO and other international organizations – in a continuing effort to establish a more humane migration regime for the benefit of all concerned.

Source: Manolo Abella, ILO.

Chapter 11
Balancing the Benefits and Costs of Skilled Migration in the Asia-Pacific Region[1]

In the end what matters is people... Labour productivity, critical for economic growth, depends on workers' knowledge, skills, motivation, and health...A well educated, healthy workforce is essential for economic growth.

INTRODUCTION[2]

Human capital is increasingly the most important form of wealth for many countries and regions, with those richest in intellectual resources tending to achieve the highest rates of economic growth and most rapid development of their science and technology sectors. Such resources not only produce wealth, they are vital in dealing with many social and environmental aspects of modern living. Yet in many developed countries, a combination of factors – high demand in certain sectors, lack of adequate training facilities, people making different career choices – has led to major skilled labour shortages. Hence the need for policies that encourage the immigration of skilled labour[3] and draw on ready-trained science and technology personnel, often from developing countries, to meet these shortages. Such policies, however, have mixed consequences for the countries of origin.

On an individual level, current policies tend to widen the opportunities for those with suitable skills to emigrate. At the macro level, these may be precisely the skilled personnel most needed in developing countries. Skilled emigration clearly has both positive and negative impacts on economies, but this is not systematically taken into account in development planning. It has been argued that, "if appropriate global development strategies were in place, then international (especially temporary migration) could be factored into (and make an important contribution to) the development process" (Appleyard, 1992).

Similarly, there is as yet insufficient policy consideration of such social issues as gender. Skilled occupations tend to be heavily male-oriented, although women now account for an increased proportion of total highly skilled migrants (Ouaked, 2002). However, there are still few analyses of their economic participation (Kofman, 2000; Raghuram, 2000).

This chapter analyses the benefits and costs for a selection of countries/regions in the Asia-Pacific of high-skilled labour mobility. It looks at the benefits that flow from skilled immigration to some of the larger immigrant receiving countries (Australia, the US, Canada, Japan and others) and the complexity of the costs and benefits for some source countries/regions at various stages of evolution of emigration management (Taiwan, China mainland,

1. *The author of this chapter is Dr Robyn Iredale, Associate Professor, School of Earth and Environmental Sciences, University of Wollongong, Australia.*

2. *For the purpose of this chapter, Asia includes the following geographic designations: China (which includes China mainland, Hong Kong Special Administrative Region of China -- hereafter referred to as Hong Kong, Macao Special Administrative Region of China -- hereafter Macao, and Taiwan Province of China -- hereafter Taiwan), the Democratic People's Republic of Korea (hereafter North Korea), and the Republic of Korea (hereafter South Korea).*

3. *Definitional issues make this a difficult area to describe accurately, but highly skilled workers are generally taken to be those who possess a tertiary qualification or have equivalent experience (Iredale, 2001). However, most of the policy interest and collection of statistical data has focused on Human Resources in Science and Technology (HRST), that has been seen as driving the demand for skilled labour. HRST covers science, engineering computing and life and health sciences.*

Vietnam, Bangladesh, India and Fiji). It also reviews the policies of these countries to counter the negative effects of skilled emigration. The conclusion highlights some key policy issues for governments and the wider international community if countries of origin are not to be seriously and permanently disadvantaged.

IMPACTS OF IMMIGRATION – GROWTH AND DEVELOPMENT

THERE has been a strong policy orientation in many developed regions towards attracting highly skilled immigrants, the "brightest and the best" on the global market. Traditional receiving countries are refining existing policies and making them more flexible in anticipation that high-skilled immigration will be a major factor in their future development. Other countries like Germany, the UK, France, the Netherlands, Japan, South Korea and Singapore are also developing new policies to attract highly skilled workers. Permanent intakes are not on the increase, but there is a significant level of temporary movement of highly skilled labour, particularly in certain sectors (IT, medicine, nursing and teaching).

One notable area of increased flexibility can be seen in the overseas student programmes. Studying abroad can lead to future migratory behaviour, and many students even go abroad with the intention of staying after completing their studies (Phillips and Stahl, 2000). In the US and Canada, this change of status has been relatively easy for some time, and Australia has also recently opened this avenue to students.

AUSTRALIA

Australia today places a high priority on skilled immigration, and has an active, flexible selection policy to capture the best for its needs, both from abroad and from foreign student ranks within Australia. Selection is on the basis of economic expediency and a points-based assessment of the propensity of migrants to settle and integrate in Australia. Selection criteria are generally objective, excluding race as a factor,[4] and focusing on such "settlement" prospect indicators as language, education, qualifications, work experience and the like. The first points system,[5] introduced in 1979, has been progressively fine-tuned to adapt the mix of migrants to evolving priorities of the government and pressures exerted by professional, training and union bodies in Australia. Consequently, educational standards among migrants have risen: between 1991 and 2001, the proportion of new immigrants with university degrees was twice as high as for persons born in Australia. According to the Longitudinal Survey of Immigrants to Australia,[6] 43 per cent of adult migrants in 1999-2000 were university graduates.

There has been a major reorientation of Australian international migration policy in recent years to include temporary as well as permanent skilled immigration. The Temporary Resident Programme increased to reach 163,700 in 2002, of which 43,300 were in the Economic Programme (OECD, 2003). This component has not been subject to the same rigorous "skills recognition" testing as for permanent entrants (except in medicine),[7] and the decision is left to employers. Much of the push for temporary entrants

4. *With the end of the White Australia Policy in the early 1970s, new selection criteria excluded race as a factor.*

5. *The points system covering skills, age, work experience, English language ability and sponsorship (if applicable) is applied in different ways to the following three major categories: Offshore General Skilled; Onshore General Skilled, and Onshore New Zealand Citizens. For full details see the DIMIA website: www.immi.gov.au/migration/skilled/index.htm*

6. *The Longitudinal Survey of Migrants to Australia (LSIA), commissioned by DIMIA, was first carried out on a sample of 6,960 primary applicants/spouses, Cohort 1, who arrived between September 1993 and August 1995. They were surveyed 6, 18 and 42 months after arrival. Cohort 2, consisting of 4,181 who arrived from September 1999 to August 2000 were also interviewed 6, 18 and 42 months after arrival.*

7. *The policy in the late 1990s-2000 to admit permanently only those with qualifications and experience 'recognized' in Australia was the most recent strategy to reduce the labour market adjustment problems of skilled migrants.*

has come from employers who want 'fast track' mechanisms to obtain workers. Despite the separate categories, there is a high degree of crossover between temporary (particularly student) and permanent entrants, with the former often becoming permanent after some time.[8]

According to the Department of Immigration and Multicultural and Indigenous Affairs (DIMIA), the benefits of these programmes to Australia include employment creation, enhancement of Australia's skill and technology base, growth of cutting edge technologies and industries, increased competitiveness and expansion of international trade and trading links.

However, their real impact needs to be measured against the increase in permanent and temporary departures of both Australia- and overseas-born in recent years. During the 1990s, there was a 146 per cent increase in permanent and a 41 per cent increase in temporary departures of persons born in Australia, of whom over two-thirds were managers, administrators, professionals and paraprofessionals. On balance, there is a net "brain gain" but some experts feel that emigration removes the "best of the best", while immigration brings in less than the best (Hugo et al., 2003). They see a disproportionate loss of Australians with superior training and skills and call for policies to attract some back, or at least encourage their circulation back to Australia.

There have also been fears about the negative impact of foreign professionals on the domestic market, in part based on research findings that skilled immigrants can reduce the relative incomes of Australians with similar skills in certain sectors (Garnaut, 2003). These and the above concerns about the emigration/immigration imbalance have led to protective or restrictive practices by national professional bodies and the government in selection and skills recognition (seen by some as potential barriers to implementing policies of diversity or non-discrimination). (See also the chapter "Oceania Migration Dynamics".)

Overall, Australia benefits from skilled migration in terms of higher average incomes (Access Economics, 2001), although not as much as it might if there were a more open attitude to other training systems. In 2001, the unemployment rate for migrants with university degrees was more than double that of graduates born in Australia (Garnaut, 2003). This is apparently due to the time necessary to adjust to the labour market, and/or to poor English language skills, but it does not fully explain the situation (Chapman and Iredale, 1993). Studies have found a clear wage differential that has disadvantaged overseas-trained university graduate workers over time.[9]

On the economic side, government-commissioned research on the economic benefits of permanent and temporary migration shows that these potentially accrue from the intake of higher skilled migrants, and range from improved living standards to increased tax revenues that can raise Commonwealth income and productivity owing to additional high-income earners (DIMIA, 2004). More broadly, large-scale migration from Asia and elsewhere has greatly benefited Australia's economic, social and political interactions with these countries. Though these gains have not been quantified, they are acknowledged as significant. They include a diversity of languages and cultures, a greater "openness" to the rest of the world and a range of attitudes, values and mores, which have all contributed significantly to Australia's culture and way of life.

Reports prepared for the government indicate little concern about the impacts of skilled migration on the countries of origin (Hugo, 2003; Garnaut, 2003). They challenge the government to achieve the "double

8. *In 2002-03 more than 50 per cent of 37,735 successful General Skilled Migration Offshore and Onshore (points-tested) applicants claimed points for an Australian qualification (DIMIA, 2004). Immediate labour market entry becomes a means to demonstrate skills and expertise and can lead to more formal recognition later.*

8. *See the study of these factors by Chapman and Iredale, 1993. Research into benefits to the Australian budget over time also shows that skilled immigrants generate greater gains than family or humanitarian entrants.*

bonus" of attracting foreign skilled people while retaining and regaining the best of Australia's own talent (Hugo, 2003). Thus, on the one hand, the government should not lose sight of the ethical and practical issues raised by the "brain drain" experienced by poorer countries (Garnaut, 2002) and, on the other, it is compelled by globalization to attract its share of talent from the rest of the world, including from among former immigrant students of Australian tertiary institutions (Garnaut, 2003).

UNITED STATES OF AMERICA (US)

The US is the first choice for many migrants. It has a more liberal approach to skilled migration, as it garners skills from a wide range of sources to fill gaps and fuel economic growth, and is less concerned about the outcomes for immigrants than meeting the needs of US employers, and stimulating growth and innovation. The 1990 *Immigration Act* aimed at broadening the focus on the economic skills and potential of immigrants, while preserving the overriding commitment to family reunion.[10] Selection in the skills categories relies heavily on:

- an offer of employment, and
- the protection of existing standards regarding wages and conditions.[11]

There have been debates on how to measure an alleged shortage and whether the government should accept employers' decisions about the best-qualified employees. In 1995-96, the former U.S. Commission on Immigration Reform (CIR) and some political leaders attempted to move to a points-based system, but this failed since it would have required a major change in immigrant selection processes and greater cooperation between business, worker advocates, government regulators and other groups.

The US has the largest temporary (non-immigrant) intake, with the major provisions for entry being:

- the H-1B visa scheme, requiring no assessment of qualifications but possession of a university degree;
- the North American Free Trade Agreement (NAFTA);
- the L-1 visa scheme for movement within multinational enterprises, and
- the O-visa category for workers of distinguished abilities.[12]

Total visas issued under these categories have consistently numbered more than half a million per annum in recent years, and in 2001 they reached over one million (OECD, 2003). As with Australia and Canada, overseas students have also become a significant source of skilled migrants in the US, and the number of university student entrants rose from 553,900 in 1998 to 689,000 in 2001 (OECD, 2003).

There have been some attempts to measure the gains from skilled migration and to quantify the benefits generated for the US economy by the ties skilled migrants maintain with their home countries. Research at the University of California at Berkeley revealed a significant correlation between the presence of first-generation immigrants and exports from California to their home country: a one per cent increase in the number of first-generation immigrants generated a 0.5 per cent increase in exports from California to the respective country. This pattern is particularly pronounced as regards the Asia-Pacific

10. *It expanded employment-based permanent immigration by increasing the annual allotment for the worker preference categories from 54,000 to 140,000 (including accompanying dependants), with an emphasis on attracting professionals and skilled workers. 179,200 people were admitted under worker preferences in 2001 (OECD, 2003).*

11. *Initially, it is determined whether there are insufficient qualified workers available in the US, and that the wages and working conditions of similarly employed US workers will not be adversely affected.*

12. *The number of H-1B visas was 195,737 in FY 2002 and most of them were taken up by males in the IT and science sectors. L-l visas allow multinationals to transfer executives, managers and employees with specialized skills from a foreign to a US location. They are easier and less costly to obtain than H-1B visas (which cost employers USD 1,000 each), employees need not be paid award wages, they allow the person to remain in the US for up to seven years and there is no limit on the numbers that may be issued. In 2002, 57,721 were issued of which around one-third went to Indian nationals. The stock of L-1 visa holders was 328,480 in 2001. A debate broke out in Florida about US firms bringing in Indian IT workers under the L-1 scheme, and then placing them with other firms.*

region (Saxenian, 2001), and compares with the findings of research commissioned by the Australian government into the economic benefits of permanent and temporary migration.

CANADA

Canada selects permanent migrants for their generic skills, but is increasingly concerned about the large number of people who are unable to enter the occupations of their training once they arrive (Tolley, 2003). Canada recently liberalized its approach to attract well-qualified, versatile migrants, and introduced a new *Immigration and Refugee Protection Act* (IRPA) in June 2002, that no longer included occupations, and instead emphasized education, knowledge of official languages (English and/or French), experience, age, arranged employment and adaptability in its points system. Canada's proximity to the US places it in a unique position to compete for skilled migrants. There is little pre-migration assessment of qualifications and no matching of occupational qualifications to jobs.

Recognizing the importance of women in the migration process, Canada is one of the few countries that apply a gender-based analysis to immigration policy (Kofman, 2003; Tolley, 2003). This adjusts selection criteria to the specific circumstances of women, making their chances of entry as skilled workers more equitable (see also the discussion on gender implications below).

Under the employment authorization scheme to attract skills in short supply the number of temporary skilled entries to Canada, including seasonal workers and re-entries, has risen from 79,800 in 1998, to 87,908 in 2002 (OECD, 2003, CIC, 2003a)., Of these, NAFTA entrants average 6,500 per year and are mostly in a defined list of professions. The proportion of temporary workers in managerial, professional and skilled/technical occupations rose to a peak of 57.2 per cent in 2002 and, though there are no statistics on the value of this intake, it clearly is a very productive addition to the workforce (CIC, 2003b). To date, Canada does not seem to have undertaken the same studies as Australia on the economic benefits of migration in terms of increases to average income, and additions to the budget and tax revenue.

JAPAN, SOUTH KOREA, TAIWAN, SINGAPORE, HONG KONG

Japan, South Korea, Hong Kong, Singapore and Taiwan are major importers of temporary skilled workers to meet specific labour market shortages and, increasingly, to gain new ideas, technologies and initiatives. The recent immigrant response to a shortage of nurses and the entry of "entertainers" has led to a feminization of these flows. In 2001, Japan admitted 141,900 temporary skilled entrants, 83 per cent of whom were "entertainers". Japan's import of "entertainers" as skilled workers, although it is generally known that many of them work in the sex industry, is a major anomaly.[13] Owing to Japan's economic slowdown, the number of visas issued to highly skilled workers declined from 3,500 in 2000 to 2,100 in 2001 (OECD, 2003). Recently, the *White Paper on International Trade in 2003*, under the subtitle "Revitalization of the Japanese Economy Through Input of Foreign Dynamism", clearly identified the need for "capable human resources from all over the world. (...) the improvement of MRA,[14] conclusion of bilateral social agreements and improvement of working environments for foreigners are essential" (Morita, 2003).

South Korea, Taiwan and Singapore all have skilled inflows to fill vacancies, though they were affected by the 1997 Asian financial crises. South Korea recently revised its *Immigration and Emigration Law* to enable unlimited stay and simplified administrative procedures for professionals. The number of entrants rose from 12,592 in 1999 to 16,000 in the first eight

13. *Note that in November 2004, the government announced plans to impose stricter work visa requirements on foreign entertainers, and lower the numbers of Filipinos on such visas (from 80,000 to 8,000 a year), in a bid to fight trafficking.*

14. *MRAs are "Mutual Recognition Agreements (MRAs). See also discussion below and ftn. 14.*

months of 2000. In mid-2003, a new Act on Foreign Workers' Employment was introduced and, since August 2004, a dual system is in place to bring low-skilled foreign workers into the country (the pre-existing industrial trainee system and an employment permit system) and to grant them equal labour rights with local workers.[15] Of the more than 380,000 foreign workers present in the country at the end of 2003, over a third were in the country irregularly and only six per cent were skilled.[16]

The new open door policy is likely to be further extended in the future (Yoo and Uh, 2001). Taiwan enables skilled workers to enter, and allows employers to make their own selection, usually through subsidiaries or business partners in Japan or elsewhere in Asia.[17] The return of overseas Taiwanese on a permanent or temporary basis is dealt with in the next section. Singapore encourages the entry of highly skilled professionals with a number of incentives, including permanent residence, and in 2000 administrators/managers and professionals accounted for 12 per cent of the 612,000 foreigners employed there. The fact that 24 per cent of the resident population (nationals and permanent residents) are in these occupations indicates that many professionals from overseas, particularly India, have acquired permanent residence (Yap, 2001).

The number of workers with special skills who had entered Hong Kong since its return to the People's Republic of China declined slightly from 16,561 in 1997 to 14,521 in 1999 (Chiu, 2001). The recession led to the increased scrutiny of entrants and, only when a vacancy cannot be filled locally and the applicant possesses "outstanding qualifications, expertise and skills which are needed but not readily available in Hong Kong", are they admitted (Chiu, 2001). Because the drop also coincided with the Hong Kong's return to China, it is not easy to clearly identify the cause of the decline.

In addition to, or in place of these movements, are flows that are likely to result from future growth of trade in services under the GATS Mode 4, or the movement of natural persons (MNP). Countries are free to choose the sectors they wish to open to foreign temporary service providers and this is most likely to happen in areas where there are skill shortages and where foreigners are less likely to compete with domestic service providers. The wages and conditions available in developed countries are likely to attract skilled service providers from developing countries, but mutual recognition agreements (MRAs) are needed to ensure transferability of qualifications and skills.[18]

The likelihood of many developing countries negotiating MRAs with more developed countries is slim, except where there are historical structural ties (e.g. among Commonwealth countries) or similar levels of development (Iredale, 2003). For example, two MRAs were due to be signed in 2004: one between Japan and Australia in engineering, after seven years of negotiations (UNCTAD, 2003), and one between the Philippines and Malaysia in architecture, also following four years of discussions (ASEAN Secretariat, 2004). This means that, if trade in services from less developed to more developed economies in the region is to increase, other mechanisms will need to be found for assessing/accrediting training and skills.

IMPACT OF EMIGRATION – GAINS AND LOSSES FROM SKILLED DIASPORAS AND RETURN MIGRATION

RESEARCH on the impact of skilled emigration, or "brain drain", has been ongoing since the 1960s. But recently the emphasis has shifted to skilled return migration and the potential benefits from "brain

15. *For more details, see the Textbox "Labour Migration in South Korea".*

16. *Ibid.*

17. *Formal qualifications must be translated and submitted to the government before a work visa is issued.*

18. *The World Trade Organization's GATS Mode 4 states that in skilled occupations MRAs should be developed between countries or groups of countries to deal with the issue of the recognition of foreign qualifications.*

circulation" for developing countries. Some argue that the "brain drain" is depriving developing countries of valuable human resources and hindering the application of new technologies, inhibiting research and development, and generally holding back development. Others argue that this is overstated, and stress the benefits of skilled emigrants for countries of origin and of destination. With this in mind, research was undertaken between 2000 and 2002 in four countries in Asia to examine the trends and the impacts of skilled migration (Iredale et al., 2003).

The study found potential benefits of emigration and eventual return migration at three levels:

a) The micro level for individual migrants, families and communities, through improvements in individual or family income, acquisition of capital to invest, development of skills through training or work experience, and improvement in family security and social status. These benefits also have second-round effects on the wider economy and society, as demonstrated by the new economics of labour migration researchers (Taylor, 1999).

b) The intermediate level for some industries/sectors, through the investment of remittances in, for example, agriculture or business activities, and the stimulation of local economies through such investment or money brought/sent home by permanent or temporary migrants and returnees. Migration networks and collectives are vital mechanisms for achieving these benefits.

c) The macro level for economies and societies as a whole, including the use of remittances to improve balance of payments, reduce foreign debt, fund imports; improved human capital at the national level; strengthened international trade and trading links, and innovative approaches to economic development through exposure to more advanced industrialized societies.

The benefits under a) and c) have received most attention in the relevant literature. The macro level is the most difficult area to analyse, as it is not easy to separate the impact of migrants on the economy and society from other exogenous influences, such as the information revolution, technology, research, and similar developments.

Few countries or regions have been able to accurately measure any of these benefits, therefore their possible magnitude can only be estimated. Many countries do not know the true volume of their skilled emigration or the return rates, either permanent or temporary. Research has shown that skilled emigration may not necessarily be replaced by immigration or return migration (often referred to as "migration transition") (Iredale et al., 2003). It is instructive to see where emigration countries like Bangladesh, Vietnam, China and Taiwan currently stand on the migration spectrum ranging from stage 1: predominantly experiencing emigration, through stage 2: emigration and start of return migration, and to stage 3: emigration, immigration and circulation.

Stage 1
- Bangladesh is still predominantly at the "brain drain" stage, and struggling to become a "globalizer".

Stage 2
- Vietnam experienced a brain drain reversal in the late 1990s, but the sluggish economy, the impact of the Asian financial crises and the slow rate of reform of both state-owned enterprises and the bureaucratic sector have all worked to discourage potential returnees (early stage 2).
- China began to experience a brain drain reversal in the mid-1990s, so that skilled return migration occurred as China's open door policies gained momentum, the economy took off and entry to the WTO had become a reality (middle stage 2).

Stage 3
- Taiwan entered stage 2 in the 1980s as the economy soared. Return did not equal outflow, but became substantial in actual numbers. The openness of the Taiwanese economy and its globalization has taken it into stage 3 in the 1990s, characterized by skilled

outflows and inflows and an increasingly high level of temporary and intermittent circulation of nationals.

Clearly the benefits/costs of skilled emigration need to be analysed on an individual country/region basis. The following case studies show that "brain drain" is no longer a major problem for Taiwan, as return migration and brain circulation have become more significant. This is increasingly the case for China mainland, although it is still a long way from repatriating the number of skilled overseas Chinese that it needs or would like. Vietnam is somewhat unique, because of the high level of government control over students going abroad and the lack of attractive work options on their return. For Bangladesh, however, the costs manifestly outweigh the benefits at this time.

India and the Philippines are also included as examples of large-scale, expanding government-backed senders of skilled workers that are currently over-training for the export markets. Fiji is also discussed, because of some analogies to Bangladesh, although it may be experiencing even greater relative costs.

TAIWAN

Taiwan is a good example of an economy that has been networking globally, largely as a result of the emigration of students since the 1950s. It has derived great benefits from attracting back highly skilled Taiwanese, although the return flow has amounted to only 20 per cent of those who left. They have been encouraged to return by a wide range of incentives and policies, as well the growth of the Taiwanese economy since the 1960s. But these policies have also provided opportunities for Taiwanese at home to better access research and academic careers (Iredale et al., 2003).

The bridges built between expatriate communities and Taiwan have enabled the return flow of capital, skills and technology. These bridges are now incorporated into wider transnational Taiwanese communities, and many social networks have led to more formal business partnerships. Taiwan now offers world-class manufacturing, flexible development and integration and access to key customers and markets in China mainland and Southeast Asia for companies based in the US (Tsay, 2003). This type of integrated or symbiotic relationship has taken 40 – 50 years to develop and is the result of foresight and appropriate policies, and close relations between the US and Taiwan over this period. The relationship is likely to intensify as Taiwan continues to provide access to the market in China mainland for US firms. Taiwan's story is unique, but its attention to long-term policies is a valuable lesson for other countries.

CHINA (PEOPLE'S REPUBLIC OF)

Since the introduction of the open-door policy in the late 1970s, the Chinese government has allowed students and scholars to study overseas in the hope that they would return to help modernize the country. As the government reports, no more than 25 per cent of the more than 700,000 overseas Chinese students returned in the period 1978-2003.[19] The seriousness of this became quite evident, but instead of trying to stem the outflow, Chinese officials began to foster the return of "overseas talent".

Cities such as Beijing, Shanghai and other coastal cities have become popular destinations for highly educated returnees, and local administrations are actively trying to attract them. In 1999, for example, the Beijing municipal government issued a provisional regulation to encourage overseas Chinese students and scholars to return to work there. Returnees were entitled to a number of benefits: simplified application and registration procedures for setting up a business; waiver of business taxes in high-tech areas; eligibility to apply for special research funding and low-interest loans to establish private businesses; eligibility to import tax-free equipment, materials and other goods for

19. *See the Textbox 6.3 "Migration in the People's Republic of China".*

research/business, and eligibility to import some durable personal items tax-free.

While many returnees have not taken advantage of the policies introduced to attract them, their return has been encouraged by the positive gestures of the Chinese government (Luo, Huang and Guo, 2003). Taking their cue from other countries, the government also created science and technology parks in Chinese cities and Special Economic Zones, many of which have become points of attraction for Chinese returnees. Returnees have also been placed in key positions in universities or research institutes and many play an important role as advisers to decision makers and policy design.

Returnees from overseas have evolved into a special category in Chinese society. This seems inevitable and is probably the only way that significant numbers can be encouraged to return home. (Luo, Huang and Guo, 2003). While not rich in financial terms, many returnees are "rich" in terms of resource channels and opportunities, and those employed by foreign enterprises or have their own business also enjoy a much higher income. Financial assistance and subsidies from employers or government programmes are much more generous than the income of their domestic counterparts. Many are granted special conditions even before signing their employment contracts, such as paid overseas visits/holidays and opportunities to attend overseas conferences. All this can create tensions between returnees and their local counterparts.[20] Many of the *émigrés* who have returned and played a major role in China's development have been those already long settled abroad who wanted to return to their roots.

Joining the World Trade Organization (WTO) is expected to improve China's economic and social environment further, and to attract more *émigrés* home to take advantage of the opportunities. Those who decide not to return frequently cite a lack of freedom and other non-economic factors as the reason for their decision. But there are also recent reports about increasingly gloomy prospects for returnees with high salary expectations after working abroad (*China Daily*, 25 June, 2004). With the economic slowdown as of mid-2004, the government will need to watch its effects on circular migration.

VIETNAM

Vietnam has a similar history to China of strict state control, but in Vietnam this lasted into the 1990s. Refugees who fled after 1975 provide a reservoir of people overseas, and some of these are returning to establish businesses or set up NGOs. Vietnam predicts that emigration will increase as its economy develops. It welcomes this trend, and in 2000 the government allocated the equivalent of USD 7 million to send students abroad. Many international organizations, universities and enterprises assist their young cadres financially to study abroad. However, a recent study shows that returnees find it difficult to adjust on their return (Dang, 2003).

Vietnam imposes an obligation on individuals whose period abroad was funded by the state or their organizations, to return to their former employers. Many work in universities, research institutions, state-owned enterprises and managerial posts. Some move from state agencies to non-governmental and international organizations in search of higher salaries, more challenging work and better working conditions.

Skilled returnees, especially scientific researchers, tend to bring back a strong sense of responsibility, a good command of foreign languages and new skills. But low salaries,[21] a certain resentment towards them and low access to decision-making in the workplace, tend to limit opportunities for promotion, dampen

20. *The popular nickname for overseas returnees, "sea turtles", reflects some resistance from the locally educated people who, on the other hand, are called "land tortoises". In public debates and the media, the terms "sea turtles" and "land tortoises" are frequently used to distinguish the place where a person received his/her formal education. This, in turn, is seen as determining their views on certain issues.*

21. *Salary scales are generally based on seniority and managerial posts rather than skills and expertise.*

any creative spirit among returnees, and generally waste their expert resources (Dang, 2003)

Vietnam's dire need for qualified scientists calls for special policies and preferential treatment to attract people back (Dang, 2003). Improved conditions will also encourage people to stay and work more effectively. In particular, women returnees face more hurdles than men in readjusting to the Vietnamese work place. Overseas Vietnamese also need to be attracted in greater numbers. Regulations and permits need to be changed to provide returning expatriates equal access and treatment to locals when opening a business. The government may also need to address the potential regional inequalities that occur if more returnees prefer to settle in the south than in the north of the country.

BANGLADESH

The situation in Bangladesh is so serious that some observers feel it is almost superfluous to analyse the benefits of emigration or of return migration.[22]

Many returnees to Bangladesh are active in the NGO sector, and most of the well known and large indigenous NGOs were founded by them in the 1970s, some directly contributing to the economic development of their home countries. Some notable returnees include Professor Mohammad Yunus, founder of the Grameen Bank, and Dr. Zafrullah Chowdhury, founder of the People's Health Centre. Others have joined university or research centres, where they bring new perspectives and attitudes to their work and their students.

The major issue of concern regarding Bangladesh is how to discourage emigration and encourage return migration. There is a desperate urge to emigrate and no incentive to return on the part of most middle class *émigrés*. The only way to begin addressing this problem is to tackle the root causes of emigration. However, there is no real plan or programme in Bangladesh, such as, for instance, the Return and Reintegration of Qualified Nationals Programme by IOM in the 1970s (Rozario and Gow, 2003).

Bangladesh is not gaining from the emigration of students and skilled personnel at this stage, and it will take a massive effort to turn this situation around. Women face more hurdles on their return than men, not just in their work, but in society generally. How they cope with this depends on many factors, but major changes to living arrangements often ensue, and female returnees become very active in civil society and in the efforts to change practices that discriminate against them. Experts have recommended some policy changes to foster targeted return programmes, high quality training institutes, incentive payments, more effective civil society operations, the engagement of international organizations, compensation or aid from countries that benefit from skilled Bangladeshi immigrants and attention to the specific needs of female returnees (Rozario and Gow, 2003). It is clear from this list that major reforms are needed, not just in relation to employment opportunities.

INDIA

India is seen as a modern success story in terms of the gains it has made from skilled emigration. From the 1980s, India targeted the IT sector as a priority in its larger development agenda, and the export of software has become the fastest-growing sector in the Indian economy. IT exports rose from USD 150 million in 1990 to USD 4 billion in 2000 (World Bank, 2004).[23] India encourages its students to go abroad to complete high-tech degrees, especially in the US, from where they bring home money, new knowledge and, above all, an "entrepreneurial bug" (Gardner, 2000). Students and researchers seek out prestigious

22. *Santi Rozario, a Bangladeshi living in Australia, writes that the "general social and political malaise makes people self-centred and relatively unconcerned with the welfare of the society at large, with no interest in the wider agenda or the future of the country" (Rozario and Gow, 2003).*

23. *A significant portion of India's IT exports involves Indian workers employed on short-term contracts with foreign firms, by means of a process known as "body shopping" in the US, Singapore, Canada, Australia, Japan and elsewhere. To these temporary workers must be added those who make the transition from a student visa to an H-1B visa or to a green card (permanent residence). This constitutes a significant number, especially among postgraduate students.*

institutions in the US and UK in order to join their elite networks (Mahroum, 2002).

Many skilled non-resident Indians (NRIs) who work or have business interests in India, do not return home permanently, partly because of differences in the standards of living, partly because of some frustrations of doing business in India. Returning Indians often experience feelings of resentment towards them – resentment related to India's long-standing hostility to foreign corporations. This makes NRIs want to "circulate" rather than return, unlike migrants from Taiwan who have increasingly returned home to start businesses or to work in established companies. Indian workers in the IT industry often serve as intermediaries, especially in the US, for the outsourcing of work to India.[24] Whether they send home remittances or not depends on whether entire families have moved with the principal workers. If they moved together, the flow of remittances tends to dry up (Khadria, 2002).

India is now actively seeking skilled labour markets for its IT workers, nurses, doctors and financial personnel. The "globalization of Indian talent and skills" is being hailed as a huge benefit for the country (Khadria, 2002). After the IT bust in the US, European Union countries were viewed as more sustainable destinations, and East/Southeast Asia also became a major destination.

Skilled workers typically come from upper-caste and upper-class families, and they benefit considerably from India's education system. Besides the economic returns mentioned above, NRIs also put their resources (money and time) into establishing organizations and networks that benefit other Indians,[25] particularly in the IT sector. But the extent to which all this helps to alleviate the high illiteracy (52%) and poverty rates (40%) in India still needs to be more closely examined.

The lack of a trickle-down effect from the IT sector to other parts of the Indian economy has caused experts to call for a major paradigm shift (Khadria, 1999). This entails replacing existing expectations about the exogenous return of resources (remittances, technology, return migration) with a new focus on enhanced productivity of the resident work force. NRIs' money, materials, skills and vision should be channelled into the health and education sectors, rather than into business and industry, work and living infrastructure or other multifarious development targets (Khadria, 1999). The World Development Report of 1996 supported the call for strategies and institutions to achieve this.[26]

In this way, the resources of NRIs "would help to restore the human capital taken away from the system and may some day even produce a break to the first generation negative effects of the brain drain" (Khadria, 2001). This long-term, societal and economy-wide outlook is quite different from the narrow focus on encouraging returnees to invest in businesses. The role of networks and associations of NRIs takes on a new dimension in terms of the contributions they could make to basic education and health services.

THE PHILIPPINES[27]

The government of the Philippines feels that the country has suffered from the negative consequences of "brain drain" for decades, a concern underscored when, in the 1990s, the "number of professional workers who went abroad *exceeded* the net additions

24. *The availability of skilled labour at home makes it feasible for NRIs to consider outsourcing from their own firms in the US, or setting up subsidiaries of American companies or their own companies in India. They act as "cultural interpreters", best able to negotiate the complex bureaucracy and infrastructure deficits of the home country (Saxenian, 2001).*

25. *One such organization, The Indus Entrepreneurs (TIE) founded in 1992 in Silicon Valley, organizes conferences, meetings and other sessions for NRIs in the US and for regional branches in Chennai, Bangalore, Hyderabad and Mumbai. The plan by TIE to contribute USD 1 billion to Indian Institutes of Technology (IITs) was based on IIT's becoming less "beholden to national caste-based affirmative action policies" (Chakravartty, 2001).*

26. *"In the end what matters is people ... Labour productivity, critical for economic growth, depends on workers' knowledge, skills, motivation, and health ... A well educated, healthy workforce is essential for economic growth" (World Bank, 1996).*

27. *For more details on the Philippines, see the chapter ""Filipinos Working Overseas: Opportunity and Challenge".*

to the professionals in the workforce" (Alburo and Abella, 2002). Many of those who emigrated, either temporarily or permanently, were already in the labour force and were therefore experienced workers. Many did not go to skilled jobs abroad, but to jobs as domestics, nurses, construction and manufacturing workers, and entertainers. Their actual professional skills were either not, or not fully utilized offshore.

The Philippines is now in a similar category with India as the country actively seeks skilled overseas labour markets. This has been called a "brain response", or the alignment of labour deployments with global needs and increased training, often in private colleges, targeting specific overseas labour markets (ibid). This deployment has mainly been in engineering, nursing and, increasingly, the computer/ICT area (60% of physicians and 30-50% of IT professionals go abroad).[28]

The implications of these trends for the domestic labour market are significant. By 1989, 11 per cent of Filipino hospital and public health positions were vacant. As many nurses left to work overseas, more nursing colleges continued to open in response to public and political pressure. But the conditions and standards were poor, many trained nurses, medical staff and deans had left and students graduated with little clinical exposure or experience (Ortin, 1994). By 2002, the National Health Scheme in the UK employed 30,000 nurses of foreign origin, including about one-quarter (7,235) from the Philippines, and the target is to recruit another 25,000 (approximately) from overseas by 2008 (OECD, 2004). The US, Canada, Australia, Japan, South Korea and others, are all looking for nurses and, as a result, some doctors in the Philippines who trained first as nurses before going on to earn their medical degree, are brushing up on their nursing skills and applying for overseas nursing positions.

Some commentators believe the situation continues to have serious consequences for the economy and that continued brain drain carries heavy social costs for the country (Alburo and Abella, 2002).[29] This is in spite of the money sent back to the Philippines as remittances each year. In 2003, the total amount of remittances received was USD 7.6 billion; this represented 16 per cent of the country's total current receipts and 10 per cent of GDP, and a rise of 6.3 per cent over 2002, even though the number of new expatriate workers declined. The amount of remittances sent by professional and technical workers, who made up 32.7 per cent of new expatriate worker intake in 2003, is not known, as separate data are not available by occupational level. Other potential gains, such as additional savings and investment, the growth of small and medium-sized enterprises and gains in human capital, are also not known. What is known is that the appropriate reintegration of skilled return migrants is limited, and many people subsequently remigrate.

The Philippines has long argued for compensation from destination countries for the skills that the latter gain from its workers. But destination countries are unwilling to cooperate, even in terms of increased aid for education and training for the source country, and this is no longer seen as a viable option. Instead, outsourcing the development of regional labour markets and enhancing management of remittances may help to mitigate some of the negative effects (ibid).

FIJI

Skilled emigration from small (island) states of Oceania, such as Fiji, is not perceived as positive, and is rather regarded as detrimental to sustainable development in the long term. Fiji loses more through the outflow of its human capital than it gains through remittances. The outflow of scarce human capital impacts on development as human resources are very limited, and demand exceeds supply (Reddy, Mohanty and Naidu, 2002). The gaps created by skilled emigrants have often been filled by less well trained

28. *See also the chapter "Filipinos Working Overseas: Opportunity and Challenge".*

29. *Despite the fact that tertiary education in the Philippines is mostly private sector driven and therefore privatized, since elementary and secondary education are predominantly publicly funded, the number of professionals among temporary migrants has increased rather than diminished the problem of the brain drain.*

people, and the impact on motivation and the quality of future human resources cannot be ignored. Skilled outflows have been heavily skewed in favour of Indo-Fijians (89%), following Indo-Fijian ethnic tensions since 1987. Professional, technical and related workers – teachers, architects, engineers and health workers – accounted for at least 15 per cent of emigrants over this period. Where such occupations are already in short supply, or where particular ethnic groups rely on professionals of their own ethnicity, this has had serious consequences.

A unique attempt has been made to quantify the economic cost of emigration for Fiji, based on all persons emigrating (5,510 per year on average) between 1987-2001 (Reddy et al., 2002). Although a more refined analysis of only skilled emigrants would have been preferable for the purposes of this chapter, it is, nevertheless, a good starting point for further analysis. The study calculated the costs of human capital in terms of:

- public education and training expenses for the migrants;[30]
- financial capital that left with the migrants;[31]
- recruitment of expatriate professionals with high wages and all other cumulative direct and indirect costs, and,
- income foregone through migration.[32]

The total loss from migration to Fiji in the short term is estimated at F$44.5m (equivalent to 4.7% of total government revenue) every year. The loss in output is some F$60.3 million per year (ibid).

The consequences of skilled emigration on civil society, the private and the public sector are estimated to be major (ibid). In particular, the quality of health care is deteriorating as patient/health worker ratios increase, and the migration of teachers, nurses and engineers has severely affected educational standards, health services and public utilities. The loss of health professionals has been raised as a matter of grave concern by the World Health Organization (WHO). Its Western Pacific Regional Office recently commissioned a study into this topic (Connell, 2001), which concluded that migration was not an "overspill" but a definite loss to the country, and the negative outcomes are both financial (loss of training costs) and social. In medical terms, the shortage or complete absence of doctors in some regions or areas of specialization will jeopardize progress towards healthy communities, possibly leading to a reversal of recent gains, especially as degenerative diseases become more prevalent. The situation is analogous to that in Africa, where the effects of the "brain drain" have been a major factor in contributing to a health workforce crisis (WHO, 2002).

GENDER IMPLICATIONS

The gender dimension requires special attention in any discussion of benefits and costs of skilled migration. In Asia and elsewhere little data or information are available on gender divisions of skilled and professional labour. Nevertheless, it is clear that women feature in skilled migration streams only when selective administrative policies are developed for their preferred occupations, e.g. the previous H-1A visa system of the US to recruit nurses and caregivers, and recent policy changes in Japan to attract nurses. Also, because women move more often as dependants, rather than as principal applicants, their skills may not be counted and they may not gain access to settlement services. When women arrive at their destination, they often face more additional accreditation and employment hurdles than men, but these are rarely documented (Iredale, 2004). In relation to qualifications and skills recognition, it has

30. *Calculated from: a) annual average national per capita expenditure (F$388.33) on health and education and, b) an assumption that scholarships were awarded to half (264) of the 528 professionals on average who left each year.*

31. *Particularly the capital and productive assets lost through business migration, an average of F$40m from 1994-2001 (figures obtained from the Reserve Bank of Fiji, quoted in Reddy et al., 2002, p. 56).*

32. *Calculated from the discounted value of the output foregone over the period in which the worker is not replaced.*

been shown that skilled women frequently sacrifice their own career for the sake of their family, or they may be disadvantaged in the recognition process due to gender bias.

In Australia in 1994, it was found that selection for immigration under the skills category was based on an interpretation of skills potentially disadvantageous to women, and that the definitions of skills needed to be re-examined to include those that more often characterize women (Fincher et al., 1994). Women were less likely to be selected in skilled migration categories in the early 1990s.[33] Major official reports on migration (including the longitudinal survey sample data) do not always include comprehensive data for eligibility categories by sex.

In the US, in fiscal year 2002, males accounted for 53.3 per cent of total non-immigrant admissions but for over 85 per cent of intra-company transferees, nearly 76 per cent of visitors for business and 75 per cent of temporary workers and trainees (USCIS, 2003).

Canada's gender-based analysis of immigration policy is a good example of how selection criteria can be actively adjusted to ensure a more equitable skills intake (Kofman, 2003; Tolley, 2003). Before 2002, the designation of (mostly) men as principal applicants relegated women to the status of dependants and devalued their occupations and qualifications. With the increase in points threshold in 2002, the following gender-related adjustments were made:[34] restrict the number of years of experience to a maximum of four years, to reflect women's greater likelihood of interrupted careers, and include spouses/common-law partners' education. Thus, while in 2001 fewer than one in four (24.53%) skilled workers were female, by 2002, women accounted for 34 per cent of the foreign worker intake.[35] There is now also a greater emphasis on education than on paid work experience, likely to be advantageous to women (Tolley, 2003), and the lack of points for specific occupations should also help make women's entry as skilled workers more equitable.[36]

At the other end of the migration spectrum, if and when skilled women return home, they often face a range of problems associated with tensions and a disjuncture between their own aspirations as highly skilled and educated returnees seeking to participate in nation-building and socio-economic transformation in their country, and local gendered expectations and gendered modes of discrimination that inhibit the realization of those aspirations (Rozario and Gow, 2003). Further research is needed into how women construct or reconstruct their gender identity in the country to which they migrate, and how they renegotiate this when they return home. Current tensions are sometimes causing women to remigrate or make an inappropriate adjustment to the labour market. In this way, human resources are lost, regardless of the outcome.

Kofman wrote in 2003 "women and men circulate differently in the global economy. At the skilled end, men overwhelmingly form the mass of those moving within transnational corporations and in the information technology and scientific sectors (HRST), upon which the notion of the highly skilled has been constructed (OECD 2002), and for whom movement was facilitated until the IT bubble burst. Women, in contrast, have tended to go into what can be broadly classified as the welfare professions (education, health, social work) which have been largely closed (with the partial exception of the UK) to migrant labour" (Kofman, 2003).

33. *In 2000-2001, the proportions of males among first-arrival primary applicants in the Points-based visa categories Business (long stay) and Business (short stay) were 77.2 per cent and 73.2 per cent respectively; and the proportion of males among independent executive primary applicant first arrivals was 80.2 per cent in 2000-01 (Khoo et al., 2003).*

34. *Based on the gender-based analysis of Bill C-11, which preceded the IRPA, 2002.*

35. *However, there is no breakdown of skill levels by sex among foreign worker arrivals, and so it is not possible to see if there were equivalent skill profiles between men and women.*

36. *In 2001, only 24.53 per cent of principal skilled worker applicants were female (Citizenship and Immigration Canada, 2002), and a slightly lower percentage of these had university degrees (77.62%) compared to men (83.2%), but female dependants of skilled workers were more educated (51.63%) than men (41.81%) (Kofman, 2003).*

The skills and knowledge of skilled women are just as valuable as those of men, but women have been underemployed and often exploited in many economies. While there are some data available on the remittance amounts attributable to women, these do not represent their real contribution, only their actual one. Their skills have been wasted, as they have mostly been hired in the "3D" jobs, or other female dominated occupations, such as nannies, entertainers and caregivers. Further research is needed to measure the extent of their wasted skills and assess the loss to sending countries in terms of unused training costs and the wages lost in receiving countries through undervaluing of workers and lower productivity.

An analysis of the different approaches to migrant selection, and the rare gender-based analyses of immigration policies, suggest that the inclusion of specific occupations or the emphasis on recent work experience in selection points schemes are likely to disadvantage women. It may still be too early to fully evaluate the impact of new immigration policies, such as those in Canada, on the presence of skilled female migrants in labour migration. But there is some evidence of an improvement in the gender balance in the temporary foreign worker intake in Canada, e.g. in 2002 over 2001. This may, however, only be in the caring occupations. In general, the collapse of the IT boom, combined with increasing global shortages in services such as education and health, should have a positive impact on the gender balance of skilled migratory flows.

GATS AND TRADE IN SERVICES[37]

While many people trumpet the gains to be made from expanding trade in services under the WTO's GATS Mode 4, the World Bank cautions that trade and flows of skilled labour can only be "complementary" to such expansion of trade. Under these circumstances, "measures to increase the mobility of skilled workers can reinforce the initial comparative advantage of the trading countries, so that skill-abundant countries become even more skill-abundant, while labour-abundant countries become even more (low-skill) labour-abundant. Trade expansion, combined with the unrestricted mobility of skilled workers, could conceivably put the accumulation of human capital beyond the reach of many developing countries" (World Bank, 2003). Some experts disagree with this and argue that skilled emigration improves the welfare of those left behind (Stark and Wang, 2001; Stark, 2004).

The World Bank's caution is important, because the apparent temporary nature of movements under GATS Mode 4 is touted as offering protection against losses. If temporary workers remit earnings and then return with enhanced human capital, this should be advantageous for countries of origin. But the key to achieving this are "changes in the trade and immigration policies of receiving countries and stepped-up efforts by sending countries to increase *return migration* of skilled workers while enhancing temporary movement of lower-skilled workers in developed country markets" (World Bank, 2003). The problem with the first part of this statement is:

- the lack of will on the part of destination countries, as pointed out in this chapter, and
- difficulties in fully integrating returnees.

There is still great resistance by developed countries to opening their labour markets under GATS Mode 4 to less skilled workers from developing countries. This renders GATS a blunt instrument for the aspirations of many labour-sending countries.

37. *See also the Textbox 9.1 "Trade and Migration – GATS Mode 4".*

CONCLUSION

THIS CHAPTER has illustrated how in the Asia-Pacific countries/regions studied, skilled migration can bring vastly different benefits and costs to source and receiving countries, as well as the migrants, depending on a range of complex, often country-specific conditions. Skilled migration is occurring on a large scale, often through globalized recruitment by the private sector, via Internet, or through student schemes. Labour markets are changing, and government policies in developed countries are adjusting accordingly, both to maximize the benefits of migrant labour and strengthen the self-sufficiency of domestic labour forces through training and development schemes.

But developing countries with labour surpluses often do not keep pace with this – and cannot complete their own transition through the "stages" identified above from simple emigration through to diversified circular migration, to fully benefit from their diaspora communities. Many Asia-Pacific countries/regions are stalled at stages 1 or 2 and experience serious losses from skilled emigration. While the long-term detrimental effects of this are more likely in countries where conditions exacerbate the basic problems that led to the emigration in the first place (Lowell and Findlay, 2001), many new countries are being added to the list of skills exporters, and the potential gains of skilled emigration cannot be guaranteed.

The case studies show that national policies need to be comprehensive if they are to address the issue to everybody's benefit; but, given the relative absence of these, there is also a need for global action. There are clearly country-specific reasons for emigration, and each source country/region must design development and other policies to address its specific economic, political, social and environmental conditions to make skilled emigration gainful for all. The strategic support of receiving countries and the international community can spread those gains across the global supply and demand spectrum.

Obvious policy options for source countries/regions include the "Six Rs": *returns*; *restricting* emigration; *recruiting* replacements; *reparation* for the loss of human capital; *resourcing* diasporas, and *retention* through education policies and economic development (ibid). While some of these are not viable at all, others are not viable for particular places. The Taiwanese experience in the region shows how, over many decades the careful planning of circular migration management, in close cooperation with the receiving country (US), can bring rewards for the migrants and their places of origin. It also shows that once there is something to which to return, rates of return increase. Others like China mainland reap benefits from the positive actions taken by the government to "re-circulate" skilled *émigrés*. For the less economically advantaged countries, more global support is needed.

Developed countries must find creative ways to support the development or replenishment of human capital in developing countries with severe skills losses, even while they are restructuring and retooling for longer-term self-sustainability of their own domestic labour markets. But most of the countries studied – at both ends of the skilled migration spectrum – are not taking these actions in a concerted way. Receiving countries accept no obligation to pay for their newly acquired human capital, and the implications of their policies for source countries receive little attention. Global policies could take account of the impacts on poor countries unable to achieve significant gains in terms of remittances, outsourcing, investments or returnees.

Since compensation has never been a viable option (Bhagwati and Humada, 1974), and increased aid packages to the source countries of many skilled migrants have not been forthcoming, attention is turning more to the possibility of "ethical migration" policies and programmes. Some specific national and international initiatives are being taken to protect certain professional sectors, like health in developing countries.[38] The UK has issued a Code of Practice for NHS Employers Involved in International Recruitment of Healthcare Professionals and several other organizations are drawing up their own codes of practice, including the Commonwealth Council of Health Ministers. The OECD calls for such codes to be global in perspective, but also predicts limited results for a range of reasons.[39] It recommends that such codes of practice be accompanied by increased development aid earmarked for human resources development in the health sectors of developing countries.

In the meantime, and considering the longer-term structural domestic reforms being considered by destination countries, developing countries suffering from "brain drain" must find ways of keeping their own people at home, encouraging more returnees and tapping their diasporas. In relation to the former, proposals have been made for country-specific training programmes that make people less internationally mobile, as well as for bonding and taxing schemes. Bonding arrangements that tie training to a longer period of service, or exchange programmes that enable overseas travel/work as a reward for domestic service could be examined. But other solutions that are not detrimental to human resource development are needed. Policies to encourage permanent or temporary return have been canvassed above. In a globalized environment, destination countries and the international community can only benefit from ensuring migration governance strength at source.

For example, the Committee on Science and Technology in Developing Countries (COSTED, 2001)[40] has proposed the establishment of an Intellectual Resources Management Fund (IRMF) to address two issues in developing countries: losses from "brain drain" and improving the standards of science and technology professionals. The concept is that monies collected from receiving countries benefiting from skilled immigration could be used towards additional training, exchanges and collaboration, and better working conditions in the developing world. The idea was not taken up in 2001, but could now be revived, as time is short for some countries. Unless this kind of global cooperation increases, the future is uncertain for those countries losing out on the international mobility of their highly skilled.

38. *For example, WHO in 2002 called for a Commonwealth Code of Practice for International Recruitment of Health Workers to overcome the crisis in Africa due to skill shortages. The OECD's* Trends in International Migration 2003 *(2004) addresses the international mobility of health professionals and points to the case of South Africa, which has lost around USD1 billion in public costs of training health professionals now working overseas. There are now major shortages in that sector, due to emigration, poor working conditions and the HIV/AIDS epidemic. To keep scarce human resources at home, South Africa has, since 1995, banned the recruitment of any physicians or nurses from SADC countries, except under specific bilateral agreements (OECD, 2004). Since 2001, this also extends to G77 and Commonwealth countries.*

39. *As "soft law", none of the codes are binding; they rule out recruitment campaigns, although recruitment still occurs over the Internet or in some other way; their scope is limited to certain countries; and surpluses will eventually run out in countries from which it is deemed "ethical" to recruit (OECD, 2004).*

40. *COSTED was part of the UN's International Council for Science until 2002.*

CHAPTER 12
FILIPINOS WORKING OVERSEAS: OPPORTUNITY AND CHALLENGE[1]

BACKGROUND[2]

ANY PHENOMENON that affects millions of people will have its share of opportunities and challenges, and overseas employment is no different. The Philippines is one of the major labour exporting countries in the world, with some seven million Filipinos, or almost nine per cent of the population, living outside the country, more than half of them on temporary contracts.[3] The rest have settled permanently, either as residents or as citizens of a country where they were not born.

Overseas Filipino workers (OFWs) are hailed as heroes, because they work hard, often under conditions that are difficult and significantly different in terms of culture and work practices they knew back home. At the same time, they risk separation and alienation from their families, a condition that goes against the grain of traditional Filipino values. It is considered a necessary sacrifice to provide a better future for the family.

For the most part, therefore, the push for contract migration is economic. While wages in the Philippines are generally higher than in comparable countries in the Asian region, the skills, training and education of Filipinos command a premium in the more developed economies, where there are skill shortages.[4] The prospect of better wages, the generally mobile character of Filipinos, as conditioned by the archipelagic character of the country and the desire for adventure and new experience, are the triggers for the decision to migrate, particularly for work of a temporary nature.

Overseas employment is driven by two essential forces: the demand for particular skills in one country, and the availability of skilled manpower in another. It may not be tied to surplus or shortages, but to requirements engendered by a specific national situation. Examples include countries emerging from conflict situations; or with educational systems that do not equip them for faster integration into the global market. Whichever condition prevails, the fact is that both for sending and receiving countries this movement of contract labour can bring mutual benefits. The receiving country gains skills for which it did not invest in terms of infrastructure and human resource development, and it enables the sending country to alleviate its unemployment levels. But, migration is not a neutral phenomenon, and it exacts a social and economic cost.

1. *This chapter was written by Dr Patricia A. Santo Tomas, former Secretary of Labor, Philippines, and currently Commissioner on the Global Commission on International Migration (GCIM). The information derives from the Department of Labor and Employment.*

2. *For the purpose of this chapter, note the following Asian geographic designations: China (which includes China mainland, Hong Kong Special Administrative Region of China -- hereafter referred to as Hong Kong, Macao Special Administrative Region of China -- hereafter Macao, and Taiwan Province of China -- hereafter Taiwan), the Democratic People's Republic of Korea (hereafter North Korea), and the Republic of Korea (hereafter South Korea).*

3. *About 80 per cent of the estimated 44,000 Filipino workers emigrating each year are land-based, and the remaining 20 per cent are seamen, constituting almost one quarter of the world's seamen on commercial vessels. Compare the Philippines population of 81 million in 2003. Destinations include Saudi Arabia, Hong Kong SAR of China, Japan, UAE, US, Canada, Taiwan Province of China, Kuwait, Singapore, Australia, Italy and others. Some 25-30 per cent of overseas workers are female domestic helpers, maids, amahs, nannies or caregivers.*

4. *There were some 2.6 million students enrolled in higher education in 2000.*

For the Philippines, the costs are in terms of family separation, which affects the very fabric of Philippine society, founded as it is on close family ties and an extended system of support and protection. This can engender cultural dysfunction that comes with assimilating into a radically different environment – extreme weather conditions, different religions, different legal systems and, in some cases, the absence of international standards or protocols on the rights of expatriate workers. There is also the risk of exploitation, an issue that shapes transnational policy and programme responses.

Given the large numbers and the spatial spread of Filipinos abroad, contract migration is an issue closely wired to the national nervous system. Any unnatural occurrence overseas – a suicide bombing in Israel, the sinking of a ship, internal strife, a train accident – alerts the national community to possible injury or death of one of its own. Such an incident often sparks a debate about whether overseas employment is good, bad or just plain ugly.

This chapter looks at the "investments" by the Philippines government in closely regulating its overseas foreign worker programme, and explores the benefits gained from this approach – for the migrants, the sending and receiving countries, and Philippine society. It draws some useful lessons for other countries embarking on this form of mutually beneficial migration management.

THE BENEFITS

CATCHBASIN FOR DOMESTIC UNEMPLOYMENT AND ECONOMY BOOSTER

The Philippines has one of the highest birth rates in the Asian region (2.34 per cent as of mid-2004). Consequently, its labour force is relatively young. A well developed education system also ensures a high percentage of graduates, who contribute annually to the country's surplus of educated unemployed. While job creation has levelled off at an average 1 million jobs per annum for the last three years, the net annual addition to the labour force has continued at 1.4 million. Unemployment has therefore remained at 11 per cent. It is clear that overseas employment has mitigated the lack of jobs locally. Ninety-five per cent of those who leave for overseas jobs have been employed in the Philippines prior to departure and, on average, have 3-5 years of local working experience. Their sally into the international job market therefore creates opportunities for new entrants, who can fill the jobs that the OFWs leave behind.

The dollar remittances of OFWs also help keep the economy afloat. Remittances, as a percentage of GNP, have grown from 2.7 per cent in 1990 to 10.2 per cent in 2003.[5] During the negative GDP growth years of 1991 and 1998, the GNP managed a small positive growth, primarily due to the dollar inflows from overseas workers. These remittances translate into money for building houses, educating children and general consumer spending. Data show that at least six per cent of Filipino families receive income from abroad, and that six out of ten of these families are located in urban areas and are relatively better off than their counterparts, who make a living from local resources.

THE GOOD LIFE

At the micro level, the favourable effects of remittances on an overseas worker's family income and savings are enormous. The remittances are acknowledged to have made it possible to send children or siblings to reputable schools, pay for relatives' medical needs, build decent houses, and to have helped with the acquisition of appliances and other amenities. OFWs and their families are looked upon as the emerging middle class, and have been accorded respect and awe by the local community. They are invited to participate in civic and church

5. *Remittances from OFWs averaged USD575 million a month in 2003, a total of USD7.5 billion for the year. They account for ca. 10 per cent of the Philippines' USD80 billion GDP. The remittances came mainly from the US, Saudi Arabia, Japan, UK, Hong Kong, Singapore and UAE.*

functions and are often courted by local politicians, or actually become local politicians themselves. They have become the new "influentials" in Philippine society.

SKILLS AND TECHNOLOGY TRANSFER

Overseas employment also facilitates skills and technology transfers to the country through the migrant workers' exposure to superior forms of work organization and state-of-the-art technology in the more industrialized host countries. Upon their return, they use their expertise to orient and train other local workers in these technologies. For some, these new skills or acquired technology provide the basis for entrepreneurial ventures, funded with the savings from their overseas employment.

TEXTBOX 12.1

RETURNING HOME

Edgar Cortes worked as a casting operator overseas for 14 years before returning to the Philippines. He set up the Pioneer Aluminium Industries by using his savings to buy machines and tools necessary for metal fabrication. He then borrowed 100,000 pesos from the Overseas Workers Welfare Administration (OWWA) and proceeded to manufacture aluminium side wheels for tricycles. Today, his shop is located in one of Manila's most depressed areas and employs four people.

Sotero Owen was a welder in Saudi Arabia until a 20 per cent cut in salary made him decide to return home. With his wife, he set up a loom weaving operation in Baguio City with the support of loans from OWWA. With income from his business, he has been able to see his children and two nephews and nieces through college. He was also able to build his house and buy a five-hectare property, on which he has started to farm.

Source: Overseas Workers Welfare Administration (OWWA) files.

THE COSTS

BRAIN DRAIN AND DE-SKILLING

The exodus of skilled and semi-skilled Filipino workers has caused some measure of brain drain for the Philippines. It has removed the talents of many highly skilled professionals, who may have been useful in the Philippines, but have chosen to work in other countries. This may include teachers, doctors, scientists and highly trained technicians. Some professionals have even "moved down" to take on jobs for which they are overqualified, like licensed doctors who attend nursing schools to gain an overseas job as a nurse. These professionals may receive higher compensation elsewhere, but the cost of training them plus the need for their services locally represent an underutilization of skills and eventual de-skilling and investment loss to the country.

THE RISKS OF THE JOB

Regardless of the economic rewards of overseas employment at the macro and micro levels, empirical studies have also shown that there are risks, costs and problems that accompany working and living in a foreign environment. The most common problems encountered by OFWs are violations of their basic rights, such as:

- lack of redress of legitimate grievances;
- discrimination at various stages of the migration process;

- fraud and deception at the recruitment stage;
- non-enforcement of contracts at the job-site;
- difficulty in adjusting to a foreign culture (e.g. language, value systems and local ethos);
- poor working conditions;
- inadequate support services at the worksite.

In addition, overseas workers often suffer suspicion and hostility on the part of their host communities, loneliness and anxiety over the families back home; and a cold reception from family members, who have been estranged from them over long periods, when they return. Those in risky occupations, like entertainers and domestic helpers, frequently also experience physical and/or sexual abuse and serious attacks on their reputation, self-esteem and morale. This is especially true in the case of undocumented or otherwise illegal workers.

The families who are left behind also have their share of suffering, not just because of anxiety over loved ones abroad, but also in terms of family displacements and juvenile delinquency. Studies and reports from welfare cases handled by the government and NGOs directly link these social problems to the long separation between spouses and from children.[6] The absence of authority figures in the home can force children into decisions that, with proper guidance, they may not normally make. Similarly, separated spouses form other relationships that may eventually break up homes and families.

The safety and welfare of its OFWs are a primary concern to the government, both as a practical and a political necessity. Since overseas workers today have absentee voting rights, they have become an important political force, possibly with as much influence and voice as the church, media, political parties and civil society.

CREATING THE APPROPRIATE GOVERNANCE STRUCTURES

WHEN overseas employment was introduced as a measure to ease domestic unemployment in the 1970s,[7] the Philippine government created agencies specifically to cater to the needs of overseas workers – the Overseas Employment Development Board (OEDB), the National Seamen's Board (NSB), and the Bureau of Employment Services (BES). In 1982, all three agencies were merged, eventually to give rise to the Philippine Overseas Employment Administration (POEA) and the Overseas Workers Welfare Administration (OWWA).

Believing that a good welfare and protection programme benefits the worker as well as the receiving country, the Philippine government has crafted a programme that looks at the employment process from beginning to end, from application for an overseas job to a worker's reintegration upon return.

RECRUITMENT AND PRE-DEPARTURE STAGE

Initially, the government sought to regulate the market by acting as the sending agency for all departing workers. It decided to downscale its placement function in 1982, realizing that market demand was so significant that intermediation would be more efficient. The government currently operates a licensing system for recruitment agencies deploying land-based workers and for manning agencies that place Filipino seafarers on ocean-going vessels.[8] Foreign employers undergo accreditation, where the Filipino labour attaché onsite verifies the existence of the principal/project and its manpower requirement. Employers who are documented as having violated the contracts of their workers, or abused or exploited

6. *This is especially problematic given the fact that women constitute the majority of migrants (60%), working as domestic helpers, caregivers and nurses, many of them on five-year contracts.*

7. *The Labor Code of 1974 was introduced as the basis for regulating the recruitment of Filipinos abroad. It established minimum standards for their work contracts and a system to verify the contracts.*

8. *There are almost 1,200 licensed recruitment agencies in the industry; they must be 70 per cent Filipino-owned.*

their workers, are suspended or eventually blacklisted, barring them from hiring Filipino workers.

POEA also regulates the placement fees charged by recruitment agencies to the workers, which have been maintained at one month's salary for every employment contract. Violation of this rule is a ground for cancellation of the recruiter's licence. POEA also holds the recruitment agency and foreign employer jointly liable for claims by OFWs, to ensure that recruitment agencies choose their principals well. Given the differences in legal systems between sending and receiving countries, this provision also enables redress of legitimate grievances in the Philippines, where the contract was signed.

All private entities wishing to engage in international manpower supply are required to place 1 million pesos in an escrow account to address workers' claims, and as a reserve fund for penalties against recruitment violations. They must maintain a minimum capitalization of 2 million pesos. Advertising for jobs, even for purposes of manpower pooling, has to be approved by the POEA to ensure that there are, in fact, job orders that need to be filled, and prospective applicants are not duped.

Applicants for skilled or semi-skilled jobs are required to submit authenticated certificates from the Technical Education and Skills Development Authority (TESDA) attesting to their level of skills and competence. Professionals submit proof of completion of the requisite course from the Commission for Higher Education (CHED). Where licensure is necessary to practise, such as for nursing or engineering, proof of having passed the requisite Board examinations is also submitted. After applicants have been selected for their skills, technical proficiency or professional credentials, they must prove that they are physically fit for the job. This is arranged through clinics or hospitals accredited by the Philippine Department of Health. After receiving their visas, which signals approval by the host country for them to work abroad, they must attend a Pre-departure Orientation Seminar (PDOS) that briefs them on the laws, customs and practices of their country of destination, their rights and obligations under the employment contracts, and how to adapt to the overseas situation.

Prospective job applicants for overseas work are also given pre-employment orientation to enable them to assess their suitability for overseas work. They learn about country-specific practices and cultural differences that need to be respected in a foreign country; and about illegal recruitment, legally permissible fees and telephone numbers available to the general public for grievances. All this helps them make an early decision about their ability to cope with these factors.

These activities are meant to protect workers who, under labour surplus conditions, may choose to take unnecessary risks to work abroad. While people continue to fall prey to illegal recruiters, the numbers have dwindled over the years, helped no doubt by a massive public information campaign. There is also a relatively low incidence of trafficking of persons from the Philippines. Overseas, employers and governments alike acknowledge that Filipinos are generally well selected and have fewer problems than some of their counterparts from other countries. At the same time, employers are assured that the workers bring the necessary credentials for the job.

Institutions accredited by the Overseas Workers Welfare Administration (OWWA), recruitment agencies and certified trainers administer these orientation sessions. Some recruitment agencies have developed in-house pre-departure orientation facilities, while NGOs have specialized in orientation courses, particularly for the more vulnerable occupations.

A standard employment contract is prescribed by POEA based on minimum standards of terms and conditions of overseas work. Some of these terms and conditions are negotiated with host countries as part of the bilateral agreements concluded with them. The peculiarities of destination countries or occupations must also be taken into account in the contracts. For instance, some contracts provide for shorter timeframes (entertainers and seafarers); others involve added risks, e.g. in war zones or in risky situations requiring the handling of chemicals. In these instances, a policy of "full disclosure" is activated, so that compensatory mechanisms like higher insurance coverage or hazard pay may be incorporated into the contracts.

The underlying premise is that in a free and open society, information is the best means to protect workers and manage their movement abroad. All workers processed through the POEA are required to be members of the OWWA, which allows them to be covered by mandatory insurance for death, disability and accident, entitles them to loans for pre-departure expenses or for money to be left behind with their families, scholarships for dependants and the worker him/herself, repatriation costs, burial benefits and initial capitalization for the funding of small business ventures as part of the reintegration process.

Still part of the regulatory mechanism is a Labor Assistance Center, which acts as an extension of the POEA at the airport to assist workers during the final checking of their documents, and provide extra protection to guard against trafficking of workers.

ONSITE OR ON-THE-JOB ASSISTANCE

Overseas, a network of more than 200 labour attachés and welfare officers worldwide provides assistance to OFWs by responding to and monitoring their problems, complaints and queries. They act as advocates for the OFWs, ensuring that the Filipino workers in their area of responsibility are treated and paid in accordance with their contract. In certain countries, a Workers' Resource Center is maintained, which serves as a halfway house for OFWs who have run away from intolerable situations. The centre also offers a social facility for Filipinos and a training venue to upgrade skills for better career mobility and compensation. Preliminary business counselling is also undertaken on the premises, particularly for returning workers.

Meanwhile, to ensure more comprehensive welfare, support and rescue services for overseas Filipino workers, whether documented or undocumented, the officers, representatives and pstaff of the Department of Labor and Employment, Department of Foreign Affairs (DFA), and other government agencies posted abroad have adopted a "one country team approach". This means that under the ambassador or the consul general, all members of the team ensure that the interests of the country and its nationals are adequately articulated and protected.

Doctors from the Department of Health (DOH) and social workers from the Department of Social Welfare and Development (DSWD) also assist overseas labour offices in responding to the workers' medical and psycho-social problems. This was particularly evident in destination countries affected by the SARS problem in 2003.

In addition to the above services, the Philippine embassies, consulates and labour offices abroad support and encourage the organization of Filipino worker communities. Experience shows that wherever Filipino workers and other compatriots band together, the support system for all Filipinos is stronger. The company of other Filipinos can mitigate the loneliness, worry and pain of adjustment and separation.

MORE ASSISTANCE OFFSITE

There are also continuous efforts to forge and upgrade bilateral or multilateral arrangements or agreements with host governments. These are pursued vigorously, despite some partner governments' apprehensions that a commitment to one labour-sending country may induce others to expect similar treatment, or to claim that this is unnecessary since their own laws adequately protect foreign workers. Experience shows that, whenever the entry of Filipino workers into a host country is governed by a bilateral agreement or arrangement, the country is able to attend more effectively to workers' complaints and problems, rendering them less vulnerable.

To date, the Philippines has negotiated 13 bilateral agreements with the Commonwealth of Northern Marianas Islands, Indonesia, Papua New Guinea, South

Korea, Taiwan, Iraq, Jordan, Kuwait, Libya, Qatar, Norway, Switzerland and the UK. These agreements commonly promote the protection and welfare of OFWs, observance of terms and conditions of the employment contracts, and regular meetings to raise issues of mutual concern. The latest agreement, signed on April 23, 2004, with the South Korean government in many ways represents a breakthrough, because it stipulates parity with Korean workers holding similar jobs, in terms of both salaries and social benefits. It also specifies recruitment through a government agency that does not charge fees for placement services. The government has also signed social security agreements with nine countries as a further safety net for Filipinos working and living abroad.

In response to the need to maintain the supply of qualified workers for both local and foreign labour markets, the public and private sectors have intensified their skills training activities and continuously develop programmes to meet the demands of labour markets. For seafarers, upgrading of skills is supported by the Maritime Training Council which includes, among others, the Philippine Coast Guard, the Maritime Industry Authority (MARINA), the Department of Education (DepEd) and the Technical Education and Skills Development Authority (TESDA), in order to reinforce the present niche carved by Filipino seamen in international seafaring.

On the other hand, in order to control the quality and quantity of Filipino entertainers going abroad, the overseas performing artists (OPAs) are required to undergo training and testing and to acquire an Artist Record Book (ARB) prior to their deployment. This requirement not only helps to upgrade the quality of entertainers going overseas, but also to minimize trafficking of women.

In April 2003, POEA established the Philippine One-Stop Shop Center (POSC) in Manila to simplify the documentation process. By grouping under one roof all government agencies that issue or process documents related to the deployment of overseas workers, it has reduced the processing time for contracts and overseas employment certificates considerably. It has since been replicated in two other provinces as an added service to OFWs in those areas.

An OFW Electronic Card – a permanent identification card for all OFWs – is also issued free of charge by the Labor Department. This serves a multitude of purposes: it proves a worker's legal status as an OFW and his/her membership of OWWA; facilitates access to OWWA benefits and services and issuance of the Overseas Employment Certificate, and exempts the OFW from airport and travel taxes. It also serves as an international ATM card or a debit card, in case the OFW decides to open an account with accredited banks, and provides a permanent ID card number, that will link OFWs to information necessary in dealing with various government and private agencies.

OWWA's emergency and medical services are part of the on-the-job assistance to OFWs. Welfare Officers are part of the Philippine Overseas Labor Office (POLO) and operate under the labour attaché.

REINTEGRATION

The government runs several economic and social reintegration programmes to address the negative effects of overseas employment on the worker and her/his family. These include:

- social counselling both for OFWs and their spouses;
- skills-training, micro-credit and business management skills development;
- educational assistance for the children and,
- on and offsite investment counselling services.

In 2002, a network of OFW families and their dependants was established that now serves as a mutual support group to facilitate access to government social services. The network, known as "family circles" helps empower families, facilitates speedier repatriation of OFWs as the need arises, and arranges psycho-social support to the returning worker to aid his/her eventual reintegration into the family and community. Family welfare officers act as links between families and government service providers, and are posted in provinces and cities with significant OFW populations.[9]

Additional services available to OFWs and other interested parties – such as researchers, policy makers, academics – are the interactive databases and the short-messaging service. The former contains the list of licensed recruitment agencies (both active, closed down and banned), job vacancies (local and abroad), pending court cases, and seafarers' certification. There are also on-line market updates regarding trends, restrictions and opportunities, new rules, laws and policies on foreign labour in host countries.[10]

ECONOMIC SECURITY UPON RETURN

Not all OFWs who spend their prime years working in a foreign land return home prepared to reintegrate into their former communities. Many are unable to sufficiently prepare for re-employment or foresee and plan for a shift in their personal economic plans. POEA and OWWA, together with the Social Security System (SSS), Pag-ibig Fund/Home Mortgage Development Fund and the Local Government Units (LGUs) have joined forces to integrate their respective welfare and social programmes for OFWs.

The SSS provides cover for overseas workers on a voluntary basis to ensure that, after finishing work abroad, they have the basic social support of old age pension, sickness benefits and access to salary and housing loans. At the same time, SSS has a special Flexi Fund available only to overseas workers, an investment fund earning higher than normal interest rates. Contributions to this fund can be withdrawn at any time. The provident fund for healthcare (Philhealth) and OWWA have also made membership available for medical and hospital care, including for catastrophes.

The Pag-ibig Fund has helped many housing efforts to tap the overseas market. Housing fairs have been conducted regularly overseas, and membership in the Pag-ibig fund allows overseas workers to tap the fund for housing loans, which can be repaid on a long-term basis. It is estimated that at least 25 per cent of new housing development in the country involves overseas Filipino workers.

Banks have also been very aggressive in supporting OFWs with, e.g. education, pension and even memorial plans. These products, and others, curtail the consumption tendencies of OFWs and force them into savings programmes that help prepare them for life after overseas employment.

The OWWA reintegration programme is premised on a number of assumptions: first, that many OFWs return to the Philippines at an age when they would have difficulty returning to productive employment; second, where they are able to find work, it is usually at much lower salary levels than they are accustomed to, and third, starting a business is not a preferred alternative, since most Filipinos are trained from an early age to take the least risky option of wage and salary work after finishing college or equivalent courses.[11] The reintegration programme of OWWA has thus shifted its focus of attention from the worker to the family left behind.

BENEFITS OF WELFARE PROGRAMMES

WHILE most countries engage in regular marketing of their available manpower, the Philippines believes that the best marketing for Filipino talent is an effective welfare and protection programme. Where workers are covered by the protective mechanisms

9. *Family welfare officers also encourage families to engage in bulk buying to benefit from discounts and commissions on all consumer goods. When family circles have gathered enough experience in bulk buying, they can access much higher interest-free loans for repayment over two years and subject to additional capitalization. They or their members may in time graduate to loans of up to a million pesos for larger business enterprises.*

10. *See www.poea.gov.ph, a phone-enabled inquiry facility for information on recruitment agencies, job vacancies, and other data on POEA and overseas employment.*

11. *There are private businesses that work to attract OFW investors, but some of them are scams. Some migrant cooperatives have been set up, but these are private initiatives on which the government only has anecdotal data.*

outlined above, they are able to work with a minimum of distractions because their basic rights are covered. A mechanism with built-in safety nets minimizes possible costs associated with unplanned events like medical emergencies, sudden deaths, or unexpected repatriation because of war, earthquakes, floods, or other events. During the wars in Iraq, or the SARS epidemic in Hong Kong, Filipinos organized programmes that focused on relocation and disease prevention and containment. This is essentially a shift to prevention rather than reactive programme interventions.

Providing comprehensive and fully integrated welfare services can benefit not just the sending country and its people, but also host countries, which may not have the requisite regulations to take care of guest workers. While ideally host countries should take responsibility for workers within their jurisdiction, overseas Filipinos enjoy the immediate protective mechanism of their own government through programmes that operate at recruitment, on the job and upon return. Likewise, the integrated welfare system and regulatory structure ensure that workers are predisposed to return at the end of their contract period.

CONCLUSION

The emigration of Filipinos to work abroad is not expected to abate for many decades yet, despite the rise in per capita income and reduction in poverty in the Philippines. OFWs will continue to be in high demand, because of their sound education, training and work ethic. In the meantime, there are lessons to be learned from the Philippine migration for work experience.

The first is that there is no substitute for good governance in migration management. Because of labour-surplus conditions in many source countries and competition among sending states, there is a need for clear regulations and appropriate structures. The Philippines takes the position that a good programme to ensure the health and wellbeing of its workers is more useful than any expensive marketing strategy. For practical and political reasons, programmes that address welfare considerations are better appreciated by officials of host and sending countries, as it minimizes tensions at both ends, and potential social costs at the receiving end.

Good governance in this case requires a "comprehensive and inclusive government" effort. While the Department of Labor and Employment may manage the deployment process itself, the Department of Foreign Affairs represents the country onsite and oversees negotiations concerning problematic areas. The education system receives inputs on manpower demand and consequently responds through curricula revisions to ensure the competitiveness of Filipino manpower. The Department of Finance looks at incentive packages for overseas contract workers, the Department of Interior and Local Government disseminates information to prospective applicants, and the Department of Justice prosecutes wrongdoers, whether illegal recruiters or erring workers.

The second lesson is that regulation must continue if the basic safety nets are to be ensured. Contract migration in the Philippines is admittedly heavily centrally managed and regulated. This situation will likely remain until international protocols or conventions respected by both sending and receiving countries are able to provide sufficient protection to people who leave their countries for fixed periods of work elsewhere. While some measure of irregular migration takes place, principally through people dissimulating their intentions by leaving as tourists, pilgrims or students, and taking on work in another country, or by overstaying beyond their contract period, the government takes the position that all Filipinos are entitled to representation and protection by their government, whatever their residence status may be.

The third lesson is that global competitiveness in the area of labour migration needs to take account of all the potential benefits of overseas employment. It cannot be achieved only through depressing working standards or lowering wages. Skills, productivity and the ability to adjust to a new workplace together with respect for its new and possibly different cultural environment are key. Anything less contributes to a perception that labour is commoditized, like consumer goods.

Thus, managing overseas migration requires collective efforts internally and internationally. Bilateral negotiations help, but they do not provide the balanced and consistent action that orderly movements of people require. It is ironic that movements of goods are covered by meticulous and detailed specifications of what is or is not allowed; or the movement of capital is covered by agreements that are binding on most countries, while people, the most vulnerable of "goods", seldom find themselves with the protective mechanisms accorded money or consumer products.

Both sending and receiving countries have significant mutual interests and benefits to derive from the highly integrated and regulated structure of the Philippines. As demonstrated above, comprehensive support at all points along the labour migration cycle ensures that migrants will return at the end of their contracts. A lack of capacity to jointly manage such critical issues to mutual benefit would be detrimental to all. Joint management efforts must both support the value of orderly movement over irregular migration, and acknowledge the increasing desire of overseas migrants to participate in the activities of their new host countries. This, without denying the right of independent states to prescribe appropriate conduct and behaviour of people seeking to settle, temporarily or otherwise, in their territories – but still giving due regard to the important new role of labour migrants in the growth and development of economies at both ends of the migration spectrum.

TEXTBOX 12.2

BILATERAL LABOUR AGREEMENTS: EFFECTIVE TOOLS FOR MANAGING LABOUR FLOWS?

Bilateral labour agreements (BLAs) can be an effective way to regulate the recruitment and employment of foreign short- and long-term workers between countries. They can take the form of formal treaties or less formal memoranda of understanding, or even very informal practical arrangements, e.g. between the national employment agencies of two countries.

Most global labour flows take place outside the scope of bilateral labour agreements, some within immigration or emigration programmes set up unilaterally by receiving countries, others through regional agreements. Many labour migration flows are irregular and clandestine in nature.

But BLAs allow for greater state involvement in the migration process and offer human resource exchange options tailored to the specific supply and demand of the countries involved. By encouraging orderly movement of labour, they promote good will and cooperation between sending and receiving countries. They can also address the thorny issue of the temporary nature of migration by including terms and procedures for return, and flexible visa arrangements where longer-term or permanent options exist.

BLAs hark back to the second half of the 20th century, when large emerging economies in the New World chose to meet their huge labour market needs via immigration. They sought bilateral agreements with countries of origin to overcome labour scarcity during the war or in its aftermath. Between 1942 and 1966, for example, the US admitted some 5 million farm workers under the Bracero programme with Mexico. Canada, Australia and Argentina also admitted large numbers on the basis of agreements with mainly European countries. In the 1950s and 1960s, European countries such as Germany and France actively recruited so-called guest workers, especially from Portugal, Spain, Turkey and North Africa. These programmes came to an end with the economic downturn of the 1970s triggered by the oil crisis.

During the last ten years, there has been renewed interest in bilateral agreements. Among OECD countries, their numbers quintupled in the 1990s, and today stand at 173. In Latin America, half of the 168 agreements signed during the last 50 years have been concluded since 1991. After the collapse of the Soviet Union, Central European, East European and Central Asian countries developed a wide range of agreements – some within the region, some with neighbouring EU countries, others with EU countries that had evolved from emigration countries to immigration countries, such as Portugal or Spain. A number were also signed with overseas countries, for example between Ukraine and Argentina.

BLAs abound between neighbouring countries (e.g. between Switzerland and EEA countries on the free movement of persons, enforced in 2002; between Argentina and Bolivia and Peru, signed in 1998), or between continents (e.g. Spain with Ecuador, Colombia and Morocco in 2001, and Dominican Republic in 2002). Asia has been less engaged in such agreements with receiving countries from other regions. As of October 2004, the Philippines, one of the major labour sending countries of the region, had managed to sign only 11 agreements with Asian destination countries, and none of them is with a main recipient of Filipino labour.

ILO has been promoting BLAs since the 1949 Migration for Employment Convention, No. 97; and offers governments a ready-made model for temporary and permanent migration (Recommendation No.86 annex (1949)), which has been used by various states ranging from Argentina to Rwanda, Tajikistan and Uruguay. ILO identifies 24 basic elements of a bilateral labour agreement (ILO, 2004), including selection procedures, entry documents, residence status, the contract, work permit, working conditions, the role of unions, remittances, family reunification and monitoring of the agreement. Some items included in the model, such as social security or irregular migration, tend to be dealt with by states in separate agreements (e.g. the bilateral social security agreement signed by the US with 20 countries, or the readmission agreements signed between several European countries and sending countries).

Receiving Country Perspective

For the receiving country, bilateral agreements can meet labour market needs quickly and efficiently – whether for low-skilled seasonal workers in the agriculture, tourism and construction sectors, or more skilled medical, educational, and other personnel needed to meet more structural labour market shortages. They can also usefully support broader regional commercial and economic relations by aiding the development of the sending country and facilitating its regional integration. Notable examples of this are the various agreements for temporary labour migration signed by Germany and other EU members with Central and Eastern European countries.

BLAs can help combat irregular migration by offering alternative legal channels to migrate for employment, which, in turn, can be a negotiation tool to secure country of origin willingness to cooperate on managing irregular migration (particularly the readmission of their nationals). In 1997, Italy and Albania signed a labour agreement in parallel with a readmission agreement, by which Albania accepts the return of its irregular nationals. Some past agreements between Argentina and its neighbours (Bolivia, Peru) also offered regularization of status for undocumented migrants.

Finally, BLAs help strengthen ties between countries that share some cultural or historical links. For example, the UK and other Commonwealth countries have mutual "Working Holiday Maker" programmes, which allow young persons to live and work part-time or casually in the other country for an extended holiday of up to two years.

Sending Country Perspective

Sending countries see BLAs as a useful vehicle to increase access to the international labour market, and to negotiate appropriate wages, living conditions, and job security for their nationals abroad. They offer the certainty of agreed definitions and terms of implementation and monitoring of workers' rights and entitlements. They can also facilitate the acquisition or enhancement of vocational skills and qualifications, e.g. through training programmes for young professionals.

Bilateral agreements can also provide a basis for sustained remittance flows, technology transfers and the general development of human capital, all of which constitute important contributions to the development of countries of origin. Sometimes the agreements include measures for return migration or the repatriation of skills and knowledge. Bilateral agreements signed by Spain with Colombia and Ecuador, for example, provide for projects to facilitate the voluntary return of temporary migrants through training and recognition of the experience acquired in Spain, as well as the creation of small and medium enterprises, the development of human resources and the transfer of technology.

Agreed quotas for highly skilled workers can also form an integral part of the sending country's human resource development strategy. They give the country a share in the international labour market, while managing the depletion of scarce human resources needed at home. In 2002, the Dutch and Polish ministers of health signed a letter of intent for the implementation of a project entitled "Polish nurses in The Netherlands, Development of Competencies", in order to prepare nurses for employment in the Dutch health care system for a maximum period of two years, and to facilitate their return and reintegration into the Polish health care system after return.

A further aim is for employers to arrange for pre-departure training of their labour immigrants in the sending country. This is reflected in agreements signed by Spain, and in second-generation agreements in Italy (these are signed after a readmission agreement).

How Effective are Bilateral Agreements?

The effectiveness of bilateral agreements is difficult to measure, as they often pursue several objectives simultaneously, and give different weight to different policy priorities. There has also been little research on the implementation and impact of such agreements.

Do BLAs improve the management of labour migration? They can create more certain, formal mechanisms by involving the key players at different stages of design and implementation of the agreement, as Italy has done by involving employers groups, trade unions and others in setting quotas. The Spain-Ecuador/Colombia agreements involve selection committees in the sending country that include embassy and employer representation. Built-in encouragements for temporary migrants to return, such as in Canada's seasonal agriculture workers programme, which allow the migrants to be selected again by the same employer, seem also to have had a positive effect on potential irregular migration (see also the chapter "Filipinos Working Overseas: Opportunity and Challenge").

Despite this, some 25 per cent of bilateral agreements in OECD countries are apparently not implemented. The most operational ones seem to be those that principally follow the demand-supply imperative, rather than just political objectives. Among them can be counted the Canadian seasonal agriculture programme and the UK agreements on foreign nurses with Spain, India and the Philippines. The extent to which employers will utilize BLAs depends on the efficiency of the system, the geographic location of the workers (if the travel cost is borne by the employer), the number of available irregular migrants, and the employer-friendly nature of other immigration programmes (e.g. despite the Spain/Ecuador BLA, Spanish employers may prefer to hire temporary workers from countries closer to Spain, such as Poland).

BLAs may thus also constrain the migrant workers, perhaps even exclude them from regular migration programmes, e.g. through age limits, quotas and language requirements. The Hungary-Romania agreement on labour seems not to have been entirely successful because, given the common border, most Romanian applicants seem to prefer quick cross-border commuting and undeclared work.

Future Prospects

In a world where labour markets are increasingly globalized, but where there are few multilateral mechanisms to deal with the massive labour flows, bilateral labour agreements are proving to be a useful way of bringing certainty and clarity to the issue. They can help all interested parties (not least the migrants themselves) to ensure that labour migration programmes are orderly, efficient and protective of the rights of migrant workers. Their well defined structures also help increase public confidence in (labour) migration. To be workable, however, they need to be realistic and flexible, and build on the lessons of past programmes.

Source: Labour Migration Service Area, IOM, Geneva.

Migration and Development

Chapter 13
Migration and Poverty: Some Issues in the Context of Asia[1]

"Migration is the oldest action against poverty. .... It is good for the country to which they go; it helps to break the equilibrium of poverty in the country from which they come."[2]

(John Kenneth Galbraith)

INTRODUCTION

There is fast growing understanding at national and international levels of the critical nexus between migration and poverty; but, as yet insufficient data exist to inform a coordinated policy approach (UK House of Commons, 2004). Migration can be both the cause and the result of poverty, while poverty itself can be both alleviated and exacerbated by population movements. But the actual respective impacts are relative and vary according to levels of development and the particular policy environment of the area under consideration.

In some locations and under certain conditions, poverty may be a root cause of migration; in others, under different conditions, the poor may be the last to move. In some areas, migration may offer a way out of poverty; in others it can make the poverty worse. The situation is further complicated by the different types of "migration" and differing levels of "poverty" that exist, each defying accurate definition or measurement. Understanding the complex interplay between migration and poverty is important for policy makers and donor agencies, particularly in their ongoing efforts at poverty reduction, and can help put migration on the development agendas of the world.

This chapter looks at some key issues at the interface between migration and poverty that need to be further pursued to fill the current data gap. All forms of human population movement are considered under "migration", or more appropriately "population mobility", including: internal and international migration; short-term circular movements, and more permanent migration. Under "poverty", distinctions are drawn between chronic, absolute poverty and the more subjective "relative deprivation".

The chapter examines the migration-poverty interface at the personal, national, regional and international levels, and cautions against drawing simple causal links between them. It shows how migration can reduce absolute poverty in some communities, and migrants abroad can act as agents of development for their home communities. It also shows how migration can increase the sense of relative deprivation in some communities, and in turn trigger more migration. It considers some policy strategies to harness the benefits of migration for poverty alleviation, including the incorporation of migration issues into national and global development agendas, such as the UN Millennium Development Goals. Finally, it highlights areas for further study in support of these strategies.

1. *This chapter has been drafted by Professor Ronald Skeldon, Professorial Fellow at the University of Sussex in the UK and Honorary Professor at the University of Hong Kong; and is a modified version of an article that first appeared in the Asia-Pacific Population Journal, vol. 17, No. 4, December 2002 (modified in consultation with IOM).*

2. *Cited in Harris, 2002, p. 119.*

For illustration, the chapter focuses mostly on the Asia-Pacific region[3] and the experiences of countries of origin like Bangladesh, China, India, Pakistan, Philippines, Thailand and Vietnam.

MIGRATION AND POVERTY: AMBIVALENT RELATIONSHIPS

IN THE 1990S, absolute poverty declined in China, the Philippines and Thailand and increased in parts of South Asia and throughout the new republics of Central Asia, with little change in poverty levels in Indonesia over the same period (ESCAP/UNDP, 2002). The figures for China need to be taken with some caution: from 1979 to 2001 some 220 million in China's rural areas reportedly came out of poverty,[4] but in 2003, the population in poverty had increased by 800,000 nationwide for the first time in the past two decades.[5] At the end of 2003, the total population in poverty was 29 million.[6] Restructuring has caused a large loss of jobs in the state sector, a trend set to continue after China's accession to the World Trade Organization in 2001. For example, some 26 million workers have been laid off from state enterprises since 1998, and the real unemployment rate in 2002 may have been in excess of 20 per cent in some sectors.[7]

Another way to look at poverty is through the proportion of a population that is undernourished. The UN Human Development Report of 2003 shows that in the decade 1990-2000 the share of the undernourished in the populations of Southeast Asia declined, indicating a trend towards poverty alleviation in those countries. In comparison with South Asia, where the improvements were not so dramatic, the data for Southeast Asia are more extensive, and show notable improvements in such long-term depressed countries as Vietnam, Lao PDR and Cambodia, although as regards the latter from a much higher base.[8]

But compared with the uncertain estimates of poverty, migration can be even more difficult to measure. Available data suggest that, despite lower relative poverty in Southeast Asia, population movement is likely to have increased from all Asian economies under consideration in the 1990s.[9] However, in several cases these figures either omit or severely underestimate the number of undocumented migrants, which for some countries is substantial.[10] In Malaysia, for example, some 2.1 million were apprehended between 1992 and 2000 (Hugo, 2002), and estimates of the stock of undocumented migrants in that country before the 1997 financial crisis were as high as 1.43 million (ILO, 1998). The vast majority of these came from neighbouring Indonesia.[11]

Even more difficult to estimate is the number of internal migrants. Data in Thailand, where poverty levels declined markedly during the 1990s, even taking into account the impact of the 1997 financial crisis, suggest that internal migration may have

3. *For the purpose of this chapter, Asia includes East Asia [China (which includes China mainland, Hong Kong Special Administrative Region of China -- hereafter referred to as Hong Kong, Macao Special Administrative Region of China -- hereafter Macao, and Taiwan Province of China -- hereafter Taiwan), the Democratic People's Republic of Korea (hereafter North Korea), Japan, Mongolia, and the Republic of Korea (hereafter South Korea)]; Southeast Asia (Brunei, Cambodia, Timor Leste, Indonesia, Laos, Malaysia, Myanmar, Philippines, Singapore, Thailand and Viet Nam); and South-Central Asia (Afghanistan, Bangladesh, Bhutan, India, Iran, Maldives, Nepal, Pakistan and Sri Lanka.*

4. *See Lu, 2001,who was then the Head of the Poverty Reduction Office of the State Council of China.*

5. *See J. Liu, 2004, currently the Head of the Poverty Reduction Office of the State Council of China.*

6. *See F. Liu, 2004, Director General of the Department of Legal Affairs of the Poverty Reduction Office of the State Council of China.*

7. *Data cited in the* Migration News, *May and July issues, 2002.*

8. *The UNDP's* Human Development Report 2003 *shows how the population proportions of undernourished persons in developing countries have changed between the periods 1990-92 and 1998-2000, e.g. Bangladesh 35 to 35 per cent; India 25 to 24 per cent; Pakistan 25 to 19 per cent; Sri Lanka 29 to 23 per cent; Cambodia 43 to 36 per cent; Lao PDR 29 to 24 per cent; Philippines 26 to 23 per cent; Thailand 28 to 18 per cent and Vietnam 27 to 18 per cent.*

9. *See the discussion of UN data on this in the chapter "International Migration Trends".*

10. *Estimates of these are likely to be based on the number of apprehensions on attempted entry or persons arrested in-country, with assumptions about the number of those escaping the official net.*

11. *Undocumented migrants are part of the large number of "illegal" migrants in Asia who do not enter a country through a formal, legal channel, which in Asia are quite limited for all except skilled migrants. Most unskilled migrants moving from one Asian country to another do so illegally.*

slowed in the 1990s. Preliminary figures from the 2000 census indicate that the percentage of the population that moved in the five years before the census was lower than in 1990, or 13.9 per cent in 2000 compared with 16.8 in 1990 (Thailand, 2002). But to conclude that a relative reduction in mobility might be conducive to a reduction in poverty would be deceptive or simply incorrect.

First, the population census only captures a part of total population movement, omitting most circulation and short-term migration. Studies in Thailand following the 1990 census showed that a change in the reference period used to define "migration" from three months (as used in the census) to one month (as per the National Migration Survey of Thailand) increased the numbers of recorded migrants by over one fifth (Chamratrithirong et al., 1995).

Second, and more critically, despite the overall drop in poverty in the 1990s, the number of poor in Thailand increased from 6.8 million at the beginning of 1997 to 7.9 million at the end of 1998 as a result of the financial crisis. This is an increase in the proportion of total population classified as poor from 11.4 to 12.9 per cent (UNDP, 1999). But it would be deceptive to conclude that this increase in poverty had caused the observed decline in internal migration in this period. More likely, the crisis stimulated an increase in precisely the types of mobility that censuses and general surveys are least able to measure, i.e. short-term mobility, as people looked for alternatives to job losses in the urban sector or market losses in the rural sector. Mobility could have increased, rather than decreased in that time, and been more of a survival strategy than a pathway to better opportunities. There are no records to prove or disprove this.

Thus any attempts to draw clear causal links between volume and patterns of migration and poverty based on existing data are likely to be problematic.

POVERTY AS A ROOT CAUSE OF MIGRATION

MIGRATION is often seen simply as a flight from poverty: there are no opportunities available locally, so people migrate in order to survive. Flight from a devastating famine appears to be the classic example of this. But such cases are generally confined to the poorest parts of the world, principally in sub-Saharan Africa. In the vast regions of Asia, they are still found in some pockets, but have become less common given the rapid economic development over the last half of the 20th century. Historic examples include the "Great Hunger" in China, 1959-1960, when millions moved in the desperate attempt to find food, although millions more were prevented from doing so by the authorities. The real impact on migration of this last great famine in China has yet to be reported, although there is some discussion of it (Becker, 1996; Banister, 1987).

Survival migration of the poorest is likely to be mainly local, or regional at most, and primarily intra-country. In apparent contradiction to the logic of survival migration, most studies of migration in non-disaster situations generally show that it is not the poorest who move, but those with access to some resources. Migration always involves some transportation costs and the abandonment of many of the few possessions the poor might have. The poorest of the poor cannot afford either risk or movement, and starvation mostly tends to occur at home. Even in the Great Famine in Ireland of 1845-1850, it was rarely the poorest who emigrated to North America. The more able-bodied could perhaps reach the United Kingdom (UK), but many among the rest perished. Emigration rates from the hardest hit countries were often significantly lower than from countries not so affected (Miller, 1985).[12]

In a different continent in a different era, the majority of those who fled from China mainland to Hong Kong,

12. *See also the chapter in this report, "International Migration Trends", which shows that emigration rates are in fact lowest in the least developed countries.*

China, after the victory of the communist forces in 1949 might have had a "well-founded fear of persecution", but over half claimed that they had moved for "economic reasons" (Hambro, 1955). They were not among the poorest in China at the time. This is not to deny that poverty is an important cause of migration, but to show that there are often other factors at play.

With the exception of particular areas and at particular times, it is often not absolute poverty *per se* that is significant in accounting for migration, but whether people *feel* that they are poor.

MIGRATION AS THE RESULT OF POVERTY

POVERTY as the root cause of migration, and migration as a result of poverty might appear to be the same thing, but there are significant differences. Migration as the result of poverty can shift the focus to the issue of feeling poor, i.e. relative rather than absolute deprivation. Migration, either of outsiders into a community, or of natives out of their community, establishes linkages between origins and destinations. These linkages spread knowledge about conditions in a wider world that can transform the characteristics of communities from "subsistence affluence" (Sahlins, 1974) to "relative deprivation", without any significant real change in the quantity of subsistence in the community.

What changes here is the less tangible, subjective sense of quality of life, where people compare their own condition to those of people living elsewhere, and the potential for migration increases with the perception. Migration of family and friends can create both the conditions that lead to people perceiving themselves as poor and further migration as they move to satisfy new-found aspirations. This process is perhaps at the root of most migration. It gives the impression that poverty is the driving force, while in reality it is the desire to better oneself according to new standards rather than the result of actual deprivation. Migration is thus both the creator and the product of poverty.

People who move are often the more innovative, better-off, better educated and hence better informed in any community, even if these qualities themselves are relative (Skeldon, 1990). In an isolated rural community, for example, the better educated might be those with basic primary education among the many with no formal education at all. Migrants are also targeted and selected by labour recruiters or other expanding urban-based groups for their relative skills and capabilities. For example, in the huge contract labour recruitment drives between South/Southeast Asia and the oil-rich countries of the Middle East, recruiters are unlikely to select the weakest or poorest members of any group (Zachariah, Kannan and Rajan 2002).[13] Whether the loss of these people contributes to poverty will be considered below. (It is also very evident from many countries that the regions producing the highest number of migrants are often not the poorest, e.g., Fujian province.)

MIGRATION AS A CAUSE OF POVERTY

THERE ARE ways in which migration can directly increase the number of absolute poor. The clearest example is where people are forced to relocate without adequate planning and support. In many cases, forced relocation is an unintended consequence of development, mainly through the creation of lakes and reservoirs resulting from the construction of dams, although displacement for roads and urban expansion is also an important trigger. For example, it is estimated that 90 – 100 million people globally were involuntarily displaced by infrastructure development projects during the last decade of the 20th century (Cernea and McDowell, 2000). In India alone, some 20 million people are thought to have

13. *In one of the most significant flows of contract labour in recent history, as at 1998 over 2 million people have moved from the State of Kerala in India alone, the overwhelming majority to the Middle East (also known as West Asia).*

been displaced over 40 years, the majority of whom became impoverished (Cernea, 2000), while in China over a similar period, more than 30 million have been thus displaced (Meikle and Zhu, 2000). The Three Gorges Project, currently under construction on the Yangtse River, is estimated to have led to resettlement well over a million people by the time it is completed.

A key factor separating forced population displacement due to development policy from other types of migration is that the numbers moving and the timing of the movements are known. Thus, if poverty is the result of forced migration, it is likely to be the fault of inadequate planning rather than of the migration itself.

There is no cogent reason for the migration to lead to increased poverty, although this often appears to be the result in Asia and elsewhere (Cernea and McDowell, 2000).[14]

BRAIN DRAIN

More difficult to assess is the loss of innovative and educated community members, or the "brain drain" that can occur at national or village levels in countries of origin. It has proven difficult to demonstrate empirically a fall in macro-level economic indicators, when there is a major exodus of educated persons at the national level. Equally, it is difficult to prove that rural-to-urban migration at the village level causes a decline in either agricultural production or productivity. Adding to this difficulty is the fact that migration is often circular. Both the educated at the national level, and workers moving from village to town, either return at a later stage, or move to extend the resource base of their families by adding new resources elsewhere.

The so-called "brain drain" argument is difficult to sustain at the macro-level in East Asia. Tens of thousands of students left Japan, South Korea, Taiwan and Hong Kong for study overseas from the 1960s at precisely the time that these economies began to grow rapidly (Skeldon, 1997a). It is difficult to prove that these economies could have grown even faster if the students had stayed home. Over time, increasing numbers returned and there clearly was a "brain gain" rather than a brain drain in these economies. In Taiwan, it is estimated that the return rate of students increased from 5 – 10 per cent in the 1950s and 1960s to 20 – 25 per cent in the 1980s (Tsai 1988), and that the number of returnees has further increased since then. The majority of them were highly educated and returned to participate in the new industrialization, particularly in the north, in Taipei, and in Shinchu City, which emerged from the late 1980s as Taiwan's Silicon Valley (Tsay and Lin, 2003).

The shift from brain drain to brain gain experienced by Taiwan is also increasingly the case in other major growing economies in Asia with significant government support for attracting back skilled émigrés, such as China, India and the Philippines. China, for example, is actively seeking to redress the massive loss of its educated in the 1980s and 1990s with government and private sector-backed incentives, such as research grants, salary supplements, housing support and educational assistance for children among others (Zweig and Rosen, 2003). The government encourages overseas Chinese entrepreneurs to open high-tech firms in China and has eased residence and other migration restrictions for returnees. These efforts have been hugely beneficial, for example the government records that more than 60 per cent of all overseas investments in China in the past two decades came from overseas Chinese investors.[15]

But this scenario is not typical of many developing countries. The loss of even relatively small numbers of educated from marginal economies can contribute to slower or even declining growth. The "brain drain" is for some the most obvious way in which migration

14. *Some experts point to the possibility that the exodus of much-needed skills may hold some governments back from structural changes necessary for development. This needs to be further examined (Ellerman, 2003).*

15. *See also the Textbox 6.3 and the chapter "Balancing the Benefits and Costs of Skilled Migration in the Asia-Pacific Region".*

can potentially harm the development prospects of a country, particularly when those providing services to the poor – doctors, nurses, teachers, etc. – leave and cause critical shortages of human capital. Some stark examples of this can be found in Sub-Saharan Africa and the Central Asian Republics (Harris, 2002).[16] In Asia, there are huge differences in losses and gains from migration, ranging from the skills drain on Bangladesh to the highly profitable brain gains of Taiwan.[17]

While the impact of the loss of highly educated and skilled persons needs to be assessed on a region-by-region basis, a critical factor will always be whether there is something for the educated to return to in their economies of origin.[18] Where there is little to return to, brain drain is more likely to occur, but where origin economies are more dynamic, a brain gain may be the result. This is country-specific, even region-specific within a country. For example, while East Asia is the most dynamic region in Asia, and China a key part of this, North Korea, and the huge hinterland of China are not, and are likely to distort any regional overviews of this issue.

At the local level, assessments of the impact of out-migration on production are equally problematic, although few studies support the idea that there is a negative impact on farm production (Simmons, 1984). An assessment in China has shown that the loss of labour due to out-migration can have a negative impact on incomes from cropping, but has no impact on crop yields (de Brauw et al., 2001). Where the impacts become intense in marginal areas, and emigration grows to such an extent that the reproductive capacity of a village is eroded, leading to ageing and declining populations, then pockets of deprivation may emerge even in the most developed societies. For example, the severely depopulating areas (*kaso*) in Japan challenge the policy makers to supply adequate services to ageing populations.[19] It is in the poorer economies that those left behind are most likely to experience "chronic poverty" (Kothari, 2002), with poverty thus a residual effect of migration.

But there is a growing awareness among countries of origin and destination that policies on labour migration from developing countries could be adjusted to:

i) better regulate the recruitment of skills that are rare and needed in these countries;
ii) create incentives to promote return migration, and,
iii) maximize the development contribution of migrant communities, including via remittances.

Some destination countries, like the UK, have established codes of conduct for recruitment in the health sector, to better engage the countries of origin and avoid a drain of essential skills. Other policy options include the establishment of guidelines for employers in destination countries regarding more ethics-based recruitment, training and skills enhancement, a global database on countries most vulnerable to skills losses and tighter regulation of international recruitment agencies and their practices.[20]

16. *Some 60,000 highly skilled workers are reported to have fled African economies during the last half of the 1980s (Ghana losing 60 per cent of its doctors) (Harris, 2002). In Central Asia, the return of large numbers of Russian or Ukrainian technicians to their "home" republics was also a likely factor in the rising poverty observed in these countries. (Note: the skilled exodus was just one migration among many in that region following the disintegration of the Soviet Union and causing suffering and deprivation (Whitlock, 2002).)*

17. *See the scale of "returns" from emigration in Asia in the chapter "Balancing the Benefits and Costs of Skilled Migration in the Asia-Pacific Region".*

18. *Some observers feel countries of origin need to make it attractive for their educated citizens to stay (or get the diaspora productively re-involved in their home country) rather than expect countries of destination to pay subsidies or compensation (Ellerman, 2003). But this may be too simple in light of the open market dynamic of globalization.*

19. *Agricultural income in these areas was 70 per cent of the national average in the mid-1990s. They covered almost half of the total land area of the country but represented only 6.3 per cent of the total population (Skeldon, 2001).*

20. *It has been suggested that education reform in sending countries could also play a key role in combating brain drain. Some strategies have been proposed, and tried, to "tie" the educated migrant to his/her home country, e.g. through a repayable education loan. But they have been hard to implement. Models to link educational reform to migration management have been debated, and warrant further investigation by policymakers (Ellerman, 2003).*

Mitigating the brain drain in sectors critical for the development of sending countries can also effectively be achieved through bilateral development cooperation projects such as IOM's MIDA Ghana Health project commenced in 2004 between the Netherlands and Ghana.[21] Such projects can help recruit migrant professionals for short-term assignments back home. Similar projects have been tried under UNDP's TOKTEN or IOM's Return of Knowledge projects in earlier years, e.g. in Thailand and the Philippines.[22] They can usefully form part of a country's human resources development strategy policy.

In sum, the brain drain issue, in particular its impact on poverty, is not as straightforward as it might appear. For one, the very developing countries experiencing crippling brain drain also urgently need to find international outlets for their surplus labour. In Bangladesh, for example, despite (or perhaps because of) the brain drain challenge, the government has set up a new ministry to deal with overseas contract labour and the diaspora, and is actively trying to reorient its education and training programmes to produce people with the necessary qualifications to enter specific foreign labour markets. For another, it is not entirely clear whether the basic health indicators in some places really show a deterioration of conditions (rising morbidity, decreasing longevity, etc.) as a direct result of the medical exodus.

International research on these issues is still too seminal to provide answers to such questions, but the answers may also not be as blindingly obvious as many may assume or hope.

URBAN POVERTY

Another key issue for countries of origin and destination is whether migration concentrates the poor in destination areas, primarily in the largest metropolitan centres of the developing world. Even if it is not the poorest who migrate from the villages, relative to city people in the destination areas they are often poor, and their ghettoization may be a further hindrance to development. Again, evidence supporting such a statement is far from conclusive. There are insufficient data to suggest that migrants are over-represented among the urban poor (but we do know they have higher unemployment rates, and that is not a bad proxy). EU-15 data show this (see EC Communication on Integration). Indeed, migrants can tend to have higher labour force participation rates than native-born in cities in the developing world.[23] This does not imply that the living conditions of all migrants in towns are satisfactory, or that they do not appear among the ranks of the urban poor.

Many occupations filled by migrants, and particularly those held by poorly educated migrant women, are badly paid, insecure and require work under appalling conditions. However, given that migration has not generally been the principal component of urban growth in the developing world (natural increase has usually been more important), and that migrants tend to have higher rates of employment than the local urban-born, the principal causes of urban poverty are to be found in the metropolitan regions themselves rather than in migration to them.

POVERTY ALLEVIATED BY MIGRATION

THE PREVAILING assumption behind much of the debate on this subject to date is that the relationship between migration and poverty is negative: migration is the result of deprivation or it leads to the impoverishment of certain areas. Developing countries of origin have responded to this with measures to reduce the outflow

21. *IOM and the Ministry of Health are working together to recruit émigré professionals abroad for temporary assignments back in Ghana, to teach, provide advisory services and logistical support to projects, mostly as medical specialists, nurses, managers, IT specialists, or finance specialists. The average assignment is 2-3 months.*

22. *The Return of Knowledge and Talent (RKT) project was begun by IOM in Manila in the late 1980s. The Thai Expert Programme (TEP) was started in 1993/1994, and by way of example, assisted some 15 to 20 Thai experts abroad to travel to Thailand inter alia to engage in technical discussions and collaboration with Thai educators, researchers and professionals at various universities, research and technical institutions around the country.*

23. *There is a huge body of literature on this, much of it summarized in Skeldon, 1990.*

of highly skilled, e.g. through exit controls or taxes (Lopes, 2002), but have found these difficult to implement. While it cannot be completely discounted, there is a lack of empirical data to support such a general negative assumption. Recent evidence by the World Bank and others supports the conclusion that population movement can significantly lower per capita and national poverty.[24]

The principal reason for this lies in the nature of the migration process itself, which is rarely just a movement from A to B, but a complex circulation between two or more destinations. Also, migrants rarely operate in a social vacuum, but are meshed into family and community networks. Rather than just being individual income maximizers, they are seen as part of a communal risk-minimizing strategy. Such an interpretation falls within the so-called "new home economics" approach to theories of migration (Massey et al., 1993; Stark, 1991).

Migration can therefore be seen as a system linking origins and destinations, in which also money and goods flow. New destinations broaden the resource base of a household, perhaps allowing a more optimal deployment of labour, as those underemployed during the slack part of the agricultural cycle can find work on a plantation or in town. Migrants can be agents of development, strengthening cooperation between home and host societies, helping to alleviate immediate poverty effects at the family and community levels through remittances, investment and the introduction of new production skills, and the like.

By extending their resource base through systems of circulation, transnational or internal, people minimize their exposure to risk and thus reduce the probability of falling into poverty. Circular/temporary migration for the poor is a basic livelihood strategy that uses migration positively to avoid the poverty trap.

DIASPORA AND REMITTANCES

More recent studies show how migrant remittances are an indispensable part of the economic survival of many countries, and at local levels can lift people out of poverty (Nyberg Sorensen, 2004; Adams and Page, 2003). But like so much about migration and poverty, this is notoriously difficult to measure accurately. Unless specialized surveys are undertaken, estimates of the amounts of money and goods remitted by internal migrants are virtually impossible to make. Some estimates of international remittances do exist, but they only reflect the official flows. Much more is transmitted informally through relatives or when the migrants return. Because of the way data are captured, remittances can be underestimated by international sources on the one hand, and overestimated by governments on the other.[25]

As discussed in greater detail in other chapters of this report, the volume and importance of officially recorded flows have more than doubled between the 1980s and the 1990s, and are likely to surpass USD 100 billion by 2005,[26] much higher than global official development assistance (ODA). If flows through unofficial channels were to be included, they would be much higher, with estimates for Bangladesh suggesting that less than half of remittances flowed through official channels (Siddiqui, 2003).

India and the Philippines were among the top three beneficiaries of migrant remittances in the developing world (alongside Mexico) in the period 1995-2000.[27] In Asia, the Philippines is the labour exporter *par excellence*, with some 7 million émigrés, of which half are estimated to be working on contract, around 60

24. *Recent World Bank research shows, for example, that on average a 10 per cent increase in the number of international migrants in a country's population can lead to a 1.6 per cent decline in per capita poverty and that a 10 per cent increase in the share of remittances in a country's GDP can lead to a 1.2 per cent decline in poverty (see the global study for the World Bank by Adams and Page, 2004).*

25. *International agencies like the International Monetary Fund (IMF) could underestimate the transfers by not including informal transactions, and official government statistics could overestimate them because other financial repatriations, including illicit ones, cannot always be distinguished from remittances. See also MPI (2003).*

26. *See also the chapter "Economic Costs and Benefits of International Labour Migration".*

27. *See World Bank statistics at: www.worldbank.org/prospects/gdf2003/gdf_statApp_web.pdf (p.198).*

per cent being women. In 2000 alone, more than USD 6 billion in foreign exchange were remitted to the Philippines (Go, 2002). For India, the annual remittances for the past five years have consistently been more than USD 9 billion, and have significantly expanded the earnings and employment opportunity of the middle class, and helped India's entry into the global economy (Newland, 2004).

But remittances are also important for many other Asian labour exporters such as Bangladesh, Pakistan and Sri Lanka. For Pakistan in the mid-1980s, they represented about 9 per cent of GDP and were an important factor in allowing Pakistan to sustain the highest growth rate in South Asia through most of the 1970s and 1980s (Addleton, 1992).[28] In the Indian state of Kerala in the 1990s, remittances accounted for 21 per cent of state income (Kannan and Hari, 2002). Even Vietnam, a relatively recent entrant into regional and global labour markets, had around 300,000 workers overseas in 2000 remitting USD 1.25 billion annually (Nguyen, 2002).

Although the important dimension of foreign exchange earnings is missing in remittances from internal migrants, these, too, are significant for communities of origin. The National Migration Survey of Thailand in 2000 shows that over one-quarter of internal migrants had sent money or goods back to their households of origin during the 12 months prior to the survey (Osaki, 2002). The numbers remitting tended to increase, as they spent more time away from home, and one-third of those who had been away for longer than 10 years were still sending money home (ibid). This is an important difference between internal migration and international migration.

Given that the number of internal migrants in any country vastly exceeds the number of those going overseas,[29] the volume of money sent back to the rural sector from cities in the developing world is significant, even if amounts sent by overseas migrants are greater on a per capita basis since, on average, they earn more than those at home. In China, households that send out internal migrants appear to increase the per capita income of those left behind by between 14 and 30 per cent (de Brauw et al., 2001). However, the marginal propensity to save appears to be generally higher in the case of remittances from international migration (Ratha, 2003) and, in the example of the State of Kerala in India, these remittances appear to have reduced the overall poverty rate in the state by three per cent, and by over six per cent among the most deprived (Zachariah, Kannan and Rajan, 2002).

More critical than the actual amounts, however, are the uses to which the monies are put, the likely impact of remittances on areas of origin of migration and, in particular, whether they actually help alleviate poverty. At one level, remittances tend to be used for conspicuous consumption rather than investment; e.g. for house construction or the sponsoring of weddings and other such purposes, rather than improvements likely to lead to increased agricultural productivity. At another level, they also pay for the education of the next generation, and that does appear to be a clear investment strategy.

Some communities use remittances more for education than others (although, as in the case of the Philippines, this education can be used by the children to better prepare future emigration for work abroad.) But expenditure on house construction can also stimulate local building enterprises and generate employment and trade in materials (if they are not imported). Even something as obvious an example of conspicuous consumption as wedding feasts generates demand for local foods, supports local musicians, etc. The Philippines can show how in some towns remittances have strengthened the local medical infrastructure and boosted banks' holdings in order to increase local loans.[30]

28. *The Asia Development Bank estimates some USD 1.6 billion remitted annually to Pakistan; the Pakistan Ministry of Finance believes it to be as high as USD 6 billion (Nyberg Sorensen, 2004); and the World Bank cites USD3.5 billion for 2002 (World Bank, 2002a).*

29. *For example, in Vietnam some 4.3 million people moved internally during 1994-1999, as compared with 300,000 who emigrated in this period (Skeldon, 2003).*

30. *See the 2001 report on the impact of remittances on the rural city of Pozorrubio, with a large émigré community abroad, which concludes: "remittances can help raise a community from poverty – often more effectively than governments"* (Wall Street Journal, 2001).

Thus, there can be important indirect benefits of remittance money to towns and villages, although there is still much information lacking on this area. The dynamics across large emigration countries can also differ widely. In China, remittances from abroad are not proportionate to the huge Chinese diaspora, when compared with the remittance performance of India or the Philippines, inter alia because of where the diaspora generally hails from (e.g. the more prosperous coastal towns). The government has also aimed its policies more at attracting direct investments and trading opportunities through its diaspora (see below).

At the family and village level, this means that there may be less direct person-to-person benefit derived from international remittances than could be expected of such a massive diaspora, and which would be so crucial for addressing immediate poverty needs at family and community levels. By contrast, recent research by China's Agriculture Ministry shows that internal migration is better able to boost economies in the poorer rural sector; and that remittances from the country's fast-growing urban labourers are likely to surpass agriculture as the biggest income generators in the rural areas they left to find work. The research found that an estimated 98 million rural residents, who worked away from their villages, sent or carried home a total of Rmb370 billion (ca. USD45 billion) in 2003, an increase of 8.5 per cent over the previous year (Kynge, 2004).

While clearly there is personal and community growth through such consumption, particularly in some rural areas (funded by internal migrants) and the more prosperous migrant-sending regions (funded by the international diaspora), the extent of actual and long-term poverty alleviation and development support from remittances remains unclear. The general conclusion about remittances is that they can boost development overall in poor countries, and subsequently benefit the poor. Migrants and their families generally tend to use their wealth wisely, and the benefits appear to more than counterbalance costs.[31] But it is likely that in many instances these do not flow directly to poor households, if the poorest do not migrate, or if supporting policies are more focused on larger, macro uses of remittances.

More information on these linkages and effects is needed; and is now, laudably, being pursued by some international donor agencies and partner governments (World Bank, DFID). For the governments, the immediate challenges will be to balance the roles to be played by the different sectors in overall national growth; and ensure that policies to leverage the effect of remittances, investment and other "returns" from their diaspora, both international and internal, help maintain that balance to the lasting benefit of both the communities and the country.

IMPACT ON SOCIO-ECONOMIC INEQUALITY

More difficult to assess is the impact of remittances on socio-economic inequality. Since many who move tend to be from the wealthier families in any community, the remittances logically flow back to those families, exacerbating or at least reinforcing existing inequalities. Poverty can be measured by the proportion of wealth controlled by the various quintiles in any population, and if the upper 20 per cent are increasing their "share" as a result of migration, and the lowest fifth decreasing their share, it could be argued that migration was indeed contributing to the intensification of poverty. Yet again, the evidence is contradictory.

In Pakistan, the distribution of remittances appears to have increased inequalities between migrant and non-migrant households, and yet spread benefits to a wider range of groups and areas that could effectively undermine the centres of traditional political and economic power (Addleton, 1992).

Migration flows do tend to be generated out of specific "niches" or areas of origin. For example, most of the migration from China comes from relatively few districts in the three coastal provinces of

31. *See the Asian examples summarized in, for example, Gunatilleke, 1986.*

Guangdong, Fujian and Zhejiang, much of the migration from India to the Gulf States is from Kerala, and almost all the migrants from Bangladesh and Pakistan to the UK come from, respectively, the districts of Sylhet and Mirpur. Hence, certain micro-regions may benefit more than those areas sending fewer migrants, thus increasing regional as well as social inequalities (Seddon et al., 2002). Nevertheless, data from Thailand show that, although the per capita amount of remittances to poor households may be much less than to wealthier families, it has a much greater relative impact and helps to alleviate poverty (Osaki, 2002).

Migration may thus help reduce absolute poverty among some communities, but at the same time increase feelings of relative deprivation among others. Overall, people may be better fed as a result of migration, but the personal sense of deprivation may still generate resentment. Thus, migration can also be a significant factor in the growth of some social and revolutionary movements, a theme that remains under-researched (Skeldon, 1987). Such movements have led in the past to destruction that in turn extended poverty on a massive scale. Illustrations are scarce here, as this remains an under-researched area, albeit important.[32]

There also remains the issue of how much remittances may be helping some governments in developing countries of origin to defer structural, labour market and educational changes essential for longer-term poverty alleviation. Some experts strike a cautionary note here, based on experiences in Latin America, as financial institutions can often have different goals for remittances than those of the migrants, their families or the government (Ellerman, 2003).

The overall question for policy makers is how to increase the impacts of remittances on poverty alleviation. There is still insufficient conclusive evidence about current actual impacts, and the differences from region to region, also rural to urban, within a country. In the Philippines, despite the massive remittances from abroad, and evidence of their positive impact in many areas, income distribution remains problematic, relative to other Southeast Asian countries, and it takes high economic growth to benefit the poor (Abella et al., 2004).[33] But the obvious question here is: how much worse would the situation be without remittances?

Increasingly, governments and finance institutions are finding ways to expedite and lower the costs of remittance transfers, which are still prohibitive for many migrants (Lowell et al., 2002).[34] In Asia, governments are trying to attract remittances through foreign currency accounts and bonds (India), pre-departure counselling to overseas foreign workers (Philippines), simpler transfer procedures and expansion of financial networks (Bangladesh) (IOM, 2003).

Economists would, finally, strike a note of caution about overestimating the "multiplier" effect of remittances. Businesses established through remittances cannot necessarily rely on their continued flow for sustainability. Remittances need to be factored into any development and growth planning as a *means* – an economic trigger – not a *way* of life.

MIGRANTS AS AGENTS OF POVERTY ALLEVIATION

A FINAL migration factor which can alleviate poverty is the behaviour of the migrants at destination and origin (after return), both domestic and international. As stated, migrants often tend to be among the more innovative and better educated members of any population. A small number of them are traders and entrepreneurs, brokers of economic exchange

32. *See the discussion of the Eritrean, Sri Lankan (Tamil) and Indian (Hindu nationalists) examples in Newland, 2004.*

33. *The 2004 CEME report on the Philippines states that globally, a 10 per cent increase in income growth means a 10 per cent gain in the incomes of the poor. In the Philippines, 10 per cent overall growth means a 4 per cent gain for the poor (Martin, 2004).*

34. *See the Chapter "Migrant Remittances as a Source of Development Finance".*

generating both wealth for themselves and employment for locals at origin and destination, which in turn generates prosperity. Entrepreneurship, often associated with particular ethnic groups, such as the Chinese or Jews, is perhaps more a function of situations and linkages resulting from migration than of particular ethnic characteristics. Entrepreneurs are the minority among the migrants (Chirot and Reid, 1997), who generate capital accumulation.

Migrants can and do contribute to the development of their home communities to varying degrees and in different ways: through remittances, as seen above, but also through new, enhanced skills acquired abroad, which they can bring back to their communities of origin, or use to train people there, on short or long-term assignments. They can also invest from abroad in community development schemes (e.g. through Home Town Associations). But they can also support democratization and human rights in their countries of origin, an area which could well engage more women in the interest of attitudinal changes towards the role of women (Newland, 2004).

The Philippines already has a well functioning, complex programme and administrative structure to encourage and support the return of its experienced diaspora.[35] China, too, has a long history of profiting from its "diaspora", also internal,[36] and has in recent years successfully attracted back large numbers of students into leading positions in China, as well as diaspora investments in Chinese enterprises.[37] The government has adapted its laws and practices to provide, i.a., tax and fee concessions to overseas investors, and this has paid off with almost half a million enterprises relying on foreign investments at October 2003, and 60 per cent of foreign investments coming from overseas Chinese investors (ibid). In India, a recent sample survey looked at IT professionals in Bangalore and their role in stimulating international mobility of Indian professionals (Khadria, 2004).[38] In Bangladesh, associations similar to the Home Town Associations in Latin America have sprung up quite independently (Newland, 2004).

While there continues to be an unfortunate lack of consolidated data on this issue, there are many stories around the world about migrants successfully operating as agents of growth and/or development for their depressed home communities.[39] But care needs to be taken about making an easy leap from development to poverty alleviation, or assumptions that diasporas are a panacea for poverty, harmoniously working (or with the potential to work harmoniously) for the good of the country. As shown above, diasporas are highly heterogeneous and can be very idiosyncratic in their relationship to the country of origin.

OTHER CONSIDERATIONS – GENDER ISSUES AND MIGRANT HEALTH

GENDER differences are an important consideration in the migration-poverty debate, particularly in parts of Asia where women are among the poorest, and are increasingly resorting to internal or international migration for economic survival (e.g. Bangladesh). In areas where males undertake most of the agricultural work, women can be released from rural households to access off-farm activities in towns and vice versa in areas where women dominate labour input into agriculture (as in much of Africa). The diversification of resource base, labour input and gender role can all

35. *See also the chapter "Filipinos Working Overseas: Opportunity and Challenge".*

36. *See Ellerman (2003) who argues that the successful "township-village enterprises" (TVEs) were the legacy of peasants who returned home with new skills after long displacements to urban areas during the Chinese Civil War.*

37. *See also the Textbox 6.3.*

38. *Khadria mentions in his paper that the results of this survey, which is part of a two-pronged survey (also on health workers), are published in an OECD STI Working Paper, 2004.*

39. *Ellerman cites the case of Slovenia, which, as a result of its technicians and engineers being forced to work in Germany during World War II was able to use the enhanced skills of its returnees to develop a high technology industry after the war, that has helped Slovenia become a leading "transition" economy today (Ellerman, 2003).*

act to alleviate poverty, where households are dependent upon a single resource at one location. But this strategy also has its costs, as migrants can be exploited at destination, and the separation of family members can cause major social disruption at origin.

These experiences are not new to Bangladesh, Sri Lanka and Pakistan, which have each variously banned or restricted the emigration of their young women, following abusive incidents abroad.[40] Today, Sri Lanka is the only one among these with an active policy to foster female labour emigration. But the problem is the much higher, immeasurable incidence of irregular migration by the women, who as uncounted statistics are highly vulnerable to abuse, exploitation, illness and death, particularly if they become victims of trafficking.

A recent study on trafficking in South Asia by the Asian Development Bank found that the most commonly identified "push" factor driving the trafficking process is poverty (ADB, 2003; 2003a). Despite this, trafficking often does not receive sufficient priority in strategies aiming to combat poverty. Trafficking is not articulated in any of the national anti-poverty country strategy papers in South Asia (ibid).

These negative consequences need to be balanced against possible improvements in the status of migrants who acquire skills or pursue education at destinations. The gender issues are significant, as women, by absenting themselves even temporarily from patriarchal structures, can improve their status through work elsewhere (Hondagneu-Sotelo,1994). Temporary absences of men can also thrust women left behind into positions of responsibility to run households, elevate their status and, indirectly or directly, reduce the incidence of deprivation. Whether they stay or leave, they can become agents of change and of development for their families and country. This has certainly been the case in the Philippines,[41] where the majority of labour migrants are women who contribute massively to remittance flows and family improvements at home.

Migrant Health is also assuming a higher priority in the work of WHO/UNAIDS, World Bank, UNDP and IOM on the nexus between migration and development. In general, there is a greater understanding of the longer-term devastation to national economies and development goals of the HIV pandemic (World Bank, 2003), particularly in Africa,[42] but increasingly also in Asia, where a report to the UNDP anticipates a pandemic potentially larger than in Africa (Iredale et al., 2004). There is an urgent call by the World Bank, UNAIDS, IOM and others for national policies and programmes to combat HIV and AIDS, also in regard to mobile populations, which are highly vulnerable, particularly where such large numbers are clandestine as in Asia, and particularly women in exploitative situations,[43] as described above.

The DFID/WB conference in London on remittances in 2003 concluded that very little is known about the gender differences in remittance behaviour. International agencies and NGOs are increasingly working together to fill the large gaps in information on both the gender and health issues, as a first step through better research;[44] and this urgently needs to target the as yet largely unknown relationship between migration and poverty.

40. *See also the chapter on "International Migration Trends and Patterns in Asia and Oceania".*

41. *Some 60 per cent of Filipino migrants are female, most of them domestic helpers, maids, nurses and caregivers.*

42. *The WB report (World Bank, 2003) anticipates that South Africa could face progressive economic collapse in several generations unless it combats the AIDS epidemic more urgently.*

43. *UNAIDS reports that today 48 per cent of all adults living with HIV are women. Refer also the UNAIDS website: www.unaids.org/EN/other/functionalities/Search.asp*

44. *The World Bank is particularly investing large amounts of money in the HIV/AIDS issue (WB, 2003).*

SOME POLICY CONCLUSIONS

THIS CHAPTER has surveyed some of the complexities of the interplay between migration and poverty, particularly in Asia. In many areas, migration can lead to improved chances of survival and an alleviation of poverty, but it can also bring exploitation and disruption, with potential costs for the migrant, society and governments. The debate weighs in favour of migration being an effective tool in the fight against poverty in less developed countries, but only where policy and programme environments can foster those benefits. Amid the uncertainty of outcome, some sensible policy directions have emerged from experience for policymakers' consideration:

i) *Facilitate migration programmes as a means of reducing poverty* in the country of origin and, where appropriate, the country of destination. Migration may not be able to eradicate all types of poverty, and may even exacerbate some; but the OECD argues that if the EU, Canada, Japan and the US allowed migrants to make up just four per cent of their labour force, the returns to origin areas could be around USD 160-200 billion a year, far more than any potential debt relief (*The Guardian*, 26 August 2002). International agencies such as the World Bank, ILO and IOM could work with states to broaden the base of such regular immigration options globally (e.g. through bilateral labour agreements).

Development concerns can be protected through better regulation of international recruitment agencies and guidelines for ethical recruitment of workers from developing countries. Some models exist, such as the UK's code of conduct for recruitment of international health workers, and regional processes could help devise and enforce such cross-cutting agreements, as, for example, the EU is trying to do at one end of the north-south migration spectrum, and the Puebla Process, "5 plus 5", MIDA, MIDWA and others are doing at the other end.

But "development-friendly" migration policies go much further than simply cautiously opening the door to immigration. They can bolster the transnational networks between origin and destination countries conducive to diaspora-based investment and growth in the former, through more effective integration programmes and flexible citizenship arrangements.

ii) *Integrate migration into broader economic and social development frameworks.* For example, insert migration into the eight Millennium Development Goals (MDGs) set by the UN to be achieved by 2015. Clever migration management strategies, as per the first point, are important for all socio-economic development goals – national and international. Within the social agendas of the MDGs, they can help strengthen gender equality, education and health. A focus on migrant health could help combat the spread of diseases such as HIV/AIDS and malaria, which seriously hamper development and poverty alleviation prospects.

This is also an injunction to both the UN and other international agencies working on migration, and on development, to combine their efforts. More coherent approaches across different arms of government and the international community are more likely to attract the right donor support.

iii) *Support and enhance the contribution of diasporas to development*, for example through remittance leveraging, diaspora networking, and sustainable return and reintegration. Only governments and the private sector working together can reduce the costs of remittance transfers, improve remittance transmission possibilities for migrants, and mobilize and channel savings through greater involvement of formal financial institutions. Strengthening ties between countries of origin and their diasporas, as China, the Philippines, India and Thailand are increasingly doing, e.g. through investment opportunities (with tax breaks), enlightened bank account policies, even social events for visiting families, can bring big returns for home communities.

Development agencies and donors should directly empower diasporas, e.g. through network strengthening, incentives and general capacity building, to encourage them to contribute in a more systematic way to poverty alleviation at home (Newland, 2004).

The Philippines, Taiwan, India and China mainland offer some diverse but useful examples of how governments can support their respective diasporas (ibid), but more research is required on the exact impacts on poverty alleviation, and why these differ from country to country or region to region within a country, depending on cultural factors, the economy, and the strategic importance of that economy globally.

All such policies should not force the diaspora into formalistic patterns of behaviour, but rather foster an enabling environment, whereby migrants choose to support development initiatives at home, and are supported in that choice. Remittances should not be seen as a replacement of international donor support for development, or an enduring form of cash flow, but as a "trigger" for other longer-term projects (Nyberg Sorensen, 2004).

iv) *Enhance understanding of the development potential of migration via Mode 4* discussions. This is more generally development-oriented, and would need some further calibration in regard to poverty alleviation. The debate is huge, complex and controversial,[45] and this chapter only seeks to link this whole topic with GATS, and ensure that the GATS debate takes account of the fact that, given the right policies, mobility of workers can reinforce the competitive advantage of labour-abundant developing countries, and leverage poverty reduction efforts.

v) *Protect migrants, both male and female, from abuse and exploitation.* The social, financial and political costs of abuse, particularly where illness or death are involved, can be huge, also in regard to poverty alleviation. Policy makers are keenly aware that the profits garnered by smugglers and traffickers are finding their way into the wrong pockets. The money could be fuelling better policies, particularly in regard to empowerment of women, human rights and alleviation of the poverty and deprivation that makes people vulnerable to the wiles of smugglers and traffickers.

vi) Importantly, *improve the quality of data on this subject by improving policy-oriented research* on the migration-poverty linkage, as the UK development agency DFID and others have begun to do.[46] Such research would need to be extended across countries and regions of origin and destination. The network should be inter-disciplinary, bringing together the perspectives and findings of national and international expert agencies in development, migration, humanitarian, labour, health, cultural and education issues.

All the above issues require more research, but without more information on the behaviour of work permit holders and migrant communities in host countries, it would be difficult to plan support strategies for diaspora and migrant networks to contribute to poverty alleviation (Findlay, 2001). Improving the quality of data on remittance flows and their impact on development is one of the key recommendations of the DFID conference on the subject in October 2003.[47] DFID is also leading the way by investing in a knowledge base on the whole issue, which may lay the foundations for future joined approaches to migration and poverty.

45. *See also the Textbox 9.1 "Trade and Migration: GATS Mode 4".*

46. *Referenced by Tamas' study, 2003, which tours other research projects undertaken or under way on the general subject of migration, development and poverty, e.g. the overview of research and policy activities in regard to this nexus by the Sussex Centre for Migration Research. DFID is also supporting the establishment of a new Migration, Globalisation and Poverty Development Research Centre at the University of Sussex.*

47. *Conference on "Migrant Remittances: Development Impact, Opportunities, and Future Prospects", sponsored by DFID, IMP and the World Bank, London, 9-10 October 2003.*

The challenge is a dual one: poverty reduction programmes should take account of, and build on, the potentially positive force of migration; and migration policies should take account of development needs and reinforce the potentially positive force of migrants to help meet these needs. This can be best achieved through the combined efforts of the international and national development and migration agencies, the migrant diaspora, and the private sector. The policy pointers in this chapter can serve all parties in this endeavour, and be tailored to the specific circumstance of the country, region or community in need.

CHAPTER 14
MIGRANT REMITTANCES AS A SOURCE OF DEVELOPMENT FINANCE[1]

Whether remittances are used for consumption or buying houses, or for other investments, they stimulate demand for other goods and services in the economy... and enable a country to pay for imports, repay foreign debt and improve creditworthiness.

INTRODUCTION

WORKERS' remittances have emerged as a major source of external development finance in recent years (Ratha, 2003; *The Economist*, July 31, 2004). Given their magnitude and potential to reduce poverty, they have gained the attention of policymakers at the highest levels.[2] This chapter discusses recent and current trends in remittance flows, highlights some of the advantages and disadvantages associated with these flows, and identifies some important issues confronting policy makers in leveraging the effectiveness of remittances for development in developing countries and regions of origin.

BACKGROUND

OFFICIALLY recorded remittances received by developing countries exceeded USD 126 billion in 2004 (**Graph 14.1**).[3] The actual size of remittances, including both officially recorded and unrecorded transfers through informal channels, was even larger. *Remittances are now more than double the size of net official flows (under USD 25 billion), and are second only to foreign direct investment (FDI) (around USD 165 billion) as a source of external finance for developing countries* (**Graph 14.1**). In 36 out of 153 developing countries, remittances are larger than all capital flows, public and private. In many countries, they are larger than their earnings from the most important export item. In Mexico, for example, they were larger than FDI, and about the same size as oil exports, in 2003. In Sri Lanka, they were larger than tea exports (Ratha 2003).

Remittances continued to grow in 2004 reaching USD 23 billion in India, USD 17 billion in Mexico, and USD 8 billion in the Philippines. In part, the surge in remittance flows can be attributed to better data recording by central banks, in response to the generally increased scrutiny of remittances flowing through alternative channels. But a reduction in remittance costs – some 60 per cent in the US-Mexico corridor since 1999 – has also stimulated a growth in flows. An increase in migrant stocks is the other factor affecting remittance flows. Finally, security concerns and heightened scrutiny by immigration authorities in many rich countries have also encouraged outward remittance of savings by undocumented migrants. Pakistan is a case in point,

1. *The author of this chapter is Dilip Ratha, Senior Economist, World Bank, Washington, D.C.; dratha@worldbank.org*

2. *The G8 Heads of State Summit at Sea Island in June 2004, for example, called for "(...) better coherence and coordination of international organizations working to enhance remittance services and heighten the developmental impact of remittance receipts".*

3. *Remittances are defined as the sum of workers' remittances, compensation of employees and migrant transfers. The workers' remittance figures from the IMF Balance of Payments Statistics are known to be under-reported in many countries. See Ratha, 2003, for a discussion of data and definition issues.*

where remittance flows to that country more than tripled between 2001 and 2003.[4]

Remittances are more evenly distributed than capital flows. Even though the top recipient countries are typically large countries such as India, Mexico and the Philippines, remittances as a share of GDP or in per capita terms are particularly large in small countries such as Tonga, Tajikistan and Lesotho. Lebanon is among the top recipients in terms of remittances per capita.

A remarkable feature of remittances is that they tend to be a stable financial flow for developing countries, and even have a counter-cyclical effect in times of economic hardship. They typically serve an altruistic purpose for the migrants. In times of need, migrants tend to send more money to help out families back home. The other distinguishing feature of remittances is that they are person-to-person flows, well targeted to the needs of the recipients, who are often poor. The sender has a fair degree of control over the use of remittances, tending to send them in several instalments over the course of a year.

GRAPH 14.1

RESOURCE FLOWS TO DEVELOPING COUNTRIES (USD BILLION)

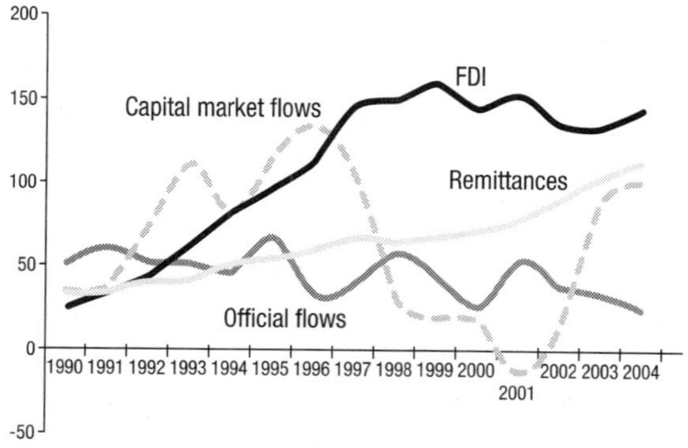

The rest of this chapter briefly addresses the following five main issues confronting policymakers interested in facilitating remittance flows and enhancing their developmental impact:

- How to strengthen the financial infrastructure supporting remittances?
- How to balance policies between combating money laundering and facilitating remittances?
- What is the developmental impact of remittances, and how can this be enhanced?
- How to improve data on remittances and migration?
- Should governments use fiscal incentives to attract remittances?

STRENGTHENING THE FINANCIAL INFRASTRUCTURE SUPPORTING REMITTANCES

EXORBITANT fees charged by money transfer agents – 13 per cent on average, and frequently as high as 20 per cent – are a drain on hard-earned remittances (**Graph 14.2**). And they especially affect poor migrants, who remit only small amounts at a proportionally higher, at times exorbitant, cost. *Reducing remittance fees would significantly increase annual remittance flows to developing countries, especially to the poor recipients.*

The remittance cost typically involves three components: the true cost of sending money, the profit component, and the foreign exchange (FX) commission. It is difficult to see why remittance fees should increase – rather than stay fixed – with the amount transferred.[5] Anecdotal evidence suggests that the true cost of sending remittances is very small. Informal channels, for example, regularly charge fees below one per cent.[6]

4. *Recent household surveys in countries like Guatemala and Colombia have shown an upward trend in remittance receipts for 2004. For example, Colombia is believed to have received over USD 3 billion in 2004 (sources: IOM Guatemala City and IOM Bogota; and IOM Press Briefing Notes, 19 November 2004).*

5. *Only one component of remittance costs, the FX commission, should be proportional to the size of remittances.*

6. *In an informal conversation, an undocumented migrant in Barcelona reported in 2004 that he saves on average 300-350 euros a month of which he remits home 250. The owner of the café down the road charges only a foreign exchange conversion fee, under 1 percent, to deliver the funds to the recipient in another country in about 24-48 hours.*

It is reported that some formal agents in Hong Kong charge a fixed fee of only USD 2.5 to transfer funds to the Philippines (Fairlamb et al., 2003). High costs are partly the result of inefficiencies in the regulatory framework. The profit component is high, as many transfer agents have been able to charge high fees without exposure to competition. To some extent, competition in the remittance industry is hindered by ad hoc rules and regulations. For example, high collateral requirements (often in excess of a million dollars in some US states) often deter new players who could compete effectively in some remittance corridors. Worse, in the US collateral requirements and compliance with regulations vary widely from one state to another, discouraging many transfer agencies from expanding their operation across states (Ratha and Riedberg, 2004).

In some countries, transfer agents need to acquire a full banking licence, even when they have no intention of providing banking services. Entry barriers also include lack of access to existing payment systems, which forces new entrants into the remittance market to build their own costly proprietary transfer systems. Frequently, some large remittance service providers have persuaded the postal network, or large banks with extensive branch networks in developing countries, to sign exclusive contracts that limit the access of competitors to these distribution networks. To address these problems adequately would require policy coordination – especially harmonizing regulatory and compliance requirements – between both source and destination countries. It would also be helpful to find ways to harmonize payment systems and increase access to existing payment systems. Use of electronic card-based products would also reduce remittance costs.

GRAPH 14.2

COSTS OF SENDING REMITTANCES ARE HIGH AND REGRESSIVE (% OF PRINCIPAL AMOUNT)

Cost of sending money from Brussels using a major money transfer operator, excluding foreign exchange commission

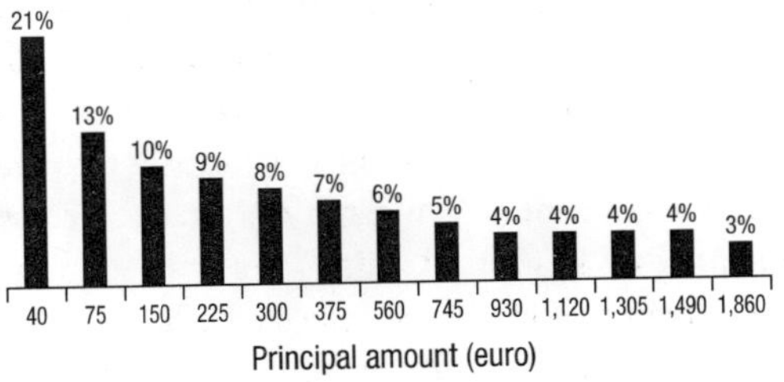

Source:
Price list obtained from various Western Union branches in Brussels and Paris.

The currency conversion fee, the third cost component mentioned above, is often in the range of 3 per cent of the principal amount. Banks with access to wholesale foreign exchange markets tend to charge a lower FX fee than money transfer operators, but banks also tend to benefit from the "float", the interest they earn by delaying delivery of funds.[7] The FX commission can be very high in countries with exchange controls and wide divergence between the official and the parallel exchange rate. In Venezuela, for example, the FX commission was nearly 40 per cent (the official rate was 1920 bolivars per dollar, the free market rate was over 3,200 bolivars per dollar) in October 2004, entailing a huge loss to remittance senders using formal channels (World Bank, 2004).

Even with the existing cost structure, there may be scope to reduce average remittance costs by bundling, i.e. enabling senders to remit more money but less frequently. In the above cost schedule, for example, if a person sends 150 euros per month for a period of six months, the total remittance cost would be 10 per cent or 90 euros. If, on the other hand, the person could send the entire 900 euros in one transaction, the remittance cost would fall to just over four per cent, or under 40 euros. The difficulty is that many poor remittance senders typically do not have sufficient

7. *For example, if a Brazilian bank received remittances on October 11, 2004, and delayed payment to the final recipient by two weeks (i.e., until after October 22, 2004), and invested the funds in the overnight money market, it would earn a float of 2.85 per cent.*

funds to be able to bundle remittances. Banks and microfinance institutions could play a role in alleviating such liquidity constraints and reducing the effective cost of remittances.

Unfortunately, a large number of migrants, especially those who are poor or undocumented, do not have bank accounts. Improving migrant workers' access to banking facilities in their host countries (typically developed countries) would not only reduce costs of remittances, it would also lead to financial development and improved intermediation of savings and investment in many receiving countries. It is observed, for example, that 14-28 per cent of non-members who came to credit unions affiliated with the World Council of Credit Unions to transfer funds ended up opening an account with them. Using existing retail financial infrastructure, such as postal savings banks, commercial banks, or microfinance institutions in rural areas could facilitate remittance flows.

To reiterate a point made above, there is a strong role for governments in setting the right policy and competition framework to ensure that private and financial sectors can be as facilitative as suggested above, also between states (such as the US-Mexican government partnership in fostering the Mexican diaspora's reinvestment in home communities). A stronger, more accommodating financial infrastructure could help the migrants help themselves, and their community and country more effectively.

BALANCING THE EFFORTS TO FIGHT MONEY LAUNDERING AND TO FACILITATE REMITTANCE FLOWS

THE REGULATORY regime governing remittances has to strike a balance between curbing money laundering, terrorist financing and general financial abuse, and facilitating the flow of funds between hard working migrants and their families back home through formal channels. It is not entirely clear that personal remittances (which are typically small in size) are an efficient way of laundering or illegally transferring sizeable amounts of funds. More importantly, informal channels owe their existence to the inefficiencies in the formal system: informal channels are cheaper, and informal agents work longer hours, operate in remote areas where there are no formal channels, and often have staff able to speak the language of the migrant customers. Informal channels, however, can be subject to abuse.

Strengthening the formal remittance infrastructure by offering the advantages of low cost, flexible hours, expanded reach and language can induce a shift in flows from the informal to the formal sector. Both sender and recipient countries should support migrants' access to banking by providing them with identification tools (as banks are now doing in regard to Mexican migrants in the US).

UNDERSTANDING THE DEVELOPMENTAL IMPACT OF REMITTANCES

ON THE POSITIVE side, *remittances are believed to reduce poverty, as it is often the poor who migrate and send back remittances.* Remittances may also help improve economic growth, especially if they are used for financing children's education or health expenses. Even when they are used for consumption, they can have multiplier effects, especially in countries with high unemployment.[8] In Morocco, as in many other countries, a large part of remittances is invested in real estate, reflecting, on the one hand, the altruistic desire of migrants to provide adequate/better housing to families left behind and, on the other, a lack of other investment instruments in the recipient community (Khachani, 2004). In Armenia, a household survey in 2002 showed that remittances seemed to go to some of the most vulnerable households in the country, and made up 80 per cent

8. *See the chapter "Migration and Poverty: Some Issues in the Context of Asia".*

of household incomes for those receiving them (Roberts, 2004).

Whether remittances are used for consumption or buying houses or other investments, they stimulate demand for other goods and services and have a positive effect on the economy. Some experts however argue that remittances may reduce recipients' motivation to work, and thus slow down growth (although reduced work effort by some individuals need not translate into low employment in an economy with a high unemployment rate). Others argue that remittances may increase income inequality in the recipient country, because it is the rich who *can* migrate and send back remittances. Also, as with all foreign currency inflows, too great a volume of remittances can result in currency appreciation, which may affect the competitiveness of exports. On the other hand, remittance receipts bring in valuable foreign exchange and enable a country to pay for imports, repay foreign debt and improve creditworthiness.

The effect of remittances on country creditworthiness is very evident in some countries. For example, for several years it was feared that Lebanon was vulnerable to a balance of payments crisis because its foreign debt stood at nearly five times the value of its exports. Yet, the fact that such a crisis did not materialize is sometimes attributed to large remittance flows. Remittances sent by its diaspora nearly equalled Lebanon's exports (about USD 2.4 billion) in 2002. The ratio of Lebanon's debt to exports is halved when remittances are included in the denominator. (Brazil and some other countries have been able to borrow from the international capital markets at lower interest and longer maturity by using remittances as collateral (Ketker and Ratha, 2001)).

In policy circles, it is often debated whether there may be ways to encourage the use of remittances for more productive purposes than consumption or purchasing real estate. While such a question may be appropriate for official aid flows, it is not exactly appropriate for personal remittance flows. If it is true that the senders and recipients rationally decide, given their economic environment and available investment instruments, to consume more and save less, then it would be hard for policy makers to induce them to do otherwise. Indeed, in such circumstances, forcing remittance recipients to save more and consume less would reduce consumer welfare. Also, such policies may exacerbate the distrust many migrants often profess towards their governments.

Nevertheless, there may be ways to indirectly increase the development impact of remittances. For example, encouraging account-to-account remittance flows instead of cash transfers would result in increased savings by recipients (and senders) and better matching (by banks) of available savings and investment demand. Improving the investment climate in the recipient community would also encourage more investment. Governments and the private sector could also ensure that other flanking measures are in place to support investment in development-related activities, such as community development projects, mortgage support, health insurance for dependants and similar allocations.

IMPROVING DATA ON REMITTANCES AND MIGRATION

Reliable data on remittances are key to our understanding of their development impact, yet the data that are available leave much to be desired. Informal remittances are large and indeterminate. Even recorded data are incomplete. Rich countries such as Canada and Denmark, for example, do not report any remittance data, not to mention several poor countries that either do not report, or report inaccurate data. Even when remittance data are available, countries often classify them incorrectly. Many report workers' remittances as "other transfers". Sometimes it is difficult to distinguish remittance flows from, say, tourism receipts or non-resident deposits. Finally, only a handful of countries report bilateral flows of remittances.

To improve remittance data would require more information to be gathered, and systematic studies to be undertaken of the relationship between migration stock and remittance flows; remittance behaviour of migrant workers in major remittance-source countries, and how remittances respond to changes in the source and destination economies. One way forward, perhaps the only way forward, would be to conduct surveys of remittance senders and recipients, to establish the size of remittance flows, their sources and destinations, the channels used, migrant motivations, and the use of the remittances. Major international coordination – among governments, private sector, international organizations and migrant/diaspora groups – is necessary for improving the data on remittances.[9]

USING FISCAL INCENTIVES TO ATTRACT REMITTANCES

THE MAJORITY of developing countries offer tax incentives to attract remittances. The side effect of such incentives, of course, is that remittances may then be used for tax evasion and money laundering. Also, some governments provide matching funds for remittance-backed projects (as in Mexico's 3-for-1 programme).[10] Again the side effect may be a diversion of scarce budgetary resources to projects favoured by non-resident nationals with the necessary means.

Many aid agencies are looking into the effectiveness of hometown associations (HTAs) to channel aid.[11] But the potential to channel any significant volumes of official funds in that way may be limited, although there is clearly a potential to use HTAs to promote community financing of infrastructure or other collective funding for community projects.

One effective policy measure to encourage remittance inflows is the application of uniform exchange rates and eliminating the black market exchange premium. Venezuela offers an interesting example in this respect. As mentioned earlier, with a current black market premium of nearly 40 per cent, the effective cost of sending remittances to Venezuela amounted to nearly half of the principal amount in the last quarter of 2004. Non-resident Venezuelans, therefore, are either discouraged from sending remittances or they are sending them through informal channels.

CONCLUSION

WHILE formulating policies on remittances, policy makers should keep in mind that remittances are *not* public money. They are personal flows, often better left to the remitters and recipients to decide how they should be spent. Efforts to tax remittances or direct them to specific investments may well prove difficult to achieve. Instead, as discussed above, policy makers may wish to improve the investment climate in the recipient communities, and the regulatory and incentives frameworks to encourage and support such investment. Remittances are more effective in generating incomes and investment when they are supported by good public policy and financial infrastructure.

9. *IOM has begun to work with governments, e.g., in Guatemala, Colombia, Argentina and Paraguay to survey patterns of remittance flows and use in those countries (sources: IOM Guatemala City, Bogota and Buenos Aires).*

10. *See the chapter "Migrant Hometown Associations: the Human Face of Globalization".*

11. *USAID, for example, has been exploring partnerships with HTAs in Mexico and other Latin American countries, see "Remittances at USAID" at www.usaid.gov/our_work/global_partnerships/.*

TEXTBOX 14.1

African Female Diaspora in France

Historically, most Africans from the sub-Saharan countries migrating to France have originated from the francophone western and central regions of the continent. There are two main discernible movements – from the Senegal River basin starting in the 1960s, and from the Gulf of Guinea and Equatorial and Central Africa in the 1980s, the latter flow dominating the African immigration scene in France from the early 1990s onwards.

Initially, the African flow was dominated by males in line with the general migration patterns of the prosperous 1960s. Young and able-bodied men, the majority from the Sahel countries (Mali, Mauritania, Senegal) came to work in France on rotation for periods between three to six years. The global economic crisis of 1974, and the resulting restrictions imposed by France on labour migration, saw fewer migrants arriving in the 1970s, with those already in the country seeking to establish themselves there more permanently. With this came the desire to have their wives and families join them. In 1976, legislation supporting family reunion helped pave the way for a large influx of women, and marked the beginnings of the gradual feminization of the African diaspora in France.

The numbers of sub-Saharan women in France more than quadrupled from 16,470 in 1975 to 73,000 in 1990, although these flows continued to be largely male-initiated. The women, mostly from the Sahel countries and of rural origin, with little formal education and poor language skills, typically saw their social role restricted to that of mother and housewife. After 1990, the second current of African migrants brought a greater demographic diversity among the incoming migrants and, by 2002, there were more than 140,000 sub-Saharan migrant women in France (see annual report of the French Ministry of Home Affairs for 2003, Titres de séjour 2002).

In this period African migrants were generally of urban origin, better educated, linguistically more proficient and showed higher levels of individual initiative, driven by economic or political motivations. Women, too, were better educated and urban-based, and tended to possess a new awareness of their status as women and a propensity for taking control of their own lives. While family reunion continued to play a major role in African female migration in the 1990s, more and more women opted for single-migrant status, be it as unattached females or as married women leaving their children behind. They were often encouraged by their spouses and families based on the popular perception that women in France now enjoyed better employment prospects than men.

Their ultimate objective was economic betterment for themselves and their families back home, which meant a sharply increased presence of independent women migrants seeking access to the French labour market. Their success depended on the ability to remit substantial portions of their income to the home country, thus replicating the traditional male migrant "provider" role.

Despite high motivation and in many cases secondary education and/or formal skills, African women seeking work in France experienced considerable difficulties and have often had to content themselves with menial jobs. The percentage of sub-Saharan women engaged in the tertiary sector (26% in 1999) is not substantially above that of migrant women in general (23% in 1999, compared with 10.5% of French-born women working in the same sector), but they appear to be over-represented at the lower end of the services category (i.e. catering, caretaking and domestic services). One in three economically active women of sub-Saharan origin was looking for work in 1999 (compared with a 25% unemployment rate for migrant women in general, and 11.2% for French-born females) (Ministère de l'emploi, du travail et de la cohésion sociale, 2002; INSEE, 2000).

However, this increase in migration was accompanied by a sharp rise in the number of women being trafficked from the region, notably from Nigeria, Ghana, Cameroon and Sierra Leone, with sub-Saharan women accounting for 10 per cent in 2000, 15 per cent in 2001, 20 per cent in 2002 and, finally, 27.5 per cent in 2003 of the total number of victims of trafficking. The central office to combat trafficking in persons, OCRTEH (Office central pour la repression du trafic des êtres humains) reported a large increase in the number of prostitutes of sub-Saharan origin during this period (Interview with Jean-Michel Colombani, Head of the OCRTEH, May 2004 (Afrik.com) *www.afrik.com/article7276.html*).

An important feature of the African female diaspora in France is their role in migrant associations that have developed and grown out of the broader migratory patterns. These generally follow a generic organization model of immigrant solidarity, known as OSIM (Organisation de solidarité internationale issue de l'immigration), although their respective structure and purpose vary widely. They often tend to follow or complement those of community organizations in the countries of origin, and aim to foster partnerships and solidarity with those countries.

OSIMs are non-profit organizations and rely on the financial and administrative support of their voluntary membership. Their operational strength depends on their members having a point of anchorage in, and a socio-cultural commitment to, both the host country and the country of origin. While initially more focused on migrant integration and welfare in the host country, in recent years OSIMs have begun to play a stronger role in economic cooperation and development outside the more formal and official foreign aid channels.

Africa-oriented OSIMs, which first appeared as natural extensions of village and inter-village associations in the home countries, are highly visible in France. It is estimated that there are more OSIMs deriving from the two currents of sub-Saharan migration than those representing all other migrant groups together. There were more than 1,000 OSIMs in France in 2000, representing some 32 countries. Of these, more than 200 are African women's associations (GREM, 2000).

While there is as yet no all-encompassing network of migrant women's associations, efforts have been made to group associations with converging aims within the African female diaspora. The most representative of these is the IFAFE (Initiatives des femmes africaines de France et d'Europe), founded as an association in 1993 and reconstituted as a federation in 1996 comprising 23 member associations. Its objectives are twofold: a) support the integration of foreigners in France, combat the negative image of foreigners (especially women) and combat racism and all forms of discrimination, and b) contribute to the development of migrant source countries in Africa and globally, especially through emergency aid in the event of natural disasters or war.

Despite limited funding, over the last five years IFAFE engaged in a variety of cooperation and development programmes, ranging from humanitarian aid (medication and school equipment), rural development projects (building wells) in Congo, Gabon and Cameroon, to vocational training for orphans or microcredit financing for farming women and small-scale businesswomen who lost their livelihood following the eruption of the Nyiragongo volcano in the Democratic Republic of Congo.

Though its work is generally modest and small-scale, IFAFE nevertheless opens the way for African female migrants to be significant players in the wider development arena. Aided and guided by OSIMs, individual migrants or groups can contribute to cooperation and development in ways that go substantially beyond the traditional transfer of remittances. They achieve this with activities ranging from fundraising in the host country or solidarity building for foreign aid programmes, to hands-on participation in skills transfers for and in their home countries.

Contributed by Sylvia Ekra, Project Officer, IOM Geneva, based on the following sources: Service de droits de femme et de l'égalité, Rapport à l'emploi des femmes immigrées et issues de l'immigration 2002, fiche 4-F, Le Point sur: Femmes immigrées et issues de l'immigration, Paris, Ministère de l'emploi, du travail et de la cohésion sociale. Daum, C. (ed.) Typologie des Organisations de solidarité internationale issues de l'immigration, 2000, Paris, GREM, Institut Panos, Ministère des affaires étrangères. Gbadamassi, F., De plus en plus de prostituées africaines en France: L'Office central pour la répression du trafic des êtres humains s'inquiète, Afrik.com 7 May 2004, Paris, L'Afrique sur l'Internet (www.afrik.com/article7276.html). National Institute for Statistics and Economic Studies, Thave, S., L'emploi des immigrés en 1999, INSEE Première no. 717, Paris, May 2000. Ministère de l'intérieur, Les titres de séjour des étrangers en France en 2002, cinquième rapport établi en application de l'article 45 de la loi du 11 mai 1998, Paris.

Chapter 15
Migrant Hometown Associations (HTAs) – The Human Face of Globalization[1]

Millions of migrants today maintain some social and familial obligations to their country of origin through remittances. Managed cleverly and in joint community ventures, these ties are increasingly helping to draw the home economies into the global economy, with migrants becoming active agents of the "globalization" of their home countries.

Immigrants are increasingly joining forces to support practical social projects back home through small grassroots organizations known as hometown associations (HTAs). Raising funds for the betterment of their places of origin, HTAs are growing in importance in Latin America and the Caribbean due to the sheer scale of support to their communities. They illustrate the close and complex relationship between development and migration at a number of cultural, economic, political and social levels (Orozco 2004a).

While primarily philanthropic in nature, HTA work sometimes overlaps with economic development activities, and in this way represents an important link between countries of origin and emigrants. It addresses the need for economic aid in migrants' home countries, strengthens cultural ties and improves the quality of life for home communities.

In Latin America and the Caribbean, migrant remittances accounted for some USD 38 billion in 2003, or 31 per cent of the global remittance levels; but the region has also become an interesting crucible for experimenting with development through collective donations for local projects (Orozco, 2002). In the US, there are thousands of Latin American and Caribbean hometown associations. According to the Mexican consulates, there are over 700 registered Mexican clubs (although government officials in Mexico and Latino community leaders estimate a much higher and increasing number). The figure below shows the increase in Mexican hometown associations based in Chicago alone over the past six years.

GRAPH 15.1

GROWTH OF MEXICAN CLUBS IN CHICAGO

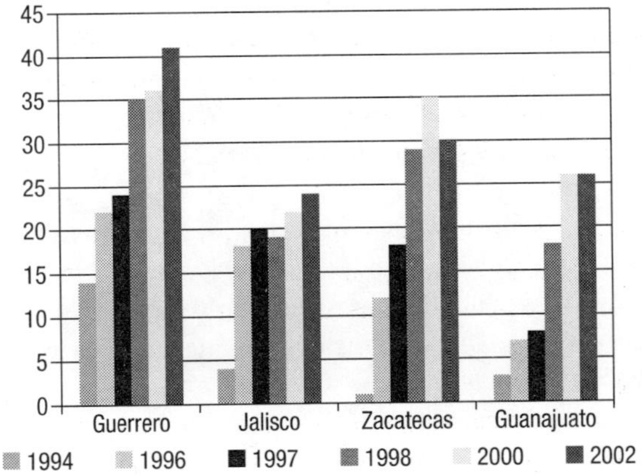

Source:
Orozco, Manuel, *Hometown Associations and their Present and Future Partnerships* (2003).

However, HTAs are not just a Mexican phenomenon. Most Latin American immigrants are organized in HTAs for the purpose of helping their communities. Salvadoran HTAs, for example, have grown in number since the 1990s; in Washington, DC, Salvadorans from eastern El Salvador are organized in more than twenty groups to raise money for assistance in areas like San Miguel province. The *Comunidad Unida de Chinameca,*

1. *The author of this text is Dr. Manuel Orozco, Senior Fellow and Project coordinator of the MIF-IFAD Remittances and Development Program, Washington, D.C.*

created in 1991, is a typical Salvadoran HTA: it began its activities in the city of Chinameca by constructing the school's water tower and 12 restrooms, and from there went on to construct a laundry facility and recreational park for the town, and painted and attached a roof to the local church. The *Comunidad* raises some USD 30,000 annually, mostly through fundraising events. During the earthquake in El Salvador in 2001, the *Comunidad* received donations of construction materials from the French Embassy to build a wall for the Red Cross, and the town participated by donating labour (Orozco 2004d).

Guyanese hometown associations focus on similar projects to those from Central America and Mexico. These associations are based in Canada and the US – New York in particular – and have long-standing organizational bases. *Guyana Watch*, founded in 1992 and based in Queens, New York, provides an annual medical outreach service in Guyana, whereby a group of 20-25 doctors and nurses travel to three different cities in Guyana (Essequibo, Demerara, and Berbice) and work at a clinic for one day, attending to between 2,500 and 3,000 people (Orozco 2004b).

HTAs vary in their level of formal organization, but most have governing boards of 10 or fewer elected members, including a president, secretary, treasurer and auditors. This core membership generally selects the hometown needs to be supported, and the projects, based on submissions to the president by any club member upon returning from a visit to the hometown. The president then initiates discussion and calls a vote among active members. Elected members also mobilize wider support for fundraising, often attracting hundreds of participants.

While HTAs are motivated by a practical desire to improve economic and social conditions in the hometown, their leaders and fund-providers argue that this strategy is also intended to reduce migration. Ironically, since these projects alone do not substantially boost development, they also do not prevent migration from continuing, at least as a matter of choice, if no longer as a necessity.

HTAs engage in a wide range of projects to improve living conditions in hometowns, including (in order of preference) in the areas of health and education (e.g. constructing or repairing health centres and school facilities, equipment donation), public infrastructure (road pavement and electrification), support to the town church or cemetery, and town beautification (such as constructing parks). They attract wide support for being concrete and assisting the town's most vulnerable populations, the elderly and children. In this way, they have both a philanthropic and developmental effect.

As shown in the table below, HTAs undergo a learning process, generating new ideas and drawing lessons from previous experiences. Older associations continue to support more traditional activities dealing with recreation or town beautification, while clubs formed after 1995 support a wider variety of projects, from church repairs to public works, health and education.

TABLE 15.2

RELATIONSHIP BETWEEN FOUNDATION OF CLUB AND TYPE OF ACTIVITY (PERCENTAGE AND NUMBERS)

	Before 1984	1985-1989	1990-1994	1995-Present	Total (% & nos.)
Church Work	13%	11%	9%	11%	100% (22)
Cemetery	0%	11%	2%	3%	100% (6)
Ornamentation of Town	9%	11%	7%	5%	100% (13)
Recreation	9%	11%	16%	5%	100% (18)
Infrastructure	9%	11%	9%	20%	100% (30)
Economic Investment	0%	11%	0%	8%	100% (10)
Health and Education	35%	11%	28%	30%	100% (57)
Other Donations	26%	22%	30%	19%	100% (47)

Source:
Orozco, Manuel *Hometown Associations and their Present and Future Partnerships: New Development Opportunities?* Washington: Inter-American Dialogue, September 2003.

HTAs are conscious of their limited fundraising base and choose activities appropriate to their resources: the majority of Mexican HTAs raise around USD 10,000 a year, although some groups generate up to USD 100,000 annually. This has a substantial impact on the rural receiving communities, as most HTAs work in rural towns with populations below 1,000, average annual per capita incomes below USD 400, and highly underdeveloped public and financial infrastructures, including the absence of commercial centres, which forces residents to travel at least 50 kilometres to purchase goods.

Where remittances occur in at least one-third of the households in a hometown, HTAs can become important for improving the quality of life of households. They can facilitate projects that would otherwise be impossible for the receiving communities to implement. In towns with fewer than 3,000 people, HTA donations represent over 50 per cent of the municipal public works budget. For localities with populations under 1,000, HTA donations can amount to seven times this budget.

TABLE 15.3

MEXICO: BUDGET ALLOCATION, HTA DONATIONS AND POPULATION (MEAN VALUES)

Population range	HTA donation (in dollars)	Ratio HTA and public works budget	Population in community
Under 999	8,648	7.1	407
1,000 to 2,999	11,999	0.5	1,686
3,000 to 4,999	8,397	0.1	4,014
5,000 to 9,999	9,602	0.1	7,328
10,000 to 14,999	11,072	0.0	12,405
Over 15,000	14,589	0.0	57,248
Total	**9,864**	**3.5**	**5,283**

Source:
Orozco, Manuel *Hometown Associations and their Present and Future Partnerships: New Development Opportunities?* Washington: Inter-American Dialogue, September 2003.

MATCHING GRANT OPPORTUNITIES

The influence of hometown associations on rural communities in Latin America, as well as their outreach to state, local and even national government officials, has led to some interesting partnerships on various community projects. Two examples are the "3 × 1" programme in Mexico, and a matching fund arrangement with the government of El Salvador.

i) "3 × 1" programme

After years of informal engagements by HTAs with various public institutions, the government of Mexico created *Iniciativa Ciudadana 3 × 1*, a programme aimed to match HTA donations with funds from the three levels of government (federal, state, municipal). In 2002, the *Iniciativa Ciudadana* projects totalled USD 43.5 million, a quarter of which came from the contributions of Mexican hometown associations, and two-thirds of which benefited the four states with high emigration and labour-intensive agricultural economies, Zacatecas, Jalisco, Guanajuato and Michoacan (see Table 15.4 below).[2]

TABLE 15.4

DISTRIBUTION OF "3X1" FUNDS BY STATE IN 2002 AND 2003 (IN THOUSANDS)

State	Amount 2002 (USD)	Percentage	Amount 2003 (USD)	Percentage
Guanajuato	2,054	4.7	1,298	3.6
Jalisco	5,199	11.9	7,720	21.4
Michoacán	4,151	9.5	2,807	7.8
Oaxaca	1,504	3.5	1,465	4.1
Puebla	557	1.3	NA	NA
San Luis Potosí	1,717	3.9	2,490	6.9
Zacatecas	16,316	37.5	13,665	37.9
Other States	12,056	27.7	6,615	18.3
Total	**43,553**	**100.0**	**36,061**	**100.0**

Amounts were converted to 2002 US dollars, and 2003 US dollars according to the year.
Source: SEDESOL, 2003, 2004.

2. *In 2003 the total dropped because Puebla did not participate in the programme.*

ii) Matching Fund Arrangements in El Salvador

The Salvadoran government has forged close partnerships with its HTAs on a range of development projects in rural El Salvador. One important example is the initiative managed by the Social Investment and Local Development Fund (FISDL) of the government through the programme "Unidos por la Solidaridad". This partnership has supported some 45 projects, at an average cost of USD 278,689 per project. The Salvadoran HTAs provide on average 16 per cent of the support, both financial and in kind; but the percentage ranges from 1 per cent in San Salvador to 57 per cent in Usulutan.

TABLE 15.5

FISDL-HTA PARTNERSHIP PROJECTS

Department	Projects	HTA funds USD	FISDL funds USD	Total project costs USD	Av. project cost USD	HTA donation %	FISDL funds %
LA UNION	11	306,317.45	2,394,216.51	3,627,382.76	329,762.07	8.4	66.0
LA PAZ	10	62,500.00	782,254.94	1,366,122.39	136,612.24	4.6	57.3
CHALATENANGO	7	109,570.15	408,652.80	682,514.28	97,502.04	16.1	59.9
CABAÑAS	3	98,787.91	778,277.68	1,133,533.85	377,844.62	8.7	68.7
SAN MIGUEL	3	66,045.69	336,622.02	446,560.89	148,853.63	14.8	75.4
CUSCATLAN	2	22,000.00	184,261.98	254,902.90	127,451.45	8.6	72.3
SAN SALVADOR	2	6,000.00	387,798.37	638,945.90	319,472.95	0.9	60.7
USULUTAN	2	1,384,221.82	1,025,048.77	2,420,699.16	1,210,349.58	57.2	42.3
AHUACHAPAN	1	4,000.00	21,000.00	40,000.00	40,000.00	10.0	52.5
LA LIBERTAD	1	14,517.89	134,586.91	149,104.80	149,104.80	9.7	90.3
MORAZAN	1	4,972.00	342,539.91	497,155.16	497,155.16	1.0	68.9
SAN VICENTE	1	36,779.00	30,092.00	66,871.00	66,871.00	55.0	45.0
SANTA ANA	1	18,298.04	93,929.94	121,986.93	121,986.93	15.0	77.0
Total/Average	**45**	**2,134,009.95**	**6,919,281.83**	**11,445,780.02**	**278,689.73**	**16.2**	**64.3**

Source:
FISDL , Proyectos de "Unidos por la Solidaridad" con Salvadoreños en el exterior, FISDL: San Salvador, El Salvador, Enero 2004.

IMPACT ON DEVELOPMENT

ALTHOUGH the contributions of HTAs are relatively small when compared to development needs or the structural transformations required to improve society, some of their philanthropic activities have a distinct developmental effect. The projects that achieve this generally possess the following qualities conducive to development:

i) They give *ownership* to individuals and the community. Projects must aim not only at collective benefits to all members, but also at transferring ownership or control of the project to the members, to legitimate the project as theirs.

ii) They reflect the real socio-economic needs of a community; particularly in the areas of health, education, public, financial infrastructure and the economic base of the community.

iii) They are *sustainable*, i.e. enable people to improve their lives over time, and continue to have a beneficial impact after the resources invested have been exhausted, without adding or constituting a burden to the beneficiary community.

iv) Finally, the development contribution of a project is complete when its attributes and functions can be *replicated* with ease and do not depend on the local and unique circumstances of a community.

Many of the thousands of HTAs referred to above give ownership of their projects to the communities, and are increasingly matching their activities more closely to the actual needs of the beneficiaries. (Not all projects correspond to the realities and priorities of a community. In some cases, a high percentage of HTA work supports church and religious activities that add little directly to the development of the community.) They are also more aware of the critical need for projects to be sustainable, and are exploring ways of ensuring longer-term commitments, and surety of support for the projects, e.g. through broader investments, to prolong the development effects. HTAs in the Americas are being watched with keen interest in other parts of the world for their potential applicability to other comparable diaspora scenarios.[3]

3. *See the 2004 report by Roberts on remittances in Armenia, which considers the possibility of HTAs for Armenia given the close relationship Armenians abroad tend to have with their home communities – particularly in regard to the "new" diaspora located mostly in Russia.*

TEXTBOX 15.1

COMMUNITY FUNDS PROGRAMME IN GUATEMALA

The Community Funds programme aims to harness the productive potential of remittances to the development needs of Guatemalan communities of migrant origin. It brings together village communities and their diaspora in the US, Canada and Mexico in joint investment ventures to benefit the home communities. The intention is to promote development in villages that are losing their inhabitants owing to poverty, by engaging the cooperation of members of the diaspora communities abroad to invest and support social projects at home to ensure the survival of vulnerable rural communities.

Many villages in Guatemala have been suffering from the economic crisis and high jobless rates, aggravated by falling coffee prices on international markets. This situation has driven many villagers, particularly the young men, to leave in search of work. The Community Funds concept draws on the income-generating capacity of the diaspora to establish grass-roots joint investment projects in the home communities to fund social, infrastructure and generally development-oriented projects. It builds on the banking capacity of migrants as a vehicle to manage their financial resources and to channel these towards the seed capital-generating small investment projects.

It is both an alternative and complementary response to the belief that Guatemala needs a New Economic Platform.

The programme aims to enable village communities to link up with local and foreign markets through business centres, and to attract investments from villagers and emigrants for local productive and social projects. The attraction of the Community Fund Programme lies in what might be paraphrased as: "think locally, act globally"; in other words, to harness overseas capacities offered by the diaspora communities for the benefit of local development and thus to:

- overcome the polarization that traditionally has isolated small producers, by aggregating their harvests, and through greater volumes strengthen their price-setting power;
- bring together local merchants to bid jointly for large aggregate purchases and obtain better prices through strengthened bargaining power;
- develop business training programmes, and
- develop credit programmes with a sound basis and realistic outlook and objectives to obtain credible access to modern commercial and marketing networks.

The productive potential of remittances is entered in an investment portfolio with a local partner bank for the purpose of financing or co-financing projects in agriculture, industry, services and community infrastructure such as roads, bridges, markets, collection centres, transportation systems and storage facilities for goods. The portfolio outlines appropriate marketing mechanisms, in this case aiming at local merchants joining forces with the aim of procuring goods in bulk to obtain better prices through their combined negotiating and purchasing power. The joint procurement strategy is complemented by a joint or aggregate marketing strategy, and the securing of better prices through strengthened price-setting and negotiating power for the goods produced under the Community Fund Programme.

The profits generated by the investment projects are to be channelled towards social projects such as hospitals, public health, schools, skills training and education. In addition, and if possible, the proceeds could also be used to help fund personal loans, emergency expenses or debts relating to migration travel costs. The programme is being implemented by IOM, which also provides support for the drafting of investment and social projects based on feasibility studies.

The programme is an experiment that complements, but does not duplicate the efforts and support by other institutions such as the Inter-American Development Bank, the IMF, the World Bank and ECLAC's surveys on trends, costs and the economic impact of remittances. Another mechanism developed for Central America and Mexico is the "Dialogue Table on Remittances and International Development Assistance", in which IOM also participates. The mechanism is coordinated by the German technical cooperation agency, GTZ, with the participation of a number of NGOs and international cooperation agencies. The Dialogue is a forum for sharing and coordinating public and private cooperative activities regarding remittances, their transfer and productive use in the Central American region.

The Community Funds Programme in Guatemala is an important experiment, and its achievements can provide a useful example for other communities experiencing high emigration rates.

Source: IOM Guatemala, *iomguatemala@iom.int*

CHAPTER 16
ENHANCING THE BENEFITS OF RETURN MIGRATION FOR DEVELOPMENT[1]

An important and insufficiently researched link between development and migration is the role that return migration can play in a country's development.[2]

INTRODUCTION

RETURN migration is a key issue in any debate about the costs and benefits of migration for development. It is often argued that one of the potential costs of migration for developing countries is the loss of skilled and qualified human resources – a "brain drain" that can act as a serious brake on development and poverty alleviation, by depriving poor countries of critical human capital in key economic and social sectors such as information technology, sciences, health, education and others.[3] Low rates of skills return can exacerbate this problem; in the case of India and China for example, only 20 per cent of their overseas graduate students have been returning on average from the US (Johnson and Regets, 1998).[4]

Such potential negative effects may be countered if developing countries can profit from migrant remittances, diaspora linkages and the return of their émigrés with enhanced skills, knowledge, ideas and capital (Lowell and Findlay, 2001). A number of measures have been devised to this end over the years, particularly to encourage the return of highly qualified professionals. Less attention has been given to encouraging the return of lower skilled workers, as it is not similarly acknowledged that less qualified returnees could also contribute to development through experience, education and contacts gained abroad (ibid).

Return migration, if not managed correctly, can also bring costs and may actually harm development, as recently reported in the UK House of Commons: "If the conditions are not right, the return of large numbers of migrants and refugees can place huge demands on a developing country, raising the potential for instability, conflict and renewed out-migration" (House of Commons, 2004, p. 27). Return migration can also mean the loss of remittances, although this can be partly offset if migrants return with substantial savings, or when return is only temporary. It can also have negative consequences, if migrants return to a situation into which they find it difficult to reintegrate.

Return migration could stimulate development, but this is more likely to occur if return is sustainable. Many migrants choose to return on their own without any special help, while others benefit from the support of an assisted return programme. Return can be voluntary, or it can be the result of expulsion or

1. *The author of this chapter is Frank Laczko, Head Research and Publications Division, IOM, Geneva. Information was also provided by the Assisted Voluntary Returns and Integration Unit, IOM Geneva.*
2. *See the report by the Government of the Netherlands (AVT, 2004, p. 61).*
3. *See also the chapter in this Report "Economic Effects of International Migration: a Synoptic Overview".*
4. *Johnson and Regets report that only some 50 per cent of overseas graduate students tend to return from the US.*

deportation (forced return).[5] Return can also be permanent or temporary: for some, marking the end of the migration cycle, for others, only an episode in that cycle.

Broadly speaking, states have adopted two types of measures to facilitate the development benefits of voluntary returns: a) incentives and inducement to encourage migrants, especially the highly qualified, to return, and b) reintegration assistance to ensure sufficient socio-economic well-being for the returnee to contribute to the development of the country.[6]

The focus of this chapter is on voluntary return migration, and assisted return programmes, and the policy measures taken to enhance their impact on development. The chapter deals with three main questions:

i) How does voluntary return migration, whether permanent or temporary, contribute to development?
ii) What can be learned from government efforts to facilitate return migration in order to promote development?
iii) What policies might be introduced in sending and receiving countries to enhance the benefits of return migration for development?

DEVELOPMENT POTENTIAL OF RETURN MIGRATION

THE IMPACT of return migration has traditionally been neglected in the migration literature (Ghosh, 2000). This is partly due to the fact that theories of migration have tended to conceptualize migration as a permanent movement for settlement. Within this paradigm, return migration is thought to occur by default, when the migrant fails to achieve the original intention to settle permanently in another country, either because of e.g. nostalgia for the home country, or social and economic integration problems. These theories tended to ignore the scale of return migration, even within migrant groups where the primary intention may have been to settle permanently in a new country. It is interesting to note, for instance, that between one-quarter and one-third of all Europeans who migrated to the US between 1908 and 1957 returned home again (Lucas 2004). Today, the increasing incidence of temporary or circular migration attracts more interest in return migration and its potential developmental effects.

It is difficult to assess the effects of return migration on development, because there is generally much less information about the return of skilled workers than the immigration of persons from developing countries (Findlay, 2001). Return migration flows that are not part of an organized programme often go unrecorded, yet they may comprise substantial numbers of migrants. As one expert pointed out: If the data on international migration are generally poor, the recording of return migration is far worse (Lucas, 2004). Even where the scale of return is established, it is often not known where the migrants returned to.

Without knowing how many and what types of migrants are returning to a country, it is also difficult for researchers to draw a representative sample of returnees (ACBF, 2004). Another weakness of research in this area is that studies are often based on relatively small samples of returnees and are usually conducted at only one point in time, making it difficult to establish the long-term effects of return migration (ibid).

Given the many different types of return migrants and movements, and their varying impact, the relationship between return migration and development is a

5. *IOM definitions of return:*
a) voluntarily without compulsion (migrants deciding at any time during their sojourn to return home on their own volition and cost, and possibly with assistance);
b) voluntarily under compulsion (persons at the end of their temporary protected status, or rejected for asylum, unable to stay and choosing to return home on their own volition);
c) involuntarily, as a result of a lack of legal status in the country (the authorities deciding, usually by law, on deportations).

6. *Reintegration assistance specifically devised to support development efforts in countries of origin should not be confused with the financial and other support provided by countries of destination to ensure sustainability of individual return, e.g. of irregular migrants.*

complex one. Some migrants return permanently to their home country, while others return temporarily. The categories of migrant also vary widely – failed asylum seekers, temporary labour migrants, highly qualified, students, seasonal workers, unskilled, refugees and persons receiving temporary protection, irregular migrants, and vulnerable groups including victims of trafficking, the elderly and children. Some return voluntarily, and others are obliged to return. Some of the categories overlap, for example, many refugees are also highly qualified.

Assessing the impact of return migration on development is not a straightforward exercise given the many different types of possible effects – social, economic, political and cultural. The impact may vary greatly over time and according to the scale of return movements. Moreover, return not only affects the migrant, but also the community of reintegration and the wider national socio-economic networks and services. It is also challenged by the fact that "development" is such a broad concept: it is more than poverty reduction and can refer to the broader social, economic and political development of a country (AVT, 2004).[7]

The impact of return migration will also vary according to the conditions in the receiving country for returnees, and on the degree to which returns are sustainable. Migrants may face many problems on their return, including lack of work, work at a lower level than before, social rejection, lack of basic health and education services, language barriers for children and the aged, and concerns about personal security.

If skilled workers left their home because of lack of job opportunities, then their return may have little positive impact on the labour market if they cannot find jobs. However, if skilled workers left in search of experience overseas and better wages, and return with their savings and increased skills, return migration may be beneficial for development. It has been argued that countries of origin are likely to gain development benefits from return migration only when three conditions are met (Ghosh, 2000):

- workers return with knowledge that is more advanced, or with better skills than they would have acquired at home;
- the knowledge and skills acquired abroad are relevant to the needs of the home country economy;
- the migrants must be willing and have the opportunity to use the skills upon return.

These conditions only refer to the return of labour migrants. But even in the case of this group, empirical evidence from different parts of the world suggests these three conditions are fully met in only a few cases (Ghosh, 2000). While there are examples of return migrants having acquired skills they can use at home, the general conclusion is less encouraging: "Overall evidence on migrants' acquisition of new skills is not encouraging, especially for low-skilled migrants. Early studies of Turkish guestworkers returning from Germany show that less than 10 per cent had received any useful training while in Germany; and recent research from Thailand shows that very few returning migrants had been employed in occupations that imparted new skills" (House of Commons, 2004).

However, for some types of occupations the benefits of return may be greater than for others. In nursing and teaching, for instance, it is reported that temporary migration can enable migrants to acquire new skills, and in many cases plays a useful role in exposing migrants, as well as host societies, to new ideas and ways of doing things, some of which may be usefully applied or adapted after the migrant's return (House of Commons, 2004).

One review concerning the benefits of return migration concludes that the sending country derives maximum benefit when highly skilled migrants leave for relatively short periods of 10-15 years, and return with financial, human and social capital (Olesen, 2003). It suggests that the benefits of this form of

7. *This is explored in more detail in the chapter "Migration and Poverty: Some Issues in the Context of Asia".*

return migration often go unrecognized, because they are unrecorded, but could be more forcefully promoted through a variety of policy mechanisms. The following discussion reviews some of the approaches that have been adopted.

POLICY APPROACHES

FOR SOME developing countries, encouraging return migration is an integral part of a comprehensive approach to planning their migrant labour export. The Philippines government, for example, expects that its nationals will eventually return and has developed measures to facilitate their reintegration (Battistella 2004).[8]

In some other developing countries, states tend to adopt a more ambivalent, if not negative, approach to return migration (Iredale et al., 2003; Black et al., 2004). A recent study, for example, found that neither Bangladesh nor Vietnam, both proactive planners of large-scale migrant labour exports, had sufficiently developed policies to encourage the return of skilled workers (Iredale, 2003). Sending countries may not wish to encourage return, if they believe returnees will have problems finding work, or if there is a risk that they will take jobs away from local workers. Sending countries which benefit from remittance flows may also not wish to promote return migration, for fear of losing these benefits, despite recognizing the significance of the brain drain (Olesen, 2003).

The approaches taken by governments in the receiving industrialized countries to return migration are also varied and somewhat ambivalent. On the one hand, more and more states encourage labour migration, particularly skilled immigration through temporary labour migration channels; and have made it easier in recent years for temporary skilled migrants to prolong their stay and eventually obtain permanent residence status (OECD, 2003). Such policies, in effect, discourage return migration. On the other hand, a number of destination countries have also experimented with incentives and reintegration packages to encourage the voluntary return through organized programmes of irregular migrants, persons with temporary protection status and refugees.

ATTRACTING BACK SKILLED MIGRANTS: GOVERNMENT INITIATIVES

SINCE 1960, a number of states that lost skilled emigrants have introduced new measures to attract them back, among them: Colombia, Ghana, India, Iran, Malaysia, Pakistan, the Philippines and Sri Lanka (Olesen, 2003; Hugo, 2003). In addition to job placement, these programmes offer such benefits as funded travel, reinsertion assistance, medical insurance and professional equipment to aid effective reintegration. The results have been mixed. Malaysia, for example, initiated a substantial scheme in 2001 targeting its 250,000 skilled workers overseas (Hugo, 2003), that included tax exemptions on income remitted to Malaysia and on all personal items brought into the country, and permanent residence status for the foreign spouses and children of returnees. It focused on six key sectors of industry overseas: information and communications technology, manufacturing, science and technology, arts, finance and medicine. Despite these efforts, only 104 expatriates returned in the first two years of the programme (ibid).

In other countries/regions in Asia, efforts to attract home skilled migrants seem to have been more successful. South Korea and Taiwan Province of China, for example, have initiated a number of programmes to encourage a reversal of brain drain, and there is some evidence that these programmes have helped increase the number of returns, although it is likely that the returns were also encouraged by the rapid economic expansion occurring in these countries (Hugo, 2003). In Taiwan, for example, a government-led initiative, the Hsinchu Science-Based

8. *See also the chapter "Filipinos Working Overseas: Opportunity and Challenge".*

Industrial Park designed to attract Taiwanese R&D professionals back to Taiwan, helped to attract 5,025 returnees in 2000, twice the figure of 2,563 in 1996 (Lucas, 2004).[9]

China pursues a strong national policy to attract back skilled expatriates. Since the mid-1990s, the Chinese government has implemented a series of programmes to attract "overseas talent" to return to China. A number of "science parks", "special development zones" and "high-tech zones" have been established in Beijing and most provincial cities, offering a range of incentives to return, including equivalent salary packages, multiple entry-exit visas and access to strictly controlled foreign exchange (Keren et. al., 2003, Hugo, 2003).[10]

As noted in the earlier chapter "International Migration Trends and Patterns in Asia and Oceania", of the more than 700,000 students who went abroad in the past 25 years, fewer than 30 per cent have so far returned – most of them obligated to do so under the agreement of their official sponsorship (Laczko, 2003, Keren et. al., 2003). However, the number of returnees has been rising; in 2002, 18,000 returned, double the number of two years earlier, of whom a high proportion held a master's degree or a doctorate, and many set up new enterprises (ILO, 2004). As in other countries in Asia, many of the returnees have assumed leading positions in government, international agencies and academic institutions (Hugo, 2003).

Apart from some media reports, few studies have been carried out in China on people who have returned (Keren et. al., 2003). An exception is a recent survey of 185 returnees conducted in Shanghai, which showed that more than a quarter of returnees claimed they did so in response to government policies or programmes. Those who returned, brought back significant savings, nearly a third with USD 50,000 or more (ibid).

There is also evidence to suggest that returns are increasing even without direct government intervention to encourage them. For example, in India several media articles in 2004 suggested that many more highly skilled migrants are returning in response to growing economic opportunities there. The *International Herald Tribune* reported in 2004 that, "what began as a trickle in the late 1990s is now substantial enough to be talked about as a "reverse brain drain". By one estimate, there are 35,000 "returned non-resident Indians in Bangalore, with many more across India" (Waldman, 2004).

INTERNATIONAL ORGANIZATIONS – DIASPORA OPTIONS

In addition to initiatives taken by developing countries, several efforts have been made over the years by international organizations, such as IOM and UNDP, to encourage the temporary or longer-term return of highly qualified workers to developing countries.

First implemented in 1974, IOM's "Return of Qualified Nationals" (RQN) programmes have been supporting the social and economic advancement of developing countries in Africa, Asia and Latin America by assisting the return and professional reinsertion of their qualified émigrés. In collaboration with relevant governments, IOM identifies suitable candidates among diaspora communities to match vacant positions not filled through the home country labour market. Supporting the return and ensuring the reintegration into both professional and personal environments of suitable applicants helps rebuild and strengthen a depleted human resource base.

The Return of Qualified African Nationals programme (RQAN), implemented for 16 years (1983-1999), helped over 2,000 highly skilled and experienced African nationals and 2,565 fellowship students in

9. *See further information on this in the chapter "Economic Effects of International Migration: A Synoptic Overview".*

10. *See also the chapters: "International Migration Trends and Patterns in Asia and Oceania" and "Balancing the Benefits and Costs of Skilled Migration in the Asia-Pacific Region".*

TEXTBOX 16.1

RETURNING TO AFGHANISTAN – IMMAM JAN'S STORY

Mr. Immam Jan returned from the UK under IOM's Voluntary Assisted Return and Reintegration Program (VARRP). He had earlier owned a successful factory producing rubber shoes in Jalalabad and wanted to get back into business on his return home.

After his return he found that there was nothing left of his previous business, so he travelled to Kabul to test the market for shoes and potential partnerships he could enter into with local producers, utilizing his managerial skills.

He found a small rubber shoe factory 10 km east from Kabul, which had good potential but needed help with the management and marketing of its products. The factory owner and Mr. Jan entered into a partnership, and through IOM's reintegration assistance and his own savings Mr. Jan was able to provide some necessary equipment for the business.

The business employs five workers from Kabul, and Mr. Jan is confident that he will be able to help increase production and expand the current market to several provinces around Kabul.

With the reintegration assistance, this project will enable Mr. Jan to sustain his return by providing an income for his family. It will also create employment for five additional Afghans.

Source: IOM Kabul.

their return and professional reintegration in public and private sector jobs in 41 countries in Africa. Evaluations of RQAN suggest that returnees did contribute to development in their home country at the micro level.

UNDP's "Transfer of Knowledge Through Expatriate Nationals" (TOKTEN) Programme has also provided opportunities for qualified professionals in the diaspora to contribute their services to home countries through short-term consultancies. In the first 20 years of its existence (1977-97), TOKTEN placed about 5,000 volunteers on assignments in 49 developing countries (Newland and Patrick, 2004).

Since policies to encourage the permanent return migration of skilled migrants have had mixed results, policy makers have in recent years turned their attention to encouraging temporary return migration, where the emphasis is on sharing and transfer of knowledge, skills, ideas and technologies, in short "brain circulation". In 2001, IOM launched a new programme: "Migration for Development in Africa (MIDA)", in Libreville, Gabon, which offers options for the African diaspora to reinvest its skills, financial and other resources in temporary, long-term or virtual returns to the home country or region.

TEXTBOX 16.2

Migration for Development in Africa (MIDA)

MIDA targets African professionals, entrepreneurs and experts in the diaspora, willing and able to contribute their skills, finances and other resources to the development efforts of their countries of origin. It is based on the notion of mobility of people and resources and, as such, offers options for reinvestment of human capital, including temporary, long-term or virtual return. Approaches are tailored to meet the needs of the origin country, without jeopardizing migrants' legal status in their host countries or newly adopted home countries.

Since its inception in 2001, MIDA has evolved from a programme to a national and regional strategy supported by many countries and the regional and international community. MIDA does not claim to address all of the economic and social problems of the countries concerned, but it contributes within a larger framework to the development process by addressing the lack of human resources and building critical skills needed in key sectors in Africa. MIDA projects span a wide range of countries, sectors and activities, including:

Mobilizing Ethiopians Living Abroad for the Development of Ethiopia

The website "Ethiopian diaspora.info" launched in 2004 and funded by the Italian government, provides timely, relevant and accurate information to the Ethiopian community abroad on how to start a business, and investment advice and announcements relevant to the diaspora.

Managing Migration of Skilled Health Personnel

IOM and the World Health Organization (WHO) launched the MIDA Health programme in 2002 to address the many urgent challenges posed to the health sector of Africa by the growing mobility of populations. Building on the lessons learned from Phase I, which established a database of health professionals in 46 African countries, IOM and WHO have extended their pilot activities to include action-oriented research and building human resource capacity in the health sector.

E-learning: a New Option for Skills Transfer

In 2003, the MIDA programme launched its pilot initiative in distance learning. The project facilitates the virtual transfer of skills, using Information and Communication Technologies (ICT) to reach a wider audience than in a traditional higher education setting. 700 second-year PhD students have so far benefited from this project funded by the Belgian Government. The project not only helps to build capacity, but also contributes to retaining trained professionals in their home country.

The Role of Remittances in MIDA

Within the framework of MIDA, IOM is encouraging the voluntary and efficient use of migrant remittances for development in countries of origin. These include initiatives that support cost saving and reliable transfer mechanisms, and the establishment of an African Diaspora Remittance Fund to encourage attractive returns on investment, efficient transfers and national development.

VOLUNTARY RETURN AND REINTEGRATION PROGRAMMES

TO ENHANCE the positive impacts of return migration, a number of countries of origin and destination have developed programmes to support the return and reintegration of certain categories of migrants. Most have been launched by destination countries in Europe and target irregular migrants, unsuccessful asylum seekers, refugees and persons receiving temporary protection (IOM, 2004).

In other parts of the world, it is the sending, rather than the receiving country which is taking the initiative to provide reintegration assistance, often as part of a package of measures designed to manage temporary labour emigration effectively. In Asia, for example, return and reintegration programmes are mainly concerned with the needs of temporary labour migrants who return to their country of origin after working on a fixed-term contract (Battistella, 2004). Experience with such programmes has been varied, and few evaluations of their impact exist (Lucas, 2004).

EUROPEAN PROGRAMMES

DURING the last decade, European countries have been hosting a growing number of unsuccessful asylum seekers. Policy approaches, focusing on involuntary return, have had limited success. As a result, there has been a new willingness by some to adopt more innovative approaches to return by linking return with reintegration assistance. For example, in the Netherlands, various civil society organizations have increasingly emphasized the importance of assisting migrants after they return to their countries of origin, to ensure effective reintegration (AVT, 2004). The stable and successful return of irregular migrants is likely to be closely linked to their effective reintegration in their country of origin (IOM, 2004).

In 2002, the European Commission reviewed a large number of return projects it had co-financed since 1997 for the voluntary return of failed asylum seekers, persons with temporary protection status and refugees (EC, 2002). Many of the projects provided job training, preparation for return through exploratory visits, information and advice on the situation in the country of origin, help in setting up small businesses and general assistance after return. The review identified a number of factors contributing to the success of these programmes (AVT, 2004), including:

- A comprehensive approach that included counselling, job training and assistance both before and after return;
- Assistance to the communities to which the migrants were returning to avoid local resentment;
- coordination with other aid initiatives in the country of origin.

Many return and reintegration schemes have been unsuccessful and have attracted low numbers of participants (Koser, 2001). For example, the Assisted Return of Rejected Asylum Seekers (GTAA) project carried out in 1997-2000 by the Netherlands was targeted at failed asylum seekers from Ethiopia and Angola. Although the Dutch government describes the programme as "a failure" (AVT, 2004), several important lessons were drawn from it:

i) The cooperation of the authorities in countries of origin is necessary, but not always forthcoming.
ii) Migrant organizations in countries of origin have an interest in discouraging return and have considerable influence on potential candidates for return as well as on governments in countries of origin.
iii) The alternative for rejected asylum seekers, staying on in the Netherlands, was too attractive.
iv) There was no serious risk of expulsion.
v) The responsible government bodies were unable to accurately estimate the numbers of candidates for return.

The Dutch authorities have learned from this experience, and active efforts have been made to secure the cooperation of the authorities in countries of origin. New programmes since then operating in Afghanistan and Angola have been described as "fairly successful" (AVT, 2004).

An earlier evaluation of several of the European return and reintegration programmes concluded that "the most successful return programmes are those that operate on a small scale, and are tailor-made for the particular circumstances of particular returnees and countries of origin" (IOM, 2001). These programmes are likely to be labour-intensive and demand a high per capita outlay of initial investment. They do not promise to deliver high numbers of returns, but they do promise to deliver sustainable and beneficial returns" (Koser, 2001, p. 44). But there have also been numerous small and large-scale projects in post-crisis scenarios like Bosnia and Herzegovina, and Kosovo, which have successfully linked individual reintegration with community rehabilitation efforts. The lessons from these programmes still need to be fully drawn and applied to the development scenarios.

THE RETURN OF MIGRANT WORKERS IN ASIA

DESPITE the fact that many countries in Asia promote the temporary labour migration of their nationals, it appears that "no adequate return migration policy has been effective anywhere in Asia", (Battistella, 2004, p. 213).

In some countries, such as Bangladesh, there has been an absence of a concrete policy framework to facilitate the reintegration of returning labour migrants (IOM, 2002). One of the few surveys of returnees' experiences conducted recently in Bangladesh found that "the process of reintegration of returnee migrants was very difficult" (ibid). This survey of 200 returnee households found a host of problems, including a lack of information on current business trends and job opportunities, and social problems with families upon their return.

Many migrants reported that they were able to bring back a considerable amount of savings, some of which was used for income-generation activities and land purchase. With regard to skills, it was found that a large number of migrant workers acquired skills while abroad, but on their return were engaged in occupations where these could not be applied. Many respondents called for more assistance to help returnees reorient themselves, and said the absence of such assistance made them more likely to re-migrate (IOM, 2002).

The Philippines is an example of a country in Asia that does run reintegration programmes to assist returning labour migrants. Studies in the 1980s found that many migrants returning to the Philippines had difficulties finding a job. Subsequently, measures were taken to assist them in this. The 1995 Migrant Workers and Overseas Filipinos Act includes a provision on return migration and the establishment of the "Replacement and Monitoring Centre", which aims at reintegration, employment promotion, and the utilization of migrant skills for development. The impact of these programmes is difficult to assess, because, like most countries in Asia, the Philippines does not have a system to collect data on returning migrants (Battistella, 2004).

But in practice, policymakers have been reluctant to provide benefits to migrants already perceived by the local population as privileged (ibid). As a result, "existing programmes have not been implemented in earnest, contingency plans for crisis-related mass returns have not been really tested, and assistance for social integration has relied only on the intervention of civil society" (ibid, p. 224). Returnees thus face many problems on their return. In the Philippines, research shows that employment is the biggest difficulty facing them, and that the skills they acquired abroad cannot be used (ibid).

CONCLUSIONS – POLICY IMPLICATIONS

THE ABOVE discussion confirms that governments need to improve the general social, economic and political conditions in migrants' home countries to create the right environment for return. Experience in different parts of the world also suggests that selective return programmes can contribute to development; and that governments have a key role to play in facilitating such return, which can sometimes be as important as economic, political and social factors (Iredale, 2003).

What are some of the measures that sending and receiving countries could take to enhance the contribution of return migration to development?

For *sending countries*, the UK has proposed the following broad measures to encourage return and reintegration (taking account of the fact that many sending countries have few explicit measures to encourage return and reintegration of their émigrés and have, at best, an ambivalent approach to return) (House of Commons, 2004):

- Be serious about welcoming migrants back.
- Make progress with improving governance and tackling corruption.
- Ensure that pay structures and progression within the civil service do not unfairly penalize migrants who have worked elsewhere and acquired useful skills.
- Help returning migrants to find suitable jobs, or to set up their own businesses.

One cautionary note drawn from experiences discussed above, would be to ensure that the return/reintegration programmes are not designed specifically for the migrants, but rather for the entire home community, to avoid resentments against returnees and hence blockage of any beneficial effects of the return migration (Batistella, 2004).

Receiving countries can also consider a range of measures to enhance the development impact of return migration. Returns can increase the opportunity for more people from developing countries to gain skills/experience in developed countries (Lowell and Findlay, 2001).

The most direct way of achieving a high rate of return is to ensure that temporary migration schemes are in fact temporary, for example through the use of incentives and sanctions (Omelaniuk, 2003), which could include:

i) In the case of students, a greater number of scholarships or bursaries, with conditions attached regarding return (to minimize the risk of brain drain).[11]
ii) Reimbursements of a portion of migrants' unused social insurance contributions once they have left the host country (House of Commons, 2004).
iii) Promotion of more circular migration, for example by opening up more avenues for regular, repeat temporary labour migration, to give the incentive of future return to the same job; making residence or dual citizenship available to certain migrants as an encouragement to productive, free exchange between the two countries (Lowell and Findley, 2001),[12] and more flexible visa regimes (Lawson et al., 2004).

There is clearly a growing recognition, especially in Europe, that more needs to be done to facilitate the reintegration of migrants returning to developing countries. The early model of simple return with some financial and travel assistance to the returnees has over the years expanded to include more complex reintegration assistance in various forms, not necessarily financial.[13] However, there is a lack of information about which factors contribute most to successful reintegration. This is one area where the usual call for more research is warranted.

Return migration policies are also more likely to be successful and to contribute to development when sending and receiving countries agree to cooperate in the design of such programmes, and where both sides agree on the need to prepare for returns at the outset of migration (Battistella, 2004). This is perhaps an indirect way of confirming that labour migration strategies should be planned together by sending and receiving countries, and that return and reintegration schemes be included as an essential component of any such programmes.

11. *OECD, Trends in International Migration, 2001, p. 115.*

12. *For example, dual citizenship has been extended to Ghanaians living abroad as an encouragement for them to return freely (Black, et.al., 2004).*

13. *This currently ranges from modest reinstallation grants to longer-term support towards employment and micro-enterprise activities involving institutional support to employers, as well as support for local community employment and development schemes.*

Migrant Integration

CHAPTER 17
BENEFITS AND COSTS OF INTEGRATION – INTERNATIONAL CONVERGENCE?[1]

Converging forces and common challenges will drive the policy choices facing developed countries. Inclusion and social stability – the need to avoid racial, religious and ethnic schisms – are key strategic priorities of all countries with significant multicultural populations.

INTRODUCTION

THE BENEFITS and costs of migration depend on a broad web of social, cultural and economic factors. As these factors vary from country to country, the benefits and costs of policy and programme interventions also vary. International comparative research[2] offers the best available tool, sometimes the only tool, to evaluate the effectiveness of policies across these variations. It can identify and examine points of convergence and divergence between countries, and draw general lessons from particular circumstances. But while often persuasive, international comparisons need to avoid the simplistic assumption that similar policies and practices will yield similar outcomes across different countries.

This chapter discusses the benefits and costs of migration and integration programmes in different national settings, and the potential for such policies to converge in the face of similar pressures and challenges. It focuses mainly on the strategies of developed countries with advanced migration and integration programmes, and the role of such critical players as ethnic communities and NGOs.[3] Its lessons also apply to other countries experiencing immigration.

Integration does not lend itself easily to a cost-benefit analysis, among other factors, because it relates closely to the individual societal models that nations set for themselves, and such imponderables as, e.g., cultural values. Hence the chapter focuses on a set of determining factors to assess the benefits and costs of institutional responses, and some broader contextual factors that are increasing the imperative for similar (or converging) policy interventions.

The chapter strikes a cautionary note for policymakers and politicians regarding the difficulty of transferring policy lessons from one setting to another – a consequence of policies producing dissimilar benefits and costs once they cross borders. But it also observes that a confluence of global pressures is smoothing away many of the differences, creating a common appreciation of the strategic challenges facing countries in the area of migration. This emerging appreciation is reshaping national perceptions and exerting a harmonizing influence over values and institutional behaviours. The end result is likely to be a convergence of benefits and costs of migration and integration policies across countries and, hence, also of the means to manage them.

1. *The author of this chapter is Meyer Burstein, international policy and research consultant, former Executive Head of the International Metropolis Project and Director General of Strategic Planning and Research for Canada, CIC; mb@meyerburstein.com, Ottawa, ON, Canada K1M 1A2.*

2. *International comparisons are at the core of international migration projects such as "Metropolis", a Canada-led international policy-research project that seeks to provide policymakers and practitioners with scientific advice on which to base decisions.*

3. *While recognizing their importance for integration, the chapter does not go into detail on the role of the migrants themselves and their countries of origin.*

WHERE TO START?

THE BENEFITS and costs of migration and integration rely on three sets of factors represented in the triangle below. The apex covers strategic goals and national values; the left angle of the triangle domestic endowments and structural features, and the right angle knowledge, experience and governance.

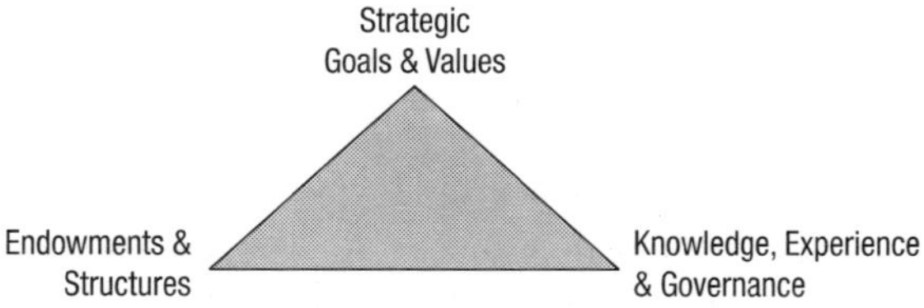

The utility of individual policies (their benefits and costs) can be triangulated as a function of these three factors – goals, endowments and knowledge. Differences between countries on any one set of factors will change the "location" of policies within the triangle and produce a different balance between migration-induced gains and losses, winners and losers, and present and future benefit streams. National management strategies must respond to the unique arrangement of factors within each country.

STRATEGIC GOALS AND VALUES

NATIONAL migration interests and pressures tend to produce policies that respond to two sets of motives. The first set is functional and purposive, the second filtering and defensive. International policy differences result from variations in the importance that countries assign to these motives and to elements thereof. Some of the differences, as the triangle suggests, are "technical", an amalgam of structural and experiential factors. These will be discussed later. The most important differences, however, result from variations in the "taste" for migration (a function of values). Such taste, or value differences, in turn affect goals and management strategies, making them more or less functional/purposive or filtering/defensive. In short, divergent values often lie at the heart of divergent policies.

For example, Australia as a young, relatively unformed and culturally open society is prepared to accept, even welcome, large numbers of migrants. Japan, on the other hand, a much older, culturally fixed and more homogeneous society insists on tightly limiting entry. The economic, social welfare and cultural policies of the two countries diverge accordingly.

If maintained, the consequences of such different migration strategies can be dramatic, not just at the cultural level. If current migration policies were to continue, in thirty years the populations of Italy and Canada would converge in size, whereas today, Italy is twice as populous as Canada. Concomitantly, the economic strength and political influence of the two countries would undergo similar transformations. The question is one of values. Countries such as Japan, Israel and Italy will, ultimately, need to choose between cultural, ethnic or religious homogeneity (which they greatly prize) and the geo-political advantages offered by a larger, more diverse, population. This choice will not offer itself as a single proposition, but rather as a series of choices and options.

Which path will societies choose? Will tastes for cultural homogeneity persist or will attitudes and policies converge? This chapter argues for convergence. Value differences will gradually diminish under the influence of unrelenting globalization, immigration pressures, converging rules governing migrant entry and entitlements, and the adoption by policymakers of similar analytic frames and interventions. Nor will these changes be limited to "western" countries. The timetables will, undoubtedly, vary but the paths will be the same in other parts of the world, because the underlying dynamics are universal.

CONVERGING FORCES AND CHOICES

Most explanations for the diversity of public attitudes towards migration and the reasons why one country's preference for migrants differs from another's invoke geography, history and culture. The problem with this is that it directs too much attention to the past and not enough to the future. The result is a discussion rooted in populism rather than strategy. Populist discussions are necessary in democratic societies; but, at political and senior bureaucratic levels, it is essential to engage a wider set of strategic goals so that critical choices can be made, and the popular discourse expanded, as opportunities present themselves.

This discussion begins by identifying several major forces profoundly affecting the volume and composition of migration to advanced industrial states. These forces are generating increased migration pressures at the same time as the capacity of states to moderate, or isolate themselves from, those pressures is being eroded. This confluence of forces is gradually raising the level of global migration and increasing the population of ethnic, cultural and religious minorities residing in developed countries.

Faced with similar pressures and tensions countries will, over time, evolve similar appreciations of the challenges they face and similar potential "solutions". Public policy plays an important role in this reconciliation: policies set the terms of public debate by framing the strategic challenges that countries face; they also exert a direct influence over attitudes by shaping intake and altering the public's experience of migrants.

COMMON PRESSURES

- The main pressure forcing migration policies to converge is globalization. All countries are affected, though timing and sensitivity differ for historical and geographical reasons. Similar (though not identical) strategic challenges confront Europe, North America, Australia and New Zealand; and parallel challenges confront countries such as the Philippines, Bangladesh, Somalia and Mexico. This chapter focuses mainly on the former group of countries.

  Economic globalization, demographic stagnation (in the developed world) and technology have contributed substantially to increase the flow of migrants to both developing and developed countries. Permanent migration, temporary labour migration, student flows and irregular migration are all growing. Huge differences in per capita income across countries have created enormous incentives for people to move; and judging by the huge increases that have occurred in traded goods, services and direct investment from the early eighties onwards, migration is likely to continue accelerating. This will be accompanied by growing concerns over how to control and channel these flows. While south-south flows dominate, it is the developed countries with elaborate social welfare systems that have invested the most in both migration restrictions and migrant integration.

  The rapid ageing of the populations in most developed countries has had major implications for labour markets and immigration. In Canada, immigrants now account for the bulk of net labour force growth, and the story is similar (or will be) for New Zealand, Australia and the US (Beaujot, 1998; DIMIA, 2004; Khawaja, 1998; Sum, 2003). In many European countries the situation is even starker, as labour markets – followed closely by population counts – are shrinking (UN Population Division, 2000). At the same time, developing countries experience an explosive upsurge in the number of young people seeking to enter labour markets unable to absorb them.

  Global technology, communications and transport networks complete the picture, making people more aware of job opportunities abroad and enabling them to move more rapidly and cheaply.

- At the same time as migration pressures are rising, some fundamental "rules" governing immigrant entry, treatment and entitlements are being relaxed. International accords, copycat jurisprudence, and converging norms for fair treatment and equity are responsible (Feldblum, 2000). Collectively, these rules constitute a migration governance system that operates to a significant extent through rights. The relaxation of rules (and extension of rights) suggests that migratory pressures will not abate, but rather increase.

The most far-reaching international instrument on migration is the Geneva Convention governing the treatment of refugees and asylum seekers. This is bolstered by other international instruments governing protection, including such relating to torture, the rights of children and smuggling and trafficking of human beings. In addition, multilateral and bilateral agreements are also contributing to convergence. The European Charter on Human Rights, treaties such as the North American Free Trade Agreement (NAFTA) and membership in the WTO all create homogeneous (though not always powerful) rules governing access and/or treatment of foreign nationals.[4]

But it is not only governments working in tandem that are responsible for the convergence of rules governing migration. National courts have also played an important role. Increasingly, the high courts of different countries have converged in their interpretation of basic human rights and their protection, through legal assistance, interpretation, appeal rights, and so forth (Schwartz, 2003). Courts have also intervened on entitlements and benefits that the state must provide to migrants (for example, educating the children of asylum seekers pending determination of their parents' claims to protection).

The last point concerns family norms. Migration to reunify families is gaining wider acceptance, as part of a larger global trend towards increased tolerance. The World Values Survey indicates that advanced industrial societies are becoming more open to diversity (notwithstanding the political situation in a number of countries and the broad media coverage this attracts). Young people are especially receptive and more apt to view migration as exotic and even stimulating (PEW Research Centre, 2004a).

More permissive, relaxed approaches to family reunification, especially in countries that do not see themselves as "immigration countries", have led to significant increases in immigration. In particular family migration, even narrowly defined as a right, has the potential to generate secondary migration flows that are potentially larger than the original ones.

- The final set of factors feeding migration pressures on developed countries is the lowering of settlement costs for migrants and the emergence of an infrastructure to facilitate migration. Improved communications, cheaper transport and the support of expatriate communities in destination countries are all helping to lower the costs and risks of relocation.

Longitudinal studies in Canada and Australia, as well as international social capital research, have revealed the critical role that ethnic communities and family play in the migration process, each wave smoothing the path for subsequent immigrants. At the same time, a sophisticated infrastructure, both legal and illegal, has sprung up to facilitate migration to developed countries. This infrastructure includes lawyers, consultants, paralegals, as well as, on the underside, traffickers and smugglers.

The end result of this process has been a substantial reduction in the cost to migrants of entering and settling in the advanced industrial societies of the West.

4. *The application and interpretation of rules follows a cyclical pattern. Currently, the prevailing ethos is restrictive; however, the overall secular trend still points towards liberalization.*

COMMON MANAGEMENT CHALLENGES

THE PRECEDING discussion sought to establish three points: south-north, east-west migration pressures are intensifying; rules governing entry and entitlements are converging, and entry and early settlement costs are falling. This makes the point that governments can no longer view immigration as an option, but as a fact. Correspondingly, migration and integration management must shift towards the centre of the policy stage.

Perceptions about migration are to a significant extent shaped by the machinery designed to manage it. In Europe, the emphasis tends to be on border controls and policing, with less attention to housing and welfare. In Canada, the US and Australia, there is greater emphasis on integration and labour issues and on the need for across-the-board institutional reform. This focus makes it easier to situate migration management in a larger strategic context.

Four critical strategic imperatives are discussed below. These are driven by the common migration pressures reshaping the labour markets and populations of developed countries. Especially noteworthy is the focus on integration as opposed to border control. It is posited that the wide differences that currently exist in national perceptions and values relating to migration and integration will converge. This will strengthen the case for exchanging policy and programme lessons. It is also posited that the productivity, well-being and security of migrant-receiving societies will depend on how well the challenges are managed.

i) *The Need to Manage Social Conflict*
Developed countries are becoming increasingly pluralistic, and social conflict is an inevitable part of this social change (Paquet, 2003; Putnam, 2003). Tensions are especially pronounced in large cities where the majority of migrants settle. There is an urgent need to develop effective conflict resolution mechanisms seen as reasonable and fair by both migrants and hosts. But this is more difficult than simply combating discrimination. Societies must learn to resolve peacefully competing claims and establish common priorities if they are to retain their capacity to act coherently and address critical issues in both the public and private spheres. Governance plays a key role in this process. Research suggests that the behaviour of public institutions can attenuate the inverse relationship between ethnic diversity and generalized trust among members of a society (Helliwell, 2003).

ii) *The Need to Foster Integration*
Social and economic integration must become national priorities. Failure to integrate immigrants and minorities can exacerbate social and economic schisms and fragment societies along ethnic, racial and religious lines. The risk lies in creating a visible minority underclass that is dysfunctional and unreceptive to policy intervention. Such an outcome would quickly erode whatever public support exists for integration, further aggravating disparities and creating a downward spiral of poverty, ghettoization and despair. Conversely, by demonstrating that migrants are productive and share the social and economic aspirations of their hosts, integration can promote tolerance and support for public assistance. This, in turn, would facilitate the economic and demographic adjustments to which immigration is able to contribute (see below). If a sense of belonging and common purpose is not fostered, it can be difficult to sustain support for migration and settlement assistance.

The path will not be easy. Research in Canada, Australia and New Zealand suggests that structural changes in the labour market have complicated the task of integrating migrants. In particular, traditional human capital and labour market factors no longer provide an adequate account of immigrant economic performance, suggesting that other factors are at play.[5] Discrimination is one – though by no means the only – explanation for the changes observed.

5. *This conclusion is derived from a series of studies conducted by the Research Branch of the Department of Citizenship and Immigration Canada as well as by the Canadian Department of Human Resources Development. The research was based on longitudinal immigration and taxfiler data and is considered to be very robust. See cic.gc.ca for research material.*

iii) *The Need to be Competitive in the Global Economy:* The future well-being of nations depends on their ability, and that of their cities, to participate and compete in the global, knowledge-based economy. In the past, this was tied to the physical capital and raw materials of a region. This is no longer the case. Many analysts now see cities as the engines of national growth, because of the human and social capital that cities assemble. Especially important is the human capital associated with creativity and innovation.

In order to succeed, countries – and cities – need to develop the capacity to attract, retain and employ the best and most creative workers. With fertility rates below replacement, this means attracting and retaining highly skilled immigrants, temporary workers and students from around the world. Recruitment from abroad will play an increasingly important role in stabilizing the labour markets of developed countries whose populations are rapidly ageing.

A close relationship is posited between corporate investment decisions and the availability of highly skilled, knowledge workers. Under the right conditions, a *virtuous* cycle of investment, attraction of skilled labour and further investment produces industrial clustering and growth. The conditions needed to induce this dynamic form an "ecosystem", a key element of which is diversity. Creating this "ecosystem" is a significant public policy challenge, requiring the dismantling of structural barriers, measures to combat discrimination and the creation of a welcoming, open environment (Florida, 2002).

iv) *The Need to Manage Actual and Perceived Threats to Safety and Security:*
Countering the threat of international terrorism and creating a safe and orderly society is an important and costly government concern. Linked to this is the need to counter the potential backlash against migrants and minorities resulting from tensions and incidents involving ethnic communities. Multicultural or pluralist policies can have a palliative influence on both.

The creation of an inclusive identity, where minority interests coincide with those of the larger community, increases the likelihood that minorities will cooperate with police and intelligence agencies in their efforts to thwart external security threats. At the same time, multiculturalism and pluralism have a prophylactic effect, reducing the ferocity of any backlash that might develop (say, as a result of a security incident) and moderating the response this would elicit from minority communities.

Similar concerns apply to issues of justice and domestic criminality, including the victimization of ethnic minorities and crimes committed by ethnic criminal organizations and youth gangs. The interaction of police and other justice agencies with members of minority groups tends to create tension in all ethnically diverse societies (Loree, 2001). Conflict can breed resentment, entrench stereotypes and degrade effective law enforcement.

Addressing safety and security concerns and breaking the destructive cycle of conflict, dysfunction, loss of support for integration and further alienation requires action on a broad front. Some of these actions are, of necessity, security and control oriented.[6] However, the critical role of integration should not be underestimated. Integration can increase the effectiveness of policing, prevent minorities from being victimized (including by members of their own ethnic group) and contribute to personal and public safety, real and perceived.

6. *See also the chapter "Managing Migration in the Wake of September 11: Implications for a Cost-Benefit Analysis".*

ENDOWMENTS AND STRUCTURES

The second angle of the triangle concentrates on institutional structures and features of social organization that affect the benefits and costs of migration and migration policies. Some of the features are fundamental to the societies in which they are found.

- *Economic Structures*
  The industrial and occupational structure of national economies plays an important role in immigrant integration, particularly in early settlement. The majority of immigrants tend to find their first jobs in the service sector, in light assembly or the building and construction sectors. Cyclical, temporary flows tend to centre on agriculture. Economies rich in these jobs allow immigrants easier entry into the labour market. Also important is the degree of unionization and the manner in which wages are determined. Societies characterized by high minimum wages, broad sectoral wage bargaining and universal welfare systems, such as exist in northern European states, do not provide ready footholds for immigrants seeking jobs. The high levels of social cohesion in these societies create exclusionary tendencies that result in substantial immigrant unemployment (much of it long-term) and a high incidence of immigrants and minorities being forced to work in the underground economy (Forsander, 2003).[7]

  Generally, it appears that states with highly organized labour markets and social welfare structures incur high welfare and housing costs when integrating immigrants. This creates resentment in egalitarian societies and makes the task of integrating immigrants even more difficult and more expensive up-front.

- *Access to Institutions:*
  What is not always recognized in comparisons between immigrant-receiving countries and more traditional societies is the extent to which integration depends on the institutional context in which it occurs. In many immigrant-receiving countries, integration is, by and large, a national effort that enjoys across-the-board institutional support. Institutional reform to give immigrants and minorities enhanced access is the norm rather than the exception for all levels of government, extending across the delivery of health services, education, justice-related services, training and welfare and benefit programmes. More recently, attention has been focused on the private sector and on eliminating barriers regarding the recognition of skills and educational credentials (Iredale, 1997; Sangster, 2001).

  The institutional orientation to service a multicultural population represents a collective investment in inclusion and social stability – a common goal for all countries. The investment produces returns (for both the host and immigrant populations) in the form of successful immigrant integration, which raises the per capita income and taxes of immigrants and offsets the cost (to the pre-existing host population) of providing health, education, welfare and policing services.

  In addition to economic returns, investment in the capacity of institutions to integrate immigrants produces a more resilient society that is better able to deal with social conflict and to withstand social "shocks". If the arguments advanced in this chapter are correct, the development of this capacity will not be a matter of choice but of necessity.

- *Fiscal Arrangements*
  The national pattern of fiscal benefits and costs from immigration depends on the governance structure, taxation powers and the distribution of migrants. Two general statements can be made:

7. *See also the chapter "Migration and the Contemporary Welfare State".*

First, macroeconomic studies in Canada, the US and Australia agree that immigration has a small but positive economic impact. This suggests that immigrants more or less pay for the public services they consume (excluding deficit financing or significant discontinuities in the public goods infrastructure). Adding the costs of settlement expenses does not significantly change this picture at the *macro* level.

Second, studies of long-term *fiscal* impact suggest that immigration has a positive net fiscal impact in the case of highly educated immigrants, but a small, negative impact in the case of less educated ones. The fiscal impact of immigration is also not evenly distributed. Benefits tend to be widely dispersed across regions or the country as a whole, accruing in the form of a more efficient allocation of labour, higher productivity and cheaper goods and services. Costs on the other hand, are concentrated in regions of heavy immigration, such as cities, which therefore bear a disproportionate share of the settlement costs.

The exact pattern of revenues and costs will depend on the level of government responsible for providing various services, the powers of taxation that each has, and the transfers that take place between regions and among governments.[8]

- *Social Institutions*

The extent to which convergent policies produce converging benefits and costs depends on the extent to which migration governance engages non-governmental entities. In the case of border management, the expected returns to public investment will be similar across countries because border control falls almost exclusively within the domain of governments. This is not the case with integration, which is both a matter of public policy and private action. The participation of social organizations and the behaviour of ordinary people towards each other have as much to do with successful integration as does public action.

In Australia, Canada and the US, public policy in the area of integration is particularly effective because it leverages enormous support from NGOs and ethnic communities. This is not the case in much of Europe or Japan, where the NGO sector dealing with migrants is active, but not as strongly developed or institutionally supported, with corresponding implications for the costs and benefits of integration policy. NGOs, with their cultural knowledge and commitment, are effective service providers and offer an efficient vehicle for government outsourcing of settlement services.

A key underpinning for the participation of social organizations is the social bridge capital that exists within a country. In the case of Canada, framework legislation such as the Multiculturalism Act plays a crucial role in creating a welcoming environment for newcomers and in establishing immigration and integration as national "projects". Direct financial support and tax relief are also responsible for the development and health of the NGO sector, but without the framework legislation the work of this sector would not be seen as in the national interest (Duncan, 2003). This would compromise the effectiveness of public action and reduce the leveraging that is currently achieved.

KNOWLEDGE, GOVERNANCE AND EXPERIENCE

THE THIRD angle of the triangle – governance, shared knowledge and institutional experience – may collectively be thought of as a form of social capital. The idea is that settlement is a holistic process requiring a complex array of supports, marshalled from public and private sources.

8. *For a detailed treatment of this complex topic, see* The Future Fiscal Impacts of Current Immigrants *in the publication* The New Americans *by the US National Research Council, 1997. Particularly interesting is the comparison of fiscal impacts at the state and federal levels. Measured in terms of net present value, the overall average fiscal impact of an immigrant is positive, with state losses (-USD 20,000) being outweighed by federal gains (+USD 80,000). States such as California and New Jersey, with large immigrant intakes incur higher net costs, especially in the case of California because of lower education levels for its immigrant population.*

The emergence of a comprehensive set of services and their coordination is an iterative process that requires time, experience, information and trust. Coordination is needed at the level of both policy and practice. This involves all levels of government – national, regional and urban – NGOs (including religious institutions) and, in some instances, business groups. Coordinating the contributions by these agencies is an organic process that evolves over time based on interests, competencies and capacities.

Research plays an important role in bringing about stakeholder collaboration by defining issues in a manner that cuts across jurisdictions. This provides incentives for agencies to collaborate at the initial stage of problem definition, as well as subsequently at the stage where remedies are identified. A commitment to evidence-based decision making also reduces ideological confrontations by emphasizing methods and outcomes as opposed to ownership. The result is a relatively neutral forum in which the focus is on ideas and practical solutions.

The social capital that is built through shared tasks and shared experiences produces benefits that increase the effectiveness and efficiency of integration services as well as lowering their costs (Reitz, 1998). The benefits accrue in the form of:

- greater policy effectiveness with fewer policy "holes", more nuanced and qualitatively better programmes and a better sense of the downstream implications of policy and programme decisions;
- greater programme efficiency due to reduced overlaps and better sharing of scarce resources;
- broader policy and programme support leading to greater policy stability, resilience and reduced vulnerability to single issues; quicker responses to crises and a reduced tendency to sidestep issues and adopt risk-verse behaviour, and
- greater capacity for public institutions to leverage private resources and control external factors by capitalizing on the attractions of culturally diverse districts to attract creative workers and corporate investment.

With time, countries that do not at present invest in integration or research, and whose agencies lack experience, will build the knowledge and relationships necessary for greater efficiency and effectiveness in delivering integration services. This will cause the benefits and costs of migration policy and practice to converge across countries, making it easier to transfer lessons among them.

CONCLUSION

This chapter began with a caution to policymakers and politicians about the dangers of uncritically transferring policies from one country to another. Three sets of factors were identified as determining the benefits and costs of interventions in different national contexts: values, institutional arrangements and knowledge and experience. Currently, significant differences exist within and between developed countries in respect to these factors, causing the benefits and costs of similar immigration policies to differ widely, depending on their location.

Notwithstanding these differences, a main tenet of the chapter is that developed countries are all facing a similar set of challenges, which create similar policy imperatives, particularly in the area of integration. These same imperatives are also causing values relating to migration to converge as nations struggle to address common tasks.

As values converge and learning takes place, many of the structural and institutional differences between countries that affect migrant integration are likely to fall away. This will result in better migrant access to institutions, the development of a robust NGO sector and the emergence of fiscal arrangements that share the benefits and costs of migrant integration more equitably among the different levels of government. (Dismantling the institutional barriers to effective integration also helps protect the rights of migrants, another value made common to all countries by converging international laws.) Some institutional differences will, of course, persist, but economic globalization may eventually grind these down as well with corresponding implications for national costs and benefits.

The final set of factors that focus on institutional coordination, knowledge and trust – a form of social capital – presents no ideological impediments to convergence between immigrant-receiving states and more traditional societies. As countries mature in their approach to migration, the capacity differences between them are likely to diminish. Benefit-cost differences associated with various integration practices should follow suit.

Significant convergence of integration policies is unlikely to happen for many decades, given the nature and pace of the economic and demographic changes driving the adjustments. This process will, however, accelerate with time. As values shift and institutional constraints are reduced, the range of options available to policymakers, particularly in Europe, will expand. Once new policies are implemented, they will have a liberalizing effect on values and on institutional behaviour, thus establishing a virtuous cycle of change, liberalization and further change. As this occurs, the benefit-cost ratios associated with implementing migration and integration programmes in different national settings will converge permitting lessons from one regime to be transposed to others with greater confidence about the likely outcomes.

TEXTBOX 17.1

INTEGRATION – EMPOWERING THE NON-GOVERNMENTAL (NGO) SECTOR

It can be argued that social integration and social inclusion generate increased social capital, while social exclusion reduces it and the levels of trust required for a vibrant economy and well functioning society.

Social capital is a public good that occurs in the relations between members of a society, and between members of a society and the institutions of that society, such as government bodies, the police, business organizations, NGOs and political organizations. It is said to be at the root of cooperation and to facilitate the development of individual human capital, smoothly functioning communities, robust and stable economies and a vibrant cultural life.[9]

Social capital theory suggests that the extent of its availability varies according to whether and to what degree civil society, including immigrants, can participate in its processes and decision making. A society characterized by social inclusion will, other things being equal, be more prosperous than one that is not. Social inclusion complements social justice mechanisms and through its broad societal reach should benefit all, not only those needing social justice supports.

NGOs Play an Important Role in Strengthening Social Capital

Governments can play a central role in promoting the social integration of migrants, but in some countries grassroots efforts in that regard still tend to be undertaken by NGOs. Canadian government programmes, for example, offer funding to NGOs for local activities

9. *See some of the standard literature on social capital such as William Coleman's* Foundations of Social Theory *(1990), Francis Fukuyama's* Trust: The Social Virtues and Creation of Prosperity *(1995), and Robert Putnam's* Bowling Alone *(2000).*

to promote social integration by settling immigrants, and assisting them to find accommodation, work and schools for their children. In principle, the best ideas submitted by the NGOs are retained for funding. This approach transfers ownership of the integration effort to the people and their communities, which in turn can create more social capital than if the government retained exclusive responsibility.

Government funding for NGOs can be an efficient means of creating social capital within immigrant communities, empowering immigrants in their own settlement and integration in ways that direct service delivery by government cannot. Such programmes signal a willingness by the government and mainstream society to trust the newcomers and regard them as members of the host society. Local administration of the programmes allows direct contact between the newcomer and the official face of their new society. (This reference relates to NGOs that deliver services, not NGOs whose primary responsibility is to advocate on behalf of groups.)

This may well support the argument for *framework* legislation rather than direct government intervention. Such a framework can provide the necessary guidance to community actors in their endeavours. Ideas for the promotion of integration are developed in greater numbers, can be designed for the particular situation of a community, and are deployed by people with a vested interest in the outcome. Frequently, government-funded programmes require that organizations work in partnership with others, including the business community, and this stimulates greater trust, greater social capital and more effective integration. In that way, framework legislation could provide both the roadmap for social integration, as well as the legitimacy, based on democratic processes, of its pursuit. The approach is similar in Australia. By contrast, in the US community groups assume a major responsibility for integration, albeit with private rather than government funding.

The motives for integration need not be just the moral imperative of social justice and the extension of human rights. In times of crisis – and many regard the post-September 11 era as such a time of crisis – social justice arguments can be supplanted by the exigencies of the moment. But, if societies are motivated to ensure general prosperity through the strengthening of social capital, and see the integration of immigrants as a necessary ingredient, they will be on firmer ground for social capital to generate longer-term economic benefits, also in non-crisis times.

Source: Howard Duncan, Executive Head, Metropolis Project.

TEXTBOX 17.2

WOMEN, DREAMS AND VIDEOS

Ana Maria Chica Coral, a journalist and migrant living in Italy, helped make the video *Dreams of Women*, which aims to improve public perceptions of migrants in Italy through the active engagement of the migrants themselves. It was conceived for *No Di (I nostril diritti – our rights)*, an association of migrant women in Italy funded by the Italian government and the EU/EQUAL programme. It forms part of a larger IOM project, "The image of migrants in Italy, through media, civil society and the labour market", which gives migrants a chance to tell their story, promote their culture and be key players in the dissemination of news and information on migration.

This is Ana Maria Chica Coral's story, freely translated from the original:

Some months ago, I participated in a seminar on the theme "identity" promoted by the Italian migrant women's association *No.Di.* When it was my turn to speak in my small working group, I realized I didn't know what to say. I remember uttering three faltering sentences without really saying anything.

Later, I thought about the difficulty I had in defining myself, and of the answers I found the one that most helped me to understand was the realization that in the last five years, since arriving in Italy, I had had to make many changes in my life. I had worked as a secretary, a Spanish teacher, cultural mediator, translator – all of which I had never done before. Changing jobs really doesn't mean changing one's identity, but you have to wear different clothes that are not yours and that often do not fit comfortably.

This might seem insignificant or superficial at first sight, but is definitely more complex than that. When one has migrated, especially from a poor to a rich country, it is very hard to put a value to one's previous working experience. Immigrants who arrived earlier advise you to forget what you were doing before and to start from scratch. Therefore, one needs to reinvent oneself. Surely this process can be enriching from a human perspective, but at the same time it is painful, because it means putting aside all that you long for and have learned, to be able to do what the new reality imposes. Compared to the many migrants who have been forced to leave their families and children behind, it might not seem very important, even trivial, but to give up a job one loved and identified with is like giving up a part of oneself.

When I was offered the chance to make this video, it was as though I could recuperate a part of myself that I had left suspended somewhere: my profession, and what it meant to work as a journalist. I finally had the chance to work on the creation of a communication tool focusing on immigrants and, more specifically, on women. It meant having a "voice" again as a journalist, and giving other women the chance to speak and to convey their experience.

Picking up journalism again meant finding people with whom to share the same professional interests and, in this case, to tell life stories of women. For Marta (my companion in work, ideas, concerns, adventures and, luckily, many good laughs) and for myself, it was clear that this was an opportunity to talk about the reasons why some women leave their country to live elsewhere, even though the conditions are not favourable. It represented a chance to talk about their faith in life, a faith so strong as to push them to choose such a risky and tough option as emigration, and of their courage to endure painful moments.

Interviewing Matsumeh, Suela, Maria Jose, Luz Maria and Adriana moved us deeply. I saw myself reflected in their answers to our questions, in their role as immigrants, women who hold on and do not give up. The only possible answer to the fear and insecurity of this new life is to work, work, and work again, partly out of necessity and partly to drown out the voices and memories in your head, and not to think.

I have many memories of this 20-minute long video. Not only of our work to produce the sound and the images, but also of the scents and tastes. The enticing perfume of Persian rice, or of the Peruvian "tanmales". Or the nostalgia of African drums and the Albanian violin played in the garden of a castle. Our main characters' accounts, their stories and the images and feelings they conveyed during these days spent together was not all they gave to us; taking time from their work they invited us to meet their families, and taste their food and listen to the music of their countries.

Surely the taste that remains and lingers on is that of friendship and female solidarity, the pleasure in doing something you believe in and the love of journalism, which, thanks to this video, I have been able to pick up again. These five life stories tell about dreams and are, in turn, a dream come true for us who filmed them.

Source: IOM Rome, Italy, 2004; *MRFRome@iom.int*

CHAPTER 18
MIGRATION AND THE CONTEMPORARY WELFARE STATE[1]

Closed borders have turned into a luxury that is rapidly becoming unaffordable.

INTRODUCTION

THE INTERNATIONAL debate on migration is often simply one about open borders versus protected societies. On the one side are those who perceive migration primarily as a threat to cherished ways of life and want to close national borders. On the other are those who clamour for open borders and see protective measures as privileges for insiders that block global economic growth. The first use communitarian arguments about the need for strong solidarity to maintain high levels of social protection, while the second use liberal arguments to posit the reverse.

But both sides may well fail to see the real dilemma. Proponents of closure often lose sight of the reality that closing borders is more likely to increase irregular migration, including human trafficking, and the universal moral standards set by international human rights treaties and national constitutions. Proponents of openness tend to downplay the challenges that market-led labour migration regimes pose for the sustainability of contemporary welfare states.

This chapter looks at the affinities between immigration and integration regimes on the one hand, and the prevailing welfare regime and the political economy on the other.[2] It is argued that there is a causal link between the way different welfare states have adapted to the challenges of post-industrialization (Esping-Andersen, 1999) and the migration policies that the states in question are pursuing.

The reasoning behind this argument is that welfare regimes are paid for from taxes or (statutory) social contributions and as such tend to increase non-wage labour costs. This, in turn, constrains employment, which imposes on businesses a strategy of mounting productivity and quality competition. This is the "high road" so much extolled by progressive literature on the subject. As wage and productivity levels rise in tandem, low- productivity labour is ultimately pushed out. Since deindustrialization forces states to find new jobs for low-skilled workers, the level of labour costs becomes crucial. Finding new employment opportunities for redundant workers while preserving the goals of equality and protection is the challenge of post-industrialization, and impinges directly on issues of migration.

The chapter looks at three well-known "worlds of welfare capitalism" (Esping-Andersen, 1990) and how differently they tackle the challenges of post-industrialization:

1. *The author of this chapter is Ewald Engelen, University of Amsterdam Faculty of Social and Behavioural Sciences, Department of Geography and Planning, Nieuwe Prinsengracht 130 1018 VZ Amsterdam, +31 20 5254059, e.r.eengelen@uva.nl.*

2. *"Political economy" here refers to the way in which the economy is politically structured. Note that this "structuring" is never solely done by the state, but always involves voluntary agencies, employer organizations and labour unions, and it impinges not only on the number of available "markets" but also on the dominant orientation among economic agents (Engelen, 2003a).*

i) In the "corporatist world" of Austria, Germany and (partly) the Netherlands, the state is highly dependent on well-organized "insiders" who are unwilling to sacrifice social equality and protection to increase employment and flexibility, and are passing the costs of post-industrial restructuring onto large numbers of "outsiders" such as women, youth and immigrants;

ii) In the "liberal world" of the UK, the US, Canada, Australia and New Zealand, where the level of equality and protection is much lower, the dominant response has been to lower the wage floor even further in an attempt to make low-production activities – primarily personal and (simple) business services – economically viable, in the process accepting ever larger degrees of income and wealth inequality;

iii) In the "social democratic world" of Sweden, Denmark, Norway and Finland, the employment effects of deindustrialization are absorbed through active labour market policies and an expansive public service sector, requiring high and ever rising levels of public spending, which raises urgent questions about the social and economic sustainability of the levels of taxation this requires (Esping-Andersen, 1999).

In the post-industrialization era, states seem to be compelled to grasp only one horn of the "trilemma" of unemployment, equality and balanced budgets at the expense of the other two (Esping-Andersen, 1999), a choice that is highly determined by the type of welfare regime.

In the light of the bitter dispute in Europe on migration issues, it is surprising that the policy tension between open borders and social protection is not discussed more in the relevant literature. The most pressing question for European states today is whether they can afford to close their borders to maintain current levels of social protection. Or, more generally, to what extent a more accommodating migration regime and a well-developed welfare regime may actually be incompatible?

The chapter describes the predicament faced by welfare regimes such as those in the US, which are strong on openness and flexibility, but much weaker on equality. It raises important questions about the need for effective integration policies to counter the segregationist tendencies current in liberal market economies. By contrast, the longer-term viability of European states' welfare regimes is threatened by the rapidly worsening demographic outlook; while their open and export-oriented economies have rendered national boundaries increasingly porous, raising doubts about the possibility and desirability of closed borders.

The chapter demonstrate how the "corporatist" and "social democratic worlds", respectively, will have different approaches to these challenges, but will both have to introduce some form of labour migration to cope with the tasks facing them. Closed borders have turned into a luxury that is rapidly becoming unaffordable.

The chapter concludes with a brief exposition on the kind of citizenship regime that could facilitate openness to migration, while still offering a modicum of social protection.

OPENNESS, FLEXIBILITY, MOBILITY AND INEQUALITY

THIS CHAPTER distinguishes between different "worlds of welfare capitalism" by the measure of "decommodification" that occurs. This criterion refers to a situation where "a service is rendered as a matter of right, and a person can maintain a livelihood without reliance on the market" (Esping-Andersen, 1990). As such, it presupposes the backdrop of a *marketized* and commodified economy. While originally meant to denote the degree of income replacement, it can also be applied to economies as a whole in order to determine the extent to which socially required goods and services are allocated by markets.

Seen in this light, a highly commodified economy is one where buying power is the main criterion of distribution; where market allocation is the dominant mechanism of coordination, and where moral restrictions on market exchange are largely replaced by the utilitarian logic of cost-cutting profit maximization (Streeck, 1997).

Liberal welfare regimes clearly betray a high level of commodification in all of these senses. Generally, they provide a low level of income replacement in case of unemployment or incapacity, link such income replacements to means tests, and prefer in kind over cash transfers. Moreover, economic success translates easily into advantages in other societal spheres, such as education, health care, and even politics. This results in a low level of protection, a high level of poverty, a wide wage spread, relatively high income and wealth inequalities, as well as high inequalities in access to politics, health care and education.

Following the above, commodification implies not only that social and economic reproduction largely occurs through market exchange, resulting in a large number of market interfaces, but also that these interfaces will be of a particular kind. The political economy of liberal welfare regimes generates a relatively high level of economic uncertainty, not only for workers but also for firms, and an adversarial, low trust business climate (Whitley, 1999). The outcome is a predominance of contractual relations, a highly litigious legal culture, an outspoken preference for individualized insurance schemes for workers and a combination of market-mediated outsourcing strategies and proprietary integration, instead of trust-based cooperation on the part of firms (Whitley, 1999).

Another crucial and closely related aspect of the liberal regime is the presence of deep and liquid equity markets. Contrary to appearances, equity markets do not serve as conduits for the aggregation, mobilization and allocation of capital. Instead, they serve as exchanges for property titles, allowing owner-managers to liquify their assets and investors to diversify their risks (O'Sullivan, 2000). As such, deep equity markets over time tend to disperse ownership, changing owner control from a personalized mode of power into a systemic one. Thus, corporate governance is increasingly effected through a shareholder-oriented ideology that is an integral part of a new, "financialized", accumulation regime, consisting of a complex mixture of non-profit and for-profit institutional investors, financial conglomerates and highly-specialized intermediaries (Scott, 1997; Clark, 2000; Lazonick & O'Sullivan, 2000; Boyer, 2000).

When combined, these attributes have resulted in high speculative portfolio building that has deflected corporate attention away from investment in production, training and education, and high performance workplaces. With this, employment relations have become ever more asymmetrical and precarious, while low union membership, precarious organization rights, and a predominance of on-the-job training have made it difficult for unions to counter the gradual shift in distribution of corporate revenues from labour to capital that is at the root of increasing economic inequality, increasing poverty, and a growing wage spread.

Moreover, unions have turned into sectional self-defence organizations, which aim to protect core workers, while placing the costs of mobility and flexibility on the peripheral worker. The result has been a multiplication of the number of available low value-added markets, creating numerous opportunities for the growth of micro firms in the personal and producer services.[3]

Because of their minimalist interpretation of citizenship rights and resultant low level of wage replacement and non-wage labour costs, liberal regimes have been able to pursue relatively generous immigration policies. Vice versa, some even believe that a generous migration policy has been an integral part of an attempt to keep workers' rights under managerial control (Burawoy, 1975; Korver, 1990).

3. *See, e.g. Sennett, 1999; Schor, 1992, 1998; O'Sullivan, 2000; Lazonick, 1991; Cappelli* et al.,*1997; Appelbaum et al., 2000; and Ehrenreich, 2001.*

The high incidence of private insurance is also accompanied by a long history of immigration (private insurance would in any case have defeated any efforts to set up European-style welfare systems). In addition, since a high degree of commodification means that there are a large number of accessible markets, liberal regimes are noted for the lack of explicit economic integration policies. The "market" is supposed to take care of that.

In summary, there are strong institutional complementarities between minimalist welfare arrangements, a low wage economy, open migrant admission policies and underdeveloped integration policies.

While the general openness, flexibility and mobility of this regime has served immigrants well, there are increasing signs that ensuring only market accessibility is not enough. The constant influx of cheap labour has reduced institutional incentives to pursue labour replacing (capital goods) or labour upgrading (training) investments. Instead, low value services absorb ever larger numbers of poorly educated immigrants, as well as natives. Should this trend continue it could ultimately result in capital replacing strategies – already visible in low-wage services and agriculture in the US (Schlosser, 2003) – which could have a downward effect on the innovativeness of some parts of the US economy in the long run. Also, the huge loss of middle-ranking jobs during the 1990s led to a rapid erosion of traditional avenues of social mobility and integration (Wright & Dwyer, 2003), resulting in a society of "segmented assimilation" described by some as "American Apartheid" (Massey & Denton, 1993).

Thus, the challenge facing the US is how to combat segmentation and segregation, while keeping the current openness and flexibility towards immigration, not only for the moral objective of ensuring equal life chances, but also for the long-term innovativeness of the American political economy. Hence the question: how long can equality be regarded as a dispensable "luxury"?

PROTECTION, EQUALITY, CLOSURE, RIGIDITY AND INTERNAL AND EXTERNAL EXCLUSION

THE SECOND, "continental" regime is known for its high level of income replacement, generous social services and corporatist political economy. Broadly, there is considerable overlap between the continental and Scandinavian regimes: both provide a high level of protection against the vagaries of the labour market, and both lean towards a "high skill/high wage equilibrium", simultaneously forcing and allowing firms to pursue capital and skills-intensive strategies based on long-term relations with capital providers (banks), suppliers, competitors and workers. As a result, the dominant mode of competition is best described as cooperative (Cooke & Morgan, 1998).

These political economies lack the mobility characteristic of the US, and hence do not have to bear the social and economic costs, or reap the benefits, of radical economic changes. Instead, they excel in incremental technical, organizational and institutional changes that require more voluntary collaboration, a less conditional type of mutual commitment and a longer-term focus.

The current modes of economic governance in Scandinavia and the European continent clearly facilitate such a collaborative, long-term logic. High quality, public vocational training systems offering portable skills shift the locus of power from the employer to the worker (Thelen & Kume, 2001; 2003). Combined with a higher level of unionism and a more cooperative polity in which governance is more frequently delegated to voluntary associations, this produces an industrial relations system in which workers tend to have far-reaching legal protections and rights, resulting in a low level of managerial discretion and consensual, horizontal management practices.

The long-term focus is also noticeable in the institutional make-up of the firm-capital nexus. Since stock markets tend to be shallow and lack liquidity, there is no well-developed market for property titles and hence no easy way out for owner/managers. As a result, a large number of firms remain outside the reach of public equity markets (Wojcik, 2002; 2003), while those firms that are publicly quoted, were, until recently, largely sheltered from shareholder speculation because of stable, long-term relations with house banks acting as large committed stakeholders (Scott, 1997).

This results in a radically different market orientation of businesses. Rather than aim for the maximization of portfolio returns, they tend to focus primarily on technical excellence, using quality rather than price as the main instrument to gain competitive advantage. This is reflected in the composition of boards of directors. Consisting overwhelmingly of lawyers and financial experts in liberal environments, board members of companies in corporatist environments tend to have a product, industry or even firm-related background, resulting in a greater emphasis on product, process and product markets over portfolio building. The upshot is less of a "shareholder culture", a limited "market for corporate control", and only a small number of (wasteful) mergers and acquisitions.

Lacking a deep equity market, the pension system in corporatist countries generally has a "pay-as-you-go" character rather than a capitalized one. This reflects the lack of liquid assets on the one hand, and the power of a well-organized labour movement on the other. Labour unions have been able to deflect attempts by employers to buy the loyalty of individual workers through firm-based pensions in order to maintain economy-wide class solidarity; while the need for employers to buy the loyalty of their workers has been mitigated by a publicly funded vocational training system. The training solves both the problem of "poaching" of highly skilled workers by competitors and of under-investment in training because of the inability of workers to take skills with them.[4] Also, the availability of earnings as a source of new productive investments is increased by the ability to use supplementary corporate pension savings as a source of cheap capital (e.g. the so-called "book reserves" in Germany and Italy),[5] and by giving firms easy access to the surpluses of corporate pension funds (as in the Netherlands).[6]

Given the high level of decommodification and collaborativeness, and the unconditional trust required of this type of political economy, there are strong insider-outsider dynamics at play. Since corporatist regimes provide ample opportunities for well-organized interests – in general highly skilled, highly paid white male workers – to block institutional changes, the effects of deindustrialization are either cushioned by labour supply reductions through generous early retirement arrangements, or externalized onto less well-organized outsiders. This results in high levels of unemployment among youth and immigrants and a stark trade-off between work and childcare for women. Since women increasingly tend to opt for (full time) labour market participation, the overall fertility trend is sloping downward, dropping below replacement level (2.1 children per woman) (Esping-Andersen, 1999).[7]

4. "Poaching problems" refer to the under-investment in general, industry-specific skills that results from the threat that some employers will free-ride on the investments in human capital of others. "Portability problems", in turn, refer to the inability of workers to take their skills with them as a result of their high firm-specificity. An emphasis on firm-specific skills, in turn, is a rational answer of the individual firm to the poaching problem. The result of the need to find individual answers to these collective action problems is a low skill environment (Crouch et al., 1999).

5. Large German and Italian firms are legally allowed to keep corporate pension savings on their books as silent reserves. This was explicitly meant by the legislator as a source of cheap capital to facilitate capital investment.

6. Although the Netherlands is the only corporatist European country with a well-developed capitalized pension system (Clark & Bennett, 2001), implying a certain distance between fund and firm, corporate pension funds have proven to be rather lax in maintaining this distance and have "donated" to their donors a total amount of € 5.6 billion in the period 1998-2000, either in the form of lump sum paybacks or in the form of "contribution holidays".

7. Fertility in the EU currently ranges from 1.19 and 1.21 in Spain and Italy respectively to 1.90 in Ireland, 1.76 in France and 1.75 in Denmark (UN 2003a). But there are enormous regional differences. In parts of Europe, couples appear to have opted for "decimation", (e.g. only 0.7 children per couple in the southern regions of Italy). Spanish and Italian fertility ratios suggest that those countries, ceteris paribus, will cease to exist 200 years from now. At current projected rates of fertility, Italy's population will decline from 57 million to 45 million by 2050.

The exclusion of domestic groups from the domestic labour market is matched by equally strong exclusion at the border. Due to rising xenophobia – in part a result of inadequate integration – both "reluctant" immigration countries such as Austria, Belgium, France, Germany, the Netherlands, Sweden and "newcomers" such as Italy and Spain have increasingly resorted to restrictive first admission policies (Cornelius et al., 1994). Currently, there seem to be only two doors left open for immigrants: general refugee programmes or family reunification programmes. Labour immigration is made up primarily of high-skilled experts from the US, other European countries and Asia, and is hence not perceived as migration at all, nor is it associated with the integration problems ascribed to post-colonial and guest worker immigration.

The convergence of first admission policies is much less obvious with integration policies. This is largely because the latter are predominantly shaped by national citizenship traditions and the structure of the polity at large, both of which reflect highly idiosyncratic political histories (Brubaker, 1992; Soysal, 1994; Castles, 1997). Hence within the group of states making up the continental model, a wide range of integration policies can be found, from "assimilationism" to "multiculturalism". Predominant across these, however, at least in practice, are "differential exclusionary" policies that include immigrants in one societal domain, mostly labour markets, and exclude them from others, mostly political citizenship (Castles, 1997). Whatever the policy, there appears to be a general trend towards assimilation in legal, cultural and religious domains and "benign neglect" in the socio-economic one.

PROTECTION, EQUALITY, CLOSURE, RIGIDITY AND EXTERNAL EXCLUSION

Despite many similarities, the Scandinavian and continental models part company on their systems of social reproduction *per se*. Continental countries have radically reversed the policy priorities of the 1950s and 1960s – valuing full employment and an egalitarian income structure over balanced budgets and low inflation – and have bought "healthy" public finances at the cost of both high unemployment and low fertility (Korpi, 2003). Scandinavian countries, on the other hand, have reacted to the challenges of post-industrialization by expanding their public sectors and absorbing displaced workers (from "brownstone industries") and large numbers of re-entering mothers.

The Scandinavian model has thus stuck to the goal of full employment, resulting both in an abundance of care facilities as part of the universal, in kind welfare arrangements characteristic of social-democratic welfare models, and relatively high levels of fertility. On the downside are rising budget deficits and increasing public indebtedness, despite high and rising tax rates. Hence, in the continental case the dominant constraint is of a demographic nature, while in the Scandinavian case it is budgetary.

Recent evidence suggests that the budgetary constraint is less prohibiting than expected. Due to the universal character of the Swedish welfare system and its high quality service provision, the socialist reversal of tax cutbacks in 1991, which threatened to erode its long-term financial viability, could count on widespread electoral support. Sweden is the only OECD member, where the general level of taxation actually rose during the 1990s (Steinmo, 2003). Whether this example can be replicated in other Nordic countries, and whether or not it requires an ethnically homogeneous population, as Steinmo suggests, bears further investigation.

The demographic constraint, on the other hand, represents a threat that is less immediate but much harder to avert, and to which not even the Scandinavian welfare regimes are immune, as demonstrated below.

Despite notorious methodological problems, it is hard to contest the UN prediction that the dependency ratio in most European countries will rise spectacularly over the next 50 years.[8] Since the number of births in most European countries will decline dramatically, and the median life expectancy will continue to rise, a declining number of workers will have to provide for a growing number of pensioners. This will drive up non-wage labour costs and erode the competitiveness of firms in world export markets. Currently there is widespread fear among Europe's ruling elites that the "greying" of the population will set in motion a downward spiral of economic decline.[9]

This issue can be "resolved" in three ways, none of them easy to implement:

i) *By incrementally adapting or radically changing current pension systems;*
With capitalized systems the level of redistribution between generations is lower than in non-funded "pay-as-you-go" systems, either because funded pensions are contribution-related (as in defined contribution plans), or because they have a double source of income: returns on investments as well as contributions (as in defined benefit plans). Hence, the more pensions are provided by capitalized funds, the less their long-term viability is endangered by demographic pressures.[10] This largely explains the growing interest among German, Italian, French and EU policy makers in funded pension systems (Clark, 2003a; 2003b; Engelen, 2003a).

ii) *By shifting the low fertility equilibrium upwards;*
This "solution" is rarely seriously debated, and is also seen by some to be at odds with the aim of increasing female labour participation. A recent study looked at the respective contributions of declining family size, on the one hand, and the postponement of births on the other, to the projected overall population decline in Europe (Lutz et al., 2003). It found that delayed maternity accounts for 40 – 46 per cent of the projected decline over a period of 10 to 40 years. This has important policy consequences; for, policies aimed at boosting the number of children per couple are not only unpalatable to Europeans and Americans, but have also proven to have limited effect (Gauthier & Hatzius, 1997). Policies aimed at reducing birth delay, however – such as day care centres, flexible working hours and part-time jobs, or work-compatible school hours and holidays – do not suffer from these constraints and have proven to be much more effective.

iii) *By implementing a policy of open borders to expand the pool of future earners.*
Even though the numbers of immigrants needed to keep the dependency ratio constant is too high to be politically feasible (UN, 1999b), a growing number of countries are considering labour migration regimes along the lines of the models offered by traditional immigrant countries. Germany is a case in point, with its recent "green card" programme for east European and Asian ICT-experts, and new Immigration Act due to be implemented in 2005. The new Act tempers Germany's infamous *ius sanguinis* with a measured dose of *ius soli*. These legislative measures were directly based on the recommendations of a high-ranking government commission (*unabhängige Kommission "Zuwanderung"*), which concluded in 2001 that Germany had in fact become an immigration country and needed regulated first admission and integration programmes.[11] This was a radical break with the exclusionary stance towards non-European immigrants that the German government had adopted in 1973 when it officially aborted its guest worker (*Gastarbeiter*) scheme.[12]

There are growing indications in Europe that political pressures for open borders will be influenced by the organization of the pension systems. Where a "pay-

8. *See Engelen, 2003b: 1360-1361 for a brief discussion of these methodological issues.*

9. *A growing number of multinational organizations have argued this since the mid-1990s, and pressed for funded pension arrangements as a solution (e.g the UN (1999a; 2002a; 2002b; 2003a; 2003b), World Bank (1994) and OECD (1995; 1996; 1998).*

10. *See Disney, 2000, Weller, 2001 and Engelen, 2003b: 1361-1364.*

11. *See www.bmi.bund.de/Downloads/Zuwanderungsbericht.pdf for its final report.*

12. *Most of its recommendations overcame substantial resistance by the opposition and passed both "Bundestag" and "Bundesrat" in 2002. But due to irregularities in the voting procedure of the German second chamber (the "Bundesrat"), the German Supreme Court struck down the new Act.*

as-you-go" system prevails, as in Germany, France and Italy, governments are likely to feel compelled, for their own survival, to create a more generous admissions policy. Where there is a more balanced mix between capitalized and "pay-as-you-go" systems, as in Sweden, Switzerland and the Netherlands, demographic arguments will generally be less convincing, resulting in a weaker political case for a more open admissions policy.

There are two qualifications: first, the margins of the option of shifting from a low to a high fertility equilibrium are not as wide as some proponents of the Scandinavian model would like. While a comparison of birth delay in Sweden and the Netherlands clearly illustrates the different "fertility effects" of the Scandinavian and Continental models,[13] there is reason to doubt the ability of the Scandinavian model to maintain its late 1980 levels of fertility. Despite some claims that Sweden is beyond "demographic stress" because of its active support of young families, and resultant birth rate at or about replacement level (i.e. 2.1) (Steinmo, 2003), the UN recently presented much lower figures (1.56 over the period 1995-2000) and ranked Sweden fifth in the top ten countries with the oldest populations, below Japan, Italy, Switzerland and Germany, but well ahead of France and the Netherlands (UN, 2003b). The reasons were worsened economic conditions, resulting in rapidly rising female unemployment from 1990 onward, and declining availability of child care for low-income earners as a result of budget cuts (Andersson, 2000).

The second qualification has to do with the viability of pension restructuring. As highlighted by the current pension panic in the UK, the US and the Netherlands caused by falling share prices (and hence declining incomes) and rising pension obligations as a result of ageing, funded pension systems also play a key role. Given the size of worldwide pension savings, the fate of pension systems has increasingly become intertwined with that of leading equity markets. It has been argued that the stock market boom of the 1980s and 1990s was largely the result of a "scarcity effect", as increasing amounts of pension savings entered the stock market and started chasing decreasing amounts of equity (Toporowski, 2000). Maturation will transform pension funds from net buyers of equity into net sellers, setting in motion a reverse flow of capital from stock markets, which is likely to have a declining effect on share prices. Hence the expectation that global stock markets are unlikely to reach the levels of the late 1990s for many decades.[14]

In other words, despite claims to the contrary, funded pension systems might also be subject to demographic stress, ultimately forcing affected governments to reconsider their migration stance and open their borders to more labour migration.

CONCLUSION

THE ABOVE discussion illustrates that all three "worlds of welfare capitalism" can be both beneficial and detrimental for migration, and that both attributes are tightly coupled. Open migration tends to go together with a high level of inequality, uncertainty and a segmented economy. A highly protected welfare regime on the other hand, tends to go hand in hand with high wage levels, a relatively impenetrable but high-quality economy, and a stark insider-outsider dynamic, both internal and external (the Continental model) or only external (the Scandinavian model).

In other words, the basic policy choice appears to be between high immigration and high inequality on the one hand, and low or limited immigration and a high level of equality on the other, raising the intriguing questions: what would a combination of the best of both worlds look like? And how could it be brought about? Do states indeed face such a stark choice, or are there sensible institutional middle courses that would combine openness and protection, mobility and security, accessibility and equality?

13. *The average child-bearing age in Sweden, is 26.3, compared to 25.9 in 1970. In the Netherlands, where childcare facilities are in limited supply and have only recently become available, the average childbearing age has soared from 24.3 in 1970 to 29.1 in 1999, one of the highest in Europe.*

14. *Dent 1998; Siegel 1998; Shiller 2001; Sterling & Waite 1998; Toporowski 2000; England 2002; Engelen 2003b.*

It is possible to avoid the stark choices analysed in this chapter and to experiment with institutional combinations of the three "worlds of welfare capitalism" that could bring about a "fourth" both more empowering and more open to entrepreneurial individuals, whatever their place of birth, helping them to reach higher levels of socio-economic participation. But the route is not an easy one. Given the current political climate in Europe and the US, it is much easier to "make" markets than to correct their outcomes.

The US faces the challenge of supplementing a relatively mobile and flexible economy with empowering mechanisms that provide immigrants with sufficient security and protection to transform the "differential exclusion" of today into the "differential inclusion" of tomorrow. The defining feature of the latter mode of incorporation is its emphasis on upward mobility.

Most European countries, on the other hand, face the opposite challenge of opening up their protective, high quality economies for entrepreneurial immigrants in a manner that does justice both to their moral (not legal!) right to better life chances as well as to the requirements of their welfare regimes.

One way to proceed is by using the available status differences between citizens, immigrants and temporary residents to construct a so-called "stairway to citizenship". According to this, newcomers could acquire rights incrementally, with each step being linked to detailed specifications about requirements, support facilities, goals and vesting periods, ultimately leading to a full set of "citizenship rights".[15] This is not to say that becoming a citizen is or should be the endpoint of all migration; the "stairway of citizenship" is not a "stairway to heaven". It is rather a case for a variety of statuses, that could be so linked as to allow individuals to reach the "rungs" they want, while ensuring that their rights and responsibilities are choices rather than fate. The development of a European concept of citizenship, located at a supranational level, goes some way toward a post-nationalization of citizenship rights – arguably a crucial first step in the construction of a "stairway to citizenship".

A policy of closed borders is rapidly becoming an unaffordable luxury, while helping newcomers to become upwardly mobile is rapidly turning into a necessity. Without realizing and acting on this, Europe could gradually turn into a "gated community" of pensioners who depend for their livelihood on the proceeds of the much younger economies in Southeast Asia and South America, while the liberal economies of the US and others may eventually turn into low-wage economies commandeered by a small number of highly skilled, affluent "masters" surrounded by vast numbers of under-privileged, low-skilled workers. Neither vision of the future is socially, economically or politically attractive.

15. *See Engelen, 2003a for an elaboration.*

TEXTBOX 18.1

Migrant Integration Policies

"Integration" refers to the level of economic and social functioning in a society, and its meaning, scope and expectations can differ widely among states. It touches on issues of culture and belonging, nationality, identity and citizenship that are critical for any society seeking to ensure social stability in an increasingly pluralistic world. It is an area of responsibility falling primarily within the domestic domain of states hosting immigrants, and has very little basis in international law, which can provide for the protection of individual rights but not obligate governments whether or how to achieve the social, economic and cultural functioning of its immigrants.

National policies on integration therefore vary widely depending on individual state policies on migration, tolerance of difference, and the perceived need for social harmony. The integration approaches tried to date invariably reflect individual state policy preferences regarding the temporary or more permanent nature of immigration within their territory. Permanent immigration programmes pursued in countries like Australia, Canada, the US, the Netherlands and Sweden have been accompanied by planned, proactive strategies to help immigrants and host communities deal in their encounters with different cultures. Temporary immigration policies, on the other hand, show less integration efforts and are mostly reactive.

Four general integration approaches exist today, aimed at permanent and regular migrants:

1. **Assimilation** – based on the expected outcome of full citizenship, and sharing of common civic values with the native population. A one-sided process of adaptation in which migrants adopt the language, norms and behaviour of the receiving society.
2. **Segregation** – does not expect migrants to assimilate into the culture of the host society, and is generally applied to temporary migrants. The temporary nature of the immigration system leads to granting migrants limited social rights.
3. **Integration,** also known as "melting pot" – a two-way process of mutual accommodation between migrants and the receiving society, where these two groups accept and contribute to a common culture. People of different cultures learn from each other's culture, while each individual or cultural group retains some sense of cultural heritage and diversity.
4. **Multiculturalism** – recognizes cultural plurality in modern societies and tries to regulate this through principles of equality. Migrants remain distinguishable from the majority population through their language, culture and social behaviour without jeopardizing national identity. It privileges a culture of tolerance for different ways of life.

Most governments introduced some basic policies and laws against discrimination and xenophobia, though in few countries is there specific legislation regarding integration, preferring administrative mechanisms that allow greater flexibility, depending on the circumstances. In some cases, integration policies come as part of immigration policies. Increasingly, countries of origin are taking an interest in the admission policies of host countries, and how their emigrants are treated abroad. The way an immigrant settles into the new country can directly affect how the individual engages with the country of origin, also in terms of maintaining productive links with the home society.

The more successful integration approaches have generally combined strong central governance and monitoring with equally strong on-the-ground cooperation of local governments, the community and the migrants. (At a joint EC/OECD conference in Brussels in 2003, Australian immigration programmes were cited as improving economic returns to the country, in part because of the highly centralized integration schemes.) Integration considerations are also increasingly factored into selection criteria for skilled immigrants, to facilitate longer-term integration planning, which, in turn, can aid the evolution from temporary to permanent status, as desired. This has been the approach by Canada and Australia with their Points Assessment Schemes for skilled immigrants; while European states have not factored "settlement propensity" into their selection criteria, but focused on ensuring that those already in the country are given appropriate language, job, education and other social support to encourage their integration.

The segregation model foresees the least possible integration of foreigners, whose presence is seen as temporary and determined by labour market needs that do not require any measures to deal with the consequences of cultural diversity. Germany, the Gulf states and Japan are examples of countries which have adhered to this model. Immigration realities and labour market needs, however, have led Germany to review its legislation, and the new German Immigration Act, to come into force in 2005, departs from this premise and includes integration provisions.

The assimilation approach, with which France is closely associated, expects that migrants will adapt and adhere to the culture of the country, while identifying themselves very little with the native culture. The US, having been shaped by immigration, embraces the integration approach in which individuals from different backgrounds and cultures accept their respective differences, while also actively engaging to develop a common culture.

All models have their shortcomings. Regardless of the approach followed by countries in the past, all of them have, for different reasons (including economic circumstances, religious considerations, terrorist threats) recently reviewed their integration approaches. The projected need for immigrants and the growing movements of people have made this imperative. Most reforms focus on cultural understanding and language skills: the Dutch government toughened its liberal integration approach by introducing mandatory courses for new migrants, and the US plans to include rigorous testing of language and culture as a precondition for gaining citizenship.

Migrant integration is now a key preoccupation of EU policy makers. The EU Council in June 2003 set out a strategy for a comprehensive and multidimensional policy on integration based on the principle of immigrant rights and obligations comparable to those of EU citizens. The November 2004 EU Council calls for the establishment of a set of common basic principles which, though non-binding, support a European framework on integration. Complementing national citizenship, also, is the EU's "Citizenship of the Union", which under Directive 2004/58/EC of 29 April, 2004, accords all EU citizens the right to move and reside freely in the territory of the member states. This provides a platform for the promotion of EU citizens' participation in public life across Europe.

In the past, integration policies were shaped more by concerns about the impact they would have on national identity. In today's globalized environment, public opinion is more likely to embrace integration and social inclusion policies that promote a sense of belonging, participation and respect for values and the rule of law, while also balancing host societies' acceptance of diversity and the migrants' commitment to participation. Successful integration will also depend on how closely connected these policies are with those targeting racism, xenophobia and discrimination.

Source: AVRI, IOM Geneva.

TEXTBOX 18.2

THE CZECH EXPERIENCE OF MIGRANT INTEGRATION

In the past few years, the Czech Republic has rapidly become a major immigration country. With an estimated 566,000 regular and irregular migrants in the country, accounting for 5.5 per cent of the total population, local authorities have made integration a high priority. The Ministry of Labour and Social Affairs is working with IOM on appropriate integration services for newcomers.

In 2003, the first year of the project, a website entitled "Home in the Czech Republic" was designed in Czech and translated into five languages (English, Vietnamese, Russian, Ukrainian and Armenian (*www.domavcr.cz*). The site offers information on, *inter alia*, residence requirements, family reunification, employment, how to set up a business, health care services, social security, education and citizenship. Links were also established with local immigrant organizations and leaders to inform them about these new services, involve them in selecting the content of the site and offer capacity building and skills development workshops. The site was expanded in 2004 to offer information in Bulgarian, Georgian and Chinese.

In a press interview a Ukrainian migrant working with the project team confirmed that the information provided is specific to the needs of each community:

Sometimes it is very hard to get any information, even for Czechs, and they speak the language... Ukrainians often do not speak the language or are not familiar with legal terminology. And, unlike the Vietnamese minority, which is concerned mainly with trade-licensing issues, Ukrainians need more information on social issues, including marriage and what rights are guaranteed by international contracts between the Czech Republic and Ukraine (Prague Post, 15 April 2004.).

Source: IOM Budapest.

Migration and Health

Chapter 19
Investing in Migration Health[1]

Well managed migration health, including public health, promotes understanding, cohesion and inclusion in mixed communities. Investing in migration health can make good economic sense and be an aid to effective integration of migrants in their communities.

INTRODUCTION

Migration can have significant health implications for migrants and affected communities alike, which, if ignored or neglected, can be costly for all involved – socially, politically and financially. Some governments with highly regulated immigration programmes routinely address migration health[2] as an integral part of migration management. But most do not. In a world of high mobility, complex transnational networking, rampant clandestine immigration and increasingly fragile health scenarios in many regions, policies about migration health have become an international imperative.

This chapter argues that it pays for governments to invest in migration health. It reviews the relationship between health and economic growth, in particular the economic impact of infectious diseases. Using health determinants specific to migrants, it also examines economic and health aspects of migration itself, and the disparities between host communities and the migrants concerning health as well as access to health care, with reference to labour and irregular migration. Finally, it offers some useful pointers linking migration and public health policies.

WHAT DETERMINES THE HEALTH OF MIGRANTS?

Health determinants are "the underlying factors which affect people's health", and can include, for instance, the health environment where they live, or travel to or from. Other factors include lifestyle (diet, tobacco, alcohol), socio-economic conditions (living and working conditions, physical and psycho-social environment) and "life chances" (how children live and grow up, educational and employment opportunities, gender discrimination).[3]

The *migration-related determinants* of health define the level of vulnerability of migrants in a society, which can in turn impede a successful migration outcome for both the individual and the affected community (Grondin, 2004). In addition to the health environment in the place of origin, transit and destination (including disease prevalence), they include patterns of mobility (regular vs. irregular) that define the conditions of the journey and their impact on health; the legal status of migrants in host societies that often determines access to health and social services; and familiarity with the culture and language of the host community. Health determinants need to be understood by policymakers when they devise migration health management policies, which then need to be factored into larger public health policies.

1. *The author of this chapter is Dr. Danielle Grondin, Director of the Migration Health Department, IOM Geneva.*

2. *Migration health is a specialized field of health science that focuses on the wellbeing of both migrants and communities in source, transit, destination and return countries and regions. In the preamble of its Constitution, WHO defines health as "a state of physical, mental and social well-being and not merely the absence of disease or infirmity"; www.who.org/about/definition/en/*

3. *See the Commission of the European Communities, 2002.*

HEALTH AND ECONOMIC GROWTH

HEALTH policies as they relate to the wellbeing of the individual and the community always have a price (Rauch-Kallat, 2003) - usually set by the state, and carried by the taxpayer. But the costs of public health and welfare can often be offset by the benefits wellbeing brings to the economy, in line with the adage that "health is wealth (...) health is a cause of progress" (Byrne, 2003).

A number of studies have demonstrated the benefits to governments of investing in the health of their peoples: better health can raise productivity and per capita income, and speed up growth of per capita GDP (**Figure 19.1**) (Bloom, 2004). It does so by raising national income, improving education, stimulating national savings and encouraging foreign investment. Life expectancy is an important denominator of income potential and capacity for savings and investments (ibid).[4] In recent decades, East Asia has illustrated the economic benefits of a larger and healthier labour force: "life expectancy increased from 39 years in 1960 to 67 years in 1990 with a concomitant decline in fertility rates; the ratio of working-age people to the dependent population rose from about 1.3 to over 2, which stimulated a much higher production level and a higher GDP per capita" (ibid). In certain circumstances, one extra year of life expectancy can raise GDP by about 4 per cent (ibid).[5] Health is thus an important factor contributing to different economic growth rates.

Investing in health enhances the quality of life and raises life expectancy by reducing the burden of disease on individuals and communities. "Health matters more (...) in low-income than in higher-income countries" (ibid). Diseases reduce individual income, public revenues and the potential for economic growth. WHO reports that the losses amount to dozens of percentage points of GNP of the poorest countries each year (WHO, 2001). A combined effort to reduce communicable diseases, malnutrition and maternal mortality, which affect the poor more than the rich in developing countries, could be an effective strategy for poverty reduction.

In its 2001 report on investing in health for economic development, WHO estimated that approximately 330 million DALYs (disability-adjusted life years) would be saved for each 8 million deaths prevented: assuming, conservatively, that each DALY saved generates an economic benefit of saving of 1 year's per capita income of a projected USD 563 in 2015, the direct economic benefit of saving 330 million DALYs would be USD 186 billion per year, and plausibly several times that amount (ibid.).

This is significant, particularly in view of the potential of ill health to reduce people's receptiveness to education, lower their earning capacity and opportunities for work and increase the risks of mental illness and social problems (**Figure 19.1**) (ibid.).

4. *Living longer is associated with higher income (Bloom, 2004). See also the table on life expectancy and rate of change in years per decade in the* World Development Indicators 2003, *World Bank, Washington.*

5. *WHO reports that an investment in health that results in a 10 per cent improvement in life expectancy at birth for each individual, could raise economic growth by at least 0.3 to 0.4 per cent a year. (The statistical example was generated using economic variables designed to account for cross-country patterns of growth, thus holds for all economies: "Standard macroeconomic analyses of cross-country growth are based on a model in which economic growth in a particular timeframe is a function of initial income (because of conditional convergence), economic policy variables, and other structural characteristics of the economy, including indicators of population health.") WHO notes that there is about 1.6 per cent difference in annual growth between a high-income country where life expectancy at birth is 77 years, and a least developed country with a life expectancy at birth of 49 years (WHO, 2001).*

FIGURE 19.1

HEALTH'S LINKS TO GDP

Poor health reduces GDP per capita by reducing both labor productivity and the relative size of the labor force.

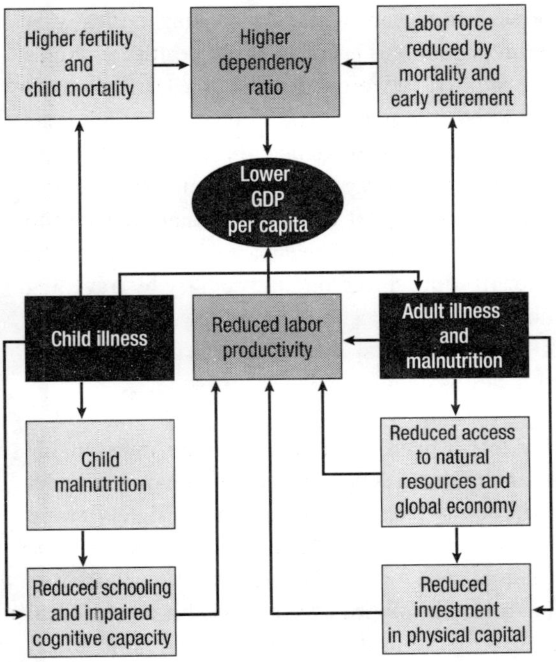

Source:
Fuger, Jennifer Prah, Dean T. Jamison, and David E. Bloom, 2001, " Health and the Economy, " page 619 in *International Public Health*, edited by Michael H Merson, Robert E. Black, and Anne J. Mills (Sudbury, Massachusetts: Jones and Barlett).

More research is needed, particularly on how well the assumption "robust health = robust economy" may apply to poorer countries with reduced employment generation prospects, and on the specific effects of health versus other social conditions that may be related to health and wealth.

INFECTIOUS DISEASES AND THE ECONOMY

The repercussions of untreated infectious diseases go well beyond individual and public health, and may affect the economy of an entire country or continent.

- The AIDS pandemic in Africa, for example, is shattering the economies of the whole continent, decimating workforces and reducing the productivity of tens of millions of working-age adults. It kills adults in their prime working years, and disables many when they fall ill. Costs for care are high, and replacement training is often unaffordable or inappropriate, which further depletes economic assets and impedes economic growth. In Eurasia, if measures are not undertaken soon to curb the disease, it is predicted that by 2025 India could lose 40 per cent of its annual economic growth, China 33 per cent and Russia 40 per cent (Behrman, 2000).

Elsewhere, other diseases have taken their economic toll:

- The recent plague in India has cost the country around USD 1.7 billion in lost tourism, transport services and exports (ibid.).
- Worldwide there were 8,096 SARS cases and 774 people have died of the disease,[6] which also had a negative impact on tourism, trade and travel.

There are a number of examples, particularly in developing countries, of the value of investing in health, particularly preventive health.

- The programme to eradicate smallpox in the late 1960's, with a return of about USD 10 for every dollar invested (Global Forum for Health Research, 2004), is still generating dividends today – a better return than many large corporate investments can generate.
- Malaria costs Africa USD 12 billion a year in production loss (ibid.). Yet anti-malarial drugs, 95 per cent effective, cost only USD 0.12 per dose, and insecticide treated bed nets, costing USD 4 a piece, can reduce child mortality by 25 per cent (ibid.). Malaria is said to lower economic growth by 1 per cent or more per year in areas of high prevalence (WHO, 2001)
- A Control Programme against Onchocerciasis (a parasitic disease also known as "river blindness), targeting 30 million people in 11 Sahelian countries, has to date cost USD 700 million. Yet it has prevented an estimated 600,000 cases of blindness

6. *See WHO on SARS www.who.int/csr/sars/country/table2004_04_21/en/ (accessed on August 26, 2004).*

and has opened up 25 hectares of agricultural land, enough to feed 17 million people a year (Global Forum for Health Research, 2004).

ECONOMIC AND HEALTH DIMENSIONS OF MIGRATION

IOM has taken the lead in migration health programmes and research globally. In cooperation with WHO, governments and other agencies, IOM takes a holistic approach by addressing the wellbeing of both migrants and communities in source, transit, destination and return countries and regions. It contextualizes migration health in the broader policy field of development, trade, security, integration, peace and human rights (Grondin, 2004). This section examines migrants' circumstances in receiving societies, the wide-ranging benefits of investing in migrant health, the socio-economic drivers of migration, and the health-related consequences of extreme forms of irregular migration such as trafficking in persons.

INVESTING IN MIGRANT HEALTH

Economic prosperity depends on a healthy workforce. As many of the wealthier receiving countries turn to immigration to help correct the effects of declining birth rates and ageing populations, they are compelled to consider ways of optimizing the wellbeing of this additional workforce. Migration brings human capital, fuels economic growth, enriches the social and cultural fabric of communities, and contributes to the technical and economic growth of both developed and developing societies.

But for many politicians, health is seen in terms of expenditure rather than investment, a cost rather than a benefit (Byrne, 2003). Some countries' immigration rules and regulations prohibit the entry of migrants with health conditions deemed to place an excessive demand on host health and social care systems (Canada and Australia). Others, faced with mounting national health care costs, are looking critically at migrant populations bringing costly health conditions to the country. The recent debate in the UK Parliament about whether to screen certain categories of migrants for the human immunodeficiency virus (HIV) before departing from source countries is an example of a selective and populist short-term financial tactic to contain cost increases. The debate does not adress the risk for HIV introduced into the country by travelling nationals, neither does it address the more complex and global financial difficulties with the national health care system.

The right to health and welfare is an unassailable entitlement of all persons (including migrants) under international laws on social, cultural, civil and political rights.[7] But the "right to health is not to be understood as a right to be healthy" (UN, 2002). The right to health implies access to health services and practices, including physical, mental and social health, delivered in a way that is culturally sensitive, non-discriminatory and non-stigmatizing. It also implies the establishment of public health policies and practices that would integrate all members of a community, including migrants, regardless of their citizenship and migration status.

Migrant integration[8] is a marker for successful immigration, and as such calls for a broader interpretation of 'migrant health', beyond just infectious disease control, to include considerations of chronic conditions, mental health, cultural beliefs and understanding of health, and human rights. Migrants in a state of wellbeing are likely to be more receptive to education and employment, and more participative in the host community. Where public health is attended to broadly, migrants may not be

7. *These rights are enshrined in, e.g., the Universal Declaration of Human Rights (1948), the International Covenant on Economic Social and Cultural Rights (ICESCR) (1996), the Migration for Employment Convention (1949), the Convention on the Legal Status of Migrant Workers (Council of Europe, 1977), the International Convention on the Protection of the Rights of All Migrant Workers and Members of their Families (1990), the Convention on the Rights of the Child (1989) and others.*

8. *Integration implies being a full member of a society with all the rights, privileges and obligations of the native born, participating and contributing to that society.*

singled out as a health threat to others, and hence would be less exposed to xenophobia and discrimination (Grondin, 2003).

Well managed migration health, including public health, promotes understanding, cohesion and inclusion in mixed communities. Investing in migration health can make good economic sense and be an aid to effective integration of migrants in their communities.

DISPARITIES IN HEALTH BETWEEN HOST COMMUNITIES AND MIGRANTS

GLOBALLY, there remain enormous disparities in health between developed and developing countries. But there are also disparities in health within countries, including rich countries, based on socio-economic groupings. Poverty is the critical health denominator for all. The poorest have poorest health (WHO, 2003). There are direct proportional relationships between socio-economic status and rates of long-standing illness (Lundberg et al., 2001), chronic diseases like cardio-vascular diseases (UK, 2004) and injuries (Graham, 2003). Confronting health disparities also means confronting the unequal distribution of wealth and socio-economic determinants (ibid.).

THE DISADVANTAGES AND VULNERABILITIES FOR MIGRANTS

Being foreign-born and from an ethnic minority state can in some cases be an independent factor related to long-term illness (Sundquist, 1995). For example, in some countries, people of different ethnic origin reportedly have a higher incidence of infant mortality and congenital malformation than the native born (Bollini, 1993; Lehman, 1990). In addition, some "first and second-generation immigrant women of reproductive age (have) an increased risk of debilitating long-standing illnesses (LSI)" (Robertson et al., 2003). Here, ethnicity can be an independent risk factor with an important link to social class, where "ethnic minority groups (...) confront a cultural barrier, new language, social devaluation, discrimination and a lack of social support, i.e. a constellation of factors that might have increased the morbidity from mental and physical diseases and self-reported LSI (ibid.). Finally, studies conducted in Europe and North America show that migrant women of different ethnic origin have poorer antenatal care than native women (15% versus 8%) and suffer more stillbirths (0.82% versus 0.67%) (Bollini 2001). Many of these problems are connected to a lack of migrant-oriented health policies and insufficient training for health professionals in caring for those from different ethnic and cultural backgrounds.

The US Center for Disease Control (CDC) has reported that foreign-born persons accounted for 53.3 per cent of new cases of TB in 2000 (USCDC, 2004). The rate of decrease in tuberculosis among the US-born population has been 3.5 times that of foreign-born persons (El Sahly, 2000)

The migration journey is an experience that encompasses the lifestyle-related health determinants often shaped by socio-economic conditions of the source, transit and hosting community. Consequently, it can expose migrants to a heightened risk of physical and mental health problems (IOM, 2003), including reproductive health (Bollini, 2001), rendering migrant populations among the most disadvantaged and vulnerable groups in most communities (Institute of Public Health, NRW, 1998).

Access to and utilization of available health and social services, as required, can decrease morbidity and mortality, improve quality of life and contribute to a potentially more productive and satisfying life. Migrants are able to access such facilities where (Bollini, 1993):

i) countries have specific health policies for immigration, such as Australia, Canada, the UK and Sweden;
ii) health care systems are comprehensive, often including services structured to meet the specific needs of ethnic communities, irrespective of legal status;

iii) there is access to political representation by migrant communities, such as in Canada, Sweden and the US.

Globally, many if not most migrants do not have such access to care. The reasons are many, but are often related to their immigration status. Irregular or undocumented migrants have the least access to health and support services. Such access also varies widely for asylum seekers, from health evaluation upon arrival for public health purposes (immunizations, detection and treatment of infectious diseases, e.g., tuberculosis), to limited access during the processing of their asylum claim, which can take months or years, or immediate access to basic health services upon arrival. The reasons for these restrictive policies vary, but they share one underlying aim: to reduce health and welfare costs. There is even a view that generous "access" policies would attract more requests for asylum.

In contrast to irregular migrants, immigrants, permanent residents and other long-term migrants often have the same access to available health and social services as the local population. Even when services are available and access is granted, irregular migrants do not use them or use them in a manner that may exclude benefits, for fear of deportation. But even migrants with legal status may not use these services because they do not know about or understand them, or the services offered are "foreign" to their cultural and religious belief.

Policymakers and health management strategists need to consider the potential for "collision of cultures" in mixed communities. Often isolated and socially excluded, migrants can face cultural and language barriers, social devaluation compared to their previous status in the country of origin, and discrimination and stigmatization. The marginalization of migrants, or their exclusion from social participation in host communities compounds the risk of poor health associated with material deprivation and relative poverty.

There are a variety of reasons for the disparity in access to and utilization of health care and social services between migrant and native populations, also at the behavioural level. The disparity has implications for the health of both migrants and communities. For example, many Africans in the UK, although they have access to all available health care and social services, are late to contact HIV care and support services, resulting in diagnoses at later stages of HIV infection (Traore, 2002). Migrant populations also often live in rented dwellings that lack the necessary safety and sanitary equipment, and where children are exposed to a higher risk of accidents and lead poisoning. If they are denied access to health care, this can have deadly and costly consequences for the migrants and the government. In France, asylum seekers who are not allowed to work while their claim is being processed, and receive less than 300 euro a month, often work underground and run the risk of exploitation and resulting ill health (Lamara, 2003).

Public health campaigns often target native populations, but fail to catch the attention of migrants. In Europe, for example, the health care agenda is not geared to services to migrants for a number of reasons, including a lack of political will, insufficient cultural sensitivity and the absence of migrant representation during the policy-making process (Edubio et al., 2001).

More research is needed to understand the complexities of access to and utilization of health care and social services in migrant populations. Access to care is not only a question of health policy and management, but also of social stability, prevention of discrimination and stigmatization, and promotion of inclusion through awareness and cultural sensitivity in health matters and empowerment of migrant communities to access services (Commission for Racial Equality, 1991; Sacks, 1983).

HEALTH DIMENSIONS OF LABOUR MIGRATION

Migration for employment is not always safe, nor always covered by regulations protecting migrant workers, employers, and economies of source and hosting countries. Labour migrants are more vulnerable to ill health than nationals working in the same occupations, with a reportedly higher incidence of accidents, illness and injuries. In Europe, occupational accident rates are about twice as high for migrant workers as for native workers (Taran, 2003). When separated from spouse and family, migrant workers are more vulnerable to risk behaviour, resulting in a higher risk of sexually transmitted infections, including HIV, and, in the case of women, rape and unwanted pregnancies (Estrella-Gust, 2001).

Social exclusion, discrimination, poor living conditions and poverty in general all impact on the mental health and social adjustment of migrants in the host community. These vulnerabilities to higher disease burdens in host working environments add to the already precarious situation of those who carry diseases from the country of origin, or acquired in transit. This can only be further exacerbated by the lack of access to health services.

It has been established that work-related stress is the second most common occupational health problem in the European Union, affecting over 40 million, 28 per cent of the population in the region, with an estimated cost of more than EUR 20 billion in lost time and health care costs.[9] But critical data on the costs of ill health of migrants are still lacking.

The growing movement of healthcare workers from developing to developed countries adds another dimension. Drawn by greater financial and career opportunities, the migration of health professionals exacerbates the shortages of health staff in the countries of origin and undermines their ability to care for the local community.[10] Developing countries are endeavouring to manage this flow, including the facilitation of return migration, through bilateral agreements, for instance those concluded between South Africa and the UK, and between Poland and the Netherlands, to name some.[11]

Mindful of the higher risk of disease among migrant workers, IOM collaborates with governments, private sector recruiters and other partners to promote better migrant health. For example, IOM has assisted in the development of audio-visual training and health awareness material for pre-departure orientation of prospective labour migrants in the Philippines; monitored the occupational health and operational aspects of a nurse exchange programme between Poland and the Netherlands, and contributed to the development of a website to inform Pakistani nurses about opportunities for work abroad, including legal requirements, occupational standards and working conditions.

Trade globalization aims for highest economic gains. This could be complemented by global efforts to reach the highest standards in social and health care of migrant workers and their communities. This is particularly necessary for low-income countries (Bhargava et al., 2001), where life expectancy is lowest and the disease burden much higher than in better-off countries.

AGRICULTURAL MIGRANT WORKERS

The International Labour Organization (ILO) recognizes construction, mining and agriculture as the three most dangerous occupations in the world,[12]

9. *See the website of the European Agency for Safety and Health at Work, as quoted in Newsletter on Occupational Health and Safety 2003; 13: pp. 32-35.*

10. *For further discussion of the costs to African and other governments of training health professionals who take their skills and training abroad see OECD, 2004, and the chapters in this report: "Migration Trends in Sub-Saharan Africa" and "Balancing the Benefits and Costs of Skilled Migration in the Asia-Pacific Region".*

11. *See also the Textbox "Bilateral Labour Agreements: Effective Tools for Managing Labour Flows".*

12. *For further information, see ILO's In Focus Programme on Safety and Health at Work and the Environment, especially in Hazardous Sectors, www.ilo.org/public/english/protection/safework/hazardwk/index.htm*

albeit essential to the economic performance of many countries, developed or developing. In the US, the USD 28 billion fruit and vegetable industry[13] is highly dependent on migrant farm workers; yet, the health of many of these workers is comparable to that in many developing countries (Leon, 2001). A great number of the migrants are either non-citizens or have no legal residence status; most earn low wages, with 60 per cent of farm worker families on incomes below the poverty level (USDOL, 2000). These persons are generally not protected by illness insurance, and absenteeism from work due to illness or injury may result in a loss of job. They rarely have access to workers' compensation (Davis, 2003), occupational rehabilitation or disability compensation. In Ontario, Canada, although migrant farm workers were paid USD 11 million in employment insurance premiums in 2000, they did not qualify to collect the benefits.[14]

Agricultural work is labour intensive, often undertaken in poor and dangerous conditions; working hours are usually long, often in harsh weather, with daily exposure to pesticides and other toxic substances, in an unfamiliar working environment where the language barrier may prevent migrants from being aware of safety recommendations or recognizing safety warnings.

MIGRANT CHILD LABOUR

Child labour is a form of slavery. It is one of the most invidious means for poor societies to fight their poverty, spur development, address labour shortages, and/or simply give vent to their greed. The numbers of children forced into slave labour can only be guessed at. Over 30 per cent (i.e. over 80 million) of the world's working children are in sub-Saharan Africa (Muchiri, 2003). Other regions also employ children, many of whom are migrants. The occupational health and other attendant risks that adult labour migrants face are compounded in the case of children, because of the impact their work has on their development and growth potential. A 2000 study of Hispanic children of migrant farm workers shows that children make up almost 25 per cent of farm labour in the US, placing them at risk of injury or even death from accidents caused by machinery. Poor access to healthcare because of family mobility, lack of health insurance, cultural barriers and lack of economic resources all threaten the health of these children (Hellier et al., 2000).

IRREGULAR MIGRATION: THE HEALTH DIMENSIONS

THE HIGHEST risk to migrant health occurs when the migration journey is irregular, not solicited or welcomed by a host country or region, and the migrant ends up undocumented. This not only poses risks to the health of the migrant, but is also a public health concern, particularly in regard to communicable disease control and surveillance, reproductive health, occupational and environmental health, and sanitation. After arrival, undocumented migrants often live in crowded, unsanitary conditions that increase their health risks (Thomas-Hope, 2003); yet their illegal status prevents them from accessing health and social services. Their unstable and marginal circumstances may contribute to mutual unease between migrant and native communities, and fuel sentiments of xenophobia and discrimination against all migrants.

There are regular reports of human rights violations against irregular migrants. Central American migrants on their way to the US face major risks when crossing Mexico, as they can be subjected to violence by groups of delinquents, and extortion by various authorities. Women migrants are more vulnerable to violence, sexual abuse and hence sexually transmitted infections than men.

13. *Refer to the National Center for Farmworker Health Inc., www.ncfh.org*

14. *See "Cultivating Health and Safety" The Migrant Agriculture Workers Support Centre found at www.whsc.on.ca/Publications/atthessource/summer2002/cultivatinghs.pdf*

UNDOCUMENTED MIGRATION AND HEALTH: THE CASE OF THAILAND

Thailand has over one million undocumented migrants, mainly from Myanmar and other neighbouring countries. Most of them are unskilled "economic" migrants, asylum seekers and trafficked persons seeking their fortune and/or protection in a country that is politically stable and in need of unskilled, low-paid labour. Thai communities with large populations of undocumented migrants have been found to have an increased risk of communicable diseases such as polio, HIV, malaria, filariasis and tuberculosis (Kittipavara, 2004). The migrants themselves are at a high risk of exposure, as illustrated by the case of the Burmese migrant workers in Thailand who have an overall HIV rate of 4.9 per cent, double the estimated rate among the Thai (2.2%) and Burmese (1.9%) populations (Srithanaviboonchai et al., 2002).

The costs of health services for migrants in Thailand, including undocumented migrants along the Thai border, have risen from 79 million THB in 1997 to 170 million THB in 2003, clearly imposing a strain on health and welfare services and the budgets for the care of Thailand's nationals (Kittipavara, 2004).

TRAFFICKING IN PERSONS AND ITS HEALTH DIMENSIONS

Trafficking in persons is a multi-billion dollar criminal industry causing huge social and financial costs for many countries, communities and families. Without going into the details of the scale of the phenomenon globally,[15] this section focuses on the health implications of trafficking, particularly within the "adult entertainment" industry, where the revenues appear to be highest.[16] The most severe consequences of trafficking in persons include the health related ones (London School of Hygiene, 2003). The impacts on trafficked persons are devastating: rape, beatings, torture, inhuman sexual abuse. The effects on mental, reproductive and overall physical health can be long-lasting, due to complications associated with malnutrition, injuries and often forced substance abuse (Javate De Dios, 1998; Raymond, 2002).

THE TRAFFICKING OF CHILDREN AND ADOLESCENTS FOR SEXUAL EXPLOITATION

The case of trafficked children and adolescents needs to be handled differently from that of trafficked adults, because behavioural patterns acquired during this early period set the pattern for adult life: some 70 per cent of premature deaths among adults are due to behaviours initiated in adolescence (WHO, 1998). Children are trafficked both for economic and sexual exploitation. The "black labour market", such as peddling and begging, seen in many large European cities, usually involves younger children, mostly boys, handed over by their poor families lured by promises of a better life for the children. Older children can be trafficked as cheap construction labour, and held in slavery-like conditions incompatible with their level of physical development. UNICEF estimates that about 1.2 million children are channelled into the sex trade every year (UNICEF, 2004); but very little is known about the true scale.

The consequences of sexual exploitation are particularly devastating for: a) mental health (anti-social behaviour, severe depression, post-traumatic stress syndrome and suicidal tendencies) and b) reproductive health (compared to adolescents worldwide, children involved in prostitution have a 6 to 16 times higher chance of contracting a sexually transmitted infection (UN, 2000)). Some 50 – 90 per cent of children rescued from brothels in Southeast Asia are infected with HIV (World Congress, 1996). Sexual exploitation of children means that children may give birth to children. Sexually active adolescent

15. *See also the statistics chapter "Counter Trafficking" of this Report.*

16. *Trafficking in women and girls for the purpose of sexual exploitation is estimated to bring profits of USD 7 billion annually (Hughes, 2001)*

girls, who do not use contraception, have a 90 per cent chance of becoming pregnant within one year. Sexually exploited children, both girls and boys, are often raped; and children are more susceptible than adults to dying from the violence associated with this.

Trafficking is costly to societies. Trafficked children are deprived of the protective environmental health determinants that promote mental and developmental wellbeing of children and adolescents: good family relationship, good peer relations, social networks, education to enhance communication skills, cognition and clear cultural and linguistic identification. ILO estimates that the economic gains from eliminating child labour, particularly sexual slavery, would be tens of billions of dollars annually, because of the added productivity that future generations of workers would bring with increased education and improved public health (ILO, 2002).

BUDAPEST CONFERENCE ON PUBLIC HEALTH AND TRAFFICKING IN PERSONS

In March 2003, a Regional Conference was held in Budapest on Public Health and Trafficking in Human Beings in central, eastern and southeast Europe.[17] It brought together public health and counter-trafficking officials, also at the ministerial level, from Albania, Belgium, Bosnia & Herzegovina, Bulgaria, Croatia, the Former Yugoslav Republic of Macedonia, Hungary, Moldova, Poland, Romania, Serbia and Montenegro (including Kosovo), Slovakia, Switzerland, Ukraine, the US, international organizations, non-governmental organizations and academic institutions. The objective of the conference was to address the public health aspects of trafficking in persons, in particular the consequences for public health of the sexually-transmitted and re-emerging infectious diseases, psycho-traumatization, and physical and emotional abuse suffered by the victims.

The conference resulted in a set of recommendations on ways to increase the standard of health assistance to trafficked victims, and a coordinated health policy approach. The Budapest Declaration builds on and complements those international instruments against trafficking of persons that cite the need to provide physical, sexual and psychological health care to trafficking victims.[18]

The conference also raised public awareness of this serious issue and paved the way for future regional cooperation among states in the region. The Declaration is the first concrete follow-up to the Brussels Declaration with regard to health issues, and could serve as a framework at regional levels, international and bilateral levels for a more comprehensive approach to victim protection and assistance, including individual health, public health and trafficking.

CONCLUSION

THIS CHAPTER has explored some of the major health-related costs of migration, and demonstrated how investing in migration health could mitigate those costs and bring economic and social gains to governments, society and the migrants. What is needed now is the intellectual acceptance of this by policy makers, and the political will for action and financial support. Investing in health is not the responsibility of health sectors alone. Since the health disparities mirror disparities in the key health determinants - i.e. socio-economic and political conditions - this investment would need to be cross-cutting, i.e. linked with other broader efforts to tackle poverty, widen education opportunities for all, regardless of gender, and facilitate employment.

17. *The conference was organized by IOM, with the support of the US Ambassador to Hungary and USAID, and in cooperation with the Ministry of Health, Family and Social Affairs of the Republic of Hungary.*

18. *These include the* Protocol to Prevent, Suppress and Punish Trafficking in Persons, Especially Women and Children, Supplementing the United Nations Convention Against Transnational Organized Crime (2000)*; the* Brussels Declaration on Preventing and Combating Trafficking in Human Beings (2002)*; and the Council of Europe's Recommendation R(2000) 11 on* Action against Trafficking in Human Beings for the Purpose of Sexual Exploitation *(19/5/2000).*

A case is made for public health policies and health management strategies to support the social and political integration of migrants, regardless of their immigration status, and respecting cultural identities. Such policies would correlate best with education, welfare, labour and justice concerns by:

i) Reducing overall risks to poverty within migrant communities by eliminating administrative barriers that limit access to employment and decent living conditions, and promoting education and training to upgrade skills.

ii) Improving access to, and utilization of, healthcare and social services through:

- "globalizing" access to health and welfare services. The ground-breaking decisions by the European Court of Justice and EU Commission to permit the cross-border access of patients to various health systems in Europe are a first step in that direction;
- overcoming cultural and language barriers, while being culturally sensitive;
- providing training and health promotion material for health literacy among migrant communities, particularly on preventive services;
- developing out-reach public health programmes (e.g. vaccinations) for migrants, who often fall through the net of public health systems because of their mobility (difficult to reach) and their lack of entitlements.

iii) Harmonizing cross-border access to, and scope of health care and welfare coverage for migrants, particularly for asylum seekers and refugees. This would decrease the "forum shopping" tendency, optimize standards for continuity of care and strengthen global public health monitoring.

iv) Involving migrant communities in setting priorities and procedures for service delivery, and to advocate for the benefits of health in migrant communities.

v) Setting a policy of non-discrimination in the provision of health care and welfare services.

At an international seminar on Health and Migration in Geneva in June 2004,[19] governments and international organizations agreed that health must be considered an integral part of migration management. They further identified a need for stronger partnership approaches to this issue between and among governments, organizations and communities at national, regional and international levels. Well managed migration health presents opportunities for improving global health to the benefit of all. Improved individual wellbeing should also support larger efforts at economic, political and cultural cooperation between countries and regions – an issue warranting further research in the interests of harmonious international relations.

19. *The seminar was organized by IOM as part of its Dialogue on Migration and was co-sponsored by WHO and the Centers for Disease Control and Prevention. It brought together health and migration officials for an exchange of views and to build capacity and understanding of the complex relationship between health and population mobility.*

CHAPTER 20
GLOBAL MOBILITY, HIV AND AIDS [1]

The failure to address HIV in relation to migration, and migration in relation to HIV, potentially entails heavy social, economic and political costs.

INTRODUCTION

IN HIV/AIDS[2] the world is facing a crucial social issue, as the pandemic threatens to undo decades of investment in health, education and human resource development. In the countries most affected by AIDS, all economic sectors are affected by a weakened and ultimately dwindling labour force. Societies must find new approaches to care for and socialize millions of children who have seen their parents fall ill and die. Along with migrant health in general, the link between HIV and population mobility is one of the most critical challenges currently confronting governments, donors and humanitarian and development agencies.

The failure to address HIV and AIDS in relation to migration, and migration in relation to HIV and AIDS potentially entails enormous social, economic and political costs; yet the field continues to be seriously under-researched and either not addressed, or only inappropriately addressed by policymakers. This chapter draws on presentations made during the International AIDS conference held in Thailand in July 2004, and on recent publications, to summarize the debates concerning global mobility and HIV, and to posit some policy actions that could make a difference.

HIV/AIDS IN GENERAL

BY 2004, virtually every country was affected by the human immunodeficiency virus (HIV) and the acquired immunodeficiency syndrome (AIDS) and between 35 and 42 million adults and children were infected with HIV. In 2003, almost 5 million people were newly infected, and almost 3 million died worldwide. About half of those infected are women and girls. Half of all new HIV infections strike people between the ages of 15 and 24 years (UNAIDS, 2004a).

What distinguishes the AIDS pandemic is its unprecedented and devastating impact on social and economic development in some of the poorest countries. If other epidemic diseases typically affect the more vulnerable, such as children and the elderly, AIDS strikes workers and parents at the height of their productivity and it strikes slowly. For the affected individuals,[3] as for households and communities, the impact of the illness is one of progressive and profound changes over many years: "by the time the wave of HIV infection makes itself felt in the form of AIDS illness in individuals, the torrent of the epidemic is about to overwhelm medical services, households, communities" (Barnett and Whiteside, 2002). AIDS is thus both an emergency and a long-term development issue.

1. *The author of this chapter is Mary Haour-Knipe, Senior Adviser. Migration and HIV/AIDS, IOM, Geneva.*
2. *Human immunodeficiency virus (HIV) and acquired immunodeficiency syndrome (AIDS).*
3. *The initial infection, which may barely be noticed, is followed by a period without symptoms, which may last 8 to 10 years in developed countries, less in developing countries. This is followed by a period of increasingly severe ill health. AIDS deaths are preceded by a period of long and debilitating illness.*

In response, intensive research has led to the development of antiretroviral (ARV) treatment to fight HIV infections, financing has increased considerably, the cost of ARV drugs has dropped, concerted efforts are making it possible to extend treatment to millions of people in low- and middle-income countries whose lives depend on it, and increased attention is being given to prevention.

However, all this is not yet sufficient to halt or reverse the epidemic and the long-term consequences of AIDS can have wide-reaching effects. If current infection rates continue and there is no large-scale treatment programme in the worst affected Sub-Saharan African countries, up to 60 per cent of today's 15-year-olds in those countries will not reach their 60th birthday. Impoverished households will break up as the orphaned children of deceased parents and grandparents migrate elsewhere; children will become more vulnerable to infection where there are no publicly supported services, and the number of health workers will be progressively depleted as they, too, become infected.

HIV/AIDS AND POPULATION MOBILITY

THE SESSION on population mobility at the XV International AIDS conference in Bangkok, July 2004,[4] was part of ongoing international effort to increase understanding of the complex relationship between migration and HIV/AIDS. Presentations given at that session form the backbone of this chapter.[5] Some of the recent data concerning HIV and migration are reviewed, and the key challenges of responding substantively to the issue are discussed. Case studies from Uganda and Thailand are used to illustrate migrant risk and vulnerability.

DATA CONCERNING HIV, AIDS AND POPULATION MOBILITY

As our understanding of HIV and AIDS increases, so does our understanding of the complex and circular relationship between HIV and population mobility. At the beginning of the epidemic before human immunodeficiency virus is prevalent, and in countries or regions with adequate epidemiological monitoring, the first cases of HIV can sometimes be traced to individuals or groups passing through, such as truck drivers, people displaced by conflict, military personnel, or returning migrant workers. But, HIV is now present in every country of the world. At later stages in the epidemic, when HIV is already entrenched in a particular area, migrants, refugees, internally displaced people (IDPs) and individuals in transit for professional or other reasons may find themselves in situations where they are at increased risk of becoming infected with the virus, and thus becoming vehicles of its further spread.

THE RELATIONSHIP BETWEEN POPULATION MOBILITY AND HIV

Work undertaken at Erasmus University in the Netherlands uses country data from demographic and health surveys to plot the correlation between the proportion of recent immigrants in urban populations and the urban HIV prevalence in Africa using sentinal surveillance data (Voeten et al., 2004). Graph 20.1 shows HIV prevalence among pregnant women by the proportion of female urban residents aged 15 to 49, who moved to their current location during the last 12 months, by country and by region, for 26 Sub-Sahara African countries. It clearly shows that, overall the higher the proportion of immigrants, the higher the HIV prevalence. For example, HIV prevalence among pregnant women was negligible in Senegal, where demographic surveys showed that less than 3% of

4. *During the symposium session organized by IOM, UNHCR and CARAM Asia, Dr Cynthia Maung, Director, of the Mae Tao Clinic, Mae Sot, Thailand, set the stage by describing HIV/AIDS risks and vulnerabilities of mobile populations, after which the Honourable Christine Amongin Aporu, State Minister for Disaster Preparedness and Refugees, Kampala, Uganda, Dr. Paul Spiegel, Senior HIV/AIDS Technical Officer, UNHCR, Geneva, Dr. Irene Fernandez, chair, CARAM-Asia, Kuala Lumpur, Malaysia, and Dr. Michael O'Dwyer, Senior Health and Population Adviser, DFID South East Asia, Bangkok, Thailand, respectively presented the views of governments, international organizations, NGOs and donors in addressing such risks and vulnerabilities.*

5. *Other recent reviews available include a brief review of AIDS and mobility in Africa, prepared by IOM for the 'Scenarios for the Future'.*

women had recently moved to their current home, but far higher in Malawi where more than 20% had done so.

The data shown in Graph 20.1 is gross, but intriguing. Another recent study examines in more depth the relationship between mobility, sexual behaviour and HIV infection in an urban population in Yaoundé, Cameroon. Among a representative sample of 1,913 urban residents, an HIV prevalence of 7.6 per cent was found among men who had been away from home for periods longer than 31 days during the previous year; 3.4 per cent among men who had been away for less than 31 days, but only 1.4 per cent among those who had not been away from home in the previous year. The association between men's mobility and HIV remained significant after controlling for other important variables, and was related to risky sexual behaviour (Lydié et al., 2004). However, there was no correlation between women's mobility and HIV infection, a finding that needs to be explored in other populations.

LABOUR MIGRATION

For labour migrants, some information on HIV is available, in part because a number of countries, particularly in Asia, systematically require HIV tests for departing, and occasionally also for returning migrants. In the Philippines, as of July 2004, the National AIDS Council estimates that 32 per cent of the 2,073 Filipinos infected with the virus were overseas workers (*Philippines Social and Environmental News*, July 14, 2004). In Bangladesh, the figure for returning migrants is around 41 per cent.[6] In both instances, the high prevalence of HIV

6. *Report of the Bangladesh AIDS Prevention and Control Programme, 1997-98, cited in UNDP, 2001.*

GRAPH 20.1

HIV PREVALENCE AMONG PREGNANT WOMEN, BY PROPORTION OF NEW IMMIGRANTS, 26 SUB-SAHARA AFRICAN COUNTRIES

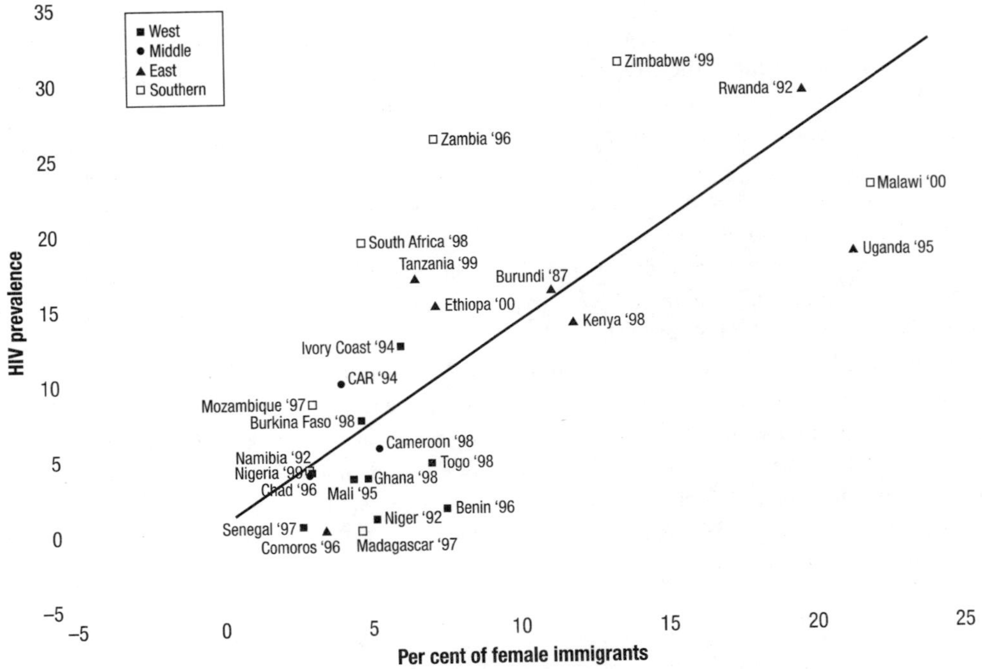

Source: Voeten et al, 2004.

among migrants may be simply because migrant workers undergo more HIV tests than non-migrants.

Several studies from Asia show that migrant women are particularly affected. In Indonesia, a support group reported that as of April 2003, 15 of the 24 individuals who had recently tested HIV positive in Banyuwangi, East Java, were women.[7] Most were migrant domestic workers and sex workers. The migrant domestic workers had been infected during employment in Taiwan and Hong Kong, some apparently through sexual contact with their employers or their employers' sons.[8]

Reports from several developed countries show that non-nationals are disproportionately affected by HIV and AIDS. In Japan, by the end of 2002 non-nationals accounted for 33 per cent of HIV cases and 72 per cent of the females infected with HIV, remarkably high rates in proportion to the 2 per cent foreign population in Japan (Japan Center for International Exchange, 2004). Several West European countries, e.g. Belgium, Norway, the UK and Switzerland, have been reporting for years that migrants were missing out on HIV prevention efforts, because they either find the efforts targeted at the 'general populations' in these countries inappropriate, or irrelevant, or because they fail to understand the relevant messages in a foreign language, and with foreign images.

When local counselling and testing facilities, and health services, fail to reach out to people of a different language and culture, these normally discover their HIV infection status later, and fail to receive early treatment (Haour-Knipe, 2000). More recently, several European countries have seen an increase in infections reported among people coming from countries with generalized epidemics, predominantly Sub-Saharan Africa (UNAIDS, 2004a), many of whom were unaware that they were infected. It is difficult to ascertain whether they arrived already infected, or became infected once in the destination countries.

It is frequently assumed that migrant men acquire HIV while away from home, and transmit the virus to their wives or partners on return. However, this assumption is being challenged by recent studies in South Africa (Lurie et al., 2003, Lurie, 2004). In a region with an advanced AIDS epidemic (at the end of 2003, South Africa reported HIV prevalence of 21.5 per cent (UNAIDS, 2004a)), studies of couples with only one infected partner revealed a surprising number where only the woman was HIV positive. The reasons have not yet been determined, but could be related to the fact that only about half of the migrant men sent money back home to their families, leaving their partners with little choice but to sell sex in order to support their families. Clearly, more research is needed to understand women's vulnerability, as both migrants and partners of migrant men.

THE INTERRELATIONSHIP BETWEEN HIV, AIDS AND CONFLICT

INCREASING attention has recently been given to the relationship between HIV and conflict situations.[9] There are several well known ways in which armed conflict can increase the risk of exposure to HIV infection, including disruption of traditional sexual norms when population displacement occurs in chaotic circumstances, and conditions of severe deprivation for women and girls, who may be coerced into exchanging sex for money, food or protection. The presence of large numbers of armed men in or out of uniform is often accompanied by the creation of a sex industry in the affected area, increasing the risk of HIV infection for both the sex workers and the men. Recourse to rape as a weapon or means of subjugation also multiplies the risk of HIV. In Rwanda, 17 per cent of the women who had been raped tested HIV positive, compared with 11 per cent of women who had not been raped (Spiegel, 2004).

7. *Reported in the Suara Pembaruan daily, a support magazine published by the NGO Yayasan Pelita Ilmu (Fernandez, 2004).*
8. *Indonesia Country Report to UN Special Rapporteur, 2003 (Fernandez, 2004).*
9. *See especially the section on AIDS and conflict, UNAIDS 2004 a, and Spiegel, 2004.*

Other risks are the result of collapsing health systems, including the breakdown of HIV prevention and care programmes, and safe blood transfusion systems. During the war in Sierra Leone, epidemiological surveillance in antenatal clinics showed that HIV prevalence rose from 4 to 7 per cent between 1995 and 1997, and that 11 per cent of the peacekeepers returning home to Nigeria from Sierra Leone were HIV positive - more than double the prevailing rate in Nigeria at the time (UNAIDS, 2004).

However, the interface between HIV and conflict is not a simple or uniform one. The factors that can increase HIV risk during conflicts are sketched in Textbox 20.1. Those that may decrease HIV transmission in such situations have received less attention. They include such structural factors as reduced mobility and accessibility (e.g. destroyed infrastructure reducing travel to high prevalence urban areas, displacement to remote locations) and, in the case of long-term post-emergency refugee camps, the possibility of improved protection, health, education, and social services. Key factors to be considered include HIV prevalence in affected communities prior to conflict, HIV prevalence in communities surrounding displaced populations, exposure to violence during conflict and flight, and the interaction between displaced persons and local communities (see **Figure 20.2**).

FIGURE 20.2

HIV RISK FACTORS: CONFLICT AND DISPLACED PERSONS

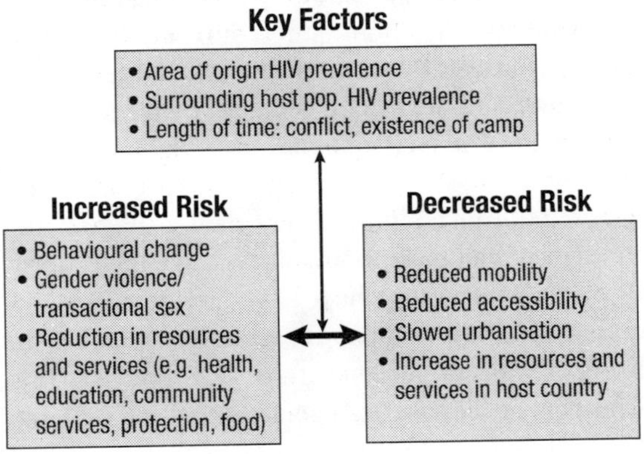

Source: Spiegel, 2004.

It is often assumed that because of the HIV vulnerability associated with conflict, refugees must have a higher rate of HIV prevalence than the surrounding host population, and that they exacerbate the epidemic. Recent studies by UNHCR are challenging this assumption, showing that globally people seeking asylum tend to move from countries of lower HIV prevalence to countries of higher prevalence. In Africa and in Europe especially, countries of asylum report levels of HIV prevalence higher than those that had prevailed in countries of origin (Spiegel, 2004).[10] A study carried out after the war in Sierra Leone in 2002 found that HIV infection levels were much lower (1-4%) than those documented during the conflict (Kaiser et al., 2002). Similarly, although Bosnia and Herzegovina was a war zone from 1992 to 1995, the country has continued to record very low HIV prevalence (0.0003% of the population in 2001) (UNAIDS, 2004a). The same appears to be true for Angola and southern Sudan.[11]

Studies of HIV prevalence among pregnant women recently carried out in more than 20 refugee camps

10. *In countries with more than 10,000 refugees, and for Africa in 2003, overall HIV prevalence was about 5.5 per cent in countries of asylum, compared with rates of just over 4 per cent in countries of origin. Figures for Europe are about one half of one per cent for countries of asylum compared to less than a quarter of one percent for the refugees' countries of origin.*

11. *Paul Spiegel, personal communication to the author.*

housing some 800,000 refugees in Kenya, Rwanda, Sudan and Tanzania show that three of the four countries' refugee populations had significantly lower HIV prevalence than the surrounding host communities.[12] Depending on their level of interaction and behaviour, refugees living for many years among a host population with higher HIV prevalence may become infected. When repatriation occurs, returning refugees may have a higher HIV prevalence than those who did not leave the country of origin; but they may have better HIV/AIDS knowledge and more consistently engage in protective behaviour than those who stayed. This appears to be the case in Angola (Spiegel and De Jong, 2003).

These counter-intuitive and paradoxical findings concerning HIV and conflict are important, as they go beyond myths and stereotypes to help increase understanding of the complex dynamics behind vulnerability. Most importantly, they point to areas where populations are liable to move between areas of different HIV prevalence, and where it will make a difference to intervene with prevention and care.

Uganda was one of the first countries to be affected by AIDS, but has managed to reduce its HIV prevalence from 18 per cent in 1990 to 6.2 per cent in 2003. It is often cited as an example of sustained success in addressing HIV and AIDS (UNAIDS, 2004). The government first established a National Committee for the Prevention of AIDS in 1985, and since then has pursued and strengthened policies to integrate HIV and AIDS awareness, counselling, treatment and prevention into all its activities. It has given strong political leadership on reducing the stigma attached to HIV and AIDS.

The right to state-provided health services is enshrined in the 1995 Constitution of the Republic of Uganda and, as of June 2004, free ARV treatment is becoming progressively available to those who need it. At the Bangkok AIDS conference, the Honourable Christine Amongin Aporu, State Minister for Disaster Preparedness and Refugees in Uganda, pointed out, however, that the country had not yet adequately integrated mobile and displaced populations into its HIV/AIDS strategies and programmes.

As of April 2004, Uganda, with a population of 26 million, counted almost two million refugees and IDPs, including over 1.6 million people displaced by the Lord's Resistance Army in north and northeastern Uganda, most of them women and children. Every evening some 44,000 children and youth leave their homes to seek safety in the towns for the night. The risks for such young IDPs are very high. They include psychological and physical trauma, hopelessness, stigmatization and lack of education when schools close and teachers flee to safer locations. HIV-related risks include rape, as well as the necessity to sell sex in exchange for food or protection. Contraceptive use is limited, fertility rates are high, and the likelihood that HIV will be transmitted from mother to child is also high as appropriate care is lacking.

The impediments to AIDS prevention in such circumstances are manifold; starting with the prioritization of immediate basic needs, that pushes AIDS to a distant level of priority. As the situation continues, poverty and chronic insecurity give rise to hopelessness and demoralization, making it less likely for IDPs to take up opportunities to receive counselling. Such opportunities can also be hampered by the difficulty of establishing programmes in insecure areas, or maintaining health units when health workers flee, and impassable roads that make the effective use of mobile clinics impossible. Funds to finance HIV and AIDS activities in refugee settlements and IDP camps are lacking, and the cost of HIV and AIDS treatment is prohibitive. Even gathering the evidence on which to base programmes may be difficult, since data regarding HIV and AIDS in camps is unreliable as IDPs frequently move on in search of safety.

12. *For example, prevalence was estimated to be 5 per cent among the 80,000 refugees in Kakuma camp in northwest Kenya in 2002, compared to 18 per cent in the surrounding Lodwar district. Among the 120,000 refugees in the Dadaab camp on the opposite side of the country, HIV prevalence was estimated at 0.6 per cent in 2003, compared with 4 per cent in neighbouring Garissa in 2002 (Spiegel, 2004).*

TEXTBOX 20.1

HIV/AIDS in Uganda

Uganda was one of the first countries to be affected by AIDS, but has managed to reduce its HIV prevalence from 18 per cent in 1990 to 6.2 per cent in 2003. It is an excellent example of sustained success in addressing HIV/AIDS (UNAIDS, 2004). The government first established a National Committee for the Prevention of AIDS in 1985, and since then has pursued and strengthened policies to integrate HIV/AIDS awareness, counselling, treatment and prevention into all its activities. It has given strong political leadership on reducing the HIV/AIDS stigma.

The right to state-provided health services is enshrined in the 1995 Constitution of the Republic of Uganda and, as of June 2004, free ARV treatment is becoming progressively available to those who need it. In her presentation at the Bangkok AIDS conference, the Honourable Christine Amongin Aporu, State Minister for Disaster Preparedness and Refugees in Uganda, pointed out, however, that the country had not yet adequately integrated mobile and displaced populations into its HIV/AIDS strategies and programmes.

As of April 2004, Uganda, with a population of 26 million, counted almost two million refugees and IDPs, including over 1.6 million people displaced by the Lords Resistance Army in north and northeastern Uganda, most of them women and children. Every evening some 44,000 children and youths leave their homes to seek safety in the towns for the night. The risks for such young IDPs are very high. They include psychological and physical trauma, hopelessness, stigmatization and lack of education when schools close and teachers flee to safer locations. HIV-related risks include rape, as well as the necessity to sell sex in exchange for food or protection. Contraceptive use is limited, fertility rates are high, and the likelihood that HIV will be transmitted from mother to child is also high as appropriate care is lacking.

KEY CHALLENGES

Key challenges to addressing HIV and AIDS within the context of migration include inadequate and inappropriate attention, stigma and discrimination, and the lack of access to prevention, care and support available to migrants.

INADEQUATE ATTENTION TO HIV/AIDS AND MIGRATION

The last few years have seen a massive increase in donor funding of HIV and AIDS initiatives. Bilateral aid has risen from USD 822 million in 2000 to USD 1.35 billion in 2002, a 64 per cent increase over three years, while multilateral aid rose from USD 314 million to USD 460 million during the same period. Contributions to the Global Fund to Fight AIDS, TB and Malaria reached USD 917 million by the end of 2002 (UNAIDS, 2004b). Encouraging as this may seem, it must be seen against other efforts taking place – or not taking place – to reduce the global inequalities that fuel the epidemic. For example, the cost of debt servicing in developing countries clearly affects the amount of money available for health and social services: Zambia, for instance, a country with almost one million HIV-positive people, spends 30 per cent more on servicing its debt than on health.[13] Cameroon spends 3.5 times as much on debt repayment as on health, and Mali spends 1.6 times as much (Oxfam, 2002).[14]

HIV rates continue to rise, and total funding is still far short of what is needed to combat the epidemic. UNAIDS recently estimated that the USD 4.7 billion committed to HIV and AIDS in 2003 would need to be doubled by 2005 to fund treatment and prevention programmes. The need will double again by 2007 (UNAIDS, 2004). Given the shortfall, efforts are being made to ensure efficient use of resources and improved coordination among donors: a recent encouraging development has been widespread support for the 'three ones' approach at country level. Key principles of the "three ones" are one agreed HIV/AIDS action framework, one national AIDS coordinating authority, and one country-level monitoring and evaluation system (ibid).

But Michael O'Dwyer, Senior Health and Population Adviser, DFID Southeast Asia, questions to what extent, if any, these rapidly growing resources are being used to address the needs of mobile and displaced populations. At the Bangkok AIDS conference, O'Dwyer pointed out that the coordinated 'three ones' approaches will not meet the needs of migrant populations, unless the needs are explicitly addressed in a national strategy and action framework. Precisely this is lacking: countries' resources have been allocated to nationals, neglecting people just passing through. Although the Declaration of Commitment by the UN General Assembly requires countries 'By 2005, (to) develop and begin to implement national, regional and international strategies that facilitate access to HIV/AIDS prevention programs for migrants and mobile workers, including the provision of information on health and social services",[15] by 2003 fewer than half had done so. Only 47 per cent of the states responding to the Secretary General's survey reported having an HIV prevention policy for cross-border migrants (UNAIDS, 2004a). In countries such as Malaysia, migrant workers do not feature in the National HIV/AIDS Strategic Plan, although more than 20 per cent of the population comprises migrants. The situation is similar for refugees.[16]

Cynthia Maung, Director of the Mae Tao Clinic, Mae Sot, Thailand, and recipient of the 1999 Jonathan Mann Award for health and human rights, brought these observations into vivid perspective at the XV AIDS conference in her discussion of the particularly marginal condition of internally displaced populations and migrant communities in Thailand, another country cited as successfully addressing AIDS. Approximately two million migrant workers from Cambodia, Laos and Myanmar live in Thailand. Most are not registered by the government and thus have no access to the Thai public health system. Such populations are overlooked in national HIV surveillance.

The HIV epidemics in China and India are expanding, but the regions bordering Myanmar face the worst localized epidemics in both countries, and Burmese communities on the Thai-Myanmar border also face a generalized epidemic.[17] The neighbouring countries of Thailand and Cambodia have reversed their HIV epidemics over the past decade through major investment in prevention strategies, in particular condom promotion, but there has been little effort to address the HIV and AIDS-related needs of communities on the other side of the borders. Lack of access to the Thai public health system hinders the communities' ability to address such public health and social issues as

13. *In 2004 the proportion of government revenue absorbed by debt was expected to rise to 32 per cent (Oxfam, 2002; World Bank/IMF/IDA, 2003, cited in UNAIDS 2004 , p. 148).*

14. *Along similar lines, Kenya spends USD 0.76 per capita on AIDS, and USD12.92 per capita on debt repayments (Kimalu, 2002, cited in UNAIDS 2004, p. 148); and the first 14 countries identified as key recipients of the United States President's Emergency Plan for AIDS Relief together spent USD 9.1 billion in servicing their debt in 2001 (Ogden and Esim, 2003, cited in UNAIDS 2004, p. 148).*

15. *Para. 50, United Nations General Assembly. Declaration of Commitment on HIV/AIDS. UN, 2001.*

16. *Of the 29 countries in Africa with more than 10,000 refugees, UNHCR has been able to review 22 National HIV/AIDS Strategic Plans. While 14 mention refugees, 8 fail to do so. Of those that do mention refugees, 4 fail to list the specific activities planned (Spiegel and Nankoe, 2004).*

17. *For example, the Mae Sot clinic, which provides antenatal services to over 2,000 people from Myanmar per year, has noted a rise in HIV prevalence among pregnant women from 0.8 per cent in 1999 to 1.5 per cent in 2004. Data from the clinic's blood donor programme show a similar trend, reaching 1.6 per cent in 2004.*

drug and alcohol abuse, gender-based violence, teenage pregnancy and unsafe abortions. When services are available, language barriers, fear of police, lack of transportation and the negative attitudes of health workers and employers can still pose significant barriers. Migrants often delay the decision to seek health care, leaving minor illnesses untreated until they become severe enough to require emergency care.

Maung pointed out that services for voluntary HIV counselling and testing for migrant workers are lacking within the Thai public health system. Grass-roots health organizations have recently begun to offer such services, but interest remains low because of community stigmatization, and the few options available for treatment. There is little job security, and migrants fear they may lose their positions if found to be HIV positive. In addition, although many of the Burmese fled their country for political reasons, they are not systematically recognized as refugees, but considered 'illegal migrant workers'. This means the host government cannot recognize the grass-roots organizations that serve them: for example, the 'back-pack' health teams working with the Mae Tao Clinic have no official status, and their training certificates are not recognized.

The long-term consequences of such marginalization are potentially grave: denied official status, the children of such unrecognized populations face the same barriers to health and education - cycles of vulnerability thus continue when the status of migrants is linked to access to health services and to education.

INAPPROPRIATE PUBLIC ATTENTION TO AIDS AND MIGRATION

It is rare in any country to find recognition of the wide range of migration issues within the HIV and AIDS discourse, in particular recognition of the ways in which migration can be an integral part of poverty alleviation and international development. Instead, there is a widespread perception that migrants consume more than their share of limited resources and contribute disproportionately to the spread of diseases. A number of factors contribute to this perception, including governments' lack of capacity to carry out the epidemiological analysis that can put HIV prevalence in perspective, and unwillingness to devote scarce resources to meet the needs of 'alien' populations.

The Bangkok AIDS conference symposium on migration stressed that stigma can be a major handicap to addressing AIDS and migration. In the words of Irene Fernandez, Chair of CARAM-Asia and recipient of the 2002 Jonathan Mann Award for health and human rights: "Migrants are seen as aliens or outsiders, as people who do not belong to our community or nation. Political leaders refer to them as 'illegals'. There is no such thing as an illegal human being on earth, but we have drawn our territorial boundaries according to countries, and the right to stay is determined by fulfilling conditions established by the countries."

Fernandez pointed out that the media in many countries often portray migrants as responsible for an increase in crime rates or diseases in the country - especially of communicable diseases. She noted that the Malaysian government, among others, carries out raids at entertainment centres, during which foreign women are arrested and detained. The result is not only stigmatization of foreign women but also arbitrary arrest, detention and deportation. Stigma and discrimination have long been recognized as a constraint to identifying the people who need prevention, care or treatment services in the first place, and to gaining access to such services thereafter. It was noted that stigmatization and discrimination against migrants are pervasive, including among health workers.

The speakers also pointed out that governments have often dealt with the issue of AIDS and migration by imposing requirements for HIV testing of immigrants. CARAM-Asia noted that many receiving countries in Southeast and Northeast Asia, as well as in the Middle East, require overseas semi-skilled and unskilled migrant workers to undergo testing for HIV and other infectious diseases. CARAM noted that such testing is often carried out with a patent disregard for good practice, including informed consent and pre- and post-test counselling.

CONCLUSION

THIS CHAPTER has explored the relationship between HIV/AIDS and migration, in particular those factors driving migration that can also increase migrants' vulnerability to HIV, such as human rights abuses, economic deprivation, social inequality and socio-economic instability.[18] It has shown how mobile persons can become vulnerable to HIV through the migration process itself, and that this can be gender-differentiated. Women may well be vulnerable as migrants and as partners of migrants, but can also become vulnerable when their partners have migrated. There is need for wider research on the situation of women migrants.

The complex relationship between conflict and HIV/AIDS has been illustrated by a case study from Uganda. Recent evidence shows that in some situations, and for reasons about which one can only hypothesize at this stage, populations isolated in regions of protracted conflict may actually be *protected* from HIV.

Government policies on HIV and AIDS have to date given limited attention to migrants.[19] In some receiving countries migrants lack access to health and social services; they may fear host country authorities, including health authorities, and often suffer from discrimination by employers, police, social services and a wide range of others, including health workers. Some key challenges in this regard are discussed in the context of Burmese migrants in Thailand.

The chapter describes AIDS as a long and slow event, hard to perceive or measure other than in retrospect (Barnett and Whiteside, 2002), thus highlighting the need to plan and react long before the full effects become apparent. Some of this planning should focus on the larger global problems, such as reducing economic imbalances, or shifting expenditure from debt servicing to public health, fostering the poverty alleviation effects of migration, and preventing and resolving conflicts. A first direct policy priority is to ensure that migration is included in national AIDS Strategic Plans and proposals to funding institutions such as the Global Fund to Fight AIDS, TB and Malaria. HIV and AIDS issues should also be factored into migration policymaking and actions to address the consequences of natural disasters, conflict, development or any other actions or events that cause population movement.

Related to this is the need to improve the evidence base by gathering HIV and AIDS epidemiological data that take account of migration, analysing social and economic factors that increase HIV vulnerability and transmission, qualitative research around some of the surprising findings presented in this discussion, and comprehensive reviews that will feed policy formulation.

Effective prevention policies begin with an assessment of who should best be targeted. For example, although women are especially vulnerable in this area, it would be unfair and inappropriate to place sole responsibility for AIDS prevention on them. Clearly, men should also be engaged. A basic policy dilemma in AIDS prevention is whether to focus on populations seen to be particularly at risk, or to expand the focus to others. The chapter gives some policy guidance on this: HIV risks created by mobility concern not only those who are mobile, but also surrounding communities and communities of origin. AIDS prevention efforts should thus address all affected parties on the migration continuum.

Another key policy challenge is how to address the 'double stigma' of the disease and the 'foreignness' of migrants. International efforts to reduce the stigma

18. *Among the many themes the chapter was unable to cover is the migration of health workers. Critically important to efforts led by WHO to assure that 3 million people in developing countries are on antiretroviral therapy by the year 2005 is the availability of health personnel to correctly administer and monitor such treatment. One way to ensure such availability would be to reverse the loss of health personnel from developing countries, recruited to work in developed countries, or in the private sector in their own countries. See also the chapters "Investing in Migration Health" and "Balancing the Benefits and Costs of Skilled Migration in the Asia-Pacific Region".*

19. *This is true even of those governments with reportedly successful HIV and AIDS policies, such as Uganda and Thailand.*

related to HIV and AIDS provide some useful lessons, among them that interventions for AIDS prevention must be rights-based, i.e. based on the principle that the right to information and protection applies to all. This can help reduce the stigmatization of particular individuals or groups for 'spreading AIDS'. It can also increase empowerment, self-esteem and confidence in health systems, leading more people to seek and receive information on HIV prevention, as well as counselling and care.

Active outreach with HIV and AIDS prevention information is important, but policy changes to reduce risk and vulnerability in the first place are even more important. Such changes may include straightforward measures to protect the safety of women and girls in refugee camps, or more complex ones such as modifying policies concerning single sex labour migration, improving access to education and housing, and supporting income generation. More fundamentally, they could address the root causes of risk and vulnerability, or help control the 'worst forms' of migration - such as trafficking and forced migration – that create situations where individuals are highly vulnerable to acquiring HIV, and unable to adopt safe behaviours.

One policy option that attracts expert consensus concerns blocking the virus from entering a country by barring access to people who are HIV-infected: WHO and UNAIDS have strongly advised in a number of UN fora and documents that HIV/AIDS-related travel restrictions have no public health justification.[20] The potential health consequences of purely control-oriented approaches are negative: they are highly unlikely to effectively exclude all HIV-infected travellers, they undermine public health efforts at HIV prevention and care by driving people underground where their clandestine status excludes them from accessing services, they encourage nationals to see HIV and AIDS as 'foreign problems', and they divert funds that could more efficiently be allocated to prevention and care programmes.

Finally, there is the critical issue of migrant access to care and treatment for HIV. World economic imbalances and inequalities create differences in access to ARV therapy, which means that death rates for HIV-infected adults in low- and middle-income countries are now up to 20 times higher than in industrialized countries. The reasons for addressing inequalities between developed and developing countries may well be ethical, but they are also practical. With easy access to information, it would be natural for those who can do so to migrate in search of the life-saving treatment they know is available elsewhere.

Migration to developed countries for access to care is a poor solution, since it can add to xenophobia, as migrants are seen as a burden on health resources. In developing countries, it can perpetuate inequalities, since it is beyond the means of most people requiring treatment. From a public health perspective such migration is even potentially dangerous, as migrants without regular status are likely to receive non-mainstream treatment that is irregular, inadequate and haphazard, ultimately leading to new strains of HIV that become resistant to ARV. These new pathogens will in turn travel, affecting more people in other places. Mobile populations, including refugees, must be included in strategies to make HIV and AIDS treatment available globally. In the words of the authors cited at the beginning of this chapter, "Health and well-being are not individual concerns: they are global issues... [they] are human rights; they are also public goods... like the road networks, clean air and clean water.(...). President Franklin Roosevelt said: "We have always known that heedless self-interest was bad morals; we now know that it is also bad economics."[21]

20. *For a review of the issues and relevant documents see 'UNAIDS/ IOM statement on HIV-related travel restrictions, June 2004'; www.iom.ch/en/PDF_Files/HIVAIDS/UNAIDS_IOM_statement_travel_restrictions.pdf or www.unaids.org/en/other/functionalities/ViewDocument.asp?href=http://gva-doc-owl/WEBcontent/Documents/pub/UNA-docs/UNAIDS-IOM_Travel-Restrictions_en.pdf>*

21. *Roosevelt (cited in Navarro, 1998). Cited by Barnett and Whiteside, 2002, p. 348.*

Institutional Measures to Manage Migration

Chapter 21
Managing Migration in the Wake of September 11: Implications for a Cost-Benefit Analysis [1]

Deterrent actions in the migration sector at a time of high concern over security may not necessarily follow the same logic as for internal management actions related to social benefits management.

INTRODUCTION

A PUBLIC survey conducted in the US in 2004 asked the question: "Should governments spend more to prevent illegal immigration?"[2] The response among the groups surveyed was divided, with over half (55 per cent) of non-immigrants, and over a third (34 per cent) of immigrants responding in the affirmative. The fact that such a question was debated publicly is instructive.

A country's citizenry usually expects some tangible results from its government's investment in migration management; and governments usually consider the costs and benefits of managing migration in financial, social and political terms. Government officials try to justify their policies and resource investments in terms of measurable benefits to society, including in the less easily "measurable" areas of social stability and national security, but also weighed against commitments to international principles of protection of migrants' and refugees' rights.

This chapter examines the rationale for governments' continual investment in certain areas of migration management, and how applicable a tool cost-benefit analysis is to evaluate these measures. It looks specifically at costs and benefits of controlling or reducing irregular migration. It concludes that, while all investments must have discernible benefits, a straightforward expenditure/benefit relationship in this area of migration management may not always be possible or expected, and that the parameters have changed since September 11 with the new focus on security. It highlights examples and suggests how these might inform policy and programming in the area of technical assistance for migration management.

WHY INVEST IN IMPROVED MIGRATION MANAGEMENT SYSTEMS?

WHAT ARE some of today's driving forces and rationales behind the ongoing investment of human, financial and political capital in managing migration? Recent events such as September 11, and several key policy papers provide some pointers on this for migration policymakers.

In the US, the terrorist attacks of September 11, 2001, led to the creation of the Department of Homeland Security (DHS) in October 2001, representing the largest government reorganization undertaken in the US since 1947. The DHS 2004 budget of USD 36.2 billion, of which USD 18.1 billion are directed to securing the nation's Borders and Transportation

1. *The authors of this chapter are Charles Harns, Head, Technical Cooperation for Migration Service Area, IOM Geneva, and Maureen Achieng, IOM Chief of Mission, Port au Prince.*

2. *Refer to the Immigration Survey, National Public Radio/Kaiser Family Foundation/Kennedy School of Government, 2004.*

Systems (BTS), and USD 1.8 billion to improving immigration services, represents an increase of 7.4 per cent over FY 2003 and over 64 per cent over FY 2002 for such activities (DHS, 2004a). Another element of this same strategy is the establishment or reorientation of some foreign assistance budget lines towards efforts to build anti-terrorism capacities in other states, with the aim of producing multiple benefits (Taylor, 2004).

Similarly, in the aftermath of the events of September 11, 2001, Citizenship and Immigration Canada (CIC) announced a five-part strategy as part of the Canadian government's Anti-Terrorism Plan, including a commitment to invest approximately CAD 49 million to, among other things, strengthen CIC's abilities to increase detention capacity and deportations. The outlay included the addition of up to one hundred new staff to enforce upgraded security at ports of entry (Government of Canada, 2001).

Looking to the European Union, the objective of its new framework for relations with its eastern and southern neighbours,[3] outlined in the Wider Europe Communication (Commission of the European Communities, 2003), is to develop a zone of prosperity and a friendly neighbourhood with which the EU can enjoy close, peaceful and cooperative relations. This Wider Europe Communication, which builds on the experience of the earlier PHARE, TACIS and INTERREG programmes,[4] seeks, inter alia, to promote stability and prosperity within and beyond the new borders of the EU in order to avoid drawing new dividing lines in Europe. It further contends that the EU's capacity to provide security, stability and sustainable development to its citizens will 'no longer be distinguishable from its interest in close cooperation with its neighbours'.

Behind the objectives of this Wider Europe Communication is the recognition of differences in living standards across the EU's borders with its neighbours, which would create challenges in various areas of governance, necessitating efficient and secure border management to protect shared borders and facilitate legitimate trade and passage. A key focus for the New Neighbourhood Instrument is more efficient border management given its recognized importance for joint prosperity and security. The principal aim is to facilitate trade and secure the EU's borders against smuggling, trafficking, organized crime, terrorist threats and irregular immigration (including in transit).

A key external relations priority of the EU is to promote stability and peace in southeastern Europe (western Balkans),[5] in order to bring the region into line with its wider objective of security and prosperity across the continent. To this end, a total of EUR 6.8 billion has been committed to that region since 1991. Starting in 2000, aid to southeastern Europe was to be streamlined through the Community Assistance for Reconstruction, Development and Stability in the Balkans (CARDS) programme.[6]

Administrative capacity building, one of six main sectors of cooperation, seeks to strengthen public institutions deemed necessary for the countries of the CARDS region to develop closer ties with the EU within the framework of the Stabilisation and Association (SAP)[7] process, and integrated border management is stated as one of several key activities.

The rationales for investing in improved migration management are remarkably consistent across countries, namely to reduce irregular movement and the influence of criminal groups in those movements,

3. *These include the western countries of the former Soviet Union, the western Balkans and the Mediterranean.*

4. *INTERREG Community Initiative: a financial instrument within the framework of the European Union's Structural Funds which supports cross-border and transnational cooperation among Member States and neighbouring countries.*
PHARE Cross-Border Cooperation (CBC) programmes: this was a pre-accession driven instrument in the candidate countries, which sought to support cross-border cooperation with Member States and between candidate countries.
TACIS Cross-Border Cooperation (CBC) programme: supports cross-border cooperation in the eastern border regions of Russia, Belarus, Ukraine and Moldova.

5. *Covering Albania, Bosnia and Herzegovina, Croatia, Macedonia, Serbia and Montenegro.*

6. *Adopted with the Council Resolution (EC) No 2666/2000 of 5 December 2000. See also the chapter "Migrants in an Enlarged Europe".*

7. *This term relates to the EU strategy for and EU membership perspectives of Albania, Bosnia and Herzegovina, Croatia, Macedonia, and Serbia and Montenegro.*

reduce security weaknesses in the migration sector, encourage migration as a tool for economic development, and ensure the protection of the most vulnerable migrants (UK Home Office, 2002b). Achieving these ends implies investments, choices based on priorities and expected outcomes, and some discernible relationship between costs and benefits.

COSTS AND BENEFITS

THE NEED to justify public spending, the limited resources resulting from governments' competing spending priorities, and the increasing focus on migration management in most countries, are all factors influencing any attempt at cost-benefit analysis in this area. Experience suggests that this may be an ambitious undertaking: a cost-benefit analysis in the area of migration management, assuming that the essential data are available, may, at best, produce approximations rather than exact ratios.

For one, there are no clear definitions of costs and benefits. What constitutes a cost in one context may not necessarily be one in another context. For instance, while erecting an electric fence to deter illegal entries obviously involves a cost, does a higher death toll resulting from migrants using more dangerous routes count equally as a cost? (The trebling of the number of agents stationed along the Mexican-US border in the 1990s is said to have resulted in an increase in the death toll related to illegal migration (Martin, 2003).) Such an exercise is further complicated by the difficulty in determining the dependent variables, including the policy goals to be achieved, and the fact that these, even in the same political context, change over relatively short periods of time (ibid).

Migration policies often pursue multiple goals, making it necessary to determine which of the competing goals is to be given highest priority, and, in turn, which costs should be factored in. Also, while it may be possible in some instances to identify benefits derived from increased enforcement, the question of how to ascribe a quantitative value to the benefit to enable a comparison of costs and benefits, is much less straightforward.

For example:
In the *US*, about half of the budget of the former US Immigration and Naturalization Service (INS) is estimated to have been spent on preventing illegal immigration in recent years. This figure grew twenty-fold in two decades, from USD 250 million in 1980 to USD 5 billion in 2000. Yet, in the same period, the estimated number of illegal foreigners rose from 3 to 9 million, despite several regularization programmes. This increase in irregular immigration, as borne out by the number of apprehensions for the same period – 910,361 in 1980, compared with 1,814,729 in 2000 (Briggs Jr., 2003) – partly explains the major increase in investment. Earlier assessments of the Border Patrol, responsible for monitoring the long borders with Mexico and Canada, had revealed chronic underfunding and understaffing, which also account in part for this significant increase in spending.

Canada appears to demonstrate a close relationship between official migration goals and actual outcomes. But this may have as much to do with the fact that Canada does not have a land border with a major emigration country, and that its immigration policy favours the admission of skilled foreigners, as it does with the effectiveness of immigration enforcement measures. This positive outlook notwithstanding, in a 2003 report on the efficiency and effectiveness of the control and enforcement measures by Citizenship and Immigration Canada[8] (CIC) the Auditor General of Canada notes that enforcement is under increasing stress and is falling behind in some areas.

The *UK*, like the US, places strong emphasis on its immigration controls at the border, more recently adding carrier sanctions to make airlines, shipping

8. *Refer the Office of the Auditor General of Canada, 2003, "Report of the Auditor General of Canada to the House of Commons", Chapter 5: Citizenship and Immigration Canada – Control and Enforcement, Ottawa.*

companies, railway and track operators bear the cost of careful screening. Its Immigration and Nationality Directorate (IND) in the Home Office spent USD 5 billion in 2002 on immigration enforcement and asylum support. Supporting the work at the borders are the internal enforcement and compliance mechanisms. One of the most pressing issues is that of in-country management, which includes benefits entitlement to migrants and removals and returns of some cases (UK Home Office, 2002a). This area of migration management may be well suited for activities to be shaped and evaluated by traditional cost/benefit analysis.

One tool used by the IND to resolve the caseload of migrants who do not qualify to be served through the asylum system or to remain in the country under another status, is the use of a Voluntary Assisted Return Programme (VARP). The goal of VARP is to provide a humane and cost-effective means of returning these migrants to their home countries. The UK finds that "VARP provided significant cost-savings for IND in comparison with the alternative of removing unsuccessful asylum seekers following the completion of the asylum process" (UK Home Office, 2002a).

The driving forces behind current priority policy and operational initiatives are many, but illegal migration and the links between weak migration management and security breaches and, from the in-country management perspective, abuses of asylum and migrant benefit systems, are two key concerns for policy makers today. Each may require a different approach to cost/benefit analysis.

COSTS AND BENEFITS OF INTERNATIONAL DETERRENCE

FOR THE PURPOSE of this discussion, international deterrence of illegal migration includes actions to build and sustain capacity for detection, interdiction and removal of migrants with no right to enter or remain in the country. The arguments for deterrence have varied over time, both in intensity and in rationale. Prior to September 11, 2001, the rationale was based largely on the perceived threats to economic and social order posed by large numbers of persons entering and, at times, taking up residence without permission, and accessing social benefits while their status was being determined. Irregular immigration did not affect all countries in the same way; it was treated as a minor annoyance by some receiving states and as a major challenge to sovereignty by others. Some major source countries saw it as neither, preferring to redefine it as the natural social order and a mechanism working towards more global economic equity and, from that perspective, essentially a human rights issue.

Few governments were consistent on the matter. Although some states felt challenged and violated by this migration, they nonetheless often gave mixed signals, for example by refusing to crack down on employers of irregular migrants. Some states promoted a human rights approach but practised questionable human rights standards for minorities in their own countries, and at times engaged in the same expulsion or deportation practices they criticized in others.

September 11 changed the entire debate considerably. National security, and the security of one's allies, became the dominant rationale for improved international deterrence systems. While the responses naturally focused most directly on the protection of the US, the implications and actions at other, more vulnerable points along migration routes across the world were an integral consideration from the start. Thus, the responses gradually became global in nature with complementing activities even in far-away locations such as Central and South Asia, East Africa, Australia and in places closer to the US, including parts of South and Central America and the Caribbean, and in all of Europe.

Rather than displace the arguments around the general challenges of illegal migration, the security agenda added a new and decisive rationale for improving measures to deter illegal entry and residence. At the same time, the possible connection between terrorism, smuggling, trafficking and other transnational organized crime exerted its influence (Reuters, 7 September 2004). Irregular border crossing and residence had to be addressed much more strongly. The 'cost' factor of this equation moved well beyond the economic arguments for or against illegal migration that preceded the terrorist attacks. The costs became as compelling as the images of the falling twin towers, and the benefits as compelling as the prevention of similar events. In this new paradigm, all reasonable action would be taken and, within that mandate, the costs would be managed as best as possible.

There are a number of striking examples of the resulting actions in this area, and each sheds light on the argument that the costs of inaction, or inadequate action, are perceived to be so high that significant investments are justified, and that a direct relationship between investment and payoff is not an appropriate measure to apply.

One example is the US effort to strengthen its capacity to identify *mala fide* persons during border checkpoint procedures. An important feature of this effort is the US-VISIT[9] programme's initiative to capture biometric indicators from most persons entering and departing through US checkpoints. While this had already been conceptualized one year prior to the September 11 attacks, the extent and speed of its implementation were strongly influenced by these events. The cost of the programme in 2004 was estimated at USD 328 million (Associated Press, 9 March, 2004). In the first nine months of its use that year, 280 persons with significant criminal records were identified as they attempted to enter the US (*International Herald Tribune*, 7 October 2004).

While the maths are easy, the basis for judging overall cost/benefit is not, nor is it meant to be a simple relationship. The US-VISIT's goals are to track the entry and exit of individuals, but it is also meant as an aid to internal enforcement of visa overstayers. The September 11 hijackers had entered the US with visas, and several had overstayed the visa timelines; thus, in addition to discovering *mala fide* travellers at the entry point, US-VISIT will be a significant tool to discover and investigate such overstayers. It is explained and defended in those terms, among others (DHS, 2004b). The costs per interdiction action in the pilot year are high and presumably will decrease over time. Sensitivity to costs is certainly part of management vision, and costs are managed in part through the usual competitive processes with the private sector firms involved. However, there is no target figure that the identification of *mala fide* travellers, including possible terrorists, must reach to justify the programme.

By comparison, cost-benefit analysis prior to September 11 did not have the weight of national security pressing on the scales, and justification in precise financial terms was more feasible and more defensible. An example of this is found in the Danish experience with airline liaison officers in the mid- to late 1990s. Starting in 1995, the Danish government decided to post immigration attachés abroad in strategically selected embassies. A few years into the experiment, a cost-benefit analysis was commissioned to assess the efficacy of this means of deterring irregular immigration into Denmark.

The costs behind all cases of impeded irregular immigration into Denmark that could be directly attributed to an immigration attaché were compared with the likely costs of asylum processing, upkeep at asylum centres and social/unemployment benefits, if

9. *"US-VISIT" is the Visitor and Immigrant Status Indicator Technology System (Department of Homeland Security).*

the attempted irregular entry had succeeded. Even though the final report pointed to significant savings as a result of the posting of immigration attachés, there was some doubt about the method of computation on the grounds that, a) it was not possible to attribute any case of impeded irregular immigration wholly to one factor (in this case the immigration attaché) and, b) the stated cost of upkeep of an irregular entrant is only an estimate, and therefore far from accurate. The ensuing discussion over the report's findings led to the eventual phasing out of the immigration attaché positions three years after they were first introduced (Afgivet af Udlændingestyrelsen, 1997).

COSTS AND BENEFITS OF INTERNAL PROCESSING AND CONTROL ACTIONS

IMPROVEMENT of the in-country control and tracking of migrants' benefits is another important pillar of migration management. These social benefits are most often linked with asylum processing and can include direct support payments alongside medical, housing and other forms of state-subsidized support. Perceived or actual abuse or mismanagement in this area often leads to calls for reform, supported by estimates of financial losses if policies, systems and procedures are not improved.

A recent example of reform activity in this area supported by cost/benefit analysis are the efforts of the IND in the UK in implementing the Immigration Biometric Identification Programme (IBI), a system to secure migrant beneficiaries' identities and manage their access to benefits. Within a remarkably short time, and still during the initial deployment phases, this system was reported to be saving GBP 120,000 per week in support payments, with a registered caseload of 40,000 claimants. Start-up costs were estimated at GBP 24 million, with GBP 15 million continuing costs (United Kingdom Parliament, 2004). Given that the initially reported savings were based on less than total deployment, and that operating costs were anticipated to decline over time, the investment is defensible in purely financial cost/benefit terms.

Another area of internal migration control is that of identifying and removing visa overstayers, particularly those working without authorization. Australia's Department of Immigration and Multicultural and Indigenous Affairs (DIMIA) is focusing increased attention on this. Noting that "locating and removing overstayers and people in breach of their visa conditions from Australia costs the taxpayer millions of dollars each year" (DIMIA, 2004), DIMIA has initiated a number of strategies, including an internet-based, real-time entitlement checking system that allows employers and licensing authorities to check a potential employee's right to work in Australia before he/she is employed. This is a free, 24-hour service. In addition, a special call-in line has been created to report persons who may be working illegally. These initiatives are too new for a cost-benefit analysis at this stage, but have a certain in-built cost-benefit rationale, also based on other deterrence-by-example experiences.[10] While they add to the immediate cost of locating and removing overstayers (by adding new administrative mechanisms), they are intended to reduce the number of such persons in the country and diminish the attractiveness of overstaying for others, thereby ultimately reducing the problem and the overall investment in this area of internal control.

CONCLUSION

THE CURRENT migration landscape compels governments across the globe to continuously examine their migration management systems at points of origin, transit or destination for their sustained ability to tackle the complex interrelationship of migration with other policy priorities, such as security.

10. *An example is the reduction in unauthorized boat arrivals in Australia in 2001-2002 following more stringent measures (see the sub-chapter "Oceania Migration Dynamics").*

Responding to this challenge requires significant investments out of limited resources, for which there are competing priorities. Against this background, the value of cost-benefit analyses in the field of migration management would seem evident if governments are to take informed decisions regarding the allocation of resource to competing areas of governance, and in view of the range of possible actions.

However, it appears that accurate cost-benefit analyses are particularly difficult to apply to the deterrence and security aspects of migration management. This seems to reduce their value as the primary basis for decision making in these areas. Rather, governments opt for the most reasonable measures in response to the immediate migration challenges, and try to ensure the lowest possible cost for these interventions through competitive bidding processes, routine reviews and *ex post* evaluations.

By contrast, for the internal management of migrant benefits and other internal control and enforcement mechanisms (e.g. assisted voluntary return as a cost-effective alternative to prolonged welfare support, detention and deportation (IOM, 2004)), there is a good case that cost-benefit analysis is both justified and possible. Essentially, this is a matter of "comparing apples with apples"; comparing financial outlays in status benefits with financial outlays for system improvements that reduce financial fraud and misuse.

In sum, deterrent actions in the migration sector at a time of high concern over security may not necessarily follow the same logic as for internal management actions related to social benefits management. As the costs of abuse of social benefits are largely financial, the remedial actions are shaped and measurable in those terms. Costs of lapses in security related to migration management are, justifiably, measured along different and multiple lines, as are the benefits to be reaped from improved security.

TEXTBOX 21.1

VISA SYSTEMS IN THE 21ST CENTURY – THE AUSTRALIAN MODEL

People today move for tourism, business or social purposes on a scale and at a speed much greater than most permanent immigration movements, putting increasing pressure on immigration authorities to facilitate this movement quickly and satisfactorily. But governments also need to ensure that migration is orderly, safe and non-threatening to society and the individual concerned. Visas are still among the most effective ways to manage cross-border movements. But how to design them to be quick, efficient yet vigilant at the same time?

The Australian Department of Immigration, Multicultural and Indigenous Affairs (DIMIA) has resorted to some useful and efficiency boosting strategies to achieve this balance.

Challenges Facing Immigration Authorities

Immigration authorities in any destination country are pulled in two directions:

To facilitate regular migration: service industries such as tourism and international education, businesses reliant on quick recruitment of overseas skilled workers, and family sponsors all want visas faster and more conveniently. Businesses are driven by the fact that, as workforces in developed countries age, global competition for mobile and highly skilled people intensifies. Governments at state and local levels are also seeking a stronger voice in migration planning, particularly skilled migration, to help boost their local economies. All this calls for greater facilitation of cross-border movement.

To control irregular migration: when legal migration increases, it is usually shadowed by more irregular movements, involving sophisticated immigration fraud (notably identity fraud and visa non-compliance). More cases are being security checked, also because of growing links between smuggling, trafficking, organized crime and terrorism. Equally, there are risks to all when mobile populations carry communicable diseases with them, particularly TB and HIV/Aids. These risks call for strengthened monitoring.

At the same time, most immigration agencies today face serious constraints on finances, IT systems, human resources and accommodation. In-country, border and overseas facilities are struggling to cope with burgeoning caseloads, and legislation and information systems cannot keep pace with the rapidly changing developments in migration.

But the consequences of not dealing adequately with these challenges are even more serious, and can lead to delayed processing of cases, backlogs, grievances by dissatisfied applicants and sponsors, diversion of resources into secondary administrative functions like inquiries and appeals, and ultimately reduced efficiency in critical areas like security checking. The consequences can be both expensive and deadly.

Some Key Strategies

Against this background, DIMIA has over recent years pursued some strategies to improve the design and delivery of visas. These are all at various stages of implementation.

i) *More Transparent and Objective Visa Criteria.* Subjective visa criteria have been replaced with more transparent and objective ones, resulting in more consistent decision making and fewer appeals to review tribunals, and a reduction of the scope for allegations of bias. Time-consuming labour market testing has been replaced by a list of skilled occupations and minimum salary levels. Moreover, specific financial and English language benchmarks for overseas students have replaced the discretionary benchmarks previously applied by government decisionmakers. All of this has enabled applicants to better assess their own chances and reduce rejection rates.

ii) *Partnerships with Expert Third Parties.* Assessing eligibility for a visa can often require subject expertise not held by immigration officials. These functions are thus out-sourced to third parties:

- assessment of skills of potential migrants (National Office of Overseas Skills Recognition (NOOSR)). This raises migrants' chances of having their qualifications recognized and being employed in Australia;
- assessment of applicants' English language skills via the International English Language Testing System (IELTS) rather than via interviews;
- testing of medical needs of Australians who sponsor migrants as caregivers.

Changes such as these have made decision making more objective, and reduced appeals and complaints against decisions. Electronic links with partner agencies will in the future ensure greater efficiency and integrity by reducing the potential for document and identity fraud.

iii) *Front-end Loading and Concurrent Processing.* "One-stop shop" processing of applications requires migrants to submit all necessary documents at the time of application, and immigration decisionmakers to undertake all relevant case checks concurrently rather than consecutively. Supported by a combination of legislative and procedural change, this has markedly lowered processing time.

iv) *Matching Visa Processing to Objective Assessments of Immigration Risk.* Objective indicators and quality data are used to better identify cases requiring additional integrity checking. Resources are thus not wasted needlessly on checking all cases, the majority of whom are non-risk. Risk indicators include non-return rates, visa non-compliance rates and rates of document fraud in the caseload. A new system ("Safeguards") will soon be introduced, to give more guidance on which cases to check and refer.

v) *Migrant Self-Assessment.* High visa refusal rates can mean that many applicants are wasting their time and money in applying, and the authorities are diverting resources into less productive work. One way of minimizing this is to place the onus of assessing their own chances of success of a visa application on applicants. This is supported by special guide booklets, contact centres and an interactive DIMIA website, which have all helped to lower the rejection rates for most visa classes.

vi) *Working More Closely with Sponsors.* In visa categories involving sponsors (parents, temporary resident doctors, sponsored business visitors, long-term temporary residents and others) officials deal directly with the sponsor, who is often more accessible than the migrant. This can greatly streamline visa processing and reduce the need for the sponsor/applicant to deal with more than one office.

vii) *Centralization/Repatriation of Administrative Aspects of Visa Processing.* Increasing caseloads can mean that the resources dedicated to administrative functions, particularly in a litigious environment, reduce the resources for integrity checking and post-arrival monitoring. To address this, DIMIA has begun to repatriate and centralize the administrative aspects of visa processing, most commonly undertaken overseas. Key benefits of this are: reduced visa processing times, resource savings that can be redirected to integrity checking and post-arrival monitoring, improved integrity of visa processing, better client services, more consistent decision making, and improved ability to address training needs of immigration officials.

viii) *Electronic Visa Lodgment and Processing.* Australia has been operating an electronic visa system for many years, and is extending this to a wider range of visa types. To date, only visitor, student, long-term temporary resident, working holidaymaker and on-shore resident return visas are electronic. By 2005, it is planned to expand this to temporary resident doctor and general skilled migration visas.

Electronic lodgment and processing supports the repatriation and centralization efforts noted above. It also improves access to DIMIA services, reduces the resources required for data entry, helps manage fees, and ensures greater accuracy of data, directly from the applicants.

ix) *Monitoring Post-arrival Compliance and Integrity Checking.* Australia's automated exit/entry control system enables it to monitor visa compliance of temporary migrants after their arrival. This can be a significant deterrent against visa abuse and help identify the conditions favouring irregular immigration, thereby improving future policy making. For some visas, it can provide the evidence for later permanent residence.

x) *Enforcement of Sponsor Undertakings.* Employers sponsoring skilled workers from overseas must sign up to a series of legally enforceable undertakings, including payment of a security bond to ensure compliance with visa conditions. These measures enable more streamlined visa processing, higher approvals and increased levels of visa compliance.

Overall Benefits

While it is always difficult to assess the impacts of such policies and measures, DIMIA reports that overall immigration outcomes improved considerably during the period since the above strategies were introduced. Examples of these include: improvement in the employment and income performance of skilled immigrants; a significant rise in approval rates for most visa categories; steady improvements in processing times and clearance of application backlogs, and a reduction in non-compliance with immigration rules.

Source: Abul Rizvi, DIMIA, Canberra; *www.immi.gov.au*

CHAPTER 22
REGIONAL AND GLOBAL CONSULTATIVE PROCESSES: TRENDS AND DEVELOPMENTS[1]

While neither set of processes follows a specific institutional format, and each has its own development path, some important commonalities are emerging that could make future migration management more efficient.

INTRODUCTION

THERE HAVE been innumerable efforts by governments and intergovernmental organizations to create cooperative mechanisms for the more efficient management of common and shared migration concerns. Regional Consultative Processes (RCPs) have emerged since the 1990s primarily out of a need for coordinated action on urgent common issues, such as irregular migration and, in particular, smuggling and trafficking of persons. Global processes, such as the Global Commission on Migration, have appeared more recently in response to a growing perception that globalization calls for more multilateral approaches. Both phenomena reflect the growing recognition by governments that migration also affects other major public policy areas such as development, labour rights, public health and security.

This chapter discusses some common orientations in migration management emerging in the evolution of RCPs and the newer global processes. By highlighting broad trends, it examines their current role in and potential benefits for migration management. While neither set of processes follows a specific institutional format, and each has its own development path, some important commonalities are emerging, that could make future migration management more efficient.

REGIONAL CONSULTATIVE PROCESSES (RCPs) – A STEADY COURSE

Informal in nature, RCPs provide venues for governments that share interests in the area of migration and migration management to exchange views and information and develop non-binding agreements, often a precursor for harmonized regional migration policies. Such *fora* operate parallel to the legal frameworks and more formal structures dealing with migration issues, such as the European Union and the United Nations.[2]

The proliferation of RCPs since 1996 reflects a major current trend in international migration management, a shift from ad hoc unilateral and bilateral approaches to regional multilateral strategies. RCPs have been initiated in North and Central America through the Regional Conference on Migration (RCM, also known as the Puebla Process), in South America through the Lima Process, in Asia through the Manila Process, in Africa through the MIDSA and MIDWA Processes and within Europe through the Budapest Process and the CIS Conference and Follow-up Process (Klekowski von Koppenfels, 2001). Cross-regional processes such as the IGC[3] for Europe, North America and Australia,

1. *The author of this chapter is Boriana Savova, with contributions from Gervais Appave, Erica Usher and Michele Klein Solomon, Migration Policy and Research Department, IOM, Geneva.*

2. *For details on the history, structure and purpose of the RCPs, see chapter 8 in* World Migration 2003, *pp. 123-139.*

3. *Intergovernmental Consultations on Asylum, Refugees and Migration Policies in Europe, North America and Australia. Its first meeting took place in 1985 and was initiated by UNHCR.*

the Bali Process for broader Asia and the ASEM Ministerial Conference for Asia and Europe[4] have emerged concurrently to tackle irregular migration globally (IOM, 2003a).

In the past few years, countries in the western Mediterranean region (southern Europe and Maghreb) have engaged in a dialogue on migration issues through the "5+5" initiative.[5] Two other regional *fora* have recently emerged, the Asian Labour Migration Ministerial Consultations, and the Regional Forum on Asylum, Migration and Sustainable Return in Southeastern Europe. These initiatives could well develop into RCPs in the future. Currently, there are 13 regional consultative mechanisms in place (IOM, 2003b).

But the increasing participation by governments in multilateral cooperation on migration through RCPs does not suggest that bilateral initiatives have become obsolete. In many cases, governments use regional consultations to strengthen bilateral cooperation through building confidence and identifying common interests. In the MIDSA process, for instance, possibilities for bilateral labour agreements between countries in the region are being investigated with a view to fostering more development through migration (IOM, 2003c). Other governments have used RCPs to similar ends.

WALKING THE TALK: THE OUTCOMES OF RCPs

At the initial stages of their development RCPs are mostly discussion *fora*, aimed at providing a venue for governments to work towards an understanding of their respective positions and priorities, and identify common ground for further cooperation. The initial meetings typically conclude with declarations in which states lay out their political objectives, agree to cooperate on certain aspects of migration management and prescribe in broad terms the actions that need to be taken. Within a year or two of their launch, RCPs tend to develop technical objectives in the form of action plans, under which concrete initiatives and projects come to life.

Some consultations, for instance the IGC (Intergovernmental Consultations) and the Bali Process, remain primarily focused on dialogue and sharing data on trends and policies. Others take a more action-oriented approach. Development and training projects, directly targeting current and potential migrant populations, have emerged within the 5+5 process. Job-creation and development activities have been launched in Algeria, Mauritania, Morocco and Tunisia,[6] in keeping with the 2003 Rabat Recommendations "to encourage social and economic development in regions with high emigration potential" (IOM, 2003d, p. 2).

The RCM in the Americas has moved beyond the enunciation of principles towards operational activities resulting in research studies, expanded training and capacity-building projects, and assistance programmes for migrants. Within the RCM general regional guidelines on safe and orderly return of migrants in the region have recently been endorsed, along with programmes to assist victims of trafficking, public information campaigns and training on ethics and integrity for public officials (RCM, 2004).

In Asia, the relatively new regional consultations of Asian labour ministers focus specifically on labour migration, and the two conferences held so far, in Colombo in 2003 and Manila in 2004, have resulted

4. *ASEM (the Asia-Europe Meeting) is an informal process of dialogue and cooperation initiated in 1996 to bring together the EU Commission and member states with ten Asian countries (Brunei, China, Indonesia, Japan, South Korea, Malaysia, the Philippines, Singapore, Thailand and Vietnam). The ASEM Summit held in Hanoi, 8-9 October 2004, included the ten new EU members and three new ASEAN countries (Cambodia, Laos and Myanmar) previously not part of the process. Migration became a topic of discussion in the ASEM context following the ASEM Ministerial Conference on Cooperation for the Management of Migratory Flows between Europe and Asia, held in Spain in April 2002 at the initiative of China, Germany and Spain. The Conference agreed on such follow-up activities as information exchange on migrant flows and migration management, cooperation on improving the quality and security of travel documents, combating document fraud, establishing networks of immigration and consular liaison officers and meetings at expert and director general level.*

5. *See the chapter "Migration Dynamics and Dialogue in the Western Mediterranean".*

6. *The PROCHE-project in Tunisia targets development of emigration areas in the country through creating sustainable employment and the development of existing local skills.*

in the completion of a number of activities,[7] as well as recommendations for further work orientation.[8] At its most recent annual conference in Palau in September 2004, the Pacific Immigration Directors' Conference (PIDC) concentrated on the increasing incidence of migrant smuggling and trafficking in the Pacific region. The PIDC has begun to develop a regional Advance Passenger Information System along ICAO standards, and fosters cooperation and technical assistance among immigration agencies within the region, particularly to strengthen the capacity to identify document fraud and other illegal activities of persons on the move.[9]

As they evolve and consolidate, most RCPs logically progress from the formulation of policy goals to strategies designed to achieve them, and final project implementation. Within more developed RCPs, continued involvement in dialogue and information exchange is often combined with developing and implementing policy goals and initiating projects.

COMPREHENSIVE APPROACH TO MIGRATION MANAGEMENT

The consolidation of RCPs often goes hand in hand with a growing awareness of the broader context affecting migration, and attempts to address migration issues holistically. Many RCPs have begun discussing classical migration concerns in regard to public health, remittances and development, migrant rights, migrant integration and other related topics. Efforts to approach migration in a comprehensive manner have evolved along two major lines – expanding RCP agendas and broadening participation in the multilateral migration dialogue.

A comprehensive approach that recognizes migration as an interdisciplinary phenomenon also complicates the formulation of migration policies. But, if well managed, this approach also offers advantages, for example the securing of broader support for the outcomes of migration dialogues by engaging a wider circle of international and national actors. A comprehensive and agreed approach also holds the promise of better informed and carefully coordinated policies, able to respond more adequately to complex migration issues.

Greater Role for International Organizations

Another feature of RCPs is their close cooperation with international organizations that have traditionally acted as secretariats of RCPs, or supported their coordinating bodies (Klekowski von Koppenfels, 2001).[10] In some cases, they have initiated the start-up of RCPs and provided non-partisan facilitation of dialogue on sensitive issues. International organizations (IO) continue to organize meetings at the request of governments on specific migratory concerns in their regions. Such meetings can develop into ongoing processes if there is enough commitment among participating states.

As many RCPs evolve from *fora* for the exchange of views to action-oriented mechanisms, IOs are increasingly called upon to provide assistance in project development and implementation in such areas as the harmonization of national and regional policy and practice, economic development in areas of high migration pressure, operational systems for migration management, and capacity building and

7. *Activities underway or completed include assessments and good practice papers in a number of priority areas; a compendium of labour migration policies and practices in the ten countries; joint training and development of curriculum and joint activities between labour sending and receiving countries in the implementation of a Migrant Resource Centre (see also footnote 8).*

8. *Recommendations from the Colombo conference concerned three main areas: 1) protection and provision of services to migrant workers, 2) optimizing benefits of organized labour migration and, 3) capacity building, data collection and inter-state cooperation. Recommendations from the Manila meeting included regulatory frameworks to prevent immigration malpractice; the establishment of Migrant Welfare Funds; pre-orientation services for the migrants and a feasibility study to establish a common Migrant Resource Centre in the Gulf Cooperation Council states.*

9. *One concrete project in the context of the PIDC is a border management assessment study by IOM for the government of Papua New Guinea, which is set to be replicated for other states in the region.*

10. *For instance, IOM has managed the secretariats of the Manila Process, the CIS Conference and Follow-up Process, MIDSA, the Dakar Process and most recently the 5+5 dialogue on migration. Other international organizations such as UNHCR, OSCE and ICMPD have similarly acted as hubs for coordinating the meetings and activities of RCMs.*

training.[11] They are also requested to conduct research and studies on topical issues, such as migration legislation, trafficking in persons, labour migration, migration and health and remittances.

RCPs often also seek the participation of UN agencies, whose representatives frequently attend RCP meetings as observers or participants. As RCP agendas expand, the need for technical expertise on a variety of topics and subjects also grows. In the future, the UN and other organizations are likely to increase their expert contributions to regional consultations.

Interaction with Economic Fora

Some RCPs are seeking to place migration issues on the agenda of regional economic groupings, which have traditionally had little interaction with migration policymakers. As these larger integration processes strive to achieve freer movement of goods and services, the challenge of liberalizing labour movements gains more prominence. A recognition of the interlinkages between labour migration, trafficking and economic development has spurred joint planning and activities between economic groupings and RCPs in recent years. Examples from Africa include the increased participation of the South African Development Community (SADC) in MIDSA's workshops and activities,[12] and the sustained involvement of the Economic Community of West African States (ECOWAS) in the 2001 Dakar Declaration Process and Follow-up Proposals. ECOWAS was one of the founders of the 2001 International Migration Policy Seminar for West Africa, which sparked the Dakar Declaration and Follow-up Proposals. It also funded technical cooperation projects on migration terminology, data sources and legislation to facilitate a meaningful dialogue on migration in the region of West Africa (IOM, 2003e).

Sustained NGO Involvement

While RCPs are governmental processes, many of them have increasingly invited regional NGOs to contribute to both policy issues and project implementation. Inclusion of civil society organizations in regional dialogue is now customary practice in more developed RCPs, like the regional conferences on migration (RCM). Sometimes, NGOs form their own *fora* within RCPs and issue declarations or make proposals that are heeded by governments or even incorporated into their Plan of Action. For instance, the Regional Network of Civil Organizations for Migration (RNCOM) emerged as part of the Puebla Process, and its proposal to assist migrants held in detention centres was adopted in the RCM Plan of Action in 2001. Similarly, NGOs have regularly participated in the MIDSA process, and a regional NGO is included in the steering committee.

Most RCPs have explicitly invited NGO participation in their declarations or recommendations. The 2003 Budapest Declaration, for example, recommended that minimum standards be established for the health care offered to victims of trafficking through a "partnership of governments, intergovernmental and non-governmental organizations, and academic institutions" (Regional Conference on Public Health and Trafficking in Human Beings in Central, Eastern and Southern Europe, 2003).[13]

Strengthening Participation in Migration Dialogue Within States

The broad range of issues discussed in RCPs has increasingly compelled governments to seek to secure concerted action on these issues within their own ranks. Recognizing that migration could no longer be dealt with single-handedly by one government agency, they have more commonly sought inputs and representation from their ministries of foreign affairs, interior, labour, trade and health. While leadership

11. *For more details see the IOM brochure on* Technical Cooperation on Migration, *2002, IOM, Geneva.*
12. *For details see IOM 2003. Annual Report to the USA: Migration Dialogue for Southern Africa (MIDSA) Phase II.*
13. *For details of the Budapest Conference, see the chapter "Investing in Migration Health".*

should lie within a single coordinating committee, the considerations of different government branches need to inform national migration policy decision making.

INTERREGIONAL COOPERATION: PROGRESS ON CREATING A FRAMEWORK OF GUIDING PRINCIPLES

As previously discussed, some of the well-established consultative processes on migration are already interregional in nature. Many RCPs are reaching out to counterparts from other regions to share experiences and best practices.

The joint IGC/APC consultation held in Bangkok in April 2001 was a first step in the direction of interregional cooperation. The first of its kind, this joint meeting offered a unique opportunity to strengthen interregional dialogue, develop a shared understanding of the variety of challenges nations face in relation to asylum, irregular migration and people smuggling, and use such dialogue as a confidence-building measure and stepping stone for future cooperation.

The development in 2002 of the Western Mediterranean Conference on Migration ("5+5") involving five southern European and five Maghreb countries of origin, transit and destination is another direct result of the desire to develop an understanding of the migration dynamics across regions. Two conferences held since then in 2003 and 2004, have moved this process further towards regional acceptance of the need for cooperative approaches, and closer collaboration with international support organizations such as IOM.

Beyond RCPs, the more recent global processes, such as the Berne Initiative launched by Switzerland in 2001, have taken the lead in bringing together governments across regions to discuss and formulate common understandings and effective practices for the management of international migration. Other calls for more global mechanisms to discuss broad migration management issues have come from IOM and the United Nations.[14] The three major global processes that have emerged in recent years at the instigation of governments, IOM and the UN – the Berne Initiative, the International Dialogue on Migration and the Global Commission on International Migration – with the goal of placing international migration on the global agenda, are reviewed below.

COMMON OBSTACLES

Limited Resources

Securing sufficient funding to carry out agreed initiatives is a serious obstacle for most RCPs. Funding may come from the annual assessed contributions of participating states, other regional, international and funding entities such as the EU, regional economic groups and international organizations (IOM 2003a). Wealthy destination countries usually make larger contributions to RCPs, which has exposed RCPs to the criticism that, while appearing to cooperate, they allow destination countries to influence migration agendas. Critics argue that as a result resources are invested in discouraging, detaining and deporting undocumented migrants and in border control measures, rather than in development, the protection of migrants' safety and human rights and improving their overall condition (Nezer, 2000).

While RCPs cannot alter the fact that countries have different bargaining powers, they leave relatively little room for "influence" by virtue of being non-binding, informal and voluntary in nature. Some states might well profit more than others from the final outcomes of RCPs, but the open dialogue offers all participating parties the opportunity to clarify their objectives and circumstances and begin exploring mutually beneficial solutions. As a result of such dialogue, many countries of destination are more willing to invest in development and capacity

14. *The UN Secretary General established the Global Commission on International Migration in 2003. UNHCR has also engaged in a broader dialogue on migration from the perspective of its refugee protection mandate in its Global Consultations on International Protection.*

building in countries of origin to address the root causes of migration. Collaboration among governments, NGOs and IOs also fosters a balance of interests and transparency in RCP proceedings. The non-partisan advice of IOs can also help to ensure that agendas are balanced.

The above criticisms are not entirely misplaced. They reflect the growing complexity, also politically, of managing mixed migration flows today. Assuring refugee protection in asylum systems and respect for the rights of migrants in the context of heightened security measures and stricter control continue to be major challenges that many RCPs are yet to address adequately.

Difficulties with Data Collection and Sharing

Data collection and meaningful information sharing have been among the first goals to appear on most RCP agendas, yet among the most difficult to accomplish. Lack of reliable data on migration trends and policies continues to hinder informed policy decision making, despite the fact that data collection and sharing have been improved in the past years. A regional database, SIEMCA, established in 2001 in the framework of the RCM, has succeeded in improving the quality and availability of information, which enabled the publication of research studies on migration flows in the Americas region. SIEMCA has proven valuable in facilitating migration negotiations and the adoption of harmonized policies.

For many RCPs, however, reliable data collection and the mechanisms to achieve this, remain absent from their agendas and plans. Information sharing is a challenge for countries participating in the MIDSA, the Budapest Process, the CIS Conference and Follow-up process and others.

Lack of Impact Evaluation Initiatives

One of the current deficiencies of RCPs, hopefully to be addressed as they consolidate further, is a lack of self-evaluation of performance and achievements. The overall impact of RCPs on migration management in their respective regions has so far not been seriously investigated. While activity reports are regularly produced, and outcomes and challenges identified, comprehensive studies of the effectiveness of RCP initiatives in the region are still sparse. Apart from the assessment of the RCM recently undertaken by Canada and Mexico, no impact evaluations have yet been completed.[15] These are difficult to carry out when funding is not stable, but remain an important means to identify deficiencies, take corrective action and confirm the credibility of RCPs.

GLOBAL PROCESSES ON MIGRATION

DESPITE the prominence of migration on international agendas for more than a decade now, efforts to achieve global consensus on its governance have proven elusive. This is partly due to the conflicting perceptions of migration among states. Instead, a myriad of interstate processes on migration have sprung up over the past decade, either bilateral or regional, as shown above. But more recently, there has also been an increasingly urgent call again by governments and agencies engaged with migration for a more global dialogue on migration. This call has been taken up by IOM with its *International Dialogue on Migration*, the Swiss government with the *Berne Initiative*, and the UN with its *Global Commission on International Migration.*

15. *Canada and Mexico submitted for the consideration of RCM members an assessment and framework for the Puebla Process for strengthening its activities in the coming years, "Strengthening the Regional Conference on Migration: Eight Years After Its Creation". It includes guidelines for the successful operation of the process, such as commitment by members to the structure of the process, adherence to the agreed meetings and working group structures, and the participation of observers, international organizations and civil society organizations. The framework was endorsed at the IXth annual meeting of the RCM in Panama in May 2004.*

INTERNATIONAL DIALOGUE ON MIGRATION[16]

IOM's Council has in recent years become a major platform for government dialogue on understanding and cooperation in managing migration at the intergovernmental level. The International Dialogue on Migration was launched in November 2001, on the occasion of IOM's 50th anniversary, in response to a request from member states for IOM to take the lead in the migration policy debate. The Council strengthened its role as a forum for migration policy dialogue through informal and interactive discussions to foster understanding of migration dynamics and policy globally, and to facilitate cooperative approaches.[17]

Each year, governments identify a theme for the Dialogue, and workshops are held around agreed topics. Since 2003, there are two additional annual intersessional workshops to allow more continuous discussion, particularly of the linkages between migration and other policy domains. For 2004, "Valuing Migration" was selected as the main theme, *inter alia*, to link the Dialogue to the *World Migration 2005* report. The aim was to strengthen understanding of the costs, benefits and challenges of migration in social, cultural, political and economic terms for all involved, including the migrants and their families. At the November/December 2004 Council session, governments discussed the "Image of Migrants in Society", both in home and host societies, and how this can affect policymaking. How can governments ensure accurate public perceptions of the complexities of migration and the positive contributions of migrants to societies?

Two intersessional workshops in 2004 engaged other key international players on the current burning issues: *Migration and Health*, co-sponsored by WHO and the Centers for Disease Control and Prevention, where health and migration officials considered, among others, the public health implications of increasingly mobile populations; and *Migration and Trade*, jointly organized by IOM, the World Bank and WTO, which explored current government mechanisms for managing temporary labour migration and the means to progress in the GATS Mode 4 negotiations to reduce barriers to the movement of service providers.

THE BERNE INITIATIVE[18]

The Berne Initiative is a state-driven international dialogue aimed at more effective management of migration at the regional and global level through enhanced interstate cooperation. At its inauguration ("Berne I") symposium in June 2001, delegates from governments, international organizations and academia encouraged the initiator, the Swiss government, to develop a non-binding international policy framework on migration. A first concept of this "International Agenda for Migration Management" was presented to governments from all regions of the world at the Berne Initiative Consultations in July 2003. The result was a non-binding international agenda for migration management comprising:

- a set of common understandings, basic shared assumptions and principles and,
- a set of effective practices drawn from government experiences.

In 2004, IOM, the secretariat of the Berne Initiative, organized four regional consultations on behalf of the Swiss government in Addis Ababa for Africa, in Budapest for Europe and Central Asia, in Guilin for Asia and the Pacific, and in Santiago de Chile for the Americas region. These were intended to move the "International Agenda for Migration Management" a step forward at the regional levels. Participants from origin, transit and destination countries in the same regions focused particularly on what united rather than divided them in this. As areas of consensus emerge, these will be compiled into a platform of

16. *For further information on IOM's Dialogue refer: www.iom.int/en/know/idm/index.shtml*

17. *As of June 2004, the IOM Council consisted of 105 member states, 27 observer states and some observer intergovernmental and non-governmental organizations.*

18. *For further details on the Berne Initiative, see IOM, 2004, and: www.iom.int/berneinitiative*

common understandings to support effective national migration policies, capacity development and interstate cooperation.

The Berne Initiative readily complements the efforts of existing regional consultative processes on migration, and can transpose the lessons learned from these into the larger global agenda. For the most recent "Berne II" conference in December 2004, participating states agreed to take stock of both the regional consultations and the future of the Berne Initiative, as mutually reinforcing efforts by states to manage migration more cooperatively.

INTERNATIONAL LABOUR CONFERENCE (ILC)[19]

In 2004, the International Labour Organization (ILO) included in its 92nd session of the ILC a general discussion on the challenges of labour migration in an era of globalization. It aimed for a more integrated approach to policies and structures for orderly migration for employment, and improving migrant worker protection through the setting of appropriate standards. The ILC concluded with a resolution for a comprehensive plan of action for migrant workers, to include a non-binding multilateral framework for a rights-based approach to labour migration.

The tripartite nature of the ILO allows greater multilateral engagement of employers, workers' associations and governments in improving the treatment and conditions of migrant workers and members of their families. Other agencies have been invited by ILO to cooperate in the elaboration of the multilateral framework, and ILO has stressed that the non-binding framework be linked to related processes such as the Global Commission on International Migration, the Berne Initiative, and the forthcoming (2006) High-level Dialogue in the United Nations General Assembly on Migration and Development.[20]

GLOBAL COMMISSION ON INTERNATIONAL MIGRATION[21]

AT THE UNITED Nations, migration was flagged as a priority issue for the UN, governments and the international community generally through the Secretary General's 2000 report on Strengthening of the United Nations: an Agenda for Further Change.[22] In 2004, the Secretary General established the UN Global Commission on Migration (GCIM) to pull together the disparate strands of international debate on migration issues, and provide coherent policy guidance.

Distinct but complementary to IOM's International Dialogue on Migration and the Berne Initiative, the GCIM is an independent entity comprising 19 migration experts, drawn from all regions of the world and bringing together a wide range of perspectives and expertise. It is co-chaired by Dr. Mamphela Ramphele of South Africa, former Managing Director of the World Bank, and Mr. Jan O. Karlsson, Sweden's former Minister for Migration and Development.

Described as a multi-stakeholder dialogue on strengthening national, regional and global governance (Langenbacher, 2004), the GCIM began its work early in 2004 with an 18-month mandate and three principal tasks:
1) promote a comprehensive dialogue on international migration among governments, international organizations, civil society, the private sector and other relevant stakeholders;
2) analyse gaps in current policy approaches to migration and the linkages between international migration and other global policy issues and,
3) present recommendations to the international community on ways to strengthen national, regional

19. *For further information on the ILC, go to: www.ilo.org/public/english/standards/relm/ilc/*
20. *See also the Text Box "ILO Action Plan on Labour Migration".*
21. *For further information on the GCIM, refer: www.gcim.org*
22. *United Nations General Assembly document A/57/387, September 9, 2002.*

and global governance of international migration, and to maximize the benefits of migration while minimizing its potentially adverse consequences.

Over the course of its term, the GCIM is organizing thematic and regional hearings and conducting analyses and research programmes. The outcomes of these activities will be presented in a report to be published in mid-2005.

CONCLUSION

IN THE PAST two years RCPs have continued to attract interest among governments and other organizations active in the field of migration as venues for international dialogue and a means for finding mutually beneficial solutions to common migration issues. While there is still no detailed assessment of the impact of RCPs on migration management, there is consensus that they can make a valuable contribution to managing migration at the regional level. Traditionally used for information sharing, RCPs have become more operational and increasingly engage in technical cooperation with intergovernmental and non-governmental organizations. While RCPs have made tangible advances in a range of functional and substantive areas over the past few years, they have yet to unleash their full potential.

The global initiatives discussed above are still in their infancy, but already show a high degree of complementarity and convergence of approach and outcome. They are all helping to bring together governments across the migrant origin-transit-destination spectrum, while supporting and dovetailing with the regional processes. The reports and studies emerging from these processes in the coming months and years will tell us more about their concrete outcomes and impacts on migration governance.

The United Nations General Assembly will devote its High-level Dialogue in 2006 to international migration and development. The dialogue will aim at maximizing the development benefits of migration; and is expected to build on the intergovernmental consultation initiatives at global, regional, and inter-regional levels discussed in this chapter.

TEXTBOX 22.1

APEC BUSINESS TRAVEL CARD – FACILITATING REGIONAL TRAVEL

It has become common in international debates on migration to reach consensus on the need for interstate cooperation. Yet, in reality there are very few successful examples of this on the ground. The **APEC Business Travel Card Scheme** is one concrete illustration of how countries in the Asia-Pacific region have achieved a special form of cooperation to facilitate business migration to their mutual benefit. It offers useful lessons on how to widen and deepen multilateral partnerships in international migration.

APEC Business Mobility Group (BMG)

The evolution of regional economic blocs such as, e.g., NAFTA, EU, APEC and ASEAN, has seen massive shifts towards facilitating regional flows of investment, trade and finance. To facilitate regional trade and investment, APEC (Asia-Pacific Economic Co-operation)[23] set up a Business Mobility Group (BMG) at its November 1996 meeting in the Philippines. One of APEC's main objectives is to stimulate economic growth in the region and reduce barriers to the free flow of trade. The challenge for the organization is how to do this without compromising national security and the integrity of national borders. The task of the BMG was to assist this process by removing barriers to the flow of business people within the APEC region (Rizvi, 2003).

The BMG became operational in 1997 and is now one of 12 expert working groups reporting to the APEC Committee on Trade and Investment. All 21 APEC countries are represented in the Group, which meets three times a year. Representatives are mainly senior immigration officers of the member states. The Group is convened by the Australian Department of Immigration and Multicultural and Indigenous Affairs (DIMIA), which also chairs the meetings. Membership of the committee has been very stable, and strong working relationships have developed. Its key objectives are (DIMIA 2003a):

- to simplify short-term entry arrangements for business visitors;
- to streamline processing for skilled persons seeking temporary residence;
- to develop transparent regulatory arrangements to allow for seamless cross-border movement.

An important initiative of the BMG was the development of the *APEC Business Travel Card Scheme*, administered by Australia on behalf of the BMG.

APEC Business Travel Card Scheme

The idea of this scheme is to simplify the entry of cardholders to the participating countries, provide flexible business travel arrangements, and reduce the time and costs for applying for entry visas and permits. In other words, to speed up business travel. The card is issued to interested persons who meet the following criteria:

23. *APEC Members include: Australia; Brunei Darussalam; Canada; Chile; China mainland; Hong Kong; Indonesia; Japan; Republic of Korea; Malaysia; Mexico; New Zealand; Papua New Guinea; Peru; The Philippines; The Russian Federation; Singapore; Taiwan Province of China; Thailand; US; Vietnam.*

- they must be a passport holder of a participating state (or permanent resident in Hong Kong (China));
- they must prove that they are a genuine business person who travels frequently within the region for trade and investment purposes;
- no criminal conviction or charges must be pending against them;
- for some countries, they must have the endorsement from a leading business organization within their country, such as a national chamber of commerce.

The card allows business people multiple entries to participating states for stays of up to 90 days. They do not need to apply for a separate entry permit or visa for each visit, and no visa labels are entered into passports. The card is the size of a credit card, and is valid for three years. Cardholders enjoy streamlined express immigration processing at airports through special APEC lines.

Business applicants submit a duly completed form, the home government checks the details of applicants against its own databases, and sends these electronically to each participating country for pre-clearance. The country receiving the details then checks them against its own alert lists and other databases used for checking arrivals. The applicant is thus pre-cleared for entry. This "double vetting" of applicant *bona fides* by the source and receiving country ensures a high degree of integrity. To date, there is no evidence of fraud in the system. Any receiving country reserves the right to refuse pre-clearance if it chooses to do so. The BMG has developed a set of principles, procedures and standards ('ABTC Operating Framework'), as a framework for implementing and managing the scheme.

Within this framework the application process should take no more than three weeks. However, some countries are still finding it difficult to meet this standard. In effect, as this process is a pre-arrival entry checking process, upon arrival it is necessary for the cardholder to produce both the card and a valid passport; and the information in the two documents must coincide.

The supporting database is maintained by DIMIA on behalf of the BMG. All member states control the data regarding their own nationals and have full access to the database.

The first trial run of the scheme took place in 1997 in three APEC member countries experiencing significant immigration – Korea, the Philippines and Australia. The evaluation took over a year, and the scheme commenced on a permanent basis in March 1997. At the end of 2003, 15 of the 21 APEC members had joined the scheme. The remaining six states are expected to join in the near future (DIMIA 2003a). All have agreed on a best endeavours basis to implement one or more of the following (Rizvi, 2003) aspects:

- visa-free or visa waiver arrangements for business people;
- participation in the APEC Business Travel Card Scheme;
- at least three years multiple entry for business people.

All APEC members have at least one of these in place.

The scheme has been recognized by APEC country leaders as a model of the "Pathfinder Approach", now being used within APEC to further other projects. This enables those countries able to move faster on some initiatives to do so and build the momentum for broader application. The approach relies on three key elements:
i) trial runs of the scheme among a few countries to prove its viability;
ii) open cooperation among members to build confidence and operational strength, and
iii) technical assistance, training and initial funding to facilitate its implementation in all countries.

As of 28 January 2004, there were 7,720 active APEC Business Travel Cards, and the success of the APEC Business Travel Card encouraged the BMG to move on to a more ambitious programme of facilitating business travel between the countries of the region.

Complementary Initiatives of the BMG

The BMG agreed on a service standard for processing applications for, and extensions of, temporary residence permits for executives, managers and specialists transferred within their companies to other APEC countries (Rizvi, 2003). Almost all APEC countries are meeting this standard. An important task of the BMG is to strengthen capacity across the region to handle international arrivals and departures. It was agreed that standards would be set for all members and that they would be implemented in both developed and developing states in the region. In addition to the standards for short-term business visitor movement and temporary residence of company transferees and specialists, states have agreed on broader standards for:

- provision of information on temporary travel arrangements;.
- travel document examination regimes and detection of travel document fraud;
- development of professional immigration services through training and streamlined practices;
- implementation of Advanced Passenger Information (API) systems.

Complementary standards have been drafted for:

- improving the security of travel documentation through workshops;
- enhancing immigration legislation infrastructure (DIMIA, 2003b).
- a feasibility study on the establishment of a pilot regional movement alert system to strengthen the capacity of border management agencies to detect stolen and fraudulent documentation and persons of concern.

Details of the work of the BMG are available on its website: *www.businessmobility.org*

Lessons learned from the APEC Business Card Scheme

A number of encouraging lessons can be drawn from this experience of interest to other countries.

1. The **development of cooperation** requires time – it should be based on a feasibility study of a few countries and the establishment of trust and confidence between countries over time.
2. **Consensus** is more easily gained for a limited, highly specific and non-threatening operational objective than for sweeping and massive intervention. Once countries realize there are benefits to be gained from cooperation, the scope of cooperation can be expanded.
3. A **phased approach** to cooperation seems to be the most successful, beginning with discussions and agreement on common principles and standards, and allowing for feasibility studies before implementation of any new system.
4. The **means and resources** for cooperation need to be assured by and for all players, especially for training of staff and installation of appropriate infrastructure. Countries with fewer resources need to be assisted by those with more experience and resources. The BMG's recognition of this and its priority to develop regional immigration personnel and infrastructure was a key lesson of the APEC Business Card Scheme.
5. Advanced computer-based information systems are essential for joint migration management. In the APEC Business Card case, activity is so high that the system will need to be upgraded in 2005. Such systems enable countries generally to manage their migration better regardless of the level of development of their economies. The API initiative, for example, which uses the international airline bookings system, helps raise countries' confidence in their management of incoming and outgoing movements.
6. Capacity building is fundamental to reforming migration policy and improving migration management and cooperation across countries. Those with more immigration experience can help support the efforts of others in a trusting, cooperative and egalitarian manner (e.g. Australia in the Asia-Pacific region).

While the card is clearly important for a highly mobile elite, it has a much wider impact by enhancing trade and investment between countries. In the contemporary international migration system, there is a clear bifurcation between high-income, skilled business people for whom international travel is increasingly facilitated, and the much larger number of poorer, less educated groups for whom international movement is constrained by receiving countries (Castles and Miller, 1998). However, schemes like the Business Travel Card can lay the foundations for broader international cooperation in migration management, with other potential spin-offs. This is a rare example of successful regional collaboration in the area of international migration, and its lessons need to be examined and learned.

Source: Professor Graeme Hugo, Federation Fellow, University of Adelaide, Australia.

SECTION 3
INTERNATIONAL MIGRATION DATA AND STATISTICS

Chapter 23
International Migration Trends[1]

INTRODUCTION

In 2000, there were 175 million international migrants[2] in the world, that is, one out of every 35 persons in the world was an international migrant.[3] This total represented more than a twofold increase from 76 million in 1960. By comparison, the world population only doubled from 3 billion in 1960 to 6 billion in 2000. As a result, international migrants represented 2.5 per cent of the world population in 1960 and 2.9 per cent in 2000.

However, a significant part of this increase worldwide was due more to the emergence of newly independent states during the 1990s than to the growing international redistribution of the population. While rising, the total number of international migrants still accounts for a small percentage of the world's population. The most significant changes in recent years have been an increased concentration of migrants in the developed world and in a small number of countries. There have also been significant shifts in the poles of attraction for labour migration, for example to East and Southeast Asia, and a remarkable contribution of international migration to the population growth of receiving countries experiencing low fertility levels.

Although data permitting the estimation of the global number of international migrants for more recent periods are not yet available, extrapolation of past trends indicates that the number of international migrants may reach between 185 million and 192 million in early 2005. That is, the growth of the international migrant stock is not likely to abate in the near future.

This chapter looks at the distribution of international migrants at the country level and in major regions of the world, teasing out recent and current trends in international mobility from United Nations estimates on the size of the migrant stock in each country. It discusses recent changes in the poles of attraction, the participation of women in international migration flows, shifts in the distribution of international migrants between developed and developing countries, labour circulation, and the contribution of international migration to population growth. This chapter provides, therefore, the statistical basis to underpin migration policy.

1. *This chapter has been prepared by the Population Division of the Department of Economic and Social Affairs of the United Nations Secretariat in New York.*

2. *International migrants in this particular case are persons living in a country other than that in which they were born.*

3. *These estimates are based on census data for 210 countries or areas out of a total of 228. The data for 156 among these relate to the number of foreign-born persons. For a further 54, the data concern the number of foreigners. For developing countries, the number of refugees as reported by UNHCR and UNRWA has been added to the number of international migrants derived from census data. In principle, censuses enumerate all persons present or living in a country at a particular time. Consequently, census counts do not necessarily exclude undocumented or unauthorized migrants. Evidence suggests that censuses generally include undocumented migrants in the counts they produce, thus providing a good basis for the estimation of all international migrants.*

GENERAL TRENDS

BETWEEN 1970 and 1980, the number of international migrants increased by 18 million, i.e. from 82 million to nearly 100 million (**Table 23.1**). In the next decade, their number rose to 154 million; but at least half of this rise was caused by the disintegration of the former Soviet Union whose effects, for the sake of comparison, have been "backdated" to 1990 in **Table 23.1**. In 1991, when the former Soviet Union disintegrated into 15 independent states, the number of international migrants increased dramatically, as people previously considered internal migrants among the Soviet republics became international migrants with the new independence of their respective countries of birth.[4] With such backdating, the stock of international migrants increased by some 21 million during 1990-2000. That is, without the disintegration of the Soviet Union, the number of international migrants worldwide would have risen by 18 million in 1970-1980, 27 million in 1980-1990, and 21 million in 1990-2000.

In addition to the geo-political factors that changed the configuration of major states during the 1990s, international migration was further propelled by the increasing interdependence among countries caused by economic liberalization, continued income disparities among nations, cheaper and more accessible means of transportation, and growing demographic disparities between developed and developing countries. As a result, there was a major shift in the distribution of increments in the stocks of international migrants between developed and developing countries. Excluding the changes involving the former Soviet Union, developed countries gained 9 million international migrants in 1970-1980, nearly 15 million in 1980-1990 and over 21 million in 1990-2000. That is, whereas in the 1970s developed countries without the Soviet Union absorbed only about half of the increase in the stock of international migrants worldwide, by the 1990s they were absorbing all the increase in international migrants and, consequently, the stock of international migrants in developing countries remained virtually unchanged.

These changes have resulted in a notable shift of international migrants towards the developed world. Whereas in 1970, 43 per cent of all international migrants lived in developed countries other than the Soviet Union, and 53 per cent lived in developing countries, by 2000, 46 per cent of all international migrants lived in the former and just 37 per cent lived in developing countries (**Table 23.1**). With the inclusion of the Soviet Union among the developed countries, the proportion of international migrants in those countries rose to 47 per cent in 1970 and 63 per cent in 2000. Notwithstanding the fact that some successor states of the former Soviet Union have been classified as developing countries, the proportion of all international migrants in the developed world remained at nearly 60 per cent in 2000.

At the regional level, increases in the share of international migrants occurred mostly in North America (from 16 per cent in 1970 to 23 per cent in 2000), and in the territory of the former Soviet Union (from 4 per cent to 17 per cent between 1970 and 2000). The share of all other regions declined, particularly in Asia, whose share dropped from 35 per cent in 1970 to 25 per cent in 2000, and Latin America and the Caribbean, whose share dropped by half in 1970-2000.

The sharp rise in the number of international migrants in North America is noteworthy, since it more than tripled during 1970-2000, from 13 million to 41 million, rising at an average rate of 3.8 per cent per year. That increase is mostly the result of the increasing foreign-born population in the US, whose numbers rose from 10 million in 1970 to 35 million in 2000. As a result of such changes, the percentage of international migrants among the total population of

4. *A similar discontinuity in the evolution of the number of international migrants occurred with the disintegration of Czechoslovakia and the former Yugoslavia, although the numbers involved are smaller. The reverse transformation also took place when, for example, the former German Democratic Republic joined the Federal Republic of Germany in late 1990.*

North America more than doubled from 5.6 per cent in 1970 to 12.9 per cent in 2000.

In Europe,[5] the number of international migrants also increased significantly, particularly in the 1990s. Between 1970 and 2000, their numbers rose from 19 million to 33 million, and their share of the total population increased from 4.1 per cent to 6.4 per cent. Thus, whereas in 1970 Europe had nearly double the number of international migrants in the US, by the end of the century, there were more in the US than in Europe. Excluding all former Communist countries from Europe, the migrant stock increased from 10 million in 1970 to 29 million in 2000, a figure still below that for the US in 2000.

In 2000, the 17 million refugees in the world constituted 9.7 per cent of all international migrants, up from 4.5 million or 5.5 per cent in 1970. The majority of these had found asylum in developing countries, particularly in Africa and Asia. In 2000, refugees accounted for 23 per cent of all international migrants in Asia and 22 per cent of those in Africa. The number of refugees under the mandate of UNHCR had risen since the late 1970s, from 2 million in 1975 to 16 million in 1990. During the 1990s, as long-standing conflicts came to an end, particularly in Africa, the repatriation of large numbers of refugees became possible. By 2000, the number reported to UNHCR had dropped to 12 million. The additional 5 million refugees in 2000 were those under the mandate of UNRWA.

Available estimates of the number of international migrants by sex show that the volume of international migration has been nearly equal for men and women. In 2000, females constituted almost 49 per cent of all migrants, up from 47 per cent in 1970 (Table 23.2). The proportion of females has tended to be higher in developed than in developing regions. In 1970, female migrants accounted for 49 per cent of the migrant stock in developed countries, and 45 per cent in developing countries. By 2000, there were slightly more female than male migrants in developed countries, but their share of the international migrant stock in developing countries had declined to just under 45 per cent.

Thus, although there has been an overall increase in the proportion of female migrants, that increase has not been universal. In particular, in Asia the share of female migrants declined from 46.6 per cent in 1970 to 43.3 per cent in 2000. In addition, the share of female migrants among the stock in North America declined somewhat from 51.1 per cent in 1970 to 50.3 in 2000. But, by the end of the 20th century, women were more numerous than men among international migrants in Latin America and the Caribbean, North America, Oceania, Europe and the former USSR, although they remained under-represented among those in Africa and Asia.

The vast majority of international migrants move in search of better economic opportunities. However, traditionally, a distinction is made between the economically active and those who move for other reasons, usually to accompany economically active migrants or to study abroad. The ILO estimates that about 50 per cent of all international migrants, that is 86 million, were economically active in 2000 (ILO, 2004).

DISTRIBUTION OF INTERNATIONAL MIGRANTS AT COUNTRY LEVEL

During the 20th century, no country remained untouched by international migration. However, in 1970, international migrants accounted for less than 1.1 per cent of the population in a quarter of all countries or areas of the world, a number that

5. *The UN estimates presented in this chapter use the following geographical delineation for the regions of Europe:* Eastern Europe – *Belarus, Bulgaria, Czech Republic, Hungary, Poland, Republic of Moldova, Romania, Russian Federation, Slovakia and Ukraine;* Northern Europe – *Channel Islands, Denmark, Estonia, Faeroe Islands, Finland, Iceland, Ireland, Isle of Man, Latvia, Lithuania, Norway, Sweden, United Kingdom;* Southern Europe – *Albania, Andorra, Bosnia and Herzegovina, Croatia, Gibraltar, Greece, Holy See, Italy, Malta, Portugal, San Marino, Serbia and Montenegro, Slovakia, Spain, and the FYROM;* Western Europe – *Austria, Belgium, France, Germany, Liechtenstein, Luxembourg, Monaco, the Netherlands and Switzerland.*

remained stable until 2000.[6] But the concentration of international migrants increased in countries with relatively high proportions, which also accounted for a quarter of all countries or areas of the world. In 1970, international migrants constituted at least 8.1 per cent of the population in each of those countries, but by 2000 their share had risen to 13 per cent. In addition, while in 1970 international migrants accounted for over 10 per cent of the population in 48 countries, by 2000 the number of countries affected had risen to 70.

In 2000, there were 7 countries or areas, where international migrants comprised more than 60 per cent of the population: Andorra, Macao Special Administrative Region of China, Guam, the Holy See, Monaco, Qatar and the United Arab Emirates.

Most of the countries or areas with a high proportion of international migrants have fewer than a million inhabitants. Among the 47 countries with more than 10 million inhabitants in 1970, in only three (Australia, Canada and France) did the proportion of international migrants surpass 10 per cent. By 2000, that number had increased to nine out of the 78 countries with 10 million inhabitants or more, namely, Australia, Belarus, Canada, Côte d'Ivoire, France, Kazakhstan, Saudi Arabia, Ukraine and the US.[7] In 1970, the three most populous countries with the largest concentration of international migrants accounted for 10 per cent of the world's migrant stock, whereas in 2000 the nine countries listed accounted for 40 per cent.

In fact, the stock of international migrants remains concentrated in relatively few countries. In 1970, just 23 countries (or 10 per cent of all countries) accounted for over three-quarters of the international migrant stock; and in 2000, 28 (or 12 per cent of all countries) did so (**Table 23.3**). There has been a marked concentration of international migrants in the US, whose share rose from 12 per cent in 1970 to 20 per cent in 2000. Other countries, whose share of international migrants increased substantially, include: Australia, Canada, France, Germany and the UK. Several countries that were not major receiving countries in 1970 became prominent in 2000, including Kazakhstan, Pakistan, the Russian Federation, Saudi Arabia and the Ukraine.

In 1970, the 22 main receiving countries included 9 in the developed world (plus the Soviet Union) and 13 in the developing world (**Table 23.3**). By 2000, the 28 major receiving countries included 11 developed countries, four successor states of the former Soviet Union and 13 developing countries. But although the distribution of major receiving countries by development group had not changed much, there had been a substantial shift in the share of international migrants in each group. Thus in 2000, the 11 major receivers in the developed world accounted for 41 per cent of all international migrants, up from the 37 per cent share of the nine developed countries listed in 1970. Concomitantly, the share of the 13 developing countries had declined markedly, from 35 per cent in 1970 to 20 per cent in 2000, with most of the gain going to the main receivers among the successor states of the USSR, whose share had risen from four per cent to 14 per cent between 1970 and 2000.

These changes point to the declining importance, in relative terms, of international migration for developing countries of destination. Although sizeable numbers of international migrants exist in a number of developing countries, their weight both as a proportion of the global migrant stock and in relation to the population of developing countries as a whole is declining. Accordingly, international migrants as a proportion of the population of developing countries dropped from 1.6 per cent in

6. *To maintain comparability, the set of countries was maintained constant from 1970 to 2000. That is, the Soviet Union was kept as a single unit throughout in these comparisons.*

7. *Note that for Germany this chapter uses the number of foreigners as a proxy for the number of international migrants. If, as Münz does in the chapter "Migrants in an Enlarged Europe", an estimate of the foreign-born population would be used instead, the number of international migrants in Germany would amount to 9.7 million accounting for 11 per cent of the population in the country. This estimate of foreign-born was obtained by Münz by adding the number of legal foreign residents born outside Germany and the estimated number of foreign-born among both all naturalized persons and ethnic German immigrants (Aussiedler).*

1970 to 1.3 per cent in 2000, a trend that contrasts with that in developed countries, where the share of international migrants in the population rose from 3.6 per cent to 8.7 per cent over the same period (**Table 23.1**).[8]

The significance of international migration in developed countries is also evidenced by the role it plays in population growth. In 1970-1975, the rate of natural increase[9] in the more developed regions as a whole was 6.8 per thousand, whereas the net migration rate was 1.0 per thousand, implying that when net migration was added to the rate of natural increase it yielded a growth rate of 7.8 per thousand (**Table 23.4**). That is, net migration contributed the equivalent of 15 per cent of natural increase to population growth in the more developed regions. In contrast, in the less developed regions, where the rate of natural increase was 24 per thousand, a net migration rate of -0.4 per thousand helped reduce the rate of natural increase by a meagre 1.7 per cent in the early 1970s. In 1995-2000, the relative impact of migration on the growth of the more developed regions had increased markedly, with net migration nearly doubling the contribution of natural increase (2.2 per thousand vs. 1.2 per thousand). In the less developed regions, net migration was still reducing the rate of natural increase by a small percentage (3.3 per cent).

In other words, although developing countries as a whole have been consistently losing population because of international migration, their overall rate of natural increase is still so high that net emigration has had only a small impact on population growth. In sharp contrast, the rising net inflows of international migrants to the more developed regions will continue to be crucial for population growth or, in some cases, to prevent population reductions. Europe, in particular, would have experienced a population decline of 4.4 million during 1995-2000 had it not been for migrant inflows: Europe added some 5 million migrants between 1995 and 2000, but increased its population by only 600,000 people. As shown in **Table 23.4**, the net migration rate of Europe in 1995-2000 (1.4 per thousand)[10] has been barely enough to offset the negative rate of natural increase of -1.2 per thousand experienced during that period.

The contribution of net migration to population growth has also increased in North America from the equivalent of 45 per cent of natural increase in 1970-1975 to 75 per cent in 1995-2000. In contrast, the relative contribution of net migration has declined in Oceania from 45 to 27 per cent of natural increase.

At the country level, Germany's population would have declined since at least 1970, were it not for the net migration gains. In the late 1990s, positive net migration has made major contributions to the population growth of countries like Austria, Denmark, Greece, Italy, Luxembourg, Spain and Switzerland, where it has at least tripled the rate of natural population increase.

In sum, international migrants are increasingly concentrated in developed countries with relatively few countries accounting for the majority of the migrants (28 in 2000). Virtually the entire growth in international migrant stocks during the 1990s has been absorbed by developed countries, in particular the US, Europe and Australia. Although in 2000 the number of countries where international migrants constituted at least 10 per cent of the population had increased markedly to 70, the vast majority of these countries have small overall populations and small numbers of international migrants. The impact of international migration is particularly important for western countries, because they attract more international migrants than the rest of the world and migration contributes significantly to raising their low or negative natural growth rates. Lastly, the

8. *As stated in footnote 3, the data used as a basis for these estimates include undocumented migrants, among them at least 7 million migrants in an irregular situation living in the US and no doubt significant numbers in other countries.*

9. *The rate of natural increase is the difference between births and deaths in the population in relation to the population at risk of experiencing those births and deaths. Natural increase does not take into account the impact of international migration on population growth or decrease.*

10. *Note that the geographic delimitation of Europe in this chapter is different from that in the chapter on "Migrants in an Enlarged Europe".*

primacy of the US as a migrant receiving country has increased markedly. In 2000, one in five international migrants lived in the US.

INTERNATIONAL MIGRATION IN WESTERN EUROPE[11]

CHANGES in the international migration landscape have been particularly dramatic in Europe since 1970. With the onset in 1973 of the recession as a result of the sharp oil price increases, governments that had encouraged the admission of foreign workers in previous decades decided to halt their recruitment, permitting the continued stay of those already on their territory and facilitating their reunification with immediate family members. The oil price shock therefore marked the beginning of a settlement phase of labour migrant populations. The overall migrant population in Europe increased from 18.7 million in 1970 to 22.2 million in 1980 (**Table 23.1**). Flow statistics for Belgium, Denmark, Germany, the Netherlands and Sweden indicate that the levels of net migration for those countries remained low or even became negative between 1975 and 1984. For most of them, negative net migration was the result of losses from other developed countries, while the gains continued to come from developing countries (Zlotnik, 1998). Family reunification contributed to maintaining positive net migration from developing countries, whereas during 1975-1984, return migration more than counterbalanced the inflows from other European countries.

By the early 1980s, the economic configuration of Europe was changing. The European Community, which had expanded in 1973 to include Denmark, Ireland and the UK, approved the membership of Greece in 1981. Although Greek workers were only granted the right to free movement in 1988, the admission of Greece into the Community was a sign that the country was no longer considered a supplier of labour. Further enlargement of the European Union in 1986, with the admission of Portugal and Spain, did not trigger an increase in emigration from those countries to other member states. In all three cases, as with Italy in the 1960s, free movement within the Community was granted when they were no longer likely to produce major outflows of workers. In fact, Italy, Spain and to a lesser extent Greece and Portugal, became poles of attraction for citizens from other EU member states and for migrants from developing countries, who often entered and stayed in an irregular situation.[12] In Europe as a whole, the number of international migrants rose by 4.1 million in the 1980s, reaching 26.3 million in 1990 (**Table 23.1**).[13]

Inflows to Europe increased and diversified in the mid-1980s, when the Communist regimes in some former East European countries[14] began to loosen their grip on travel abroad, or became more lenient towards the emigration of certain ethnic groups (e.g. Jews or ethnic Germans). Germany, in particular, registered major increases in the net intake of migrants from the former Soviet Union, mainly *Aussiedler or* ethnic Germans, who had the right to German citizenship upon entry into Germany. Most *Aussiedler* originated in Kazakhstan, Poland and the Russian Federation. During 1985-1989, Germany added an annual average of 284,000 persons through the return of "ethnic Germans" who obtained citizenship after their return, and migrants from Eastern Europe; by 1990-1994, that number had risen to about half a million (Zlotnik, 1998). By the late 1990s, the net inflow from these countries dropped again to about 280,000 persons annually, as the number of ethnic Germans abroad declined and the government took measures to slow the inflow. Other ethnic flows of relative importance were Greeks from

11. *See footnote 5 for a list of the countries covered.*

12. *In Italy, for instance, the number of foreigners increased from 183,000 in 1980 to 781,000 in 1990, while in Spain the increase in foreigners occurred mostly in the 1990s, rising from 279,000 in 1990 to 1.1 million in 2001.*

13. *Compare these with the generally higher figures presented in the chapter on "Migrants in an Enlarged Europe", which uses censuses and other sources to estimate the number of international migrants.*

14. *See footnote 5 for a listing of the countries covered under Eastern Europe.*

Albania and the successor states of the former Soviet Union, Hungarians from Romania and Slovakia (some from Serbian Vojvodina) and, above all, ethnic Russians after the republics they lived in became independent.

In addition, between 1990 and 2000, western Europe received more than 2 million asylum applications from citizens of the former Eastern bloc countries. The disintegration of former Yugoslavia – the war in Croatia in 1991 and the confrontation that began in Bosnia and Herzegovina in 1992, in particular – generated outflows of almost half a million persons a year between 1990 and 1994 (UN, 2002). Although refugee status was granted to only a small number of applicants, many were allowed to stay for humanitarian reasons.

But flows of asylum seekers had become controversial as the main armed conflicts subsided and the reasons for admitting large numbers waned. Although most EU member states had tightened their asylum regulations by the mid-1990s, countries like Belgium, France, the Netherlands, Sweden and the UK experienced increases in asylum applications in the late 1990s that continued until the early part of the 21st century because of ongoing conflicts in Afghanistan, Western Asia and parts of sub-Saharan Africa. These trends, together with developments in the former Soviet Union, significantly increased the proportion of refugees among international migrants in Europe and the former Soviet Union from 2.3 per cent in 1990 to 3.9 per cent in 2000 (Table 23.5).

As a result of these developments and the improved economic climate in most western European countries in the late 1990s, the number of international migrants on the continent rose by 6.5 million in the 1990s and reached 32.8 million by 2000. Increases occurred not only in terms of the foreign-born population, but also in respect of those who remained foreigners (i.e. non-citizens) in their countries of residence. Increases in the number of foreigners were particularly marked after 1990, especially in countries that had not been major importers of labour in the 1960s. Between 1990 and 2000 the stock of non-citizens more than doubled in Finland, Ireland, Italy, Portugal and Spain. Increases of at least 50 per cent were observed in Austria, Denmark, Luxembourg and the UK. In contrast, the stock of foreigners remained unchanged or declined in Belgium, France, the Netherlands and Sweden (UN, 2004).

In all these countries, both return migration and naturalization contributed to this trend. In Germany, the country with the largest number of foreigners in Europe, the growth of foreign stock depends not only on international migration but also on natural increase, because persons born in Germany did not have the right to German citizenship before the adoption of a new nationality law in 2000.[15] Between 1995 and 2001, about one million foreigners acquired German citizenship through naturalization, and 1.4 million naturalizations were registered in France between 1990 and 2001. Thus, both the reduction of foreign stock in France and its modest growth in Germany owe much to the large number of naturalizations that took place in the 1990s.

There have also been significant changes in the countries of origin of international migrants in Europe. One way of assessing these is to consider the countries of citizenship of the majority of foreigners in each of the major receiving countries. For example, in the period 1980 to 2001, the number of Poles in 16 major European receiving countries[16] tripled, the Moroccans rose by 74 per cent, and British citizens, Turks and citizens from the successor states of former Yugoslavia increased by about 40 per cent each. In contrast, very small increases or even reductions were evident among the expatriate populations of Greeks, Italians, Portuguese or Spaniards, nationalities that in the 1960s and 1970s accounted for the bulk of migrant workers in other European countries. Little change was also observed in the number of Algerian and US citizens (ibid).

15. *Under the 2000 law, naturalization is possible after a period of 8 years of continuous legal residence compared to 15 years prior to 1 January 2000.*

16. *Austria, Belgium, Denmark, Finland, France, Germany, Ireland, Italy, Luxembourg, Netherlands, Norway, Portugal, Spain, Sweden, Switzerland, UK.*

Also in the period 1980 to 2001, the sum of all the major nationalities of origin accounted for a decreasing proportion of the total foreign population in Western Europe, implying that there is an increasing diversification of the origins of migrants to those countries. More detailed information suggests that the numbers of migrants from Brazil, China, the Dominican Republic, Peru, Senegal, Sri Lanka and Romania have been rising (ibid).

Despite the growing diversification of sources of international migrants, there has not been a comparable diversification of destinations. OECD shows that in 2000 virtually all Algerian migrants were in France, while most Greeks, Poles and Turks were in Germany. There is somewhat greater diversification in the European destinations of migrants from Italy, Morocco, Portugal, Spain, former Yugoslavia or the US. Yet over half of all Portuguese migrants and 45 per cent of all Moroccans were in France, and over 40 per cent of Italians and citizens from the successor states of former Yugoslavia were in Germany. Spaniards were somewhat more evenly distributed between France and Germany, as were citizens of the US between Germany and the UK (OECD, 2004). The tendency for nationalities to cluster in a few destinations reflects the strong migration – often historical – ties between countries and suggests that diversification needs time to evolve.

Although migration to most European countries continues to be restricted, foreign workers remain an important part of the labour force of many of those countries. Foreign workers constituted at least 5 per cent of the labour force in eight of the sixteen major European receiving countries in 2001 (OECD, 2004). Not surprisingly, in small Luxembourg, 61 per cent of the total labour force is foreign (although many of these are commuters from neighbouring countries), but in more populous Switzerland 18 per cent is foreign and in Austria 11 per cent. In virtually all countries with trend data, the proportion of the labour force comprising foreign workers increased between 1990 and 2000. That increase was particularly marked, in relative terms, among the newer countries of destination – Ireland, Italy, Norway, Portugal and Spain.

INTERNATIONAL MIGRATION FROM COUNTRIES WITH ECONOMIES IN TRANSITION

THE COMBINATION of political instability, ethnic conflict, economic hardship and the opening of borders following the end of communist rule in the former eastern bloc and Soviet Union prompted a new wave of international migration, both among the affected countries and from there to the West. Emigration from the former had begun to rise in the 1980s, but reached unprecedented levels during 1990-1994, when over one million persons migrated to the "Western bloc" destinations. International migration among the countries of Eastern Europe and the former Soviet Union was even higher and estimated at between 1.5 million and 2 million annually (UN, 2002). The disintegration of Czechoslovakia, the USSR and Yugoslavia contributed to this increase, as persons belonging to some of the newly independent states, but residing in others, repatriated. These movements were often fuelled by rising ethnic tensions, especially in former Yugoslavia and some of the successor states of the Soviet Union. The ensuing protracted conflicts, particularly in former Yugoslavia, caused massive population displacements.

Aside from the emigration of ethnic Germans to Germany, Pontian Greeks to Greece and Jews to Israel and the US, most migrants originating in the successor states of the former Soviet Union moved to other countries in that group, particularly to the Russian Federation. Thus, from 1992 to 1998, the Russian Federation received a net inflow of 3.7 million migrants from other members of the Commonwealth of Independent States (CIS)[17] and the Baltic States. Nearly 80 per cent of the migrants

17. *The Commonwealth of Independent States (CIS) includes 12 of the 15 independent states which constituted the former Soviet Union. Western CIS refers to Belarus, Ukraine and Moldova. See also the sub-chapter "Migration in Eastern Europe and Central Asia".*

received by the Russian Federation during this period were ethnic Russians.

In the 1990s, certain countries in Eastern and Central Europe began attracting new types of migrants. For example, the Czech Republic, Hungary and Poland found themselves acting as countries of transit for migrants headed west or as destinations of short-term travellers often engaged in unauthorized economic activities, including trading. While mostly unrecorded, these movements appear to be an important source of income for the inhabitants of neighbouring countries (Okólski, 1998).

The enlargement of the EU through admission of ten new members on 1 May 2004 (Cyprus, the Czech Republic, Estonia, Hungary, Latvia, Lithuania, Malta, Poland, Slovakia and Slovenia) has opened the possibility of freer flows of workers from East to West. Recent studies conclude that enlargement will likely have a moderate impact on migration flows within the EU, with the stronger effects being felt in those regions of Austria and Germany bordering the newly admitted states. Wages and employment are not expected to be much affected by the temporary increase in migration flows.[18] Nevertheless, accession treaties for the new member states include transitional clauses restricting the mobility of workers within the expanded EU; and requirements exacted from new members prior to their accession reduce the migration incentives for their nationals.

THE TRADITIONAL COUNTRIES OF IMMIGRATION

Australia, Canada, New Zealand and the US are among the few countries in the world admitting immigrants for permanent settlement. As expected, the number of immigrants in these four countries increased markedly during 1970-2000, rising from 15.9 million to 46.4 million. The US registered the major increase of over 25 million migrants and a rise in its foreign-born population from 9.7 million to 35 million.[19] Canada registered a net gain of 2.6 million migrants during this period, Australia 2.2 million and New Zealand 0.4 million. By 2000, Canada was hosting 5.8 million foreign-born residents, Australia 4.7 million and New Zealand 0.8 million.

Immigration to these countries has been determined by their respective admission policies. In 1965, the US modified its admission system by eliminating the quotas by region of origin used until then and substituting selection criteria based mainly on family ties with US citizens or permanent US residents. In the 1970s, Australia and Canada followed suit, eliminating their selection systems based on national origins and adopting their respective versions of a "points system" for economic migrants, under which the different attributes of prospective immigrants are graded and weighted for admission. As a result of these changes, all three countries experienced a diversification of immigration flows. Yet, there are significant differences in the admission policies of each (Table 23.6). Although Australia and Canada, together with western Europe, registered fairly low immigration levels in 1975-1984, since 1985 their intake diverged significantly: in 2000-2002, immigration to Canada rose above the previously recorded levels to an annual average of 238,000 (i.e. above the planned range of 200,000 – 225,000, while the annual average intake of immigrants in Australia remained below 100,000 throughout the 1990s.

Trends in the US were different: between 1970 and 1995, the average annual number of immigrants admitted increased steadily. The slight decline recorded in 1995-2000 is due to delays in the processing of applications. During the 1990s, the US admitted an annual average of over 750,000 immigrants, and by the early 21st century that number had grown to nearly a million immigrants per year. The actual number of immigrants processed

18. *See the chapter on "Migrants in an Enlarged Europe".*

19. *These numbers differ from those normally reported in US sources because they include the number of foreign-born persons enumerated in the US who were US citizens by birth (that is, children born abroad to to US parents).*

during the period 1989-1994 was higher than that listed in **Table 23.6**, because the table excludes the 2.7 million immigrants whose status was regularized as a result of the Immigration Reform and Control Act (IRCA) of 1986, 75 per cent of whom were Mexican. As a result of that regularization, the number of migrants in an irregular situation in the US declined from an estimated 4 million in 1986 to 2.5 million in 1989. However, irregular immigration appears to have continued unabated during the 1990s, especially as the US economy boomed. The number of unauthorized migrants in the US in January 2000 was estimated at 7 million,[20] 4.8 million of whom were Mexican (US Immigration and Naturalization Service, 2003).

In all three countries, immigrant flows have diversified in terms of origin. The proportion of immigrants from developing countries increased in all of them; especially in Australia, registering an increase from 20 per cent in 1970-1974 to 60 per cent in 1990-1994, and Canada, where a rise from 42 per cent to 78 per cent for the same time period was registered. In the US, migrants from developing countries already accounted for 70 per cent of the immigrant intake in 1970-1974. That proportion rose to 87 per cent in 1985-1989 and has remained close to 80 per cent since 1990. If regularized migrants were included in the statistics for the early 1990s, the proportion originating in developing countries would rise considerably.

There has been a tendency for the proportion of immigrants originating in the former Eastern bloc countries to increase in all three countries, but the rise occurred earlier in Canada (early 1980s) than in Australia or the US (1990s). In addition, in Australia the proportion of immigrants originating in developed countries rose after 1995.

Immigrants from Asia accounted for a growing share of the immigrant intake in all three countries of immigration, but particularly in Canada, where over half of the immigrants admitted since 1995 originated in Asia. In Australia, the highest relative levels of Asian migration were recorded in 1990-1994, while in the US they occurred in 1980-1984 when important contingents of refugees from Indo-China were being resettled. Immigrants from Latin America and the Caribbean have generally constituted very high proportions of the immigrant admissions to the US. During the 1990s, they surpassed the share of Asian migrants, especially if the admissions resulting from the IRCA regularization are taken into account. Even in the absence of that regularization, Mexico would have been the major source of immigrants to the US since at least 1980.

There is considerable diversity in the countries of origin of immigrants to the countries of destination. However, Canada and the US have tended to have a more diversified immigrant intake than Australia. Among the immigrants admitted during 1990-1994, 26 countries accounted for three-quarters of those admitted by the US, 24 for those admitted by Canada and just 12 for those received by Australia. A major component of immigration to Australia is the free movement of citizens from neighbouring New Zealand and from other countries or areas in Oceania.

A common feature of the traditional countries of immigration is the importance of family ties in the selection of immigrants. Admissions on the basis of family reunification are, therefore, a major component of the immigrant intake in those countries. Nevertheless, as **Table 23.7** shows, there are wide differences regarding the importance of family reunification among them. In the US, family reunification accounts for 70 per cent or more of total immigration, while its share in Canada is somewhat higher than 60 per cent and in Australia it is considerably below 50 per cent. Furthermore, a comparison with European countries indicates that Denmark, France and Sweden also admit around 60 per cent of their long-term migrants on the basis of family reunification. Because refugees also represent a high proportion of the migrant intake of those countries, the share of economically motivated

20. *Other estimates have put the total number of unauthorized migrants in the US in 2000 at 8.5 million (Passel, 2001 and 2002). Today, that estimate has risen over 9 million (see also the chapter "Economist Costs and Benefits of International Labour Migration").*

migration (the admission of workers) is relatively low, ranging from 2 per cent in Sweden to between 20 – 30 per cent in Denmark and France. The pattern of admissions is different in Switzerland and the UK, where the proportions of long-term immigrants admitted for work are high and the share of those admitted for family reunification is generally below 50 per cent. Furthermore, trends in these countries are similar to those in Australia, in that the share of family-based admissions has declined in favour of workers, mostly skilled immigrants. Thus, not only is there considerable variation among the traditional countries of immigration in the types of immigrants admitted, but the variability of circumstances resembles that found among European countries.

The admission of skilled workers is another area of convergence among receiving countries in the developed world. The numbers and percentages of persons formally admitted as skilled immigrants by the traditional countries of immigration have tended to increase between the early and the late 1990s, and similar trends have characterized admissions of skilled personnel in Sweden and the UK. By 2001, skilled immigrants and their family members constituted over half the immigrant intake in Australia, Canada and New Zealand, and nearly one-third of long-term immigrants admitted to the UK (**Table 23.8**). This trend appears to be continuing, indeed increasing.

Lastly, another means of having recourse to foreign skilled workers is by admitting them under temporary visas or permits. All traditional countries of immigration allow such temporary admission and, as shown in **Table 23.9**, they have admitted a growing number of skilled workers. Increases in the temporary admission of skilled persons are also evident in France and the UK. However, there are also striking differences among the admissions levels of various countries, with over half a million being reported in the US in 2000, over 100,000 each in Australia and the UK, slightly less than 100,000 in Canada and nearly 50,000 in New Zealand. France, with less than 10,000, appears as an anomaly.

Although lack of comparability may be the cause of such diversity, it is clear that the temporary migration of skilled workers is very significant and a major contribution to the migration intake of the main receiving countries of the developed world.

LABOUR MIGRATION IN ASIA

In 1970, Asia[21] accounted for 35 per cent of the world's migrant stock (**Table 23.1**). By 2000, that share had declined to 25 per cent, although Asia experienced a major increase in refugees from 2 million in 1970 to 9.8 million in 2000, and had seen the share of other international migrants increase from 26.1 million in 1970 to 33.9 million in 2000 (**Table 23.5**). In particular, international labour migration from and within Asia expanded rapidly from 1970 onwards. Following the sharp increase in the oil price in 1973, the oil-producing countries of Western Asia accelerated the intake of foreign workers, initially for the construction of needed infrastructure. The migrant stock in the six member states of the Gulf Cooperation Council (GCC: Bahrain, Kuwait, Oman, Qatar, Saudi Arabia and the United Arab Emirates) rose from an estimated 1 million in 1970 to 4 million in 1980, and to 9.6 million in 2000, of which 5.3 million resided in Saudi Arabia (**Table 23.10**). It is estimated that by 2000 international migrants constituted 38 per cent of the population in Bahrain, 49 per cent in Kuwait, 26 per cent in Oman, 70 per cent in Qatar, 24 per cent in Saudi Arabia and 68 per cent in the United Arab Emirates (UN, 2004). As migration increased, workers were recruited from more distant origins. While in the 1970s migrant workers had mostly been imported from other Arab countries, by the late 1970s they were being recruited from Bangladesh, India and Pakistan, and soon also from several East and Southeast Asian countries, especially the Republic of Korea, the

21. *Note that the United Nations uses a geographical delineation of regions of Asia where the Central Asian Republics are part of South-Central Asia; and the Caucasian countries of Armenia, Azerbaijan and Georgia plus the countries of the Middle East and the Gulf Cooperation Council are part of Western Asia.*

Philippines and, later, Thailand, Sri Lanka and Indonesia.

Iraq's invasion of Kuwait in August 1990 had a significant effect on the foreign population in the GCC. During the first four months of the invasion, more than 2 million foreigners are estimated to have left Iraq, Kuwait and Saudi Arabia (Russell, 1992). Soon after the end of the war in 1991, foreign workers began to return to Kuwait and Saudi Arabia. However, changes in political alignments during the crisis led to the repatriation of important groups of foreigners, such as Jordanians, Palestinians and Yemenis, and to the recruitment of workers from Egypt and the main sending countries in East and Southeast Asia to fill the jobs vacated by those departing.

During the past 30 years, labour migration to the GCC countries evolved in terms of occupations and the participation of women. Once the construction of infrastructure was over, migrant workers began to move from the construction to the services sector. As part of the rising demand for service workers, women began to be recruited as migrant workers, mainly as domestic workers. Hence their numbers rose while the foreign labour force in the GCC countries remained primarily male. By the early 1990s, women constituted 25 per cent of the foreign labour force in Kuwait, 10 per cent in Oman and 9 per cent in Qatar (UN, 2003b, **Table 23.10**).

In the 1980s, sustained economic growth in Japan and the newly industrialized countries of East and Southeast Asia began to attract foreign workers from less prosperous countries in the region. Hong Kong and Singapore, which had long been importers of migrant workers, as well as Japan, Malaysia, the Republic of Korea and Taiwan, provided an alternative destination for unskilled workers from countries such as China, Indonesia, the Philippines or Thailand. As in other settings, migrant workers inserted themselves mostly in construction and certain manufacturing industries, such as the automotive industry in Japan or the electronics sector in the Republic of Korea or Taiwan. Labour migration within East and Southeast Asia involved a high participation of women, who found employment mainly in the service sector, typically as domestic workers.

Japan deserves special attention because, until the early 1980s, it had achieved rapid economic growth without resorting to foreign workers. However, as Japanese workers became more affluent and shunned certain low-paying jobs, foreign workers flowed in to fill them. Between 1975 and 2001, the number of legally resident foreigners in Japan more than doubled from 750,000 to 1.8 million (OECD, 1990 and 2004). Increases in the number of foreigners of Japanese descent, originating mostly from Brazil and Peru, accounted for almost half the growth of migrant stock in Japan between 1985 and 1995. But a major part of that growth stemmed from the admission of citizens from other Asian countries as trainees or foreign students allowed to work part-time. In addition, by 2001 there were over 250,000 foreigners in an irregular situation in Japan (Japan, Ministry of Justice, 2001).

The Republic of Korea also began to experience labour shortages in certain sectors of the economy during the 1980s, thus becoming a magnet for both legal and undocumented migrant workers. By 1988, there were 45,000 foreigners in the Republic of Korea and the number of employment related visas issued in 1989 reached 162,000. By 2001, the number of foreign residents had more than quadrupled to 230,000, 129,000 of whom were in the labour force (OECD, 2004). In addition, Korean authorities estimated that the number of migrants in an irregular situation had risen from 65,500 in 1992 to 148,000 in 1997 (Uh, 1999) and, despite a reduction following the financial crisis of 1997, had continued to grow after 1999 to reach an estimated 255,000 in 2002. To control undocumented migration, a regularization drive was carried out in 2002, and the government undertook to deport all those who still remained in an irregular situation in 2003 (OECD, 2004).

Taiwan also had to resort to foreign labour to maintain its economic expansion. In 1991, it recruited 3,000 contract workers, all destined for the construction industry. By 1993, the number of admitted contract workers had risen to 98,000, 74 per cent employed in the manufacturing industry. The number of contract workers admitted annually increased steadily, reaching 316,000 in 2000, with 58 per cent working in manufacturing, 12 per cent in construction and 30 per cent, mostly women, in health and domestic services. In 2000, the major countries of origin of contract workers were Thailand (46%), the Philippines (36%) and Indonesia (17%). Most of the workers in the service sector were Filipino (Tsay, 2000; Tsay and Lin, 2001).

Malaysia has a long history of reliance on foreign workers, mostly from neighbouring Indonesia, to work in the plantations. By 1993, the total foreign workforce in Malaysia was estimated at 1.2 million, constituting about 15 per cent of the total labour force in the country (Lim, 1996). During the 1997 Asian financial crisis, many undocumented Indonesian workers had to return home. Nevertheless, the migrant population in Malaysia is estimated to have reached nearly 1.4 million in 2000. As a result of the financial crisis, several receiving countries in the region introduced measures to restrict the admission of foreign workers; but, as in Malaysia, the constraining effect of the crisis on the flows of workers to these countries was only temporary (UN, 2003b).

INTERNATIONAL MIGRATION IN AFRICA

During 1970-2000, Africa was host to the second-largest share of all international migrants in the developing world, after Asia; but this has since declined. In 1970, its share of 9.9 million constituted 12 per cent of the world's international migrants, but by 2000 that share had changed to 16.3 million international migrants, or just 9 per cent of the global migrant stock (**Table** 23.1). One consistent characteristic of international migration in Africa has been the high proportion of refugees. Already in 1970, the one million refugees in Africa accounted for 10 per cent of the continent's total migrant stock (**Table** 23.5). In 1990, when the number of refugees in Africa reached a high of 5.4 million, they represented 33 per cent of all international migrants in the region. By 2000, the number and share of refugees had declined to 3.6 million and 22 per cent, respectively, largely as a result of voluntary repatriations made possible during the late 1990s by the resolution of long-standing conflicts. Nevertheless, political instability and conflicts still affect many African countries, and the forces generating refugees and forced migration in general are not expected to subside in the region in the near future.

Although movements of refugees have been an important aspect of international migration in Africa, other types of migration have accounted for the bulk of international migrants in the region but, as **Table** 23.5 shows, the numbers changed slowly during 1970-1990 from 8.9 million to 10.9 million. A more important increase took place during 1990-2000, when the number of non-refugee international migrants in Africa rose by nearly 2 million to 12.7 million in 2000.

International migration originating in certain parts of Africa has mostly been oriented to other world regions. Thus, migrants from North Africa have tended to go to Europe and the oil-producing countries of the GCC. Within the region, Egyptians and Tunisians have worked, over different periods, in the Libyan Arab Jamahiriya, but fluctuations in international relations among the countries involved have prompted major return flows at different times.

In West Africa, migration has been largely shaped by agricultural workers, including seasonal workers, moving from the landlocked countries bordering the Sahel to those bordering the coast. A major receiving country, Côte d'Ivoire has attracted migrants from surrounding countries, especially Burkina Faso and Mali, to work in its cocoa and coffee plantations or as domestic workers. According to censuses, the foreign population in Côte d'Ivoire increased from nearly 1.5 million in 1975 to 3 million in 1988 and to 4 million in 1996. However, deteriorating economic conditions in the 1990s caused significant return migration to the countries of origin (CERPOD, 1995). Also in the late 1990s, the government of Côte d'Ivoire adopted measures to disenfranchise migrants and deport those in an irregular situation. These measures, together with the waves of violence against foreigners in the early 2000s and the political unrest begun in 2002, have led to major return flows. By 2000, Burkina Faso had become a major receiver of international migrants, largely because of the return of its foreign-born citizens.

Other countries in West Africa host substantial numbers of international migrants. Among them, Ghana and Nigeria were poles of attraction in the 1960s and 1970s, respectively, but, as their economic situation deteriorated, both resorted to mass expulsions of international migrants in an irregular situation. Ghana did so in 1969 and Nigeria in 1983 (UN, 1985). Recent information on the number of international migrants in those countries is lacking; however, Ghana is estimated to have had about 600,000 foreign-born persons in 2000 and Nigeria about 750,000 (UN, 2004).

Gabon, a country rich in natural resources, hosted more than 100,000 international migrants in the early 1990s, but stringent laws enacted in 1995 requiring foreigners to pay residence fees led to the expulsion of more than half of those migrants (IOM, 2000).

In South Africa, the mining industry used to rely heavily on migrant workers from neighbouring countries, recruiting an annual average of 308,000 in the early 1970s; but this dropped to around 200,000 in the 1980s and early 1990s (South Africa, Chamber of Mines, 1987 and 1993). This reflected both a decision by South Africa to cut its dependence on migrant workers, and restrictions on emigration imposed by some countries of origin. South Africa also attracted white settlers from a variety of origins; yet, according to census information, its foreign-born population declined from 1.9 million in 1985 to 1.2 million in 1991. Recent evidence suggests that the inflow of migrants may have increased after the end of apartheid in 1994. The strictly regulated migration of workers for specific industries is now accompanied by substantial irregular migration of unskilled workers, and the authorized inflow of skilled professionals. The number of migrants in an irregular situation is claimed to be very high. A 1997 estimate put the figure at between 3 and 5 million (South Africa, Ministry of Home Affairs, 1999).

Migration among African countries is perhaps the least well documented in the developing world. The rapidity with which some movements start or reverse themselves implies that they are seldom reflected properly in censuses. Furthermore, recent censuses have not been producing as much data on the foreign-born population as earlier ones. Hence, recent trends in the migrant stock of African countries are often only a matter of conjecture. Nevertheless, they suggest that the 1990s witnessed a modest increase in the international mobility of Africans within the continent.

INTERNATIONAL MIGRATION IN LATIN AMERICA AND THE CARIBBEAN

IN CONTRAST to Africa, most countries in Latin America and the Caribbean have relatively comprehensive data on the foreign-born population derived from censuses. Hence, the finding that the number of international migrants in the region declined from 7 million to 5.9 million during 1990-2000 bears highlighting (**Table 23.2**). This drop is largely the result of the successful repatriation of refugees in Central America in the early 1990s. As Table 23.5 indicates, the 1.2 million refugees reported by Latin American countries in 1990 had disappeared by 2000. Excluding refugees, the stock of international migrants in the region has changed minimally since 1980, oscillating between 5.8 million and 6 million.

International migration in the Americas is dominated by flows to the US and, to a lesser extent, Canada. Migration between Latin American countries is low in comparison. Mexico dominates the flows to the US. In 1964, when the *Bracero* programme came to an end, the US admitted about 40,000 Mexican immigrants annually. In the late 1980s, that number had risen to

73,000, even without the Mexicans legalized under IRCA. By the late 1990s, annual legal immigration to the US from Mexico averaged 139,000 persons per year, again excluding IRCA legalizations. In addition, over 2 million Mexicans became legal immigrants as a result of IRCA. According to US censuses, the Mexican-born population in the US increased from 750,000 in 1970 to 4.3 million in 1990, and to nearly 10 million in 2000 (US Census Bureau, 2001). Despite the substantial legal immigration from Mexico, it is estimated that about half the Mexican-born population in the US in 2000 (4.8 million) was in an irregular situation (US Immigration and Naturalization Service, 2003). Despite the hope that the 1994 North American Free Trade Agreement might result in lower emigration from Mexico to the US, the flows have increased.

In Central America the conflicts and other socio-political disruptions affecting several countries during the 1980s led to major outflows of displaced persons and refugees, and a sharp increase in the number of international migrants in the region from 0.6 million in 1980 to 1.9 million in 1990 (UN, 2004). During that decade, the number of international migrants in Costa Rica, Guatemala, Honduras and Mexico rose by 1.2 million. The resolution of conflicts in the 1990s prompted the voluntary repatriation of a large number of persons, particularly to El Salvador, Guatemala and Nicaragua. As a result, the migrant stock in the four major receiving countries of the region declined by 0.7 million during 1990-2000. By 2000, Central America had 1.1 million international migrants, with over half a million in Mexico and more than 300,000 in Costa Rica. The main countries of origin in the region remained El Salvador, Guatemala and Nicaragua (Villa and Pizarro, 2001).

In South America, Argentina and Venezuela were important countries of immigration in the early 20th century, and were poles of attraction for migrant workers from neighbouring countries. While Argentina has been the main destination for migrants from the southern cone, particularly from Bolivia and Paraguay, but also from Brazil, Chile and Uruguay, Venezuela attracted migrants from the Andean region, especially neighbouring Colombia during the 1970s oil boom. However, in the late 1980s and the 1990s, the return to Europe of former European immigrants and their descendants led to a reduction in the foreign-born population in both countries.

In the Caribbean, the small populations of the countries or areas in the region, coupled with long traditions of international mobility, imply that migration has had a considerable impact on their population composition. In half the Caribbean countries or areas, international migrants constitute more than 10 per cent of the population, and more than a third in Aruba, the British Virgin Islands, the Cayman Islands and the US Virgin Islands (UN, 2004). The majority of migrants in the Caribbean originate in other Caribbean countries (Villa and Pizarro, 2001). Emigration from the Caribbean is also important, with most of it directed to the US, especially from Cuba, the Dominican Republic, Jamaica and Haiti. In 2000, there were 873,000 Cuban-born persons in the US, 688,000 born in the Dominican Republic, 553,000 from Jamaica and 419,000 from Haiti.

CONCLUSION

Over the course of the 20th century, population mobility increased markedly, and a large part of that increase occurred in the last decades of the century. As this chapter has shown, one measure of international mobility, the stock of international migrants, rose from 82 million in 1970 to 175 million in 2000, more than doubling over the course of thirty years. Yet, a major contributor to that increase was not population mobility per se, but rather the emergence of newly independent states after the disintegration of the Soviet Union. Without this, the number of international migrants in 2000 would have been some 27 million lower, and the rate of increase in their numbers during the latter part of the century would not have been as pronounced.

The data presented also show that the number of international migrants did not grow at the same rate in every region of the world. Even without the effect of the break-up of the Soviet Union, the growth rate of the stock of international migrants was more rapid in the developed than in the developing regions. In fact, estimates for the 1990s indicate that the number of international migrants in developing countries as a whole hardly changed.

Regarding the participation of women in international migration, current estimates show that 48.6 per cent of all international migrants are female, a slight increase over the 47.2 per cent estimated in 1970. Thus, the participation of women in international migration has been high for a long time, especially when directed to developed countries. In fact, available estimates indicate that the female share of the international migrant stock declined somewhat in the developing world from 45.7 per cent in 1970 to 44.6 per cent in 2000. Increases in the female share of international migration are therefore neither uniform nor universal, and are small compared to the high proportion of females estimated in the 1970s. This perspective belies the claim that international migration is becoming increasingly feminized. While it is true that the participation of women in certain types of flows, and from certain countries, has risen, the main finding is that, already by 1970 overall female migration had nearly reached parity with male migration.

The late 20th century did witness some key changes in international migration trends, though they are not as dramatic as often portrayed. For one, the steady and rapid increase in the number of international migrants in the developed world has led to a greater concentration of international migrants in developed countries. The US, in particular, now accounts for one in every five international migrants in the world. Most of the international migrants remain concentrated in a few countries (28 at last count) and, while that number has been growing, it has done so slowly.

International migrants do represent a high proportion (a quarter or more) of the population of an increasing number of countries or areas, but most of these have small populations (under 8 million in 2000) and have had high proportions of international migrants since the 1970s. There are, however, some important shifts in the major poles of attraction within some regions. Perhaps the most significant was the transformation of the rapidly industrializing countries of East and Southeast Asia into destinations for migrant workers in the late 1980s and the 1990s. A number of these had themselves been important sources of emigrants just a decade before. In fact, some, for instance Malaysia or the Republic of Korea, experience both significant outflows of citizens and inflows of foreign workers, and in this regard are similar to a number of European countries that since the 1970s, have been registering net losses of citizens and net gains of foreigners.

International migration has never been a one-way street, although the general lack of data on emigration often leads to the false assumption that countries receiving migrants are not themselves also the origin of migrant outflows. Even the US, the major attraction pole in the world, is estimated to lose 200,000 emigrants annually, and there are significant populations of American expatriates in a number of European countries and elsewhere.

The transformation of flows in Europe should also be underscored. During the 1980s, the former labour-sending countries of southern Europe, especially those newly admitted to the EU, became key destinations for international migrants seeking employment. In addition, East-West migration flows increased with the changes in former communist countries, and became a major part of the migrant intake of a number of western countries, especially after the disintegration of the Soviet Union or former Yugoslavia. Family reunification of refugees and migrants became a significant part of migrant inflows to western Europe. Concomitantly, the opening of borders among former "Eastern bloc" countries and the break-up of the Soviet Union caused movements among those countries, driven in part by the "un-mixing" of nationalities as certain ethnic groups sought to return to their republics of origin.

In the 1990s, developed countries either commenced or redoubled efforts to attract temporary skilled workers from abroad to satisfy the demand in particular sectors of their economies. Consequently, temporary admissions of workers grew in number both in the traditional countries of immigration, such as Australia and the US, and in a number of European countries. This has led to some diversification of major source countries of migrants to the main receiving countries in the developed world.

In the developing world, especially Africa and Latin America and the Caribbean, migration to destinations outside the region is more voluminous than that occurring within the region. The reduction in refugees during the 1990s led to the slow growth in international migrants in Africa and their decline in Latin America. In both regions, some of the earlier important poles of attraction have themselves been experiencing economic or political difficulties, that resulted in sizeable return flows of former migrants or the outright emigration of their citizens.

Clearly, international migration evolves as the economic, social and political situation of countries changes. With more independent states, the possibilities for international migration increase. Furthermore, because there continue to be wide economic disparities among countries, there is ample room for population movements to respond to the opportunities available in the better-off countries, be they in developed or the more prosperous developing countries. Differences in demographic dynamics also play a part, as the better-off countries tend to be those where fertility rates are lower and population ageing is accelerating. International migration is already helping to prevent or slow down the population decline in a number of countries in the developed world, and it is expected to continue to play that role in the future (**Tables 23.11 and 23.12**).

TABLE 23.1

EVOLUTION OF THE NUMBER OF INTERNATIONAL MIGRANTS IN THE WORLD AND MAJOR AREAS, AND SELECTED INDICATORS REGARDING THE STOCK OF INTERNATIONAL MIGRANTS, 1970-2000

Major area	Number of international migrants (millions)				Average annual rate of growth of the number of international migrants (percentage)			International migrants as a percentage of the population		Percentage distribution of international migrants by region	
	1970	1980	1990	2000	1970-1980	1980-1990	1990-2000	1970	2000	1970	2000
World	81,5	99,8	154,0	174,9	2,0	4,3	1,3	2,2	2,9	100,0	100,0
Developed countries	38,3	47,7	89,7	110,3	2,2	6,3	2,1	3,6	8,7	47,0	63,1
Developed countries excluding USSR	35,2	44,5	59,3	80,8	2,3	2,9	3,0	4,3	8,3	43,2	46,2
Developing countries	43,2	52,1	64,3	64,6	1,8	2,1	0,0	1,6	1,3	53,0	36,9
Africa	9,9	14,1	16,2	16,3	3,6	1,4	0,0	2,8	2,0	12,1	9,3
Asia[a]	28,1	32,3	41,8	43,8	1,4	2,6	0,5	1,3	1,2	34,5	25,0
Latin America and the Caribbean	5,8	6,1	7,0	5,9	0,7	1,3	-1,7	2,0	1,1	7,1	3,4
Northern America	13,0	18,1	27,6	40,8	3,3	4,2	3,9	5,6	12,9	15,9	23,3
Oceania	3,0	3,8	4,8	5,8	2,1	2,3	2,1	15,6	18,8	3,7	3,3
Europe[b]	18,7	22,2	26,3	32,8	1,7	1,7	2,2	4,1	6,4	22,9	18,7
USSR (former)	3,1	3,3	30,3	29,5	0,5	22,3	-0,3	1,3	10,2	3,8	16,8

a. Excluding Armenia, Azerbaijan, Georgia, Kazakhstan, Kyrgyzstan, Tajikistan, Turkmenistan and Uzbekistan.
b. Excluding Belarus, Estonia, Latvia, Lithuania, the Republic of Moldova, the Russian Federation and Ukraine.

Source: United Nations, *Trends in Total Migrant Stock*: The 2003 Revision (POP/DB/MIG/2003/1 and ESA/P/WP.188), data in digital form.

TABLE 23.2

PROPORTION FEMALE AMONG THE STOCK OF INTERNATIONAL MIGRANTS BY MAJOR AREA, 1970 AND 2000

Major area	1970	2000
World	47,2	48,6
Developed countries	49,0	51,0
Developed countries excluding USSR	49,0	50,6
Developing countries	45,7	44,6
Africa	42,7	46,7
Asia[a]	46,6	43,3
Latin America and the Caribbean	46,8	50,2
Northern America	51,1	50,3
Oceania	46,5	50,5
Europe[b]	48,0	51,0
USSR (Former)	48,0	52,1

a. Excluding Armenia, Azerbaijan, Georgia, Kazakhstan, Kyrgyzstan, Tajikistan, Turkmenistan and Uzbekistan.
b. Excluding Belarus, Estonia, Latvia, Lithuania, the Republic of Moldova, the Russian Federation and Ukraine.

Source:
United Nations, *Trends in Total Migrant Stock: The 2003 Revision* (POP/DB/MIG/2003/1 and ESA/P/WP.188), data in digital form.

TABLE 23.3

COUNTRIES HOSTING THE LARGEST NUMBER OF INTERNATIONAL MIGRANTS, 1970 AND 2000

		1970					2000		
Rank	Country or area	Migrant stock (millions)	Percentage of the world's migrant stock	Cumulated percentage	Rank	Country or area	Migrant stock (millions)	Percentage of the world's migrant stock	Cumulated percentage
1	United States	9,7	11,9	11,9	1	United States	35,0	20,0	20,0
2	India	9,1	11,2	23,1	2	Russian Federation	13,3	7,6	27,6
3	France	5,2	6,4	29,5	3	Germany	7,3	4,2	31,8
4	Pakistan	5,1	6,3	35,8	4	Ukraine	6,9	4,0	35,8
5	Canada	3,3	4,0	39,8	5	France	6,3	3,6	39,4
6	USSR (former)	3,1	3,8	43,6	6	India	6,3	3,6	43,0
7	United Kingdom	2,9	3,6	47,2	7	Canada	5,8	3,3	46,3
8	Germany	2,6	3,2	50,4	8	Saudi Arabia	5,3	3,0	49,3
9	Australia	2,5	3,0	53,4	9	Australia	4,7	2,7	52,0
10	Argentina	2,3	2,8	56,2	10	Pakistan	4,2	2,4	54,4
11	Poland	2,1	2,6	58,8	11	United Kingdom	4,0	2,3	56,7
12	China, Hong Kong SAR	1,7	2,1	60,9	12	Kazakhstan	3,0	1,7	58,4
13	Dem. Rep. of the Congo	1,4	1,7	62,6	13	China, Hong Kong SAR	2,7	1,5	59,9
14	Israel	1,4	1,7	64,3	14	Côte d'Ivoire	2,3	1,3	61,2
15	Brazil	1,3	1,6	65,9	15	Iran (Islamic Republic of)	2,3	1,3	62,5
16	Indonesia	1,2	1,4	67,3	16	Israel	2,3	1,3	63,8
17	Côte d' Ivoire	1,1	1,4	68,7	17	Poland	2,1	1,2	65,0
18	Switzerland	1,1	1,4	70,1	18	Jordan	1,9	1,1	66,1
19	South Africa	1,0	1,2	71,3	19	United Arab Emirates	1,9	1,1	67,2
20	Uganda	1,0	1,2	72,5	20	Switzerland	1,8	1,0	68,2
21	Italy	0,9	1,1	73,6	21	Occupied Palestinian Terr.	1,7	1,0	69,2
22	Occupied Palestinian Terr.	0,9	1,1	74,7	22	Italy	1,6	0,9	70,1
23	Sri Lanka	0,8	1,0	75,7	23	Japan	1,6	0,9	71,0
					24	Netherlands	1,6	0,9	71,9
					25	Turkey	1,5	0,9	72,8
					26	Argentina	1,4	0,8	73,6
					27	Malaysia	1,4	0,8	74,4
					28	Uzbekistan	1,4	0,8	75,2
	World	81,5	100,0	100,0		World	174,9	100,0	100,0

Source:
United Nations, *Trends in Total Migrant Stock: The 2003 Revision* (POP/DB/MIG/2003/1 and ESA/P/WP.188), data in digital form.

TABLE 23.4

CONTRIBUTION OF NET INTERNATIONAL MIGRATION TO POPULATION GROWTH OR DECREASE, 1970-1975 AND 1995-2000

	1970-1975				1995-2000			
Major area	Net migration rate (per 1,000)	Rate of natural increase (per 1,000)	Population growth rate (per 1,000)	Net migration as percentage of natural increase	Net migration rate (per 1,000)	Rate of natural increase (per 1,000)	Population growth rate (per 1,000)	Net migration as percentage of natural increase
More developed regions	1,0	6,8	7,8	14,7	2,2	1,2	3,4	183,3
Less developed regions	-0,4	24,0	23,6	-1,7	-0,6	16,7	16,1	-3,3
Africa	-1,2	27,8	26,6	-4,3	-0,5	24,0	23,5	-2,1
Asia	-0,1	33,9	33,8	-0,3	-0,4	14,5	14,1	-2,8
Latin America and the Caribbean	-1,1	36,5	35,4	-3,0	-1,2	16,8	15,6	-7,1
Northern America	3,0	6,7	9,7	44,8	4,6	6,1	10,7	75,4
Europe	0,3	5,6	5,9	5,4	1,4	-1,2	0,2	..
Oceania	6,4	14,3	20,7	44,8	3,0	11,1	14,1	27,0

Source:
World Population Prospects: The 2002 Revision, Volume I: Comprehensive Tables, United Nations publications, Sales No. E.03.XIII.6, 2003.

TABLE 23.5

ESTIMATES NUMBER OF REFUGEES AND OF OTHER INTERNATIONAL MIGRANTS BY MAJOR AREA, 1970 TO 2000

Major area of asylum	Number of international migrants excluding refugees (millions)				Number of refugees (millions)				Percentage of refugees			
	1970	1980	1990	2000	1970	1980	1990	2000	1970	1980	1990	2000
World	77,2	90,2	135,0	158,3	4,3	9,5	19,0	16,6	5,3	9,6	12,3	9,5
Developed countries	37,1	46,2	87,6	107,1	1,2	1,5	2,0	3,2	3,1	3,1	2,2	2,9
Developing countries	40,1	44,0	47,4	51,2	3,1	8,1	17,0	13,5	7,3	15,5	26,4	20,8
Africa	8,9	10,5	10,9	12,7	1,0	3,6	5,4	3,6	10,1	25,6	33,0	22,0
Asia	26,1	28,0	31,3	33,9	2,0	4,3	10,4	9,8	7,1	13,3	25,0	22,5
Under UNHCR	..	..	..	..	0,2	2,0	7,4	5,1	0,6	6,1	17,7	11,6
Under UNRWA	..	..	..	..	1,9	2,3	3,1	4,8	6,6	7,2	7,3	10,9
Latin America and the Caribbean	5,6	6,0	5,8	5,9	0,1	0,1	1,2	0,0	1,9	2,4	17,1	0,8
Northern America	12,5	17,4	27,0	40,2	0,5	0,6	0,6	0,6	4,0	3,6	2,1	1,6
Oceania	3,0	3,4	4,6	5,8	0,0	0,3	0,1	0,1	1,5	8,4	2,3	1,1
Europe and former USSR	21,2	24,9	55,4	59,8	0,6	0,5	1,3	2,4	2,9	2,1	2,3	3,9

Source: United Nations, *Trends in Total Migrant Stock: The 2003 Revision* (POP/DB/MIG/2003/1 and ESA/P/WP.188), data in digital form.

TABLE 23.6

AVERAGE ANNUAL NUMBER OF ADMISSIONS OF IMMIGRANTS TO AUSTRALIA, CANADA AND THE UNITED STATES AND DISTRIBUTION BY REGION OF ORIGIN, 1970-2001

Receiving country	1970-1974	1975-1979	1980-1984	1985-1989	1990-1994	1995-1999	2000-2002
Average annual number of immigrants (thousands)							
Australia	142	71	95	115	99	87	92
Canada	159	130	114	138	236	204	236
United States	385	462	565	606	770	746	993
Percentage from developing countries							
Australia	20	41	39	53	60	55	53
Canada	42	56	62	71	78	78	78
United States	70	81	85	87	79	82	81
Percentage from economies in transition							
Australia	12	5	7	5	7	9	6
Canada	5	5	9	10	11	12	12
United States	5	3	4	4	11	11	11
Percentage from developed countries							
Australia	69	55	53	42	32	36	41
Canada	52	40	29	19	11	10	10
United States	25	19	11	10	10	7	8
Percentage from Asia							
Australia	12	29	31	41	51	43	40
Canada	22	32	44	40	49	54	54
United States	29	37	45	43	41	33	30
Percentage from Latin America and the Caribbean							
Canada	15	17	13	16	13	8	8
United States	40	41	35	40	35	42	42

Sources: United Nations, *South-to-North International Migration* (POP/1B/MIG/2001/1), data in digital form. OECD, *Trends in International Migration. SOPEMI 2003.* Annual Report. 2003 Edition. Paris: OECD. *United States Department of Homeland Security, Office of Immigration Statistics. 2002 Yearbook of Immigration Statistics.*

TABLE 23.7

COMPARISON OF THE COMPOSITION OF IMMIGRANT OR LONG-TERM MIGRANT ADMISSIONS BY CATEGORY, SELECTED DEVELOPED COUNTRIES, 1991 AND 2001

Receiving country	Workers		Family reunification		Refugees	
	1991	2001	1991	2001	1991	2001
Australia	45	55	47	33	8	12
Canada	18	26	64	62	18	12
United States	10	19	75	70	15	11
Denmark	20	22	60	53	20	25
France	27	20	58	69	15	11
Sweden	2	2	62	65	36	33
Switzerland	47	55	51	42	2	3
United Kingdom	49	54	42	35	9	11

Sources:
OECD, *Trends in International Migration*: SOPEMI. Annual Reports 1998 and 2003, Chart I.2.

TABLE 23.8

NUMBER OF IMMIGRANTS IN THE SKILLED CATEGORIES OF SELECTED COUNTRIES, 1991, 1999 AND 2001

	Number of immigrants in skilled category (thousands)			As percentage of total immigrants		
Country	1991	1999	2001[d]	1991	1999	2001[d]
Australia[a]	41	35	54	37	42	60
Canada[b]	41	81	137	18	47	55
New Zealand	..	13	36	..	47	68
United States[c]	12	57	175	18	22	17
Sweden	0	3	4	6	8	10
United Kingdom	4	32	40	7	33	32

a. The skilled category includes family members with certain professional qualifications and linguistic aptitudes
b. The skilled-worker category includes assisted relatives who are not point-tested.
c. Employment-based preferences category includes family members of skilled workers.
d. The data for the United States refer to 2002.

Sources:
OECD, *Trends in International Migration. SOPEMI. Annual Reports 1992, 2001 and 2004; OECD, International Mobility of the Highly-Skilled.* United States Department of Justice, Immigration and Naturalization Service, *Statistical Yearbook of the Immigration and Naturalization Service*, 1991 and 1999. United States Department of Homeland Security, 2002 *Yearbook of Immigration Statistics.*

TABLE 23.9

NUMBER OF TEMPORARY WORKERS ADMITTED UNDER THE SKILLED-BASED CATEGORIES (THOUSANDS)

Country	1992	1997	1998	1999	2000
Australia	41	82	93	100	116
Canada	70	75	80	85	94
New Zealand	..	27	30	39	48
United States[a]	143	..	343	423	505
France	5	5	4	6	8
United Kingdom	54	80	89	98	124

a. The statistics reflect the number of admissions under H-IB visas, not the number of persons. Double-counting is possible if a person enters the United States more than once during a fiscal year.

Sources:
OECD, *Trends in International Migration. SOPEMI. Annual Reports 1992, 2001 and 2004; OECD, International Mobility of the Highly-Skilled.* United States Department of Justice, Immigration and Naturalization Service, *Statistical Yearbook of the Immigration and Naturalization Service*, 1991 and 1999. United States Department of Homeland Security, 2002 *Yearbook of Immigration Statistics.*

TABLE 23.10

ESTIMATED NUMBER OF INTERNATIONAL MIGRANTS IN THE MEMBERS OF THE GULF COOPERATION COUNCIL, 1970-2000

Country	1970	1980	1990	2000
Bahrain	38	103	173	254
Kuwait	468	964	1 560	1 108
Oman	40	180	450	682
Qatar	63	157	345	409
Saudi Arabia	303	1 804	4 220	5 255
United Arab Emirates	62	737	1 556	1 922
Total	**974**	**3 946**	**8 305**	**9 630**

Sources:
United Nations, *Trends in Total Migrant Stock: The 2003 Revision* (POP/DB/MIG/2003/1 and ESA/P/WP.188), data in digital form.

TABLE 23.11

PROJECTED POPULATION WITH AND WITHOUT INTERNATIONAL MIGRATION BY REGION, 2000 AND 2050.

Major area	Population in 2000 (millions)	Population in 2050 (millions)		2000-2050		Difference between medium and zero-migration variants	Migration effect as a percentage of natural increase[a]
		Medium variant	Zero-migration variant	Medium variant	Zero-migration variant		
More developed regions	1 194	1 220	1 032	26	- 162	187	(116)
Less developed regions	4 877	7 699	7 837	2 822	2 960	- 138	-5
Africa	796	1 803	1 817	1 008	1 022	- 14	-1
Asia	3 680	5 222	5 303	1 542	1 623	- 81	-5
Latin America and the Caribbean	520	768	806	247	286	- 38	-13
Northern America	316	448	314	132	- 2	134	(6763)
Europe	728	632	589	- 96	- 139	43	(30)
Oceania	31	46	40	15	9	6	67

a. The figures in parenthesis represent the effect of migration in reducing negative natural increase.

Source: *World Population Prospects:* The 2002 Revision, Volume I: Comprehensive Tables, United Nations publications, Sales No. E.03.XIII.6, 2003.

TABLE 23.12

PROJECTED POPULATION TO 2050 WITH AND WITHOUT MIGRATION FOR SELECTED COUNTRIES AND DEPENDENCY RATIOS WITH AND WITHOUT MIGRATION.

Country or area	Population in 2000 (millions)	Population in 2050 (millions)		Difference between medium and zero-migration variants	Dependency ratio (per 100)		Dependency ratio in 2050 (per 100)		Difference between medium and zero-migration variants
		Medium variant	Zero-migration variant		1950	2000	Medium variant	Zero-migration variant	
United States of America	285	409	287	122	54	52	66	61	5
Germany	82	79	64	16	49	47	85	76	9
Canada	31	39	27	12	60	46	79	70	9
United Kingdom	59	66	54	12	49	54	72	65	7
Afghanistan	21	70	62	7	83	86	53	53	0
Australia	19	26	19	7	53	49	73	67	6
Saudi Arabia	22	55	50	4	83	73	49	47	2
Spain	41	37	33	4	52	46	100	93	7
Japan	127	110	106	4	68	47	101	98	2
France	59	64	61	4	52	53	73	73	0
Russian Federation	146	101	98	4	54	44	72	71	1
China, Hong Kong SAR	7	9	6	4	49	37	101	79	22
Italy	58	45	42	3	53	48	90	90	0
Netherlands	16	17	15	2	59	47	72	68	4
Kuwait	2	5	3	2	64	39	59	57	1

Source: *World Population Prospects: The 2002 Revision*, Volume I: Comprehensive Tables, United Nations publications, Sales No. E.03.XIII.6, 2003.

CHAPTER 24
IOM STATISTICS ON INTERNATIONAL MIGRATION[1]

INTRODUCTION

IOM routinely collects statistics relating to its operational programmes and projects in over 165 countries. These cover a range of different migratory movements including the **repatriation** and **resettlement** of refugees, and the **returns** of such migrant categories as highly qualified persons, victims of trafficking, stranded transit migrants, internally displaced persons, unsuccessful asylum seekers, and soldiers as part of demobilization programmes.

Operational statistics are essentially collected for project development, evaluation and management purposes. They are useful for research, and also enable the Organization to report on its activities to Member States and donors. More recently, efforts have been made to improve data collection in order to assist IOM in policy analyses and to achieve a better understanding of both regular and irregular migratory flows.

IOM's statistics relate mainly to programmes rather than types of migratory flows. For example, some return programmes include different categories of returnees, such as temporary protected persons, unsuccessful asylum seekers and trafficked migrants, making it difficult to analyse individual types of return movements. Some programmes include both return and resettlement movements. The regular return and resettlement programmes developed by IOM in Western Europe at the end of the 1970s and the early 1980s were designed to provide both kinds of assistance.

IOM data refer primarily to flows rather than stocks of migrants and refugees. Until recently, relatively little information has been collected on the post-arrival experiences of groups, such as returning migrants, and their ability to reintegrate. However, increased efforts are being undertaken to monitor the experiences of migrants returned by IOM, especially those belonging to vulnerable groups who may require special assistance.

IOM's statistical files cover all operations since the founding of the Organization in 1951 up to the end of 2003. Some 12.3 million people have been helped to move over that period. The electronic database contains statistics for IOM's movements from 1992 to date. During the ten-year period 1994-2003, covered in the overall movement statistics presented below, IOM assisted in moving nearly five million (4,942,255) individuals. More than three million people were assisted in **emergency** situations, and nearly two million under **standard** resettlement operations. Together, these five million represent 40 per cent of the total 12.3 million people assisted.

Emergency operations mainly respond to immediate needs for the rapid, safe and orderly evacuation of people, and relocation of refugees. This type of support is key to the effective implementation of humanitarian responses, either to manmade emergencies or natural disasters, and in instances where it is necessary to respond quickly to the plight

1. *This chapter has been prepared by the Research Unit, MPRC Department, IOM Geneva.*

of vulnerable populations. Emergency movement assistance is typically provided at embarkation, during movement and upon arrival. IOM and its UN and NGO partners deliver different types of logistical and movement assistance at these points.

Standard operations refer to movements carried out in more stable conditions, where IOM provides reliable transfer of individual migrants for resettlement, employment, studies or any other purposes of orderly migration. Most of IOM's standard operations include selection, processing, language training, orientation, medical examinations and other relevant activities to facilitate reintegration. Movement activities are designed and established on a bilateral basis with the governments, and with the help of migrants and supporting NGOs. Emergency and standard categories refer to the urgency of programmes and not to types of movements that are described in the following sections.

I. TYPES OF MOVEMENT COVERED BY IOM STATISTICS

Resettlement. IOM assists with the resettlement of persons accepted under regular immigration programmes through the processing of relevant documentation, performing medical screening and arranging safe, reliable and economical means of transportation. Of the 209,000 people assisted by IOM as part of its movement operations during 2003, more than 70,000 were resettled, about half of them to the USA. Other important countries of resettlement during that period were Canada, Australia, Denmark, Norway and Sweden. IOM statistics provide information on the socio-economic profile and the health status of persons being resettled.

Emergency/Post-emergency Movement (Repatriation). One of the major programmes implemented by IOM is to organize and facilitate the repatriation of refugees and other groups, such as IDPs, during and after emergencies. IOM statistics relating to this form of assistance fall under two broad headings: "Repatriation of refugees" and "Post-emergency movement assistance". The first category refers to the voluntary repatriation of refugees organized in accordance with UNHCR's protection concerns and procedures. The second category includes persons who may not be refugees, such as IDPs and soldiers involved in demobilization programmes.

Assisted Voluntary Return. IOM statistics distinguish a third major type of return programme, "Return Assistance to Migrants and Governments". IOM's regular ongoing return programmes, such as "Reintegration or Emigration of Asylum Seekers from Germany" (REAG) and "Reintegration or Emigration of Asylum Seekers from Belgium" (REAB) fall under this heading. Persons assisted under these programmes include a high proportion of unsuccessful asylum seekers, but also persons receiving "temporary protection".

Migration Health. The Migration Health Services (MHS) department of IOM specializes in the medical assessment and treatment of refugees and migrants. Though personal medical information is strictly confidential, IOM produces analyses of the non-personal health-related data that it collects. The majority of health assessments in the last years were conducted in eastern Europe and Central Asia, followed by south-eastern Europe, Southeast Asia, Africa and South Asia.

Counter-trafficking. It is widely accepted that it is extremely difficult to obtain reliable data on the scope and magnitude of migrant trafficking. Governments mainly rely on estimates that can vary widely. In recent years, IOM has expanded its counter-trafficking programmes and these provide a rare source of international data on trafficking based on information obtained directly from victims of trafficking assisted by IOM. IOM collects both qualitative and quantitative data on trafficking, such as the number of victims assisted, their country of origin, age, travel route, and how they were trafficked. Where available, information is also collected on the nationality and the methods used by the traffickers.

The **Graph 24.1** shows the annual numbers of individuals assisted by IOM under Standard or Emergency Operations during the ten-year period 1994-2003.

The significant peaks in emergency operations in 1994-96, shown best in the graph, relate to IOM's emergency operations in Africa, mainly movement assistance to displaced populations of hundreds of thousands of people following the genocide in Rwanda, and repatriations of large numbers of Mozambican refugees from neighbouring countries, or those displaced inside the country. The large-scale operations continued in Rwanda up to 1996.

After the peak years (and with the exception of the large-scale post-conflict assistance to 160,000 Angolans in 1997) the emergency figures clearly declined in the later 1990s, to surge again in 1999 and 2000 following the displacements caused by conflicts in Kosovo and Timor Leste. Assistance to some 350,000 Afghans (refugees and IDPs) returning after the ousting of the Taliban regime, created the latest peak in 2002.

GRAPH 24.1

PERSONS MOVED BY IOM UNDER STANDARD OR EMERGENCY OPERATIONS, 1994 – 2003

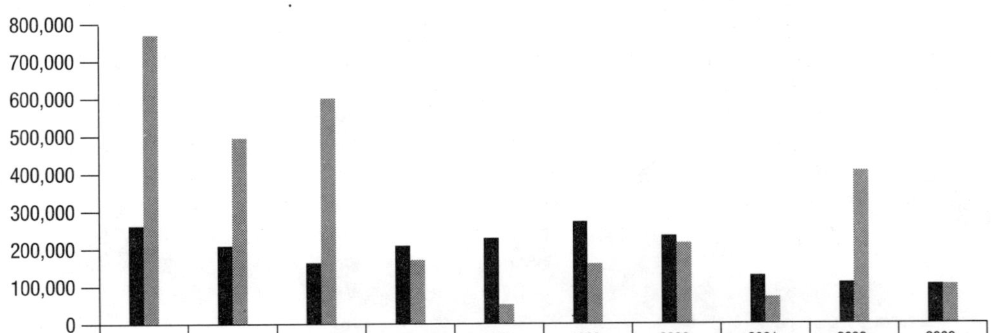

	1994	1995	1996	1997	1998	1999	2000	2001	2002	2003
Standard	262,383	209,170	163,644	209,102	229,085	272,996	235,464	127,885	109,737	104,918
Emergency OPS	770,708	495,881	601,787	170,527	25,260	158,925	215,274	70,515	404,756	104,238

Source: IOM.

Table 24.2 shows that most of the IOM-operated movements take place within a given region, usually in the neighbourhood of conflict areas. In the standard interregional movement operations during the decade covered, the US continued to figure as the most important resettlement country, followed by Canada and Australia.

After the events of September 11, 2001, new procedures and constraints by governments of resettlement countries have significantly slowed down and reduced IOM's standard resettlement activities, particularly to the US. However, the numbers were expected to pick up in 2004, following the inclusion of security and procedural changes into routine processing.

TABLE 24.2

MIGRANTS ASSISTED BY IOM BY REGIONS OF DEPARTURE AND DESTINATION, 1994-2003

Region of Departure	Region of Destination	1994	1995	1996	1997	1998	1999	2000	2001	2002	2003	Total
Africa	Africa	755,326	394,265	595,273	158,777	386	1,762	7,708	45,135	38,348	30,877	2,027,857
	Americas	5,403	7,730	11,185	9,580	8,555	16,205	22,428	17,937	6,286	18,198	123,507
	Asia	147	12	17	38	400	187	45	86	35	24	991
	Europe	3,159	3,230	3,054	2,756	2,869	2,921	2,834	3,249	4,423	3,942	32,437
	Oceania	1,422	1,342	1,027	1,284	1,663	1,135	1,286	1,916	2,198	4,067	17,340
Africa Total		765,457	406,579	610,556	172,435	13,873	22,210	34,301	68,323	51,290	57,108	2,202,132
Americas	Africa	302	276	272	178	109	126	26	4	14	3	1,310
	Americas	25,470	19,076	13,077	18,846	18,642	14,497	11,710	9,493	7,639	6,802	145,252
	Asia	445	249	102	169	157	100	114	26	78	41	1,481
	Europe	2,444	2,774	2,963	3,691	4,092	7,750	4,343	2,961	4,196	3,589	38,803
	Oceania	752	952	803	520	414	365	305	350	256	135	4,852
Americas Total		29,413	23,327	17,217	23,404	23,414	22,838	16,498	12,834	12,183	10,570	191,698
Asia	Africa	1,623	181	148	82	136	58	56	49	31	4,493	6,857
	Americas	66,198	52,760	28,851	19,518	21,215	16,891	18,943	17,335	15,771	13,441	270,923
	Asia	57,337	102,842	14,398	8,681	24,389	99,671	208,550	18,249	377,853	70,267	982,237
	Europe	5,462	5,041	5,575	9,726	8,020	10,329	7,873	9,706	9,605	6,468	77,805
	Oceania	8,335	7,802	10,764	3,228	1,992	2,226	1,787	1,243	1,645	2,447	41,469
Asia Total		138,955	168,626	59,736	41,235	55,752	129,175	237,209	46,582	404,905	97,116	1,379,291
Europe	Africa	4,421	3,927	2,359	2,175	1,996	1,681	898	678	880	1,438	20,453
	Americas	63,354	53,937	50,135	59,211	59,387	71,706	45,167	32,216	20,517	15,323	470,953
	Asia	5,054	4,827	4,323	5,380	5,588	10,315	4,332	4,177	4,803	7,454	56,253
	Europe	23,881	40,440	15,192	68,599	88,910	162,758	107,728	31,235	16,901	18,630	574,274
	Oceania	2,362	3,297	3,611	2,775	5,377	6,611	3,636	2,178	2,171	1,045	33,063
Europe Total		99,072	106,428	75,620	138,140	161,258	253,071	161,761	70,484	45,272	43,890	1,154,996
Oceania	Africa	10	3	10		9	9	1	2	3		47
	Americas	98	82	2,212	4,375	19	4	1	13	11	2	6,817
	Asia	71		1	1	2	993	719	20	348	243	2,398
	Europe	12	1	59	12	5	3,460	203	1	24	13	3,790
	Oceania	3	5	20	27	13	161	45	141	457	214	1,086
Oceania Total		194	91	2,302	4,415	48	4,627	969	177	843	472	14,138
Grand Total		1,033,091	705,051	765,431	379,629	254,345	431,921	450,738	198,400	514,493	209,156	4,942,255

Source: IOM.

ASSISTED VOLUNTARY RETURN TO KOSOVO AND RETURN OF QUALIFIED AFGHANS

ASSISTED *Voluntary Return (AVR)* has become an indispensable part of contemporary migration management practice. It offers logistical return assistance, counselling and financial support to migrants who cannot, or do not want to, remain in a host country.[2] It is a more humane and cost-effective alternative to forced return, and as such helps to maintain the integrity of regular immigration and asylum processes and foster cooperative forms of migration management among countries of origin, transit and destination. It can also ensure that home communities benefit from the newly acquired or enhanced skills and experience of returning migrants (see chapter on "Enhancing the Benefits of Return Migration for Development").

IOM has been operating AVR programmes for 25 years, mostly in Europe,[3] and today manages over 100 such projects globally. In the past decade, more than 3.61 million migrants have been assisted in returning home through AVR, over 131,000 of them in 2003. The AVR to Kosovo programme illustrated below, involving over 190,000 returns from 37 countries between June 1999 and June 2004, is one of the most important examples of this kinf of programme.

A complementary form of return migration is the *Return of Qualified Nationals (RQN)* programme, which targets expatriate nationals with particular professional skills and knowledge needed in the country of origin, willing to return temporarily or permanently to support reconstruction and socio-economic development there. They can also usefully act as a catalyst for further voluntary return. The Afghan RQN programme, presented in this section, is an important example of this.

ASSISTED VOLUNTARY RETURNS TO KOSOVO, 1999-2004

SINCE THE END of the conflict in Kosovo, major asylum destination countries, particularly in Europe, have funded large-scale return programmes to the province, coupled with support to facilitate rehabilitation there. In the post-conflict period, 1998-2000, asylum applications from the then Federal Republic of Yugoslavia (FRY), particularly Kosovo, were among the highest in many industrialized countries.[4] Germany and Switzerland were the largest recipients of these applications during and immediately after the conflict, and as a result also accounted for some of the largest subsequent returns (**Graph 24.3**).[5] IOM's operational network in Kosovo helped facilitate these returns from neighbouring and other countries in cooperation with local authorities, UNMIK, UNHCR and others.

GRAPH 24.3

TOTAL ANNUAL IOM ASSISTED RETURNS TO KOSOVO, JULY 1999 - JUNE 2004

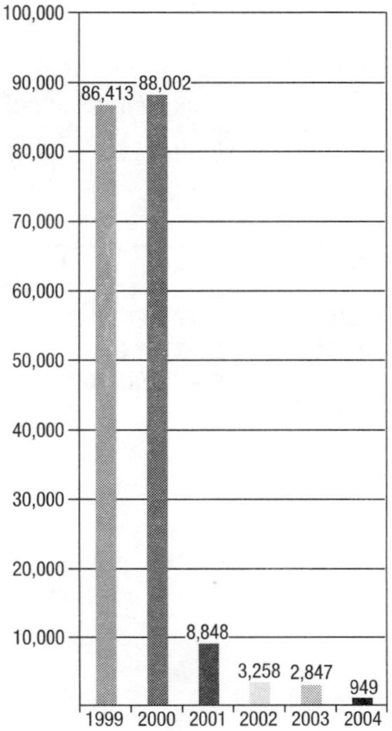

Source: IOM Office in Kosovo.

2. *AVR services also include facilitation of cooperation among countries of origin, transit and destination.*

3. *The first AVR programme began in Germany in 1979 (REAG programme), and became the model for further such programmes, adjusted to national circumstances, in the Netherlands, Belgium, Switzerland and others, including the EU Member States. IOM today operates over 20 AVR programmes.*

4. *See UNHCR,* 2002 Annual Statistical Report: Serbia and Montenegro.

5. *Between January 1998 and June 1999 Germany accounted for about 30 per cent of a total of 221,941 asylum applications lodged in industrialized countries by FRY nationals, while Switzerland accounted for 22 per cent.*

The majority of Kosovars who fled to neighbouring countries returned of their own volition to the province after conclusion of the peace agreement on 10 June 1999. Similarly, over 90 per cent of IOM's return caseload to date occurred shortly after the end of hostilities. In the first 18 months of operation, between July 1999 and December 2000, IOM assisted almost 175,000 Kosovars to return to the province under the Kosovo Humanitarian Return Assistance Programme (KHRP). 90 per cent of these returns were from non-adjacent countries and the remaining 10 per cent from neighbouring countries. As of 30 June 2004, IOM had assisted a total of 190,317 Kosovars to return to the province (**Graph 24.3**).

The majority of returns between 1999 and 2004 were from Germany (44%) and Switzerland (17%) (**Graph 24.4**). Some 55 per cent of returnees were male and 45 per cent female, and about 40 per cent of the total number of returnees were accompanying dependants.

Returns were mainly to the capital Pristina (approx. 40%), followed by Ferizaj and Peja (**Graph 24.3**). Some violent incidents in 2003 unsettled conditions in certain Serb and other minority communities, and limitations on the freedom of movement of minorities in regions such as Peja and Pristina encouraged returns to areas where conditions were more favourable (Gjilani and Prizreni).

Since the intense mass returns of 1999-2000, the priority has shifted from returns as such towards post-conflict rehabilitation. The return programmes are now more focused on longer-term solutions for an economy in transition, and include such components as reintegration of minorities, processing of property claims, creation of employment opportunities and the development of local infrastructure. The programmes are tailored to better respond to the needs of both returnees and the wider community, and include initiatives with local authorities to create environments conducive to the sustainability of returns. Sustainable return programmes in Kosovo are thus part of a broader reconstruction process.

Though mass returns have now ended, a more modest rate of return has continued steadily in recent years as the slow pace of recovery in the province continued to spur emigration, which in some cases necessitates voluntary return assistance. In the transition from humanitarian to rehabilitation and development assistance, a comprehensive migration management strategy is applied, combining, for example, capacity building with ongoing reintegration and community development assistance, as illustrated above, to facilitate sustainability of returns.

GRAPH 24.4

TOTAL IOM ASSISTED RETURNS TO KOSOVO BY COUNTRY OF RETURN, JULY 1999 - JUNE 2004

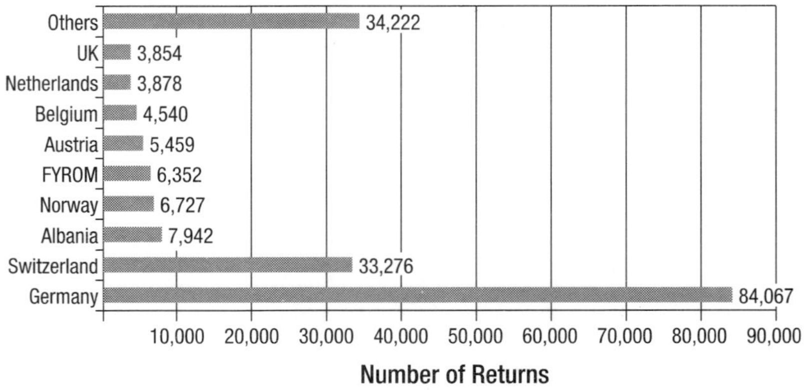

Source: IOM Office in Kosovo.

FIGURE 24.5

IOM ASSISTED VOLUNTARY RETURNS TO KOSOVO, BY MUNICIPALITY, JULY 1999 - JUNE 2004

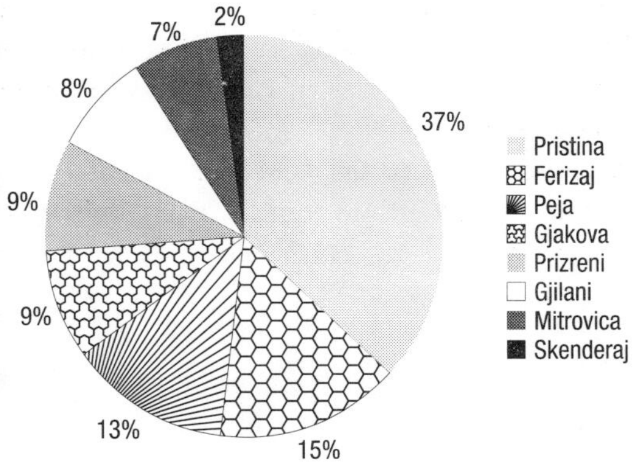

Source: IOM Office in Kosovo.

RETURN OF QUALIFIED AFGHANS (RQA), 2001-2004

IOM's Return of Qualified Nationals (RQN) programmes have a long history, both globally and in Afghanistan.[6] The RQA programme was initiated in December 2001 (following the conflict that toppled the Taliban regime) as a pilot programme to facilitate the progressive transfer of skills from Afghan nationals residing abroad, particularly in Pakistan and Iran. By the end of the pilot phase in March 2002, the programme had placed 170 highly qualified expatriate Afghan nationals, 31 per cent of them women, in key positions within 14 ministries of the Afghan Interim Administration, 22 non-governmental organizations (NGOs), and international and other organizations operating in Afghanistan. 150 of these returns were permanent.

The current RQA programme builds on this initial experience and operates alongside a general AVR programme. Its objective is to fill local human resource gaps and enhance the reintegration chances of returning migrants through the temporary transfer of highly skilled Afghans. Participants may choose employment for either six or 12 months, and are matched to positions in key public-sector areas, particularly the Afghan Transitional Authority (ATA), or international, non-governmental, and private organizations operating in the country.

A self-employment component has also recently been added to the RQA programme to assist and provide grants to individuals wishing to start small businesses. The recruitment of qualified Afghan women is encouraged through an additional monthly supplement to help redress gender imbalances in employment and salary levels.

In 2002, there were an estimated 400,000 Afghans in Europe,[7] and the EU announced extensive plans to encourage the return of qualified human resources to facilitate reconstruction and capacity building in Afghanistan.[8] One such initiative is the EU-RQA project funded by the European Commission and implemented by IOM since March 2003, and planned to continue until March 2005.

Between December 2001 and July 2004, 4,448 candidates from 42 countries had registered in the global RQA database, 604 of whom had been successfully returned and placed in jobs, representing 14 per cent of the registered candidates. 62 per cent of the returnees came from Pakistan. Included in the global figure were 614 applications under the EU programme, of which 123 had been successfully returned and placed in jobs (**Graph 24.6**). As of May 2004, 58 had been assigned to positions in the public sector.

6. *For more details on the Return of Qualified African Nationals (RQAN) programme, see the chapter "Enhancing the Benefits of Return Migration for Development". IOM's programmes in Afghanistan date back to the 1990s, with the Return and Reintegration of Qualified Afghans (RQAfgN) programme. It was implemented simultaneously with humanitarian and return assistance to refugees from neighbouring countries such as Pakistan and Iran in 1990 (e.g. IOM returned some 160,000 refugees from Iran and Pakistan between 1999 and 2000, together with UNHCR).*

7. *IRIN/OCHA,* Afghans React Strongly to EU Repatriation Initiative, *12 October 2002.*

8. *Council of the European Union,* Return Plan for Afghanistan, *28 November 2002.*

Profiles of Applicants and Returnees[9]

The majority of applicants for the RQA programmes are from Pakistan (48%), Iran (16%), the US (7%), Germany (4%) and Tajikistan (4%). These statistics are a fair indication of the distribution of Afghans abroad. UNHCR estimates suggest that there are some 3.5 million Afghans living in Pakistan and Iran, while Germany is reported to have the largest Afghan diaspora community in Europe.[10]

Within the EU-RQA programme, Germany (33%), the Netherlands (19%) and the UK (13%) have the highest number of RQA applicants (**Graph 24.7**). The majority of returnees are aged between 40 and 60 years, indicating that they belong to the first generation who emigrated after the political turmoil of the late 1970s and have now been living abroad for up to 25 years.

The programme strongly encourages the return of qualified women and as of July 2004, 16 per cent (708) of all those registered in the database were female, compared to 18 per cent (109) of all returnees. Women in the EU-RQA programme accounted for 7 per cent of all returnees.

By July 2004, five returnees had been assisted to establish small enterprises in Afghanistan under the EU-RQA programme, which aims to ultimately assist 30 Afghan nationals in this way.

Main RQA Trends

- Neighbouring countries (Pakistan and Iran) yield the majority of applicants and returnees, although there are high numbers also from North America and Europe (**Graph 24.6**).
- Qualified Afghan returnees have been successfully placed in key positions in public administration, education, health, public infrastructure sectors (e.g. agriculture, construction, transportation) and international and non-governmental organizations (**Figure 24.9**).
- Education and training, construction and engineering, and health are among some of the frequently cited areas of expertise of returnees (**Table 24.8**).
- Approximately 80 per cent of RQA participants remain in Afghanistan after the expiration of their initial contract.[11]

GRAPH 24.6

IOM'S RETURN OF QUALIFIED AFGHANS (RQA) PROGRAMME: APPLICANTS AND PARTICIPANTS (RETURNEES) BY COUNTRY/REGION OF RESIDENCE, DECEMBER 2001 - JULY 2004

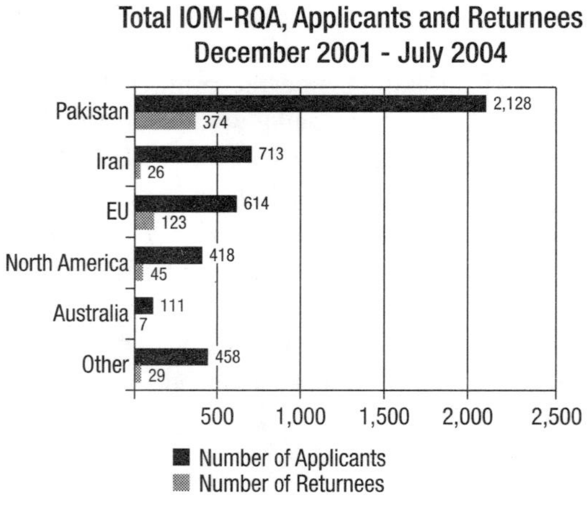

Source: IOM Mission in Afghanistan.

9. *Applicants or candidates refer to those currently registered in the database. Returnees or participants refer to those who have been successfully placed in jobs and have returned to Afghanistan.*

10. *According to the German Federal Ministry of Economic Cooperation and Development (BMZ) about 100,000 Afghans live in Germany, making them the largest Afghan diaspora community in Europe.*

11. *Current estimates are based on the number of requests for assistance to return to the host country. More accurate statistics will become available after the final project assessment.*

GRAPH 24.7

EU APPLICANTS AND PARTICIPANTS (EU-RQA) OF THE IOM RETURN OF QUALIFIED AFGHANS (RQA) PROGRAMME BY COUNTRY OF RETURN, DECEMBER 2001 - JULY 2004

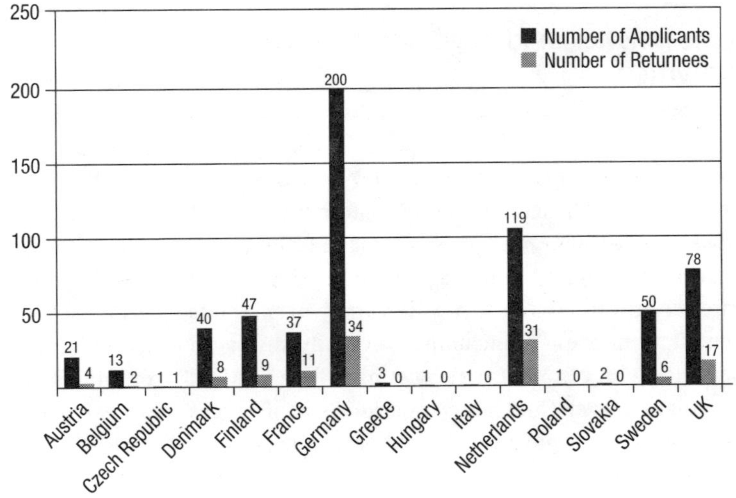

Source: IOM Mission in Afghanistan.

TABLE 24.8

RETURN OF QUALIFIED AFGHANS (RQA) PROGRAMME - APPLICANT AND PARTICIPANT PROFILES BY TOP 10 FIELDS OF EXPERTISE, DECEMBER 2001 - JULY 2004

Field of Expertise	Number of Applicants	Percentage	Number of Returnees	Percentage
Education/Training	1,903	43	274	45
Construction/Engineering	992	22	114	19
Health	975	22	130	22
Admin./Managerial	902	20	109	18
Telecomm./Media	421	9	53	9
Finance/Banking	393	9	44	7
Agricultural	386	9	45	7
Manufacturing/Production	221	5	13	2
Law	217	5	49	8
Information Technology	121	3	12	2

Notes:
1) Total number of applicants – 4,448.
2) Total number of returnees – 604.
3) Figures do not tally as some applicants indicated multiple fields of expertise.

FIGURE 24.9

RETURN OF QUALIFIED AFGHANS (RQA) PROGRAMME: RETURNEE PROFILES BY EMPLOYMENT CATEGORY, DECEMBER 2001 - JULY 2004

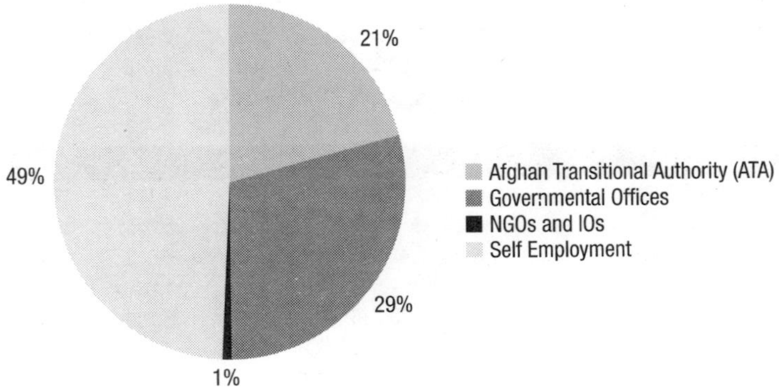

Source: IOM.

IOM STATISTICS OF KEY MIGRATION HEALTH ACTIVITIES[12]

IOM promotes migrant health and develops migration health related research, policies and projects. It advocates for migrants' physical, mental and social health and directly delivers comprehensive health care services to migrants. A wide variety of migrants benefit from these – including internally displaced persons, refugees, returnees, victims of trafficking, irregular migrants, and labour migrants – at all stages of the migration process, viz. pre-departure, transit, arrival in host community, and return. The key areas of service delivery include migration health assessments, post-emergency migration health assistance, mental and psycho-social health and migration, irregular migration and health, and HIV/AIDS and migration (see also the chapters "Investing in Migration Health" and "Global Mobility and HIV and AIDS").

MIGRATION HEALTH ASSESSMENTS

Since 1951 IOM has been conducting large-scale migration health assessments in the context of its migrant resettlement programmes carried out on behalf of mainly traditional immigration countries such as Australia, Canada and the US. These pre-departure health assessments serve to detect conditions that, if left untreated, could have a negative impact on the migrants' health and/or the public health of the host communities. In addition to offering large-scale pre-departure treatment of high prevalence conditions like malaria and intestinal parasites, IOM treats migrants with tuberculosis, and certain treatable sexually transmissible infections (STI), immunizes for preventable conditions and ensures pre and post-test HIV counselling.

Table 24.10 and the related graph illustrate the trend in the number of health assessments provided by IOM since 1990. The sharp decline in Southeast Asia since 1991 reflects the final years of the Comprehensive Plan of Action (CPA),[13] which promoted the orderly

12. *Source: Migration Health Department (MHD), IOM Geneva, which is also responsible for policy/programme development and quality service delivery by IOM in this area globally.*

13. *United Nations High Commissioner for Refugees. The Indo Chinese exodus and the CPA. Special Report, Geneva, June, 1996.*

TABLE 24.10

HEALTH ASSESSMENT OF MIGRANTS (REFUGEES AND IMMIGRANTS) ASSISTED UNDER IOM'S RESETTLEMENT PROGRAMMES BY REGION OF ORIGIN, 1990-2003

Region	1990	1991	1992	1993	1994	1995	1996	...
Southeast Asia	145,709	174,867	151,468	108,237	81,092	46,724	40,292	...
South-Eastern Europe	0	0	0	0	840	2,237	4,559	...
Eastern Europe Central Asia	8,010	83,614	76,638	63,580	49,115	50,174	44,220	...
Africa	0	0	0	3,929	788	458	0	...
Total	**153,719**	**258,481**	**228,106**	**175,746**	**131,835**	**99,593**	**89,071**	...
Refugees (%)	n/a	n/a	n/a	n/a	n/a	n/a	n/a	...

Region	...	1997	1998	1999	2000	2001	2002	2003	Total
Southeast Asia	...	16,796	23,138	14,195	11,980	13,262	12,119	10,935	836,619
South-Eastern Europe	...	8,518	12,598	26,658	13,478	13,694	15,471	12,664	84,059
Eastern Europe Central Asia	...	41,421	36,973	40,513	42,257	40,487	35,143	33,386	605,018
Africa	...	4,000	286	1,644	8,555	8,396	15,706	22,929	65,047
Total	...	**70,735**	**72,995**	**23,138**	**76,270**	**75,839**	**78,439**	**79,914**	**1,590,743**
Refugees (%)	...	74	67	62	55	47	45	43	300,914

Source: Migration Health Department (MHD), IOM Geneva.

resettlement of Indo-Chinese refugees under the Orderly Departure Programme, and ended in 1996.[14]

IOM offers health assistance during the process of resettlement to both refugees and immigrants. In 2003, refugees represented 43 per cent of the assisted population. However, there were differences between various country programmes, where refugee groups represented two-thirds of the assisted migrants bound for the US, and 8-15 per cent for other countries.

Table 24.11 presents the IOM-assisted and medically assessed population in 2003, broken down by destination country and gender. The US was the destination for 55.1 per cent in 2003. Overall, with 53.3 per cent women made up the majority in this population.

Certain conditions detected in the pre-departure health assessment can expose an applicant to being excluded pending adequate treatment. While the conditions being tested for vary from country to country, the main conditions liable to lead to exclusion are infectious tuberculosis, STIs, including HIV infection, leprosy, behavioural disorders that pose a risk to self or others, substance abuse, and certain chronic illnesses. However, only a very modest number of migrants (1.0% of all persons examined) had such a "potentially excludable condition" in 2003.

Medical escorts are arranged for those who have received medical clearance to travel (found to be free of "potentially excludable condition") but who need assistance and care *en route* to ensure their travel proceeds without undue hardship to themselves or

14. *In June 1989, 10 years after the first Indochinese refugee conference, 70 governments adopted a new regional approach, known as the Comprehensive Plan of Action (CPA), to resolve the Vietnamese refugee problem in a multilateral way. This included refugee determination and resettlement in third countries as appropriate, and return and reintegration to home countries for those not found to be refugees.* In 1991, the CPA finally brought an end to the flow of Vietnamese asylum seekers.

TABLE 24.11

DISTRIBUTION OF MIGRANTS ASSESSED BY IOM PER COUNTRY OF DESTINATION (YEAR 2003)

	Sex		Total	Dest.country	Refugees		Immigrants		Total	
Country of destination	Female	Male		%	n	%	n	%	n	%
Australia	6,064	5,092	11,156	14.0	916	8.2	10,240	91.8	11,156	100.0
Canada	12,482	10,445	22,927	28.7	3,510	15.3	19,417	84.7	22,927	100.0
New Zealand	707	767	1,474	1.8	168	11.4	1,306	88.6	1,474	100.0
USA	23,153	20,856	44,009	55.1	29,336	66.7	14,673	33.3	44,009	100.0
Other (mainly Norway)	187	161	348	0.4	327	94.0	21	6.0	348	100.0
Total	42,593	37,321	79,914	100.0	34,257	42.9	45,657	57.1	79,914	100.0

Source: Migration Health Department (MHD), IOM Geneva.

GRAPH 24.12

TRENDS IN THE NUMBERS OF IOM HEALTH ASSESSMENTS

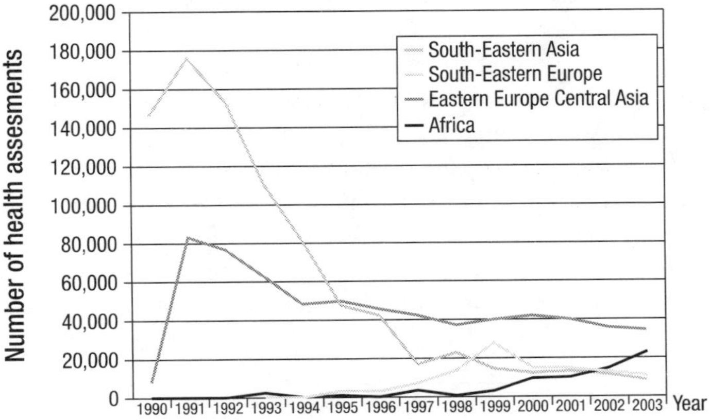

other travellers. In 2001-2003 some 2,807 persons (4.6% of all IOM assisted migrants during the period) were escorted in this way, mainly because of a heart condition, psychiatric, neurological, respiratory or endocrinological disorders, or old age.

EXAMPLES OF IOM'S SPECIAL PROGRAMMES ON MIGRATION HEALTH

Mental and Psychosocial Health and Migration Example: National Mental Health Programme, Cambodia

Although migration as such does not threaten mental health, it can create vulnerabilities and pressures liable to affect mental health if combined with additional risk factors such as war, famine or human rights violations. The National Mental Health Programme in Cambodia aims at restoring the country's mental health and psychiatric services destroyed during the Khmer Rouge regime, and assisting the population after decades of conflict, sanctions, human rights violations and consequent internal displacement. Since 1994, IOM has assisted the Government of the Kingdom of Cambodia to re-establish mental health training and services, for example by training the first 20 Cambodian psychiatrists after the end of the Pol Pot regime, and an additional 20 psychiatric nurses.

Since its start in 2002, the National Mental Health Programme has provided capacity building to Cambodian psychiatrists and nurses and delivered mental health services at eight outpatient clinics in the country, including seven in the provinces and one in Phnom Penh. In 2002, 11,797 new patients (of whom 70% cent were women) visited the clinics, and 50,779 psychiatric consultations were provided. In addition, six psychiatrists and nine nurses started post-graduate training in psychiatry (three years for doctors and 18 months for nurses). Short-term training was also provided to 40 general practitioners and 57 nurses in the country. In contrast to previous IOM mental health programmes in Cambodia, this programme is almost entirely managed by IOM-trained Cambodian professionals.[15]

TABLE 24.13

CLINICAL DIAGNOSIS AMONG NATIONAL MENTAL HEALTH PROGRAMME, CAMBODIA, 2002-2003

Diagnosis ICD 10*	Frequency	Percentage
Neurotic, stress -related and somatoform disorders	5,163	43.8%
Mood [affective] disorders	3,306	28.0%
Schizophrenia, schizotypal and delusional disorders	2,219	18.8%
Epilepsy	364	3.1%
Mental and behavioural disorders due to psychoactive substance use	334	2.8%
Organic, including symptomatic, mental disorders	191	1.6%
Observation for suspected mental and behavioral disorders	106	0.9%
Behavioural syndromes associated with physiological disturbances and physi cal factors	30	0.3%
Mental retardation	28	0.2%
Disorders of adult personality and behaviour	28	0.2%
Other diagnosis	28	0.2%
Total	11,797	100%

* Diagnosis following the WHO International Statistical Classification of Diseases and Related Health Problems, Tenth Revision.

IRREGULAR MIGRATION AND HEALTH

Migrants in an irregular situation can be at risk of poor health due to poverty, powerlessness, discrimination, vulnerability to labour exploitation, and lack of access to health care and social services. Even if social and health services are available without charge, irregular migrants often hesitate to seek such services for fear of being reported to immigration officials, or deported.

Persons trafficked for sexual and labour exploitation are a particularly vulnerable group that today poses one of the most serious and urgent challenges to migration policymakers around the world. Besides other assistance to trafficked persons, IOM supports

15. *The Programme is financed by the Norwegian Agency for Development Co-operation (NORAD).*

them through health examinations and diagnostic assistance, treatment for conditions such as STIs, psychological and psychiatric counselling/treatment, HIV pre and post-test counselling, and counselling on reproductive health matters. These services are usually provided in close collaboration with governmental and non-governmental partners at rehabilitation centres and shelters accommodating trafficked victims. A useful example of this is IOM Kyiv's Rehabilitation Centre for Trafficked Persons.

392 trafficked persons were received by the Kyiv centre in the two-year period 2002-2003. All those assisted were women, the vast majority of them between 20 and 30 years of age. Almost 80 per cent of the victims stayed one or more nights in the centre. 95 per cent of all assisted victims accepted and received health assessments by IOM. 50 per cent of the conditions diagnosed among the trafficked population upon arrival concerned reproductive health, and 33 per cent mental health. 4 out of 5 victims were found to be in need of some therapeutic treatment, and 75 per cent of victims received such treatment directly from IOM.

POST-EMERGENCY MIGRATION HEALTH ASSISTANCE

Emergency and post-emergency migration health programmes are designed to assist countries and communities during and after emergency situations, by managing the safe and rapid mass movement of people, arranging medical evacuations for those requiring locally unavailable treatment, and organizing safe return transport. In addition to travel-related health assistance, post-emergency programmes assist in the reconstruction of damaged, or incomplete, health infrastructures. Initial assistance may include short-term solutions to cover immediate needs, but the long-term goal is to rebuild the country's sustainable health care capacity through training of national personnel. IOM has run emergency and post-emergency health programmes, for example during and after conflicts in Africa, in the Former Yugoslavia and in Iraq.

COUNTER TRAFFICKING

IOM COUNTER-TRAFFICKING DATABASE

Trafficking in persons[16] is a clandestine phenomenon that remains largely unreported.[17] However, such authorities as the police and border guards, and agencies that assist victims of trafficking, increasingly keep statistics of the cases they deal with. While such datasets remain fragmentary and cannot illustrate the full magnitude of the criminal activity at national or global levels, they are often the most solid information available to guide policymakers and counter-trafficking workers.

Since 1999, IOM has been collecting data from persons assisted in the Organization's counter-trafficking programmes. The Counter Trafficking Module Database (CTM) is meant to facilitate management of assistance and voluntary return/reintegration activities for the victims. It also increases understanding about the causes, processes, trends and consequences of trafficking, thereby assisting IOM in its policy and project development, research, monitoring and evaluation. The CTM informs about the victims' background, trafficking experience and need for assistance. It is also a useful tool for coordination between IOM missions on the follow-up of individual cases.

Since the data collection first began with the assistance programmes in the Balkans, its content is still weighted

16. *According to the Protocol to Prevent, Suppress and Punish Trafficking in Persons, Especially Women and Children, Supplementing the United Nations Convention Against Transnational Organized Crime, trafficking in persons is defined as "the recruitment, transportation, transfer, harbouring or receipt of persons, by means of the threat or use of force or other forms of coercion, of abduction, of fraud, of giving or receiving of payments or benefits to achieve the consent of a person having control over another person, for the purpose of exploitation. Exploitation shall include, at a minimum, the exploitation of the prostitution of others or other forms of sexual exploitation, forced labour or services, slavery or practices similar to slavery, servitude or the removal of organs."*

17. *The 2004 Trafficking in Persons Report of the US Department of State estimates that each year 600,000 to 800,000 men, women, and children are trafficked across international borders. Other estimations of international and non-governmental organizations place the number much higher.*

towards that region, where Moldova, Ukraine and Romania predominate as countries of origin. It has since been expanded to cover other regions, but, given its IOM programme focus, it is in all likelihood not broadly representative. The total population of trafficked persons in a given country is not known.

Some examples drawn from the database are presented below. The indicators used for such background variables as age, training, employment and general socio-economic conditions support many hypotheses and conclusions that, in the broader research on trafficking to date, have often been based on anecdotal evidence, or at best on survey samples much smaller than the database.

The information in IOM's counter-trafficking database can serve trafficking research and the development of more targeted and effective counter trafficking measures. IOM is continuing to expand the database and develop new and wider uses for it in the counter-trafficking work globally.

INFORMATION FROM THE DATABASE

In July 2004, the database contained data on 2,791 victims, representing some 35 nationalities (for 44 victims, or 1.6 per cent of the total, the nationality was unknown). The indicators presented below relate to the six most common countries of origin/ nationality in the database. These are Moldova, Romania, Ukraine, Belarus, Bulgaria and Dominican Republic, which account for 88 per cent of the data. The four most important destination countries or regions where victims were referred to IOM for assistance are the Former Yugoslav Republic of Macedonia (FYROM), Bosnia and Herzegovina, Kosovo and Albania.

Almost 59 per cent of the victims in the database are in the 18 – 24 year age bracket (72% under 24 years), which would seem to correspond to the educational levels of the victims: relatively young, many completed only the obligatory school education, whereas the largest group had obtained secondary level education.

Given the relative youth of the victims, combined with the high unemployment in many former communist states, as many as 30 per cent had had no work experience at all. 57 per cent had had some work experience, but only 50 per cent of all victims worked at the time of recruitment. Of those that worked, 70 per cent claimed to be a private or public employee, 6.9 per cent were self-employed or employed by their families, 3 per cent were domestic workers, and 1.2 per cent had worked in the sex industry prior to recruitment. 6.4 per cent had had other occupations, while information about the nature of work was not available for 11.7 per cent of those 1,276 persons claiming to have worked at the time of recruitment.

TABLE 24.14

AGE RANGE OF VICTIMS BY TOP SIX NATIONALITIES

Categories	MOLDOVA	ROMANIA	UKRAINE	BELARUS	BULGARIA	DOMINICAN REPUBLIC	Overall DB Total
Below 14 years	0,09%	0,57%	0,00%	0,00%	0,00%	0,00%	0,97%
14 to 17 years	8,57%	20,57%	0,00%	4,12%	6,54%	1,69%	12,11%
18 to 24 years	62,38%	64,71%	48,50%	58,24%	64,49%	22,03%	58,51%
25 to 30 years	22,19%	11,00%	37,22%	15,88%	12,15%	18,64%	19,20%
Over 30 years	6,00%	2,43%	13,16%	7,65%	14,02%	57,63%	7,35%
N/A	0,77%	0,71%	1,13%	14,12%	2,80%	0,00%	1,86%
Total (by nationality)	100,00%	100,00%	100,00%	100,00%	100,00%	100,00%	100,00%

Source: IOM Counter-Trafficking Database.

But for those who had work, the salaries were extremely low. Income data was not available for 37 per cent of the database, but 45 per cent of all victims said that before being recruited they had earned less than USD50 per month, 12 per cent said USD50-100, 5.25 per cent USD101-500, and only 0.3 per cent earned more than USD500 a month. In spite of the unavailability of much salary information, the data give a strong indication of poverty and under-employment experienced by many victims in their countries of origin. This is confirmed by the fact that for the great majority of the victims of the top six nationalities their income was the sole household income.

The data in **Table 24.17** support the observation of earlier research that a relatively large share of trafficked women had children, whom they supported without a spouse. In IOM's database, 815 of all 2,791 victims, or 29.2 per cent, had one or more children. Of the 266 Ukrainian victims, 107 had children, and of these, as many as 86 women, or 80.4 per cent, were sole supporters. In Moldova, 417 of the 1,167 victims had children, and 309 of these (74% of those with children, or 26.5% of all Moldovan victims) were single mothers. In the group of 59 Dominican victims in the database, 54 had children and 43 of them, no less than 72.9 per cent of the whole group, were single

TABLE 24.15

EDUCATION LEVEL BY TOP SIX NATIONALITIES

Categories	MOLDOVA	ROMANIA	UKRAINE	BELARUS	BULGARIA	DOMINICAN REPUBLIC	Overall DB Total
College/University	5,23%	0,57%	4,51%	20,00%	4,67%	1,69%	4,66%
Highschool	21,51%	24,57%	27,07%	19,41%	28,97%	8,47%	22,04%
Middle/Elementary school	24,42%	23,57%	16,54%	14,12%	22,43%	18,64%	21,28%
N/A	10,45%	12,57%	15,79%	5,88%	1,87%	0,00%	11,25%
None	0,51%	1,00%	0,00%	0,00%	4,67%	6,78%	2,04%
Other	3,43%	0,71%	1,50%	1,18%	0,93%	0,00%	2,11%
Primary school	18,94%	26,43%	7,14%	1,18%	30,84%	61,02%	21,14%
Trade/Technical/Vocational school	15,51%	10,57%	27,44%	38,24%	5,61%	3,39%	15,48%
Total (by nationality)	100,00%	100,00%	100,00%	100,00%	100,00%	100,00%	100,00%

Source: IOM Counter-Trafficking Database.

TABLE 24.16

MARITAL STATUS OF VICTIMS OF TRAFFICKING AMONG THE TOP SIX NATIONALITIES

Categories	MOLDOVA	ROMANIA	UKRAINE	BELARUS	BULGARIA	DOMINICAN REPUBLIC	Overall DB Total
Common law	1,29%	1,86%	1,88%	0,00%	1,87%	6,78%	1,50%
Divorced	12,34%	7,86%	18,80%	10,00%	0,93%	3,39%	10,64%
Married	11,40%	5,43%	10,15%	13,53%	3,74%	11,86%	8,96%
N/A	9,68%	12,29%	13,53%	7,06%	2,80%	0,00%	10,00%
Separated	7,88%	5,29%	8,65%	0,59%	12,15%	10,17%	6,63%
Single	56,13%	66,86%	45,86%	67,65%	75,70%	66,10%	61,13%
Widowed	1,29%	0,43%	1,13%	1,18%	2,80%	1,69%	1,15%
Total (by nationality)	**100,00%**	**100,00%**	**100,00%**	**100,00%**	**100,00%**	**100,00%**	**100,00%**

79.5 per cent of all victims in the database were either single, separated, divorced or widowed, and only 10.4 per cent were married or in a common-law marriage.

Source: IOM Counter-Trafficking Database.

supporting mothers. This information points out even more concretely than earlier research that women in cumulative poverty, with low education, poor income, if any, underemployment, one or more children (or other family members) to look after alone, should be especially targeted for prevention measures in countries of origin (e.g. information, child support, job creation).

The database confirms that trafficking is not run by male criminals alone, but that women traffickers figure prominently at least at certain stages of the process, and that women act as recruiters almost as often as men. Of the 2,791 trafficking cases in the database, the gender of the recruiter was known in 85 per cent of cases. Of these, 46 per cent were female (1,092 persons). In Moldova, 56.1 per cent of the known recruiters were female; in the Dominican Republic as many as 76.5 per cent, or three out of four, of the known cases were recruited by a female trafficker. Among the six nationalities under review, male recruiters predominated in Romania (77.5% of the 621 cases) and Bulgaria (65.3% of the 95 recruiters).

Table 24.19 illustrates the relationship of the recruiter to the victims. This is not known in 30 per cent of cases, but among the known cases, the categories "stranger" (60%) and "friend" (30%) predominate, and others such as "relative" and "partner" account for smaller shares.

While the type of exploitation was not known for 481 cases, or 17 per cent of the whole database, *2,094 victims (75% of total caseload) were exploited in sex work and 196 (7%) through other forms of forced labour.* Apart from sex work, forced labour and "illegal activities" (20 cases altogether among the Moldovan and Romanian victims), military service (0 cases) and organ removal (0 cases in the database) the type of exploitation was still "other" than those mentioned in no fewer than 481 cases, or 17 per cent of the whole database.

TABLE 24.17

VICTIMS OF TRAFFICKING WHO ARE MOTHERS OR SINGLE MOTHERS

Categories	MOLDOVA	ROMANIA	UKRAINE	BELARUS	BULGARIA	DOMINICAN REPUBLIC
Total	1,167	700	266	170	107	59
Victims with children	417	154	107	50	29	54
Single mothers among them	309 (74%)	123 (79.90%)	86 (80.40%)	30 (60%)	24 (82.80%)	42 (79.60%)
Single mothers in total (%)	26.50%	17.60%	32.30%	17.60%	22.40%	72.90%

Single mothers (sole supporters) are either unmarried, divorced, separated or widowed.

Source: IOM Counter-Trafficking Database.

TABLE 24.18

GENDER OF THE RECRUITERS OF THE TOP SIX NATIONALITIES OF VICTIMS

Categories	MOLDOVA	ROMANIA	UKRAINE	BELARUS	BULGARIA	DOMINICAN REPUBLIC	Overall DB Total
Female	47,73%	28,71%	43,61%	32,35%	30,84%	66,10%	39,13%
Male	37,28%	60,00%	42,11%	45,88%	57,94%	20,34%	45,90%
Unknown	15,00%	11,29%	14,29%	21,76%	11,21%	13,56%	14,98%
Total (by nationality)	100,00%	100,00%	100,00%	100,00%	100,00%	100,00%	100,00%

Source: IOM Counter-Trafficking Database.

In profiling victims in countries of destination, the database helps to profile potential victims in their countries of origin. This enables IOM to better target its information campaigns in those countries. For example, in Moldova one of the components of a prevention project was a summer mobile information centre/minibus, which travelled to 52 carefully targeted locations over four weeks, stopping at summer camps, villages and major towns. Specially trained IOM interns provided information about legal migration, risks of illegal migration and dangers of trafficking. They also conducted interviews and gathered views about the need for more information on migration. The nationwide media campaign included a 4-minute music video, "Undeva," by the rock band The Snails, and a 30-second advertisement to maximize cross-promotion of the toll free 24-hour a day hotline (0-800-77777) and website www.migratie.md. In the first six weeks of operation, the website received more than 4,900 visitors, averaging over 100 visitors per day. Calls to the toll-free hotline operated by IOM partner La Strada doubled compared to the same period the last year. About 70 per cent of the calls came from rural areas, particularly from young women, a primary target group for traffickers.

TABLE 24.19

RELATIONSHIP TO RECRUITER BY SIX TOP NATIONALITIES

Categories	MOLDOVA	ROMANIA	UKRAINE	BELARUS	BULGARIA	DOMINICAN REPUBLIC	Overall DB Total
Family	0,26%	0,00%	0,00%	0,00%	0,00%	0,00%	0,36%
Friend	22,79%	25,57%	22,18%	11,18%	23,36%	33,90%	23,47%
N/A	25,28%	20,00%	21,05%	16,47%	25,23%	35,59%	22,57%
Other	2,40%	1,86%	3,76%	0,59%	0,00%	3,39%	3,62%
Partner	1,37%	2,14%	1,88%	0,00%	3,74%	0,00%	1,86%
Pimp	0,86%	0,00%	0,38%	0,00%	0,93%	0,00%	0,43%
Relative	1,97%	2,86%	0,75%	1,76%	8,41%	0,00%	2,47%
Stranger	45,07%	47,57%	50,00%	70,00%	38,32%	27,12%	45,22%
Total (by nationality)	100,00%	100,00%	100,00%	100,00%	100,00%	100,00%	100,00%

Source: IOM Counter-Trafficking Database.

TABLE 24.20

TYPE OF EXPLOITATION EXPERIENCED BY THE TOP SIX NATIONALITIES OF VICTIMS

Categories	MOLDOVA	ROMANIA	UKRAINE	BELARUS	BULGARIA	DOMINICAN REPUBLIC	Overall DB Total
Sexual exploitation	77,55%	79,00%	81,95%	78,82%	71,03%	69,49%	75,03%
Forced labour	5,83%	5,71%	3,01%	7,06%	20,56%	22,03%	7,02%
Illegal activities	1,20%	0,14%	0,00%	0,00%	0,00%	0,00%	0,72%
Other	15,42%	15,14%	15,04%	14,12%	8,41%	8,47%	17,23%
Total (by nationality)	100,00%	100,00%	100,00%	100,00%	100,00%	100,00%	100,00%

Source: IOM Counter-Trafficking Database.

ANNEXES

INTRODUCTION

Annan, K.
2003 "Emma Lazarus Lecture on International Flows of Humanity", Columbia University, N.Y., 21 Nov.

Battistella, G. and M. M. B. Asis (Eds)
2003 *Unauthorized Migration in Southeast Asia*, Quezan City, Philippines, Scalabrinin Migration Center.

Chamie, Joseph
2003 "Knock, Knock ...Who's There? Many Migrants!", *Yale Global*, 5 August.

Dustmann, C. and I. Preston
2004 "Racial and Economic Factors in Attitudes to Immigration", *CReAM* discussion paper No. 1.

Economist, The
2004 "Migration and Development", 6 May.
"Out of Africa", October 9, pp. 37-38.

Hugo, G., D. Rudd and K. Harris
2001 *Emigration from Australia: Economic Implications*, CEDA Information Paper, No. 77, June, Australia.

Kofman, E.
2003a "Skilled International Female Migrants: migratory strategies and settlement experiences", *Report Canadian Faculty Research Program* Grant.

Newland, K.,
2004 *Beyond Remittances: The Role of Diaspora in Poverty Reduction in their Countries of Origin*, a study for the UK Department for International Development (DFID), MPI, Washington.

Papademetriou, D.
2003 "Reflections on Managing Rapid and Deep Change in the Newest Age of Migration", Migration Policy Institute, Washington D.C., April.

Richardson, S. and L. Lester
2004 *A Comparison of Australian and Canadian Immigration Policies and Labour Market Outcomes*, Report to DIMIA, National Institute of Labour Studies, Flinders University, September.

UK, House of Commons, International Development Committee
2004 *Migration and Development: How to Make Migration Work for Poverty Reduction 1*, Report, together with formal minutes, The Stationery Office, London.

UN
2003 "The Doyle Report", background report on migration prepared for the senior management group, United Nations, N.Y., March.
2004a *Trends in Total Migrant Stock: The 2003 Revision. Diskette Documentation*, United Nations Department of Economic and Social Affairs Population Division Working Paper No. ESA/P/WP.188.
2004b *World Economic and Social Survey 2004. International Migration*, November; *www.un.org/esa/policy/wess/index.html*

World Bank
2004 "Enhancing the Developmental Effects of Workers' Remittances to Developing Countries", in *Global Development Finance 2004*, Annex A, Washington, D.C.

CHAPTER 1 – MIGRATION: AN OPPORTUNITY FOR AFRICA?

Baker, J.
1995 *The migration experience in Africa*, Uppsala.

De Bruijn, M., R. van Dijk, D. Foeken,
2001 "Mobile Africa: changing patterns of movement in Africa and beyond", Leiden.

Eurostat
2002 *European Social Statistics, Migration*, Luxembourg.

French Economic and Social Council:
2001 "De l'exode à la mobilisation des compétences dans le cadre d'un véritable co-développement", Paris.

Immigration and Naturalization Service (INS)
2002 *Statistical Yearbook of the Immigration and Naturalization Service*, Washington, D.C. Mbembe, A.
1999 "Africa's frontiers in flux. Migration of peoples, Disintegration of States", Le Monde diplomatique/ English edition mondediplo.com, *www.mondediplo.com/1999/11/12africa*

Ratha, D.
2003 "Workers' Remittances: An Important and Stable Source of External Development Finance", in The World Bank: Global Development Finance, Washington, D.C

UNPD (United Nations Population Division)
2001 World Urbanization Prospects: The 2001 Revision, Department of Economic and Social Affairs, NY.
2002 World Population Prospects: The 2002 Revision, Department of Economic and Social Affairs, NY.

TEXTBOX 1.1
The Role of (Migrant) Women in Post-conflict Reconstruction and Development

Cohen, R.
1998 "Protecting Internally Displaced Women and children", in *Rights Have no Borders, Internal Displacement Worldwide*, (Ed. W. Davies), Norwegian Refugee Council/Global IDP Survey, ISBN 82-7411-064-1

Rehn, E. and E.J. Sirleaf
2002 "Women, War and Peace: The Independent Experts' Assessment on the Impact of Armed Conflict on Women and Women's Role in Peace-building", UNIFEM, New York

United Nations Economic and Social Council
2003 "Report of the UN Secretary General on Women's equal participation in conflict prevention, management and conflict resolution and in post-conflict peace-building", E/CN.6/2004/10, 22 December, 2003, N.Y.

GENERAL WEBSITES
Women Waging Peace Web Portal, A Programme of Hunt Alternatives Fund: *www.womenwagingpeace.net*

GENERAL BIBLIOGRAPHY

CHAPTER 2 – MIGRATION TRENDS IN SUB-SAHARAN AFRICA (SSA)

ACBF (The African Capacity Building Foundation)
2004 *An Analysis of the Market for Skilled African Development Management Professionals: Towards Strategies and Utilization in Sub-Saharan Africa.*

Adepoju, A.
1998 "Emigration Dynamics in Sub-Saharan Africa", in: Appleyard, R. (ed.) *Emigration Dynamics in Developing countries, Volume I: Sub-Saharan Africa.*

Adepoju, A.
1995 "Migration in Africa", in: Jonathan Baker and Tade Akin Aina (eds.) *The Migration Experience in Africa.*
2004a "Changing Configurations of Migration in Africa", (*www.migrationinformation.org*).
2004b "Trends in international migration in and from Africa", in: Massey, D. Taylor (Eds). *International Migration Prospects and Policies in a Global Market. Oxford University Press.*

African Union
2002 "Migration and HIV/AIDS in Sub-Saharan Africa", for the Fourth General Assembly of the African Population Commission, Addis Ababa, Ethiopia, February
2004 Report on the seminar on "The impact of HIV/AIDS on socio-economic development in Africa", Cotonou, Benin, April.
2004 "Report of the Chairperson of the Commission on Conflict Situations in Africa", at the Executive Council, Fifth Ordinary Session, Addis Ababa, Ethiopia, 25 June - 3 July.
2004 "Vision and Strategic Plan 2004-2007", African Union, Addis Ababa.

Al Ali, N.
2004 The Relationship between Migration within and from the Middle East and North Africa and Pro-Poor Policies: A Report by the Institute of Arab and Islamic Studies, University of Exeter for the Department of International Development, University of Exeter, Exeter.

Boubakri, H.
2004 Transit Migration between Tunisia, Libya and Sub-Saharan Africa: Study based on Greater Tunis, paper presented at the Council of Europe Regional Conference on Migrants in Transit Countries: Sharing Responsibility for Management and Protection, Istanbul, 30 September - 1 October.

Castles, S. and M. Miller
2003 *The Age of Migration: International Population Movements in the Modern World*, 3rd rev. and updated edition, Palgrave, Houndmills.

Curtin, P.
1997 "Africa and global patterns of migration", in: Gungwu (ed.), *Global History and Migrations* (Boulder: Westview).

DFID (Department for International Development)
2004 "Migration and pro-poor policy in Sub-Saharan Africa", Development Research Centre on Migration Globalisation and Poverty, August.

ECA (Economic Commission for Africa)
2004 "Assessing Regional Integration in Africa", Policy Research Report.

Eriksson, M., P. Wallensteen and M. Sollenberg
2003 "Armed Conflict, 1989-2002", in Journal of Peace Research, Vol. 40, No.5, pp. 593-607.

Europa Publications
2003 *The Middle East and North Africa 2004* (ed. L. Dean), from the series *Regional Surveys of the World*, 50th edition, London

GTZ
2003 *Study on Trafficking in Women in East Africa: A Situational Analysis including Current NGO and Governmental Activities, as well as Future Opportunities to Address Trafficking in Women and Girls in Ethiopia, Kenya, Tanzania, Uganda and Nigeria*, GTZ, Eschborn.

Gugler, J. (Ed.)
1996 The Urban Transformation of the Developing World, Oxford University Press, NY.

HRW (Human Rights Watch)
2003 "Bordering Slavery: Children in Togo", Vol. 15, N.8 (A).

ILO (International Labour Office)
2004 "Issues Paper: African Union Extraordinary Summit of Heads of State and Government on Employment and Poverty Alleviation in Africa", Ougadougu, Burkina Faso, September.

Institute for Security Studies
2003 *African Security Review*, Volume 12, Number 4.

IOM
2003 *Seduction, Sale and Slavery: Trafficking in Women and Children in Southern Africa*, 3rd ed., Pretoria.

IOM and UNAIDS
2003 "Mobile Populations and HIV/AIDS in the Southern African Region", Reports on Mobile Populations and HIV/AIDS, Vol. 1.

Koser, K. (Ed.)
2003 New African Diasporas, Routledge, London (Global Diasporas).

Lachaud, J.P.
1999 "Envoi de fonds, inégalité et pauvreté au Burkina Faso", Working Paper, Centre d'Economie du Développement de l'Université Montesquieu-Bordeaux IV, Bordeaux, (*www.ced.montesquieu.u-bordeaux.fr/ceddt40.pdf*)

Lahlou, M. et al.
2002 "Rapport de l'enquête migrants menée au Maroc", *Cahiers des Migrations Internationales*, 54 F, BIT, Genève.

Ricca, S.
1989 *International Migration in Africa: Legal and administrative aspects.* ILO, Geneva.

Sander, C. and S. Munzele Maimbo
2003 *Migrant Labor Remittances in Africa: Reducing Obstacles to Development Contributions.* World Bank, Washington, DC (African Region Working Paper Series, No. 64).

Simone, A. M.
2003 "Moving Towards Uncertainty: Migration and the Turbulence of African Urban Life", (*www.princeton.edu/pumconference/papers/2-Simone.pdf*).

SAMP (Southern African Migration Project)
2004 *"Migration, Sexuality and the Spread of HIV/AIDS in Rural South Africa", Migration Policy Series* No. 31.

South African Institute of International Affairs
2003 "Africa's Health Care Crises", September, Braamfontein.

Stilwell, B. et al (Khassum Diallo, Pascal Zurn, Mario R. Dal Poz, Orvill Adams, James Buchan
2004 Human Resources for Health: Developing evidence-based ethical policies on the migration of health workers: conceptual and practical challenges, (*www.human-resources-health.com/content/1/1/8*).

Swindell, K.
1995 "People on the move in West Africa: from pre-colonial polities to post-independence states", in: Cohen R. (ed.) *The Cambridge Survey of World Migration.*

Todaro, M.P.
1997 "Urbanization, Unemployment, and Migration in Africa: Theory and Policy", in: Todaro, M.P, Economic Development in the Third World.

UNCHS (United Nations Centre for Human Settlement)
2001 The State of the World's Cities Report 2001, UNCHS, Nairobi.

UNDP (United Nations Development Programme)
2003 Human Development Report 2003 – Millennium Goals: A Compact among Nations to End Human Poverty, Oxford University Press, New York.

UNESCO (United Nations Educational, Scientific and Cultural Organization)
1998 "International Migration and Africa: Trends and Prospects for the 21st Century". Regional Meeting of Experts Final Report, Gaborone, Botswana, 2-5 June.

United Nations
2003 "Côte d'Ivoire Plus Five: Consolidated Inter-Agency Appeal – April to December 2003", OCHA, Geneva.
2004 "Liberia 2004: Mid-Term Review - Consolidated Appeals Process", OCHA, Geneva.
2004 "International Migration Trends", forthcoming chapter from the UN Population Division, (Department of Economic and Social Affairs) for World Migration 2005 (Chapter 24 in this volume).

United Nations Division for the Advancement of Women
1999 *World Survey on the Role of Women in Development: Globalization, Gender and Work,* N.Y.

USCR (US Committee for Refugees)
2003 *World Refugee Survey 2003: An Annual Assessment of Conditions Affecting Refugees, Asylum Seekers, and Internally Displaced Persons,* USCR, Washington, DC.

Wallenstein et al.
2003 "Armed Conflict, 1989-2002", in *Journal of Peace Research, Vol. 40,* No. 5, pp. 593-607.

Weiner, M.
1995 The Global Migration Crisis: Challenge to States and to Human Rights, HarperCollins College Publishers, N. Y.

Zlotnik, H.
2004 "International Migration in Africa: An Analysis Based on Estimates of the Migrant Stock". *(www.migrationinformation.org).*

CHAPTER 3 – MIGRATION IN THE MIDDLE EAST

ABC
2001 "The Iraqi Brain Drain", news.com, 16 February 2001.

AFP
2001 "French Military in Boatpeople Rescue", 1 December.

Al-Ahram
2002 "800 Illegal Asylum Seekers from the Horn of Africa Caught on the Yemeni Shore", 26 November.

Al-Najjar S.
2002 "Women Migrant Domestic Workers in Bahrain", International Migration Papers 47, ILO. *www.ilo.org/public/english/protection/migrant/download/imp/imp47e.pdf.*

Arab News Daily, **Jeddah**
2003 "Indonesian maid attempts suicide" January 9.

Awad, M.
2002 "Arab Organization for Human Rights", CARAMASIA Regional Summit on Foreign Domestic Workers, August: *caramasia.gn.apc.org*

Badil
2002 "UNHCR, Palestinian Refugees and Durable Solutions", Information and Discussion Brief No. 7.

BBC News
2002 "Millions forced into slavery", 27 May.
2003 "Social Customs Hide Child Sex Abuse", 21 January.

Bhagwandas
2001 "Smuggling of Camel-Kids to Gulf States on the Rise", Dawn, 23 March.

Blanchet, T.
2002 *Beyond Boundaries, a Critical Look at Women's Labor Migration and the Trafficking Within,* Dhaka.

Center for Women's Research (CENWOR)
2004 Women Migrant Workers of Sri Lanka, Colombo, Sri Lanka *www.cenwor.lk/migworkersstat.* accessed 8 July 2004.

Chatelard, G.
2002 *Iraqi Forced Migrants in Jordan: Conditions, Religious Networks, and the Smuggling Process,* European University Institute.

Dorai, M.
2000 *Migration in the Arab Middle East: Policies, Networks and Communities in the Context of Globalization,* Research Program CERMOC, Beirut/Amman, Konrad Adenauer Foundation.

ad-Dustour
2003 Arabic daily newspaper, Amman, 27 September.

ECOSOC
2003 *International Migration 2002,* Population Division, NY.

Economic and Social Commission for Western Asia
2004 "Where Do Arab Women Stand In The Development Process?" *www.escwa.org.lb/information/publications/sdd/docs/sdd-04-booklet.1.pdf*

Farsakh, L.
2001 "Palestinian Labor Migration to Israel since Oslo and Beyond", paper presented at the Middle East Studies

Association Conference 2001, School of Oriental and African Studies, University of London.

Fergany, N.
2001 *Aspects of Labor Migration and Unemployment in the Arab Region*, Almishkat Center for Research, Egypt: *www.almishkat.org* (accessed February 2001).

Human Rights Watch
2000 "Discrimination Based On Origin and Status: The Bidun", Report Kuwait: *www.hrw.org/reports/2000/kuwait/kuwait-04* (accessed on 14 May 2004).
2003 "Iraq: Forcible Expulsion Of Ethnic Minorities" *www.hrw.org/reports/2003/iraq0303/*

Icduygu and Toktas
2002 "How Do Smuggling and Trafficking Operate?", *International Migration* 4(6), Blackwell Publishers, Malden and Oxford.

ILO Committee of Experts
2002 ILO Conference, Committee on the Application of Standards, 2002.

International Monetary Fund (IMF)
2003 *Balance of Payments Yearbook.*

IOM
2003 *Migration Policy Issues*, No. 2, March, Geneva.

IOM and League of Arab States
2004 "Arab Migration Patterns: The Mashreq" in *Arab Migration in A Globalized World*, Geneva.

Inter Press Services News
2002 "Detention of 150 Sri Lankans en route to Italy by Means of Illegal Migration" Al-Ahram 18 November, "Sri Lanka: Detained Would-be Migrants Live in Limbo".

Jordan Times
2002 "Six Egyptians on trial for spying, 'smuggling tourists'", November 14.

Jureidini, R.
2002 "Women Migrant Domestic Workers in Lebanon", International Migration Papers 48, ILO; *www.ilo.org/public/english/protection/migrant /download/imp/ imp48e.pdf*
2003 Migrant Labor: Xenophobia, Indenture and Trafficking in the Gulf States. European University Institute; *www.iue.it/RSCAS/RestrictedPapers/conmed2003free /200303JureidiniO5.pdf*
2004 "The Domestic Labor Market: the Case of Sri Lankan Maids in Lebanon" Research Program CERMOC/Konrad Adenauer Foundation, Amman: *www.lb.refer.org/cermoc/migration/projetseng /RayJureidini*

Kapiszewski, A.
2001 *Nationals and Expatriates Population and Labor Dilemmas of the GCC States*, Ithaca Press.
2003 "Arab Labor Migration to the GCC States", *Arab Migration in A Globalized World*, IOM and League of Arab States, Geneva.

Khalaf, M. C.
2003 Women International Labor Migration in the Arab World: Historical and Socio-Economic Perspectives, United Nations, N.Y.

www.un.org/womenwat ch/daw/meetings/consult/CM -Dec03-EP5.pdf

Al Khouri, R.
2004 "Arab Migration Patterns: The Mashreq", *Arab Migration in A Globalized World*, IOM and League of Arab States, Geneva.

Lawyers for Human Rights
2002 *Trafficking of Pakistani Children to UAE for Camel Jockeying.*

Mannan, M.
2000 "Boy Kidnapped from Pakistan Rescued by Ansar Burney", *Khaleej Times*, 13 September.

Mattar, M. and J. Borkholder
2002 "Domestic Service as a Form of Trafficking in Persons in the Middle East", delivered at the First World Congress for Middle Eastern Studies, Mainz, Germany, 12 September.

Middle East Times
2002 "Diplomat arrested in Israel Smuggling Case", November 17.

Milch, B.
1998 *Rights of Migrant Workers and their Families*, Stanford University: *www.stanford.edu/group/smun/oldversion/oldversion/s imun98/briefings/migrant*

Norwegian Refugee Council
2002 "Profile of Internal Displacement: Lebanon" NRC/Global Displacement Project, June 2002.
2003 "Internal Displacement in the Middle East", Global IDP Project: *www.idpproject.org/regions/Middle_East_idps*
2004 "Profile of Internal Displacement: Iraq": *www.db.idpproject.org/Sites/idpSurvey.nsf/wCountries/I raq/$File/Iraq%20-February%202004.pdf*

Raghavan, C.
1996 "Asian Female Migrant Workers Require Protection, Says ILO": *www.twnside.org.sg/title/ilo1-cn*

Ruppert Bulmer, E.
2001 "The Impact of Future Labor Policy Options on the Palestinian Labor Market", World Bank; *www.lnweb18.worldbank.org/mna/mena.nsf/Attachme nt s/WP+24/$File/WP24—main.pdf*

Sabban, R.
2002 "Migrant Women in The United Arab Emirates: The Case of Female Domestic Workers", *GENPROM* Working Paper No. 10, Series on Women and Migration. International Labour Office. 2002. *www.ilo.org/public/english/employment/gems/download /swmuae.pdf.*

Thompson, G. and K. Grey,
2003 *Foreign Correspondent*, Australian Broadcasting Corporation, 25 February.

Trabelsi, H.
2004 *Gulf states aim to halt camel jockeys trafficking*, Middle East Online, 27 January.

United Nations Commission on Human Rights
2004 Sub-Commission on the Promotion and Protection of Human Rights, Working Group on Contemporary Forms of Slavery, 28th Session.

UNDP

1997 "A Profile of Sustainable Human Development in Lebanon", Chapter 3K, *The Displaced and Development*, N.Y. *www.undp.org.lb/programme/governance/advocacy/nhdr/nhdr97/chpt3k.pdf*

2002 *Arab Human Development Report: 2002: Creating Opportunities for Future Generations*: *www.undp.org/rbas/a hdr/englishpresskit2002*

2003 *Arab Human Development Report 2003: Building a Knowledge Society*: *www.undp.org/rbas/a hdr/english2003 p 138*

UNIFEM

2000 *Migrant Workers in Jordan: A concept paper on the situation of female domestic migrant workers in Jordan*, August.

UNHCR

2001 *Global Report: The Middle East.*

UNRWA

2002 "Number of Registered Refugees as of 30 June": *www.unrwa.org* (accessed on 22 April 2003).

USCR

2002 Country Report: Jordan: *refugees.org/world/countryrpt/mideast/jordan*

2003 "Middle East Report", *World Refugee Survey 2003*, *www.refugees.org/do wnloads/wrs03/Middl.East.pdf*

US Department of State

2001 *UAE Country Report on Human Rights Practices 2001.*

2003 *Trafficking in Persons Report*, June.

Xinhua News Agency

1998 21 Trafficked Children Recovered in Bangladesh, 5 October.

ISRAEL: A COUNTRY OF IMMIGRATION

Cohen S. and D. Paserman

2002 "Mass migration to Israel and natives' employment outcomes", *Falk Institute working paper.*

Geva-May, I.

2000 "On impacts of comparative policy analysis. Immigration to Israel: What other countries can learn", *International Migration, 38(1)*, 3-45.

Gruenpeter Gold, L. and Ben Ami, N.

2004 "National NGOs report to the annual UN Commission on Human Rights: Evaluation of National Authorities activities and Actual facts on the Trafficking in Persons for the purpose of prostitution in Israel," *UN Commission on Human Rights, 60th session, 15 March-23 April 2004.*

Leshem, E. and M. Sicron

1998 "The absorption process of immigrants from the Former Soviet Union, 1990-1995", main findings in Sicron M. and Leshem E. (eds.), *Profiles of an immigration wave*, Jerusalem: The Magnes Press.

Menahem G. and M. Lerner

2001 "An evaluation of the effect of public support in enhancing occupational incorporation of Former Soviet Union immigrants to Israel: A longitudinal study", *Journal of Social Policy, 30(2)*, 307-331.

Raijman, R. and M. Semyonov

1998 "Best of times, worst of times and occupational mobility: The case of Soviet immigrants in Israel", *International Migration, 36(3)*, 291-310.

Razin, Assaf.

2002 "Israel and the Globalized World Economy." *10th Caesaria Conference on Globalization.* July 2002 *www.tau.ac.il/~razin/globalization.ppt*

Semyonov, M. and N. Lewin-Epstein

2003 "Immigration and ethnicity in Israel: Returning diasporas and nation building", in Rainer Münz (ed.), *Diasporas and ethnic migrants in 20th century Europe.* London: Frank Cass.

WEBSITES

Ministry of Absorption, Israel: *www.moia.gov.il*
The Central Bureau of Statistics, Israel: *www.cbs.gov.il*
United Nations High Commissioner for Refugees: *www.unhcr.ch*

CHAPTER 4 – MIGRATION DYNAMICS AND DIALOGUE IN THE WESTERN MEDITERRANEAN

Al Amn-Alam

2004 Review of Libya's General Committee of the People for Security, Tripoli, June.

Brand L.A.

2002 "States and their Expatriates: Explaining the Development of Tunisian and Moroccan Emigration-Related Institutions", Working Paper No. 52, University of California, San Diego.

Collinson S.

1996 Shore to Shore. The Politics of Migration in Euro-Maghreb Relations, The Royal Institute of Foreign Affairs, London.

Commission of the European Communities

2004 "European Neighboring Policy, Country Report: Tunisia", Commission Staff Working Paper , Brussels.

Council of the European Union (CIVIPOL)

2003 "Feasibility study on the control of the European Union's maritime borders"– Final report – Brussels.

El Yazami D. and R.Schwartz

2001 "*Rapport à la création d'un Centre national de l'histoire et des cultures de l'immigration*", La Documentation Française, Paris.

Eurostat (1998) (2000), *Evolution démographique récente en Europe*, Luxembourg.

Fargues P.

2002 "Migration Policies in the Western Mediterranean: Context, Contents, Perspectives", Tunis. Report prepared for the IOM on the occasion of the Ministerial Conference on the 5+5 Migration Dialogue, held in Tunis in 2002.

Gillespie R.

2002 "Regionalism and Globalism in the EMP: The Limits to Western Mediterranean Co-operation" (not published). Speech delivered at the conference: The Convergence of Civilizations? Constructing a Mediterranean Region (Fundação Oriente), 8-9 June, Setúbal, Portugal.

IMF
2001 Balance of Payments Yearbook, Washington, DC.

INED
2000 *Population and Sociétés: Maghreb: la chute irrésistible de la fécondité*, No. 359 (July-August), Paris.

INSEE
2003 "*La population française immatriculée à l'étranger est en forte hausse*", No. 919, Paris.

IOM
2000 "International Migration", jointly published with the United Nations Organization, Switzerland.
2001 "The Role of the Regional Consultative Process in Managing International Migration", IOM Migration Research Series, No. III, Geneva.
2004 Irregular Migration in the Western Mediterranean. 5+5 Forum, Introductory Note (not published), Geneva.

Khachani M.
1999 "*La femme marocaine immigrée dans l'espace économique des pays d'accueil. Quelques repères*", Records of the international colloquy on Women and Migrations and special issue of the Legal, Political and Economic Journal of Morocco (published by the Faculty of Legal, Economic and Social Sciences of Rabat), Morocco.

Lahlou M. and BARROS, L.; Escoffier C.; Pumares, P.; Ruspini P.
2002 "Report of the survey on migrants conducted in Morocco", International Migration Papers, 54 F, ILO, Geneva.

Lebon. A.
2002 « *Immigration et présence étrangère en France en 2002* », coll. La Documentation Française, Paris.

OTE
2000 *Tunisiens à l'étranger: transferts de fonds et investissements en Tunisie (éléments de comparaison)*, OTE Report, Tunis.

Pastore F.
2001 "Nationality Law and International Migration", in Hansen, R. and Weil, P. (2001), Towards a European Nationality Law in the EU, UK.

Pumares P.
2002 "Sub-Saharan immigration and Spanish migration policy", International Migration Papers, 54 F, ILO, Geneva, p. 88.

Rubio, J.
1974 "*La emigración española a Francia*", Ariel, Barcelona.

Salt, J.
2000 *Current Trends in International Migration in Europe*, Council of Europe, London.

Sayad, A.
1999 "*La double absence. Des illusions de l'émigré aux souffrances de l'immigré*", Paris. Also published in English as: A. Sayad (2004), The suffering of the immigrant, translated by David Macey, Polity Press.

Tapinos, G.
1975 "*L'immigration étrangère en France*", Institut national d'études démographiques (INED), Cahier No. 71, p. 61, Paris.

UNDP
2002 *Human Development Report: Deepening Democracy in a Fragmented World*, Oxford University Press, New York/Oxford.
2002 *World Development Report: Making Services Work for Poor People*, Oxford University Press, New York/Oxford.

CHAPTER 5 – MIGRATION TRENDS AND PATTERNS IN THE AMERICAS

Alba, F.
2003 "Mexico: A Crucial Crossroads", Migration Information Source, Washington, D.C., July.

BBC News
2003 "Spain Relaxes Citizenship Laws", 9 January.

Beach, C., A. Green and J. Reitz (Eds.)
2003 *Canadian Immigration Policy for the 21st Century*, McGill-Queen's University Press, London.

Belgrave, R.
2004 "Fixing Immigration Key for Harper", *Brampton Guardian*, 11 June.

Bloland P. and H.Williams
2002 *Malaria Control During Mass Population Movements and Natural Disasters*, The National Academies Press, Washington D.C.

Bronfman M., R. Leyva, M.Negroni (Editores)
2004 *Movilidad poblacional y VIH/SIDA, contextos de vulnerabilidad en México y Centroamérica. Instituto Nacional de Salud Pública de México*, México. Available at: *www.insp.mx*

Center for Migration and Development
2004 "Neoliberal Hopes Stir up Growing Inequalities: Evidence from Latin America", *Points of Development*, Princeton University, Princeton, NJ, January.

Consejo Nacional de Población (CONAPO)
2000 "Inmigrantes Residentes en México por Características Seleccionadas, Según Principales Países de Origen, 2000", *XII Censo General de Población y Vivienda*, Mexico City, Mexico.

Diario de la Sociedad Civil
2004 "Argentina Regularizará a Inmigrantes Ilegales", 5 January.

Economic Commission for Latin America and the Caribbean (ECLAC)
2002 "Social Panorama of Latin America, 2001-2002": *www.eclac.cl/publicaciones/Desarollosocial/3/LCG2183 PI/Capitulo_I_2002_Ing.pdf*

El Comercio **newspaper**
2003 Quito, 23 June 2003.

Friscolanti, M.
2004 "Fewer Refugees Seeking Asylum Inside Canada", *National Post*, 18 June.

IMPSIDA (Prevención del SIDA)
2004 "Annual Progress Report Period reported: January – December 2003", Organización Internacional para las Migraciones, Sistema de Información Estadística sobre

las Migraciones en Centroamérica (SIEMCA): *www.siemca.iom.int*

IDB (Inter-American Development Bank)
2004 "Remittances to Latin America and the Caribbean: Goals and Recommendations", Multilateral Investment Bank and Inter-American Development Bank conference on Remittances as a Development Tool, Lima, Peru, 27 March.

International Herald Tribune
2004 "Sending Money Home", 11 May.

IOM
2004a "Population Mobility and HIV/AIDS – IOM brochure 2004". Available at: *www.iom.int//DOCUMENTS/PUBLICATION/EN/IOM_HIV_brochure_July_2004.pdf*
2004b Position Paper on HIV/AIDS and migration. Available at: *www.iom.int/DOCUMENTS/GOVERNING/EN/Mcinf252.pdf*

Izquierdo, A.
2002 «Panorama de la Inmigración en España al alba del siglo XXI», *Colección Mediterráneo económico: procesos migratorios, economía y personas*, N 1, Madrid.

Jachimowicz, M.
2003 "Foreign Students and Exchange Visitors", *Spotlight*, Migration Information Source, Washington, D.C., 1 September.

Jachimowicz, M. and R. McKay
2003 "Revamped Homeland Security Department to Incorporate INS Duties", *Policy Beat*, Migration Information Source, Washington, D.C., 1 March.

Kashiwazaki, C.
2002 "Japan's Resilient Demand for Foreign Workers", Migration Information Source, Washington, D.C., 13 May.

Kerr-Pontes L., F. Gonzalez, C. Kendall et al.
2004 "Prevention of HIV infection among migrant population groups in Northeast Brazil", *Cad Saude Publica* 20(1):320-8.

Liberal Party of Canada
2004 "Multiculturalism is the bedrock of our society, says Martin", 19 June.

Lichtblau, E., J. Peterson and Times Staff Writers
2002 "US Ends Argentines' Ability to Avoid Visas", *Los Angeles Times*, 21 February.

Massey, D., J. Arango, G. Hugo, A. Kouaouci, A. Pelligrino and J. Taylor
1998 *Worlds in Motion: Understanding International Migration at the End of the Millennium*, Clarendon Press, Oxford.

Meyers, D.W.
2003 "Does 'Smarter' Lead to Safer? An Assessment of the Border Accords with Canada and Mexico", *Insight No.2*, Migration Policy Institute, Washington, D.C., June.

Migration Information Source
2004 Chart titled: "United States: Stock of foreign-born population by country of birth, 1995 to 2003 (in thousands)", Global Data Center: *www.migrationinformation.org/GlobalData/countrydata/data.cfm*

Ministry of Immigrants Absorption
2004 "Current Immigration Data: Immigration from Argentina": *www.moia.gov.il/english/netunim/yachas.asp?KodTeur=4&KodShemDoch=9&ezor=0*

Mogollón A., M. Vázquez, and M. García
2003 Health-Related Needs of the Displaced Population Due to Armed Conflict in Bogotá. Rev Esp Salud Publica 77(2).

MPI staff
2002 "A New Century: Immigration and the US", Migration Information Source, Washington, D.C., May.

Organización Internacional para las Migraciones (OIM)
2004 "Sistema de Información Estadística sobre las Migraciones en Centroamérica (SIEMCA)", *Inmigración y emigración en Centroamérica a inicios del siglo XXI: sus características e impacto*, Mayo.

Papademetriou, D. K. and Hamilton
2000 *Reinventing Japan: Immigration's Role in Shaping Japan's Future*, Carnegie Endowment for International Peace, Washington, DC.

PAHO (Pan American Health Organization)
2002 *Health in the Americas, a Scientific and Technical Publication*, No. 587.
2003 *Status Report on Malaria Programs in the Americas*, Washington D.C. 2003.

Perkins, D.
2004 "Business", *World Magazine*, 26 June.

Programa Estado de la Nación
1999 State of the Region Report on Sustainable Human Development in Central America. 1999 and 2003, Programa Estado de la Nación, San José, Costa Rica (*www.estadonacion.or.cr/InfoRegion/english1/prologue.html*).

Solimano, A.
2002 "Governance Crises and the Andean Region: A Political Economy Analysis", Paper presented in Santiago, Chile as part of the Second Workshop on the Project on Political Economy of Andean Countries sponsored by ECLAC and the Inter-American Dialogue, 11 August.

Sopemi
2002 *Trends in International Migration*, OECD, Paris.

Statistics Canada
2003 "Immigrant Population by Place of Birth and Period of Immigration", *Census of Population 2001*, Ottawa, Ontario, 13 May.

Suro, R.
2003 "Latino Remittances Swell Despite US Economic Slump", Migration Information Source, Washington D.C., February.

The News
2003 Mexico City, 12 June 2003

Thomas-Hope, E.
2002 "Trends and Patterns of Migration to and from Caribbean Countries", Paper prepared for the *Simposio*

sobre migracion internacional en las Americas, Sponsored by the United Nations, CEPAL, and ECLAC, San José, Costa Rica, September.

UNAIDS
2004 "Report on the global AIDS epidemic", Joint United Nations Programme on HIV/AIDS (UNAIDS) Geneva.

United Nations High Commissioner for Refugees (UNHCR)
2004 *Statistical Yearbook 2002*, UNHCR, Geneva.

United Nations Population Division
2003 "International Migration 2002 Wallchart", (ST/ESA/SER.A/219), United Nations, New York.

U.S. Census Bureau Report
2001 "The Profile of the Foreign-Born Population in the United States: 2000", U.S. Government Printing Office, Washington, D.C.

Valiente, R.
2003 "La migración dominicana hacia España, factores, evolución y desarrollo." *Revue Européenne des Migrations Internacionales*,Vol 19, No.1.

Villa, M. and Pizarro, Martínez, J.
2002 "Trends and Patterns of International Migration in Latin America and the Caribbean", Paper prepared for the *Simposio sobre migracíon internacional en las Americas*, Sponsored by the United Nations, CEPAL, and ECLAC, San José, Costa Rica, September.

Waterman, S.
2004 "U.S./Mexico Tuberculosis (TB) Border Health Card: Bilateral TB Referral and Treatment Initiative", CDC, USA. IOM/CDC /WHO Seminar on migration health, Geneva, June.

CHAPTER 6 – INTERNATIONAL MIGRATION TRENDS AND PATTERNS IN ASIA AND OCEANIA

Akaha, T.
2003 *Cross-Border Migration as a new Element of International Relations in North Asia*, Monterey Institute of International Studies, Monterey.

Asis, M.
2003 "Asian Women Migrants: Going the Distance, But Not Far Enough", Migration Information Source, Washington, D.C., 1 March.

Bloomberg News
2004 "Fukui Pledges to G-7 Japan Will Keep Rates Near Zero", 24 April.

Charny, J.
2003 "North Korean Refugees In China: The Current Situation and Strategies for Protection", Testimony to the Senate Committee on Foreign Relations, Washington, D.C, 4 November.

China Daily
2003a "Historic level of economic growth", 17 October.
2003b "Jobless situation to stay grave for many years", 5 November.

China Education and Research Network
2002 *Chinese Universities Become Popular Among Thai Students*, China Education and Research Network, February.

Curtis, P.
2003 "Fall in US Overseas Student Market", Guardian Newspapers Limited, 4 November.

Deng, F.
2000 *Internal Displacement: A Global Overview*, Presentation, Conference on Internal Displacement in Bangkok, Thailand: *www.brook.edu/dybdocroot/fp/projects/idp/conferences /asia200002/post*

Department of Immigration and Multicultural and Indigenous Affairs (DIMIA)
2004 Population Flows: Immigration Aspects, Economic and Demographic Analysis Section, Migration Branch, Australia, March.

Economic and Social Commission for Asia and the Pacific
2003 "Migration Patterns and Policies in the Asian and Pacific Region", *Asian Population Studies Series* 160, New York.

Education Travel
2002 "Australia flies high", Issue 1.
2004 "Slowdown in US Market", Issue 2.

Esfandiari, G.
2004 Coping with the World's Highest Rate of Brain Drain, March; *www.iranexpert.com/2004/drain8march.htm.*

Gazdar, H.
2003 "A Review of Migration Issues in Pakistan", paper presented at the Regional Conference on Migration, Development and Pro-poor Policy in Asia, organized jointly by RMMRU, Bangladesh and DFID, 22-24 June 2003, Dhaka, Bangladesh.

HDN Key Correspondent Team/Rapporteur
2003 "Team Moving Across Borders", 2nd APCRSH: 6 - 10 October, Bangkok, Thailand; *correspondents@hdnet.org*

Hugo, G.
2002 "Indonesia's Labor Looks Abroad", Migration Information Source, Washington D.C., September.

Human Rights Watch
2000 "Thousands of Thai Women Trafficked to Japan: Japanese Government Unresponsive, Says Report", Press Release, New York, 21 September: *www.hrw.org/press/2000/09/japan0921.htm*
2000a "Owed Justice, Thai Women Trafficked into Debt Bondage in Japan", New York, Washington, London, Brussels, September.

Human Rights Watch
2002 "The Invisible Exodus, North Koreans in the People's Republic of China", North Korea 14(8).

IDP Project
2003 "Myanmar (Burma) Summary", Norwegian Refugee Council, November.
2004 "Internal Displacement in Asia and the Pacific", Norwegian Refugee Council, January.

ILO
2004 "Youth Unemployment at all time high, doubles in SEA in the past decade", Press Release, Geneva.

Institute for International Education
2003 Open Doors Report 2003, November.

IOM
2003 "Understanding Migration between China and Europe", International Migration, vol. 41 (3) Special Issue 1/2003, Blackwells, Oxford.
2004 World Migration 2003, Volume 2 - IOM World Migration Report Series, Geneva.

Inter Press Service
1998 "Population Asia: Economic Crisis Spurs Illegal Immigration", Geneva, 15 June.

Japan Times, The
2004 March 12: *www.202.221.217.59/print/news/nn03-2004/nn20040312b5.htm*
2004 "Tougher visa requirements planned for entertainers", November 24. *www.japantimes.co.jp/cgi-bin/getarticle.pl5?nn20041124a2.htm*

Ji-Young, S. and Y. Donho
2003 "Illegal Aliens Force Mass Deportation", Korea Times, 17 June.

Laczko, F.
2002 "Human Trafficking: the Need for Better Data", Migration Information Source, Washington, D.C., 1 November.

Manila Times
2004 "Maids as slaves: Asia's hidden shame", June 3.

Manning, C.
2000 "Labor Mobility, Business Migration and Economic Development in the APEC Region", conference paper entitled *Trade Facilitation in the Asia Pacific: New Directions and the Development Challenge,* Hotel Meritus Negara Singapore, 13-14 September.

Migration Information Source
2004 *Global Data Center: www.migrationinformation.org/GlobalData/*

Migration News
2001 "Thailand, Malaysia", University of California, Davis, October 1.
2002 "China, Hong Kong, Taiwan", University of California, Davis, 1 March.
2003 "China, Hong Kong, Taiwan: Migrants", University of California, Davis, October.

Newland, K.,
2004 Beyond Remittances: The Role of Diaspora in Poverty Reduction in their Countries of Origin, a study for the UK Department for International Development (DFID), MPI, Washington.

Norwegian Refugee Council
2004a Afghanistan Summary, February.
2004b NRC Starts Operations in Sri Lanka, 23 April.

OECD
2001 Trends in International Migration, Organization for Economic Co-operation and Development, Paris.
2004 Trends in International Migration, Paris.

Omelaniuk, I., P. Martin
2004 Best Practices to Manage Migration: China, report for the Cooperative Efforts to Manage Emigration (CEME) project, University of California, Davis.

Rees-Gildea, P. and H. Higashiura
1999 "Bangladesh: Floods", Situation Report no. 5, International Federation of Red Cross and Red Crescent Societies, March 16.

Robinson, C.
2004 "Minimizing Development-Induced Displacement", Migration Information Source, Washington D.C., January 1.

Sizan, Ambassador D.
2003 Deployment of Overseas Filipino Workers, Presentation, Embassy of the Republic of Philippines: (*www.mofa.go.jp/policy/economy/event/sympo0301-2.pdf*)

SRV Official Gazette
2004 "Handling and Prevention of Vietnamese Citizens' Illegal Exit, Entry and Residence in Foreign Countries", Directive No. 14/2004/CT-TTg, No. 6, 2 April.

The Star
2004 "Crackdown on plantations hiring illegal foreign hands", 29 January 2004.

Steil, S. and D. Yuefang
2002 "Policies and practice in Three Gorges resettlement: a field account", Forced Migration Review, Refugee Studies Center, Issue 12, January.

UNAIDS
2002 *www.unaids.org/EN/Geographical+Area/By+Region/South_South_East+Asia.asp*

UNIFEM
The Jakarta Recommendations for Action on Recognizing, Protecting and Empowering Women Migrant Workers in Asia", from the Regional Workshop on "Protecting Women Migrant Workers: Meeting the Challenges", 9-11 December, Jakarta.

United Nations
2002a International Migration Report, New York.
2002b "Strengthening of the United Nations: an agenda for further change, Report of the Secretary-General", A/57/387, United Nations General Assembly, 9 September.

United Nations High Commissioner for Refugees (UNHCR)
2001 Report of the Workshop on the "Impact of Globalisation on the full Enjoyment of Economic, Social and Cultural Rights and the Right to Development", Kuala Lumpur, 8-10 May.
2002a Country Report: Bangladesh: *www.refugees.org/world/countryrpt/scasia/bangladesh.htm*
2002b Country Report: Nepal: *www.refugees.org/world/countryrpt/scasia/nepal.htm*
2002c Country Report: India: *www.refugees.org/world/countryrpt/scasia/india.htm*
2003a "Refugees by Numbers 2003", Geneva.
2003b "Country Operations Plan:. Country Afghanistan", Geneva, May.
2004a "Afghan refugees to resolve disputes before leaving Iran", 21 May.
2004b "2003 Global Refugee Trends", Population Data Unit, Geneva, June 2004.

United Nations Regional Profile
2003 "Human Trafficking: Regional Profile", 11 March.

US Centers for Disease Control and Prevention
2004 *www.cdc.gov/nchstp/od/gap/countries/vietnam.htm*

US Committee for Refugees
2003a "Afghanistan Country Report", World Refugee Survey 2003, Immigration and Refugee Services of America, Washington, D.C.
2003b "Thailand Country Report", World Refugee Survey 2003, Immigration and Refugee Services of America, Washington, D.C.

United States Department of State
2004a China (Taiwan Only)—Country Reports on Human Rights Practices, Bureau of Democracy, Human Rights and Labor, Washington, D.C., 25 February.
2004b Trafficking in Persons Report. U.S. Department of State, Washington, DC.

Vietnam Investment Review
2004a "Trade in Women, Children Growing", May 31-June 6.
2004b "Human Chattel", Vietnam Investment Review Website, No. 680, release date Oct. 25.
2004c "The Quiet Spread of HIV/AIDS", May 17-23.

Wickramasekera, P.
2002 "Asian Labour Migration: Issues and Challenges in an Era of Globalization", International Migration Papers 57, International Labour Organization, Geneva, August.

Wille, C. and B. Passl (Eds.)
2001 Change and Continuity: Female Labour Migration in South East Asia, Asian Research Centre for Migration, Bangkok.

World Bank
2004 "Addressing HIV/AIDS in East Asia and the Pacific", *www.lnweb18.worldbank.org/eap/eap.nsf/0/00A1B68CE1D6FEDA85256ECA0058DC8E?OpenDocument.*

World Health Organization (WHO)
2001 "Setting priorities for Tuberculosis and HIV/AIDS in high burden countries in S and SEA", Third Annual Asia Development Forum, June 11-14, Bangkok, Thailand, wc.whothi.org/EN/Section 3/Section39.htm.
2003 "WHO case definitions for Surveillance of Severe Acute Respiratory Syndrome (SARS)", revised 1 May; *www.who.int/csr/sars/casedefinition/en/.*
2004 "Interim Guidelines for National SARS Preparedness (4 April 2003)", Western Pacific Regional Office.

ZHU Guohong
1999 "Emigration from China in Modern Times: 1840-1949", in Xue Shu Jiang Zuo Hui Bian (No. 18) (Chinese), Wang Kuancheng Education Foundation, China.

Zlotnik, H.
2003 "The Global Dimensions of Female Migration", Migration Information Source, Washington, D.C., 1 March.

ECONOMIC MIGRATION IN SOUTH ASIA

Afsar, Rita
2003 "Internal migration and development nexus: the case of Bangladesh", paper presented at the Regional Conference on *Migration, Development and Pro-poor Policy in Asia* jointly organised by RMMRU, Bangladesh and DFID on 22-24 June, Dhaka.

Anh, D.N.
2003 "Migration and poverty in Asia: with reference to Bangladesh, China, the Philippines Development: Opportunities and Challenges for Poverty Reduction in the ESCAP Region on 27-29 August.

Battistella, G.
2001 "International Migration in the ESCAP Region", ESCAP 2001, presented at the Ad Hoc Expert Group Meeting on Migration and Development: Opportunities and Challenges for Poverty Reduction in the ESCAP Region.

INSTRAW-IOM
2000 Temporary Labour Migration of Women: Case Studies of Bangladesh and Sri Lanka.

IOM
2003 Labour Migration in Asia: Trends, Challenges and Policy Responses in Countries of Origin, Geneva.
2004 Migration Initiatives 2004, Geneva.

K.C, B.K.
2003 "Migration, poverty and development in Nepal", ESCAP, paper presented to the Ad Hoc Expert Group Meeting on Migration and Development: Opportunities and Challenges for Poverty Reduction in the ESCAP Region on 27-29 August.

Kuddus, U.
2003 Channelling Diaspora Remittance into the Securities Market of Bangladesh, Internship Report, Institute of Business Administration, University of Dhaka. New Era
2000 "Migration Policy in Nepal", June.

Rajan S. I.
2003 "Dynamics of international migration from India: it's economic and social implications", ESCAP, paper presented on the Ad Hoc Expert Group Meeting on *Migration and Development: Opportunities and Challenges for Poverty Reduction in the ESCAP Region* on 27-29 August.

Siddiqui, T.
2004 Institutionalising Diaspora Linkage: The Emigrant Bangladeshis in UK and USA, IOM, Geneva.

Skeldon, R.
2003 "Migration and Migration Policies in Asia: a Synthesis of Selected Cases", paper presented at the Regional Conference on Migration, Development and Pro-poor Policy in Asia jointly organised by RMMRU, Bangladesh and DFID on 22-24 June, Dhaka, Bangladesh.

UNDP
2001 Human Development Report 2001: *www.undp.org/hdr2001/indicator/indic_31_1_1.html.*

Waddington, C.
2003 "International Migration Policies in Asia", paper presented at the Regional Conference on Migration, Development and Pro-poor Policy in Asia jointly organised by RMMRU, Bangladesh and DFID on 22-24 June, Dhaka, Bangladesh.

TEXTBOX 6.3
Migration in the People's Republic of China

Chen Yujie (Director of the Overseas Chinese Affairs Office of the State Council)

2003 Interview with reporter of Qiao Bao in the US on 6 November and published in Qiao Bao (Chinese) 07 Nov.

China Ministry of Public Security

2003 *www//edu.sinohome.com/oversea/papers/2793.htm*, China Radio International: *www.fpon.cri.com.cn/773/2003-2-6/118@153822.htm*

China National Statistics Bureau (CNSB)

2003 Floating population in the whole country reached 121,070,000, (information from Population and Social Science Department, CNSB) published by Happyhome net (Chinese) January 3. *www.happyhome.net.cn/read.asp?subjectid=212&infoid=7996&forumid=18508*

McKinley, B.

2004 "Chinese Workers Abroad Send Back HKD 78 Billion", *Hong Kong Economic Daily*, 13 November.

Zhang Feng

2004 Study on the 2004 Prospects of Chinese Economy, Beijing Chen Bao (Chinese), 22 January.

Nan Ke

2003 "Interview with a senior Official of the State Administration of Foreign Exchange on the Status of Income and Expenditure" (in Chinese), 16 October 2003, published on Chinamoney net. *www.chinamoney.com.cn/content/zongheng/yanjiu*

Li Peilin

2003 "Issues for the Economic Development of China in 2004", published in Zhongguowang (Chinese) on 19 December, Beijing. *www.bj.edu21cn.com/web_news/news.asp?id=1183&type=703*

Zhu Guohong

1999 "Emigration from China in Modern Times: 1840–1949", published in *Xue Shu Jiang Zuo Hui Bian (No. 18)* (Chinese), Wang Kuancheng Education Foundation, China.

GENERAL WEBSITES

China National Tourism Administration: *www.cnta.com/chujing/chujing.htm*

Ministry of Public Security: *www.mps.gov.cn/webpage/shownews.asp?id=710&biaoshi=bitGreatNews*

Xinhuanet: *www.qingdaonews.com/gb/content/2004-03/25/content_2908986.htm*

OCEANIA - MIGRATION DYNAMICS

Australian Bureau of Statistics

2004 *Australian Social Trends 2002 Population - Population Composition: New Zealanders in Australia*: *www.abs.gov.au/Ausstats/abs@.nsf/0/6abbe003a85d6c9dca256bcd008272ef?OpenDocument*, accessed 23 July 2004.

2004 *Australian Social Trends, International Population: www.abs.gov.au/Ausstats/abs@.nsf/0/f40a4516936226d4ca256e9e002989c0?OpenDocument*, accessed 1 October 2004.

Commonwealth of Australia

2002 *Intergenerational Report 2002-03*, Budget Paper No. 5: *www.budget.gov.au/2002-03/bp5/html/01_BP5Prelim.html*, accessed 24 July 2004.

2003 "A Pacific engaged: Australia's relations with Papua New Guinea and the island states of the southwest Pacific", Senate Foreign Affairs, Defence and Trade Committee Report: *www.aph.gov.au/Senate/committee/fadt_ctte/png/report/*, accessed 14 October 2004.

DIMIA (Department of Immigration, Multiculturalism and Indigenous Affairs)

2003a *The People of Australia: Statistics from the 2001 Census*: *www.immi.gov.au/research/publications/people_of_australia.pdf*, accessed 21 July, 2004.

2003b "Overview of Skilled Migration to Australia", Fact Sheet No. 24: *www.immi.gov.au/facts/24overview_skilled.htm*, accessed 25 May 2004.

2003c "Temporary Entry: an Overview", Fact Sheet No. 46: *www.immi.gov.au/facts/46temporary_entry.htm*, accessed 25 May 2004.

2004a "New Zealanders in Australia", Fact Sheet No. 17: *www.immi.gov.au/facts/17nz.htm*, accessed 23 July 2004.

2004b "Working Holiday Maker Program", Fact Sheet No. 49: *www.immi.gov.au/facts/49whm.htm*, accessed 21 July 2004.

2004c "Australia's Refugee and Humanitarian Program", Fact Sheet No. 60: *www.immi.gov.au/facts/60refugee.htm*, accessed 24 July 2004.

2004d "Commonwealth Presence in the Torres Strait", Fact Sheet No. 72: *www.immi.gov.au/facts/72torres.htm*, accessed 15 October 2004.

2004e "Unauthorised Arrivals by Air and Sea", Fact Sheet No. 74: *www.immi.gov.au/facts/74unauthorised.htm*, accessed 24 July 2004.

2004f "New Measures for Temporary Protection And Temporary Humanitarian Visa Holders", Fact Sheet No. 64a; *www.immi.gov.au/facts/64protection.htm*

2004g "New Onshore Visa Options for Temporary Protection and Temporary Humanitarian Visa Holders", Fact Sheet No. 64d: *www.immi.gov.au/facts/64d_mte.htm*, accessed 15 October 2004.

2004h *Population Flows: Immigration Aspects 2002-03 Edition*: *www.immi.gov.au/statistics/publications/popflows2002_3/ch1_pt1.pdf*, accessed 24, July 2004.

Hugo, G., D. Rudd and K. Harris

2001 *Emigration from Australia: Economic Implications*, CEDA Information Paper No. 77, Adelaide University, Australia.

New Zealand Government

2003 "Population and Sustainable Development 2003", government report, June.

NZIS

2003 "General Trends in Residence Approvals", Issue Paper Volume 3, September.

2004a *www.immigration.govt.nz/community/general/general-information/statistics/nzisfactpack.htm*

2004b *www.trcnz.govt.nz/Surveys/International+Visitor+Survey/Data+and+Analysis/Australia*

New Zealand Ministry of Health

2004 Refugee Resettlement in New Zealand: *www.asylumsupport.info/publications/mohnewzealand/handbook/two.pdf*, accessed 23 July 2004.

New Zealand Ministry of Tourism

2004 "The Tourism Industry": *www.tourism.govt.nz/aboutus/au-tourismindustry.html*

PIDC (Pacific Immigration Directors' Conference)

2004 "People Smuggling, Trafficking and Illegal Migration in the Pacific: A Regional Perspective 2004", Annex A, 8th Pacific Immigration Directors' Conference, Palau, September.

Ruddock, P.

2002 Ministerial Press Statement MPS 078/2002: *www.minister.immi.gov.au/media_releases/ruddock_media02/r02078.htm*

Statistics New Zealand

2004a "Births and Deaths (June 2004 quarter)", Information Release; *www.stats.govt.nz/domino/external/pasfull/pasfull.nsf/web/Hot+Off+The+Press+Births+and+Deaths+June+2004+quarter?open* accessed 4 October 2004.

2004b "External Migration (June 2004)", Information Release, *www.stats.govt.nz/domino/external/pasfull/pasfull.nsf/web/Hot+Off+The+Press+External+Migration+June+2004?open* accessed 4 October 2004.

Tourism Research Council New Zealand

2004 "International Visitor Arrivals: August 2004"; *www.trcnz.govt.nz/Surveys/International+Visitor+Arrivals/Data+and+Analysis/*

United Nations

2003 Trends in Total Migrant Stock: The 2003 Revision, (POP/DB/MIG/2003/1 and ESA/P/WP.188).

UNHCR

2002 "Summary Conclusions on the Concept of 'Effective Protection' in the Context of Secondary Movements of Refugees and Asylum-Seekers": *www.unhcr.ch/cgi-bin/texis/vtx/home/+MwwBm8je-6mwwwwrwwwwwwwhFqA72ZR0gRfZNtFqrpGdBnqBAFqA72ZR0gRfZNcFqGPo5xdDa2d1DmBwxcnDzmxwwwwwww/opendoc.pdf*

UNPD (United Nations Population Division)

2001 *World Urbanization Prospects: The 2001 Revision*, Department of Economic and Social Affairs, NY.; *www.esa.un.org/unpp*, accessed on 1 October 2004.

2002 *World Population Prospects: The 2002 Revision*, Department of Economic and Social Affairs, NY.

2003 *www.esa.un.org/unpp/definition.html#Oceania*, accessed on 1 October 2004.

Vanstone, A.

2004 *Work and Holiday Visa Arrangement between Australia and Thailand*, Press Release VPS 095/2004: *www.minister.immi.gov.au/media_releases/media04/v04095.htm*, accessed 25 July 2004.

Vitorino, A.

2004 *The Future of the European Union Agenda on Asylum, Migration and Borders* SPEECH/04/435 given at Conference of the European Policy Center and King Baudouin Foundation, Brussels, 4 October: *www.europa.eu.int/rapid/pressReleasesAction.do?reference=SPEECH/04/435&format=PDF&aged=0&language*

CHAPTER 7 – MIGRANTS IN AN ENLARGED EUROPE

Alvarez-Plata, P., H. Brücker and Boris Silverstovs

2003 *Potential Migration from Central and Eastern Europe into the EU-15. An Update*, European Commission/DG Employment and Social Affairs, Brussels.

Bade, K., M. Bommes and R. Münz (Eds.)

2004 *Migrationsreport 2004*, Frankfurt/M.-New York: Campus.

Baldwin-Edwards, M.

2004 "The Changing Mosaic of Mediterranean Migrations", *Migration Information Source*, Migration Policy Institute, Washington DC: *www.migrationinformation.org/Feature/display.cfm?id=230*

BMA (British Medical Association)

2001 *The Medical Profession and Human Rights: Handbook for a Changing Agenda*, British Medical Association, 2001, London.

Carvel, J.

2000 "Child minders. Charity call to protect young refugees", *The Guardian*, 20.09.

Einaudi, L.

2004 *Historical Approaches to Legal and Illegal Migration for Employment in Italy and France*, Paper presented at the 2nd Stockholm Workshop on Global Mobility Regimes, IFS, Stockholm.

European Commission

2000 Communication from the Commission to the Council and the European Parliament On a Community Integration Policy, COM (2000) 757 final. Brussels.

2002 Communication from the Commission to the Council and the European Parliament. Integrating Migration Issues in the European Union's Relations with Third Countries, COM (2002) 703 final. Brussels

2003 Communication from the Commission to the Council and the European Parliament *On immigration, integration and employment*, COM (2003) 336 final, June 3, EC, Brussels.

2004 Communication from the Commission to the Council and the European Parliament. First Annual Report on Migration and Integration, COM(2004) 508 final. Brussels

2004 "*A single roof for asylum in the European Union. www.europa.eu.int/comm/justice_home/doc_centre/asylum/doc_asylum_intor_en.htm*

European Commission/DG Employment and Social Affairs

2003 *Employment in Europe 2003 – Recent Trends and Prospects*, EC, Brussels.

2004 *Employment in Europe 2004*. Luxemburg: EC, Brussels.

European Commission/DG Justice and Home Affairs
2004 *Freedom, Security and Justice*: *www.europa.eu.int/comm/justice_home/doc_centre/intro/doc_intro_en.htm*

European Commission/Eurostat
2002 The Social Situation in the European Union 2002. Luxembourg: EC.

European Council Directive:
2003a 2003/86/EC of 22 September 2003 on the right to family reunification, *Official Journal of the European Union*, L 251/12 3 October 2003: 12-18.
2003b 2003/109/EC of 25 November 2003 concerning the status of third-country nationals who are long-term residents, *Official Journal of the European Union*, L16/44, 25 November 2003: 44-53.

Fassmann, H. and R. Münz and F. Laczko, I. Stacher, and A. Klekowski von Koppenfels (Eds.)
2002 "EU Enlargement and East-West Migration in Europe", *New Challenges for Migration Policy in Central and Eastern Europe*, IOM, Geneva: 59-86.

InburgerNet
2004 *Traject*: *www.inburgernet.nl/traject/index.html*

IOM
2003 *World Migration 2003*, IOM, Geneva.
2003a *Migration Health Newsletter*, IOM MHS, Vol. 1, Geneva.
2004a "Counter Trafficking Handbook" (in press), chapter 4, Geneva.
2004b "Migration trends in selected EU application countries", Vol. V, IOM Vienna.

König, K. and B. Perchinig and J. Niessen, Y. Schibel and R. Magoni (Eds.)
2003 "Austria", *EU and US approaches to the management of immigration*, Migration Policy Group, Brussels: *www.migpolgroup.com/uploadstore/Austria.pdf*

Krieger, H.
2004 *Migration Trends in an Enlarged Europe*, European Foundation for the Improvement of Living and Working Conditions, Dublin.

London School of Hygiene and Tropical Medicine
2003 "The health risks and consequences of trafficking in women and adolescents, findings from a European study", London: LSHTM.

Ministry of Integration (Denmark)
2002 *Bill amending the Aliens Act, the Marriage Act and other Acts (Abolishment of the de facto refugee concept, streamlining of the asylum proceedings, more stringent conditions for the issue of permanent residence permits and tightening of the conditions for family reunification, etc.)* 28 February 2002 File No. 2001/7310-81: *www.inm.dk/images Upload/dokument/aliens_act_amending.pdf*

Ministry of Justice (the Netherlands)
2001 *Een nieuw bestaan in Nederland: inburgeren voor nieuwkomers (A new life in the Netherlands: Integration procedure for newcomers)*, The Hague.

Münz, R. and M. Jandl and I. Stacher (Eds.)
2004 "The Demography of International Migration: Facts, Assumptions, Gaps", *Towards a Multilateral Migration Regime* (Special Anniversary Edition dedicated to J. Widgren), International Center for Migration Policy Development, Vienna: 119-124.

Münz, R. and H. Fassmann
2004 "Migrants in Europe and their Economic Position: Evidence from the European Labour Force Survey and from Other Sources", Paper prepared for the European Commission, DG Employment and Social Affairs, EC, Brussels; HWWA, Hamburg(*www.migration-research.org*).

Münz, R. and R. Ulrich and R. Alba, P. Schmidt and M. Wasmer (Eds.)
2003 "The ethnic and demographic structure of foreigner and immigrants in Germany", *Germans or Foreigners?*, Palgrave-Macmillan, New York, Basingstoke: 19-44.

Organization for Economic Co-operation and Development
2004 *Trends in International Migration: Sopemi 2003*, OECD, Paris.

Österreichischer Austauschdienst,
2003 *Entry and Residence Regulations Nationals of other countries (third countries)*: *www.oead.ac.at/_english/austria/entry/integration.htm*

United Nations Population Division
2002 *International Migration Report 2002*, UN, New York.

United Nations Population Division
2002 *World Population Prospects - The 2002 Revision*, UN, New York.

US Department of State
2002 Statement of Ambassador Nancy Ely-Raphel, Senior Advisor to the Secretary, Office to Monitor and Combat Trafficking in Persons on the release of the 2002 *Trafficking in Persons Report*, European Women's Lobby: *The Gender Divide in the EU* (Statistics).

van Selm, J. and E. Tsolakis
2004 "The Enlargement of an 'Area of Freedom, Security and Justice': Managing Migration in a European Union of 25 Members", *Policy Brief No. 4*, Migration Policy Institute, Washingtom DC: *www.migrationpolicy.org/pubs/eu_enlargement.pdf*

Willis B.M. and B.S. Levy
2002 "Child prostitution: global health burden, research needs and interventions", *The Lancet*, Apr 20; 359 (9315): 1417-22.

MIGRATION IN EASTERN EUROPE AND CENTRAL ASIA (EECA)

Government of the Russian Federation
2004 "Country Report: Russian Federation", Report prepared for the High-level Review Meeting on "Refugees, Migration and Protection", follow-up to the 1996 Geneva Conference on the Problems of Refugees, Displaced Persona, Migration and Asylum Issues, organized jointly by UNCHR, IOM, OSCE and the Council of Europe, Minsk, 26-28 May.

IOM
2002 *Migration Trends in Eastern Europe and Central Asia; 2001-2002 Review*, Geneva.

2003 "Analysis of Institutional and Legal Frameworks and Overview of Cooperation Patterns in the Field of Counter-trafficking in Eastern Europe and Central Asia", Report by IOM Vienna.

Kelly, L.
2002 *Journeys of Jeopardy: A Commentary on Current Research on Trafficking of Women and Children for Sexual Exploitation Within Europe*, paper commissioned by IOM for the EU/IOM European Conference on "Preventing and Combating Trafficking in Human Beings: A Global Challenge for the 21st Century".

US Department of State
2004 *Trafficking in Persons Report 2004*. Available at *www.state.gov/g/tip/rls/tiprpt/2004/*.

World Bank
2004 *Challenges and Opportunities of International Migration for the EU, its Member States, Neighbouring Countries and Regions: A Policy Note*, Social Protection Discussion Paper Series No. 0411, Social Protection Unit, Human Development Network, Washington D.C.

MIGRATION IN TURKEY: FACING CHANGES AND MAKING CHOICES

Futo, P. and M. Jandl (eds.)
2004 *2003 Year Book on Illegal Migration, Human Smuggling and Trafficking in Central and Eastern Europe: A Survey and Analysis of Border Management and Border Apprehension Data from 19* States, ICMPD, Vienna.

Icduygu A
2000 "The Politics of International Migratory Regimes: Transit Migration Flows in Turkey", *International Social Science Journal*, 165: 357-367.

Icduygu, A.
2002 "Irregular Migration in Turkey", IOM Migration Research Series, No. 12, Geneva.
2003a SOPEMI Report for Turkey, 2002-2003, Koc University, Istanbul.
2003b "Irregular Migration in Turkey", in *IOM Migration Research Series*, No. 12, IOM, Geneva.

Icduygu, A. and S. Toktas
2002 "How Do Smuggling and Trafficking Operate via Irregular Border Crossings in the Middle East?", *International Migration*, 40 (6): 25-54.

Icduygu, A. and S. Koser-Akcapar
2004 "Labor Outcome of Irregular Migration and Human Trafficking in Turkey", ILO Working Paper, Geneva.

Kirisci, K
2001 *Justice and Home Affairs, Issues in Turkish-EU Relations*, Istanbul: Tesev Publications.

UNHCR
2004 *Statistics at a Glance*, Geneva; *www.unhcr.ch/statistics*

CHAPTER 8 – ECONOMIC EFFECTS OF INTERNATIONAL MIGRATION: A SYNOPTIC OVERVIEW

Adams, R.H.
1998 "Remittances, Investment and Rural Asset Accumulation in Pakistan", Economic Development and Cultural Change, University of Chicago Press, Chicago, pp. 155-173.
2003 *International Migration, remittances and the brain drain: A study of the 24 labour-exporting countries*, World Bank Policy research Working Paper 3069, World Bank, Washington D.C.

Adams, R.(Jr.) and J. Page
2003 "The impact of international migration and remittances on poverty", Paper prepared for the DFID/world Bank Conference on Migrant Remittances, London, October.

Adepoju, A.
1991 "South-North migration: The African experience", *International Migration* XXIX (2), IOM, Geneva, pp. 205-221.

Baker, M. and D. Benjamin
1993 *The receipt of transfer payments by immigrants*, University of Toronto, Canada.

Biers, D. and S. Dhume
2000 "In India, a bit of California", *far Eastern Economic Review*, 2 November.

Böhning, W.R. and M.L. Schloeter-Paredes
1994 *Aid in Place of Migration*, ILO, Geneva.

Borjas, G.J.
1994 "The economics of immigration", *Journal of Economics Literature* 23, December.
2003 "The labour demand curve is downward sloping: Re-examining the impact of immigration on the labour market", *The Quarterly Journal of Economics* 118(4).
2004 *Increasing the supply of labour through immigration, measuring the impact on native-born workers*, Center for Immigration Studies.

Brücker H.
2002 Can International Migration Solve the Problems of European Labour Markets?
paper presented at the UNECE Economic Analysis Division's Spring Seminar Labour market challenges in the ECE Region.

Brücker, H., G. Epstein *et al.*
2002 "Managing migration in the European welfare state", in *Immigration Policy and the Welfare System*, Oxford University Press, Oxford, England.

Choucri, N. and S. Lahiri
1983 *Short term energy economy interactions in Egypt*, MIT, Cambridge, Mass, US.

Coulombe, J-F et al.
2004 *Literacy scores, human capital and growth rates in 14 OECD countries*, Statistics Department, University of Ottawa, Canada, Ottawa.

DeFreitas, G.
1986 *The impact of immigration on low-wage workers*, mimeo.

De New, J. and K.F. Zimmermann
1994 "Native wage impacts of foreign labor: A random effects panel analysis", *Journal of Population Economics* 7.

Desai, M., D. Kapur and J. McHale
2001 "The fiscal impact of the brain drain: Indian emigration to the US", *Weekly Public Economy Discussion Paper*, Harvard University.

Devan, J. and P. Tewari
2001 "Brains Abroad", *The Mckinsley Quarterly*.

DIEE
1998 *Annual Report of the National Skills Task Force: Skills Needs in Great Britain and Northern Ireland*, London.

Dustmann C., C.F. Fabri and I. Preston
2004 "The local labour market effect of immigration in the U.K", CReAM discussion paper No. 2.

Economist, The
2000 "A continent on the move", 4 May.
2002 "Outward bound", 28 September.
2004 "Myths and Reality", 26 February.
2004 "Skill shortages seen as key in outsourcing", 31 March.

Financial Times
2000 "Europe's leaders warned over IT skills gap", 7 March.
"A ladder out of the low-skills economy", 6 September.
2004 "IT Services gear up as outsourcing row wages", 31 March.
"Top companies trawl a global talent pool", 1 July.
"Exodus of medical staff hampers Aids programmes throughout Africa", 16 July.
"The bureaucracy crippling India", 17 August.

Ghosh, B.
1992a "Migration, trade and international co-operation; Do the inter-linkages work?", *International Migration, 3/4.*
1992b "Migration-development linkages: some specific issues and practical policy measures", *International Migration, 3/4.*
1996 "Economic Migration and the Sending Countries" in Julien van den Broek, *The Economics of Labour Migration*, Edward Elgar, Cheltenham, UK.
1997 *Gains from Global Linkages:Trade in Services and Movement of Person*, Macmillan Press, London; St. Martins Press, New York.
1998 *Huddled Masses and Uncertain Shores: Insights into Irregular Migration*, Kluwer Law International, The Hague, Boston, London.
2004 "Harnessing development potential of migrants' remittances", Paper presented to the meeting of the financial sector organised by the Club of The Hague, The Hague, July.

Ghosh, B. (Ed.)
2000 *Managing Migration: Time for a New International Regime?*, Oxford University Press, Oxford, England.

Goldfarb, R., O. Havrylyshyn and S. Magnum
1984 "Can remittances compensate for manpower outflows: the case of Philippine physicians", Journal of Development Economics, Elsevier Sciences, Amsterdam, pp. 1-17.

Gott, C. and K. Johnston
2002 "The migrant population in the UK: Fiscal effects", RDS Occasional Paper 77, London.

Haisken-DeNew, J. and K.F. Zimmermann
1995 "Wage and mobility effects of trade and migration", CEPR Discussion Paper 1318, London.

Hamilton, B. and J. Whalley
1984 "Efficiency and Distributional Implications of Global Restrictions on Labour Mobility", *Journal of Developmental Economics* 14, pp. 61-75.

Hanson, G., K.F. Sheve *et al.* **and T. Boeri, G. Hanson and B. McCormick (Eds.)**
2002 "Immigration and the US economy: Labour market impacts, illegal entry and policy choices", *Immigration Policy and the Welfare System*, Oxford University Press, Oxford, England.

IADB (Inter-American Development Bank)
2003 *Sending Money Home: An International Comparison of Remittance Markets*, Washington D.C.

IOM
2003 *World Migration Report 2003*, Geneva.
2004 *Return Migration: Policies and Practices in Europe*, Geneva.

ILO
1981 *Employment, Trade and North-South Co-operation*, Geneva.
1999 *Migrant Workers*, Geneva.
2004 *Towards a fair deal for migrant workers in the global economy*, Geneva.

ILO/UNDP
1988 *Agenda for Policy: Asian Migration Project*, ILO, Bangkok.

IMD (International Institute for Management Development)
1999 *Brain drain: survey results*, Lausanne.

Kim, S.
1983 "The labour migration from Korea to the Middle East: its trends and impacts on the Korean economy", paper presented to the conference on Asian labour Migration in Sri Lanka.

Korale, R.B.M. and G.D.C. Gunapala
1985 "Dimensions of Return Migration in Sri Lanka", paper presented to the Policy Workshop on International Migration in Asia and the Pacific, Bangkok, October.

Korner, H.
1987 "The experience in the main geographical OECD areas - European sending countries in OECD", *Future of Migration*, OECD, Paris.

Lowell, B.L., A. Findlay and E. Stewart
2004 Brain strain: optimising highly skilled migration from developing countries, Institute for Public Policy Research, London (Asylum and Migration Working Paper 3).

Luo, Y.L. and W.J Wang
2001 "High-skill migration and Chinese Taipei's industrial development", paper presented at International Mobility of Highly Skilled Workers: From Statistical Analysis to the Formulation of Policies Seminar, organized by OECD, Paris, 11-12 June.

Martin, P. and E. Midgley
1994 "Immigration to the United States: Journey to an uncertain destination", *Population Bulletin* 49(2), Washington D.C.

McCormick, B. and J. Wahaba
2002 "Return Migration and geographical inequality " (mimeo.), University of Southampton.

Migration News
1996 Vol. 3, No. 8, August.
1997 Vol. 4, No. 2, February.

Meeus, W. and D. Sanders
2003 "Pull factors in international migration of health professionals", presented at the Public Health 2003 Conference, Public Health Association of South Africa (PHASA), Cape Town, 24-26 March.

Meyer, J-B and M. Brown
1999 "A new approach to the brain drain", Discussion paper no. 41, World Conference on Science, UNESCO-ICSU, Budapest, June-July.

New York Times
2004 "U.S. is linking status of aliens to hospital aid", 10 August.

OECD
1993 *Trends in International Migration*, Paris.
1998 *Trends in International Migration*, Paris.
2002a "International mobility of the highly skilled", policy brief, Paris.
2002b "The brain drain: old myths, new realities", Paris.

NRC (National Research Council)
1997 *The New American: Economic, Social and Fiscal Effects of Immigration*, Washington D.C.

Papademetriou, D.G. and P.L. Martin (Eds.)
1991 *The Unsettled Relationship: Labour Migration and Development*, Greenwood Press, New York.

Puri, S. and T. Ritzema
1999 *Migrant worker remittances, micro finance and informal economy*, Working Paper 21, Social Finance Unit, ILO, Geneva.

Rodrik, D.
2002 *Feasible Globalizations*, Kennedy School of Government, Working Paper Series RWPO 2029, July.

Rubenstein, H.
1992 "Migration, development and remittances in rural Mexico", *International Migration* 30(2).

Simon, J.
1989 *The Economic Consequences of Immigration*, Basil Blackwell, Oxford, England.

Smith, J. and B. Edmonston
1997 *The New Americans: Economic, demographic and fiscal effects of immigration*, National Academy Press, Washington D.C.

Sum, A. et al.
2003 *New Immigrants in the Labor Force and the Number of Employed New Immigrants in the U.S. from 2000-2003: Continued Growth Amidst Declining Employment Among the Native Born Population*, North Eastern University.

Taylor, J.
1999 "The new economics of labor migration and the role of remittances", *International Migration* 37(1).

UN
1997 *World Population Monitoring*, New York, New York.

UNHCR
1992 *Refugees*, No. 90, July, Geneva.

US Commission for the Study of International Migration and Cooperative Economic Development.
1990 *Unauthorized Migration: An Economic Development Response*, Government Printing Office, Washington.

Van Doorn, J.
2003 "Migration, remittances and development", *Labour* 129, Geneva.

Venables, A.
1999 "Trade liberalisation and factor mobility: an overview" in R.Fani et al. (ed.) *Migration: The Controversies and The Evidence*, Cambridge University Press, London.

Weintraub, S. and S. Diaz-Briquets,
1994 "The use of foreign aid for reducing incentives to emigrate from Central America" in W.R Bohning and M.L. Schloeter-Paredes , *Aid in Place of Migration*, ILO, Geneva.

Williamson, J.
1996 "Globalization and trends in inequality", American Economic Association.

World Bank
1995 *World Development Report*, Washington, D.C.
1997 *World Development Indicators*, Washington, D.C.
2003 "Workers' remittances: an important and stable source of external development finance", by D.Ratha in *Global Development Finance 2003*, Washington D.C.

CHAPTER 9 – ECONOMIC COSTS AND BENEFITS OF INTERNATIONAL LABOUR MIGRATION

Borjas, G.J.
1994 "The Economics of Immigration", *Journal of Economic Literature* 32(4), pp. 1167-1717.

Dugger, C. W.
2004 "In Africa, an Exodus of Nurses" in New York Times, July 12.

Ellerman, D.
2003 Policy Research on Migration and Development. Mimeo.

Fisher, S.
2003 "Globalization and its Challenges", American Economic Review 93.

Hamilton, B. and J. Whalley
1984 "Efficiency and Distributional Implications of Global Restrictions on Labour Mobility", Journal of Developmental Economics 14, pp. 61-75.

Hinojosa-Ojeda, R. and S. Robinson
1991 Alternative Scenarios of U.S.-Mexican Integration: A Computable General Equilibrium Approach, Working Paper 609, Department of Agricultural and Resource Economics, University of California, Berkeley.

Hufbauer, G. and J. Schott
1992 North American Free Trade: Issues and Recommendations, Institute for International Economics, Washington.

Johnson, H. and W. Adams (Ed.)
1968 "An 'Internationalist' Model", The Brain Drain, Macmillan, New York, pp. 69-91.

Krueger, A. B.
1999 "Measuring Labor's Share", AEA Papers and Proceedings, Vol. 89, No. 2, May. *www.irs.princeton.edu/krueger/working_papers.html*

Martin, P.L.
1993 Trade and Migration: NAFTA and Agriculture, Institute for International Economics Washington, D.C.

Mayer, J.
1996 Implications of New Trade and Endogenous Growth Theories for Diversification Policies of Commodity-Dependent Countries, United Nations Conference on Trade and Development (UNCTAD).

OECD
2004 *Trends in International Migration SOPEMI 2003*, Annual Report, 2003 Edition, Paris.

Passel , J. S., R. Capps and M. E. Fix
2004 *ndocumented Immigrants: Facts and Figures*; *www.urban.org/url.cfm?ID=1000587*

Patinkin, D. and W. Adams (Ed.)
1968 "A 'Nationalist' Model", *The Brain Drain*, Macmillan, New York, pp. 92-108.

Ratha, D.
2003 Workers' Remittances: An Important and Stable Source of External Development Finance", Global Development Finance 2003, World Bank, pp. 157-170; *www.worldbank.org/prospects/gdf2003/*

Rodrik, D.
2001 Comments at the Conference on Immigration Policy and the Welfare State, Trieste, June 23: *www.ksghome.harvard.edu/~.drodrik.academic.ksg/papers.html*

Smith, J.P. and B. Edmonston (Eds.)
1997 The New Americans: Economic, Demographic and Fiscal Effects of Immigration, National Academy Press, Washington.

Taylor, J.E. and P.L. Martin and B. Gardener and G. Rausser (Eds.)
2001 "Human Capital: Migration and Rural Population Change", Handbook of Agricultural Economics 1, Elsevier Science, Amsterdam: *www.elsevier.nl/*

Tsuda, T.
2003 Strangers in the Ethnic Homeland; Japanese Brazilian Return Migration in Transnational Perspective, Columbia University Press: *www.columbia.edu/cu/cup*

UNDP
1992 Human Development Report, Global Dimensions of Human Development, NY.

Williamson, J.
1998 "Globalization, Labour Markets and Policy Backlash", Journal of Economic Perspectives 12.

US Commission for the Study of International Migration and Cooperative Economic Development.
1990 *Unauthorized Migration: An Economic Development Response*, Government Printing Office, Washington.

World Bank
2003 "Remittances to Select Countries 1995-2001", Table in *www.worldbank.org/prospects/gdf2003/gdf_statApp_web.pdf*

CHAPTER 10 – DESIGNING VIABLE AND ETHICAL LABOUR IMMIGRATION POLICIES

Baldwin, R. and Martin P.
1999 "Two Waves of Globalisation: Superficial Similarities, Fundamental Differences", *NBER Working Paper*, No. 6904.

Borjas, G.
1995 "The Economic Benefits from Immigration", *Journal of Economic Perspectives* 9(2): 3-22.
2001 "Does Immigration Grease the Wheels of the Labour Market?", *Brookings Papers on Economic Activity* 1, pp. 69-133.
2003 "The Labor Demand Curve *Is* Downward Sloping: Reexamining the Impact of Immigration on the Labor Market", *The Quarterly Journal of Economics* 118(4), pp. 1335-1374.

Card, D.
2004 "Is the New Immigration Really So Bad?", *IZA Discussion Paper* No. 1119, Bonn.

Carens, J.
1996 "Realistic and Idealistic Approaches to the Ethics of Migration", *International Migration Review* 30(1), pp. 156-170.

Castles, S.
1986 "The Guest-Worker in Western Europe - an Obituary", *International Migration Review* 20(4), pp. 764-778.
2004 "Why Migration Policies Fail", *Ethnic and Racial Studies* (forthcoming)

Cornelius, W.
2004 *Controlling Unwanted Immigration: Lessons from the United States, 1993-2004*, mimeo: *www.compas.ox.ac.uk*

Dustmann, C., F. Fabbri, I. Preston, and J. Wadsworth
2003 "The Local Labour Market Effects of Immigration in the UK", *Home Office Online Report 06/03*, London: *www.homeoffice.gov.uk/rds/pdfs2/rdsolr0603.pdf.*

European Commission
2002 *Commission's Action Plan for Skills and Mobility*, Brussels: *www.europa.eu.int/comm/employment_social/news/2002/feb/ap_en.html*

Fisher, L.
1953 *The Harvest Labor Market in California*, Harvard University Press, Boston.

Ghosh, B.
2003 *Elusive Protection, Uncertain Lands*, IOM, Geneva.

Goodhart, D.
2004 "Too Diverse?", *Prospect Magazine*, February, London. *www.prospect-magazine.co.uk/ArticleView.asp?P_Article=12394*

Goodin, R.
1988 "What Is So Special About Our Fellow Countrymen?", *Ethics* 98(4), pp. 663-686.

Gott, C. and K. Johnston
2002 "The Migrant Population in the UK: Fiscal Effects", Home Office Occasional Paper 77, London; *www.homeoffice.gov.uk/rds/pdfs/occ77migrant.pdf*

Hanson, G. and A. Spilimbergo
2001 "Political Economy, Sectoral Shocks, and Border Enforcement", *Canadian Journal of Economics* 34(3), pp. 612-638.

Hatton, T. and J. Williamson
1998 *The Age of Mass Migration. Causes and Economic Impact*, Oxford University Press, Oxford.

Home Office
2003 *Control of Immigration: Statistics United Kingdom 2002*, TSO, London.

Huntington, S.
2004 "The Hispanic Challenge", *Foreign Policy*, March/April, Washington DC: *www.foreignpolicy.com*

International Labour Organisation
2004 *Towards a Fair Deal for Migrant Workers in the Global Economy*, Report VI prepared for the International Labour Conference 2004, ILO, Geneva.

Klekowski, A.
2001 "The Role of Regional Consultative Processes in Managing International Migration", *Migration Research Series* 3, IOM, Geneva.

Martin, P.
2003 *Managing Labour Migration: Temporary Worker programs for the 21st Century*,
Special lecture on migration, International Institute for Labour Studies, International Labour Organisation (ILO), Geneva:
www.ilo.org/public/english/bureau/inst/download/migration3.pdf

Martin, P. and M. Miller
2000 "Employer Sanctions; French, German and US Experiences", *International Migration Papers* 36, International Labour Office (ILO), Geneva.

Martin, P. and A. Olmstead
1985 "The Agricultural Mechanization Controversy", *Science* 227, pp. 601406.

Martin, P. and M. Teitelbaum
2001 "The Mirage of Mexican Guest Workers", *Foreign Affairs* 80(6), pp. 117-131.

Nozick, R.
1974 *Anarchy, State and Utopia*, Basic Books, New York.

Nussbaum, Martha, et al.
1996 *For Love of Country: Debating the Limits of Patriotism*, Beacon Press, Boston.

Nye, J.
2002 "The American National Interest and Global Public Goods", *International Affairs* 78(2), pp. 233-44.

Rodrik, D.
2002 "Feasible Globalizations", *Working Paper* 9129, National Bureau of Economic Research, Cambridge, Mass.

Ruhs, M.
2003 "Temporary Foreign Worker Programmes: Policies, Adverse Consequences and the Need to Make Them Work", *Perspectives on Labour Migration* 6, International Migration Branch, International Labour Organisation (ILO), Geneva.

Ruhs, M. and H-J. Chang
2004 "The Ethics of Labor Immigration Policy", *International Organization* 58(1), pp. 69-102.

Scheffler, S. (Ed.)
1988 *Consequentialism and Its Critics*, Oxford University Press, Oxford.

Spencer, S.
2003 Introduction in *The Politics of Migration*, edited by Sarah Spencer, Blackwell Publishings, Oxford.

Taran, P.
2000 "Human Rights of Migrants: Challenges of the New Decade", *International Migration* 38(6), pp. 7-52.

Taylor, A.
1996 "International Capital Mobility in History: the Savings-Investment Relationship", *NBER Working Paper*, No. 5743.

Trefler, D.
1997 "Immigrants and Natives in General Equilibrium Trade Models", *Working Paper* 6209, National Bureau of Economic Research, Cambridge, Mass.

United Nations Conference on Trade and Development
2001 *World Investment Report 2001*, Geneva.

United Nations Population Division
2002 *International Migration Report 2002 (ST/ESA/SER.A/220)*, UNPOP, New York.

Walzer, M.
1983 *Spheres of Justice*, Basic Books, New York.

Weil, P.
2002 "Towards a Coherent Policy of Co-Development", *International Migration* 40(3), pp. 41-55.

Weinstein, E.
2002 "Migration for the Benefit of All", *International Labour Review* 141(3), pp. 225-252.

Wickramasekara, P.
2003 "Policy Responses to Skilled Migration: Retention, Return and Circulation", *Perspectives on Labour Migration* 5, International Migration Branch, International Labour Organisation (ILO), Geneva.

Williamson, J.
2002 "Winners and Losers Over Two Centuries of Globalization", *NBER Working Paper*, No. 9161.

CHAPTER 11 – BALANCING THE BENEFITS AND COSTS OF SKILLED MIGRATION IN THE ASIA-PACIFIC REGION

Access Economics
2001 *Impact of Immigrants on the Commonwealth Budget, Summary Report, 2000-2001 Update*, Department of Immigration and Multicultural Affairs, Canberra.

Alburo, F.A. and D.I. Abella
2002 "Skilled Labour Migration from Developing Countries: Study on the Philippines", *International Migration Papers 51*, International Labour Office, Geneva.

ASEAN Secretariat
2004 Personal meeting with staff, Jakarta, 15 February.

Auriol, L. and J. Sexton
2002 "Human resources in science and technology: measurement issues and international mobility", *International Migration of the Highly Skilled*, OECD, Paris, pp. 13-38.

Appleyard, R.T.
1992 "Migration and Development: A Global Agenda for the Future", *International Migration, Special Issue*, 30(1), pp. 17-32.

Bhagwati, J. and K. Hamada
1974 "The brain drain, international integration of markets for professionals and unemployment: a theoretical analysis", *Journal of Development Economics*, 1(1), pp. 19-42.

Chapman, B. and R. Iredale
1993 "Immigrant Qualifications: Recognition Rates and Relative Wages", *International Migration Review*, 27(2), pp. 359-387.

Chiu, S.W.K.
2001 "Hong Kong (China)", *Migration and the Labour Market in Asia: Recent Trends and Policies*, OECD, Paris, pp. 141-170.

CIC (Citizenship and Immigration Canada)
2002 *Citizenship and Immigration Canada 2002, Facts and Figures 2001: Immigration Overview, www.cic.gc.ca*, accessed 30 November 2003.
2003a *Citizenship and Immigration Canada 2003, Facts and Figures 2002: Immigration Overview, www.cic.gc.ca*, accessed 21 May 2004.
2003b *Citizenship and Immigration Canada 2003, Facts and Figures 2002: Statistical Overview of the Temporary Resident and Refugee Claimant Population*, CIC website, *www.cic.gc.ca*, accessed 21 May 2004.

COSTED (Committee on Science and Technology in Developing Countries, International Council for Science).
2001 *International Mobility of S&T Professionals: Demand and Trends, Impact and Response*, Central Secretariat of COSTED, Chennai, India.

Connell, J.
2001 *The Migration of Skilled Health Personnel in the Pacific Region*, School of Geosciences, University of Sydney, Sydney.

Dang, A.N. and R. Iredale, F. Guo and S. Rozario (Eds.)
2003 "Vietnam: Emergence of Return Skilled Migration", in *Return Migration in the Asia Pacific*, Edward Elgar Publishing, Cheltenham, UK and Northampton, US, pp. 136-168.

DIMIA (Department of Immigration and Multicultural and Indigenous Affairs)
2004 *Population Flows: Immigration Aspects 2002-03 Edition*, Commonwealth of Australia, Canberra: *www.immi.gov.au/migration*

Fincher, R., L. Foster and R. Wilmot
1994 *Gender Equity and Australian Immigration Policy*, Australian Government Publishing Service, Canberra.

Garnaut, R.
2002 *Migration: Benefiting Australia Conference Proceedings, Part 3: Social and economic participation of migrants*, Commonwealth of Australia, Canberra: *www.immi.gov.au/cgi-bin/AT-immisearch.cgi*
2003 *Migration to Australia and Comparisons with the United States: Who Benefits?*, Report prepared for the Department of Immigration and Multicultural and Indigenous Affairs,: Commonwealth of Australia, Canberra: *www.immi.gov.au/publications/index.htm*

Hugo, G. and M. Crock and K. Lyon (Eds.)
2000 "Migrants and Demography: Global and Australian Trends and Issues for Policy Makers, Business and Employers", *Nation Skilling: Migration, Labour and the Law*, Desert Pea Press, Sydney, pp. 84-116.

Hugo, G., D. Rudd and K. Harris
2003 "Australia's Diaspora: Its Size, Nature and Policy Implications", *CEDA Information Paper* No. 80: *www.immi.gov.au/cgi-bin/AT-immisearch.cgi*

Iredale, R.R.
2001 "The Migration of Professionals: Theories and Typologies", *International Migration*, 39(5), pp. 7-24.
2003 "Accreditation of the qualifications and skills of developing country service providers (Mode 4)", Paper presented at *UNCTAD expert meeting on GATS Mode 4*, 29-31 July, Geneva.
2004 "Gender, Immigration Policies and Accreditation: Valuing the Skills of Professional Women Migrants", *Geoforum*, forthcoming.

Iredale, R., F. Guo, and S. Rozario (Eds.)
2003 *Return Migration in the Asia Pacific*, Edward Elgar Publishing, Cheltenham, UK and Northampton, US.

Khadria, B.
2002 "Skilled Labour Migration from Developing Countries: Study on India", *International Migration Papers* 49, International Labour Office, Geneva.

Khoo, S-E., C. Voigt-Graf, G. Hugo and P. McDonald
2003 *Temporary Skilled Migration to Australia, The first five years of arrivals in the 457 visa sub-class*, Unpublished Report to DIMIA, Australian Centre for Population Research, Australian National University, Canberra.

Kofman, E.
2000 "The invisibility of skilled female migrants and gender relations in studies of skilled migration in Europe", *International Journal of Population Geography*, 6(1), pp. 1-15.
2003a "Skilled International Female Migrants: migratory strategies and settlement experiences", *Report Canadian Faculty Research Program* Grant.
2003b "Women Migrants in the European Union", Paper presented at *The Economic And Social Aspects Of Migration Conference* jointly organized by The European Commission and the OECD, Brussels, 21-22 January 2003.

Lowell, B.L. and A. Findlay
2001 "Migration of Highly Skilled Persons from Developing Countries: Impact and Policy Responses", *International Migration Papers* 44, ILO, Geneva.

Luo, K., P. Huang, and F. Guo and R. Iredale, F. Guo and S. Rozario (Eds.)
2003 "China: Government Policies and Emerging Trends of reversal of the Brain Drain", *Return Migration in the*

Asia Pacific, Edward Elgar Publishing, Cheltenham, UK and Northampton, US, pp. 88-111.

Moore, R.
1994 *An Administrative History of the Assessment of Skills and Qualifications of Migrants of Non-English Speaking Background and Equal Opportunity – From the Second World War Until 1990*, Working Paper No. 111, Department of Economics, Murdoch University, Western Australia.

Morita, M.
2003 "The Current Situation and Future Prospects of Japan from the Perspective of the Japanese Private Sector", Paper presented at *UNCTAD expert meeting on GATS Mode 4*, 29-31 July, Geneva.

OECD
2003 *Poverty and Health in Developing Countries: Key Actions*, OECD Observer Policy Brief, OECD, Paris.
2004 *Trends in International Migration: SOPEMI 2003 edition*, OECD, Paris.

Ortin, E.
1994 "The exodus of Filipino nurses: An action agenda", *Asian Migrant*, 4(4), pp. 126-145.

Phillips, M. and C.W. Stahl
2000 *Internationalisation of Education, Training and Professional Services: Trends and Issues*, Centre for Asia Pacific Transformation Studies, Working Paper, University of Wollongong.

Ouaked, S.
2002 "TransAtlantic Workshop on High Skilled Migration", *International Migration*, 40(4), pp. 153-164.

Raghuram, P.
2000 "Gendering skilled migratory streams: implications for conceptualizations of migration", *Asian and Pacific Migration Journal*, 9(4), pp. 429-457.

Reddy, M., M. Mohanty and V. Naidu and K. Lyon and C. Voigt-Graf (Eds.)
2002 "Economic Cost of Human Capital Loss from Fiji: Implications for Sustainable Development", *5th International APMRN Conference, Fiji 2002: Selected Papers*, Working Paper No. 12, University of Wollongong, Wollongong, Australia, pp. 49-63.

Rozario, S. and J. Gow and R. Iredale, F. Guo and S. Rozario (Eds.)
2003 "Bangladesh: Return Migration and Social Transformation", *Return Migration in the Asia Pacific*, Edward Elgar Publishing, Cheltenham, UK and Northampton, US, pp. 47-87.

Saxenian, A. and W.A. Cornelius, T.J. Espenshade and I. Salehyan (Eds.)
2001 "Silicon Valley's New Immigrant Entrepreneurs", *The International Migration of the Highly Skilled*, Centre for Comparative Immigration Studies, University of California, San Diego, pp. 197-234.

Stark, O.
2004 "Rethinking the Brain Drain", *World Development*, 32(1), pp. 15-22.

Stark, O. and Y. Wang
2001 *Inducing Human Capital Formation: Migration as a Substitute for Subsidies*, Reihe Ökonomie Economics Series 100, Institute for Advanced Studies, Vienna.

Taylor, J.E.
1999 "The New Economics of Labour Migration and the Role of Remittances in the Migration Process", *International Migration, Special Issue: Migration and Development*, 37(1), pp. 63-88.

Tolley, E.
2003 "The skilled worker class: selection criteria in the Immigration and Refugee Protection Act", *Metropolis Briefing* 1.

Tsay, C-L and R. Iredale, F. Guo and S. Rozario (Eds.)
2003 "Taiwan: Significance, Characteristics and Policies on Return Skilled Migration *Return Migration in the Asia Pacific*, Edward Elgar Publishing, Cheltenham, UK and Northampton, US, pp. 112-135.

UNCTAD Expert Meeting on GATS Mode 4
2003 Presentation by Japanese Delegation, 29-31 July, Geneva.

USCIS (U.S. Citizenship and Immigration Services)
2003 *Characteristics of Specialty Occupation Workers (H-1B); Fiscal Year 2002: uscis.gov/graphics/shared/services/employerinfo/h1b.htm* (accessed on 21 May 2004).

World Bank
2003 "Labor Mobility and the WTO: Liberalizing Temporary Movement", *Global Economic Prospects 2004*, World Bank, Washington, pp. 143-76.

World Health Organization Regional Office for Africa
2002 *Building Strategic Partnerships in Education and Health in Africa*, Report on Consultative Meeting, 29 January-1 February.

Yap, M-T
2001 "Singapore", *Migration and the Labour Market in Asia: Recent Trends and Policies*, OECD, Paris, pp. 281-288.

Yoo, K-S and Uh, S-B
2001 "Korea", *Migration and the Labour Market in Asia: Recent Trends and Policies*, OECD, Paris, pp. 215-230.

CHAPTER 12 – FILIPINOS WORKING OVERSEAS: OPPORTUNITY AND CHALLENGE

IOM
2003 *Labor migration in Asia: trends, challenges and policy responses in countries of origin: www.iom.int//DOCUMENTS/PUBLICATION/EN/LabourMigAsia.pdf* (15 April 2004).

Montañez, J. T.
2003 *Pains and Gains: A Study of Overseas Performing Artists in Japan – from Pre-Departure to Reintegration*, Development Action for Women (DAWN), Manila.

Philippine Department of Labor and Employment
1995 *White Paper on Overseas Employment Program*, DOLE, Manila. Various Speeches of different senior officials, Manila.

POEA (Philippine Overseas Employment Agency)
2004 *www.poea.gov.ph* (last accessed 15 April 2004).

Soriano, M.T.
2003 *Managing overseas migration program under a globalized regime: is it any different?* Paper presented at the OECD-World Bank-IOM Seminar on Trade and Migration, 12-14 November 2003, Palais Des Nations, Geneva.

Watkins, F.
2002 *International migration in policy and practice in South Asia*, ID21 Development Research Reporting Service: *www.id21.org/society/ s10cfw1g1.html* (15 April 2004).

GENERAL WEBSITES
OWWA (Overseas Workers' Welfare Administration, Department of Labor and Employment) : *www.owwa.gov.ph*

TEXTBOX 12.2
Bilateral Labour Agreements: Effective Tools for Managing Labour Flows?

Abella, M.
Sending Workers Abroad, ILO, Geneva.

International Labour Office (ILO)
2004 "Towards a fair Deal for Migrant Workers in the Global Economy", Report VI, International Labour Conference, 92nd Session, Geneva.
2004 "Acuerdos Bilaterales de Migraci'on de Mano de Obra: Modo de empleo, Edouardo Geronimi, Estudios Sobre Migraciones Internacionales, n. 65.

IOM
2003 *World Migration report 2003*, Geneva.

OECD and IMES (Swiss Federal Office of Immigration, Integration and Emigration)
2003 "Bilateral Labour Agreements and other Forms of Recruitment of Foreign Workers", joint seminar, Montreux , 19-20 June.

CHAPTER 13 – MIGRATION AND POVERTY: SOME ISSUES IN THE CONTEXT OF ASIA

Abella, M., P. Martin and E. Midgley
2004 *Best Practices to Manage Migration: The Philippines*, a report for the Cooperative Efforts to Manage Emigration (CEME) project, University of California, Davis.

Adams, R.H. and J. Page
2003 *The Impact of International Migration and Remittances on Poverty*, Paper presented at the DFID/World Bank Conference on Migrant Remittances, London, pp. 9-10 October, 2003.

Addleton, J.S.
1992 *Undermining the Centre: the Gulf Migration and Pakistan*, Oxford University Press, Karachi.

ADB (Asia Development Bank)
2003 *Combating Trafficking of Women and Children in South Asia: Regional Synthesis Paper for Bangladesh, India, and Nepal*, Manila.
2003a *Combating Trafficking of Women and Children in South Asia: Guide for Integrating Trafficking Concerns into ADB Operations*, Manila.

Banister, J.
1987 *China's Changing Population*, Stanford University Press, Stanford.

Becker, J.
1996 *Hungry Ghosts: China's Secret Famine*, John Murray, London.

Cernea, M.M.
2000 "Risks, safeguards, and reconstruction: a model for population displacement and resettlement", *Risks and Reconstruction: Experiences of Resettlers and Refugees*, The World Bank, Washington, pp. 11-55.

Cernea, M.M. and C. McDowell and C. McDowell and M.M. Cernea (Eds.)
2000 "Reconstructing resettlers' and refugees' livelihoods", *Risks and Reconstruction: Experiences of Resettlers and Refugees*, The World Bank, Washington, pp. 1-8.

Chamratrithirong, A, K. Archavanitkul, K. Richter, P. Guest, V. Thongthai, W. Boonchalaksi, N. Piriyathamwong and P. Vong-Ek
1995 *National Migration Survey of Thailand*, Publication No. 188, Institute for Population and Social Research, Mahidol University, Salaya.

Chirot, D. and A. Reid
1997 *Essential Outsiders: Chinese and Jews in the Modern Transformation of Southeast Asia and Central Europe*, University of Washington Press, Seattle.

de Brauw, A., J.E. Taylor and S. Rozelle
2001 *Migration and incomes in source communities: a new economics of migration perspective from China*, a paper produced in the Department of Agriculture and Resource Economics, University of California, Davis.

de Haan, A.
2002 *Migrants, livelihoods, and rights: the relevance of migration in development policies*, Social Development Working Paper No. 4, Department for International Development, Social Development Department, London.

Ellerman, D.
2003 *Policy Research on Migration and Development*, World Bank Working Paper 3117.

Findlay, A.
2001 *From Brain Exchange to Brain Gain: Policy Implications for the UK of recent Trends in Skilled Migration from Developing Countries*, ILO, Geneva.

Go, S.P.
2002 *Recent trends in migration movements and policies: the movement of Filipino professionals and managers*, paper presented at the Workshop on International Migration and Labour Market in Asia, Japan Institute of Labor and OECD, Tokyo, 4-5 February.

Gunatilleke, G.
1986 *Migration of Asian Workers to the Arab World*, United Nations University, Tokyo.

Hambro, E.
1955 *The Problem of Chinese Refugees in Hong Kong* (Leiden, A. W. Sijthoff).

Harris, N.
2002 *Thinking the Unthinkable: the Immigration Myth Exposed*, I. B. Tauris, London.

Hodagneu-Sotelo, P.
1994 *Gendered Transitions: Mexican Experiences of Immigration*, University of California Press, Berkeley.

Hugo, G.
2002 "Introduction", *Migration and the Labour Market in Asia: Recent Trends and Policies*, OECD, Paris: pp. 7-16.
2003 *Migration and Development: A Perspective from Asia*, No. 14, IOM Migration Research Series, Geneva.

IOM
2003 *International Development Committee Inquiry into "Migration and Development"*, written evidence from the IOM, November 2003.

ILO
1998 *The Social Impact of the Asian Financial Crisis*, Regional Office for Asia and the Pacific of the International Labour Organization, Bangkok.

Iredale, R., Swati Ghosh, Sung Ho Ko, Jungwan Lee, Quiang Ren, Tasneem Siddiqui, Joe Weeramunda, Zhenzhen, zheng.
2004 "Migration and HIV Vulnerability in South and North East Asia: A Background Paper" by Asia-Pacific Migration Research Network (APMRN) for UNDP.

Kannan, K.P. and K.S. Hari and K.C. Zachariah, K.P. Kannan and S. Irudaya Rajan (Eds.)
2002 "Kerala's Gulf connection: remittances and their macroeconomic impact", *Kerala's Gulf Connection: CDS Studies on International Migration from Kerala State in India* Centre for Development Studies, Thiruvananthapuram, pp. 199-230.

Kothari, U.
2002 *Migration and chronic poverty*, Working Paper No. 16, Chronic Poverty Research Centre, Institute for Development Policy and Management, University of Manchester.

Kynge, J.
2004 "China's urban workforce fuels rural economy", *Financial Times*, 25 February.

Liu F.
2004 Interview with Dong Qian of CCTV, published on 30 July, see also *www.gdxy163.com/ReadNews.asp?NewsID=5549*

Liu J.
2004 Presentations held at the Symposium on "Intellectual Assistance for Poverty Reduction in China", Beijing, 16 July; see also *www.news.china.com/zh_cn/social/1007/20040730/11808849.html*, and *www.bdly.heagri.gov.cn/default3.aspx?id=352*

Lopes, C.
2002 *Connecting Migration, Brain Drain and Capacity Development*, UNDP Bureau for Development Policy.

Lowell, L.B. and Garza, R. de la
2002 *Sending Money Home: Hispanic Remittances and Community Development*, Rowman and Littlefield, Oxford.

Lu F.
2001 Presentations at the International Conference On Poverty Reduction by NGOs, Beijing, 28 October; see also *www.china.org.cn/chinese/pinkun/75358.htm*

Martin, P.L.
2004 "Best Practices to Manage Migration: The Philippines", *Cooperative Efforts to Manage Emigration (CEME)* Project, February 2004, University of California, Davis: *plmartin@ucdavis,edu*

Martin, P.L. and J. Widgren
2002 "International migration: facing the challenge", *Population Bulletin*, 57(1).

Massey, D.S., J. Arango, G. Hugo, A. Kouaouci, A. Pellegrino, and J. Edward Taylor
1993 "Theories of international migration: a review and appraisal", *Population and Development Review*, 19(3), pp. 431-466.

Meikle, S. and Z. Youxuan and M.M. Cernea and C. McDowell (Eds.)
2000 "Employment for displaces in the socialist market economy of China", *Risks and Reconstruction: Experiences of Resettlers and Refugees*, World Bank, Washington, pp. 127-143.

Migration Policy Institute
2003 "Remittance Data", Migration Information Source, 1 June, Washington DC.

Miller, K.A.
1985 *Emigrants and Exiles: Ireland and the Irish Exodus to North America*, Oxford University Press, New York.

Newland, K.,
2004 *Beyond Remittances: The Role of Diaspora in Poverty Reduction in their Countries of Origin*, a study for the UK Department for International Development (DFID), MPI, Washington.

Nguyen, N.X.
2002 *International migration of highly skilled workers in Vietnam*, paper presented at the Workshop on International Migration and Labour Market in Asia, Japan Institute of Labor and OECD, Tokyo, 4-5 February.

Nyberg Sorensen, N.
2004 *The Development Dimension of Migrant Remittances*, working paper for the Migration Policy Series, IOM, Geneva.

Osaki, K.
2002 *Internal migration and remittances in Thailand: economic necessity or social institution?*, paper presented at the IUSSP Regional Population Conference, Bangkok, Thailand, 11-12 June.

Ratha, D.
2003 "Workers' remittances: an important and stable source of external development finance", *Global Development Finance 2003: Striving for Stability in Development Finance*, The World Bank, Washington, pp. 157-175.

Russell, S.
1992 "Migrant remittances and development", *International Migration*, 30(3,4): 267-287.

Sahlins, M.
1974 *Stone Age Economics*, Tavistock, London.

Seddon, D., J. Adhikari and G. Gurung
2002 "Foreign labor migration and the remittance economy", *Critical Asian Studies*, 34(1), pp. 19-40.

Siddiqui, T.
2003 "Migration as a livelihood strategy of the poor: the Bangladesh case", Department for International Development, London: www.livelihoods.org

Simmons, A.B.
1984 "Migration and rural development: conceptual approaches, research findings and policy issues", *Population Distribution, Migration and Development*, ST/ESA/SER.A/89, Department of International Economic and Social Affairs, United Nations, New York, pp. 156-192.

Skeldon, R.
1987 "Protest, Peasants and the Proletariat", in Ghose, R. (ed.), *Protest Movements in South and South-East Asia*, Centre for Asian Studies, University of Hong Kong, pp. 3-18.
1990 *Population Mobility in Developing Countries: A Reinterpretation*, Belhaven, London.
1997a *Migration and Development: A Global Perspective*, Longman, London.
1997b "Rural-to-urban migration and its implications for poverty alleviation", *Asia-Pacific Population Journal* 12(1), pp. 3-16.
2001 "Ageing of rural populations in South-East and East Asia", *The World Ageing Situation: Exploring a Society for All Ages*, ST/ESA/271, Department of Economic and Social Affairs, United Nations, New York, pp. 38-54.
2003 "Interlinkages between internal and international migration and development in the Asian region", paper presented at the Ad Hoc Expert Group Meeting on Migration and Development organized by ESCAP, Bangkok, 27-29 August 2003.

Stark, O.
1991 *The Migration of Labor*, Blackwell, Oxford.

Tamas, K.
2003 "Mapping Study on International Migration", Institute of Future Studies, Stockholm.

Thailand National Statistical Office
2002 Advance results from the *Population and Housing Census 2000* at *www.nso.go.th/pop2000/report/adv_e.htm*

Tsai, H-C
1988 "A study on the migration of students from Taiwan to the United States: a summary report", *Journal of Population Studies* 12, pp. 91-120.

Tsay, C-L and J-P Lin and R.Iredale, C.Hawksley and S.Castles (Eds.)
2003 "Return migration and reversal of brain drain to Taiwan: an analysis of 1990 census data", *Migration in the Asia Pacific: Population, Settlement and Citizenship Issues*, Elgar, Cheltenham, UK, pp. 273-292.

UK, House of Commons, International Development Committee
2004 *Migration and Development: How to Make Migration Work for Poverty Reduction* 1, Report, together with formal minutes, The Stationery Office, London.

UNDP
1999 *Human Development Report of Thailand 1999*, United Nations Development Programme, Bangkok.
2003 *Human Development Report 2003*, Oxford University Press, New York.

Wall Street Journal
2001 "For a Philippine Town, Monthly Allowances Pave a Road to Riches – Third World Gets Huge Sums From Relatives Abroad; Some Call it Dependence – Pozorrubio's Lights Go On", Tuesday, May 22, by Robert Frank, New York.

Whitlock, M.
2002 *Beyond the Oxus: The Central Asians*, John Murray, London.

World Bank
2003 *The Long-Run Economic Costs of AIDS: Theory and an Application to South Africa*, Washington DC.
2003a *Global Development Finance*, Washington D.C.

Zachariah, K.C., K.P.Kannan and S.I.Rajan (Eds.)
2002 *Kerala's Gulf Connection: CDS Studies on International Labour Migration from Kerala State in India*, Thiruvananthapuram, Centre for Development Studies.

Zweig, D. and S. Rosen
2003 *How China trained a new Generation Abroad*: *sciDev.Net*

CHAPTER 14 – MIGRANT REMITTANCES AS A SOURCE OF DEVELOPMENT FINANCE

Economist, The
2004 "Monetary Lifeline", July 31, p. 66.

Fairlamb, D., G. Smith and F. Balfour
2003 "Can Western Union Keep On Delivering? Wiring money overseas has been a hugely profitable business. But now, rivals are elbowing in, driving the fees down", in *Business Week*, October 22, 2003.

IOM
2004 "Colombia – Remittances on the Increase", Press Briefing Notes, 19 November.

Khachani, M.
2004 "Transferts de revenues par les immigres et developpement", paper presented at the World Congress on HMI, Barcelona, September 2-5.

Ketkar, S. and D. Ratha
2001 "Development Financing during a Crisis: Securitization of Future Receivables", World Bank, Policy Research Working Paper 2582.

Ratha, D.
2003 "Workers' remittances – an important and stable source of external development finance" by Dilip Ratha, in *Global Development Finance 2003*, chapter 7. *www.worldbank.org.*

Ratha, D. and J. Riedberg
2004 "How to lower remittance costs: conversations with remittance service providers", World Bank, Washington, D.C.

Roberts, B.and K. Banaian

2004 "Remittances in Armenia: Size, Impacts, and Measures to enhance their Contribution to Development", special study for USAID/Armenia, Bearing Point, October.

USAID

2004 "Remittances at USAID", REVISED 08/26/04, at *www.usaid.gov/our_work/global_partnerships/*.

World Bank

2004 "Enhancing the Developmental Effects of Workers' Remittances to Developing Countries", in *Global Development Finance 2004*, Annex A, Washington, D.C.

CHAPTER 15 – MIGRANT HOMETOWN ASSOCIATIONS (HTAS) – THE HUMAN FACE OF GLOBALIZATION

FISDL (Fondo de Inversión Social para el Desarrollo Local)

2004 "Proyectos de "Unidos por la Solidaridad" con Salvadoreños en el exterior", San Salvador, El Salvador, Enero.

Orozco, M.

2002 "Globalization and Migration: The Impact of Family Remittances in Latin America", *Latin American Politics and Society.*

2003 "Hometown Associations and their Present and Future Partnerships: New Development Opportunities?", Inter-American Dialogue, Washington.

2004a "Diasporas, Development and Social Inclusion: Issues and Opportunities for the Caribbean", Washington, DC: the World Bank. Policy brief commissioned by the World Bank.

2004b "Distant but close: Guyanese transnational communities and their remittances from the United States", Inter-American Dialogue, Report commissioned by the U.S. Agency for International Development, Washington, DC.

2004c "Mexican Hometown Associations and Development Opportunities", *Journal of International Affairs* 57(2).

2004d "The Salvadoran diaspora: remittances, transnationalism and government responses", paper commissioned by the Tomas Rivera Policy Institute, Washington.

Roberts, B. and K. Banaian

2004 "Remittances in Armenia: Size, Impacts, and Measures to Enhance Their Contribution to Development", Special Study for USAID/Armenia, Bearing Point, October.

SEDESOL (Secretaría de Desarrollo Social de México)

2004 *Programa Nacional de Desarrollo Social 2001-2006*, Mexico City.

CHAPTER 16 – ENHANCING THE BENEFITS OF RETURN MIGRATION FOR DEVELOPMENT

ACBF (The African Capacity Building Foundation)

2004 *An Analysis of the Market for Skilled African Development Management Professionals: Towards Strategies and Utilization in Sub-Saharan Africa*, ACBF, Harare.

AVT

2004 *Development and Migration: Policy Memorandum*, Government of the Netherlands, The Hague (unofficial translation from the Dutch original text).

Battistella, G.

2004 "Return Migration in the Philippines: Issues and Policies", in: Massey, D.S. and J.E. Taylor (Eds.) *International Migration: Prospects and Policies in a Global Market*, Oxford University Press, Oxford.

Black, R. (Ed.)

2004 *Migration and Pro-Poor Policies in Africa*, Sussex Centre for Migration Research, University of Sussex, Brighton.

European Commission

2002 *Green Paper on a Community Return Policy on Illegal Residents*, Brussels, COM(2002), p. 175.

Ellerman, D.

2003 *Policy Research on Migration and Development*, World Bank, Washington D.C. (World Bank Policy Research Working Paper, 3117).

Ghosh, B. (Ed.)

2000 *Return Migration: Journey of Hope or Despair?* UN, IOM, Geneva.

Hugo, G.

2003 *Migration and Development: A Perspective from Asia*, IOM, Geneva (IOM Migration Research Series 14).

House of Commons, International Development Committee

2004 *Migration and Development: How to Make Migration Work for Poverty Reduction: Sixth Report of Session 2003-04, Volume 1*, London, Stationery Office.

Iredale, R., F. Guo and R. Santi (Eds.)

2003 *Return Migration in the Asia Pacific*, Edward Elgar, Cheltenham.

IOM

2000 *Evaluation of Phase III of the Programme for the Return of Qualified African Nationals*, Office of Programme Evaluation, Geneva.

2002 *Contribution of Returnees: an analytical survey of Post Return Experience*, Geneva.

2004 *Return Migration: Policies and Practices in Europe*, for the Advisory Committee on Aliens Affairs, The Netherlands, Geneva.

IOM and UNDP

2004 *Towards a Fair Deal for Migrant Workers in the Global Economy*, ILO, Geneva. (Report VI, International Labour Conference, 92nd Session.

Johnson, J.M. and M.C. Regets

1998 *International Mobility of Scientists and Engineers to the U.S.: Brain Drain or Brain Circulation?* National Science Foundation, Arlington. (NSF Issue Brief, pp. 98-316).

Laczko, F. (Ed.)

2003 *Understanding Migration Between Europe and China.* International Migration 41(3): Special Issue 1/2003, Blackwell, Oxford.

Lawson, S., R. Purushothaman S. Schels

2004 *Making the Most of Global Migration*, Goldman Sachs, London. (Global Economics Paper No. 115),

Lindsay Lowell, B., A. Findlay, E.Stewart
2004 *Brain Strain: Optimizing Highly Skilled Migration from Developing Countries*, Institute for Public Policy Research, London. (Asylum and Migration Working Paper 3).

Lindsay Lowell, B. and S. G. Gerova
2004 *Diasporas and Economic Development: State of Knowledge*, September 13, 2004, Institute for the Study of International Migration, Georgetown University, Washington, D.C.

Lucas, R.E.B.
2005 Report from the EGDI Seminar "International Migration Regimes and Economic Development," Stockholm, May 13, Stockholm Ministry for Foreign Affairs and Expert Group on Development Issues (*www.egdi.gov.se/seminars6.htm*)

Newland, K. and E. Patrick
2004 *Beyond Remittances: the Role of Diaspora in Poverty Reduction in their Countries of Origin*, Migration Policy Institute, Washington, D.C.

OECD
2003 *SOPEMI - Trends in International Migration: Annual Report 2002*, OECD, Paris.

Olesen, H.
2003 "Migration, Return and Development: An Institutional Perspective", in: N. van Hear and N. Nyberg-Sorensen (Eds.) *The Migration-Development Nexus*, IOM, Geneva, pp. 133-158.

Omelaniuk, I.
2003 "Dealing with Overstaying", Paper presented at the OECD-World Bank-IOM Seminar on Trade and Migration, Geneva, November.

Saxenian,A.L.
2001 *The Silicon Valley Connection: Transnational Networks and Regional Development in Taiwan, China and India*, University of Pennsylvania, Institute for the Advanced Study of India, Philadelphia.

Waldman, A.
2004 "In a 'Brain Gain', India's Westernized Émigrés Return Home", *International Herald Tribune*, Neuilly-sur-Seine, 26 July *(www.iht.com/articles/531044.html)*

CHAPTER 17 - BENEFITS AND COSTS OF INTEGRATION - INTERNATIONAL CONVERGENCE?

Beaujot, R.
1998 *Immigration and Canadian Demographics: State of the Research*, Population Studies Centre, University of Western Ontario, London.

Department of Immigration and Multicultural and Indigenous Affairs (DIMIA)
2004 *Number 15: Population Projection*, Canberra.

Duncan, H.
2003 "The Opportunity and Challenge of Diversity: A Case for Social Capital?", Conference Presentation at *Managing Migration and Diversity: The Case for Social Capital* Conference, OECD and Policy Research Initiative, Montreal.

Feldblum, M. and T.A. Aleinikoff and D. Klusmeyer (Eds.)
2000 "Managing Membership: New Trends in Citizenship and Nationality Policy", *From Migrants to Citizens*, Carnegie Endowment for International Peace, Washington.

Florida, R.
2002 *The Rise of the Creative Class*, Perseus Books Group, Boulder.

Forsander, A.
2003 "The Opportunity and Challenge of Diversity: A Case for Social Capital?", Conference Presentation at *Managing Migration and Diversity: The Case for Social Capital* Conference, OECD and Policy Research Initiative, Montreal.

Gertler, M.
2002 *Competing on Creativity: Placing Ontario's Cities in North American Context*, Report for the Ontario Ministry of Enterprise, Opportunity and Innovation and the Institute for Competitiveness, Productivity and Economic Progress, Toronto.

Helliwell, J.
2003 "The Opportunity and Challenge of Diversity: A Case for Social Capital?", Conference Presentation at *Managing Migration and Diversity: The Case for Social Capital* Conference, OECD and Policy Research Initiative, Montreal.

Iredale, R.
1997 *Skills Transfer: International Migration and Accreditation Issues*, Wollongong.

Khawaja, M. and I. Richards
1998 *New Zealand Labour Force Projections*, Christchurch.

Loree, D.
2001 *Police Role and Relationships in Minority Communities: Some Canadian Issues*, paper prepared for Sixth International Metropolis Conference, Royal Canadian Mounted Police, Ottawa.

Paquet, G., and P. Reid
2003 "Are There Limits to Diversity?", *Optimum* 33, no.1, Ottawa.

PEW Research Centre
2004 *A Global Generation Gap: Adapting to a New World*, PEW Research Centre, Washington.

PEW Research Centre
2004a "Whose Culture is Best" and "Putting the Brakes on Immigration", in the *World Values Survey*.

Putnam, R.
2003 "The Opportunity and Challenge of Diversity: A Case for Social Capital?", Keynote Address at *Managing Migration and Diversity: The Case for Social Capital* Conference, OECD and Policy Research Initiative, Montreal.

Reitz, J.
1998 *Warmth of the Welcome: Causes of Economic Success for Immigrants in Different Nations and Cities*, University of Toronto, Toronto.

Sangster, D.
2001 *Assessing and Recognizing Foreign Credentials in Canada - Employers' Views*, Ottawa.

Schwartz, H.
2003 "The Internationalization of Constitutional Law", *Human Rights Brief* 10, no. 2, Washington College of Law, Washington.

Sum, A. et al.
2003 *New Immigrants in the Labor Force and the Number of Employed New Immigrants in the U.S. from 2000-2003: Continued Growth Amidst Declining Employment Among the Native Born Population*; North Eastern University, Boston.

United Nations (UN)
2000 *Replacement Migration: Is It a Solution to Declining and Ageing Populations*, UN Population Division, New York.

US National Research Council
1997 "The Future Fiscal Impacts of Current Immigrants", in the publication *The New Americans*, Washington.

CHAPTER 18 – MIGRATION AND THE CONTEMPORARY WELFARE STATE

Andersson, G.
2000 "The Impact of Labour-Force Participation on Childbearing Behaviour. Pro-Cyclical Fertility in Sweden During the 1980s and the 1990s", *European Journal of Population* 16: pp. 293-333.

Appelbaum, E., T. Bailey, P. Berg, and A. Kalleberg (Ed.)
2000 *Manufacturing Advantage. Why High Performance Work Systems Pay Off*, Cornell University Press, Ithaca, London.

Boyer, R.
2000 "Is a Finance-Led Growth Regime a Viable Alternative to Fordism? A Preliminary Analysis", *Economy and Society* 29, No. 1: pp. 111-145.

Brubaker, Rogers
1992 *Citizenship and Nationhood in France and Germany*, Harvard University Press, Cambridge.

Burawoy, M.
1975 "The Functions and Reproduction of Migrant Labor. Comparative Material from Southern Africa and the United States", *American Journal of Sociology* 81, No. 5: pp. 1050-1087.

Capelli, P., L. Bassi, H. Katz, D. Knoke, P. Osterman and M. Useem
1997 *Change at Work*, Oxford University Press, New York.

Castles, S. and V.M. Bader (Ed.)
1997 "Multicultural Citizenship. The Australian Experience", *Citizenship and Exclusion*, MacMillan, Houndmills: pp. 113-138.

Clark, G.
2000 *Pension Fund Capitalism*, Oxford University Press, Oxford.
2003a "Pension Security in the Global Economy. Markets and National Institutions in the 21st Century", *Environment and Planning A* 35, No. 8: pp. 1339-1356.
2003b *European Pensions and Global Finance*, Oxford University Press, Oxford.

Clark, G. and P. Bennett
2001 "Dutch Sector-Wide Supplementary Pensions. Fund Governance, European Competition Policy, and the Geography of Finance", *Environment and Planning A* 33: pp. 27-48.

Cooke, P. and K. Morgan
1998 *The Associational Economy. Firms, Regions, and Innovation*, Oxford University Press, Oxford.

Cornelius, W., P. Martin and J. Hollifield (Ed.)
1994 *Controlling Immigration. A Global Perspective*, Stanford University Press, Stanford, CA.

Crouch, C., D. Finegold and M. Sako
1999 *Are Skills the Answer? The Political Economy of Skill Creation in Advanced Industrial Economies*, Oxford University Press, Oxford.

Dent, H.
1998 *The Roaring 2000s*, Simon and Schuster, New York.

Disney, R.
2000 "Crises in Public Pension Programmes in OECD. What Are the Reform Options?", *The Economic Journal*, No. 110: pp. 1-23.

Ehrenreich, B.
2001 *Nickel and Dimes. On (Not) Getting by in America*, Metropolitan Books, New York, NY.

Engelen, E.
2003a "How to Combine Openness and Protection? Citizenship, Migration and Welfare Regimes", *Politics and Society* 31, No. 4: pp. 503-536.
2003b "The Logic of Funding. European Pension Restructuring and the Dangers of Financialisation", *Environment and Planning* A 35: pp. 1357-1372.

England, R.S.
2002 *Global Aging and Financial Markets. Hard Landings Ahead?*, Center for Strategic and International Studies.

Esping-Andersen, G.
1999 *Social Foundations of Postindustrial Democracies*, Oxford University Press, Oxford.
1990 *Three Worlds of Welfare Capitalism*, Polity Press, Oxford.

Gauthier, A. and J. Hatzius.
1997 "Family Benefits and Fertility. An Econometric Analysis", *Population Studies* 51: pp. 295-306.

Korpi, W.
2002 "The Great through in Unemployment. A Long-Term View of Unemployment, Inflation, Strikes, and the Profit/Wage Ratio", *Politics and Society* 30, No. 3: pp. 365-426.

Korver, T.
1990 *The Fictitious Commodity. A Study of the U.S. Labor Market, 1880-1940*, Greenwood Press, New York.

Lazonick, W.
1991 *Business Organization and the Myth of the Market Economy*, Cambridge University Press, New York, NY.

Lazonick, W. and O'Sullivan, M.
2000 "Maximizing Shareholder Value. A New Ideology for Corporate Governance", *Economy and Society* 29, No. 1: pp. 13-35.

Lutz, W., B. O'Neill and S. Scherbov
2003 "Europe's Population at a Turning Point", *Science* 299: 1991-1992.

Massey, D. and N. Denton
1993 *American Apartheid. Segregation and the Making of the Underclass*, Harvard University Press, Cambridge.

OECD
1996 *Ageing in oecd Countries. A Critical Policy Challenge*, OECD, Paris.
1998 *Maintaining Prosperity in an Ageing Society*, OECD, Paris. 1995 *The Transition from Work to Retirement*, OECD, Paris.

O'Sullivan, M.
2000 *Contests for Corporate Control. Corporate Governance and Economic Performance in the United States and Germany*, Oxford University Press, Oxford.

Schlosser, E.
2003 *Reefer Madness. Sex, Drugs, and Cheap Labor in the American Black Market*, Houghton and Mifflin, New York.

Schor, J.
1998 *The Overspent American. Why We Want What We Don't Need*, Basic Books, New York, NY.
1992 *The Overworked American. The Unexpected Decline of Leisure*, Basic Books, New York, NY.

Scott, J.
1997 *Corporate Business and Capitalist Classes* (2nd Ed.), Oxford University Press, Oxford.

Sennett, R.
1998 *The Corrosion of Character. The Personal Consequences of Work in the New Capitalism*, Norton, New York, NY.

Siegel, J.J.
1998 *Stocks for the Long Run* (2nd Ed.), McGraw-Hill, New York.

Shiller, R.
2000 *Irrational Exuberance*, Broadway Books, New York.

Soysal, Y.
1994 *Limits of Citizenship. Migrants and Postnational Membership in Europe*, The University of Chicago Press, Chicago.

Steinmo, S.
2003 "Bucking the Trend? The Welfare State and the Global Economy. The Swedish Case up Close", *New Political Economy* 8, No. 1: pp. 31-48.

Sterling, W. and S. Waite
1998 *Bommernomics. The Future of Your Money in the Upcoming Generational Warfare*, Ballantine, New York.

Streeck, W. and J.R. Hollingsworth and R.Boyer (Eds.)
1997 "Beneficial Constraints. On the Economic Limits of Rational Voluntarism", *Contemporary Capitalism. The Embeddedness of Institutions*, Cambridge University Press, Cambridge: pp. 197-219.

Thelen, K. and I. Kume and W.K. Yamamura and Streeck (Eds.)
2003 "The Future of Nationally Embedded Capitalism. Industrial Relations in Germany and Japan", *The End of Diversity? Prospects for German and Japanese Capitalism*, Cornell University Press, Ithaca: pp. 183-211.
2001 "The Rise of Nonliberal Training Regimes. Germany and Japan Compared", *The Origins of Nonliberal Capitalism. Germany and Japan in Comparison*, Cornell University Press, Ithaca: pp. 200-27.

Toporowski, J.
2000 *The End of Finance. Capital Market Inflation, Financial Derivatives and Pension Fund Capitalism*, Routledge, London.

UN
1999a *The World at Six Billion*, United Nations, New York.
1999b *Replacement Migration. Is it a Solution to Declining and Ageing Populations*, United Nations, New York.
2002a *Completing the Fertility Transition*, United Nations, New York.
2002b *World Population Ageing, 1950-2050*, United Nations, New York.
2003a *World Population Prospects. The 2002 Revision*, United Nations, New York.
2003b *World Population Prospects. The 2002 Revision. Annex Tables*, United Nations, New York.

Weller, C.
2001 *Programs without Alternatives. Public Pensions in the OECD, www.insead.fr/cgep.*

Whitley, R.
1999 *Divergent Capitalism. The Social Structuring and Change of Business Systems*, Oxford University Press, Oxford.

Wojcik, D.
2003 "Change in the German Model of Corporate Governance. Evidence from Blockholdings 1997-2001", *Environment and Planning A* 35, no.8: pp. 1431-1458.
2002 "The Länder Are the Building Blocks of the German Capital Market." *Regional Studies* 36, no. 8: pp. 877-895.

World Bank
1994 *Averting the Old Age Crisis. Policies to Protect the Old and Promote Growth*, Oxford University Press, New York.

Wright, E.O. and R. Dwyer
2003 "The Patterns of Job Expansions in the USA. A Comparison of the 1960s and 1990s", *Socio-Economic Review* 1, No. 3: pp. 289-325.

CHAPTER 19 – INVESTING IN MIGRATION HEALTH

Behrman G.
2000 "The Cost of AIDS in Asia," Newsweek International Edition, July 19.

Bhargava A, Jamison, D., Lau L., and Murray C.J.L.
2001 "Modelling the Effects of Health on Economic Growth", Journal of Health Economics, Vol. 20 (May), pp. 423-40.

Bloom D.E., Canning D. and Jamison D.T.
2004 "Health, Wealth, and Welfare", Finance and Development, IMF Quarterly Magazine, Vol.41, No. 1 (March), pp. 10-15.

Bollini P.
1993 "Health for Immigrants and Refugees in the 1990s. A Comparative study in Seven Receiving Countries", Innovation, Volume 6, No. 1.

2001 "The Reproductive Health of Immigrant Women", IOM Newsletter Migration and Health, 2.

Byrne D.
2003 "Health equals Wealth", speech given during a plenary session of the 6th European Health Forum, Gastein, Austria, 1-4 October 2003, and published in the Congress Report "Health and Wealth: Economic and Social Dimensions of Health", 2004, pp. 34-40. Also available on website: *ww.ehfg.org*

Commission for Racial Equality
1991 "NHS. Contracts and Racial Equality", London.

Commission of the European Communities
2002 "Communication on the Health Strategy of the European Community", 2000/0119/COD, Brussels.

Davis S.
2003 "Improving Farmworker Access to Workers Compensation Benefits", Migrant Health Newsline, Buda, Tx; National Center for Farmworker Health, November/December.

Edubio A. and Sabanadesan R.
2001 "African Communities in Northern Europe and HIV/AIDS. Report of Two Qualitative Studies in Germany and Finland on the Perception of the AIDS Epidemic in Selected African Minorities", European Project AIDS and Mobility, October.

El Sahly H.M., Adams G.J., Soini H., Teeter L. and Musser J.M.
2000 "Epidemiologic Differences between United States and Foreign Born Tuberculosis Patients in Houston, Texas", Journal of Infectious Diseases, 183(3), pp. 461-8.

Estrella-Gust D.P.
2001 "Globalization and Asian Women: The Philippine Case", in Asia-Pacific Newsletter on Occupational Health and Safety, 8, pp. 66-70.

European Agency for Safety and Health at Work
2003 Newsletter on Occupational Health and Safety, 13, pp. 32-35

Global Forum for Health Research
2004 The 10/90 Report on Health Research 2003-2004, Switzerland, available on *www.globalforumhealth.org.*

Graham H.
2003 "Instruments and best practice: Health inequalities – underlying factors and different ways of addressing them", speech given during a forum session of the 6th European Health Forum, Gastein, Austria, 1-4 October 2003, and published in the Congress Report "Health and Wealth: Economic and Social Dimensions of Health",2004, pp.45-53. Also available on website: *www.ehfg.*

Grondin D.
2004 "From Migration towards Mobility: Need for a New Model of Migration Health Policy", Swiss FORUM for Migration and Population Studies, No. 3, pp. 27-32.

2003 "MHS Annual Report 2002, Introduction", IOM, pp. 4-5.

Hellier Wilson A., Lupo Wold J., Spencer L., Pittman K.
2000 "Primary Health Care for Hispanic Children of Migrant Farm Workers", Journal of Pediatric Health Care, 14, pp. 209-215.

Hughes D.M.
2001 "The 'Natasha' Trade: Transnational Sex Trafficking", *National Institute of Justice Journal*, 246: pp. 9-15.

ILO
2002 "Investing in Every Child, An Economic Study of the Costs and Benefits of Eliminating Child Labour", International Programme on the Elimination of Child Labour, Geneva, December.
2003 2004 "In Focus Programme on Safety and Health at Work and the Environment, especially Hazardous Sectors", last accessed August 26, 2004; *www.ilo.org/public/english/protection/safework/hazardwk/index.htm*

Institute of Public Health, NRW (North-Rhine Westphalia)
1998 "Report on Socio-economic Differences in Health Indicators in Europe: Health Inequalities in Europe and the Situation of Disadvantaged Groups, prepared for the European Commission; *www.europa.eu.int/comm/health/ph_projects/1998/monitoring/fp_monitoring_1998_annexe1_06_en.pdf*

IOM
2003 Position Paper on Psychosocial and Mental Well-being of Migrants, MC/INF/271, November.

Javate De Dios A.
1998 "Macro-economic Exploitation and Their Impact on Sexual Exploitation and Trafficking of Women and Girls: Issues, Responses and Challenges", Coalition Against Trafficking in Women - Asia-Pacific, Malaysia.

Kittipavara C.
2004 "Solving Health Problems for Migrants in Thailand," speech given during the IOM's International Dialogue on Migration, 9-11 June, IOM, Geneva.

Lamara F. and N. Djebarat N.
2003 "Réseau européen d'échanges et de coopération sur l'exclusion sociale et la santé des migrants: Autriche, Espagne, France, Grèce, Portugal", RESEAU SESAME,rapport conjoint, IOM, Paris, presented at the International Metropolis Conference, Vienna, September.

Lehmann P., Mamboury C., Minder C.E.
1990 "Health and Social Inequities in Switzerland", Social Science and Medicine, 31, pp. 369-86.

Leon E.
2001 "The Health Condition of Migrant Farmworkers", Julian Samora Institute, Michigan State University.

London School of Hygiene and Tropical Medicine
2002 "The Health Risks and Consequences of Trafficking in Women and Adolescents – Findings from a European Study", London.

Lundberg O, Diderichsen F., Yngwe M.A.
2001 "Changing Health Inequalities in a changing societies? Sweden in the mid-1980s and mid-1990s", Scandinavian Journal of Public Health, 29 (suppl. 55), pp. 31-39, Taylor and Francis, London.

Migrant Agriculture Workers Support Centre
2002 "Cultivating Health and Safety", Learnington, found on: *www.whsc.on.ca/Publications/atthessource/summer2002/cultivatinghs.pdf*

Muchiri F.K.
2003 "Occupational Health and Development in Africa: Challenges and the way forward", in Newsletter on Occupational Health and Safety 13, pp. 44-46.

OECD
2004 *Trends in International Migration: SOPEMI 2003*, Paris.

Rauch-Kallat M.
2004 "Health and Wealth", speech given during a plenary session of the 6th European Health Forum, Gastein, Austria, 1-4 October 2003, published in the Congress Report "Health and Wealth: Economic and Social Dimensions of Health", 2004, pp.18-23. Also available on website: *www.ehfg*.

Raymond J., D'Cunha J., Ruhaini Dzuhayatin S., Hynes P., Ramirez Rodriguez Z. and Santos A.
2002 "A Comparative Study of Women Trafficked in the Migration Process", Coalition Against Trafficking in Women.

Robertson E., Iglesias E., Johansson S.-E., Sundquist J.
2004 "Migration status and limiting long-standing illness", European Journal of Public Health, Volume 13(2), June, pp. 99-104.

Sacks L.
1983 "Evil Eye or Bacteria; Turkish Migrant Women and Swedish Health Care", University of Stockholm, Department of Social Anthropology.

Srithanaviboonchai K., Choi K., van Griensven F., Hudes E.S., Visaruratana S., Mandel J.S.
2002 "HIV-1 in Ethnic Shan Migrant Workers in Northern Thailand", AIDS, 16(6), 929-31.

Sundquist J.
1995 "Ethnicity, social class and health: a population-based study on the influence of social factors on self-reported illness in 223 Latin American refugees, 333 Finnish and 126 south European labour migrants and 841 Swedish controls", Social Science and Medicine, 40(6), pp. 777-87.

Taran, P.
2003 "Migration, Public Health and Protection", paper presented at the International Migration Policy Conference, Addis Ababa, June.

Thomas-Hope E.
2004 "Irregular Migration and Asylum Seekers in the Caribbean", UNU/WIDER Discussion Paper No. 2003/48, Tokyo, Japan; available at: *www.unu.edu/hq/library/collection/PDF_files/WIDER/WIDERdp2003.48.pdf*

Traore C.E.
2002 "Promoting Knowledge of HIV status amongst Africans in the UK", poster at the XIV International AIDS Conference, Barcelona, July.

UK Office for National Statistics
2004 "Living in Britain: Results from the 2002 General Household Survey", the Stationery Office, Norwich.

UNICEF
2004 "Trafficking and Sexual Exploitation", Child Protection Unit *www.unicef.org/protection/index_exploitation.html* (last accessed 9 November, 2004).

United Nations (UN)
2000 "Sexually abused and sexually exploited children and youth in the greater Mekong sub-region: a qualitative assessment of their health needs and available services", Economic and Social Commission for Asia and the Pacific", Geneva, ST/ESCAP/2074.
2002 UN Committee on Economic, Social and Cultural Rights, 2002.

US Centers for Disease Control and Prevention
2004 "TB Rates Remain High for Foreign-Born, Racial and Ethnic Minority Populations in United States despite Overall Decline", CDC Factsheet, Atlanta, GA.

USDOL (US Department of Labor)
2000 "National Agricultural Workers Survey", March 2000.

WHO (World Health Organization)
2001 "Macroeconomics and Health for Economic Development: Investing in Health for Economic Development", Report of the Commission on Macroeconomics and Health, 2001, Geneva.
2003 "Mobilization of Domestic and Donor Resources for Health: A Viewpoint", in Increasing Investments in Health Outcomes for the Poor, Second Consultation in Macroeconomics and Health, Geneva, October.

World Bank
2003 *World Development Indicators 2003*, Washington, D.C.

World Congress Against Commercial Sexual Exploitation of Children
1996 "Impact Factsheet", United States Embassy, Stockholm, August.

GENERAL WEBSITES
US National Center for Farmworker Health Inc.; *www.ncfh.org*.

CHAPTER 20 – GLOBAL MOBILITY AND HIV/AIDS

Barnett, T. and Whiteside A.
2002 *AIDS in the Twenty-First Century: Disease and Globalisation*, Palgrave Macmillan, Basingstoke.

Fernandez, Irene
2004 "Challenging Exclusion and Stigmatization for Mobile and Displaced Populations: Challenges for NGOs", presentation at the XV International AIDS Conference, Bangkok, July.

Globe and Mail
2004 "Coming to Canada with dreams and HIV" (Robert Remis), Toronto, 2 October.

Haour-Knipe, M.
2000 "Migration et VIH/Sida en Europe", *INFOTHEK*, 2000(5): pp. 4-14

Japan Center for International Exchange
2004 Japan's response to the Spread of HIV/AIDS. Tokyo.

Kaiser, R., Spiegel P., Salama P., Brady W., Bell E., Bond K. and Downer M.
2001 HIV/AIDS Sero-prevalence and Behavioral Risk Factor Survey in Sierra Leone, Centers for Disease Control and Prevention, Atlanta, April.

Kimalu, P.
2002 "Debt Relief and Health Care in Kenya", WIDER Discussion Paper No.2002/65, United Nations University, Finland.

Lurie M.
2004 "The Association Between Mobility and HIV/AIDS", presented at the Bangkok AIDS conference-related session on 'The Role of Mobility in the Spread and Control of HIV', organized by the Department of Public Health, Erasmus University Medical Center, the Netherlands, 11 July.

Lurie M. et al.
2003 *The impact of migration on HIV-1 transmission in South Africa. Sexually Transmitted Diseases*, 30(2).

Lydié, N., Robinson N.J., Ferry B., Akam E., De Loenzien M. and Abega S.
2004 "Mobility, Sexual Behaviour, and HIV Infection in an Urban Population in Cameroon", *Journal of Acquired Immune Deficiency Syndromes* 35(1): pp. 67-74.

Ogden, J. and Esim S.
2003 *Reconceptualizing the Care Continuum for HIV/AIDS Programmes in Botswana, Lesotho, Mozambique, Swaziland, and South Africa*, Human Sciences Research Council, South Africa, October.

Oxfam
2002 "Debt Relief and the HIV/AIDS Crisis in Africa: Does the Heavily Indebted Poor Country (HIPC) Initiative Go Far Enough?", Briefing Paper No. 25, Oxford.

Philipines Social and Environmental News
2004 "In 5 years, more OFWs seen to have HIV/AIDS", Bayanihan, Wednesday, July 14; *www.bayanihan.org/html/public_html/article.php?story=20040714154646042* (last accessed Nov. 15, 2004)

Spiegel, P.
2004 "HIV/AIDS among Conflict-Affected and Displaced Populations: Dispelling Myths and Taking Action", *Disasters*, 28(3): pp. 322-339.

Spiegel, P. and De Jong E.
2003 HIV/*AIDS and Refugees/Returnees: Mission to Luanda, Angola*, UNCHR, Geneva.

Spiegel, P. and Nankoe A.
2004 "UNHCR, HIV/AIDS and Refugees: Lessons Learned", *Forced Migration Review*, 19: pp. 21-23.

Tenaganita
2000 *Vulnerable – A Case Study of HIV/AIDS and Bangladeshi Migrant Workers in Malaysia*, CARAM Malaysia, April.

UN
2001 *United Nations General Assembly Declaration of Commitment on HIV/AIDS*, A/RES/S-26/2, New York.

UNAIDS
2003 *Progress Report on the Global Response to the HIV/AIDS Epidemic*, Geneva.
2004(a) *Report on the Global AIDS Epidemic: 4th Global Report*, Geneva, July.
2004(b) *Funding for AIDS*, Fact Sheet, Geneva, July.

UNAIDS/IOM
2004 "UNAIDS/IOM Statement on HIV/AIDS-Related Travel Restrictions", Geneva; *www.iom.int/en/PDF_Files/HIVAIDS/UNAIDS_IOM_statement_travel_restrictions.pdf*

UNAIDS/UNHCR
2003 *HIV and STI Prevention and Care in Rwandan Refugee Camps in the United Republic of Tanzania*, UNAIDS/03.16E, Geneva, March.

UNDP HIV and Development Project: South and South West Asia
2001 *HIV Vulnerability and Migration: A South Asia Perspective*, New Delhi, October.

Voeten, H., Gregson s., Zaba B., White R. and Habbema D.
2004 "Ecological Association between Migration and HIV Prevalence in African Cities", submitted for publication and presented at the Bangkok AIDS conference-related session on 'The Role of Mobility in the Spread and Control of HIV', organised by the Department of Public Health, Erasmus University Medical Center, the Netherlands.

World Bank/IMF/IDA
2003 *HIPC Initiative – Statistical Update*, available at *www.worldbank.org/hipc/*.

CHAPTER 21 – MANAGING MIGRATION IN THE WAKE OF SEPTEMBER 11: IMPLICATIONS FOR A COST-BENEFIT ANALYSIS

Afgivet af Udlændingestyrelsen
1997 Rapport om udlændingeattachér, København, Juni.

Associated Press
2004 "Senators want to hasten US-VISIT programme", 9 March; *www.Foxnews.com*

Briggs, Jr., V. M.
2003 "*Mass Immigration and the National Interest: Policy Directions for the New Century*", M.E. Sharpe, Armonk, N.Y. ;London (3rd Ed.).

Commission of the European Communities
2003 "Paving the Way for a New Neighbourhood Instrument", Communication from the Commission, Brussels. *www.see-educoop.net/education_in/pdf/comm-from-com-oth-enl-t02.pdf*

DHS (Department of Homeland Security)
2004a "2004 Budget in Brief", Washington, D.C. *www.dhs.gov/interweb/assetlibrary/FY_2004_BUDGET_IN_BRIEF.pdf*
2004b "Secretary Tom Ridge Launches the New US-VISIT Program", Media Briefing, 5 January. *www.vodium.com/mediapod/us_visit/*

DIMIA (Australian Department of Immigration and Multicultural and Indigenous Affairs)
2004 "Overstayers and People in Breach of Visa Conditions", Factsheet 86, September.

Government of Canada,
2001 News Release "Strengthened Immigration Measures to Counter Terrorism," Niagara Falls *www.cic.gc.ca/english/press/01/0119-pre.html*

ILO (International Labour Organization)
2004 "Towards a Fair Deal for Migrant Workers in the Global Economy", Report VI, International Labour Conference, 92nd Session, Geneva.

IOM (International Organization for Migration)
2003 *World Migration Report 2003*, Geneva.
2004 *Return Migration: Policies and Practices in Europe*, report to the Advisory Committee on Aliens Affairs, the Netherlands, Geneva.

International Herald Tribune
2004 *"US says new controls stopped 280 at border"*, International Edition, 7 October, p. 20

Office of the Auditor General of Canada
2003 "Report of the Auditor General of Canada to the House of Commons", Chapter 5: Citizenship and Immigration Canada - Control and Enforcement, Ottawa. *www.oag-bvg.gc.ca/domino/reports.nsf/html/20030405ce.html/$file/20030405ce.pdf*

Martin, P.
2003 Bordering on Control: Combating Irregular Migration in North America and Europe, IOM Migration Research Series, No. 13, Geneva.

National Public Radio/Kaiser Family Foundation/Kennedy School of Government
2004 Immigration Survey, USA *www.kff.org/kaiserpolls/pomr100604pkg.cfm*

Reuters
2004 "Italy study sees Al Qaeda link to Human Trafficking." (L. Baker), 7 September.

Taylor, F. X. (Amb.)
2004 "Diplomatic Security's Mission in the Age of Terrorism", before the House International Relations Committee, 9/11 Commission, August 19.

United Kingdom Parliament
2004 "Visas and Residence Permits", Letter from Caroline Flint MP, to the Chairman, 5 January; *www.publications.parliament.uk/pa/ld200304/ldselect/ldeucom/140/140we110.htm*
UK Home Office
2002a "The Voluntary Assisted Returns Programme: an Evaluation", in *Findings 175*, London. *www.homeoffice.gov.uk/rds/pdfs2/r175.pdf*
2002b "Secure Borders, Safe Haven: Integration with Diversity in Modern Britain", presented to Parliament by the Secretary of State for the Home Department by Command of her Majesty, February. HMSO, Norwich; *copyright@hmso.gov.uk*

CHAPTER 22 – REGIONAL AND GLOBAL CONSULTATIVE PROCESSES: TRENDS AND DEVELOPMENTS

IMP (International Migration Policy Programme)
2002 "Global and Regional Migration Policies: Recent Developments Towards Strengthening International Cooperation on Migration", paper prepared by IMP for its regional meetings with senior government officials.

IOM
2003a "Managing Migration at the Regional Level - Strategies for Regional Consultation." *World Migration Report 2003*, pp. 123-138.
2003b "IOM's role in Enhancing Regional Dialogues on Migration." Council Document MC/INF/266, Geneva.
2003c "Recommendations of MIDSA Workshop on Extraregional Irregular Migration and Migrant Smuggling to, through and from the SADC Region." Johannesburg, South Africa, 25-27 June, 2003.
2003d "Conclusion of the Chairmanship", 5+5 Dialogue, Second Ministerial Conference on Migration in the Western Mediterranean, Rabat, 22-23 October (informal translation).
2003e "Migration Data and Legislative Implications for ECOWAS Member States", IOM project document, Geneva.
2004 "IOM will organize the Berne Initiative Regional Consultations." IOM, Belgium; *www.belgium.iom.int/index.asp?News_ID=178*

Klekowski Von Koppenfels, A.
2001 The *Role of Regional Consultative Processes in Managing International Migration*, IOM Migration Research Series, No. 3, IOM, Geneva.

RCM (Regional Conference on Migration) ("Puebla Process")
2004 Report on the IX Regional Conference on Migration, Panama, 17-21 May.

Regional Conference on Public Health and Trafficking in Human Beings in Central, Eastern and Southern Europe
2003 Budapest Declaration on Public Health and Trafficking in Human Beings, available at *www.iomskopje.org.mk/CT/pdf/budapest_dec.pdf*

Langenbacher, Dominik Ambassador (Delegate for Migration Dialogue Federal Office for Refugees)
2004 Statement at the European Population Forum, 14 January, Geneva.

Nezer, Melanie.
1999 "The Puebla Process: US Migration Controls Move South of the Border", Worldwide Refugee Information. *www.refugees.org/world/articles/wrs99_migrationcontrols.htm*

OTHER SOURCES CONSULTED

Amnesty International
2003 Bali Ministerial Conference on People Smuggling, Trafficking in Persons and Transnational Crime must address human rights concerns, Press release, April 8.

IGC (Intergovernmental Consultations on Asylum, Refugees and Migration Policies in Europe, North America and Australia)
2003 Powerpoint Presentation. Workshop on Approaches to Data Collection and Data Management, Sept. 8-9, Geneva.

IOM (some sources may be internal only)
"Managing Migration at the Regional Level: Strategies for Regional Consultation", Round table on Managing Migration at the Regional Level, June 2002.
2002 *Significant International Statements on Migration: a Thematic Compilation.*
2002 "Illustration of Multilateral, Regional and Bilateral Cooperative Arrangements in the Management of Migration".
2003 "An Overview of IOM Partnership with Maghreb Countries".

2003 SIEMCA (Powerpoint presentation). Workshop on Approaches to Data Collection and Data Management, Sept. 8-9, Geneva.

2003 Statements, 86th Council, 18-21 November, 2003.

2003 Final Report, Labour Migration Ministerial Consultations for Countries of Origin in Asia, 1-2 April, Colombo, Sri Lanka.

2003 "Sri Lanka -Asian Labour Migration Ministerial Consultations", press briefing notes, April 1.

2003 "Trends, Characteristics, Policy and Interstate Cooperation", in *Labour Migration in Asia: Trends, Challenges and Policy Responses in Countries of Origin*, Geneva.

2004 "Kenya-Regional Workshop on Labour Migration", press briefing notes, May 4.

2004 Essentials on Migration Management for Policy Makers and Practitioners, Section 1.7: International Cooperation, *Course Manual.*

MARRI-Migration, Asylum, Refugee Regional Initiative

2004 "MARRI-The Way Ahead in 2004-2005"; *www.stabilitypact.org/marri*

RCM (Regional Consultation on Migration) ("Puebla Process")

2003 "Activity and Financial Report of the Technical Secretariat for the period June-December 2003".

2003 "Summary Report", VIII Regional Conference on Migration. Declaration, Cancun, Mexico, May 29, 2003.

TEXTBOX 22.1

APEC Business Travel Card – Facilitating Regional Travel

Castles, S. and Miller, M.J.

1998 *The Age of Migration: International Population Movements in the Modern World*, (Second Edition), Macmillan, London.

DIMIA (Department of Immigration and Multicultural and Indigenous Affairs)

2003a "APEC Business Travel Card: Operating Framework", unpublished document, Canberra.

2003b "Regional Trade Facilitation Initiatives - APEC Business Travel Card Scheme", OECD-World Bank-IOM Seminar on Trade and Migration, Geneva, Palais des Nations, 12-14 November.

Rizvi, A.

2003 *SOPEMI 2004: Australia*, report by Australia's Correspondent to the OECD, November.

CHAPTER 23 – INTERNATIONAL MIGRATION TRENDS

Borjas, George J.

1994 "The economics of immigration", *Journal of Economic Literature (Nashville, Tennessee)*, 77(4): 531-553.

Centre d'Études et de Recherche sur la Population et le Développement (CERPOD)

1995 *Migrations et Urbanisation en Afrique de l'Ouest (MUAO): Résultats Préliminaires*, CERPOD, Bamako, Mali.

Duleep, H.O. and M.C. Regets and B.R. Chiswick (Ed.)

1992 "Some evidence on the effect of admission criteria on immigrant assimilation", *Immigration, Language and Ethnicity: Canada and the United States*, American Enterprise Institute, Washington.

International Labour Organization (ILO)

1936 *World Statistics of Aliens: A Comparative Study of Census Returns 1910-1920-1930*, Studies and Reports, Series O (Migration), No.6, International Labour Organization, Geneva.

2004 *Towards a Fair Deal for Migrant Workers in the Global Economy*, Report VI, International Labour Conference, 92nd Session, 2004, International Labour Organization, Geneva.

IOM

2000 *World Migration Report 2000*: UN Sales No. E.00.III.S.3.

Japan, Ministry of Justice

2001 *Immigration Control*, Tokyo.

Kramer, R.G.

2003 *Development in international migration to the United States: 2003, Immigration Policy and Research*, Working Paper 38, U.S. Department of Labor, Bureau of International Labor Affairs.

Lim, L.L.

1996 "The migration transition in Malaysia", *Asian and Pacific Migration Journal* 5(2;3), Manila: 319-337.

OECD

1990 *Trends in International Migration: Continuous Reporting System on International Migration. SOPEMI*, Annual Reports, OECD, Paris.

1995 *Trends in International Migration: Continuous Reporting System on International Migration. SOPEMI*, Annual Report, 1994 Edition, OECD, Paris.

2001 *International Mobility of the Highly Skilled*, OECD Paris.

2004 *Trends in International Migration SOPEMI 2003*, Annual Report, 2003 Edition, OECD, Paris.

Passel, J.S.

2001 *Estimates of undocumented immigrants living in the United States: 2000*, Research Report, The Urban Institute.: *www.urban.org* (April 2004)

2002 "New estimates of the undocumented population in the United States" (mimeo.), *Migration Information Source*, Feature Story No. 19, 22 May 2002: *www.migrationinformation.org*. (April 2004)

Russell, S.S.

1992 "International migration and political turmoil in the Middle East", *Population and Development Review* 18(4), New York: 719-728.

South Africa, Chamber of Mines

var. *Statistical Tables 1987 and 1993*, Johannesburg.

South Africa, Ministry of Home Affairs, Task Team on International Migration

1999 "White paper on international migration": *www.gov.za/whitepaper/1999/migrate/htm* (April 2004)

Tsay, C-L

2000 "Trends and characteristics of migration flows to the economy of Chinese Taipei", *Proceedings of the International Workshop on International Migration and Human Resources Development in the APEC Member Economies. Chiba, Japan, 20-21 January 2000*, Institute of Developing Economies, Chiba, Japan: 131-166.

Tsay, C-L and J-P Lin and Y. Hayase and C-L Tsay (Eds.)
2001 "Impacts of labour importation on the unemployment of local workers: An exploration based on survey data", *Proceedings of the International Workshop on International Migration and Structural Change in the APEC Member Economies. Chinese Taipei, 19-20 October 2000*, Institute of Developing Economies, JETRO: 307-332.

Uh, SB
1999 "Immigration and labour market issues in Korea", *Migration and Regional Economic Integration in Asia*, OECD, Paris: 153-164.

UN
1985 *World Population Trends, Population and Development Interrelations and Population Policies*, 1983 Monitoring Report, Vol. 1, Population Trends: Sales No. E.85.XIII.1.
2001 *Replacement Migration: Is It a Solution to Declining and Ageing Populations?*: Sales No. E.01.XIII.19.
2002 *International Migration from Countries with Economies in Transition: 1980-1999*, United Nations Department of Economic Affairs Population Division Working Paper No. ESA/P/WP.176.
2003a *World Population Prospects. The 2002 Revision. Volume I: Comprehensive Tables*: Sales No. E.03.XIII.6.
2003b *Levels and Trends of International Migration to Selected Countries in Asia*: Sales No. E.03.XIII.2.
2003c *World Population Monitoring 2003. Population, Education and Development* (Draft), United Nations Department of Economic and Social Affairs Population Division Working Paper No. ESA/P/WP.179.
2004 *Trends in Total Migrant Stock: The 2003 Revision* (POP/DB/MIG/2003/1) (database in digital form).
2004 *Trends in Total Migrant Stock: The 2003 Revision. Diskette Documentation*, United Nations Department of Economic and Social Affairs Population Division Working Paper No. ESA/P/WP.188.

United States Census Bureau
2001 "Profile of the foreign-born population in the United States: 2000", *Current Population Reports*, Series P23-206, U.S. Government Printing Office , Washington D.C.

United States Department of Homeland Security, Office of Immigration Statistics
2003 *2002 Yearbook of Immigration Statistics*, US Government Printing Office., Washington D.C.

United States Immigration and Naturalization Service
2003 *Estimates of the unauthorized immigrant population residing in the United States: 1990 to 2000*, Office of Policy Planning: *www.uscis.gov/graphics/shared/aboutus/statistics/III_Report_1211.pdf.*

Villa, M. and J.M. Pizarro and Y. Hayase and C-L Tsay (Eds.)
2001 "Trends and patterns of international migration in Latin America and the Caribbean", *Proceedings of the International Workshop on International Migration and Structural Change in the APEC Member Economies. Chinese Taipei, 19-20 October 2000*, Institute of Developing Economies, JETRO: 39-69.

Zlotnik, H.
1998 "International migration 1965-96: An overview", *Population and Development Review* 4(3), New York: 429-468.

admission: The granting of entry into a state.

alien: A person who is not a national of a given state. See also foreigner

amnesty: A general pardon, for 'legalization', that deals with people who can show residence in a country for which the amnesty is granted, despite the fact that such residence was illegal.

assimilation: Adaptation of one ethnic or social group – usually a minority – to another, involving the subsuming of language, traditions, values and behaviour or even fundamental vital interests and an alteration in the feeling of belonging.

assisted voluntary return: Logistical and financial support to rejected asylum seekers, trafficked migrants, stranded students, qualified nationals and other migrants unable or unwilling to remain in the host country, who volunteer to return to their countries of origin.

asylum seekers: Persons seeking to be admitted into a country as refugees and awaiting a decision on their application for refugee status under relevant international and national instruments.

biometrics: The study of measurable biological characteristics. "Biometric identifiers" (BIs) are pieces of information that encode a representation of a person's unique biological make up (e.g. fingerprints, retinal scans or voice scans).

border control: A state's regulation of the entry of persons to its territory, in the exercise of its sovereignty.

border management: Facilitation of authorized flows of business people, tourists, migrants and refugees and the detection and prevention of illegal entry of aliens into a given country.

brain drain: Emigration of trained and talented individuals from the country of origin to a third country, due to causes such as conflict or lack of opportunities .

brain gain: Immigration of trained and talented individuals from a third country into the receiving country. Also called reverse brain drain.

carrier liability law: A law imposing fines upon carriers who bring into the territory of a state persons without valid entry documents.

change of status: Procedure whereby an alien lawfully present in a state may seek a different immigration status.

citizen: See national

citizenship: See nationality

clandestine migration: Secret or concealed migration in breach of immigration requirements.

consular officers: Government officials representing the State abroad in visa and residency issues (See Art. 1(d), Vienna Convention on Consular Relations, 1963).

country of destination: The country that is a destination for migratory flows (legal or illegal).

country of origin: The country that is a source of migratory flows (legal or illegal).

country of transit: The country through which migratory flows (legal or illegal) move.

dependant: A person who relies on another for support. In the migration context, a spouse and minor children are generally considered 'dependants', even if the spouse is not financially dependent.

deportation: The act of a state in the exercise of its sovereignty in removing an alien from its territory to a certain place after refusal of admission or termination of permission to remain.

detention: Restriction on freedom of movement, usually through enforced confinement, of an individual by government authorities.

diaspora: People or ethnic populations that leave their traditional ethnic homelands, being dispersed throughout other parts of the world.

discrimination: A failure to treat all persons equally where no reasonable distinction can be found between those favoured and those not favoured. Discrimination is prohibited in respect of "race, sex, language or religion" (Art. 1(3), UN Charter, 1945) or "of any kind, such as race, colour, sex, language, religion, political or other opinion, national or social origin, property, birth or other status" (Art. 2, Universal Declaration of Human Rights, 1948).

displaced person: A person who flees his/her state or community due to fear or dangers other than those which would make him/her a refugee.

economic migrant: A person leaving his/her habitual place of residence to settle outside his/her country of origin in order to improve his/her quality of life.

emigration: The act of departing or exiting from one state with a view to settle in another.

entry: Any entrance of an alien into a foreign country, whether voluntary or involuntary, legally or illegally.

exclusion: The formal denial of an alien's admission into a state.

expulsion: An act by an authority of the state with the intention and with the effect of securing the removal of a person or persons (aliens or stateless persons) against their will from the territory of that state.

family reunification: Process whereby family members already separated through forced or voluntary migration regroup in a country other than the one of their origin.

feminization of migration: The growing participation of women in migration (some 49 per cent of all migrants are women).

forced migration: A migratory movement in which an element of coercion exists, including threats to life and livelihood, whether arising from natural or man-made causes (e.g. movements of refugees and internally displaced persons as well as people displaced by natural or environmental disasters, chemical or nuclear disasters, famine, or development projects).

forced return: The compulsory return of an individual to the country of origin, transit or third country, on the basis of an administrative or judicial act.

fraudulent document: Any travel or identity document that has been falsely made or altered in some material way by anyone other than a person or agency lawfully authorized to make or issue the travel or identity document on behalf of a state; or that has been improperly issued or obtained through misrepresentation, corruption or duress or in any other unlawful manner; or is being used by a person other than the rightful holder (Art. 3(c), UN Protocol Against the Smuggling of Migrants by Land, Sea and Air, supplementing the United Nations Convention against Transnational Organized Crime, 2000).

host country: See receiving country

human rights: Those liberties and benefits which, by accepted contemporary values, all human beings should be able to claim "as of right" in the society in which they live; e.g. as contained in the Universal Declaration of Human Rights, 1948 and the International Covenants on Economic, Social and Cultural Rights, and on Civil and Political Rights, 1966 and developed by other treaties. from this core.

illegal entry: Act of crossing borders without complying with the necessary requirements for legal entry into the receiving state (Art. 3(b), UN Protocol Against the Smuggling of Migrants by Land, Sea and Air, supplementing the United Nations Convention against Transnational Organized Crime, 2000).

MIGRATION TERMINOLOGY

illegal migration: See irregular migration

immigration: A process by which non-nationals move into a country for the purpose of settlement.

integration: The process by which immigrants become accepted into society, both as individuals and as groups.

interception: Any measure applied by a state outside its national territory to prevent, interrupt, or stop the movement of persons without required documentation from crossing borders by land, air or sea, and making their way to the country of prospective destination.

internal migration: A movement of people from one area of a country to another for the purpose or with the effect of establishing a new residence.

internally displaced persons/IDPs : Persons or groups of persons who have been forced or obliged to flee or to leave their homes or places of habitual residence, in particular as a result of or in order to avoid the effects of armed conflict, situations of generalized violence, violations of human rights or natural or human-made disasters, and who have not crossed an internationally recognized State border *(Guiding Principles on Internal Displacement, UN Doc E/CN.4/1998/53/Add.2.).*

international migration: Movement of persons who leave their country of origin, or the country of habitual residence, to establish themselves either permanently or temporarily in another country.

irregular migrant: Someone who, owing to illegal entry or the expiry of his or her visa, lacks legal status in a transit or host country.

irregular migration: Movement that takes place outside the regulatory norms of the sending, transit and receiving countries.

jus sanguinis (latin): The rule that determines a child's nationality by its parents' nationality, irrespective of the place of its birth.

jus soli (latin): The rule that determines a child's nationality by its place of birth (although it can also be conveyed by the parents).

labour migration: Movement of persons from their home state to another state for the purpose of employment.

lookout system: A state's official list, usually (but not necessarily) automated, of persons who should be prevented from entering the country or who should be arrested upon arrival.

migrant flow: The number of migrants counted as moving or being authorized to move, to or from a country for employment or to establish themselves in a defined period of time.

migrant stock: The number of migrants residing in a country at a particular point in time.

migrant worker: A person who is to be engaged, is engaged or has been engaged in a remunerated activity in a state of which he or she is not a national *(Art. 2(1), International Convention on the Protection of the Rights of All Migrant Workers and Members of Their Families, 1990).*

migration: A process of moving, either across an international border, or within a state. It includes migration of refugees, displaced persons, uprooted people, and economic migrants.

migration management: A term used to encompass numerous governmental functions and a national system of orderly and humane management for cross-border migration, particularly managing the entry and presence of foreigners within the borders of the state and the protection of refugees and others in need of protection.

national: A person, who, either by birth or naturalization, is a member of a political community, owing allegiance to the community and being entitled to enjoy all its civil and political rights and protection; a member of the state, entitled to all its privileges.

nationality: Legal bond between an individual and a state. Under *Art. 1, Hague Convention on Certain Questions Relating to the Conflict of Nationality Laws, 1930* "it is for each State to determine under its own laws who are its nationals. This law shall be recognized by other States in so far as it is consistent with international conventions, international custom, and the principles of law generally recognized with regard to nationality."

naturalization: Granting by a state of its nationality to an alien through a formal act on the application of the individual concerned.

net migration: See total migration

orderly migration: The movement of a person from his/her usual place of residence to a new place of residence, in keeping with the laws and regulations governing exit of the country of origin and travel, transit and entry into the host country.

permanent residence: The right, granted by a host state to a non-national, to live and work therein on a permanent (unlimited) basis.

protection: All activities aimed at securing respect for individual rights in accordance with the letter and spirit of the relevant bodies of law (namely, Human Rights Law, International Humanitarian Law, Migration Law and Refugee Law).

quota: In the migration context, a quantitative restriction on the number of immigrants to be admitted each year.

readmission agreement: Agreement which addresses procedures for one state to return aliens in an irregular situation to their home state or a state through which they passed en route to the state which seeks to return them.

receiving country: Country of destination or a third country. In the case of return or repatriation, also the country of origin.

re-emigration: The movement of a person who, after having returned to his/her country of departure, again emigrates.

refoulement: The return by a state of an individual to the territory of another state in which his/her life or liberty would be threatened, or s/he may be persecuted for reasons of race, religion, nationality, membership of a particular social group or political opinion; or would run the risk of torture.

refugee (mandate): A person who meets the criteria of the UNHCR Statute and qualifies for the protection of the United Nations provided by the High Commissioner, regardless of whether or not s/he is in a country that is a party to the Convention relating to the Status of Refugees, 1951 or the 1967 Protocol relating to the Status of Refugees, or whether or not s/he has been recognized by the host country as a refugee under either of these instruments.

refugee (recognized): A person, who 'owing to well-founded fear of persecution for reasons of race, religion, nationality, membership of a particular social group or political opinions, is outside the country of his nationality and is unable or, owing to such fear, is unwilling to avail himself of the protection of that country' *(Convention relating to the Status of Refugees, Art. 1A(2), 1951 as modified by the 1967 Protocol).*

regional consultative processes: Non-binding consultative fora, bringing representatives of states, civil society (Non Governmental Organizations (NGOs)) and international organizations together at the regional level to discuss migration issues in a cooperative manner.

regularization: Any process by which a country allows aliens in an irregular situation to obtain legal status in the country.

reintegration: Re-inclusion or re-incorporation of a person into a group or a process, e.g. of a migrant into the society of his/her country of origin.

remittances: Monies earned or acquired by non-nationals that are transferred back to their country of origin.

repatriation: The personal right of a refugee or a prisoner of war to return to his/her country of nationality under specific conditions laid down in various international instruments *(Geneva Conventions, 1949 and Protocols, 1977,the Regulations Respecting the Laws and Customs of War on Land, Annexed to the Fourth Hague Convention, 1907, the human rights instruments as well as in customary international law).*

resettlement: The relocation and integration of people (refugees, internally displaced persons, etc.) into another geographical area and environment, usually in a third country.

residence: The act or fact of living in a given place for some time; the place where one actually lives as distinguished from a domicile.

return migration: The movement of a person returning to his/her country of origin or habitual residence usually after at least one year in another country. The return may or may not be voluntary.

sending country: A country from which people leave to settle abroad permanently or temporarily.

skilled migrant: A migrant worker who, because of his/her skills, is usually granted preferential treatment regarding admission to a host country.

slavery: The status or condition of a person over whom any or all the powers attaching to the right of ownership are exercised *(Art. 1, Slavery Convention, 1926 as amended by 1953 Protocol).*

smuggler (of people): An intermediary who is moving people by agreement with them, in order to illegally transport them across an internationally recognized state border.

smuggling: The procurement, in order to obtain, directly or indirectly, a financial or other material benefit, of the illegal entry of a person into a State Party of which the person is not a national or a permanent resident *(Art. 3(a), UN Protocol Against the Smuggling of Migrants by Land, Sea and Air, supplementing the United Nations Convention against Transnational Organized Crime, 2000).*

state: A political entity with legal jurisdiction and effective control over a defined territory, and the authority to make collective decisions for a permanent population, a monopoly on the legitimate use of force, and an internationally recognized government that interacts, or has the capacity to interact, in formal relations with other entities.

technical cooperation: The sharing of information and expertise on a given subject usually focused on public sector functions.

temporary migrant workers: Skilled, semi-skilled or untrained workers in the receiving country for definite periods under a work contract with an individual worker or a service contract with an enterprise.

terrorism: Any act intended to cause death or serious bodily injury to a civilian, or any other person not taking an active part in the hostilities in a situation of armed conflict, when the purpose of such act is to intimidate a population, or compel a government or an international organization to do or abstain from doing an act *(Art. 2(1)(b), International Convention for the Suppression of Financing of Terrorism, 1999).*

total migration/net migration: Total migration is the sum of the entries or arrivals of immigrants, and of exits, or departures of emigrants; net migration is the balance resulting from the difference between arrivals and departures.

trafficker, human: An intermediary who is moving people in order to obtain an economic or other profit by means of deception, coercion and/or other forms of exploitation.

trafficking in persons: The recruitment, transportation, transfer, harbouring or receipt of persons, by means of the threat or use of force or other forms of coercion, of abduction, of fraud, of deception, of the abuse of power or of a position of vulnerability or of the giving or receiving of payments or benefits to achieve the consent of a person having control over another person, for the purpose of exploitation *(Art. 3(a), UN Protocol to Prevent, Suppress and Punish trafficking in Persons, Especially Women and Children, Supplementing the UN Convention Against Organized Crime, 2000).*

travel documents: All documents which are acceptable proof of identity for the purpose of entering another country. Passports and visas are the most widely used forms of travel documents.

unaccompanied minors: Persons under the age of majority who are not accompanied by a parent, guardian, or other adult who by law or custom is responsible for them.

undocumented migrant workers/ migrant workers in an irregular situation: Migrant workers or members of their families not authorized to enter, to stay or to engage in employment in a state.

visa: An endorsement by a consular officer in a passport or a certificate of identity that indicates that the officer, at the time of issuance, believes the holder to fall within a category of non-nationals who can be admitted under the state's laws.

voluntary return: The assisted or independent return to the country of origin, transit or another third country based on the free will of the returnee.

vulnerable groups: Any group or sector of society at higher risk of being subjected to discriminatory practices, violence, natural or environmental disasters, or economic hardship, than other groups within the state; any group or sector of society (such as women, children or the elderly) that is at higher risk in periods of conflict and crisis.

working permit: A legal document giving authorization required for employment of migrant workers in the host country.

xenophobia: While no universally accepted definition of xenophobia exists, it can be described as attitudes, prejudices and behaviour that reject, exclude and often vilify persons based on the perception that they are outsiders or foreigners to the community, society or national identity.

A

B

J

K

L

R

S

T

ACRONYMS AND ABBREVIATIONS

ABS	Australian Bureau of Statistics
ACBF	African Capacity Building Foundation
ACP	African, Caribbean and Pacific countries
ADB	American Development Bank
AEC	African Economic Community
AHDR	Arab Human Development Report
ALO	Airline Liaison Officer
AMU	Arab Maghreb Union
APEC	Asia-Pacific Economic Cooperation
API	Advanced Passenger Information
APP	Advanced Passenger Processing
ARB	Artist Record Book (Philipines)
ARV	Antiretroviral
ASEAN	Association of South-East Asian Nations
ASEM	Asia-Europe Meeting
AU	African Union
AVR	Assisted Voluntary Return
BES	Bureau of Employement Services (Philippines)
BFBA	Bureau for foreigners, Borders and Asylum (Turkey)
BLA	Bilateral Labor Agreement
BMA	British Medical Association
BMET	Bangladesh Bureau of manpower, Employement and Training
BMG	Busines Mobility Group
CAFTA	Central Amercian Free Trade Association
CARICOM	Caribbean Community
CARDS	Community Assistance for Reconstruction, Development and Stability in the Balkans
CDC	Centre for Disease Control (USA)
CEME	Cooperative Efforts to Manage Emigration
CENSAD	Communauté Economique des États du Sahel et du Sahara
CENWOR	Center for Women's Research
CHED	Commission for Higher Education (Philippines)
CIA	Central Intelligence Agency
CIC	Citizenship and Immigration Canada
CIS	Commonwealth of Independent States
COMESA	Common Market for Eastern and Southern Africa
COMPAS	Centre on Migration, Policy and Society (UK)
CONAPO	Consejo Nacional de Población (Mexico)
COSTED	Committee on Science and Technology in Developing countries
CPA	Comprehensive Plan of Action
CTM	Counter-Trafficking Module
DALY	Disability-Adjusted Life Years
DFID	Department for International Developement (UK)
DHS	Department of Homeland Security (USA)
DIMIA	Dpt of Immig. and Multicultural and Indigenous Aff.
DOH	Doctors from the Department of Health (Philippines)
DRC	Democratic Republic of the Congo
DSWD	Department of Social Welfare and Development
EAC	East African Community
ECA	Economic Commission for Africa
ECOSOC	Economic and Social Council (UN)
ECOWAS	Economic Community for West African States
EEA	European Economic Area
EECA	Eastern Europe and Central Asia
EMP	Euro-Mediterranean Partnership
ESCWA	Economic and Social Commissionfor Western Asia
ESS	European Social Survey
ETA	Electronic Travel Authority (Australia)
EU	European Union
FDI	Foreign Direct Investment
FHI	Family Health International
FX	Foreign Exchange
FYROM	Former Yugoslav Republic of Macedonia
GATS	General Agreement on Trades and Services
GCC	Gulf Cooperation Council
GCIM	Global Commission on International Migration
GDP	Gross Domestic Product
GMG	Geneva Migration Group
GMS	Greater Mekong Subregion
GNP	Gross National Product
GTZ	Gesellschaft für Technische Zusammenarbeit (Germany)
HIV/AIDS	Human Immunodeficiency Virus/Acquired Immune Deficiency Syndrome
HRHC	Human Rights High commissioner
HRST	Human Resources in Science and Technology (Australia)
HTA	Hometown Associations
IGC	Intergovernmental Consultations
IND	Immigration and Nationality Directorate (UK)
IADB	Inter-American Development Bank
ICAO	International Civil Aviation Organization
ICMPD	International Centre for Migration Policy Development
IDB	International Development Bank
IDPs	Internally Displaced Persons
IELTS	International English Language Testing System
IGAD	Intergovernmental Authority on Development
ILC	International Labour Conference
ILO	International Labour Organization
IMF	International Monetary Fund
IMPSIDA	Iniciativa Mesoamericana para la Prevención del SIDA
IND	Immigration and Nationality Directorate (UK)
INED	Institut National d'Etudes Démographiques
INS	Immigration and Naturalization Service (US)
INSTRAW	UN International Research and Training Institute for the Advancement of Women
IOM	International Organization for Migration
IPEC	International Programme for the Elimination of Child Labour
IRCA	(Mexicans legalized under ....)
IRD	Institute of Research for Development
IRMF	Intellectual Resources Management Fund
KHRP	Kosovo Humanitarian Return Assistance Programme (IOM)
LFS	European Labour force Survey
LGU	Local Government Unit (Philippines)
LHRLA	Lawyers for Human rightsd and Legal Aid
LRA	Lord's Resistance Army (Uganda)
LSHTM	London School of Hygiene and Tropical Medicine
LSI	Long-standing illnesses
LSIA	Longitudinal Survey of Migrants to Australia (Australia)
MARINA	Maritime Industry Authority (Philippines)
MDGs	Millennium Development Goals
MHS	Medical Health Services (IOM)
MIDA	Migration for Development in Africa
MIDSA	Migration Dialogue for Southern Africa
MoD	Ministry for the Displaced
MOGE	Ministra of Gender Equality (Korea)
MOU	Memorandum of Understanding
MPI	Migration Policy Institute
MPS	Ministry of Public Security (Vietnam)
MRA	Mutual Recognition Agreements (Japan ??)
MRF	Mission with Regional Functions (IOM)
MWC	Migrant Workers Convention (UN)

NAFTA	North American Free Trade Agreement
NEPAD	New Partnership for Africa's Development
NGO	Non-Governmental Organization
NHS	National Health Service (UK)
NIC	Newly Industrializing Country (Taiwan)
NOORS	National Office of Overseas Skills Recognition (UK)
NORAD	Norwegian Agency for Development Cooperation
NRC	National Research Council (USA)
NRI	Non-Resident Indians
NSB	National Seamen's Board (Philippines)
NSEERS	National Security Entry-Exit Registration System
NZIS	New Zealand Immigration Service
OAS	Organization of American States
OAU	Organization of African Unity
OCAM	Organización Centroamericana de Migración
ODA	Overseas Development Assistance
OECD	Organization for Economic Cooperation and Development
OEDB	Overseas Employment Development Board (Philippines)
OFW	Overseas Filipino Workers
OHCHR	Office of the High Commissioner for Human Rights
OPA	Overses Performing Artists (Philippines)
OPT	Occupied Palestinian Territories
OSCE	Organization for Security and Cooperation in Europe
OWWA	Overseas Workers Welfare Administration (Philippines)
PAHO	Pan American Health Organization
PDOS	Pre-departure Orientation Seminar (Philippines)
PIDC	Pacific Immigration Directors' Conference
PNG	Papua New Guinea
POEA	Philippine Overseas Employment Administration
POLO	Philippines Overseas Labor Office
POSC	Philippine One-stop Shop Center
PRSP	Poverty Reduction Strategy Paper
QIZ	Qualifying Industrial zone
RCM	Regional Conference on Migration
RCP	Regional Consultative Processes
REAB	Reintegration or Emigration of Asylum Seekers from Belgium (IOM)
RECs	Regional Economic Communities
RKT	Return of Knowledge and Talent (IOM Manila)
RMMRU	Refugee and Migratory Movements Research Unit (Bangladesh)
RNCOM	Regional Network of Civil Organizations for Migration
RQA	Return of Qualified Afghans (IOM)
RQAN	Return of Qualified African Nationals
RQN	Return of Qualified Nationals
SAARC	South Asia Association for Regional Cooperation
SADC	Southern African Development Community
SAP	Stabilization and Association Process
SARS	Severe Acute Respiratory Syndrome
SBS	Sector Based Schemes (UK)
SEVIS	Student and Exchange Visitor Inforamtion System
SIEMCA	Sistema de Información Estadística sobre las Migraciones en Central America
SLBFE	Sri Lanka Bureau of Foreign Employment
SMC	Skilled Migrant Category
SSA	Sub-Saharan Africa
SSS	Social Security System (Philippines)
STI	Sexually Transmitted Infections
SYNA	Society of Iranian Youith News Agency
TCNs	Third Country Nationals
TEP	Thai Export Programme (IOM Manila)
TESDA	Technical Education and Skills Development Authority (Philipines)
TFWP	Temporary Foreign Worker Programmes
TICAD	Tokyo International Conference on African Development
TOTKEN	Transfer of Knowledge Trhought Expatriate Nationals (UNDP)
TPV	Temporary Protection Visa
TTTA	Trans-Tasman Travel Arrangements (Australia)
TVE	Township-Village Enterprise (Philippines)
UAE	United Arab Emirates
UK	United Kingdom
UN	United Nations
UNAIDS	Joint United Nations Programme on HIV/AIDS
UNCCP	United Nations Conciliation Commission for Palestine
UNCHS	United Nations Centre for Human Settlements
UNCTAD	United Nations Conference on Trade and Development
UNDP	United Nations Development Programme
UNECA	United nations Economic Commission for Africa
UNEP	United Nations Environment Programme
UNESCO	United Nations Educational, Scientific and Cultural Organization
UNFIP	United Nations Fund for International Partnerships
UNFPA	United Nations Population Fund
UNHCR	United Nations High Commissioner for Refugees
UNHCS	United Nations Human coordinator for Sudan
UNIAP	United Nations Inter-Agency Project on Human Trafficking the Greater Mekong Sub-Regionregion
UNICEF	United Nations Children's Fund
UNIFEM	United Nations Development fund for Women
UNODC	United Nations Office on Drugs and Crime
UNRWA	United Nations Relief and Works Agency
USCR	US Committee for Refugees
VAMAS	Vietnam Association for Manpower Supply
VARP	Voluntary Assisted Return Programme (IOM)
VARRP	Voluntary Assisted Return and Reintegration Programme (IOM)
VISIT	Visitor and Immigration Status Identification Technology System
WHO	World Health Organization
WTO	World Trade Organization

LIST OF GRAPHS, FIGURES AND TABLES

Maps

MAP 1 **TOTAL AND MIGRANT POPULATION BY REGION, IN 2000**

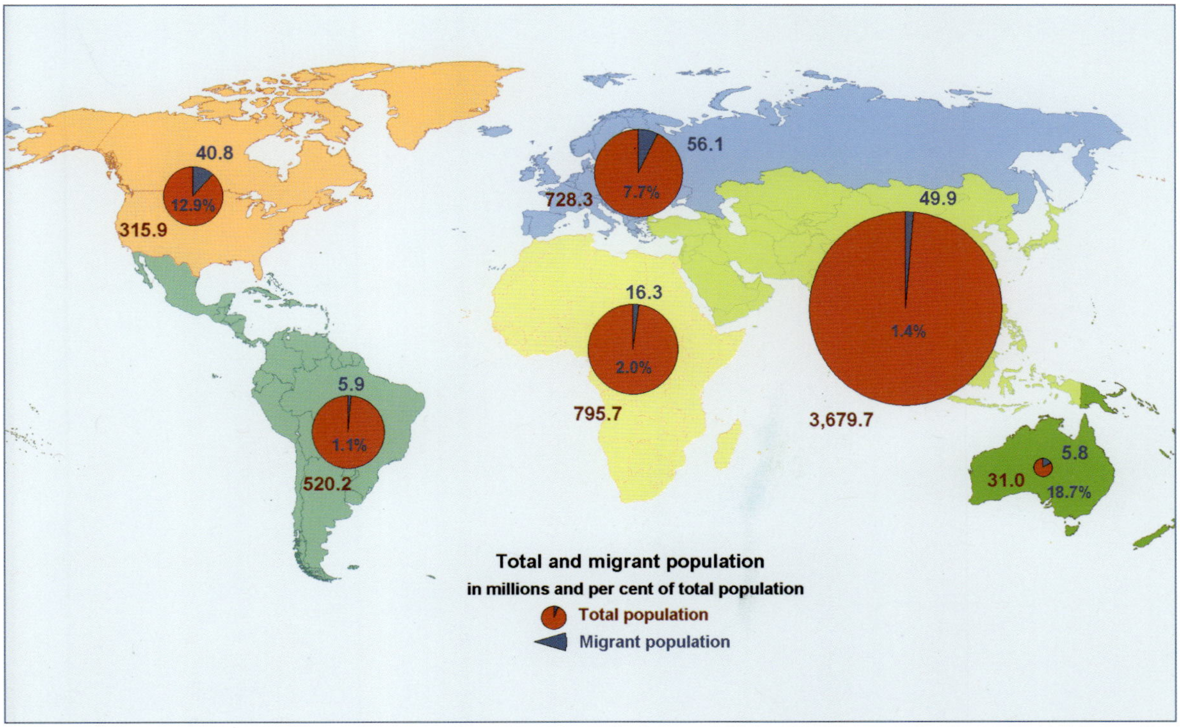

Source: United Nations, *Trends in Total Migrant Stock: the 2003 Revision.* Database maintained by the Population Division of the Department for Economic and Social Affairs, 2003. POP/DB/MIG/2003/1/*Trends in total Migrant Stock by Sex 1990-2000.*

In 2000, Europe hosted the largest migrant population of all world regions, over 56 million (including the *European* part of the Former Soviet Union), followed by Asia with nearly 50 million (including the *Asian* part of the Former Soviet Union) and North America with just over 40 million immigrants. Among these three regions, North America had the highest proportion of migrants in the population, 12.9 per cent, and Asia the lowest with only 1.4 per cent. Among all regions, Oceania's 5.8 million immigrants represented the highest share at 18.7 per cent of the total population of the region.

(Note that these global statistics for 2000 are derived from the UN Population Division's 2003 revision of "Trends in Total Migrant Stock", which uses two different regional constellations for Europe. The one illustrated in Map 1 places the countries that were part of the Former Soviet Union (FSU) either in Europe or in Asia. The other (reflected in Table 23.1 provided by UNPD in Chapter 23) classifies the Former Soviet Union as a region in itself, with 29.5 million migrants, leaving Europe with an estimated 32.8 million and Asia with 43.8 million migrants in 2000.) The UN's depiction of Asia in this map also includes central and west Asia (compare chapter 6, which excludes these sub-regions).

MAP 2 **POPULATION IN- AND OUTFLOWS FOR SELECTED OECD COUNTRIES**

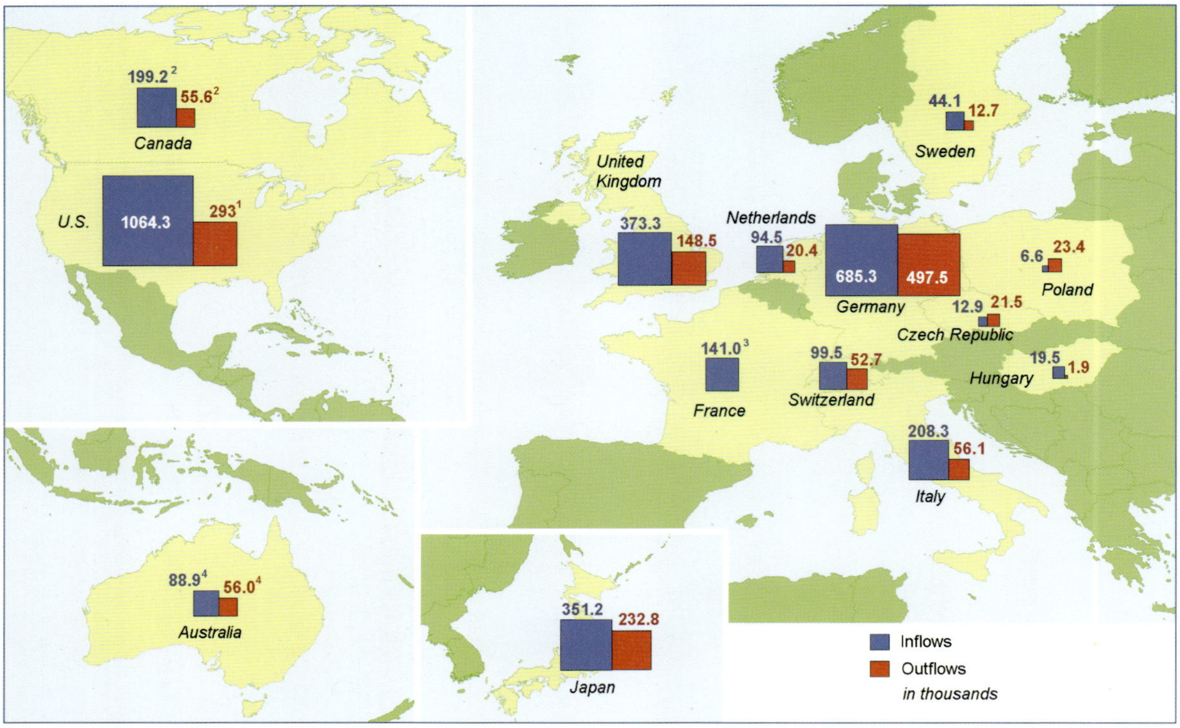

Source: OECD, *Trends in International Migration*, 2004.

Footnotes: **[1]** Source: US Census Bureau, 2000. Figure is a projected estimation. **[2]** Data refer to period from July 2002 to June 2003. **[3]** Data not available due to lack of population register in France. **[4]** Data refer to period from July 2001 to June 2002.

Map 2 shows that even states traditionally thought of as "immigration countries" are also countries of emigration. Each year countries such as Australia, Canada, and the US report significant outflows of persons from their territories. For example, in 2001, while the US accepted more immigrants than any other country (over 1 million), nearly 300,000 persons also emigrated. Of the three traditional immigration countries, the ratio of outflows (56,000) to inflows (88,900) was highest in Australia, which registered two persons leaving for every three persons who migrated into the country.

In Europe, Germany, the country receiving the largest number of immigrants (over 685,000) in 2001 also reported significant outflows of persons. For every three immigrants, two persons moved out of the country leaving a net migration balance of 188,000 persons. In Switzerland, the ratio of outflows to inflows was one migrant for every two newcomers, and in the UK two emigrants for every five immigrants. The map also shows how the migration situation has changed in Central Europe where immigration levels are rising. Hungary, formerly a country of emigration, now records more immigration than emigration.

MAP 3 **FOREIGN STUDENTS IN HIGHER EDUCATION IN SELECTED COUNTRIES**

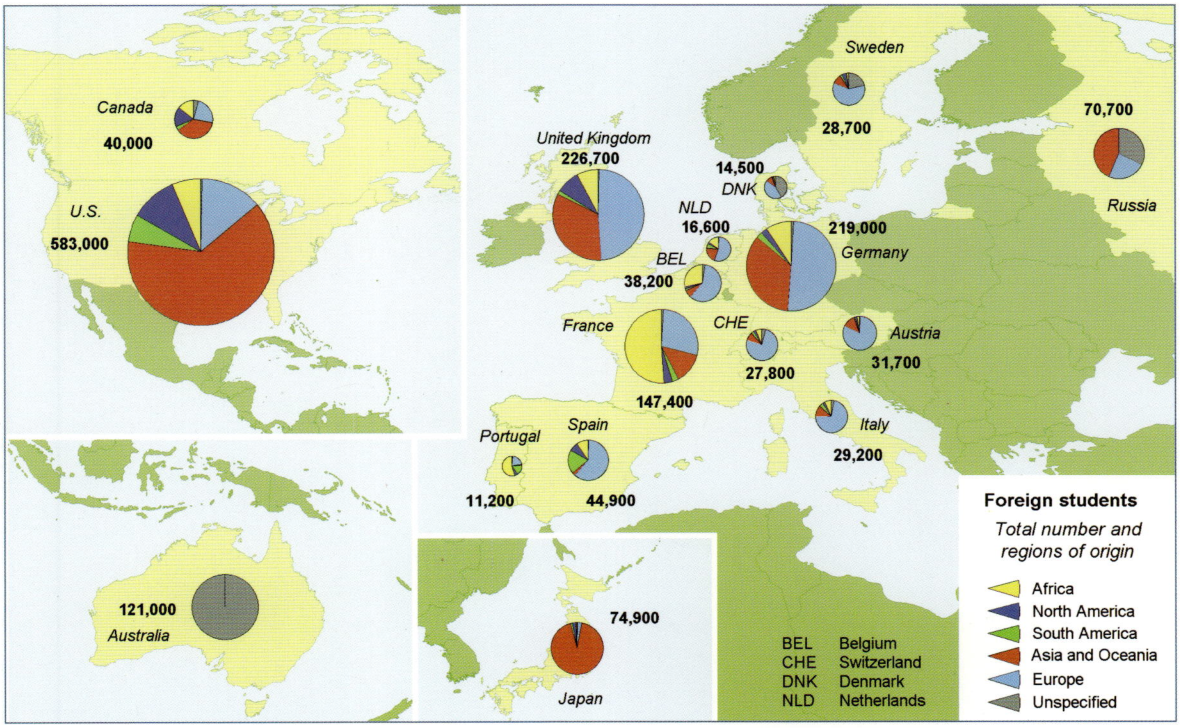

Source: UNESCO, *Global Education Digest 2004:* Comparing Education Statistics Across the World, UNESCO, 2004, Montreal.

Map 3 shows the distribution of foreign students living in selected OECD countries and in the Russian Federation by region of origin. It is difficult to obtain comparable data for the same period of time, because school years are scheduled differently in different countries. The data in this map primarily refer to the 2000 - 2001 school year.

The US, the UK, Germany, France, and Australia have the largest numbers of foreign students; the highest number in 2001-2002 being in the US (582,996). The US figure is twice that of the UK, (225,722), and slightly higher than the combined numbers in Germany, (219,039), France, (147,402), and Australia, (120,987). Relative to population size, the US figure is lower than that for other observed countries. Australia hosted the largest number of foreign students per capita in 2001-2002. In the US, only 4 per cent of all students were foreign students in 2001-2002. In Japan, foreign students represented only 2 per cent of the total number of students. In Europe, the proportion of foreign students is much higher in several countries (UK and Germany over 10%; Belgium 11%, and Switzerland 17%), largely because many students from EU countries are able to study in another EU Member State. Half the foreign students in Germany and the UK are from other parts of Europe. In North America, most foreign students (61%) come from Asia. More than 90 per cent of foreign students in Japan are from the Asian region. (The source used provides no breakdown by region of origin for foreign students in Australia).

MAP 4 **INTERNALLY DISPLACED PEOPLE**

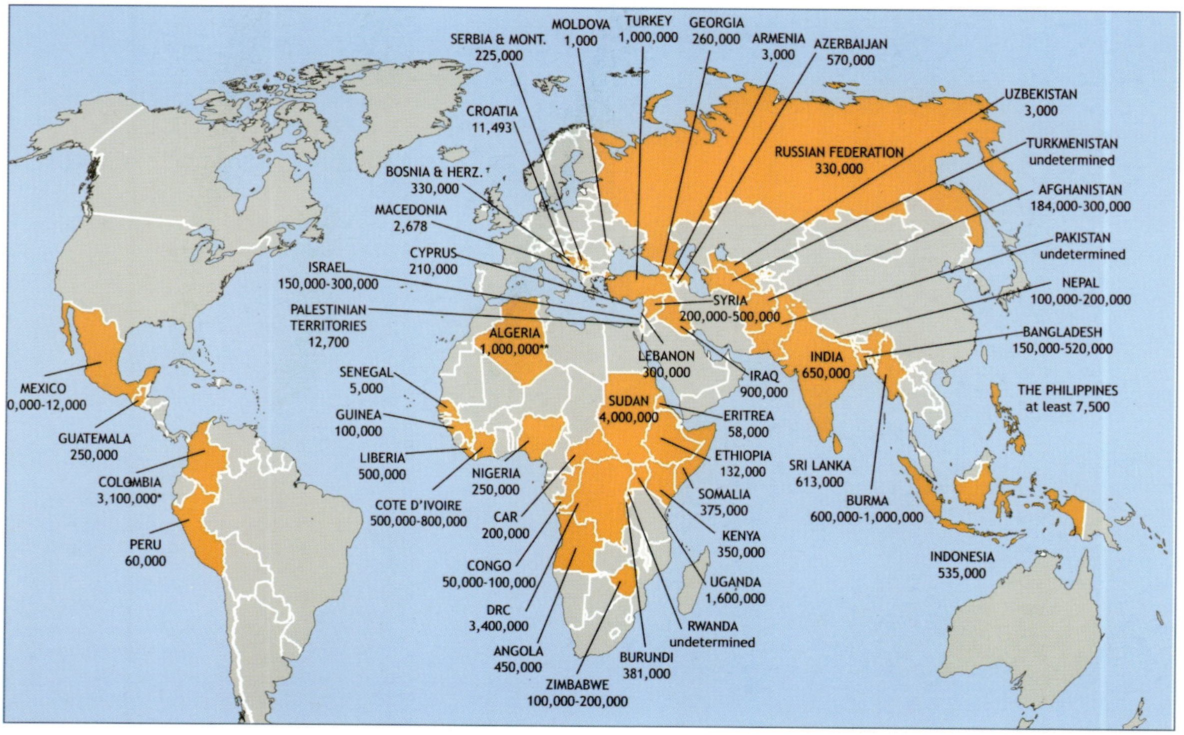

Source: *Global IDP Project*. Norwegian Refugee Council, Geneva. Website: www.idpproject.org

The estimated global figure for internally displaced persons (IDPs) has in recent years remained close to 25 million, with Africa in 2003 hosting just over half of all IDPs (some 12.7 million), the Asia-Pacific region 3.6 million, the Americas 3.3 million, Europe about 3 million and the Middle East some 2 million IDPs. According to the report of the Representative of the Secretary General on IDPs submitted in March 2004, more than three million persons were newly displaced in 2003, mostly in Africa (notably in Burundi, the Democratic Republic of Congo, Liberia, the Sudan, and Uganda), whereas 3 million persons were able to return home in countries such as Angola, Afghanistan, Bosnia and Herzegovina and Indonesia.

MAP 5 WORLD'S REFUGEES BY REGION OF ORIGIN AND REGION OF ASYLUM, 2003

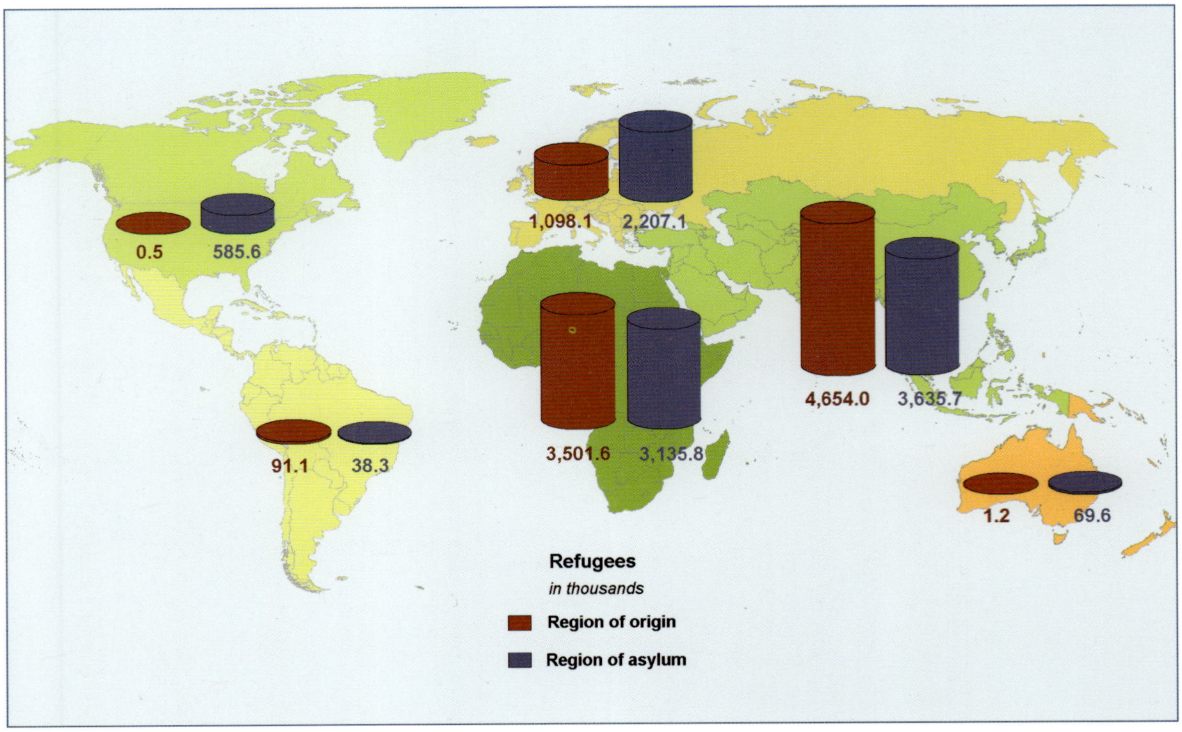

Source: UNHCR, *2003 Global Refugee Trends*, 2004

Complementing Map 4 on IDPs, Map 5 shows that most of the world's international refugees stay in the same region after having fled their own countries. Most refugees can be found in the developing world. Thus, Africa and Asia, while sending significant numbers of refugees to other continents, also host large refugee populations, both over 3 million in 2003, respectively. Europe and North America are the most important net receivers of refugees.

MAP 6 **PROPORTION OF WOMEN MIGRANTS IN THE WORLD REGIONS 1960 - 1980 - 2000**

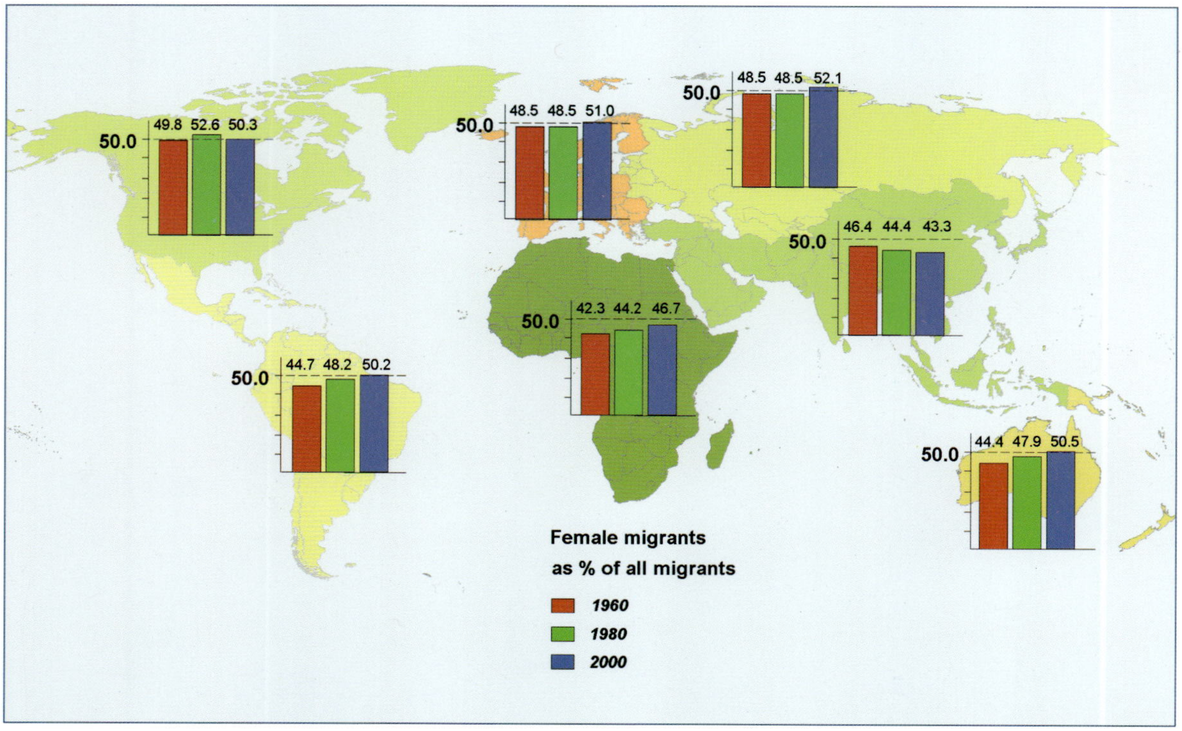

Source: United Nations, *Trends in Total Migrant Stock:* the 2003 Revision. Database maintained by the Population Division of the Department for Economic and Social Affairs, 2003. POP/DB/MIG/2003/1.

Map 6 shows the proportion of women migrants residing in different world regions in the period 1960 to 2000. This proportion rose by less than two per cent, from 46.7 per cent in 1960 to 48.6 per cent in 2000; the steepest rises being recorded in Latin America and Oceania. In both regions, the share of female migrants climbed by about 6 per cent to over 50 per cent of all recorded migrants. Asia was the only region where the female migrant share declined during this period, down from 46.4 per cent to 43.3 per cent. North America saw a rise between 1960 to 1980, followed by a decline. By 2000 just over half of all migrants in North America were female.

MAP 7 **POPULATION CHANGE IN THE CURRENT 25 EU COUNTRIES IN 2003**

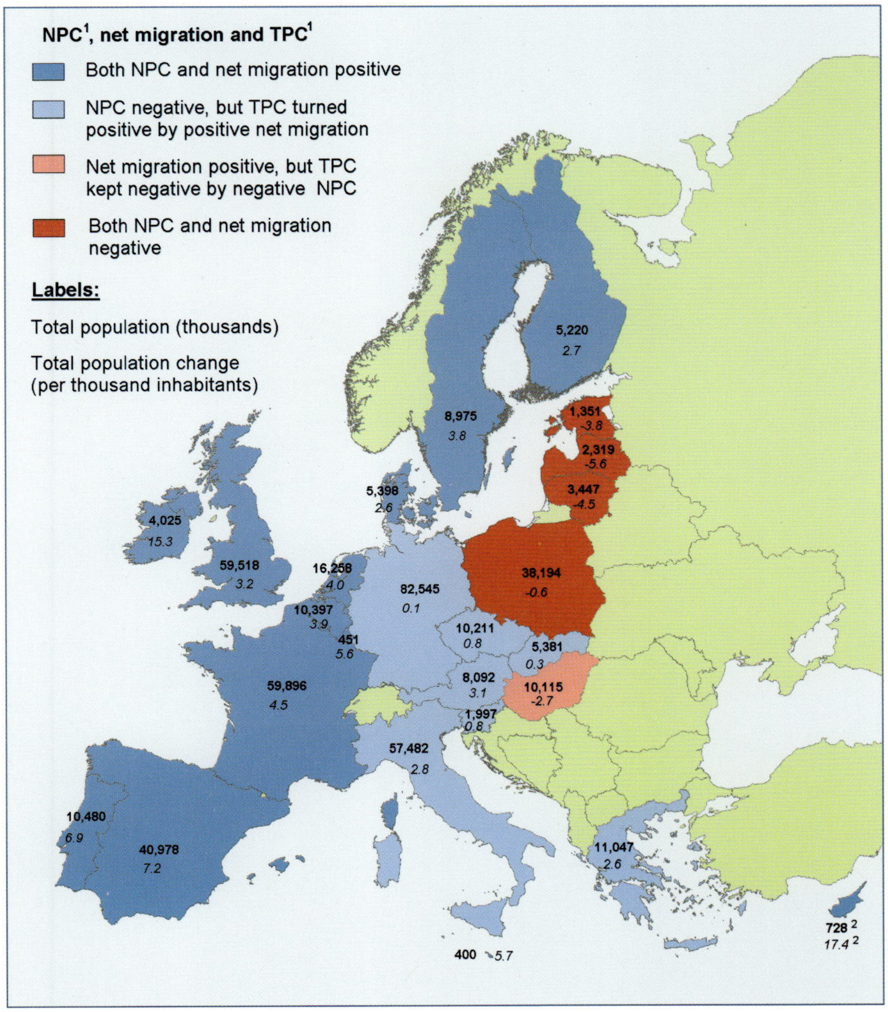

Source: EUROSTAT Chronos database, cited in Chapter 7 of this report.

Footnotes: **[1]** The abbreviation NPC used on the map means Natural Population Change = fertility minus mortality in a given year, per thousand inhabitants. TPC means Total Population Change = NPC plus net migration, per thousand inhabitants. **[2]** The Greek area of Cyprus only.

Map 7 illustrates the demographic indicators for the current 25 EU Member States in the year 2003, and refers to Table 1 in Chapter 7 of this report. The map shows that the natural population change (births minus deaths) and net migration were both positive in 12 of the 25 EU Member States in 2003. For eight of the current members, the natural population change was zero or negative, but the total change was towards growth through positive net migration. Italy, Germany, Greece, the Czech Republic and Slovakia belonged to this group. For Hungary, the strongly negative natural change kept the total change in red, in spite of the clearly positive net migration. For Poland and the three Baltic states, both components were on the negative side. (The figures on Cyprus cover the Greek area only.)

IRREGULAR MIGRATION

MAP 8 **MAIN REGULARIZATION PROGRAMMES IN SELECTED OECD COUNTRIES**

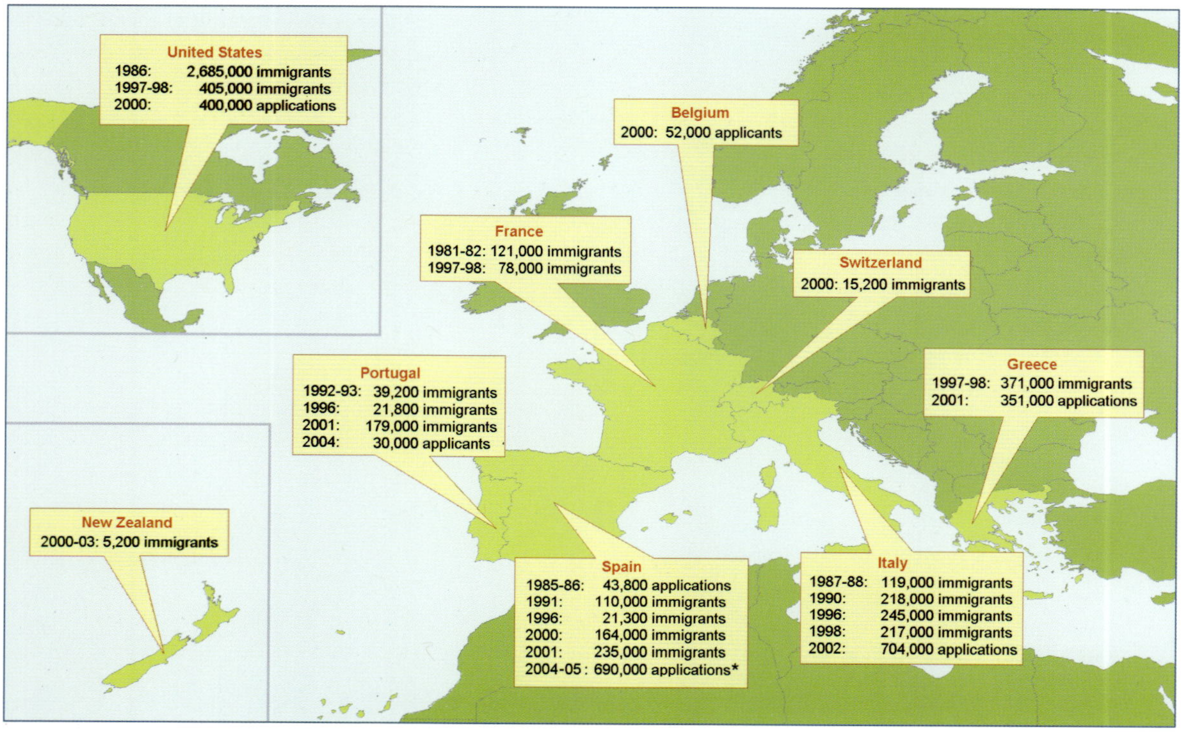

Source: OECD, *Trends in International Migration,* 2004; Government of New Zealand; Government of Portugal.
* ABC, Madrid.

It is difficult to obtain reliable indicators of the scale of irregular migration and the profile of irregular migrants. One useful indicator is the number of persons participating in regularization or amnesty programmes, which enable irregular migrants to acquire legal status. Not all irregular migrants can benefit from these measures, as regularization often depends on the number of years a person has lived in a country. The figures in map 8 are only indicative of the number of irregular migrants residing in a country. Migrants who do not fulfil the regularization conditions may not take part in an amnesty programme. Other factors limiting participation in such programmes are that employers may not wish to reveal their use of illegal labour, or may prefer to keep workers undocumented so that they can pay lower wages. Furthermore, the regularization frequently does not offer permanent status. Many fall back into an illegal status owing to the insecurity or short duration of the status offered under such programmes and the burdensome administrative procedures involved in renewing their legal status (OECD, 2003).

COMPARABILITY OF DATA

It is important to note that the regularization figures published by governments can refer either to the number of applications for, or the number of persons granted regular status. Each country has its own individual system for collecting data. For instance, the Belgian figure for 2000 counts the number of applications received and the dependants named therein. The 1986 figure for the US counts the number of persons granted residence permits, which excludes dependants.

Countries on the northern shores of the Mediterranean (Portugal, Spain, France, Italy, Greece) have carried out successive regularization programmes, which principally target undocumented immigrant workers. Belgium and Switzerland carried out regularization programmes aimed at asylum seekers in 2000. The US regularization programmes have principally targeted agricultural workers (1986), Nicaraguans and Cubans (1997-98) and irregular aliens (2000). New Zealand's regularization programme targeted overstayers.

The majority of regularization applicants in Spain are from South America; in Portugal they are from Brazil; in Belgium from the Democratic Republic of Congo, and in France they are from the Maghreb region. Many irregular migrants also originate from Central and Eastern Europe and China. In many countries, China ranks among the top five countries of origin. In the last amnesty in Italy, most came from Romania and Ukraine (OECD 2004). Another regularization was announced in Spain in late 2004, and was expected to offer hundreds of thousands of undocumented migrants the possibility to legalize their status if they "were able to demonstrate an authentic labour relationship".

IRREGULAR MIGRATION

MAP 9 — AMNESTY PROGRAMMES IN ASIA

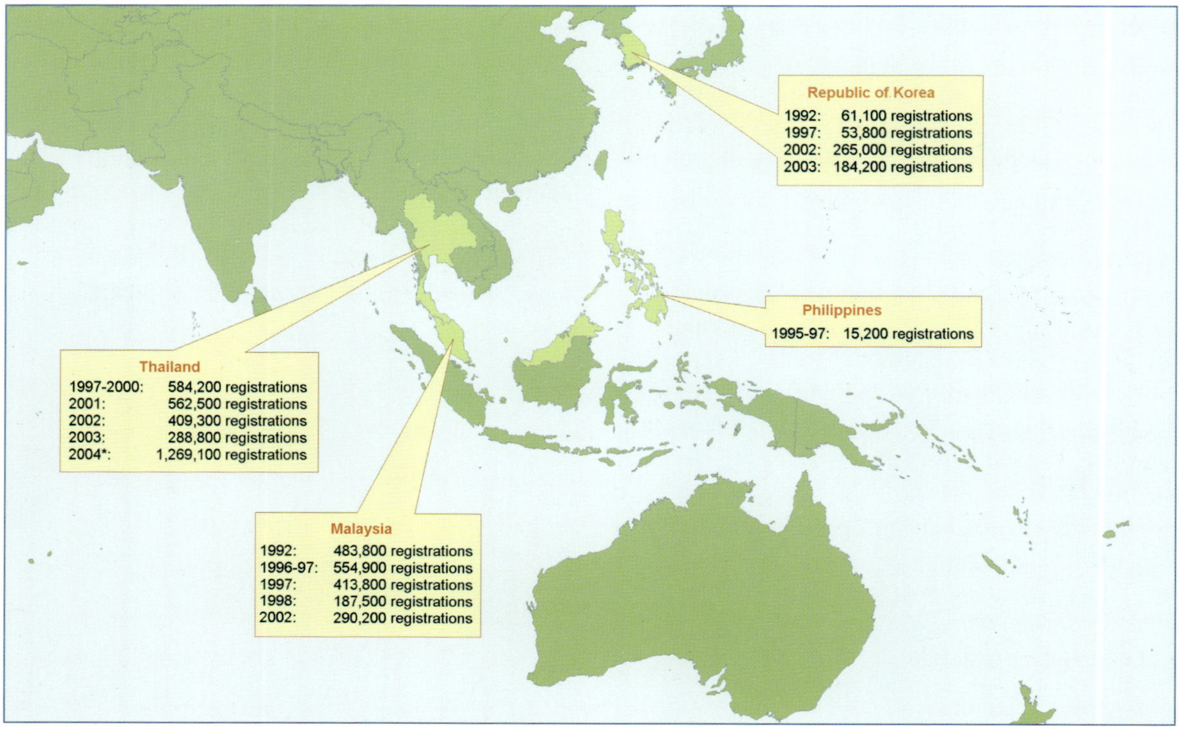

Source: Thailand: Ministries of Labour and Interior; The Philippines: Ministry of Labour; Korea: Ministry of Justice; Malaysia: OECD; Migration News.

In many Asian countries periods of rapid economic growth have resulted in significant importation of immigrant workers, not all of which have immediately been furnished with requisite documentation for residence and work. Therefore, the labour importing countries in the region have repeatedly offered the possibility for undocumented immigrant workers to register themselves and obtain valid documentation.

MIGRATION AND DEVELOPMENT

MAP 10 **REMITTANCES AND FOREIGN AID BY REGION, 2002**

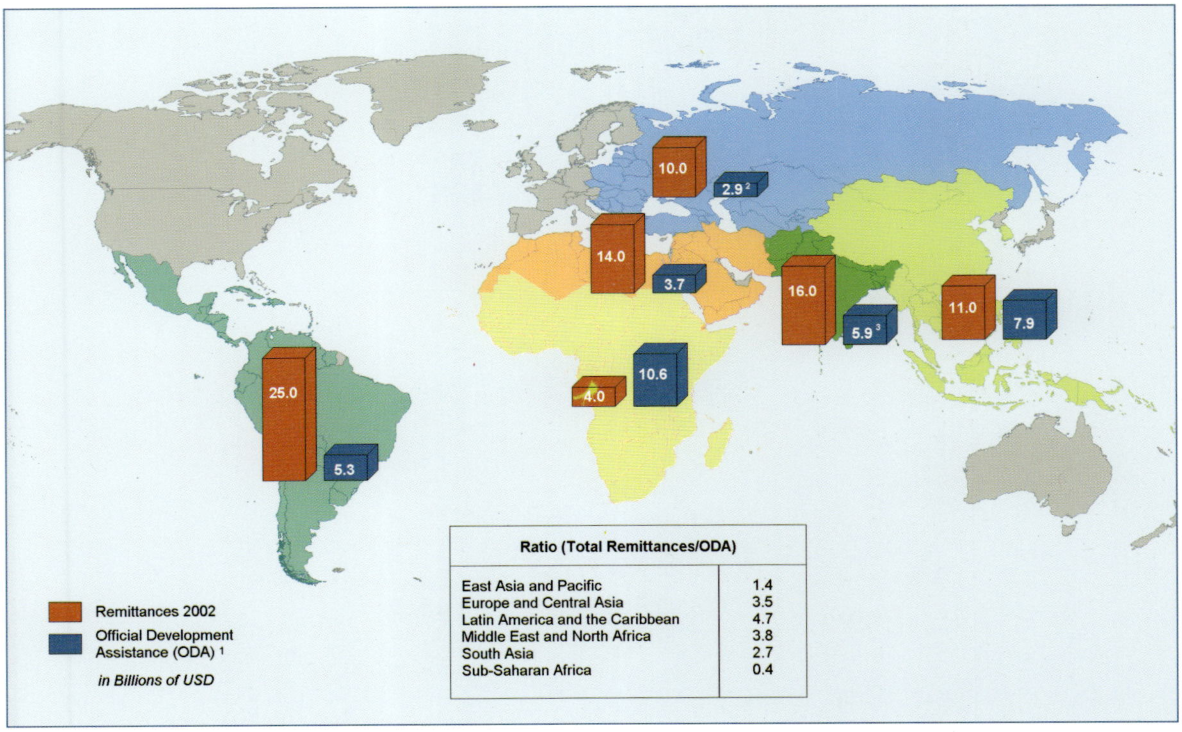

Source: The World Bank, *Global Development,* 2003; OECD, 2004.

Footnotes: [1] Official Development Assistance (ODA). Figures represent 2001-02 average gross bilateral ODA received by developing countries, as defined by the OECD's Development Assistance Committee (DAC). **[2]** Does not include Central Asia. **[3]** Includes Central Asia.

In 2002, migrants living and working in developed countries sent more than USD 88 billion back to their families in the developing world.[1] In 2002, official development assistance (ODA) was just over half that amount, USD 44.4 billion, which highlights the importance of remittances as a source of income for developing countries.

The economic importance of migrant remittances varies across the globe. Some developing countries and regions receive considerably higher amounts of remittances than ODA, while in other regions ODA plays a larger role in development. In the Latin American and Caribbean region, remittances were 4.7 times higher than ODA received in 2002. In the Middle East and North African region, remittances were 3.8 times higher than development assistance. By contrast, sub-Saharan Africa (SSA) was the only developing region where ODA exceeded remittances in 2002. As SSA received the smallest nominal amount of remittances, the region received the highest percent of development aid (23.8% of total ODA). Total remittances thus only accounted for 0.4 times the amount of ODA.

According to World Bank estimates, the total amount of remittances to developing countries increased to some USD 93 billion in 2003.

1. *The World Bank, Global Development Finance, 2003 and 2004 Editions.*

MIGRATION AND DEVELOPMENT

MAP 11 **REMITTANCES TO SELECT AFRICAN AND MIDDLE EAST COUNTRIES, 2002**

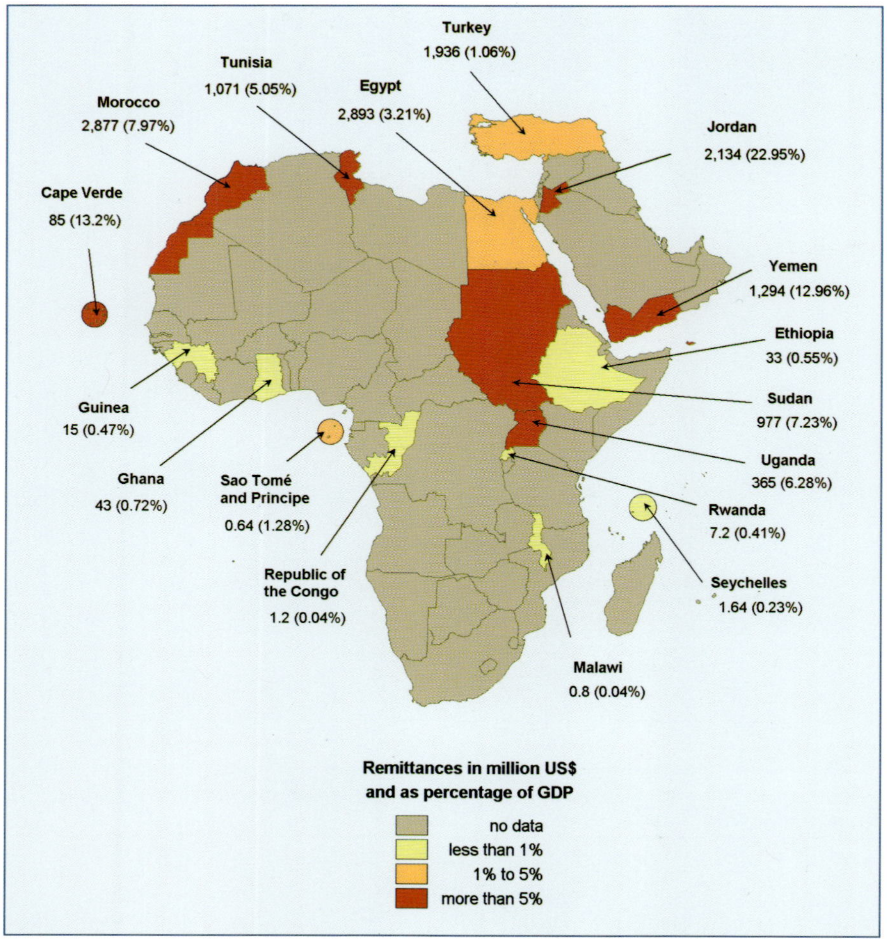

Source: World Bank, *Country at a Glance Tables, 2003;* IMF, *Balance of Payment Statistics Yearbook 2003,* 2003

Total migrant remittances in 2002 to Africa (including the Maghreb countries) and the Middle East in 2002 amounted to USD 18 billion.[1] Morocco scored high among these countries, with the second-highest monetary remittances of USD 2,877 million, the equivalent of 8 per cent of the country's GDP. Egypt received the highest amount of remittances - USD 2,893 million - but this only accounted for 3.22 per cent of national GDP. Both Egypt and Morocco have traditionally been large receivers of migrant money transfers.

Measured against the countries' yearly GDP, remittances were highest in Jordan (equal to almost 23 per cent of GDP) and in Cape Verde (13.8%) in 2002. As remittance data are not collected in most regions, definitive conclusions on larger regional trends and total money flows cannot be drawn at present.

1. *The World Bank, Global Development Finance, World Bank, Washington DC, 2003.*

MIGRATION AND DEVELOPMENT

MAP 12 **REMITTANCES TO SELECT LATIN AMERICAN COUNTRIES, 2002**

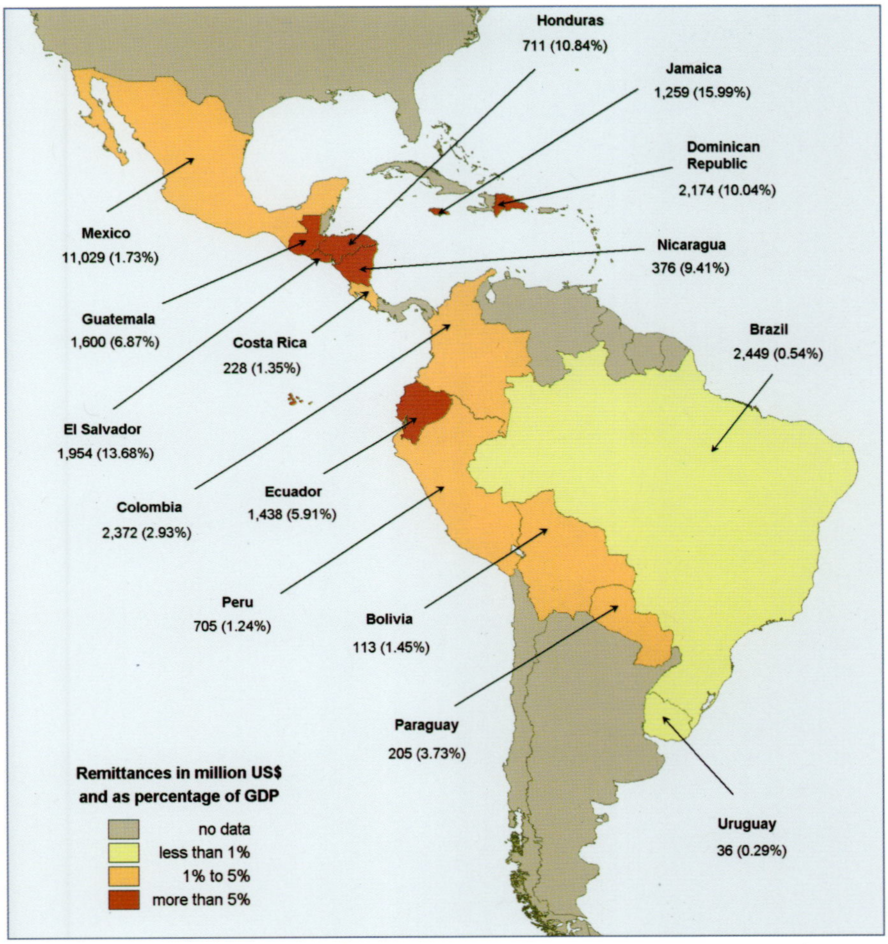

Source: World Bank, *Country at a Glance Tables, 2003;* IMF, Balance of *Payment Statistics Yearbook 2003*, 2003.

Total migrant remittances to the Latin America and Caribbean region in 2002 amounted to USD 25 billion,[1] of which almost 40 per cent was received by Mexico, the world's number one receiver of migrant money transfers. Mexico's officially registered annual amount of USD 11,029 million equalled 1.73 per cent of its GDP in 2002. The next largest receivers in the region were Colombia and the Dominican Republic. Remittances accounted for the highest proportion of GDP in Jamaica, El Salvador and Honduras, where the shares of GDP ranged between 10 and 16 per cent, while in Nicaragua and the Dominican Republic they fell just under 10 per cent.

1. *The World Bank, Global Development Finance, World Bank, Washington DC, 2003.*

MIGRATION AND DEVELOPMENT

MAP 13 **REMITTANCES TO SELECT ASIAN COUNTRIES AND NEW ZEALAND, 2002**

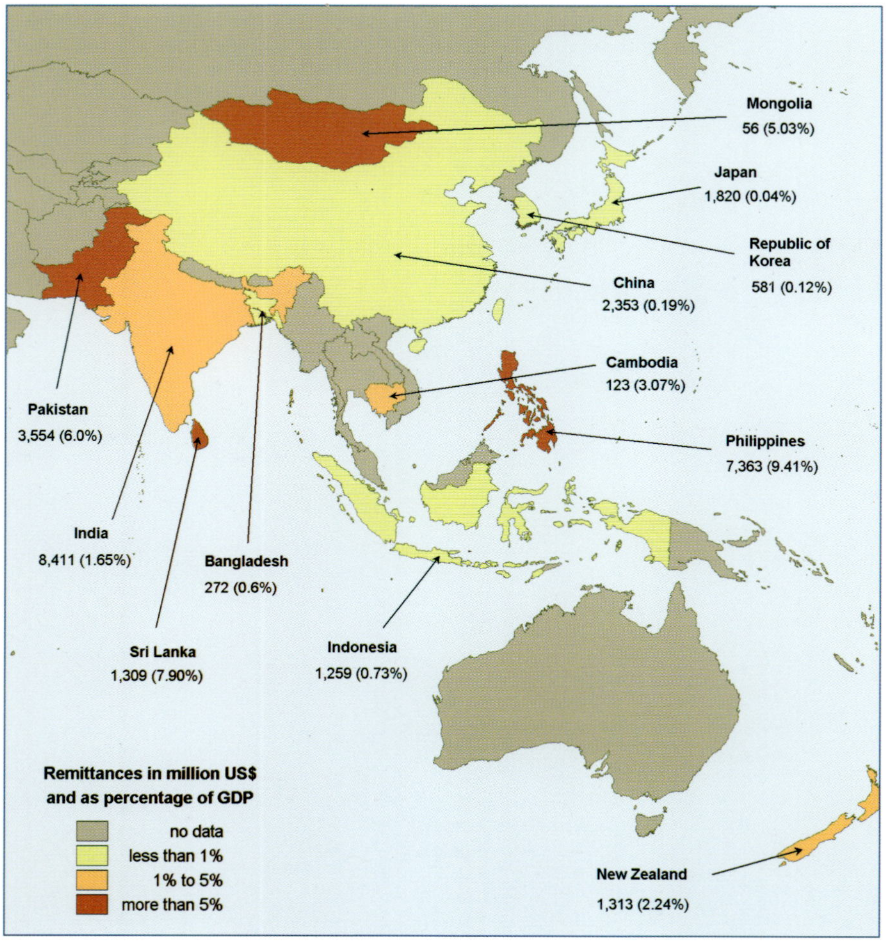

Source: World Bank (2003), *Country at a Glance Tables;* IMF (2003) *Balance of Payment Statistics Yearbook 2003.*

In 2002, the Asia-Pacific region received a total of USD 27 billion in migrant remittances.[1] India has consistently been one of the top receivers with (globally) the second-largest sum of remittances, USD 8,411 million in 2002, and USD 8,159 million in 2001.[1] The Philippines also recorded a high figure with USD 7,363 million, or 9.45 per cent of the country's GDP. Pakistan received about half the amount received by the Philippines, but this accounted for some 6 per cent of GDP, which in the region was only surpassed by Sri Lanka (with USD 1,287 million received, the equivalent of 7.9 per cent of its GDP in 2002).

1. *The World Bank, Global Development Finance, World Bank, Washington DC, 2003.*